2005

W9-ACT-632

The Cambridge Companion to Ovid

Ovid was one of the greatest writers of classical antiquity, and arguably the single most influential ancient poet for post-classical literature and culture. In this *Cambridge Companion* chapters by leading authorities from Europe and North America discuss the backgrounds and contexts for Ovid, the individual works, and his influence on later literature and art. Coverage of essential information is combined with exciting new critical approaches. This *Companion* is designed both as an accessible handbook for the general reader who wishes to learn about Ovid, and as a series of stimulating essays for students of Latin poetry and of the classical tradition.

CAMBRIDGE COMPANIONS TO LITERATURE

CAMBRIDGE COMPANIONS TO CULTURE

THE CAMBRIDGE
COMPANION TO
OVID

EDITED BY
PHILIP HARDIE

*University Reader in Latin Literature
in the University of Cambridge,
and Fellow of New Hall*

PUBLISHED BY THE PRESS SYNDICATE OF THE UNIVERSITY OF CAMBRIDGE
The Pitt Building, Trumpington Street, Cambridge, United Kingdom

CAMBRIDGE UNIVERSITY PRESS
The Edinburgh Building, Cambridge CB2 2RU, UK
40 West 20th Street, New York, NY 10011-4211, USA
477 Williamstown Road, Port Melbourne, VIC 3207, Australia
Ruiz de Alarcón 13, 28014 Madrid, Spain
Dock House, The Waterfront, Cape Town 8001, South Africa

http://www.cambridge.org

© Cambridge University Press 2002

This book is in copyright. Subject to statutory exception
and to the provisions of relevant collective licensing agreements,
no reproduction of any part may take place without
the written permission of Cambridge University Press.

First published 2002

Printed in the United Kingdom at the University Press, Cambridge

Typeface Sabon 10/13 pt.   *System* LATEX 2$_\varepsilon$ [TB]

A catalogue record for this book is available from the British Library

Library of Congress Cataloguing in Publication data

The Cambridge companion to Ovid / edited by Philip Hardie.
p.   cm. (Cambridge companions to literature)
Includes bibliographical references and index.
ISBN 0 521 77281 8 (hardback) ISBN 0 521 77528 0 (paperback)
1. Ovid, 43 BC–17 or 18 AD – Criticism and interpretation – Handbooks, manuals, etc.
2. Epistolary poetry, Latin – History and criticism – Handbooks, manuals, etc.
3. Didactic poetry, Latin – History and criticism – Handbooks, manuals, etc.   4. Love
poetry, Latin – History and criticism – Handbooks, manuals, etc.   5. Mythology,
Classical, in literature – Handbooks, manuals, etc.   I. Title: Companion to Ovid.
II. Hardie, Philip R.   III. Series.
PA6537 .C28   2002
871′.01–dc21   2001037923

ISBN 0 521 77281 8 hardback
ISBN 0 521 77528 0 paperback

871
C.178

$41.60

12&T

3/24/05

CONTENTS

Contents

Contents

ILLUSTRATIONS

CONTRIBUTORS

CHRISTOPHER ALLEN is an art historian and writer who lives in Sydney and teaches at the National Art School. He held two postdoctoral appointments at the Collège de France between 1994 and 1996, and has recently finished writing a volume on *French Seventeenth-Century Painting* for Thames and Hudson (World of Art). He is also the author, in the same series, of *Art in Australia: From Colonization to Postmodernism*. He is currently co-editing an edition with commentary of Charles-Alphonse Dufresnoy's Latin didactic poem on the art of painting, *De arte graphica* (1668).

ALESSANDRO BARCHIESI is Professor of Latin at the University of Siena at Arezzo. His research focuses in particular on Augustan poetry and on the interaction between classics and contemporary criticism and theory. He has published a commentary on Ovid's *Heroides* 1–3 (1992), a book on Virgil and papers on Horace and Petronius. His recent books include *The Poet and the Prince* (1997) and *Speaking Volumes* (2001), and he has co-edited *Ovidian Transformations* (1999) and *Iambic Ideas* (2001). He is the general editor of a complete commentary on Ovid's *Metamorphoses* to be published by the Fondazione Valla. He has been a Nellie Wallace Lecturer in Oxford (1998), a Gray Lecturer in Cambridge (2001) and is currently working on his 2002 Jerome Lectures for the University of Michigan and the American Academy in Rome.

COLIN BURROW is a Senior Lecturer in the Faculty of English at the University of Cambridge, and a Fellow and Tutor of Gonville and Caius College. He has published extensively on relations between classical and European literatures in the Renaissance. His publications include *Epic Romance: Homer to Milton* (1993), *Edmund Spenser* (1996), and *The Complete Sonnets and Poems* for the Oxford Shakespeare (2002).

JEREMY DIMMICK is a College Lecturer in English at St Catherine's College, Oxford, having previously been a Junior Research Fellow of Gonville and Caius College, Cambridge. He works on Gower and Lydgate, and is writing a book on Ovid in the Middle Ages.

ANDREW FELDHERR is Assistant Professor of Classics at Princeton University. He has published *Spectacle and Society in Livy's History* (1998) and articles on Virgil, Ovid and Catullus. He is currently working on a book-length study of the *Metamorphoses*, focusing specifically on the relationship between politics and narratology in the poem.

FRITZ GRAF is the Andrew Fleming West Professor in the Department of Classics at Princeton University, having previously held the chair of Latin Philology and Religions of the Ancient Mediterranean at the University of Basel. His publications include *Nordionische Kulte* (1985), *Greek Mythology* (1985; English translation 1993), *Magic in the Ancient World* (1997) and *Der Lauf des rollenden Jahres. Zeit und Kalender in Rom* (1997). He is currently working on a study of Greek and Roman festivals in the eastern half of the Roman empire, also the topic of his 2000 Gray Lectures at the University of Cambridge.

THOMAS HABINEK is Professor of Classics at the University of Southern California. He is the author of *The Politics of Latin Literature* (1998) and co-editor of *The Roman Cultural Revolution* (1997). His research considers the social and political dimensions of classical Latin poetry and prose.

PHILIP HARDIE is Reader in Latin Literature at the University of Cambridge, and a Fellow of New Hall. He is the author of *Virgil's Aeneid: Cosmos and Imperium* (1986), *The Epic Successors of Virgil* (1993), an edition of Virgil's *Aeneid* Book IX in the Cambridge Greek and Latin Classics series (1994) and *Ovid's Poetics of Illusion* (2002), and co-editor of *Ovidian Transformations* (1999). He is currently contributing to the complete commentary on Ovid's *Metamorphoses* to be published by the Fondazione Valla. He is a General Editor of the Cambridge Greek and Latin Classics series and a Fellow of the British Academy.

STEPHEN HARRISON is Fellow and Tutor in Classics at Corpus Christi College, Oxford, and Reader in Classical Languages and Literature at the University of Oxford. He is the author of a commentary on Virgil's *Aeneid* 10 (1991) and of *Apuleius: A Latin Sophist* (2000), and is completing a book on genre in Augustan poetry.

STEPHEN HINDS is Professor and Chair of Classics at the University of Washington, Seattle. He is the author of *The Metamorphosis of Persephone: Ovid and the Self-Conscious Muse* (1987) and *Allusion and Intertext: Dynamics of Appropriation in Roman Poetry* (1998), and co-editor of *Ovidian Transformations* (1999). He is also co-editor (with Denis Feeney) of the Roman Literature and its Contexts series published by Cambridge University Press. He is currently preparing a commentary on Ovid's *Tristia* Book 1 for the Cambridge Greek and Latin Classics series.

DUNCAN F. KENNEDY is Reader in Latin Literature and the Theory of Criticism at the University of Bristol. He is the author of *The Arts of Love: Five Studies in the Discourse of Roman Love Elegy* (1993) and *Rethinking Reality: Lucretius and the Textualization of Nature* (2001).

RAPHAEL LYNE is a Newton Trust Lecturer at the University of Cambridge, and a Fellow of New Hall. He is the author of *Ovid's Changing Worlds: English Metamorphoses 1567–1632* (2001) and of articles on Renaissance literature and classical imitation.

CAROLE NEWLANDS is Professor and Chair of Classics at the University of Wisconsin, Madison. She has published *Playing with Time: Ovid and the Fasti* (1995) and *Statius' Silvae and the Poetics of Empire* (2002) and has general research interests in Roman studies and imperial and late Antique poetry.

ALESSANDRO SCHIESARO has taught at the University of Wisconsin, Madison and Princeton University and is currently Professor of Latin at King's College, London. He has written on didactic poetry, and is the author of *Simulacrum et imago: gli argomenti analogici nel* De rerum natura (1990); he has also published on Virgil, Ovid, Seneca, Apuleius and Leopardi. He has co-edited *Mega Nepios* (1993) and *The Roman Cultural Revolution* (1997), and has recently completed a monograph on Seneca's *Thyestes*.

ALISON SHARROCK is Reader in Classics at the University of Manchester. Her research interests cover a range of topics in Latin literature, around the epicentre of Ovid's amatory poetry. Previous books include *Seduction and Repetition in Ovid's Ars Amatoria II* (1994) and (co-edited with Helen Morales) *Intratextuality: Greek and Roman Textual Relations* (2000). A book entitled *Fifty Key Classical Authors* (co-authored with Rhiannon Ash) is forthcoming with Routledge. In preparation is a book-length revision of her 1999 W. B. Stanford Memorial Lectures entitled *Fabulous Artifice: Poetics and Playfulness in Roman Comedy*.

RICHARD TARRANT has taught at the University of Toronto and at Harvard University, where he is currently Pope Professor of the Latin Language and Literature and Harvard College Professor. He has published commentaries on Seneca's *Agamemnon* (1976) and *Thyestes* (1985), and is one of the co-authors of *Texts and Transmissions: A Guide to the Latin Classics* (1983). He has recently completed an Oxford Classical Text of Ovid's *Metamorphoses*, and his next project is a commentary on Virgil's *Aeneid* Book XII for the Cambridge Greek and Latin Classics series. He is a General Editor of the Cambridge Classical Texts and Commentaries series.

GARETH WILLIAMS is Associate Professor of Classics at Columbia University. He has published *Banished Voices: Readings in Ovid's Exile Poetry* (1994) and is currently producing an edition of selected dialogues of Seneca for the Cambridge Greek and Latin Classics series.

PREFACE

Ovid is arguably the single most important author from classical antiquity for the post-classical western tradition. This *Companion* aims to locate Ovid's dazzling *œuvre* within the history of ancient Roman culture and literature, and also to illustrate some of the many ways in which his texts have been used by later writers and artists. It is designed both as an introduction to basic aspects of Ovid's works and their reception, and as a sample of the range of approaches that have emerged during what has been nothing less than an explosion of critical and theoretical studies of Ovid in recent years, after a period of neglect; we hope that the volume may also provide signposts for future work. Our intention is to stimulate as much as to inform.

I am grateful to all the contributors for their good-humoured responsiveness to a sometimes importunate editor, and also to our copy-editor, Muriel Hall. For their expertise and understanding I owe especial thanks to Pauline Hire of Cambridge University Press, who first suggested that I might undertake this volume, and to her successor at the Press, Michael Sharp.

The quotation from *Tales from Ovid* by Ted Hughes printed in the epigraph to the Introduction has been reproduced with permission from Faber and Faber Ltd, London and Farrar, Strauss & Giroux Inc., New York.

PHILIP HARDIE

Introduction

Descend again, be pleased to reanimate
This revival of those marvels.
Reveal, now, exactly
How they were performed
From the beginning
Up to this moment.[1]

As the twentieth century drew to its close Ovid's star shone brightly in the sky, at least of the Anglo-Saxon world. Two volumes of adaptations of stories from the *Metamorphoses*, published by Faber & Faber, turned out to be bestsellers.[2] One of these, *Tales from Ovid* (1997), was the last but one collection published before his death by the Poet Laureate Ted Hughes, to be followed by *Birthday letters* (1998), poems written to his wife Sylvia Plath over the decades following her suicide. The juxtaposition has a certain irony. *Birthday letters*, addressed to one of the heroines of modern poetry, is written in a confessional mode that caters to a continuing post-Romantic craving for a literature of sincerity and truth to life. *Tales from Ovid* reworks the most self-consciously fictive poem of a white male poet, dead for almost two millennia. His works were to become a byword for a playful detachment from the serious business of life, and as a result went into a critical eclipse during the nineteenth and much of the twentieth centuries.

Life, it might be said, caught up with the poet when Ovid was sent into exile on the shore of the Black Sea in AD 8. Thereupon he did turn to a plangent self-expression in the verse letters from exile. But even so Ovid could not win, for these confessional works in the first-person singular were for long dismissed as inferior; their repetitive self-obsession was not read sympathetically as the history of a soul in pain, but taken as an index of Ovid's expulsion from the fertile garden of poetic feigning.

---

[1] Hughes (1997) 3, translating *Met.* 1.1–4.
[2] Hofmann and Lasdun (1994); Hughes (1997).

With the recent flood of scholarly criticism of the exile poetry, the reanimation of Ovid's poetic *corpus* has been completed, at least in the academic world. One of the fruits of the intense cultivation of the exile poetry has been an appreciation of the complex links between the poetry of after AD 8 and the earlier works, a continuity bridging the drastic change in the poet's circumstances consequent on his removal from the metropolitan centre to an outpost of the Roman empire. With a hindsight to which Ovid himself steers us, all parts of his dazzlingly varied and shape-shifting poetic career seem to form themselves into a single plan, beginning with an elegy of erotic complaint in which the lover attempts to gain entry to the locked door of his girlfriend, and ending with the elegies of an exile vainly (as it turned out) trying to win the right to return to Rome.[3] Stephen Harrison (chapter 5) traces the change-in-continuity of Ovid's elegiac career.

Both bodies of first-person elegy, the youthful *Amores* and the late exile poetry, are concerned to relate the private experiences of the poet to the wider worlds of Greek mythology and of Roman history and politics, worlds explored more directly in the works of the central section of Ovid's career, the *Heroides*, *Metamorphoses*, and *Fasti*. As Richard Tarrant (chapter 1) and Gareth Williams (chapter 14) show, the exile poems construct themselves by superimposing the 'facts' of Ovid's exile on features, both of form and content, from all three of these earlier works (at least one of which, the *Fasti*, continued to be revised in exile). Most striking is Ovid's conversion of his own exile into a real-life example of the kind of incredible story told in the *Metamorphoses*. Ovid complains that in exile he has lost the powers that enabled the poetic triumph of the *Metamorphoses*, yet this dissembles the fact that business continues as usual. From hexameter mythological epic to first-person elegiac letters from exile seems an almost inevitable progression.

Perhaps Ted Hughes' apparently disparate closing brace of poetry books also has an Ovidian logic. An easy way to trace continuity would be to lean on Ted Hughes' own location of the secret of Ovid's enduring popularity in the fact that 'Above all, Ovid was interested in passion.'[4] Raphael Lyne points out that Hughes' version of the *Metamorphoses* ends with the Pyramus and Thisbe story, and with two lovers 'closed in a single urn' (chapter 15, p. 263). But consider the following: a collection of fantastic mythical tales, followed by a collection of letters prompted by the fact of an irreversible loss, and including as addressee a wife whom the writer will never see again. Is the author Ovid or Ted Hughes?

---

[3] On the unity of the work of Ovid as elegist see also Holzberg (1999) 60 'It is actually possible to read Ovid's works from the *Heroides* through to his exile poetry as a series of "metamorphoses" of the elegiac discourse found in the *Amores*.'

[4] Hughes (1997) p. ix.

Hughes himself perhaps never saw things in this way. Is it then illegitimate for the reader aware of the Ovidian pattern to discern it in the shape of Hughes' œuvre? That would at least be a highly Ovidian appropriation. Of all ancient poets Ovid is perhaps the most aware of the rewards and hazards of his own reception. The *Metamorphoses* closes with a reworking of Horace's ode on his own monumental fame (*Odes* 3.30), in which Ovid looks forward to an eternity in which 'I shall be read on the lips of the people' (*Met.* 15.878). The Latin words, *ore legar populi*, could also be translated 'I [i.e. my soul] shall be gathered on the lips of the people', hinting at an image of poetic tradition and transmission as a Pythagoreanizing re-embodiment of dead poets in the bodies of living poets – or living readers.[5] Metempsychosis allows texts to have a life of their own after the death of their original owners and producers. The history of Ovid's reception starts with Ovid himself, who after the figurative death of exile rereads and redeploys his own unfinished *Metamorphoses* to reflect his own altered circumstances. 'By *rewriting* its opening lines, Ovid will force us to *reread* the entire poem in a slightly different way.'[6] But an interest in his own reception predates the exile: Duncan Kennedy (chapter 13) shows that the uncertainty of the legendary writers of the *Heroides* as to whether their letters will ever reach their destination, and, if they do, what reception they will find, figures Ovid's own concern for an appropriate readership. This is the poet who addresses one of his own missives from exile to 'posterity' (*Trist.* 4.10.2).

Colin Burrow (chapter 18) considers further aspects of Ovid's self-imitation and auto-reception. Ovid's concern for his standing with posterity is of a piece with his constant awareness of previous literary tradition and of his place within that tradition, as discussed by Richard Tarrant (chapter 1). The urge to shape his own career into an overarching unity is motivated not just by the wish to assert some kind of control over the caprices of external fortune, but by the desire to forge for himself a literary stature comparable to that of his immediate and greatest predecessor, Virgil, whose three major works became a model of the poetic career apparently prescribed according to a sequential structure of unity in diversity, imitated by poets such as Spenser and Milton.[7] Raphael Lyne shows how the sequence of the several personae of the Ovidian career offers an alternative model to the Virgilian for post-classical poets' self-fashioning (chapter 17).

Burrow suggests that one reason for Ovid's popularity with Renaissance poets was that he offered these writers ways of handling their own place within the classical tradition, with the dominant model of continuity in

---

[5] See Hardie (1999b) 268 n. 44. [6] Hinds (1985) 25, discussing *Trist.* 1.7.
[7] See Theodorakopoulos (1997).

change, or metamorphosis. In the earlier twentieth century the titular subject of the *Metamorphoses* was often seen as little more than an excuse for bizarre tales in an Alexandrian vein, and, even as that, often marginal to the poem's real concerns.[8] Recently metamorphosis has moved to centre stage as a dominant trope of Ovidian criticism, a way of thinking about change and continuity not just in linguistic and literary areas such as genre, allegory and personification, allusion and intertextuality, and reader response, but also in Ovid's dealings with the extratextual worlds of psychology, culture, history and ideology: a number of these areas are discussed by Andrew Feldherr (chapter 10).

As academic classicists have found new and (for us) compelling ways of talking about Ovid's construction of his place within literary traditions, for the wider readership it may be increasingly difficult to recapture the Renaissance conviction that the relationship of the present to a classical past, perhaps to tradition of any kind, is central to a modern cultural awareness. In the rest of this 'Introduction' I point to some of the other features of the Ovidian texts that have brought about nothing less than a sea-change in their critical fortunes over the past few decades, and restored them to something approaching the centre of the cultural mainstream.

What formerly was seen as superficial wit and an irredeemable lack of seriousness has been reassessed in the light of a postmodernist flight from realism and presence towards textuality and anti-foundationalism.[9] 'Parody', a term often used in dismissive acknowledgement of Ovid's entertainment value, has moved to the theoretical centre of studies of allusion and intertextuality. Ovid exults in the fictiveness of his poetry, that written in the first person singular quite as much as self-evidently tall tales like that of the beautiful girl Scylla changed into a hideous sea-monster (*Met.* 13.732–4). At the heart of the *Metamorphoses* we come across a debate on the truth or fiction of stories of metamorphosis, conducted by fictional characters at the dinner-table of a river-god, himself a shape-shifter (*Met.* 8.611–19).[10]

The later twentieth-century novel saw a significant shift from the prevailing nineteenth-century realist tradition that concealed its own devices, back towards the seventeenth- and eighteenth-century self-conscious novel, defined by Robert Alter as 'a novel that systematically flaunts its own condition of artifice and that by so doing probes into the problematic relationship between

---

[8] For an early exercise in widening the scope of metamorphosis from subject matter to a 'functional principle' see Galinsky (1975) 42–70.

[9] Don Fowler was unmatched as a postmodernist critic of Latin literature, and also for his ability to bring popular culture into his scholarship; he published little on Ovid, but there is a gem in his 'Pyramus, Thisbe, King Kong: Ovid and the presence of poetry', in Fowler (2000) 156–67.

[10] Discussed by Feeney (1991) 229–32; on the general issues see also Feeney (1993).

real-seeming artifice and reality'.[11] The line of Cervantes, Sterne, and Diderot may be traced back directly to the ancient prose novel, but also to Ovid. The Ovidian line surfaces explicitly, for example, in Chaucer's *House of Fame*, in eighteenth-century novels by Fielding and others, to flow into the magic realism of recent novels such as Salman Rushdie's *Satanic verses*, as Duncan Kennedy shows (chapter 19). Narrative self-consciousness is matched on the dramatic stage by metatheatricality: famous Shakespearean moments such as the masque in the *Tempest*, or Prospero's final abjuration of his powers, or the statue scene in *The Winter's Tale* have specific Ovidian models. We should not forget that Ovid was the writer of an acclaimed tragedy, the *Medea*, now lost; the dream-god Morpheus who comes close to being a personification of the principle of fiction in the *Metamorphoses* (11.633–70) is an actor, as well as a fabricator of narratives and visual images.[12]

The uncertain relationship between text and what lies outside the text is foregrounded in other ways by Ovid. Perhaps his most instantly recognizable quality, strikingly uniform throughout his career, is his style, insistently calling attention to the linguistic surface of the texts.[13] A wide array of types of verbal repetition[14] impose a pointed linguistic articulation on the messy and amorphous flux of the pre-linguistic world, beginning with the repetitions that characterize the primal chaos (*Met.* 1.15–17):

> utque erat et tellus illic et pontus et aer,
> sic erat instabilis tellus, innabilis unda,
> lucis egens aer; nulli sua forma manebat.

> But earth, and air, and water, were in one.
> Thus air was void of light, and earth unstable,
> And water's dark abyss unnavigable.

> (Dryden)

Other kinds of verbal wit, such as the pun and syllepsis (e.g. 'At once from life and from the chariot driv'n' (Phaethon), Addison's translation of *Met.* 2.312–13) collapse conceptual boundaries and introduce disorder into a neatly ordered world. An awareness of the way in which we construct the world through language, always in danger of revealing itself as nothing but language, comes through in Ovid's dealings with personifications, vividly imagined presences that call attention to the emptiness at their core, culminating with the personification in *Metamorphoses* 12 of *Fama*, 'rumour',

---

[11] Alter (1975) p. x.   [12] Pointed out by Tissol (1997) 78–9.
[13] For brief further discussion of Ovid's style see ch. 2, pp. 42–5.
[14] The 'Index locorum' in Wills' (1996) remarkable book on repetition in Latin poetry gives a ready impression of the ubiquity of Ovidian repetition.

'fame', 'tradition', the power of language itself. *Fama* is a 'person' who sees and reports everything, but is herself invisible, an absent presence in the world over which she rules.

A long-standing tendency among classicists to dismiss Ovid's verbal pyrotechnics as so much empty 'rhetoric' has been overtaken by a rise in the theoretical and literary-critical stock of rhetoric. Philip Hardie (chapter 2) and Alessandro Schiesaro (chapter 4) develop approaches to the rehabilitation of Ovidian rhetoric. *Amores* 1.9, a notable example of Ovidian rhetoric, takes the form of a declamation exercise developing the paradox 'the lover is a soldier'; the opening couplet flaunts a rhetorical figure of repetition, *conduplicatio*:[15]

> Militat omnis amans, et habet sua castra Cupido;
> Attice, crede mihi, militat omnis amans.

> Every lover is a soldier, and Cupid has his camp; believe me, Atticus, every lover is a soldier.

But this poem merely trumpets to the winds the secret that Latin love elegy constantly murmurs into a ditch, like Midas' servant, that the subjectivity of the lover is a discursive construct, and the lover a stagey role-player, topics given full airing by Alison Sharrock in her discussion of both the first-person love elegies, the *Amores*, and the parodic didactic poems which give instructions in how to fall in and out of love, the *Ars amatoria* and *Remedia amoris* (chapter 9). To confine the spontaneity of passion within the method of didactic poetry is at once a paradox and a demonstration that love also has its rules and conventions.

Narcissus comes to a tragic realization of love's superficiality, when he is trapped by what he sees on the surface of a body of water. His reaction to his reflection prompts some of Ovid's most pointed repetitions, a reflexive parody almost of the self-love of his own talent of which Quintilian[16] was to accuse the poet, *Met.* 3.425–6:

> se cupit imprudens et qui probat ipse probatur,
> dumque petit petitur, pariterque accendit et ardet.

Golding's translation loses the snappy compression, but preserves the repetitions:

> He is enamored of himselfe for want of taking heede,
> And where he lykes another thing, he lykes himself in deede.
> He is the partie whome he wooes, and suter that doth wooe,
> He is the flame that settes on fire, and thing that burneth tooe.

---

[15] For full details on the rhetorical contexts of the poem see McKeown ad loc.
[16] Quintil. *Inst. or.* 10.1.89 *nimium amator ingenii sui.*

These repetitions translate to the verbal plane issues of visual representation. Does a verbal repetition signal identity, or does a gap open up in the space between two instances of the same word? What is the relationship between reality and representation?[17] One of Ovid's big topics is visual illusionism and the relationship between art and nature. Narcissus' erotic delusion merges into artistic illusion. At *Metamorphoses* 3.419 Narcissus transfixed by his reflection is compared to a marble statue. The simile offers the reader a verbal image of the scene, but this is also the visual image perceived by Narcissus, since the object of his gaze, as a reflection of the statuesque viewer, also looks like a statue. A reflection in a still pool is the ultimately lifelike image, yet the gap between this image and reality is as unbridgeable for Narcissus as the gap that always divides art from the reality which it represents.

Ecphrasis, the verbal description of something seen, and (in current usage) more specifically the description of a work of art, offers Ovid recurrent opportunities to explore the links between word and image. In chapter 8 Stephen Hinds expands the discussion of Ovidian artistic ecphrasis in a far-reaching exploration of Ovidian landscapes and their afterlife. In chapter 20 Christopher Allen makes soundings in the extremely rich area of Ovid's influence on the visual arts. Ovid's well-developed visual sense makes him a fertile source for later painters and sculptors (not to mention landscape gardeners), both as a treasury of vividly imagined subject matter, and as a stimulus to visual artists to reflect on their own representational strategies.

Metamorphosis as a narrative device occupies an uneasy space between art and nature. The *Metamorphoses* is a gigantic repertory of aetiologies for phenomena in the natural world, a world that is at once an image of the one in which we live, and also a pointedly artificial and fictive remaking and doubling of that world. Andrew Feldherr (chapter 10) discusses the way that metamorphosis is enlisted by Ovid as part of his wider thematization of representation. Alessandro Barchiesi (chapter 11) concludes his innovative contribution to another major area where Ovid has proved remarkably responsive to modern theory, as the magical story-teller turns out also to be a highly qualified narratologist, with the suggestion that the study of narrative technique must escape a formalist straitjacket to realize its implications for the act of representation.

Narcissus is Ovid's most comic parody of the elegiac lover, but this uniquely unfortunate dupe of erotic error is also a strangely unsettling example of the insatiability of desire. His love for his insubstantial image, as we have seen, is a figure for the reader's or viewer's desiring relationship to a text or work of art as much as is Pygmalion's love for his statue, an episode intimately

---

[17] For these issues as they touch Ovid's *Amores*, and love elegy in general, see Kennedy (1993) ch. 1 'Representation and the rhetoric of reality'.

connected with the story of Narcissus.[18] But in terms of sexual desire too, Narcissus' delusion is only a special case of the universal truth about the emptiness of desire for another, as luridly described by Lucretius in the diatribe against love in *De rerum natura* 4, a passage to which Ovid's Narcissus narrative makes sustained allusion.[19]

Ovid has often been accused of mocking and trivializing love, and in effect bringing about the death of love elegy. This might seem strange for a poet described by Chaucer as 'Venus' clerk' (*House of Fame* 1487). Recent theorizations of desire offer opportunities to move beyond the stereotype of Ovid the cynical realist. The teasing revelation that the elegist's object of desire, Corinna, may be no more than an effect of the text confronts us with an awareness of our own investment of desire in the process of reading. 'Reading about desire provokes the desire to read.'[20] Ovid complains that he has prostituted his girl-friend to the reader in his poems (*Am.* 3.12.5–8). In the *Metamorphoses* Ovid offers virtuoso experiences of a Barthesian 'plaisir du texte'. An episode like the story of Mercury's enchantment of Argus (*Met.* 1.668–723) thematizes the model of reading as seduction.[21]

Peter Brooks puts Freudian theories of desire to work in analyses of the workings of texts, both in the dynamic of desire and repetition that structures narrative plots, and in the inscription of meaning on desired bodies within such narratives, the 'semioticization of desire'.[22] Ovidian narrative repetition lends itself readily to the former kind of analysis; with regard to the latter a body like that of Daphne, in the archetypal erotic narrative of the *Metamorphoses* (1.452–567), is transformed into a multiply determined site of signification, the deposit of a desire whose satisfaction is for ever deferred. Lacan's analysis of the structures of desire according to a linguistic model offers another handle on the Ovidian textualization of desire, for example in Micaela Janan's study of Apollo's literal inscription of his grief on the flower into which his dead boyfriend Hyacinthus metamorphoses, or in Don Fowler's reading of the Pyramus and Thisbe story as a dramatization of the incommensurability of the Lacanian Symbolic and Imaginary.[23]

Freudian and Lacanian accounts locate repetition and loss at the heart of desire. Ovid revitalizes the conventional elegiac association of love and grief; the powerful narratives of erotic grief in such episodes in the *Metamorphoses* as Apollo and Hyacinthus or Ceyx and Alcyone feed naturally into the

---

[18] On the erotics of the gaze see Elsner (1996b); on the connections between Ovid's Narcissus and Pygmalion see Rosati (1983).
[19] Hardie (1988).   [20] Sharrock (1994a) 296.
[21] On narrative erotics see Nagle (1988a), (1988b).   [22] Brooks (1984), (1993).
[23] Janan (1988): Fowler (2000) (n. 9 above).

repetitive expressions of grief in the exile poetry. In exile Ovid makes of his own situation a special case of the universal connection between desire and loss. The undervaluation of the exile poetry has been recent and transient: the image of the exiled poet was of constant fascination to the Middle Ages (see Jeremy Dimmick, chapter 16), and Ovid's unique exile later came to be universalized as a figure for the situation of the humanist exiled from the ancient world whose presence he craves (see Raphael Lyne, chapter 17), and, more recently still, as a figure for the sense of alienation that the twentieth-century intellectual came to feel as almost his or her birthright.

Finally to history and politics. According to an older account Ovid was an essentially apolitical creature, who began his career by playfully putting on the persona of the love elegist debarred by enslavement to love from the public-spirited pursuits of a young upper-class Roman. After exhausting the possibilities of this game, he turned to Greek mythological subjects in the *Heroides* and *Metamorphoses*. His mind was seriously directed to the realities of politics only by the thunderbolt of his exile in AD 8. In this account little attention was paid to the *Fasti*, the poem on the Roman religious calendar whose rise in critical esteem has been one of the most recent events in Ovidian criticism. The sharp division between text and history implied in this account has been eroded through brands of criticism associated with New Historicism and cultural materialism, which start from the premise that no hard line can be drawn between texts and historical processes. From the very beginning not only can Ovid not escape from the discursive universe out of which emerges the 'reality' of the Augustan order, but he is a very knowing manipulator of the political and cultural discourses of his time. Ovid's god of love is an out-and-out imperialist, swiftly moving at the beginning of the *Amores* (1.2.19–52) to celebrate a triumph, the pageant in which Roman power most ostentatiously manifests itself through shows and fictions. Augustus himself was as adroit an image-maker as the poet. The name 'Augustus' itself is a mask, whose etymological resonances include *auctoritas*, the 'authority' of an *auctor*, a word with many meanings that include 'guarantor', 'person of authority', 'city-founder', 'empire-builder', and also (literary) 'author'.[24] Near the end of the *Metamorphoses* Jupiter prophesies to Venus, distraught at the imminent murder of Julius Caesar, the forthcoming glory of Augustus; at a certain point this divine character within Ovid's text is given words that seem to mimic the words of another text, the *Res gestae* of Augustus himself, the authoritative imperial statement

---

[24] Galinsky (1996) explores the analogy between political and literary *auctoritas*, but with a conviction that not all would share that there is a graspable historical reality outside the texts, whether they be the *Aeneid* or the *Res gestae*. On the polyvalence of *auctor* in Ovid see Barchiesi in this volume, p. 196.

of Augustan *auctoritas*.[25] Ovid draws attention to the fact that works of imperial autobiography, themselves potent tools of policy, are no less textual constructs than is a fiction like the *Metamorphoses*.

But all this leaves room for disagreement as to whether Ovidian texts align themselves with, or highlight faultlines within, the imperial Roman discourse. Alessandro Schiesaro, discussing Ovid's engagement with various kinds of official knowledge and expertise crucial to the emperor's cultural control of Rome (chapter 4), and Carole Newlands writing on the *Fasti* (chapter 12), both emphasize ways in which Ovid's poems foreground the contested nature of all kinds of authority, and so tend to undermine the monolithic edifice of Augustanism. Thomas Habinek (chapter 3) presents a provocative, and currently minority, argument for an Ovid profoundly in tune with the Augustan imperialist agenda. The debates on authority staged and enacted within the Ovidian texts made them and their author of absorbing interest to medieval authors engaged on their own explorations of political, cultural, and religious authority, as Jeremy Dimmick shows in chapter 16.

One of the gains of recent work on Augustan ideology has been the dissolution of any simple dichotomy between 'public' and 'private'. Ovid offers much for the student of personal politics, particularly in the area of gender, discussed by Alison Sharrock (chapter 6). For a male Roman poet Ovid spends an unusual amount of time talking about or giving voice to female experience. Whether his interest is that of the voyeur or of a proto-feminist remains as fiercely disputed as does the question of whether Ovid's early imperial fascination with violence, whether inflicted on the body of woman, man, or beast, reflects the point of view of spectator in the arena or of one whose sympathies lie with the victim (on amphitheatrical violence in Ovid see Hardie, chapter 2).

It might be an exaggeration to claim that we have entered a new *aetas Ovidiana*, the label given by Ludwig Traube to the twelfth and thirteenth centuries. Nevertheless, the current revival of interest in Ovid gives some reason to suppose that the depreciation of his poetry that set in during the eighteenth, and continued through the nineteenth and much of the twentieth centuries, will come to be seen as a blip in the longer history of his central and dominating place within the western classical tradition. Whether the recent flurry of interest in the wider cultural marketplace heralds a lasting restoration of Ovid to the 'lips of the people', to use his own confident estimate of his reception, it is too early to predict.

---

[25] Hardie (1997) 192.

I

CONTEXTS AND HISTORY

I

RICHARD TARRANT

Ovid and ancient literary history

Poets are fascinated by literary history, above all by their own place in it. In that respect Ovid is like his Roman predecessors and contemporaries, only more so: his references to other writers, and to his work in relation to theirs, are more numerous than those of any other Roman poet. To a degree this might be expected given the length of Ovid's poetic career – more than forty years, from roughly the mid-20s BC to the late teens of the first century AD – and the variety of poetic forms he cultivated, forms as diverse as love elegy and tragedy, mock-didactic and epic-scale narrative, epistles of mythological heroines and letters from exile.

But Ovid's literary-historical references do more than track the stages of his literary career, as is arguably the case with Horace, his nearest rival in longevity and generic versatility. By comparison Ovid's outlook is both more wide-ranging and more fluid. Whatever the form with which Ovid is engaged, his eye takes in the full sweep of Greco-Roman poetry, and the story he tells about his work is always being rewritten. If 'literary history' connotes a stable record of writers' careers and of their relations to one another, Ovid is an anti-historian, who delights in reshuffling the data and producing constantly new accounts. For Ovid literary history is a species of rhetoric, a way of showing how a thing can be made to look depending on the perspective adopted or the effect desired.

The exact chronology of Ovid's works is beyond recovery, but his career falls into three main periods.[1] The first (mid- to late 20s BC to AD 2) includes his literary debut, the *Amores*, originally published *seriatim* in five books and later[2] reissued in a unified three-book format, the single letters of the *Heroides*, the lost tragedy *Medea*, and the didactic cycle comprising

---

[1] Two lost works cannot be dated: a Latin version of Aratus' *Phaenomena*, which Ovid never mentions and which he may have dismissed as apprentice work, and the intriguing *Liber in malos poetas* referred to by Quintilian *Inst.* 6.3.96.

[2] One traditionally fixed point is that the revised edition of the *Amores* must precede Book 3 of the *Ars amatoria*, since line 343 of that work speaks of 'three books' of *Amores* (*deue tribus libris titulus quos signat AMORVM*, 'of the three books entitled AMORES'); the crucial word

the *Ars amatoria* (published in two stages, Books 1–2 addressed to men and Book 3 to women), the partially preserved work on cosmetics *Medicamina faciei femineae*, and the *Remedia amoris*. The brief second period (AD 2 or somewhat earlier to AD 8) was devoted to two large-scale compositions, the *Metamorphoses* and the *Fasti*, and ended abruptly with Augustus' sentence of banishment to Tomis on the Black Sea. The years of exile (AD 8–17 or 18) produced five books of *Tristia*, four books of *Epistulae ex Ponto*, the invective poem *Ibis*, and perhaps the double letters of the *Heroides*.[3]

Belatedness and canonicity

Ovid's political belatedness is well known: born in 43, the year following Julius Caesar's assassination, he was still on the threshold of adulthood in 27, when the title 'Augustus' was conferred on the victor of Actium. The literary consequences of Ovid's birthdate are no less significant. The thirty years preceding his first poetic efforts had been a period of creative energy without parallel in Latin literature. In the 50s Catullus and the other so-called *poetae noui* began an intense engagement with the traditional genres of Greek poetry seen through the filter of Hellenistic poetics, with their stress on erudite allusiveness and exquisite artistry.[4] The results set new standards of refinement in Latin poetry, and with the following generation (represented above all by Virgil and Horace), new levels of poetic ambition. The notion of Roman 'classics' that could stand beside the canonical Greek texts became not only thinkable but real, at least in the eyes of the Roman poets themselves. By the mid-20s distinguished Roman exemplars of Theocritean pastoral, Hesiodic didactic, Archilochean iambic, and Attic tragedy had appeared, and attempts on lyric and Homeric epic were in progress, in Horace's *Odes* and Virgil's *Aeneid*. The period was also marked by generic innovation and cross-fertilization, of which the most vigorous product was a subjective 'love elegy' that combined conventional elements from New Comedy and Hellenistic epigram with the emotional seriousness of Catullus; first given definition as a genre by Cornelius Gallus in the 40s, love elegy was soon taken up by two writers of genius, Tibullus and Propertius, each of whom published a first collection of elegies in the early 20s.

tribus, however, is a manuscript variant in a textually uncertain passage, and is rejected by Kenney (1994).

[3] Ovid's authorship of the double letters has been questioned, but see Kenney (1996) 20–6. Doubts have also been raised about the authorship of some of the single letters, most notably the letters of Sappho (*Her.* 15, see n. 78), Deianira (*Her.* 9), and Medea (*Her.* 12, see n. 21). For still more sweeping scepticism see n. 76.

[4] On this process see Clausen (1987) 1–14.

The excitement of these years for a young poet is vividly conveyed in the mini-autobiography of *Tristia* 4.10. Ovid claims to have revered the established poets of his youth as though they were gods,[5] but the ebullience of his early work suggests that he was exhilarated rather than abashed by the presence of so much poetic talent, and confident of earning a place of honour even in such distinguished company. At this time the concept of a poetic 'place of honour' had been given a newly tangible meaning by Augustus' Temple of Apollo Palatinus, with its twin libraries of Greek and Roman literature. When Horace speaks of Maecenas 'inserting' him among the canonical Greek lyric poets,[6] or when Ovid hopes that his name may 'mingle' with those of his predecessors,[7] the physical imagery operates at a literal as well as a metaphorical level.

I've got a little list

Ovid's characteristic literary-historical gesture is the list. Extended lists of authors appear at *Am.* 1.15.9–30, *Ars* 3.321–48, *Rem.* 361–96, 757–66, *Trist.* 2.359–468, 4.10.43–54, *Pont.* 4.16.5–44, and references to clusters of poets at *Am.* 3.9.21–6, 61–6, 3.15.7–8, *Ars* 3.535–8, *Trist.* 5.1.17–19. In addition, the catalogue of passionate women in *Ars* 1.283–340 and its inverted counterpart in *Rem.* 55–68 function as implicit lists of poets who have treated those legends.[8]

These catalogues of poets have been assimilated to other lists in Ovid's poetry (such as rivers in love or hunting dogs), or even cited to prove his alleged lack of self-restraint.[9] They are more revealing than such judgements suggest. Several appear in the last poem of a book, where a Roman poet usually defines his place within a genre or tradition (*Am.* 1.15, 3.15, *Trist.* 4.10, *Pont.* 4.16). But each of Ovid's concluding poems looks beyond a strictly elegiac framework, and each does so in a different way. *Amores* 1.15 surveys all major genres of Greek and Roman poetry, while 3.15 singles out Catullus and Virgil for bringing fame to Verona and Mantua, as Ovid will to Sulmo; *Tristia* 4.10 recalls the poetic Rome of Ovid's youth, *Ex Ponto* 4.16 that of the years before his exile. Ovid's other literary lists are similarly

---

[5] *Trist.* 4.10.41–2 *temporis illius colui fouique poetas, | quotque aderant uates, rebar adesse deos*, 'I cultivated and courted the poets of that time, and I thought that the bards were so many gods on earth'.

[6] *Odes* 1.1.35 *quod si me lyricis uatibus inseres.*

[7] *Ars* 3.339 *forsitan et nostrum nomen miscebitur istis.*

[8] Ovid is also given to listing his own works: *Am.* 2.18 is the most remarkable example, including a partial table of contents of the single *Heroides*, also *Ars* 3.341–8 (*Ars, Amores, Heroides*), *Trist.* 2.547–56 (*Fasti, Medea, Metamorphoses*).

[9] Wilkinson (1955) 73, 'Ovid could rarely refrain from sowing with the sack instead of the hand.'

diverse: the *Ars amatoria* and *Remedia amoris* offer reading lists designed to induce or counteract erotic feelings, and the encyclopedic catalogue of *Tristia* 2 attempts to dilute the scandal of the *Ars* by reviewing all of Greek and Roman poetry *sub specie amoris*.[10]

A closer look at Ovid's earliest canon of poets, in *Amores* 1.15, illustrates the issues raised by these lists. To support the claim that poetry confers lasting fame, Ovid adduces a roll-call of Greek and Roman writers: Homer and Hesiod, Callimachus, Sophocles, Aratus, and Menander on the Greek side, and in Latin Ennius, Accius, Varro of Atax, Lucretius, Virgil, Tibullus, and Gallus. Only Tibullus and Gallus are exponents of love elegy, the genre of the *Amores* itself. The poem thus reflects the breadth of Ovid's poetic horizon rather than his claims for this particular collection.

The closest parallel in previous Latin poetry is the last elegy of Propertius' second book (2.34), a wide-ranging poem that refers to eminent Greek poets in various genres (Homer, Aeschylus, Antimachus, Callimachus and Philetas), pays tribute to Virgil and heralds the completion of the *Aeneid*, and concludes with a Roman poetic genealogy for love elegy (Varro of Atax, Catullus, Calvus, and Gallus), a precursor of the succession of Gallus, Tibullus, Propertius, and Ovid that Ovid himself would make canonical.[11] *Amores* 1.15 integrates the Greek and Roman dimensions of Propertius' poem while introducing a radically different perspective. Propertius evaluates all non-elegiac writers from the vantage point of the love poet, for whom genres such as epic and tragedy represent the poetic 'other'. For Ovid this distinction does not exist, probably because even in the *Amores* he does not fully identify himself as a love poet.

The panoramic scope and triumphal tone of *Amores* 1.15 are also re-markable given the poem's subordinate position. By contrast, 3.15, which concludes the whole collection, is a much slighter poem focusing on Ovid's abandonment of love elegy in favour of tragedy, a move foreshadowed in 2.18 and in the opening poem of Book 3. The choice of tragedy, rather than the usual epic, as the higher form that lures Ovid away from love elegy must be related to the fact that Ovid did compose a tragedy, a *Medea*.[12] The date of the play is not known, but it is plausible that it was written between the appearance of the books of *Amores* in their original form and their republication; if so, the progression toward tragedy seen in the extant *Amores* could be a product of Ovid's revision, designed to update the collection by making it 'predict' the turn taken by Ovid's career in the intervening years. The

---

[10] As nicely put by Conte (1994b) 357.

[11] *Ars* 3.535–8, *Rem.* 763–6, *Trist.* 4.10.53–4, 5.1.17–18, Quintilian *Inst.* 10.1.93.

[12] The scepticism of Holzberg (1997b) 15–18 on this point is stimulating but not in my view persuasive.

references in *Amores* 2.18 to the *Heroides* and, perhaps, the *Ars amatoria*[13] would also be part of this process. To speculate further, if 1.15 originally concluded the fifth book of *Amores* by celebrating Ovid's achievement as a love elegist, its less prominent place in the three-book revision reflects the subsequent growth of Ovid's poetic ambitions.

Amores 1.15 thus exemplifies both inclusiveness and fluidity – useful co-ordinates for looking more generally at Ovid's literary-historical outlook.

In omnes ambitiosus

An inclusive approach to poetic composition informs Ovid's treatment of many literary-historical issues, of which the following will be singled out here: the range of traditional poetic forms, the potential of individual genres, and the Greco-Roman literary tradition as a whole.

The *Amores* opens with a version of the Callimachean primal scene, the poet embarking on an epic who is deflected into a less exalted genre by divine intervention. Ovid gives the motif two twists. The god is Amor rather than Apollo, which lightens the mood and foreshadows the erotic nature of the poetry Ovid will be forced to write. There is also no hint that Ovid is unsuited to epic or that epic is an inappropriate choice of genre; in turning Ovid's second hexameter into an elegiac pentameter Amor seems to be playing a mischievous joke rather than directing Ovid to his proper poetic vocation.

The same message is conveyed by Ovid's distinctive impersonation of the lover-poet. In Propertius and Tibullus the lover's professed fidelity to the mistress mirrors the poet's adherence to elegy. Ovid's vaunted susceptibility to other women is the erotic analogue to his generic ambitions; cf., e.g., *Am.* 2.4.47–8 *denique quas tota quisquam probat Vrbe puellas,* | *noster in has omnes ambitiosus amor.* ('there's beauty in Rome to please all tastes, | and mine are all-embracing.')[14] In *Amores* 1.1.14 *ambitiosus* is a reproach addressed by Ovid to Amor, who refuses to remain within his proper sphere; by later applying the word to himself Ovid suggests that he shares Amor's disregard for normal limits.

Sheer generic ambition is a possible motive (indeed perhaps the most credible one) for Ovid's venture into tragedy, the most confining of literary forms and the one most remote from his accustomed subject and mood. The *Medea* was apparently Ovid's only tragedy; one was enough to make

---

[13] The meaning of *artes ... amoris* in line 19 is disputed; for even-handed discussion see McKeown (1998) 385–6.

[14] Translation from Lee (1968); 'all-embracing' for *ambitiosus* also in Humphries (1957).

the point. The work elicited even Quintilian's grudging admiration,[15] and it and Varius' *Thyestes* were conventionally regarded as the pre-eminent specimens of Roman tragedy.[16] Ovid often dealt with tragic plots and characters in his later work, but usually in ways that transmuted them into a distinctly non-tragic form and ethos.

It was customary, especially after Virgil, for a Roman poet to aspire to a *magnum opus*. In hindsight Ovid could lay claim to three, each generically distinct – *Fasti, Medea, Metamorphoses*.[17] Other writers, such as Virgil's friend Varius, had written both epic and tragedy, but this constellation of genres was unprecedented, and does not include the other forms of elegy that had established Ovid's reputation.[18]

Each of Ovid's works adopts a comprehensive approach to its subject, and several enlarge more limited treatments of their themes by other writers. The *Amores* depicts the full range of a lover's experience, from infatuation through attempts at disengagement to renunciation – a trajectory more orderly than anything in Propertius or Tibullus, and perhaps made more obviously so in the revised edition. The germ of the *Heroides* is present in an elegy of Propertius (4.3), a letter written by a Roman wife to her husband, a soldier on campaign. Ovid made the letter writers famous women of mythology and turned a single specimen into a multi-faceted collection.[19] The *Ars amatoria* elaborates motifs of erotic instruction found in single elegies of Propertius and Tibullus into an insanely systematic manual, then expands itself by a dialectic of opposition: advice to men in *Ars* 1–2 generates its counterpart addressed to women (*Ars* 3), and the entire *Ars* calls forth its antidote in the *Remedia amoris*. The *Fasti* and the *Metamorphoses* each projects its theme onto an all-inclusive temporal framework, the Roman sacred calendar and the history of the world. Each also represents a quantum leap in scale compared to earlier treatments, such as the various Hellenistic collections of metamorphosis-stories or the elegies of Propertius' fourth book dealing with Roman rituals. The desire to mine the full potential of a theme also marks the poetry of exile: the eventual total of nine books of *Tristia* and *Epistulae ex Ponto* dwarfs the elegiac output of Propertius and Tibullus, and in sheer volume creates an exilic counterpart to Ovid's amatory corpus.

Inclusiveness of this kind is Ovid's particular form of novelty: innovation for him consisted less in free invention than in seeing richer possibilities in

---

[15] *Inst.* 10.1.98.   [16] Tac. *Dial.* 12.6.   [17] *Trist.* 2.547–62.

[18] Ennius' generic versatility may have been even greater than Ovid's, but by Ovid's time Ennius was known primarily as the epic poet of the *Annales* and secondarily as a writer of tragedy.

[19] Jacobson (1974) 319–48 usefully surveys the literary background to the *Heroides*, but underestimates the importance of Propertius 4.3.

existing material. In fact Ovid applies the rhetoric of invention to his poetry only once, about the *Heroides* (*Ars* 3.346 *ignotum hoc aliis ille nouauit opus* 'this kind of poem, unknown to others, he pioneered'), and even here his originality lay in relocation and elaboration rather than in creation *ex nihilo*.[20]

Ovid has often been seen as occupying a transitional place in Roman literary history, between a 'Golden' and a 'Silver' Age (concepts critically examined by Philip Hardie in the following chapter). This depiction in part arises from another aspect of Ovid's inclusiveness: he is the first and the last Roman poet to combine a broad knowledge of Greek literature with an intimate awareness of the new Latin 'classics'. For later writers such as Seneca and Lucan, Roman and specifically Augustan predecessors – notably Ovid himself – largely replace the Greeks as the models for emulation.

This all-encompassing perspective is visible as early as the *Heroides*: the collection begins with figures from Homer (Penelope (1), Briseis (3)) but also includes well-known characters of Greek tragedy (Phaedra (4), Hypsipyle (6), perhaps Medea (12)),[21] Hellenistic poetry (Phyllis (2)), and the most memorable heroines of Latin poetry to date, Catullus' Ariadne (10) and Virgil's Dido (7). The *Ars amatoria* presents a more complex interplay of genres. Its basic strategy draws the serious associations of didactic poetry into a clash with the situations of erotic elegy, evoking humour at the expense of both. But Homeric epic is also implicated through constant use of the Troy story as a source for erotic example, and Ovid's catalogues of exemplary figures (*Ars* 1.283–340 and *Rem.* 55–68) extend his frame of reference to tragedy, Hellenistic poetry, and its Latin successors, as in Ovid's hilarious treatment (*Ars* 1.289–326) of the Pasiphae of Virgil's sixth *Eclogue*.

The *Metamorphoses* most clearly embodies Ovid's global outlook, subsuming all major forms of Greek and Latin literature into a unique and transforming synthesis. This range is advertised in the first book, which also shows that the incorporation of earlier literature will offer a counterpoint to the illusion of chronological progress. The poem opens with a Hesiodic theme (creation and the four ages), but defers its closest Homeric encounters to Books 12 and 13, while some of the most modern (i.e. neoteric and elegiac) episodes in their poetic colouring, such as the stories of Apollo and Daphne and Jupiter and Io, are placed immediately after the opening cosmological sequence. In addition, hardly any episode maintains a one-to-one relation

---

[20] Ovid more often highlights internal novelty, signalling a venture that is new or surprising for him, as at the beginning of the *Metamorphoses* (1.1–2) and *Fasti* (2.3–8).

[21] Against Ovid's authorship of *Heroides* 12, Knox (1986a); in favour, Hinds (1993) and Bessone (1997).

with a single poetic form; most fuse elements from several into a novel amalgam. For example, in recounting Polyphemus' courtship of Galatea Ovid engages in dialogue with Theocritean and Virgilian pastoral, love elegy, and Homeric and Virgilian epic.[22]

Ovid's inclusive outlook marks him as a quintessentially Augustan figure. His creative synthesis of diverse traditions has analogies in Augustan architecture, historiography, and political ideology.[23] More piquant are the parallels between Ovid's ambitions and those of Augustus himself. Ovid aspired to hold all available poetic distinctions just as the *princeps* prided himself on adding one civil, military, or religious office after another to his array of titles. Ovid's fondness for lists as a means of documenting his achievements is another trait he shares with the author of the *Res Gestae*.

The same, only different: revising and rewriting

To prove the value of *facundia* (fluency) in attracting women, the *praeceptor* of the *Ars* cites the example of Ulysses, who responded to Calypso's unending desire to hear the story of Troy by relating the same events in everchanging form (*Ars* 2.128 *ille referre aliter saepe solebat idem*). Alison Sharrock remarks that 'Ovid's comment on Ulysses' rhetorical skills could almost be a programmatic statement of his own',[24] and it is indeed telling that Ovid links Ulysses' traditional mental agility to his skill as a narrator, and locates the narrator's challenge in giving new shape to familiar material.[25]

Rewriting permeates Ovid's poetry and supplies the controlling dynamic for several of his works. Many individual poems of the *Amores* contain ironizing rewritings of elegies of Propertius and Tibullus, and the originality of the collection as a whole consists in the novel slant it gives to well-worn themes.[26] The letters of the *Heroides* offer elegiac takes on canonical, usually non-elegiac, stories, now told from the heroine's perspective. In transforming Propertius 4.3 into the *Heroides*, Ovid characteristically turned pure fiction into retelling: Propertius' Arethusa and Lycotas have no history outside that poem, but each of Ovid's heroines does, and that history is an essential element of her Ovidian *persona*.[27]

---

[22] Farrell (1992).   [23] Galinsky (1999) 107–110.
[24] Sharrock (1994a) 2; Galinsky (1975) 4–5 applied the line to Ovid's procedure in the *Metamorphoses*.
[25] Homer's Odysseus had no fondness for repeating a tale once told, see *Od.* 12.452–3, cited by Sharrock (1987) 407. Sharrock also notes (411) that the scene in the *Ars* reworks material from the *Heroides* (1.31–6), thus exemplifying the Ulyssean technique it describes.
[26] See Morgan (1977), O'Neill (1999), most fully Boyd (1997).
[27] Barchiesi (1993), Hinds (1993); see below, p. 25, on the Dido of *Heroides* 7.

The concept of rewriting is fundamental to the *Metamorphoses*, where every story retells an earlier version or versions. Ovid follows no single pattern in these reworkings. Traditional epic material is in general subverted, usually by being subordinated to erotic motifs, as in Ovid's account of the Calydonian Boar Hunt.[28] But an inverse process of aggrandizing is also present, e.g., where Hellenistic authors had deflated Homeric or Hesiodic material, as with Callimachus' Erysicthon or Theocritus' Cyclops. Ovid's liberal use of internal narrators offers a more subtle means of reshaping earlier narratives, as familiar myths are filtered through the idiosyncratic or self-interested perspective of the storyteller in the poem. So, for example, Calliope's song of the Rape of Proserpina in the singing contest of Book 5 is coloured throughout by its dual function as a *Preislied* and a vindication of the gods.[29]

Three authors have a special place as objects of Ovid's revisionary efforts: Callimachus, Virgil, and himself.

Ingenio non ualet, arte ualet

Propertius had aspired to be the *Romanus Callimachus* (4.1.64). Ovid has a stronger claim to the title, but he would have found it too narrow, and regarded its explicit statement as lacking in sophistication. Ovid's Callimacheanism goes beyond specific imitations to a basic communality of temperament. Ovid shares Callimachus' erudite allusiveness, his fondness for oblique and ironic statement, his innovative treatment of myth, his stylistic versatility, and his acute sensitivity to his status as a poet – though the *persona* Ovid projects is more genial and, at least before his exile, less easily nettled by adverse criticism. Ovid's engagement with Callimachus spans his entire career, from the opening scene of the *Amores* to that bizarre product of exile, the curse-poem *Ibis*, Ovid's most overtly Callimachean (and least-read) work.[30] Even the 'facts' of Ovid's life can have a Callimachean origin: Ovid's statement that he began writing poetry 'when my beard had been cut once or twice' (*Trist.* 4.10.58) echoes a similar self-description in Callimachus.[31]

Callimachus' prominent position in Ovid's literary universe is evident from the canon of *Amores* 1.15, where he appears out of chronological order immediately after Homer and Hesiod. But the following descriptive tag – 'not strong in inspiration, he is strong in technical skill' – shows that Ovid's admiration ended far this side of idolatry. This discriminating view is partly

---

[28] Horsfall (1979).
[29] The episode is also a prime specimen of Ovid's self-rewriting; see below, p. 29.
[30] The re-evaluation by Williams (1996) may help remedy this long-standing neglect.
[31] McKeown (1987) 74.

the product of chronology. Callimachus' poetics had been bracingly novel for Catullus and his contemporaries, but by the 20s these writers were gone from the scene, along with the resident Greeks such as Parthenius who had initiated them in Alexandrian poetic ways. Callimachean literary values were now conventional, and Ovid's way of maintaining a Callimachean lightness of spirit is to treat them with irony. Consequently Ovid's references to Callimachean catchwords are either offhand[32] or wittily skewed. Callimachus praised the 'slender Muse'; Ovid accordingly shrinks the *Amores* from five to three books and promises that the pain of reading them will now at least be lightened (*leuior*).[33] The hackneyed motif of the poet's divine inspiration is toyed with in the *Amores* and jettisoned in the *Ars*, where the *praeceptor* breezily disavows any guidance from Apollo or the Muses (1.25–30). The claim to be guided by *usus*, experience, might seem provocatively anti-Callimachean but is in fact a ruse, since much of the wisdom dispensed by the *praeceptor* has been gathered from poetry, and even parts of his own erotic history turn out to be reminiscences of the *Amores*.[34]

At a more fundamental level, Ovid's understanding of Callimacheanism was shaped by developments of the previous generation. For Catullus (as apparently for the young Virgil) adherence to Callimachean ideals precluded poetry in larger forms, but the *Aeneid* had shown that a Callimachean poet could write at epic length.[35] The *Metamorphoses* also responds to this challenge, but reconciles the competing claims in an entirely different way, by weaving hundreds of discrete episodes into a thematically and chronologically ordered whole. Ovid's proem implies that the work will be both *perpetuum* ('continuous, unbroken') and *deductum* ('fine-spun'), thereby defining its distinctive quality in terms of Callimachean poetics and their Roman reception.[36]

Ovid's use of Callimachus is in fact most sustained in his longest poems. The *Metamorphoses* and *Fasti* draw on the narrative technique of Callimachus' longer poems, the *Aitia* and the *Hecale*, in ways that suit their differing structures: in the *Fasti* the poet adopts the *persona* of a researcher questioning informants, as Callimachus had conversed with the Muses in

---

[32] For example, *Ars* 2.285 *uigilatum carmen*, evoking the sleeplessness expected of the diligent poet.

[33] *Epigr.* 4 *leuior demptis poena duobus erit*; see McKeown (1989) 2.

[34] See n. 61. Clauss (1989) finds a more complex instance of such irony in an episode of *Metamorphoses* 6 in which the goddess Latona attempts to drink from a pool and is thwarted by a crowd of farmers. The passage teasingly evokes the imagery of water as a symbol of poetic inspiration but refuses to resolve along Callimachean lines.

[35] An aspect of the *Aeneid* highlighted by Clausen (1987).

[36] *Met.* 1.4 *ad mea* <u>*perpetuum*</u> <u>*deducite*</u> *tempora carmen*, 'spin a continuous song down to my own times'. On the Callimachean resonances of the proem see Kenney (1976), Heyworth (1994) 72–6, Wheeler (1999) 8–30.

the *Aitia*,[37] while some of the most intricately nested sections of narrative in the *Metamorphoses* develop Callimachus' procedure in the *Hecale*.[38]

In one respect Ovid is strikingly at odds with both Callimachus and his previous Roman followers: he shows no interest in restricting his work to the attention of a cultivated few. Instead, from the outset Ovid sought the favour of a large public. The frame poems of the *Amores* mention no individual addressee, and in *Amores* 2.1 he envisages his poems being read by lovers of both sexes. In the *Ars*, Ovid has the *praeceptor* address himself to the entire *populus*; similarly, the epilogue to the *Metamorphoses* predicts that Ovid will be ever 'on the lips of the people' (15.878 *ore legar populi*). Here too Ovid is heir to an evolution within Roman Callimacheanism: Roman poets first contracted the scope of their intended readership and then, with the *Aeneid* and Horace's *Odes*, expanded it outward to a potentially national audience.[39] Ovid adopts this post-Virgilian outlook – which might also be called the Augustan outlook in light of Augustus' projection of political-ideological messages to the *populus Romanus* – but applies it to conspicu-ously non-Augustan ends. Ovid's populist view of his audience takes on a new edge in his exile poetry, where he hopes for favour from 'the hands of commoners' (*plebeiae … manus*, *Trist.* 3.1.82) to offset his official disgrace and exclusion.[40]

Vergilium uidi tantum

'Virgil I only saw.' Ovid's terse disclaimer of personal acquaintance in *Trist.* 4.10.51 belies his lifelong fascination with Virgil's poetry and his even greater fascination with Virgil's place in Roman literary history. Ovid clearly admired Virgil's work; 'il lungo studio e 'l grande amore' is as true of him as it is of Dante. But Virgil's standing also spurred Ovid to an intense form of *aemulatio*, and this rivalry will be the focus of attention here.

In hindsight Virgil's generic ascent from the *Eclogues* through the *Georgics* to the *Aeneid* would seem natural, a sort of literary *cursus honorum*, but to contemporaries like Horace, and to younger poets such as Propertius, the evolution was unpredictable and surprising.[41] By contrast, at the start of his career Ovid could contemplate Virgil's *oeuvre* as a whole – it is no accident that the first word of the *Amores* is *arma* – and could measure his progress against what Virgil had achieved.

Ovid's pre-exilic career can be interpreted as an attempt both to replicate and to surpass Virgil's. Ovid may at first have channelled his own generic

---

[37] Fantham (1998) 11–18. [38] See Keith (1992a) on *Met.* 2.531–835.
[39] Citroni (1995) 31–56 and 207–69.
[40] Videau-Delibes (1991) 456–9, Citroni (1995) 440–2. [41] See Thomas (1985).

ascent within an elegiac framework – from *Amores* to *Heroides* to *Ars* and *Remedia*[42] – but the inclusion of didactic surely points to the *Georgics*, and from there the further step to epic would appear natural. When that step was taken is not clear. In the *Remedia* Ovid claims to have done as much for elegy as Virgil had for epic (395–6), and speaks of the further growth of his reputation in elegiac terms;[43] but by then he was almost certainly contemplating what would become the *Metamorphoses*, and may even have begun drafting the poem. Ovid may have stressed his involvement with elegy to heighten the impact of his coming transformation into a writer of epic; also, once the *Metamorphoses* had given Ovid equal standing with Virgil in epic, his contributions to elegy would make him the more widely accomplished of the two. Ovid clearly meant the *Metamorphoses* to be his counterpart to the *Aeneid*, but he could not have foreseen that Augustus would abet his plan by banishing him, allowing Ovid the operatic gesture of burning his unrevised *magnum opus*.

Ovid specifically responds to Virgil's canonical status with a variety of self-assertive manoeuvres. One of these is shameless appropriation of Virgil's language. Virgil was said to have remarked that it is easier to steal Hercules' club than a line of Homer.[44] Ovid stages a series of daring daylight robberies, quoting signature lines of the *Aeneid* in shockingly discordant contexts. The Sibyl's warning to Aeneas about returning from the Underworld, *hoc opus, hic labor est* (*Aen.* 6.129), becomes a statement from the *praeceptor* of the difficulty of sleeping with a woman without giving her presents first (*Ars* 1.453). At least the Sibyl's words are allowed to retain their original meaning; when Ovid speaks of Virgil bringing Aeneas to Dido's bed (*Trist.* 2.534 *contulit in Tyrios arma uirumque toros*), he turns the opening words of the *Aeneid* into an obscene hendiadys.[45] The element of pure cheek in such transgressive quotations is undeniable, but they also show that Virgilian epic language can be redirected to Ovidian erotic ends and that all poetic language is open to reuse by a sufficiently strong reader/writer.[46]

Quotation of a more subtle sort belongs to the Hellenistic cult of learnedness. *Metamorphoses* 13.258 *Alcandrum Haliumque Noemonaque Prytanimque* is identical with *Aeneid* 9.767, which itself translates *Iliad*

---

[42] See Harrison below, pp. 80–4.

[43] Especially 390 *maius erit* [sc. *nostrum nomen*], *tantum, quo pede coepit, eat*, '[my name] will be greater, if only its feet continue on the path on which it began', with the common play on *pes* (= 'metre').

[44] *Vit. Donat.* 46, Macrob. *Sat.* 5.23.16.

[45] *Arma uirumque* ('arms and a man') = *uirum armatum* ('an armed (i.e., erect) man'); for *arma* in a sexual sense Adams (1982) 19–22, 224.

[46] On Ovid's 'consistent and calculated' adaptation of Virgil's language see Kenney (1973), especially 118–28.

5.678. Homer's line enumerates Lycians killed by Odysseus, transformed by Virgil into victims of Turnus; in Ovid the speaker is Ulysses, who is thus allowed to reclaim his Homeric triumphs.[47] Callimachean erudition and intertextual play are here applied to the Latin Homer.

In defending the *Ars amatoria* to Augustus, Ovid mischievously claimed that no part of the *Aeneid* was as widely read as the story of Dido and Aeneas' 'illicit affair'.[48] Certainly no other book of the *Aeneid* received as much attention from Ovid, and the variety of his responses encapsulates his treatment of Virgilian material.

Heroides 7 (Dido to Aeneas), a pre-suicide letter of some 200 lines, constitutes one of the earliest surviving reactions to the *Aeneid*, and one of the boldest. Ovid revises both Dido's character, making her more loving even at the end, but also more scathing about Aeneas, and also her language, transposing her Virgilian rhetoric into a relentlessly epigrammatic mode, as in her epitaph, *Praebuit Aeneas et causam mortis et ensem*, 'Aeneas gave both cause and means of death' (197). The resulting loss of nuance is deliberate, since from the standpoint adopted by Ovid complexity is just a way of excusing Aeneas.

Ovid's Dido may not have read the *Aeneid*, but she displays a clarity about herself that results from her curious position, at once pre-Virgilian (in the fictive moment of her writing) and post-Virgilian (in the experience of Ovid's readers).[49] Recalling Aeneas' narrative of his past, she wryly observes that he had already shown his faithlessness by abandoning Creusa at Troy (83–5). When she reflects on her encounter with Aeneas in the cave, Ovid gives her an awareness of the event's meaning that in Virgil is reserved to the narrator (93–6, cf. *Aen.* 4.169–72), and even allows her to 'correct' the facts as related in the *Aeneid*, if only at the rhetorical level ('I thought it was the nymphs howling' – as Virgil says it was – 'rather the Eumenides were giving the signal for my doom'). Virgil's Dido lamented that she had no 'little Aeneas' to console her for the loss of her lover (*Aen.* 4.327–30); Ovid, ever the realist, knew that certainty on that score was not possible, and has his Dido warn Aeneas that her death could doom his unborn child (133–8). At least once, though, Ovid plays on his character's ignorance of Virgil to pathetic effect, when she predicts that Aeneas will yield 'unless you are more unbending than the oak-trees' (52); a famous simile (*Aen.* 4.441–9) comparing Aeneas to an oak that is battered but stays firm would have shown her the futility of that hope.

---

[47] Hardie (1994) on *Aen.* 9.767, Smith (1997) 47–9.
[48] *Trist.* 2.536 *non legitimo foedere iunctus amor.* Ovid affects a censorious tone that contrasts sharply with his slant in *Heroides* 7 and *Metamorphoses* 14, where Aeneas is depicted as an absconding husband.
[49] Desmond (1993).

In *Metamorphoses* 14, Dido's story is dispatched in a single loaded sentence (78–81): *excipit Aenean illic animoque domoque | non bene discidium Phrygii latura mariti | Sidonis, inque pyra sacri sub imagine facta | incubuit ferro deceptaque decipit omnes.* ('There the Sidonian queen welcomed Aeneas in heart and home, destined ill to bear the parting from her Phrygian husband: on a pyre, built under pretence of holy rites, she fell upon his sword and, herself deceived, deceived all.')[50] Radically abbreviating a story can show deference to an earlier version by implying that it has left nothing more to be said: examples are Medea's murder of her children (*Met.* 7.394–7) and Ariadne's abandonment by Theseus and rescue by Bacchus (*Met.* 8.174–9), which nod respectfully to Euripides and Catullus, and also to Ovid himself (*Medea* and *Heroides* 10). Cumulatively, however, Ovid's reduction of this and other major episodes from the *Aeneid* is hardly respectful, since it implies a set of values in which the public concerns of the *Aeneid* merit only passing mention.

Ovid also asserts his control over Virgil's most famous creation by redistributing language associated with Dido to other parts of his poem. Ovid's Medea fantasizes about Jason as her husband (*coniunx*, *Met.* 7.68), then rebukes herself for cloaking her offence (*culpa*) in fair-seeming terms (*speciosa nomina*); she seems to have learned from Dido's whitewashing of *culpa* as *coniugium* (*Aen.* 4.172) and can catch herself in the same misuse of language.[51] The dying Procris echoes Dido's appeal to Aeneas (*Aen.* 4.314–19) in pleading with her husband Cephalus not to bring his (in fact nonexistent) mistress into their home (*Met.* 7.852–6). Most surprisingly of all, in a transformation so thorough that it has gone unnoticed by commentators, Dido's agonizing death-throes (*Aen.* 4.688–92) are reimagined as Sleep's droll efforts to wake himself up (*Met.* 11.618–21).[52]

Finally, we must take note of Ovid's influence on Virgil, or in less paradoxical terms on our reading of Virgil.[53] Part of the effect of Ovidian rewriting is to alter our response to the work being rewritten. Stephen Hinds has shown how Ovid's handling of the Aeneas legend in the *Metamorphoses* makes us more aware of stories of metamorphosis present in the *Aeneid* but there kept in the background.[54] For me at least, Ovid's distanced account in *Metamorphoses* 10 of Orpheus' descent to the Underworld and his almost

---

[50] Translation from Hinds (1998) 105.

[51] Readers thus alerted to the Dido parallel may notice the much subtler reworking of the line endings of *Aen.* 4.54–6 (*amore* – *pudorem* – *aras*) in *Met.* 7.72–4 (*pudorque* – *Cupido* – *aras*); Smith (1997) 101–2.

[52] Dido unexpectedly appears outside the *Metamorphoses* as well: her wish to hear the story of Aeneas' travails again and again (*Aen.* 4.77–9) lies behind Calypso's repeated requests to Ulysses (*Ars* 2.127), on which see above, p. 20. Both passages contain a doubled *iterum*, which in Ovid becomes a way of marking repetition of a motif from an earlier text.

[53] On this aspect of intertextuality see Fowler (2000) 130.

[54] Hinds (1998) 104–22.

matter-of-fact description of the loss of Eurydice can make the emotively charged narrative in the *Georgics* seem overwrought and melodramatic. One might also ask whether by defining himself in opposition to Virgil in matters relating to Augustus Ovid did not help to create the image of Virgil the pure 'Augustan' that much recent criticism has been at pains to complicate.

Self-refashioning

> The friends who have it I do wrong
> When ever I remake a song
> Should know what issue is at stake:
> It is myself that I remake.
>
> (Yeats)

Even in his own lifetime Ovid was criticized for not knowing when to leave well enough alone.[55] This judgement targets the alleged overabundance of Ovid's style, but it can also draw attention to his extraordinary capacity for revising his work. Self-revision is not rare among Greek and Latin poets – Callimachus and Virgil are apposite examples[56] – but Ovid is unusual in the degree and variety of modes with which he pursued it. Ovid acts as his own strong reader, constantly seeing new possibilities in apparently finished work. Such an interest in revising suits a poet who repeatedly dramatized the transformation of his *persona*: elegist into tragedian, lover-poet into *praeceptor amoris*, writer of light elegy into writer of epic and aetiological poetry, and, finally, all of the above into the poet of exile.[57]

Several of Ovid's works are extant in a revised or expanded form: most clearly the *Amores* and the *Fasti,* probably the *Heroides,* possibly the *Ars amatoria.*[58] In his exile poetry Ovid describes the *Metamorphoses* as both unfinished and unrevised, even though the transmitted text, unlike that of the *Aeneid*, gives no clear sign of incompleteness or lack of polish. Ovid may have spoken in this way to heighten the parallel with Virgil, but another factor may have been his reluctance to see any of his works as 'closed'.

Some of this revision is the result of altered circumstances, such as the changes made in the *Fasti* to update the poem after the death of Augustus.[59] In other cases the character of the work itself prompted its extension. Thus the single *Heroides* led naturally to the double letters, and indeed a circumstantial argument for regarding the double letters as genuine is that the step

---

[55] Sen. *Contr.* 9.5.17 (quoting Mamercus Aemilius Scaurus) *nescit quod bene cessit relinquere.*
[56] Zetzel (1983) 101, 105 n. 34.   [57] Holzberg (1997b) 5.
[58] Syme (1978) 13–20 proposed (not to my mind convincingly) a date of 9–6 BC for a first edition of *Ars* 1–2.
[59] Fantham (1998) 1–4, also Feeney (1992) 15–19 on other possible post-exilic revisions.

from single to double letters is such a characteristic step for Ovid to have taken. In a similar way the elaboration of erotic advice from *Ars* 1–2 to *Ars* 3 and then to the *Remedia amoris* reflects the habit of arguing both sides of a case that Ovid absorbed from his training in declamatory rhetoric. Only with the *Amores* does dissatisfaction with the first form of the work seem to have been a cause for revision, and even here other motives may have been more compelling.

At a more specific level, Ovid often recasts his writing by incorporating it into a subsequent work. Recycling of this kind is not the result of flagging inspiration: part of its attraction surely lay in giving existing material a new meaning by placing it in a new context. So, for example, incidents presented in the *Amores* as the lover-poet's own experience become in the *Ars amatoria* the material for lessons in seduction.[60] In one case the *praeceptor* claims to remember (*memini, Ars* 2.169) tearing his mistress' hair, as his *Amores* self had done; the use of memory as a trope for literary allusion[61] links two stages in Ovid's evolving *persona*. The Ovid of the *Amores* is recalled in a more complex way in *Metamorphoses* 1.454–65, when Apollo mocks Amor's bowmanship and is punished by being made to fall in love with Daphne. By re-enacting his own earlier transformation by Amor from aspiring epic poet to elegist, Ovid implies that his actual epic will bear an elegiac and erotic rather than a martial stamp.[62]

More extensive self-reworking can be seen in episodes of the *Metamorphoses* (Daedalus and Icarus, Cephalus and Procris) that retell myths narrated in the *Ars Amatoria*. Even where the two versions are close in wording, the later account introduces a shift of focus and/or function. In the *Ars* Minos' failure to thwart Daedalus' winged escape ironically parallels the task of the *praeceptor*,[63] while in *Metamorphoses* 8 Ovid highlights the dynamic of father and son to link the story to other destructive parent-child relationships narrated in that book (Scylla–Nisus, Althaea–Meleager, Erysicthon–daughter).[64] The *Amores* offers the most thoroughgoing instance of reuse of earlier work. The details are necessarily speculative, since the nature and degree of revision will never be known, but it seems beyond doubt that the three-book collection in some way tells a different story from

---

[60] *Am.* 1.4 and *Ars* 565–606, *Am.* 1.7 and *Ars* 2.167–76, *Am.* 3.2 and *Ars* 1.135–62. The *Ars* reworkings are often criticized as inferior, but see Dalzell (1996) 140–44.

[61] See Miller (1993), also Conte (1986) 57–63 on Ovid's Ariadne remembering her Catullan self.

[62] Nicoll (1980).

[63] *Ars* 2.98–9 *non potuit Minos hominis compescere pennas,* | *ipse deum uolucrem detinuisse paro,* 'Minos could not restrain the wings of a man; | I try to hold down the winged god'; cf. Ahern (1989).

[64] The accounts can be distinguished in other ways; see the full discussion in Sharrock (1994a) 87–195.

the original five books, and highly likely that many individual poems, while remaining verbally unchanged, were given a new function in the masterplot by being relocated.[65]

The revision of the *Amores* is atypical in that it condenses and suppresses the earlier form of the work. Elsewhere Ovid proceeds by supplementation: the *Remedia* does not cancel the *Ars*, but sets up an ironic counterpoint to it, in which each work affects how the other is read. So also with the most complex case of intra-Ovidian revision, the reciprocal rewriting of the Rape of Proserpina effected by the different accounts in *Metamorphoses* 5 and *Fasti* 4: though each version is intelligible in isolation, when read against each other (as they were probably written), each makes the emphases and silences of the other more meaningful.[66]

For Ovid all writing entails rewriting; all reading, rereading. In contemporary critical parlance, Ovid recognized the inherently intertextual element of literary meaning.[67] The prominence of rewriting/rereading in Ovid's work also creates another dimension of multiple meaning, since connections between a text and its 'source' texts will be interpreted differently by individual readers. Ovid's poetry has proven so hospitable to postmodernist forms of criticism because Ovid himself was so sensitive to the ambiguities and slippages inherent in all communication between poet and reader.

The view from Tomis

Ovid's exile poetry was long regretted as a dreary epilogue to a brilliant career. Recent criticism has shown how – especially at the outset – Ovid embraced exile as a fresh poetic subject to which he applied all his gifts of invention. The notion that Ovid's years in Tomis are entirely a fiction of the poet, though it cannot be right, itself reveals how thoroughly Ovid transformed the facts of his situation into a new poetic *persona*.[68]

In this last phase all of Ovid's literary-historical preoccupations take on new definition. In particular, exile reactivates the process of self-revision, as Ovid recasts his whole earlier career from this new perspective. The refocusing is signalled by having the first collection of exile poems (*Tristia* 1)

---

[65] See above, pp. 16–17.
[66] The classic study by Heinze (1919) in terms of 'epic' and 'elegiac' narrative modes was given a more nuanced rereading by Hinds (1987).
[67] See Conte (1986) 29, Fowler (2000) ch. 5.
[68] For the idea see Fitton Brown (1985) and the comments of Williams (1994) 3–8. The many references to a vindictive Augustus would have been fatally offensive if Ovid were still in Rome.

meet its 'brothers' in Ovid's library back in Rome.[69] It proceeds with minor-key rewritings of earlier programmatic statements. For example, the *Ars amatoria* opens with an expansive address to the Roman people (*si quis in hoc artem populo non nouit amandi* 'if anyone in this populace does not know the art of loving'), which reappears at the start of the *Tristia* in a tentative and pathetic form (1.1.17–18 *si quis, ut in populo, nostri non immemor illic, si quis, qui, quid agam, forte requirat, erit* 'if anyone there, as can happen in a large populace, has not forgotten me, if anyone should chance to ask what I am doing'). At *Trist.* 5.1.17–19 Ovid reverses his usual claim to be one of the canonical *quadriga* of elegists (19 *utinam numero non nos essemus in isto* 'how I would wish not to be in that company'). The list of Ovid's 'serious' works at *Trist.* 2.547–56 (*Fasti, Medea, Metamorphoses*) replaces the erotic reading list in *Ars* 3.341–8 (*Ars, Amores, Heroides*).[70]

Ovid's most dramatic revision of previous work is directed at the *Metamorphoses*. Sending the opening poem of the *Tristia* to Rome in his stead, Ovid orders a place to be found for himself in the *Metamorphoses* as an instance of good fortune transformed to ill.[71] In *Tristia* 1.7 Ovid provides a new preface introducing the *Metamorphoses* as the work of the exiled poet and begging the reader's pardon for its flaws. But as with Ovidian self-revision in general, this reinterpretation of the *Metamorphoses* does not exclude others: in the same poem (*Trist.* 1.7.15–22) Ovid casts the epic in the role of his *Aeneid*, while at *Trist.* 2.557–62 he speaks of it as though it consisted largely of praise for Augustus and his house.

Ovid can now aspire to new, more rueful, forms of canonicity: he can boast that his misfortunes would fill a whole *Iliad*,[72] rank himself alongside Actaeon and Odysseus among the victims of angry divinities, and claim that his wife surpasses the heroines of legend in virtue and misfortune – thus deserving pride of place in the *Heroides*.[73]

Separation from Rome sharpened Ovid's concern for his place in literary history. 'Place' again functions literally as well as figuratively, since Ovid now fears that all his works, not just the condemned *Ars amatoria*, will be refused admission to Rome's public libraries.[74] It is therefore understandable that the poetry of exile contains Ovid's most extensive literary-historical statements:

---

[69] Hinds (1985) remains basic for this and other exilic reinterpretations of Ovid's earlier poetry.

[70] For other revisions of earlier themes see Galinsky (1969) 102–3 (triumph descriptions), Nagle (1980) 45–70 (erotic diction and motifs), 120–1 (*recusatio*), Claassen (1999) 32–5, 211–14. See also Williams, below, pp. 243–4.

[71] *Trist.* 1.1.117–22.

[72] *Pont.* 2.7.34 *Ilias est fati longa futura mei.* 'An *Iliad* of woes' is proverbial, but Ovid's phrasing dolefully echoes Propertius' boast that his erotic struggles with Cynthia create *longas ... Iliadas* (2.1.14).

[73] Hinds (1999a) 124–8.   [74] *Trist.* 3.1.65–74, 3.14.1–10, *Pont.* 1.1.5–10.

the exculpatory survey of Greek and Latin poetry in *Tristia* 2, the poetic autobiography of *Tristia* 4.10, and the catalogue of contemporary poets in *Ex Ponto* 4.16. Each passage, in addition to its immediate function, reasserts Ovid's standing in the Roman literary world.

But even as Ovid repeats his claim to poetic recognition, the terms of the claim become significantly more modest. Whether as a form of *captatio misericordiae* or because of a genuinely chastened outlook, the poet who had asserted equality with Homer and Virgil now asks only to be accepted among the poets of his time. In *Trist.* 4.10.125–8 Ovid says that fame was 'not unkind' (*non ... maligna*) to his talent and that he is regarded as 'not inferior' (*non minor*) to many writers whom he ranked above himself, while in *Pont.* 4.16.45–6 he asks indulgence for stating only that 'my poetry was of good repute and worthy to be read in this company' (*claro mea nomine Musa | atque inter tantos quae legeretur erat*).[75] The minimalist rhetoric of these passages is painfully moving.

Ovid's final collection of poems ends with his most remarkable list of poets, a *tour d'horizon* of Roman literary life in the years preceding Ovid's banishment. A handful of the thirty writers mentioned qualify for footnotes in modern literary histories of Rome, but most are mere names, known only from their appearance in this poem. Is Ovid pretending to be impressed by this throng of nonentities? Or is he nostalgically recreating the literary scene from which he had been ejected? Perhaps Ovid could afford to be generous to his fellow-poets, leaving his readers to regret that the greatest poet of the time had been reduced to lamenting his exile. To the extent that *Ex Ponto* 4.16 recalls Ovid's account in *Tristia* 4.10 of his early years as a poet, the poem also maps in crushing detail the decline in poetic talent (except for Ovid himself) between the start of Augustus' principate and its final decade.

From Ovid rewriting to rewriting Ovid

Ovid's 'dialogic' engagement with earlier poetry (including his own) helps to define the type of imitation Ovid's work has inspired. With the possible exception of the *Heroides*, no work of Ovid was ever imitated as a whole; Ovid's talent for exhausting the possibilities of a theme may have rendered his poetry immune to straightforward replication. But many of his works were expanded and supplemented by others, both in his own lifetime and in later antiquity and the Middle Ages.[76] Ancient examples include

---

[75] Translation from Kenney (1982) 454.
[76] Zwierlein (1999) alleges that all of Ovid's works survive in a form extensively revised and expanded by Julius Montanus, a poet-rhetorician of the time of Tiberius. The evidence for this

Amores 3.5,[77] the *Letter of Sappho* (=*Heroides* 15),[78] the *Nux* (elegiac complaint of a walnut tree),[79] and a hexameter didactic poem on fish, the *Halieutica*.[80] The apparent ease of Ovid's style is usually cited as the main factor for such emulation, but Ovid's evident fondness for reopening already finished work was probably another stimulus. 'Adding to Ovid's *Metamorphoses*' is a motif that begins with Ovid himself and is then taken up in Seneca's *Apocolocyntosis*, where the apotheosis of Claudius is regarded as incredible enough to merit inclusion;[81] at least one medieval reader of the poem was inspired to create an original transformation story that blends elements of the *Metamorphoses* and the *Fasti*.[82] A form of rewriting that might have given Ovid wry pleasure is that which turns his work in a radically different direction. The medieval allegorizing interpretations of the *Metamorphoses* are the best-known case,[83] but an especially neat example is the fifth-century *Commonitorium* of Orientius, which deploys the language and rhetorical strategies of the *Ars amatoria* to enjoin chastity.[84]

More broadly, Ovid's demonstration that all stories can be retold – and that therein lies their vitality – has helped make his writing endlessly appealing to storytellers in all media. Like Ovid himself in his relation to other writers, Ovid's poetry thrives on retelling and reinvention.

FURTHER READING

Since one aim of this chapter is to provide an overview of Ovid's poetic career, it may in that respect be supplemented by several book-length treatments, such as Wilkinson (1955) in an older style or the more up-to-date Holzberg (1997a, soon to be available in English). Zingerle (1869–71) is still useful for documenting Ovid's verbal indebtedness to earlier and contemporary Roman poets, and also as an example of an earlier form of scholarship that defined literary influence almost exclusively in terms of verbal borrowings. More recent approaches to the issue of literary relatedness are illustrated by Hinds (1998). Fantham (1996) briefly discusses Ovid's place in the evolution of Roman literary culture (see also Quinn (1982)); a fuller treatment in Citroni (1995, in Italian). Cameron (1995) is an important (and avowedly controversial) re-examination of Callimachus' literary views and their Roman reception.

Discussions of individual works. Boyd (1997) treats the *Amores* with emphasis on Ovid's innovative treatments of elegiac motifs. On literary allusion in the *Heroides* see Barchiesi (1993); there is also useful material in Jacobson (1974). Dalzell (1996)

---

radical hypothesis, which among other claims would attribute all the *Heroides* to Montanus, has yet to be fully presented.

[77] Kenney (1969a).   [78] Tarrant (1981), but see Rosati (1996b).

[79] Lee (1958), Richmond (1981) 2759–67.   [80] Richmond (1981) 2746–59.

[81] *Apocol.* 9.5.   [82] Anderson (1976).

[83] See Allen (1970) 163–99, Hexter (1987), Coulson (1991); Dimmick in this volume, pp. 278–82.

[84] Vessey (1999) 165–71.

considers the *Ars* in relation to the traditions of didactic poetry. Fantham (1998) 4–25 conveniently reviews the varied generic background to the *Fasti*. On the exile poetry as a reinterpretation of Ovid's earlier work see Hinds (1985), Williams (1994), Claassen (1999).

Knox (1986b) is good on the learned and specifically Callimachean dimension of the *Metamorphoses*. See also O'Hara (1996) for a particular aspect of Ovid's learning, his use of etymological word-play. On the *Metamorphoses* as a response to the *Aeneid* see in general Hardie (1993) and Hinds (1998); Kenney (1973) considers Ovid's language in relation to Virgil's. For Ovid's reworking of earlier versions of individual stories in the *Metamorphoses* the Appendix in Otis (1970) is an accessible starting-point. Useful treatments of individual episodes from this perspective include Horsfall (1979), Keith (1992a), and Farrell (1992). Ovid's use of tragic material is studied by Gildenhard and Zissos (1999), who promise a monograph on this subject.

Finally, Myers (1999) helpfully surveys recent critical work on several of the topics discussed in this chapter.

2

PHILIP HARDIE

Ovid and early imperial literature

'He was writing at a major point of change in Roman literature, and was himself no small part of that change. Some of his work...can be read as putting the finishing touches to earlier types of poetry; but the major part of it looks unmistakably to the future.'[1] Gordon Williams' statement is typical of a literary history that places Ovid at a point of transition between two periods of Latin literature, frequently conceived in evaluative terms as a transition from a 'Golden', Augustan, to a 'Silver', Imperial, age, or from a classical to a post-classical period that is sometimes labelled 'mannerist' or 'baroque', on the analogy of the periodization of Renaissance art.[2] These aesthetic labels have political and moral implications: 'Augustanism' is seen as the spirit of a golden age of political and cultural stability and harmony, followed by a descent into an oppressive autocracy, under which literary activity becomes detached from a constructive symbiosis with political and cultural reality, a literature either of escapism or of protest.[3]

Ovid's dates conveniently fit this scheme: he was born in 43 BC, the year after the assassination of Julius Caesar, and his first works appeared in the bright days of the early Augustan principate, a celebration, albeit on Ovid's own terms, of the prosperity and sophistication that flourished in the *pax Augusta*. Ovid lived on into the reign of Tiberius, detached now physically by exile from the centres of political and cultural life. The change from Golden to Silver is often located not at the succession from Augustus to Tiberius, but within the reign of Augustus himself, as he mutates from approachable *princeps* into suspicious autocrat. The death of Horace in

---

[1] Williams (1978) 52.

[2] On the Renaissance origins of the application of the ages of metals to Latin literary history see Klein (1967); the use of 'mannerist' derives from Curtius (1953), ch. 15. Johnson (1970) 137–48 takes Ovid as an example of the 'counter-classical', a 'poetry of disenchantment' in contrast to a classical aesthetic characterized by harmony and optimism.

[3] Williams (1978) 100 for the rhetoric of 'retreat' from politics, into Roman antiquarianism (safety of the past), Greek mythology (safety of another culture), and fulsome imperial panegyric (safety of flattery).

8 BC is taken as a watershed;[4] thereafter Ovid was without serious poetic rivals, tracing a lonely course into a postlapsarian Silver Age, to undergo his own personal fall into exile in AD 8. Ovid's exile is then simply an extreme case of the new reality for imperial writers, constantly exposed to the oppressive and potentially dangerous presence of the arbitrary power of the emperor.[5]

Periodization is always hazardous. For example, the picture sketched above rests on a particular view of the essentially serious and homogeneous nature of the culture of the early Augustan principate. Karl Galinsky offers a revisionist account of Augustan culture as a whole, in which features of Ovid's poetry, such as his pluralist mixing of genres, a tendency to the episodic, and a preference for Greek mythological over Roman historical themes, are all seen as centrally Augustan rather than marks of transition to a 'Silver' period.[6] Again, so far from pointing towards the future, Ovid's predilections for recherché Greek myth, and for extreme emotional situations and the bizarre, are often seen as a retreat to the late-Republican Alexandrianism of the neoteric poets, the reaction of an essentially apolitical poet to Augustan earnestness rather than a defence mechanism against autocracy. The picture of an apolitical Ovid has been extensively revised recently, but it is worth reflecting that modernity may be constructed out of a bricolage of the past.

Ovid himself contributes to the myth of decline through the obsessive complaints in his exile poetry that his poetic powers are failing. Stephen Hinds observes that '[Ovid's exilic] narrative of "Silver" history, although in some respects peculiar to Ovid ... in its tale of the victimization of a poet by an autocratic *princeps* has been felt to be broadly symptomatic; so that the *Tristia* and *Epistulae ex Ponto* have been seen as foundational texts of the age of decline.'[7] Hinds and others have shown, however, that Ovid's exile poetry shows little diminution in the ingenuity and subtlety displayed in the earlier works. Indeed, one sticking-point for a view of Ovid as a poet transitional between periods is the remarkable consistency in style and poetics between his earliest and latest works, spanning some forty years.

---

[4] Brink (1982) 523–72 offers an elaborate essay in the subdivisions of periods within 'Augustanism', which he suggests ends in 8 BC: (572) 'Kept at bay while Horace was still writing, the Silver Age has now begun.'

[5] Citroni (1995) 462. On Ovid at Tomi 'as an early paradigm for the gallery of imperial exiles handled in palace-curial politics and annalysed in fascinated detail by historians through Tacitus as the cutting edge of autocracy' see Henderson (1997) 142.

[6] Galinsky (1989) and (1996) 261–9, 360.

[7] Hinds (1998) 89. See Williams in this volume pp. 238–9.

Rhetoric

One of the negative labels most frequently applied to early imperial literature is 'rhetorical', denoting a literature of empty verbal display, as opposed to one seriously engaged with issues in the extratextual world; a literature that aims at immediate emotional and sensationalist effects, as opposed to the subtle and allusive crafting of verbal structures. The supposed prevalence of an empty rhetoric in the first century AD is linked to two specific, inter-linked, historical conditions: firstly the triumph of rhetoric in the Roman higher educational system, and secondly the withering of Republican political oratory under the imperial autocracy, driving the rhetors into their schools to sharpen up their skills and those of their pupils on far-fetched and fantastic topics, where success was measured by the level of applause rather than by the ability to persuade a jury or political assembly.[8] This retreat from reality is symbolized in the two enclosed spaces associated with early impe-rial verbal performance: the declamation hall in the rhetorical school, and the recitation hall, which became the main theatre for the oral 'publication' of early imperial literature after the introduction to Rome of the practice of public recitation by C. Asinius Pollio in the 30s BC.[9] Literary culture, on this view, returns to a predominantly oral mode, with the consequence that, as well as being empty and detached from reality, it is also 'a literature of immediate impact', rather than one intended for meditation and reflection over the written page.[10] Orator and poet converge. Yet this is at best only a part of the story: Ovid's texts are unusually self-conscious of their status as *books* to be circulated and read, and Ovid has some claim to be the inventor of the generic 'dear reader', reflecting developments in the book trade and readerships that are determinative for the early empire.[11]

Ovid appears prominently in the Elder Seneca's reminiscences of the decla-mation schools of the early Augustan period, the *Controversiae* and *Suasoriae*, published in Seneca's old age (it is all too easy to forget that our key surviving examples of rhetorical ingenuity and display in fact go back to the beginning of the Augustan period).[12] According to the Elder Seneca (*Controv.* 2.2.8–12), in his student days Ovid was held to be a good

---

[8] On the rhetorical system of education see Duff (1964) Part 1 ch. 2; Bonner (1949) is still the best account of early imperial Roman declamation (150–6 on Ovid). On other aspects of the rhetorical in Ovid see Schiesaro in this volume, pp. 70–4.

[9] Recitation: Williams (1978) 303–6; Ovid and recitation: McKeown (1987) 63–73, according to whom (68) 'The *recitatio* not only stimulated Ovid to present his love-elegies in a dramatic manner, it also, and perhaps more significantly, stimulated him to exploit his rhetorical training.'

[10] Williams (1978) 231.

[11] On these issues see Citroni (1995) ch. 8; Fowler (forthcoming) *Unrolling the text* ch. 4.

[12] In general see Higham (1958).

declaimer; we are given excerpts from one of his exercise speeches, on a theme of marital devotion and paternal strictness whose elements could be readily paralleled from Ovid's poetry. Seneca comments on the cleverness of Ovid's treatment, 'except that he ran through the commonplaces in no fixed order'. Here we see the beginnings of a stereotype of excessive ingenuity (*ingenium*) combined with lack of self-discipline and judgement (*iudicium*), that will frequently be applied both to Ovid and to writers of the later first century AD.

The Elder Seneca also offers an example of the influence of declamation on Ovid's poetry (*Controv.* 2.2.8):

> He was so keen a student of Latro [one of the famous declaimers] that he transferred many epigrams [*sententiae*] of his to his own verse. On the Judgement of Arms, Latro had said: 'Let us hurl the arms at the enemy – and go to fetch them.' Ovid wrote [*Met.* 13.121–2]:
>
>> Let the hero's arms be hurled into the enemy's midst;
>> Order them to be fetched – from there.

These lines come from the contest between Ajax and Ulysses as to who should be awarded the arms of the dead Achilles, at nearly 400 lines one of the longest episodes in the *Metamorphoses*. Ovid recasts the famous deeds of epic tradition as verbal skirmishing, with an acute sense for the anachronistic effect of endowing Homeric heroes with the debating skills of the declamation hall. But this is not an arid exercise in rhetorical point; rather the point is precisely the dissolution of the famous actions of the heroic tradition into a contestation of words, concluding in the triumph of words over deeds (13.382–3): *quid facundia posset, | re patuit, fortisque uiri tulit arma disertus* ('the event revealed the power of eloquence, and the orator carried off the arms of the brave man'), with more than a hint of a celebration of the poet Ovid's own powers. The claim can be formulated more strongly, in terms of the *priority* of words over deeds; Ovid lets out the secret that epic and historical traditions are not simply faithful mirrors of things done (the model of the poet as the passive conduit for the omniscient and objective Muse), but partial constructions of a version of reality, or two versions, in the case of a debate such as that between Ajax and Ulysses.

The priority of words over things, of opinions over facts, has been claimed by many strands of postmodern thinking.[13] Recent rehabilitation both of Ovid and of post-Ovidian authors of the early empire has embraced the rhetorical, self-reflexive, and anti-foundationalist tendencies of these texts,

---

[13] For an excellent survey of the general issues see Fish (1990).

whose status *as* texts is boldly advertised. Ovidian 'shallowness' and 'insincerity' are recuperated, for example, in Richard Lanham's intervention in the ancient debate between philosophy and rhetoric in order to formulate two 'fundamental strategies' that determine man's view of himself in the world. In one corner is Plato, champion for a view of a unique central core of individuality within the person, the ultimate standard of reality and sincerity. In the other corner is Ovid, champion of a view of man as an actor, a role player, manipulating words in order to construct his relationship with the outside world, and hence to construct an identity for himself.[14] Rather than choosing sides in this contest, Lanham seeks to rewrite the history of western literature 'as precisely the symbiotic relationship of the two theories of knowledge, theories of style, ways to construct reality'.[15]

Cultures of display in early imperial literature

Ovidian textuality and self-reflexivity can be seen as a consequence of a renewed engagement with Hellenistic literary culture. The self-consciousness of a Callimachus has much to do with the Alexandrian sense of its relationship to the past glories of Greek literature; Ovid, like his first-century successors, is equally self-conscious of the need to negotiate his relationship to the now canonical monuments of Augustan literature, Virgil's poetry above all.[16] But certain aspects of Ovid's self-consciousness – his foregrounding of rhetoric as an art of verbal display and as performance, his awareness of the opacity of the relationship between words and things – may also be understood within the very contemporary context of the early principate.

Verbal and visual displays. The spectacular. Appearance and reality

Recent studies have emphasized the role of display in early imperial culture, above all in the visual sphere.[17] The relationship between emperor and subjects is expressed in highly visible ways. The emperor puts on shows for the people in the theatre and amphitheatre, where the emperor himself is on show in his box. Architectural and sculptural monuments provide more permanent forms of imperial display. Verbal display in the form of speeches addressed to and by the emperor will also have been important, although by an accident of survival we have no complete specimens of imperial rhetoric before Pliny

---

[14] Lanham (1976): ch. 2 'The fundamental strategies: Plato and Ovid'.
[15] Lanham (1976) 34.   [16] On Ovid's emulation of Virgil see Tarrant, in this volume pp. 23–7.
[17] See Bartsch (1994); Coleman (1990); on Livy see Feldherr (1998). On display in the visual arts see Elsner (1998) Part I; Hinds in this volume pp. 136–40.

the Younger's massive *Panegyricus* of AD 100, addressed to Trajan. It is an oversimplification to state that with the coming of the principate rhetoric retreats into the schools.

Imperial shows figure large in the historical works of Tacitus and Suetonius; particular shows, pageants, and monuments are celebrated in short but showy occasional poems such as Statius' *Silvae* and Martial's *Epigrams*. Ovid offers examples of the poetry of showmanship in descriptions of chariot races in the Circus (*Amores* 3.2; *Ars* 1.135–62); of various religious festivals in the *Fasti*; of a future triumph at *Ars* 1.205–28, and of triumphs both present and prospective, but viewed from a distance, in the exile poetry.[18] Far from Rome, Ovid sketches out the project of an occasional poetry of the city, with the emperor at its centre, and with the poet himself ideally present as spectator and participant – a project for court poetry that will be realized by writers such as Statius and Martial.[19] Like so much else in early imperial poetry, this occasional court poetry has Alexandrian precedents, in the poetry celebrating the power and culture of the Ptolemaic court.

In imperial literature the spectacular develops into a general or figurative 'spectacularity', independent of specific shows or pageants, as in Lucan's *Bellum civile*, where civil war is recurrently presented to the reader in terms of a spectacle in the amphitheatre.[20] Imperial epic and historiography work overtime in what had always been a central goal of these genres, the verbal evocation of striking visual impressions (*enargeia*). In his exile poetry Ovid has an urgent personal need for a visual illusionism that might conjure up visions of distant Rome, but a heavy investment in the gaze also marks his earlier works, above all the *Metamorphoses* which strives to give the reader a vivid sense of viewing the bizarre events unfolding in often sensual landscapes, through a variety of techniques, including empathy with the emotional reactions of internal spectators. This 'spectacularity' is closely connected with the illusionism that characterizes realist aesthetics throughout antiquity, but which reaches a height of intensity in the early empire in writers like Pliny the Younger and Statius.[21]

Make-believe and violence in the arena and in the text

Ovid's interest in the spectacular also touches on the public forms of spectacle in Rome, as in the amphitheatrical imagery applied to the deaths of

---

[18] Ovid and the triumph: Galinsky (1969) 91–107.
[19] For the project see Labate (1987) 103–8, with the nuances of Barchiesi (1997a) 36–7, with n. 34; and also Citroni (1995) 461–3.
[20] See Leigh (1997).
[21] The best treatment of the 'spettacolarità' of the *Metamorphoses* is Rosati (1983).

Actaeon (*Met.* 3.237–52) and of Orpheus (*Met.* 11.25–7).[22] The story of Orpheus is one of those mythological subjects that were later in the first century AD staged in amphitheatrical shows in which the deaths of the mythological characters were acted out by condemned prisoners in real deaths.[23] The shocking transgression in such 'fatal charades' of the boundary between illusion and reality reflects a wider concern in the early empire about the limits of the real, focused on the person of the emperor and his interaction with the other orders of the Roman state, an interaction which recent students of the period have come increasingly to see in terms of role-playing or acting.[24] Nero's appearances on the real stage were unacceptable not just because of Roman attitudes to the social status of actors, but because such an unambiguous entry into the world of the actor threatened the delicate suspension of disbelief that governed the roles played by emperor and subjects in the world of Roman politics. Make-believe, it might be said, is projected out of the realm of the aesthetic into the political and social. Commenting on the ambiguity between the imaginary and the real in the mythological dramas mentioned above, Paul Plass notes 'Such "reality in the second degree" is implicit also in Tacitus' concept of sham as a major political phenomenon, e.g. in Petronius "life of vice – or an imitation of it" (*Ann.* 16.18.2).'[25]

Ovid, supreme poet of illusionism and fictionality, introduces the reader to a looking-glass world that bears more than a passing likeness to the delusory and unstable world of appearances in Tacitus' picture of imperial Rome. This quality marks the whole of Ovid's *œuvre*, from the games with the reality or unreality of his elegiac girl-friend in the *Amores* and with the instability of the boundary between fake passion and true love in the *Art of Love*, to the uncertainty about the identity of Augustus in the exile poetry – ordinary mortal or Jupiter in person? – but it is a quality developed above all in the shifting world of the *Metamorphoses*.[26] 'You would have thought that the bodies of the Athenian women [Procne and Philomela] were suspended on wings; they were suspended on wings' (*Met.* 6.667–8): but of course this is all just a story, and the limits of appearance and reality within the narrative are framed by the boundary between the fictional and extra-fictional worlds.

---

[22] On the death of Actaeon see Feldherr (1998) 42–4, detecting in the story of Actaeon elements both of the amphitheatrical *venatio* and of the declamation hall. For further amphitheatrical elements in the *Metamorphoses* see Hinds (1987) 33–5.

[23] See Coleman (1990).

[24] Bartsch (1994) chs. 1 and 2, on Nero; Woodman (1998) ch. 11 'Amateur dramatics at the court of Nero'; Edwards (1994).

[25] Plass (1988) 136.

[26] Rosati (1983) again gives the best account of Ovid's dealings with illusion and reality, esp. ch. 2.

Spectacle in the amphitheatre presents to the gaze scenes of extreme violence and bodily fragmentation. The amphitheatre was not an invention of the empire, and an interest in death and dismemberment was always a defining feature of the genres of epic and tragedy, but early imperial Latin literature is notorious for a fascination with grotesque forms of pain and violence. Once dismissed as gratuitous exercises in sensationalism, pandering to a taste jaded by the routine experience of death in the arena, such writing has now been subjected to more sympathetic analysis, helped by the readiness of modern literature and theatre to explore the limits of the violent and grotesque.[27] In this area, too, Ovid sets a trend. Taking as its subject 'shapes changed into new bodies', the *Metamorphoses* by definition deals with extreme vicissitudes of the human body and with the accompanying emotions. The theme of change includes not just supernatural transformation, but the alterations wrought on the body by violence. The reader is often invited to gaze on the resultant spectacle, as in the flaying of Marsyas (*Met.* 6.387–91):

> clamanti cutis est summos direpta per artus,
> nec quidquam nisi uulnus erat; cruor undique manat
> detectique patent nerui trepidaeque sine ulla
> pelle micant uenae; salientia uiscera *possis*
> et perlucentes *numerare* in pectore fibras.

As he shouted the skin was torn off the surface of his limbs; he was nothing but a wound. The blood oozes all over, his sinews are uncovered and laid bare, and his pulsing veins quiver freed from the skin. You could have counted the throbbing entrails and the fibres glistening on his breast.

While the satyr in his agony is transmuted from human shape into just one big wound, we are calmly asked to count the quivering fibres in the exquisitely anatomized body. This aestheticization of violence is effected through a simile in the description of Pyramus' death-wound at *Met.* 4.121–4:

> cruor emicat alte,
> non aliter quam cum uitiato fistula plumbo
> scinditur et tenues stridente foramine longe
> eiaculatur aquas atque ictibus aera rumpit.

The blood spurted up high, just as when a pipe with a flaw in the lead splits, and shoots out afar a fine jet of water through the hissing hole and bursts through the air in pulses.

---

[27] For a representative view of early imperial violence as decadent see Williams (1978) 184–90; 254–61; more sympathetic treatments in Most (1992) and Segal (1998).

Here the incongruence between the violence of the wound and the detachment of the image is mirrored by the anachronistic mismatch of exotic legend with Roman plumbing.

In other cases the narration of violence contributes to thematic structures, as in the tale of Tereus and Philomela (*Met.* 6.424–674). Here the rape of Philomela, excision of her tongue, and butchering of Itys to feed to his father Tereus, contribute to an exploration of tyrannical excess and male sadism, and of the confusion of boundaries in a household undergoing violent meltdown. Tereus' banquet is a model for the 'Thyestean banquet' in Seneca's *Thyestes*, in which the legendary Atreus' self-realization as tyrant through the revenge exacted on his brother mirrors Roman anxieties and fantasies about the transgressive powers of the bad emperor.

From Ovidian metamorphosis-through-violation of bodily boundaries a direct line runs to Lucan's lingering descriptions of the weird transfigurations by snake-bite of the Roman soldiers led through the African desert by Cato in book nine of the *Bellum civile*. This complex episode combines an outrageous humour with a contrast between the vulnerability of the body and the self-sufficiency of the upright soul of the Stoic Cato. Early imperial violence often tests the ability of philosophical virtue to withstand the tyrant's arbitrary control over the body. Ovid provides one model for such scenes in the death of the Trojan princess Polyxena, who asserts her moral freedom by a defiant acceptance of her sacrifice at the tomb of the implacable Achilles (*Met.* 13.453–80). Something very Roman is here produced through an unusually faithful reproduction of a Greek model, Euripides' *Hecabe*; in turn Ovid's narrative of Hecuba and Polyxena is extensively reworked in the *Troades* of the younger Seneca, whose tragedies are permeated with Ovidian allusion and language.[28]

Form and content. Paradox and wit

Ovid, like later 'Silver Latin' writers, has been criticized for his empty cleverness and wit, and for elevating form over content. The Elder Seneca's reprimands of Ovid are echoed by later critics of the 'corrupt style', such as Tacitus (through the mouthpiece of Messalla in the *Dialogus*), the younger Seneca, and Quintilian.[29] Such criticism continues down the centuries, as in Dryden's charge that Ovid 'often writ too pointedly for his Subject ... so

---

[28] On the *Troades* see Fantham (1982) 30–4; in general on Ovid's influence on Senecan tragedy see Tarrant (1978) 261–3.

[29] See Fantham (1982) 26–30. Summers (1910) pp. xv–xli 'The pointed style in Greek and Roman literature' is still an excellent formal survey of its subject.

that he is frequently witty out of season'.[30] But Dryden, like the younger Seneca and Tacitus, is himself a master of the pointed manner, betraying a guilty self-defensiveness in these puritanical strictures. With the coming of the principate literary Latin seems to experience a loss of innocence and an anxiety about the uses of language, a neurotic intensification of a national distrust of the clever speaker, symbolized in the fear of the Elder Cato, the archetypal old-fashioned Roman, that clever Greek words might corrupt Roman plain dealing. Cato's advice to the orator was to 'keep a grip of the subject-matter, and the words will follow'.

The modern reader is not condemned to repeat the moralizing of the ancient critics. For one thing, the model of decline from a 'Golden Age' obscures the lines of continuity between late Republican/early Augustan and late Augustan/first-century literature. Paradox and oxymoron are already marked features in the style of the great 'classical' writers Virgil and Horace.[31] Hyperbole is often taken as a sign of stylistic bankruptcy, as ever increasing resources are devoted to the production of diminishing effects, but Virgil is one of the great poets of hyperbole.[32]

Virgilian hyperbole matches stylistic resources to an inherently hyperbolical subject matter (*Aen.* 1.33 'such an enormous task it was to found the Roman race'). The pointed style's insistence on drawing attention to its own artifices does not preclude a deeper connection between word and concept. A typical example of Ovidian wit is the description of Althea, the mother of Meleager who has killed his uncles, at the moment that she inclines to avenge her brothers' death through the death of her son (*Met.* 8.476–7): *et, consanguineas ut sanguine leniat umbras,* | *impietate pia est* ('in order to appease with blood her blood-relatives' shades, she is pious in her impiety'). A modern commentator describes the pointed jingle in *consanguineas . . . sanguine* as 'a forced and almost pointless word-play', and finds 'the oxymoron [of 'pious in her impiety'] . . . characteristic of our poet even if not very pleasing'. But the repetition in *consanguineas . . . sanguine* highlights the fact that the blood shed in revenge is almost as closely akin to Althea's as is the blood of those avenged. These pointed formulations focus the underlying conflict in the episode between competing duties, a dilemma of a kind that informs the plots of many Attic tragedies, as well as the plot of the *Aeneid* where, in the poem's final action, Aeneas' killing of Turnus realizes a *pietas* towards

---

[30] *Preface* to *Ovid's Epistles*, quoted by Hopkins (1988) 169.
[31] On oxymoron and puns in Horace see Commager (1962) 101–2; on paradox in Virgil see Hardie (1996). Summers (1910) discovers significant examples of the pointed style in the early Cicero and in Varro and Livy.
[32] Hardie (1986) ch. 6 'Hyperbole'.

the dead Pallas and his father Evander, but at the cost of ignoring Turnus' final appeal that respect be paid to his own father's grief for a son.

The *Metamorphoses* has a subject-matter of inherent paradox and emotionality well suited to a pointed manner. But already in his erotic poetry Ovidian wit points up the conventional paradoxes of the elegiac situation: the free Roman male citizen as the slave of a woman; the soft life of love as a kind of warfare; the boy-god of love, at home in the bedroom, as a world-dominating imperialist. The Neronian epic poet Lucan is perhaps the showiest exponent of the pointed style, but his use of hyperbole and paradox is no more than the appropriate expressive form for a poem whose subject is the titanic convulsions of Roman civil war, and the confusions of category and value that follow when Roman *virtus* is turned against itself. The pointed style is an apt vehicle for an epic on the World Upside Down, in which the familiar world of Rome is subjected to bizarre kinds of metamorphosis.[33] Ovid finally entered his own private World Upside Down in exile at Tomi, a mutation of personal circumstance that might seem tailor-made as a new theatre for the display of his pointed style.

But to reduce the verbal foreground to invisibility by a demonstration that style matches content would be false to the experience of reading writers like Ovid, Seneca, Lucan, and Tacitus. One should not underestimate the pleasure afforded to writers and their audiences by the exuberant play of language. In an age like ours when traditional verbal skills are increasingly marginalized, it may be hard to imagine an élite entertainment industry based on the word. Furthermore the foregrounding of linguistic texture also makes points about the relationship between language and reality. Two typically Ovidian figures operate at the boundary between language and extralinguistic reality. Syllepsis (e.g., 'an exile from his wits and home') forcibly links the literal and the figurative within a single word; and personification lends concrete and bodily form to a linguistic abstraction. As transgressive and shifty uses of language syllepsis and personification are thoroughly at home in a poem on shifting and unstable boundaries, such as the *Metamorphoses*, many of whose tales of change can be understood as the literalization of metaphor (the tyrant Lycaon is 'wolfish' in his savagery; Lycaon turns into a literal wolf).[34] Ovid plays a key role in the development of personification allegory, paving the way for the Middle Ages.[35] Political personifications were to become an essential tool of the Roman emperor's self-representation, and

---

[33] On Lucan see Martindale (1976); Bartsch (1997) ch. 2 'Paradox, doubling, and despair'.

[34] See Tissol (1997) ch. 1 'Glittering trifles: verbal wit and physical transformation', one of the most important recent contributions to an understanding of Ovidian wit.

[35] On Ovid's use of personification see Feeney (1991) 241–8; 364–91 (on Statius); on the later history of personification allegory see Lewis (1936).

for a hostile audience an obvious place to locate a gap between appearance and reality. More generally, the way in which language can be manipulated to create a version of reality becomes an obsession of much early imperial historiography, which represents the principate as a political theatre of the absurd, a system based on contradiction and maintained through play-acting and repression, and given appropriate expression in the language of wit and jokes, a language whose very artificiality is an index of the artificial emptiness of the system that it describes.[36]

Ovid is at once a major Augustan poet and the first in the line of post-Augustan, early imperial, writers. Master of the art of deceptive transitions, he would no doubt have enjoyed the embarrassment of literary historians who try to pin him down within a neat scheme of periods. He might also have derived an ironic satisfaction from the thought that his own downfall would be taken as the epoch of an age of literary decline. Yet it is hard to believe that he would have agreed that writers like Seneca, Lucan, Statius, and Martial were the products of a decadent age, rather than rivals of his own poetic intelligence.

FURTHER READING

For a typical view of the development of 'Silver Latin' in older literary histories see Wight Duff (1964); Williams (1978) attempts to reinstate a history of literary decline, determined by political and cultural factors, but this has been widely contested. For a wider historical view of the development of the concept of a 'Silver Age' see Mayer (1999). More sympathetic accounts, from differing viewpoints, of Ovid's place in literary history are found in Galinsky (1989), and Johnson (1970).

On Ovid and rhetoric see Higham (1958); in general on Ovid's 'rhetorical' world-outlook Lanham (1976) is very stimulating.

The best discussion of spectacle and illusion in Ovid is in Italian, Rosati (1983). Stimulating new approaches to spectacularity are offered in Feldherr (1997).

On Ovidian wit and wordplay see Tissol (1997), especially ch. 1; Frécaut (1972). On Ovid's style in general Kenney (1973) is indispensable.

---

[36] For a penetrating analysis see Plass (1988).

3

THOMAS HABINEK

Ovid and empire

Born in 43 BC, Ovid enjoyed the benefits of the Augustan principate without witnessing the struggles that brought it into being. As a result, the political and social concerns that find their way into his poetry differ from those that preoccupy his predecessors, such as Virgil, Horace, and Propertius. This generational difference, while routinely acknowledged by Ovidian criticism, is not always given the weight that it deserves, inasmuch as it is still possible to read of an 'anti-Augustan' Ovid, or an Ovid who endorses *libertas* in its republican connotation of free political speech. At the same time, the fact that Ovid neither experienced nor shaped the transformation of Rome from republic to principate does not entitle us to interpret his poetry as apolitical, either in intention or impact. Romantic Ovid is as anachronistic as Romantic Virgil or Lucan. The political commitments of Ovid's poetry differ from those of his predecessors (and successors), but they are no less complex and consequential. Indeed, much as the principate, during Ovid's lifetime, evolved from a set of institutional arrangements and personal loyalties into a broadly based cultural hegemony that incorporated new or revised discourses of authority, sexuality, and religion, and new conceptions of space and time, so too does Ovid's poetry raise the stakes on his predecessors, moving outward from the quintessential early Augustan concern with the refoundation of Rome to a late Augustan survey of empire.[1] At the risk of overschematization, we might say that whereas Virgil, Horace, and Propertius are by and large politically introspective, focusing on Roman history and on the inner workings of Roman society, Ovid's poetry is concerned with prospects: from a seat in the theatre to the show down below; from Rome to its distant possessions; and finally, in the last lines of the *Metamorphoses*, from the immutable heavens to the ever-changing earth. Because Ovid's position as both

---

[1] On the cultural transfomations of the Augustan period see Habinek and Schiesaro (1997), especially the essay by A. Wallace-Hadrill entitled '*Mutatio morum*: The idea of a cultural revolution.' On the 'spectacularity' of Ovidian poetry see Hardie, this volume, chapter 2, and Feldherr (1997).

subject and object of the imperial gaze in many ways resembles our own, exploration of his politics invites uncomfortable self-scrutiny on the part of the critic – a consideration that may explain why most studies of Ovidian politics limit themselves to examining the degree to which the poet distances himself from the *princeps* rather than considering the extent to which his writing is implicated in Roman imperialism.

Ovid casts his first glance (so to speak) at his own body. The opening poem of the *Amores* presents Ovid as the victim of Cupid. He is a would-be epic poet, transformed by Cupid's arrow into a veritable love-machine, alternately erect and flaccid (*cum bene surrexit ... attenuat neruos, Am.* 1.1.17–18) in keeping with the cadence of elegiac verse. Far from exciting Ovid, or inspiring him, Cupid appears as conqueror and colonizer of Ovid's self. His victory over Ovid is presented as an illegitimate extension of jurisdiction (*quis tibi ... dedit hoc in carmina iuris?*, 5), an instance of political expansionism (*sunt tibi magna ... nimiumque potentia regna*, 13), and a form of sexual dominance (*cur opus adfectas ambitiose nouum?*, 14).[2] Ovid is but the victim of Cupid's universal ambitions (*an, quod ubique, tuum est?*, 15). Framed as a *recusatio*, saying farewell to war and its attendant epic poetry, the poem in fact describes the disarming of one who can no longer act in his own defence. Whereas earlier elegists had explored the metaphor of *seruitium amoris*, imagining the lover as slave to the beloved, and thereby sought to negotiate the position of male aristocrats newly subordinated to a system and an emperor not entirely beholden to their whims, Ovid now imagines himself as the conquest of love: a substitution of territorial alterity for hierarchical.

Amores 1.2 compresses the first poem's metaphors of conquest and expropriation into the spectacle of Love's triumph, in which the poet becomes the spoils (*praeda*, 19 and 29) on display in the triumphal procession. It turns out that the encounter with Cupid in poem 1 had an impact after all: the poet still feels the slender arrows in his heart (*haeserunt tenues in corde sagittae*, 7); 'wild Love works the heart it occupies'. The last translated phrase, *et possessa ferus pectora uersat Amor* (1.2.8), marks the shift from conquest to colonization, with Love inducing the defeated to undertake his bidding willingly. This act of acquiescence on Ovid's part opens the way to Amor's triumph, one in which multiple accoutrements of the historical

---

[2] On the sexual overtones of this and other passages see Kennedy (1993) 46–63. Cahoon (1988) reads the imagery of love and war throughout the *Amores* as an 'exposé of the competitive, violent, and destructive nature of *amor*': I agree, but am not as inclined as she is to interpret this exposé as intentionally critical on Ovid's part; even less so with respect to the language of empire in *Metamorphoses* 5, which another critic (Johnson (1996)) regards as expressly anti-Augustan. There the association of Venus with the wicked Sicilian governor Verres and the failure of characters to achieve sexual justice within the context of the household both call to mind problems actively addressed by Augustus in his administrative and judicial reforms.

triumph are present: captive youth, an admission of defeat, joyous comrades, cheering crowd, proud mother, chains, roses, the implicit threat of further violence, and finally, an appeal for clemency on the model of Caesar, whose gracious treatment of those he has conquered is to serve as an example for Amor in his dealings with Ovid and his ilk.[3]

The images of war and conquest, slavery and imperialism, clemency and triumph carry over into poem three and shade our reading of its otherwise attractive evocation of personal loyalty and the power of poetry. At the out-set, the poet seeks a truce (*iusta precor*, 1.3.1), not with Cupid, as we might expect, but with a girl who has just now preyed upon him (*quae me nuper praedata puella est*, 1.3.1). Structuring his request around the commands 'take' (*accipe*, 1.3.5) and 'give' (*praebe*, 1.3.19), the poet proposes an ama-tory exchange that will generate poetic offspring: take me, despite my lack of family and wealth, offer yourself, as fertile resource for my songs, and songs will be forthcoming that are worthy of their source. It is a marriage of sorts that Ovid proposes, with poems to constitute the promised love-children. But the mythological *exempla* offered as evidence of the power of song form a poor wedding-hymn: Io, Leda, and Europa were all vic-tims of rape, by Jove no less, and were never wed to one who offered *pura fides*, or 'unadulterated trust'. What is more, their appearance extends the geographical horizons of what is otherwise a rather domestic poem: Io is known for her wanderings in Egypt, and Europa is here described precisely through her precarious journey across the sea. No sooner has Ovid listed these victims than he declares that 'we too will be sung throughout the world as equals and always my name will be yoked to yours' (*nos quoque per totum pariter cantabimur orbem | iunctaque semper erunt nomina nostra tuis*, Am. 1.3.25–6). The joke, whereby Ovid and the beloved are yoked (*iuncta*), as the heifer Io or Jupiter in bovine form might be to their respec-tive partners, cannot entirely dispel certain deeper problems.[4] In what way are Ovid and the anonymous addressee to be sung 'as equals'? What is the relationship between his victimization, as *praeda*, both here and in the pre-ceding poem, and her identification with victims of rape by Zeus? There is just the hint that their equality stems from shared oppression, not shared elevation. In addition, the extended geographical horizons of this poem, cul-minating in the reference to song 'through all the world' (*per totum orbem*), respond to and reverse the inward geographical movement of poem 2, which

---

[3] Buchan (1995) discusses *Amores* 1.1–1.5, and this passage in particular, providing a good example of the kind of reading that seeks out possible ambiguities in the poet's language con-cerning Augustus while passing over the numerous other ways in which the poems articulate an imperialist position.

[4] Yoking is also a metaphor for marriage. See Deianira's words to Hercules at *Her.* 9.29–30.

describes the triumph, or quintessential celebration of the resources of the world moving into Rome. As a lover Ovid promises good press for love. As a Roman he exchanges *carmina* for the goods acquired through conquest.

The opening three poems of book 1 of the *Amores* thus exemplify a number of features that characterize the Ovidian corpus more generally in its relationship to events and practices of the later Augustan era: namely, the assimilation of male emotional distress to the sexual and economic oppression of women; the creation of a correlation between human bodies, both male and female, and the projects of imperialism; the unquestioned assumption that empire consists of an asymmetric relationship between one part and the whole, including the objectification of the conquered; the use of extended metaphors from political and social institutions such as the triumph in which the disturbing aspects of the vehicle severely problematize the tenor; and the casual incorporation of Caesar into seemingly non-political contexts. Such inferences we draw from following Ovid's self-inspection in poems 1–3. When he looks outward in the remaining *Amores* his eye is equally caught by images of empire. If he looks at his girlfriend (*Am.* 1.14), he sees borrowed German hair: 'Now Germany will send to you its captive hair, | Your appearance will be rescued thanks to the gift of a triumphed-over race' (*nunc tibi captiuos mittet Germania crines;* | *tuta triumphatae munere gentis eris,* 1.14.45–6). If he inspects his rival, he sees a rich man who has achieved his wealth through wounds, acquired his equestrian status through blood (*ecce recens diues parto per uulnera censu, Am.* 3.8.9). Each body part calls to mind the rival's history – his head a reminder of his helmet, his groin (*latus*) of the sword that hung nearby, his left hand of the shield it bore, his right of the blood it shed (3.8.9–17). In contrast to Livy's 'old veteran', whose scarred body advertises his citizen status and mutely appeals to the state for fair treatment, Ovid's veteran is an ugly reminder of the source of Rome's wealth, to be repudiated in favour of the pure (intact, uninjured) priest of the Muses and Apollo (3.8.23).[5] One cannot help thinking, here and elsewhere, of Mary Louise Pratt's observations concerning the efforts of nineteenth-century European scholars and artists to differentiate themselves from 'real' imperialists, i.e. soldiers and bureaucrats.[6]

Other citations of earlier literature are also adapted to the imperial context. Catullus' Lesbia mourns a dead sparrow, origins unknown: Ovid's girl laments the parrot imported from India, land of the dawn (*Am.* 2.6). All desirable girls have guardians in Roman love-poetry: Corinna's is an Armenian eunuch, Bagoas by name (*Am.* 2.2). In the *Aeneid* the blush of the Italian princess Lavinia, when she hears Aeneas' name, is like crimson

---

[5] Livy 2.2.25, with an insightful analysis by Way (1998).   [6] Pratt (1992).

THOMAS HABINEK

smeared on Indian ivory or roses mixed with lilies (*Aen.* 12.67–9), images
vivid enough to send Turnus into a self-destructive frenzy and pave the way
for the founding of Rome. Ovid's Corinna blushes like early dawn; no, like
a bride spotted by her new husband; no, like the moon at eclipse; no, like
Assyrian ivory tinted by a Lydian woman in order to prevent longterm discol-
oration (*aut quod, ne longis flauescere possit ab annis,* | *Maeonis Assyrium
femina tinxit ebur, Am.* 2.5.39–40). A spontaneous emotional response is
best described in terms of crafts and commodities made available by empire.
The literary resonance of the passage – the adjective *Maeonis* points to the
Homeric antecedent of the Virgilian image – is inseparable from the imperialist dimension: Maeonia is a real place, the status of its inhabitants a topos
of Augustan-era scholarship.[7]

In *Medicamina faciei femineae*, a poem dedicated to the fine art of 'putting
it together', the connection between empire and wealth is explored through
consideration of female adornment. Girls of olden times were happy to work
hard tending flocks and fire, but today's mother will raise a tender daughter eager for gold-embroidered clothing, perfumed hair, jewelled hands, a
necklace from the Orient, and a weighty gem for each ear. And why not?
She's worth it! (*nec tamen indignum*, 23) Especially since the menfolk are
dandies these days themselves. So (the voice of the poet/adviser declares)
when you've shaken the sleep from your limbs, get going and apply that
barley from Libya, cummin seed from Etruria, iris from Illyria, honey from
Attica, and African spice. Here the age-old anxieties about women as con-
sumers (think of Hesiod's Pandora, or Cato the Elder's speech on the Oppian
law) are cast aside in favour of a celebration of the imperial cornucopia.
Sumptuary laws and other strategies of élite 'auto-conservation' are unnecessary in the new global economy.[8] *Cultus* becomes an end in itself, whether
it's planting, pruning, grafting, covering, or dyeing – your face. In years to
come, the association between womanly desire and imperial autocracy will
necessitate the rhetorical elimination of both, as in Tacitus' assimilation of
the promiscuous Messallina to an out-of-control empire.[9] But in the heyday
of the *pax Augusta*, *cultus* (that is, adornment, cultivation, make-up) is both
the agent and the outcome of empire. The extension of Roman culture, of

7 Philip Hardie rightly points out that by introducing the adjective *Maeonis* Ovid points to
the Homeric antecedent (*Il.* 4.141–2) of the Virgilian image – a passage that contains the
word and is ascribed to a poet sometimes known as the offspring of Maeon. On Maeonia
in Roman times, see Strabo 13.625, 679 and Diod. Sic. 3.58.1. From the Neronian period
onward survive inscriptions referring to the political institutions of Maeonia: see *RE* 14
(1930) 582–4. It is the choice of modern scholars, and not necessarily of ancient readers, to
notice only the literary antecedents and to ignore the imperialist dimension, as, for example,
McKeown (1998) 100.
8 Clemente (1981); Habinek (1998) 60–1.   9 Joshel (1997).

which Ovid's poetry is an important exponent, makes possible the continuing cultivation of provincial resources to Rome's advantage.[10]

In the ceremony of the triumph – whether historical or literary – the body of the captive is displayed as one of the resources expropriated from newly conquered territory. This political/ritual practice, described at the outset of the *Amores*, continues to shape and structure Ovid's relationship to empire throughout his love poetry, as the passages just cited suggest. The central figure that organizes the political references of these early works is the movement of people and goods from exotic locales to the consumer-city of Rome. As Ovid puts it in the *Ars amatoria*, when advising would-be seducers to look no further than Rome, 'everything that used to be in the world is now here' (*haec habet . . . quicquid in orbe fuit, Ars* 1.56). A different set of political rituals characterizes the opening of the *Metamorphoses* and anticipates a different political dynamic in that poem. Scholars have long understood how Ovid presents the council of the gods in *Metamorphoses* 1 in such a way as to call to mind the meeting of the Roman senate as well as the primacy of Augustus, as *princeps*, within it.[11] Jupiter's description of Lycaon's misbehaviour as a threat on the scale of the giants' earlier assault on Olympus works both within the narrative as an argument from precedent directed by Jupiter toward the other gods, and beyond the immediate context as a link to Augustan ideology, since the victory of Augustus over foes of various sorts had for some time been represented in poetry and art as comparable to the Olympian gods' defeat of the Titans.[12] But scholars have been less alert to the connection between Jupiter's rationale for his assault on all humankind and conventional Roman foreign policy, or between the timing of his narrative and the after-the-fact justifications of victorious generals. For Jupiter does not in fact propose to destroy Lycaon for his wickedness: he has already destroyed him by the time the council is called. Nor does he acknowledge Lycaon as a genuine threat to himself or his order: rather, it is those lesser beings in the *tutela*, or protection, of the Olympians whose security is at risk. 'Those demigods, those rustic presences, nymphs, fauns, and satyrs, wood and mountain dwellers, we have not yet honoured with a place in Heaven, but they should have some place to live in peace and safety', declares Jupiter (*Met.* 1.192–5).[13] And so, in order to protect the nearer reaches of his empire, Jupiter expands it; and in order to take vengeance on a single evildoer, he destroys an entire race, or *gens*: both classic strategies of Roman foreign policy based as it was on the maintenance of buffer zones and the application

---

[10] For further discussion of (literary) art and empire, see Habinek (1998) 131ff.
[11] Buchheit (1966); Muller (1987); Feeney (1991) 188ff. – among others.
[12] Hardie (1986) and Buchheit (1966).   [13] Translation from Humphries (1955).

of swift, terrifying vengeance in the case of real or perceived assaults.[14] The description of Jupiter's imperial policy in terms of the actual policy of Rome sets the stage for a poem in which the whole world both already exists and yet needs to be achieved. Critics often speak of the *Metamorphoses* as a poem of ceaseless transformation and suggest thereby that its narrative pattern undermines the ambition of Augustus and other Romans to achieve permanent control. But ceaseless transformation is an inaccurate description of the activity of the poem, since in fact each metamorphosis is final: once Daphne becomes a laurel, she stays a laurel; once Aesculapius moves to Rome, he stays there; once Caesar reaches the heavens he doesn't return to earth. In Johannes Fabian's words, 'The important thing in tales of evolution remains their ending.'[15] From the standpoint of the poem the only changes that matter are those that produce the world as currently configured.

What is ceaseless – or better, seamless – at least within the confines of the poem, is the movement from story to story. Each story recounts a distinct metamorphosis and has a distinct emotional or psychological component, and yet one story flows, almost effortlessly, into the next. In literary-historical terms, Ovid has situated the fine-spun short poem favoured by Alexandrianism within the narrative framework of epic. Outside the narrowly literary sphere, his achievement finds more precise parallels, which in turn bring to light certain political investments. One parallel is to the realm of dance. Lucian tells of a dance called 'string of beads', in which rows of young men and young women one-by-one adopt the postures appropriate to male and female adulthood in the community.[16] The dance communicates both the particular schemes, which are appropriate to some males and some females at any given time, and the movement within a lifespan from the schemes adopted earlier (e.g. in boyhood) to the schemes adopted later (as when a young man goes to war). One sees both the product, that is the necklace or *hormos*, and the process of stringing the beads. The adoption of sequential postures seems to have been an important element of ancient dance, as indicated by Lucian's argument elsewhere (*On the Dance*, 19) that

---

[14] Mattern (1999). Lycaon perhaps most closely resembles an unruly client-king, neither fully subject to Jovian rule, as are the gods of Olympus (*uos habeoque regoque*, *Met.* 1.197), nor in a state of *tutela*, as are the nymphs and satyrs (192–6). His failure to acquiesce leads to the destruction of all humanity and the assignment of its territory to a more compliant race – a drastic version of 'ethnic cleansing'. On non-Ovidian versions of the story of Lycaon, see Feldherr (this volume p. 171).

[15] Fabian (1991) 193, commenting more generally on the relationship between categories of temporality and cultural imperialism.

[16] Lucian, *On the Dance* 12, translations throughout as in the Loeb edition. Galinsky (1996) 265–6 briefly discusses the connection between Ovid's *Metamorphoses* and Lucian's history of dance, suggesting that dance may be a model or parallel for the episodic structure of Ovid's poem.

the mythological figure Proteus was originally just a very skilled dancer who could change shapes or *skhemata* on cue, and by his remarkable claim that a dance virtuoso must know all the schemes from Chaos to Cleopatra (*On the Dance*, 37). This last remark suggests that the association between the *Metamorphoses* and dance is far from incidental, since Ovid's poem, in effect, covers the same time span, starting with Chaos and ending with the reign of Augustus, with the death of Cleopatra being among the historical events mentioned last in the poem. And indeed, many of the dances listed by Lucian correspond to stories recounted by Ovid: Deucalion, Theseus and Aegeus, Medea, Scylla (together with Minos and Nisus of the purple lock), Pentheus, Niobe, Io, Perseus and Andromeda, Hyacinthus and Apollo, Aeneas and Dido, Daedalus and Icarus, Glaucus, Atalanta and Meleager, 'Orpheus, his dismemberment and his talking head that voyaged on the lyre', Pelias and Jason, 'Phaethon and the poplars that are his sisters, mourning and weeping amber... [H]e will not fail to know all the fabulous transformations, the people who have been changed into trees or beasts or birds, and the women who have turned into men; Caeneus, I mean, and Tiresias, and their like' (*On the Dance*, 39–58). Not only does Lucian describe a dancer's repertoire that corresponds closely in general and specifics to the metamorphoses of Ovid's poem; he also articulates an underlying principle of geographical organization that is not entirely lacking in Ovid either. Lucian's myths, like Ovid's, describe cycles of events from Assyria and Babylon, the different communities of Greece (i.e. Athens, Megara, Corinth, Sparta, Crete, and Thrace); but also Asia, Italy, Phoenicia, even Macedonia, once its rule was established. Only Egypt is set to the side (as it is in Ovid), on the grounds 'that Egyptian tales are somewhat mystic, so the dancer will present them more symbolically' (59).

Lucian tells us that although dance is as old as the universe and came into being along with Eros or Desire, it did not achieve its current beauty until the reign of Augustus (34). In other words the art form reached its apogee at the time Ovid was composing his poem, and its repertoire consists of pantomime stories that run only as late as the death of Cleopatra after Actium: an event repeatedly interpreted as foundational for the Augustan principate. The history of dance and history as danced culminate just as Ovid's poem does. (This although Lucian was writing 150 to 200 years later.) Again, the metamorphoses of dance and song are continuous but not ceaseless. 'The important thing in tales of evolution remains their ending.' The connection between dance and Ovid's song not only clarifies the formal arrangement of Ovid's sequence of metamorphoses; it also suggests a close connection between such form and an ideology of cosmic convergence on the Roman empire as constituted by Augustus.

Indeed, there is another tale of evolution implicit in the *Metamorphoses* (as in Lucian's treatise), and that is the story of the transfer of empire, or *translatio imperii*.[17] This theme had preoccupied historians at least since Polybius, who interpreted Rome's defeat of Carthage as an instance of the transfer of empire on the scale of Alexander's conquest of Persia. In subsequent years Timagenes of Alexandria and others used the concept to articulate the hope that empire would be transferred from the Romans. As Momigliano points out, slave revolts in Italy, the insurrection of Aristonicus in Asia Minor, the expansionist policies of Mithradates, and Cleopatra's alliance with Mark Antony were all accompanied by prophecies of the return of power from Rome to the East. The theme of *translatio imperii* and the genre of universal history that articulated it thus carried potentially contradictory political implications. On the one hand, calling attention to the rise of other empires retroactively served as justification for the emergence of Rome. At the same time, recognition that power had been held, in succession, by Assyria, Persia, Macedonia, and Rome implicitly suggests the impermanence of Rome. The movement of Ovid's great poem, temporally from Chaos to Cleopatra and geographically from East to West (with stories based first in Phoenicia, Babylon, Asia Minor, and Greece and only later in Italy) reproduces the literary structure of universal history in the face of alternative models for presentation of cross-cultural material. (Nepos, Atticus, and Varro in the generations before Ovid had all described the historical evolution of Greece and Rome as moving on parallel rather than sequential courses, as Denis Feeney recently reminds us.)[18] Does Ovid's universal history also carry the ideological duality of the genre?

Here again, the finality of the metamorphoses described by Ovid tends to foreclose rather than open the type of reading that is hostile to Rome. Everything changes, but not forever. The transfer of empire to Rome is the topic of the final book of the *Metamorphoses* not only because that is as far as history has come but because this change has been authorized and validated by the heavens. In the famous final lines of the poem Ovid imagines not

---

[17] Momigliano (1987) 31–57 discusses *translatio imperii* as a constitutive theme of universal history. See also Luhr (1980). On Ovid and universal history see Galinsky (1996) 262 and Ludwig (1965).

[18] Feeney (1999); see also Habinek (1998) 94–8. Feeney emphasizes Ovid's rejection of 'canonical' (more accurately, Republican) time-schemes, and argues that this rejection creates a space for 'uncertainty, for contingency, for unreality, for a different construction of the individual self in time' (25). True enough, but it does so at the expense of acceptance of the simultaneity of non-Roman time. Ovidian individuality depends upon a political scenario in which the cultural Other is always conveniently Past. In a similar manner, Venus' transformation into a fully Augustan deity at the end of the *Metamorphoses* is facilitated by her absorption of Alexandrian cultural models – as represented in allusions to poetry that predates Ovid by about two centuries! (on which see now Barchiesi (1999)).

only his own immortality, carried by a work that neither Jupiter's wrath nor fire, nor steel, nor long time can erode; he also envisions an empire without rival, and thus, at least by implication, without successor. 'My name will be indelible,' he writes, 'where Roman power lies open because the lands have been conquered' (*nomenque erit indelebile nostrum, | quaque patet domitis Romana potentia terris*, 15.876–7). The Latin word *patet* ('lie open') should give pause. While commentators and translators have usually taken the word to mean something like 'extend', the implied reference being to Rome's continuing expansion, in fact the word more generally describes something that is unprotected, or easy of access: doors, nostrils, escape routes, unguarded fields, an unwalled city, open minds are all used as the subject of the verb *pateo*, to lie open, to be accessible, to permit entrance.[19] To say that Roman power lies open, or is accessible, indicates that it brooks no rival, it has no reason to surround itself with guards, it is open to all; and the expression *domitis terris* would seem to explain why – because the lands have been not just conquered but mastered, pacified, domesticated. Once again Johannes Fabian's recent ruminations on space-time fusions in imperialist thought seem apropos: '. . . ways of life, modes of thought, and methods of survival that exist now, but not here, are related to our own now and here as past. Instead of confronting other ways here and now as challenges to our own ways of life, modes of thought, and methods of survival – something that would require us to acknowledge otherness as present – we incorporate them as omens into our stories of fulfilment. What, then, are the chances for us to establish meaningful relations with other cultures and societies that could be the foundation of just and rational politics if we already start out with a surplus of meaning that determines our very perception of cultural difference?'[20] In Ovid's version of universal history, the transfer of empire from one locale to the next is but an omen that finds its fulfilment in Rome. The problem of succession is resolved by the openness of Roman power. The beads of the dance are strung according to a preordained pattern.

But a different kind of succession preoccupies the poet in the final years of his career, and has preoccupied scholars as well, and that is the succession from Julius to Augustus Caesar that led to the formation of the Roman principate, and the succession from Augustus to the next *princeps* – Tiberius as it turns out – which resonates in both the last book of the *Metamorphoses* and in Ovid's letters from exile. The whole question of Ovid's relationship to Augustus has received a great deal of attention in recent years, without the emergence of a clear scholarly consensus. In the years before his exile by Augustus, the poet's relationship to the *princeps* seems to have been one

---

[19] Examples found in *Oxford Latin Dictionary*.   [20] Fabian (1991) 200

of neither support nor opposition nor ambivalence, but rather of detached engagement. On the one hand, the pervasiveness of the efforts of cultural restoration during the period in question made it impossible not to be implicated to one degree or another in the projects of Augustanism; on the other hand, the internal logic of the literary system made the *princeps*, in Barchiesi's formulation, an aesthetic problem.[21] How was one to acknowledge and represent accurately the position of the *princeps* without allowing him to overwhelm the poetry in which he appeared? How was one to write of the traditional Roman religious calendar, as Ovid did in the *Fasti*, without acknowledging the novelty of Augustus' insertion of himself within it?

Recognizing the limitations of the critical dichotomy pro- and anti-Augustan is not the same as saying that literature has no politics or that Latin poetry's politics cannot be described.[22] Partisanship and politics are not coextensive. Indeed, the impasse that Barchiesi and others identify in the political criticism of Latin literature may be due not to a failure of critical methods but to a failure of political understanding. As I have already intimated, shifting our attention to such issues as concepts of self and other, practices of oppression and exploitation, relationship to luxury goods, organization of time and space, conventions of naming, emergence of an ideology of individual autonomy, etc., allows us to develop a rich and nuanced sense of the political commitments and consequences of Latin poetry. In particular, a return to Kristeva's notion of intertextuality as a way of 'orienting the text to its sociohistorical signification' via the ideologeme, i.e. 'the communal function that attaches a concrete structure (like the novel) to other structures (like the discourse of science) in an intertextual space' would seem a healthy antidote to the enervated concept of intertexuality as a kind of glamorous but non-political version of literary history that prevails in Latin literary studies.[23] Indeed, the over-attention to the relationship between poet and *princeps* that characterizes much recent work on Ovid comes close to being an avoidance of politics altogether, since it accepts uncritically the notion that what really matters about the events of Ovid's lifetime is the development of a symbolic focus of empire in the person of the *princeps*, rather than changes in provincial governance, gender relations, class structure, expert discourse, cultural patterns, and the like. Even a reading of Ovid as resistant can overlook the obvious in its obsession with Augustus. For example, if the critical depiction of the gods throughout the *Metamorphoses* applies to Augustus as in some sense human counterpart of Jupiter, should it not also apply to Ovid's élite audience, as counterparts of the rest of the Olympians? How can

---

[21] Barchiesi (1997a) 43–4, 69ff.   [22] Kennedy (1992).
[23] Godard (1993) citing and translating Kristeva (1968).

we separate doubts about Jupiter from doubts about other divinities who are just as wilful and self-absorbed as he?

Aetiological poetry inevitably addresses issues of causation and temporality for purposes of explaining the here and now. In the *Metamorphoses* the chain of aetiological myths, each explaining how some component of the world came to be, culminates in present-day Rome, with the result that the preceding myths are retroactively interpreted as pointing toward the current situation. In the *Fasti*, as the opening words of the poem put it, *tempora* are linked with *causae* (*Tempora cum causis Latium digesta per annum | lapsaque sub terras ortaque signa canam*, 1.1–2, 'times with their causes arranged over the Latin year, and the stars that set and rise over the earth, shall be my song'); but here the times of the Roman state calendar provide the organizing principle, with *causae* introduced on the appropriate days. In either case, the interesting thing about evolution is the outcome – whether with the *Metamorphoses* we follow the evolution to the outcome, or with the *Fasti* we work back from the outcome to the evolution. As a poem, the *Fasti* has a narrative momentum and asks to be read sequentially.[24] But observing this phenomenon is not sufficient basis for neglecting the ideological import of a poem that organizes itself in accordance with state religious and political festivals. Indeed, over and over again throughout the *Fasti* Ovid describes himself as being 'hailed' by the institutional framework of the calendar to speak of some matter or other: 'the occasion itself demands...' (*exigit ipse locus*, 4.417); 'now I am bidden' (*iam iubeor*, 6.651); 'behold Janus is at hand' (*ecce Ianus adest*, 1.63–4); 'the song itself has led us to the Altar of Peace' (*ipsum nos carmen deduxit Pacis ad aram*, 1.709). While Barchiesi is no doubt correct to point out that the claim of compulsion in fact allows the poet to write on a wide variety of topics in a sequence that would otherwise appear highly disorganized, I do not agree that such invitations are in any sense 'neutral' – deceptively or not.[25] They draw into the poem the full apparatus of the state, with all of its power to beckon, command, and define.[26] Indeed, they invite the reader to evaluate the Roman state as an explicitly cultural, as opposed to military or economic, arrangement – a point further emphasized by the fact that it is the political calendar, commencing in January, rather than an agricultural or military calendar, commencing in March, that shapes Ovid's poem.[27]

Far from resisting the hailing of the state calendar, Ovid himself participates in the process of turning his readers into proper Romans. The *Fasti*

---

[24] Hinds (1992) is helpful on this point.   [25] Barchiesi (1997a) 73ff.
[26] I.e., they 'interpellate' the poetic ego, as defined by Althusser (1971).
[27] What is more, it is a calendar that has achieved normalcy only in AD 8, as Ovid was at work on the *Fasti*. See Herbert-Brown (1994) 25.

opens with an invitation/command to Germanicus to take up this work and to read of his ancestors Julius and Augustus Caesar (*excipe*, 1.3; *legendus*, 1.10). And the impression he is to obtain of Caesar is of a specific sort. Not Caesar the warrior, but Caesar the culture-hero, founder and restorer of temples and priesthoods (*Caesaris arma canant alii: nos Caesaris aras | et quoscumque sacris addidit ille dies*, 1.13–14). Just as other features of the contemporary world will find their antecedents throughout the poem, so the tension between Caesar of the arms and Caesar of the altars is implicitly explained with the immediate juxtaposition of Romulus and Numa, the first and second kings of Rome. Romulus, according to the proem, understood weapons better than stars, and left the Roman state with an inadequate number of months: it was up to Numa to regularize the cycle of twelve (1.28–44) Is it any wonder then that throughout the poem Romulus is a highly problematic figure, while Numa is, in Barchiesi's terms, 'the most likeable and provident among the characters that appear recurrently in the *Fasti*'?[28] Ovid's preference for Numa is neither pro- nor anti-Augustan: rather it highlights a different aspect of rulership that can be understood to be more appropriate under current circumstances. Thus I cannot follow the logic of scholars who argue that 'to diminish the figure of Romulus' is potentially harmful to 'the Augustan cause' simply on the grounds that on some occasions Augustus and his supporters linked him with the city's founder.[29] To repudiate the idea of exemplary kings of any sort – that might do disservice to the Augustan cause. But reminding the readers of the religious and institutional components of the first Roman founding, and of its dependence on a single wise ruler, seems more helpful than hurtful to the cause of empire, whoever and of whatever sort the current ruler might be.

While Ovid's politics in the broad sense seem not to change in the poetry from exile, he certainly – and understandably – adopts a narrowly partisan position in favour of himself. His relationship to the *princeps* takes on a very practical quality as he seeks to effect a recall to Rome. And his references to other members of leading households come fast and furious as he works to position himself on the winning side of the struggle over succession. Indeed, one of his final poems celebrates his own involvement in the public ceremony of oath-taking to the new emperor Tiberius.[30] But now, in exile, instead of looking at the frontier from afar, he sees it up close. In his early love poetry he insisted that the greatest testament of love is the willingness to follow the beloved to the ends of the empire. The trope is anticipated in

---

[28] Barchiesi (1997a) 131. For a positive evaluation of Numa see also Hinds (1992) who assumes that a positive evaluation of Numa constitutes a negative assessment of Augustus.

[29] Barchiesi (1997a) 81.

[30] *Ex Ponto* 4.13; for discussion see Habinek (1998) 160–1.

Amores 1.3's reference to heroines of the frontier, and made explicit (among other places) in 2.16 where the poet's imagination takes him from his home in Sulmo on a veritable inspection tour of the imperial frontier, i.e., the Alps, Libya, the Peloponnese; Scythia, Cilicia, and Britain. An attractive prospect, until of course Augustus intervenes and allows Ovid to live the dream – in exile, without wife (or even mistress), among 'real' barbarians, who can profit from his illumination. Why leave the city when the whole world comes here, the *praeceptor amoris* asks of his readers near the opening of the *Ars*. The unacknowledged (until later) answer is 'because someone must do the work of empire'.

In the exile poems, as I have argued in detail elsewhere, that someone is Ovid.[31] Empires depend on the internalization of the imperial project by the colonizing agents, on the creation of an appropriately colonialist subjectivity not just in the conquered peoples, but even more so among the conquering peoples who are displaced to far-off lands to do the difficult work of pacification. In the Roman world enculturation via literature is a crucial strategy of subject-formation; and so Ovid provides in the form of poetic letters continuing dispatches from the contact zone of Pontus. Through his fictionalization of the cultural realities of Pontus he enforces a divide between overseas Roman and barbarian Tomitan in need of pacification. His poetry becomes one of the mechanisms through which the Roman system of governance is transformed from 'merely a squeeze' to a new world order, with colonizing Romans and colonized Tomitans appropriately positioned therein.

The exile poetry, like the earlier love poetry, presents a story of unrequited love, of a desire for integration foiled by the requirements of honour. In the *Amores* and *Ars amatoria*, the expressed longing for equal love, shared pleasure, simultaneous orgasm, is continually undermined by the conviction that if one is not in charge, one is under control.[32] Thus the figure of the poet on display in the triumph is not just a figure relating the resources of empire to empire's central authority; it is also an expression of a state of mind that cannot conceive of equality. One is either conqueror or conquered, *triumphator* or *praeda*. So too, in the exile poetry, where the interconnections among the characters are more overtly political – i.e. Ovid the Roman in relationship with his Getan hosts and neighbours, Ovid the exile in failed relationship with Rome – the sentiments are nonetheless eroticized. The format of the exilic corpus – elegiac letters from afar – calls to mind the frustrated effusions of the heroines of the *Heroides*, separated from the male figures who guarantee their well-being. And in describing his

---

[31] Habinek (1998) 151–69. For specifics on the political context of the exile poems see Wiedemann (1975) and Syme (1978).
[32] Habinek (1997), esp. 37–8.

contacts with the Getans, Ovid describes frustration from a different, but still eroticized, perspective: he depicts himself as 'planting his seed in sterile soil' (*Pont.* 1.5.33–4), 'tilling a dry shore with a sterile plough' (*Pont.* 4.2.16), and begetting books as motherless children, sick, like him, from contact with the indigenes (*Trist.* 3.14.13–17). Whereas the mistress of love-poetry, through her very desirability, could provide fertile matter (*materiem felicem, Am.* 1.3.19) for poetic composition, the Getans cannot replace the loss of Rome or inspire even a self-consciously literary love.

And so the final image of the exile poetry, indeed of all of Ovid's poetry, returns us to the spectacle of the poet's body. Ovid addresses *Liuor*, a personification of envy, and insists that his lacerations will have no effect. The poet's name will endure. Therefore, *Liuor*,

> cease to slash at me . . .
> > or to scatter my ashes.
> I have lost everything. Only so much life remains
> > that I might experience the loss.
> What does it profit to plunge the iron into dead limbs?
> > I no longer have room for blows.
> > > (*Pont.* 4.16.47–52)

> ergo . . . proscindere, Liuor,
> > desine, neu cineres sparge, cruente, meos.
> omnia perdidimus: tantummodo uita relicta est
> > praebeat ut sensum materiamque mali.
> quid iuuat extinctos ferrum demittere in artus?
> > non habet in nobis iam noua plaga locum.

The image is of a defeated gladiator, waiting for the final blow. Nothing will be gained, says Ovid, by finishing me off. But whose profit (*iuuat*) is at stake, and who is to do the slaying or to refrain from slaying? Is it *Liuor*, imagined in earlier lines as a sore winner? Is it the crowd of spectators, who in the Roman games praise or blame the defeated gladiator for the honour of his performance? Is it the editor of the gladiatorial *munus* – sometimes, but not always, the emperor himself? Or is it just possibly Ovid who must decide to plunge or not to plunge – like St Perpetua years later who must help her trembling executioner to apply the sword to her throat?

In the allegory of Love's triumph (*Am.* 1.3), each role is carefully assigned. Here the vagueness of the overall scenario focuses our attention on the body so abused it has no room for another blow, so dead (*extinctus*) it cannot die but must remain forever in a state of feeling loss. Ovid has left us with a perfect image of incapacitation through dishonour, one that sums up the exile poetry as a whole, which repeatedly laments the inability to lament.

But it also valorizes a psychology of honour that negates the possibility of love: conquer or be conquered, penetrate or be penetrated. Here and throughout his works, Ovid lays bare not only the politics of empire but also the psychology that sustains it.

FURTHER READING

Already in his 1975 study *Ovid's Metamorphoses: An Introduction to its Basic Aspects*, Karl Galinsky took to task those critics who find in the discrepancy between Ovid's references to Augustus and earlier laudations evidence of resistance to Augustanism, attributing the differences instead to the literary challenge posed by the emperor's longevity and the need to find original ways to speak of his accomplishments. But the search for subtle repudiations of Augustan themes and programmes persists: see for example Hinds (1992) and Johnson (1996). Discussion of Ovid's relationship to the *princeps* has focused in particular on the deification of Augustus as presented in *Metamorphoses* 15. For example Holzberg (1997a) sees the incorporation of Augustus into a poem about transformation as problematizing the principate, while Salzman (1998) reads the accounts of deification as essentially laudatory. A major study by Barchiesi (1997a) has received a great deal of attention for its treatment of court-poetry as a literary problem and for its insistence on the polysemous nature of all discourses – propaganda, ideology, as well as poetry. Galinsky (again) in a 1996 study, *Augustan Culture: An Interpretive Introduction*, discusses the fluid and playful nature of Augustan culture more generally, arguing that the love of contradiction and wit that characterizes Ovidian poetry is very much of the spirit of the Augustan age. Not seeming overly enthusiastic or simple-minded about Augustus might thus be seen as placing Ovid in the camp of the Augustans. My own work, in the present essay and elsewhere (1997, 1998) tries to draw attention away from the figure of Augustus and toward the broader transformations in ideology and practice that characterize the years of his reign. Like Galinsky, I see Ovid as in tune with the spirit of the age, even responsible for shaping it. But unlike Galinsky, I am inclined to call attention to the bleaker aspects of the age, especially those that are otherwise mystified by the glamour of Ovidian verse. In my view, literature is an important component of the cultural hegemony that, for better or for worse, sustained Roman power for centuries; an important task of the critic is to bring to light the contradictory aspects of power that a given text seeks to suppress. I am happy to acknowledge that I have been anticipated in certain aspects of this endeavour by feminist readers of Ovid, e.g. Cahoon (1988, 1996).

Readers seeking a concise description of the historical and cultural developments of Ovid's lifetime should consult Gruen (1996). Syme (1978), as is to be expected, brilliantly illuminates a wide variety of otherwise obscure historical references in the poetry of Ovid without presuming, however, to tease out their cultural or ideological implications. Classicists still suffer from a sense of the incommensurability of the objects of their affection: but as one addicted to comparison, I have found two works on imperialism in more recent literature especially satisfying, viz. Said (1993), and Pratt (1992).

4

ALESSANDRO SCHIESARO

Ovid and the professional discourses of scholarship, religion, rhetoric

'Ovid is not a researcher,' claimed Concetto Marchesi nearly a century ago,[1] a remark recently echoed by John Scheid: 'Ovid is not a colleague.'[2] Undoubtedly. Yet Ovid's poetry is permeated with knowledge, from the religious and aetiological focus of *Fasti*, ostensibly the result of dogged antiquarian investigation,[3] to the mythological feats of the *Metamorphoses*, but also in the abundance of, for instance, legal vocabulary[4] in his love poetry or of recherché anecdotes in *Ibis*. It is hardly surprising that Ovid's encyclopedic aspirations gained a telling, if dubious, recognition: he was considered the author of the *Halieutica*, a rather detailed poem on the art of fishing, as well. Equally, it is perhaps unfair further to complain that modern scholars have unduly exploited Ovid as a wealthy repository of information, since didacticism is a fundamental component of his narrative strategy even in the unexpected form it takes in the *Ars amatoria* and *Remedia*. Indeed, throughout his *oeuvre* Ovid plays extensively with the well-established traditions of Greek and Roman didactic poetry. On his profound knowledge of, and admiration for, the masters of the genre – Empedocles, Lucretius, Virgil[5] – he builds a radical revision of the objectives and strategies of a form of poetry which was supposed to provide an authoritative interpretation (or at the very least a compelling description) of the universe and its fundamental principles. The *Ars*, *Fasti* and *Remedia* resort to the structure and syntax of didacticism to describe (and, to a lesser extent, prescribe for) a world of uncertainty dominated more by mutable desires (human and divine) and elusive memories than by unyielding natural or providential laws.

Upon closer inspection it becomes apparent that Ovid's knowledge is as vast and technically proficient as it appears, but riven by tensions and uncertainties. He is the last in an impressive sequence of poets who explored

Thanks to the Editor and to Ingo Gildenhard for their valuable comments.
[1] Marchesi (1910) 110 (=(1978) 761).   [2] Scheid (1992) 118.
[3] Cf. *Fasti* 1.7 *sacra recognosces annalibus eruta priscis*.
[4] Kenney (1969b).   [5] And Aratus: see now Gee (2000).

relentlessly the nexus between poetry and knowledge and elaborated quite different theoretical positions and practical recommendations. Lucretius, if by nothing else than his choice of topic, foregrounds the aims and objectives of didactic poetry, and offers as authoritative and solid a model as possible. Poetry is the medium that best conveys the eternal truths of Epicurean physics and grounds all human affairs in the lucid understanding of the underlying physical reality of the universe. Virgil's *Georgics*, on the other hand, recoil from the liberating potential of *De rerum natura* by depicting a human world firmly in the grasp of divine agents who somewhat begrudgingly hand out well-defined and carefully selected items of knowledge thanks to a pious demiurge. The didactic poet's task is thus parallel to that of the paternalistic, authoritarian *princeps*, as they both convey unquestionable truths and norms validated by divine authority. Ovid effectively rejects both models. Lucretian certainties are not for him, for all that the language of atomism is occasionally put to use. Similarly, a strong theological approach is out of the question. Gods do exist and intervene in human affairs, but they are distinctly unreliable purveyors of certainty in ethics, politics, and physics – not to mention theology itself.[6] Ovid, I argue, problematizes further the very notion of knowing, and drowns his predecessors' fundamentalist certainties in a whirlwind of competing accounts and elusive contradictions. His 'knowledge' will eschew Lucretius' atomistic foundationalism and Virgil's theodicy, and will be shown to be based, if anything, on the powers and perils of rhetoric.

In the *Fasti*, Ovid's highly original contribution to the genre of Roman didactic poetry,[7] the breadth and depth of Ovidian learning is by now amply recognized, as is his originality in selecting, adapting or innovating available information.[8] Etymology represents a peculiarly fruitful field of investigation where all these characteristics shine through. Ovid was both fully abreast of contemporary scholarship and original in his approach.[9] An investigation of Ovid's connection with, for instance, the work of Varro or Verrius Flaccus, the two researchers and intellectuals who dominate the world of knowledge in the first century BC,[10] reveals, *mutatis mutandis*, the same attitude that we can discern in his relationship to philosophical doctrine – in-depth knowledge of different traditions and very little inclination to adopt wholesale a

---

[6] The very first episode of the *Metamorphoses* advertises the intrinsically contradictory nature of Ovid's theodicy: Anderson (1989).

[7] On the didactic nature of the poem see Miller (1992b).

[8] The most extensive treatment is Porte (1985).

[9] A full treatment in Porte (1985) 197–264, 501. See Wallace-Hadrill (1997) for a persuasive interpretation of the role of technical expertise in the Augustan age.

[10] In general see Rawson (1985).

coherent view of the world.[11] The main focus of interest, therefore, must be on how knowledge is articulated and presented, and what epistemological protocols emerge from such articulation.

The first few words of the *Fasti* – *tempora cum causis* ('times and their causes') – highlight the most significant concern of the poem. *Causae* clearly refers, on the one hand, to Callimachus' *Aitia*, whose importance as a model for Ovid's project is unquestionable, but on the other situates the poem and its object of study within a specifically Roman tradition. The most important programmatic passage of Virgil's *Georgics* famously identifies two possible approaches to didactic poetry, one directed at understanding the causes of phenomena and in so doing liberating mankind from the grip of superstition, the other content with 'knowledge of the rural gods': *felix qui potuit rerum cognoscere causas|... | fortunatus et ille deos qui nouit agrestis* (2.490–3 'blessed is he who has been able to acquire knowledge of the causes of things/.../happy, too, is he who knows the woodland gods'). Causal knowledge defines Lucretius' unrelenting exploration of the *ratio* underlying phenomena, while the *Georgics* extol the ethical virtues of a non-scientific, more traditional approach.[12] Ovid's *Fasti* can be read as an attempt to combine Lucretius's interest in *causae* with Virgil's ethical and religious concerns. Ovid's *causae*, in fact, are rooted in history and tradition,[13] not in the eternal laws of nature celebrated in *De rerum natura*, and are thus ultimately less absolute and less reliable, and less disruptive of traditional religious observance.

Readers of the *Fasti* soon realize how difficult it is to identify dependable points of reference in a poem where many, perhaps too many, sources of information are given a chance to parade their competence. Janus is the most eloquent example.[14] He appears at the beginning of book 1 as the ideal informant, solicitous, approachable, experienced, altogether a far cry from the reluctant Proteus of the *Georgics*. But doubleness is indelibly inscribed in Janus' name and character, and thus he is fully involved in the shifty dialectics of meaning which emerges as perhaps the most pervasive characteristic of a poem whose organicity is always threatened by its episodic structure. In general, it would be impossible to grant the gods of the *Fasti* (let alone the *Metamorphoses*) an indisputable claim to authority and truth. They are, for one thing, as much characters of the poem as their human counterparts, fully involved in the action of the plot.[15] They do not live in the epistemic

---

[11] See Myers (1994) for a convincing analysis. [12] Cf. Schiesaro (1997a).

[13] Newlands' essay in this volume (ch. 12) deals extensively with this issue.

[14] On Janus see Miller (1983) 166; Harries (1989); Hardie (1991); Barchiesi (1991) and (1997a) 230–5; Newlands (this volume, ch. 12).

[15] In general see Feeney (1991).

equivalent of *intermundia* ('the spaces between worlds'), unperturbed by events and passions, but like humans they are subject to hatred and desire. Furthermore, their authority is regularly invoked on matters that touch them very closely, and where they have, inevitably, a biased point of view. Thus, for instance, Romulus offers a blatantly subjective and self-serving view of Remus' death (4.807–62).[16] Just after invoking Carmenta's help in reconstructing the origin of her cult (1.465–68) the narrator lets in the cautionary remark *de se si creditur ipsi* (1.469, 'if one is to be believed when one talks about oneself'), which indirectly affects the goddess's credibility as well. The authoritarian model of *ipse dixit*, which is in different forms at work both in Lucretius and in Virgil, is neatly turned on its head: it is precisely because *ipse* can offer a very personal version of events that any sense of ultimate certainty is taken away from her pronouncements. The place of authority is thus conceptually occupied by rhetoric, by the discursive arrangements which articulate reality according to variable points of view rather than ultimate truth.[17]

In many expositions of alternative causes Ovid follows a pattern which had been successfully codified by Callimachus' *Aitia*. A list of possible explanations is drawn up, and at the end the narrator or the speaker may or may not point out the one he favours.[18] This method may well reveal the poet's multifarious doctrine,[19] but it also opens up the space for contradictory accounts and choices, especially because some of Ovid's alternative explanations are in fact mutually exclusive: is the Roman tradition of taking up the *toga uirilis* on Bacchus' festivities due to the fact that the god is eternally young, or, on the contrary, that he is a father figure?[20] Both explanations would have been conceivable in a cultural context where *lucus* ('grove') can be derived from *non lucendo* ('because there is no light') – it is not Ovid's technical competence which is in doubt – but their juxtaposition shows that 'explaining causes' is a more open-ended and manipulative operation than it ever was in different didactic contexts. The multiplicity of points of view on offer is most fully visible in the Muses' belated and puzzling appearance at the beginning of book 5 (1–110),[21] when they offer contrasting and irreconcilable accounts, as the narrative explicitly acknowledges (9 *dissensere deae*, 'the goddesses were in disagreement'), about the origin of the name of their month, May.

Callimachus' role as an advocate of multiple explanations, a practice well known to Roman antiquarians as well,[22] should not obfuscate the specifically

---

[16] Harries (1989) 170; Barchiesi (1997a) 161–4.   [17] See below, pp. 70–4.
[18] See esp. Miller (1982b) and (1992).
[19] Harries (1989) 184–5. His positive assessment of the technique may be predicated on a partial view of the phenomenon (cf. 184 n.96).
[20] *Fasti* 3.771–6, with Barchiesi (1997a) 193.   [21] See Harries (1989) and Barchiesi (1991).
[22] Feeney (1998) 27–31.

Roman development of the method offered by Lucretius in accordance with Epicurean epistemology. Lucretius rigorously confines use of the so-called *pleonachos tropos* 'multiplicity of explanations'[23] to specific topics of knowledge, those dealt with in books 5 and 6 of *De rerum natura*. Certain physical phenomena can be explained in a variety of equally plausible ways, none of which stands out as the only correct one. Such indeterminacy, however, is precisely the point: what is at stake for the Epicurean student is the explicability of phenomena, which warrants the absence of divine intervention in their unfolding. *Pleonachos tropos* is used when it does not matter which specific explanation is true, provided a number of plausible ones can be advanced; but Lucretius would never resort to this method when the fundamental physical truths of Epicureanism are at stake. The role of this practice in the *Fasti*, once read against the Lucretian model, reveals that the distinction between ultimate truths and phenomena subject to multiple explanations is no longer possible, and all *causae* inhabit a more relativistic universe.[24]

This strongly relativistic approach does not mean, however, that Ovid betrays the supposedly uniform rigour of religious expertise. Rather, he avails himself to the full of a potential that was always inscribed in calendars and religious rituals, that of putting forth his own selection and interpretation of the material, of pushing his own exegetical agenda.[25] His own rearrangement of the *fasti* tradition in the *Fasti* should not be evaluated against the objective impersonality of a standard calendar, but side by side with similar, conflicting accounts of the matter at hand. Ovid's technique in this respect is unsurprisingly sophisticated, because on the one hand he celebrates the undeniable reliability that the Caesarean reform of the calendar, based on firm astronomical data, introduces into a previously murky area, but on the other he avails himself liberally of the arbitrary freedom which characterized the activity of the priests of old.[26] He shows that tradition and aetiology are inextricably linked ingredients of any attempt to make sense of the physical, mythical and historical universe we inhabit, and that both Lucretius' and Virgil's epistemologies are too monolithic. Each of them, in its own way, is excessively confident that a well-defined and unique truth (be it scientific or 'traditional') may emerge from the turbulent waters of phenomenological experience.

The *Metamorphoses* would seem to provide an interesting contrast vis-à-vis the orderly structure of the *Fasti*. The opening of the *Fasti* celebrates the

---

[23] Epicurus, *ad Pyth.* 87.2, Lucr. 5.526–33.
[24] A pointed departure from Lucretian practice is to be found at a crucial juncture in *Met.* 1, where the narrator declines to adjudicate between two radically different explanations of the creation of man, each introduced by *siue* (78–81).
[25] Scheid (1992), Phillips (1992).   [26] Cf. Beard (1985).

ruling house's intellectual achievement in devising a new, scientific structure of the calendar which superseded the unreliable ten-month year introduced early on by Romulus, clearly more at ease with *arma* ('weapons') than with *sidera* ('stars') (1.29).[27] Caesar's reform of 46 BC, in which he finally brings to an end the 'uncertainty' (Macr. *Sat.*1.14.1 *inconstantiam temporum*) typical of the old calendar, remains in the background, but Ovid explicitly praises Germanicus' expertise in such matters, indeed he is a *doctus princeps* (1.19–20, 'learned ruler') ideally suited to favour a learned poet (1.25 *uates rege uatis habenas*, 'a poet, guide a poet's reins'). In the world of the *Metamorphoses*, however, chronology loses much of its structuring potential. The proem does at one level hold out the promise to proceed in an orderly fashion from the very creation of the world down to the poet's (and emperor's) present, but it actually reveals the existence of an undetermined past occupied by Chaos whose boundaries are in all senses elusive. After the four-line preface the first word is not, for instance, *principio*,[28] but *ante* (1.5), which introduces a distinctive element of confusion into the plan to begin from the beginning. From then on, things only get more entangled, as the primordial creation unexpectedly figures in two encores, albeit partial. The escape from Chaos at 1.21–4 is short-lived, since at 291 the primordial confusion between elements is reintroduced, and this time on Jupiter's orders: *iamque mare et tellus nullum discrimen habebant* ('already there was no distinction between sea and land'). Chronological linearity is thus challenged early on, and never regains the upper hand. Consider the first extended narrative section after the second creation. Among the first creatures to emerge from the earth after the flood is Python, an enormous snake killed by Phoebus, who then introduced the Pythian games in memory of his triumph. But winners at the games could not be adorned with the laurel, which did not yet exist because Phoebus had not yet fallen in love with Daphne . . . A string of verbs in the imperfect flattens out any sense of meaningful chronological distinction. The primordial creation of Python is followed immediately by the games, then by the story of Phoebus' passion for Daphne, without any clear-cut separation between human and mythical times, nor between different stages of human development. Since most of the stories are then joined together by often rather flimsy connections, even the internal sense of chronology disappears. The virtuosic fugue of inset narratives further undermines the attempts of any reader interested in keeping track of the chronology, absolute or even relative, of the poem. Significantly, the vague

---

[27] Ovid uses the Julian *Fasti*: Wallace-Hadrill (1987) 224.
[28] Cf. for instance Lucr. 5.783, at the beginning of the section about the inception of life on Earth.

adverb *nuper* is one of the favourite chronological indicators throughout the *Metamorphoses*.[29]

Analepsis and prolepsis are of course crucial ingredients of narrative, but in the *Metamorphoses* we witness a more pervasive and disruptive phenomenon. Jumping from one point of the mythical fabric to another without any apparent concern for time or space, Ovid has constructed an image of the universe which is almost monodimensional, and stands as a challenge to the careful articulation of chronology ostensibly celebrated in *Fasti*.[30] What he offers is not so much a direct denial of that particular cultural construction, but an alternative option which under the circumstances he finds equally appealing: the history of the world, and, for that matter, of Rome, can be couched in the (at least superficially) reassuring structure of the religious calendar, or reassembled by free association following the chaotic thread of the *Metamorphoses*. The alternative, however, reveals that even chronology, for all that it is by now the domain of academic specialists retained by powerful rulers,[31] is, after all, a matter of point of view. The proem of *Fasti*, too, contains a trace of relativism. Romulus is (cheerfully) reproached for his astronomical incompetence, but the praise shortly after bestowed on Numa is somewhat disingenuous. True, Numa *nec Ianum nec auitas praeterit umbras* (1.43, 'but Numa did not overlook Janus or the ancestral shades'), and dutifully adds January and February to the year, but his failure to establish a reliable solar calendar paves the way for a long period of chronological chaos which only Caesar will eventually bring to an end.

Ovid's erotic poetry, though thematically very different from other parts of Ovid's production, shares some of the most distinctive features outlined so far. The *Amores*, *Ars* and *Remedia* naturally form a group, but erotics is no less central a concern of *Fasti* and *Metamorphoses*. More importantly, erotic poetry is fully involved in the dialectics of knowledge we have sketched so far. Catullus and Lucretius had already displayed a full awareness of erotic discourse's potential to foreground issues of knowledge and understanding. Love and its verbal expressions present endless opportunities for interpretation, for decoding the lovers' signs and hints (even silences),[32] and thus stand as a constant reminder of the intrinsic difficulties of attaining unambiguous knowledge. In matters of love words can forever be bent and rearranged, and

---

[29] Ovid finds a Hellenistic, and specifically Callimachean, precedent in *néon*: see Hollis (1990) 235, on Call. *Hec.* fr. 70.10.

[30] Recent work on Ovidian times: Schiesaro (1997a), Zissos and Gildenhard (1999), Feeney (1999), Hinds (1999b).

[31] Wallace Hadrill (1997) 16–18.

[32] *Ars* 1.572 *saepe tacens uocem uerbaque uultus habet* ('often a silent face has a voice and words').

superficially true statements readily conceal unspeakable situations. When questioned by Cinyra about the young woman who fancies him, Myrrha's nurse replies with a literally correct, yet profoundly ambiguous statement: *quaesitis uirginis annis,* | *'par' ait 'est Myrrhae'* (10.440–1, 'when he asked the maiden's age, she said: "The same as Myrrha's"').

Ovid makes all these issues central to his erotic poetry. Lovers communicate through carefully arranged signs, whose shifting nature is evident even as they do occasionally enable contact and understanding. The potential for disaster is always paramount, emblematically so in the story of Pyramus and Thisbe.[33] Their forbidden love can be communicated only through a small fissure in the wall which keeps them apart (73–85); they agree to elope, and meet at night under a tree near Ninus' tomb, but when Pyramus arrives, and finds Thisbe's scarf soaked in blood next to the traces of a wild beast, he resolves to join his beloved by killing himself. His interpretation of the evidence, however, is flawed: Thisbe let her stained scarf fall behind in her flight, but was never attacked or wounded. The main focus of this poignant story is Pyramus' faulty reading of *uestigia* (105, 'traces'), a word which since Lucretius has acquired privileged status in the technical vocabulary of investigation and knowledge. In the Epicurean system *uestigia* can unfailingly be decoded in the light of general principles which by their permanence and pervasiveness guarantee the ultimate legibility of the physical world. In the *Metamorphoses*, on the contrary, such is the state of uncertainty and impermanence that it would actually be surprising if *uestigia* were anything but unreliable. The lioness' *uestigia* are clearly legible,[34] and so, ominously, are the blood-stains. The connection between these two items, however, proves fatally elusive, as the space of Lucretius' unfailing causality is occupied by the ambiguity of interpretation: in the absence of firm natural laws the interpretation of *uestigia* inevitably becomes a hit-or-miss affair.

At the centre of Ovid's erotics, however, stands, more often than not, a void. Here again Lucretius might have represented an influential suggestion, since one of the most powerful sections of *De rerum natura* book 4 concentrates on the intrinsic impossibility of attaining what the lover supposedly craves – his beloved. The *rabies* ('rage') and *furor* ('fury') (4.1117) of love stem from the technical impossibility, from an atomistic point of view, of lovers' desire for one another being satisfied. Much as they cling to each other, join their lips and even bite each other, lovers 'can rub nothing off, nor can they penetrate and be absorbed body in body' (1110–11).

---

[33] *Met.* 4.55–166. On this episode see now Fowler (2000) 156–167.
[34] Indeed, they are *certa* (106). In Virgil's *Georgics* signs are very often 'certain', because they are guaranteed by a higher authority. Ovid's 'certainty' is only superficially useful. Cf. Schiesaro (1997a) 70.

Desire is born of *simulacra* (4.1095), incorporeal images that tease the mind and are easily snatched away by winds (1096). Ovid does not emulate Lucretius in his lengthy explanation of this impossibility,[35] and in his Pygmalion episode he gives a very novel twist to the notion that *simulacra* are inevitably incorporeal[36] as Pygmalion's beloved woman-statue actually comes to life. Yet this fundamental sense of unattainability is central to so many Ovidian descriptions of pursuit, especially in the *Metamorphoses*. Lovers are beholden to appealing *simulacra*, and often fall in love, literally, at first sight.[37] But pursuit yields no result, because fleeting *puellae* (and the occasional *puer*) more often than not have a way of transforming themselves into something else, inanimate objects whose connection with their human antecedents is (again) predicated on aetiology, a story, a discourse. Born as the child of sight, love ultimately comes to rest in words and symbols.

In his treatment of love objects Ovid displays the same tendencies to fragmentation and rearrangement that dominate in his view of physical and historical phenomena. Bodies are dissolved into their constituents and rearranged fetishistically as objects of desire whose sum is less than the addition of their parts, and whose identity is thus terminally challenged.[38] Ovid's time and space remind modern readers of the cubists' diffraction of reality,[39] and even more so do Ovid's bodies, whose original features are not completely obliterated but violently displaced into new and perturbing wholes. In the poem that declares from the outset its intention to sing of 'changed shapes', *mutatas ... formas* (1.1), bodies are thus the privileged signifiers of this unrelenting entropy.

The soundings I have offered on how Ovid's poetry deals with technical knowledge and with the form of knowledge involved in the pursuit of erotic objects of desire share common characteristics. Most prominently, they foreground the relativistic nature of knowledge and the shifting, ultimately unseizable nature of its object. The outside world does not possess an essential, permanent shape, but is constantly shaped and reshaped by desire and interpretation, by the gaze and words of the beholder. Thus the issue of Ovid's 'rhetoricity' becomes, in a very fundamental sense, central to all the issues I have dealt with so far. The label 'Ovid the rhetorician'[40] may be unfair as an aesthetic judgement, but rhetoric, the technique of shaping reality and

---

[35] Cf. Hardie (1988).   [36] As explained at length at Lucr. 4.1084–1104.

[37] The motif is established early on, in the story of Apollo and Daphne: *Phoebus amat uisaeque cupit conubia Daphnes* (1.490, 'Phoebus falls in love, and craves union with Daphne as soon as he sees her').

[38] I draw here on the seminal treatment developed by Brooks (1993), esp. 88–122.

[39] Schiesaro (1997b) 99.   [40] Higham (1958) 41.

its interpretation according to shifting points of view and more or less pre-ordained patterns, can indeed be seen as the unifying *episteme* of Ovid's poetry.

Ovid's 'rhetoricity' has traditionally been explained, and invariably criticized, as the result of the author's early exposure to forensic training, described in some detail by the Elder Seneca.[41] It is hardly surprising that Ovid received such training, although a coherent biographical argument should also admit that Ovid explicitly differentiates between himself and his brother, much keener on *eloquium* and literally 'born' *fortia uerbosi ... ad arma fori* (*Trist.*4.10.17–8, 'for the strong weapons of the word-arena'). If Seneca's strictures have enjoyed a longevity well beyond the author's credentials as a literary critic,[42] it must be because they can be seen to dovetail quite neatly with some large-scale characteristics of Ovid's poetic style. I will try shortly to show that they can be read in quite a different way.

A particularly strong connection has been established between Ovid's early training and the style and structure of the many speeches which can be found in his poetry. It is very difficult, however, to detect in these speeches more numerous or more conspicuous declamatory elements than are generally found in supposedly less 'rhetorical' authors such as Virgil (or, for that matter, Homer). Effective speeches had to be structured according to recognizable strategies of persuasion, and Virgil himself was indeed used as a model for orators.[43] The *Heroides* have been considered the 'most rhetorical work' of a 'rhetorical poet'[44] partly because of their supposed resemblance to declamatory exercises. The heroines' letters have been repeatedly read as literary versions of a specific type of declamation, the *suasoria*,[45] or of *ethopoiia*, a standard declamatory exercise in which the student was asked to compose the speech that a famous character would have given under specific circumstances. The forced identification of the *Heroides* with such exercises not only underestimates the poems' rich and varied texture, but, incidentally, also presupposes a somewhat tendentious view of *ethopoiiai* themselves.[46]

A close association between the *Heroides* and *suasoriae* is of course meant to be damning. Even in a resolutely pre-Romantic conception of art, too close a relationship between poetry and declamation is not altogether flattering, and it is not by chance that the *Heroides* have been among the last of Ovid's

---

[41] A thorough and sensible discussion in Higham (1953). On the 'rhetorical' qualities of Ovid's poetry see also Hardie in this volume, pp. 36–8.
[42] Cf. Tarrant (1995) 63.   [43] See especially Farrell (1997); Pennacini (1988).
[44] Jacobson (1974) 322.
[45] A view fully refuted by Oppel (1968) 37–67, but see now Knox (1995) 16.
[46] The view goes back to Richard Bentley. A full discussion in Jacobson (1974) 325–9.

works to undergo a thorough critical revaluation. A less apologetic argument may be proposed. The charge of 'excessive' rhetoricity would probably not have been levelled against the *Heroides* if the entire collection did not ostentatiously display serial repetition as an organizing principle. Here is an extensive gallery of female lovers captured by the post-elegiac poet at the same stage of their love life, as they write impassionate if doomed appeals to their absent beloveds. The impact of seriality is all the more striking when one considers that the programmatic foundation of elegy is represented by the uniqueness of the lover's passion for a highly individualized counterpart. Similar self-limitations operate in other Ovidian works. Each book of the *Fasti* encapsulates a single month, thus remotivating the predilection of Roman epic for poems of six or twelve books. A different, yet comparable constraint operates as the organizing principle of the *Metamorphoses*, where what is in effect a comprehensive mythological *summa* is parcelled out into a vast number of individual stories all of which must accommodate a metamorphosis. All these arrangements, which, of course, exist in addition to the numerous usual conventions of Latin poetry, can indeed be labelled as 'rhetorical' in so far as they obey a set of arbitrarily chosen, yet faithfully respected, external constraints of a rather artificial nature. Although such constraints do not reach the surreal extreme of some contemporary experimentation with 'mechanical' writing, they do gesture towards a strikingly modern form of 'artificiality'. Serial music, pop-art, and permutational art, for instance, have promoted a more favourable aesthetic appreciation of the poet's struggle with predetermined constraints, and have reassessed in modern terms the aesthetic potential of self-imposed discipline. In all these forms of expression the author wagers that externally imposed rules maximize the ability to display differentially his originality. Precisely because they almost obsessively repeat a familiar theme, the *Heroides* produce a peculiar aesthetic effect and meaning. They bring to an extreme a fundamental quality of poetry based on mythical plots – their predictability – and by so doing force the reader to confront the implicit conventions of that form of poetry. *Omnia iam uulgata* (Virg. *Georg*.3.4, 'all is trite') was felt to be an appropriate comment already in Virgil's times. Ovid takes his illustrious predecessor at his word, and proceeds to explore the expressive potential of repetition and predictability, of viewing the world without any illusion that a direct take is possible, but with the belief that artificiality can, paradoxically, heighten original perception. The whole of the *Heroides* stands as a (serial) remake of the elegiac experience of Catullus and Tibullus, of Propertius and even Ovid himself.

Once we are alerted to the potential of rhetoric as a form of perception and interpretation of reality we can perhaps go back to Seneca's infamous remarks at *Contr.2.2.8–12*.[47] Three criticisms are made of Ovid's youthful declamatory exercises, all of which have traditionally been seen as early indications of the 'vices' in which he later indulged: (i) his treatment was episodic and fragmentary (9 *sine certo ordine per locos discurrebat*); (ii) he eschewed argumentation (12 *molesta illi erat omnis argumentatio*); (iii) he was emotionally unable to repress his *licentia* (12).

All these features can be mapped onto Ovid's poetic production, but they describe, rather than a lack of proper stylistic discipline, a set of coherent epistemic assumptions. In this respect the avoidance of a *certus ordo* that undoubtedly characterizes the *Metamorphoses*' rhapsodic structure emerges as an effective indictment of organicity. The meandering 'disorganization' of the poem must be seen as one of the most effective ways to represent the fluidity and flux of the universe Ovid describes. A lack of interest in the subtleties of argumentation has invariably been considered as a weakness, as if the poet Ovid opted for the easy attractiveness of *pathos* without risking any deeper involvement with philosophical and logical rigour. Again, failure to engage in arguments can be redescribed as a sign that much of what reality offers ultimately defies rational analysis. If the world of the *Metamorphoses* is one of flux and instability, that of the *Fasti*, as we have seen, is dominated by contradictory and often puzzling explanations. Or, again, the *Heroides* show the intrinsic inability of rhetoric and logic (or at least of what count as 'rational' entreaties on the part of abandoned lovers) to develop a successful argument. But here Ovid is not so much taking an easy way out of philosophical engagement, as following and indeed sharpening a scepticism towards the virtues of argumentation that had been theorized explicitly in the *Georgics*, where Virgil puts to rest Lucretius' passion for *cognoscere causas* ('knowing the causes') and stops in front of the eternal mysteries of revealed religion. As we noticed before, Ovid exploits Virgil's lack of faith in the power of rational explanation, and then turns against his preferred solution as well, showing that gods are hardly more reliable purveyors of truth.

In other passages Seneca the Elder remarks unfavourably on Ovid's excessive indulgence in the use of *sententiae*, the quick, witty repartees which form an anthology of memorable quotes, often comparable to declamatory models.[48] Accusing *sententiae* of shallowness, however, is tautological, because the defining characteristic of *sententiae* is their rejection of analytic argumentation in favour of a compressed argument from authority which deliberately does not lend itself to analysis or deconstruction.[49] *Sententiae*,

---

[47] The passage is analysed at length by Higham (1953) 34–5 from a different yet equally unprejudiced point of view.

[48] Cf. Bonner (1949) 150–5, esp.150–2.

[49] The sociological implications of *sententiae* are now well discussed by Sinclair (1995).

therefore, do not represent a failure of logic, but the most appropriate form of expression in a non-rational, non-organic, non-explainable and often paradoxical world.

In different ways and across very different domains Ovid's poetry emphasizes repeatedly the indeterminacy and unreliability of knowledge, be it religious, aetiological or amorous. Knowledge is actively, sometimes even relentlessly, pursued, but its limitations have ultimately less to do with the weakness of epistemic protocols than with the intrinsic elusiveness of the objects it would like to apprehend. In a universe where the laws of physics do not play a significant role, and in which the gods are mired in the same contradictions and partialities as humans, knowledge can be entrusted only to a variety of accounts, fragmentary and biased as they inevitably are. As he selects lesser-known versions of famous mythical stories, or privileges tendentious details, Ovid reconnects Callimachean sophistication to a more comprehensive world view which can be reasonably seen as hopelessly decentred.

In this respect, as I suggested at the beginning, Ovid's knowledge can be labelled 'rhetorical', if rhetoric is the art of putting a case in the best possible form irrespective of its intrinsic claim to truth, and is thus taken, somewhat metaphorically, as symbol of the prevalence of *verba* over *res*. As a specialized *techne*, however, even rhetoric fares no better than others, since the most rhetorically sophisticated examples of speeches which Ovid offers in his poetry unfailingly miss their mark: Apollo sets a dangerous precedent when he fails to persuade Daphne in *Metamorphoses* 1, and Ovid himself fares no better in the *Tristia* and *Ex Ponto*.[50] The value of this and other forms of technical competence is necessarily relative.

The reflection on knowledge and its boundaries that animates poets from Lucretius and Virgil to Ovid is necessarily a reflection on power and authority. Lucretius offers a set of potentially liberating formulas, while Virgil retreats from this freedom in the name of an authoritarian, if paternalistic, approach. Ovid, unsurprisingly, cannot quite bring himself to accept either model. His unquenchable passion for all that is relative, fluid, epistemologically elusive, is hardly the ideal breeding ground for authority and norm. It is tempting, indeed, to read these overarching passions as a sophisticated indictment of the increasingly authoritarian penchant displayed by the Augustan regime. Yet in a world dominated by different accounts of events, all vying for plausibility, the powers-that-be, too, have a chance to construct their own version of 'the truth' and appeal for credibility. If ultimate authority is unreachable anyway, genealogies and aetiologies

---

[50] As pointed out by Tarrant (1995).

can all be somewhat misleading, and yet compete effectively in the public arena.

FURTHER READING

Rawson (1985) offers an invaluable overview of Ovid's intellectual background; for a powerful interpretation of the relationship between specialist knowledge and power Wallace-Hadrill (1997) is unsurpassed. On Lucretian and Virgilian epistemology see Schiesaro (1997a). Aetiology is the specific focus of two monographs, Porte (1985) on the *Fasti* and Myers (1994) on the *Metamorphoses*, but many recent works, especially on the *Fasti*, deal with this and similar issues: cf. Harries (1989), Hardie (1991), Miller (1982) and (1992b), Barchiesi (1997a). Additional bibliography on these aspects of the *Fasti* can be found in Newlands' contribution to this volume (ch. 12). For the *Metamorphoses* the reader is directed especially to Hardie (1995) and (1997). On time and its importance for an understanding of Ovid's poetics, see now Schiesaro (1997b), Feeney (1999), Zissos and Gildenhard (1999), Hinds (1999b).

2

THEMES AND WORKS

5

STEPHEN HARRISON

Ovid and genre: evolutions of an elegist

Introduction: genre and supergenre

'Within elegy [Ovid] achieved an unparalleled variety of output by exploiting and extending the range of the genre as no poet had done before.'[1] This consistently inventive and radical expansion of a highly conventional poetic kind suggests that 'supergenre' might be a better term than 'genre' in discussing the extraordinary Ovidian use of the elegiac form, beginning with traditional erotic discourse but expanding and diversifying to include practically every poetic topic. Ancient genres are often classified by features such as metre and vocabulary, thematic concerns, and generic codes and models;[2] in all but the first, the Ovidian elegiac output shows a remarkable and highly self-conscious variety. Here as so often, Ovid's work confounds and subverts conventional categories.

The choice of elegy, even redefined as a supergenre, nevertheless needs to be set within the broad range of genres available for Roman poets in the first century BC, and against the ideological and literary factors influencing that choice. First, the impact of the evident political pressure for encomiastic epic for Augustus encountered by all the major Augustan poets: like Horace and Propertius, Ovid avoids this by a firmly non-epic generic policy until the *Metamorphoses*, though some of his elegiac poems show concern with epic and (the poet later claimed) with political conformism.[3] Second, partly under this same ideological pressure, elegy had already shown signs of developing from its basic amatory form into a broader genre which could encompass a variety of themes including antiquarianism and politics; this is clear already in the third book of Propertius, which probably emerged at much the same time as Ovid's earliest *Amores* in the late 20s BC. This flexibility and consequent potential richness became the basis of the

I am most grateful to Stephen Heyworth for his many helpful and stimulating comments.
[1] Hinds (1996) 1086.
[2] See most importantly Conte (1986) and (1994a).   [3] Cf. *Trist.* 2.547–66.

variety and development of the Ovidian elegiac output. Finally, elegy had been untouched by the two greatest Augustan poets, Virgil and Horace: given the strong Ovidian sense of 'belatedness',[4] the choice of a genre where a latecomer could still have literary space to operate was surely a key factor.

The increasingly broad concerns of Ovidian elegy made it a natural arena for continual metageneric reflection and debate. In its constant staging of deliberate and instructive confrontations between elegy and other literary traditions, Ovidian elegy reflects and continues a key feature of earlier Augustan poetry.[5] This is my central concern in what follows, set within a diachronic structure which attempts to track something of the poet's development.

Defining and exhausting love-elegy – *Amores*

The *Amores* are a useful starting-point, both because of their early date and because they look firmly (if with some parodic amusement) to the Ovidian starting-point of 'traditional' love-elegy as earlier established by Gallus, Propertius and Tibullus (cf. *Trist*. 4.10.51–4). In the three extant books of *Amores*, apparently condensed from an original five according to a prefatory epigram,[6] Ovid's contribution to 'traditional' love-elegy is confronted and eventually superseded by elements of other genres. It is instructive to read the collection in a linear fashion. Generic issues are foregrounded and contested right from the start of the *Amores*. 1.1 begins by repeating the first word of Virgil's *Aeneid*, *arma*, 'arms', creating the expectation of epic.[7] Cupid's intervention, a clever variation on Virgil's sixth *Eclogue* (epic diverted by Apollo into pastoral),[8] diverts epic into erotic love-elegy (1.1.27–30), wittily recalling that love-elegy too can be described as war (see *Amores* 1.9): this is indeed war, but of the bedroom rather than the battlefield. The second book announces more of the same, still under the direction of Cupid (2.1.1–3) and once again the poet represents himself (2.1.11–18) as diverted from grander, epic themes (here a Gigantomachy) by pressing erotic concerns (here the closing of the mistress's door).

But it is at the end of this book that the theme of deviation from the core model is most stressed: in *Amores* 2.18, surely written for the later, three-book edition,[9] the poet again contrasts his occupation of elegy with

---

[4] See Tarrant, ch. 1 in this volume. [5] See Conte (1986) 97–129 and (1994a) 105–28.
[6] On the second edition of the *Amores* (doubted by some scholars) see Cameron (1968) and McKeown (1986) 76–7.
[7] So McKeown (1987) 72.
[8] Both passages also of course look back to Callimachus' *Aitia*-prologue; on the literary allusions and generic stance of *Amores* 1.1 see also Keith (1992b) and McKeown (1989) 7–11.
[9] See the discussion of Hollis (1977) 150–1.

other potential genres, specifying both epic (2.18.11–12), rejected again for the erotic 'war' of elegy, and tragedy, in which the poet claims already to have achieved distinction, though returning to elegy thereafter (13–14; this looks like a reference to the lost tragedy *Medea*).[10] The poem then points for the first time to other erotic works which diversify elegiac themes: 2.18.19 'arts of love' surely refers to the *Ars amatoria*,[11] while 2.18.21–6 clearly refers to the single *Heroides*, 1–15 (and the following lines about the replies to them composed by Sabinus strongly suggest that the double *Heroides* 16–21 are as yet unwritten). In its rhetorical context, this presentation of diversification within the Ovidian poetic *oeuvre* is understandable, since the poem argues, perhaps even with some plausibility, that its addressee, the epic poet Macer (lines 1–2), may yet take up elegy (39–40), thereby in some degree resembling this Ovidian versatility.[12]

For the mention of the writing of tragedy in 2.18.13–14, as well as the general idea that the poet of the *Amores* is capable of generic diversification, plainly prepares the ground for the generic dialectic visible in the two poems which frame the third and last book. In *Amores* 3.1 we find a fully-dramatized generic debate, with a personified Tragedy seductively urging the poet to greater things (3.1.24 'begin a greater work'), and an equally anthropomorphic Elegy arguing for the poet's continued loyalty to his first love (3.1.59–60). The poet's diplomatic compromise between his two mistresses is one more book of love-elegies before turning to tragedy (61–70), and in the last poem of the book he duly marks the transition, asking Venus, mother of the *Amores*, to find another elegist (3.15.1–2), and looking ahead to the greater scope of tragedy (17–18). Here the tragedy of 2.18 reappears in force, taking over from elegy as the poet's central genre. The loss of the Ovidian *Medea* so fully prepared for here is itself one of the greatest tragedies for Augustan literary history.

This last book of *Amores* contains further signs of generic discontent and elegiac diversification. Aptly for a last book of elegies, 3.9, the elegy for Tibullus, not only buries a love-elegist and his themes but also reclaims elegy for one of its original functions, lamentation.[13] Likewise, 3.13 presents a scenario in which the poet, accompanied by his wife (the only reference to the poet's married status in the *Amores*), attends a religious festival at Falerii: this presents a poet 'maturing' both thematically, already interested in the

---

[10] So Hollis (1977) 150–1, McKeown (1998) 393–4.
[11] Though some argue for the *Amores*: see McKeown (1998) 385–6.
[12] It is not impossible that Ovid's Macer is identical with the Macer said to be abandoning love (elegy?) for war (epic?) in Tibullus 2.6: for bibliography and a sceptical view cf. Murgatroyd (1994) 239–40.
[13] For lamentation as an original function of archaic Greek elegy see Alexiou (1974) 104, West (1974) 4–5.

religious antiquarianism of the *Fasti*, and sociologically, no longer a 'poet of wickedness' (*Amores* 2.1.2) canoodling with a mistress but a respectable married man engaged in conjugal tourism. Two crucial points emerge. First, Ovid's close exploitation of conventional love-elegy is now complete, as foreshadowed in 2.18 with its indication of other generic possibilities both within and outside the elegiac form. Second, following Virgil in the *Eclogues* and *Georgics*, the poet of the *Amores* is clearly constructing a poetics of generic ascent,[14] from love-elegy to tragedy, while suggesting the existence of other forms of erotic and learned elegy. This provides an uncannily close prediction of Ovidian poetic output for the next decade or two, not least because it is quite likely that by the time of the publication of the second, three-book edition of the *Amores*, such a prediction would have been largely a prophecy after the event.

Diversifying love-elegy – *Heroides, Ars amatoria, Remedia amoris*

These works, completed in and just after the last decade BC,[15] show a clear strategy of diversification in erotic elegy. The single *Heroides* 1–15, perhaps three original books,[16] give a (purely lamenting) voice to the (powerless) abandoned woman where elegy commonly presents only the male speaker, and add both an element of rhetorical persuasion and the framework of epistolarity (both elements of interaction with prose genres).[17] All three of these characteristics are already found in Propertius 4.3, in another book of generic experimentation within love-elegy.[18] Some element of generic ascent is indicated by the greater length of these elegies (between 100 and 220 lines) and their elevated literary sources in epic (1,3,6,7), Attic tragedy (4,8,9,11,12,14), and Hellenistic or neoteric narrative poetry (2,5,10,13), the last two genres being the natural source for the complaining mythological heroines sometimes mentioned in brief examples in traditional love-elegy.[19]

---

[14] For a recent discussion of the Virgilian poetic 'career' see Theodorakopoulos (1997).

[15] See e.g. Syme (1978) 1–20. For *Heroides* 16–21 as post-exilic see n.55 below.

[16] *Heroides* 1–5 as they stand contain 752 lines, 6–10 802 lines, 11–15 858 lines; these are ideal numbers of poems and lines for Augustan poetry-books. But the issues of the distribution of the poems into books and the authenticity of several of the poems (esp. *Heroides* 15) are highly controversial: for these issues see Knox (1995) 5–14.

[17] On the connection of the *Heroides* with declamation see Knox (1995) 15–17. The use of an epistolary framework in a whole poetry-book (as opposed to the one-off poem Propertius 4.3) had already been a prominent feature of Horace's *Epistles* 1 and possibly of some lost Tibullan erotic epistles, if the information of the *vita Tibulli* attributed to Domitius Marsus is reliable (see Lee (1990) 163).

[18] Speech is also given to the mistress in Propertius 1.3 and 3.6, and a number of other poems in Propertius 4 apart from 4.3 present a female voice (4.4, 4.5, 4.7, 4.8, 4.9 and 4.11).

[19] It is also of course relevant to the *Heroides* that lamentation was perceived as one of the functions of elegy from the earliest times – see n.13 above.

The three pairs of double epistles (*Heroides* 16–21) add the further element of letters from male heroes paired with replies from heroines, yielding opportunity for rhetorical and even legalistic debate; this second collection was perhaps stimulated by the (lost) male replies written by Ovid's contemporary Sabinus to the single *Heroides* (*Amores* 2.18.27–34, *Ex Ponto* 4.16.13–14), but was no doubt also intended to give a novel twist to a sequel to a successful collection. Here we might see the reinsertion of the male as prime erotic mover as a reversion in some sense to traditional love-elegy, but the generic move upwards from the *Amores* is maintained overall in the continuing dramatic and mythological framework, with material again derived from epic, tragedy and Hellenistic narrative poetry.[20] In particular, the combination of scenic and erotic elements in all the *Heroides* can be significantly linked with the debate between elegy and tragedy staged in the third book of *Amores* (see p. 81 above).

A didactic element had been inherent in traditional love-elegy from the beginning (cf. Propertius 1.7, Tibullus 1.4), with its concern to narrate the events of the life of love to a youthful audience which might find such material useful as well as congenial. In the *Ars amatoria* such precepts are codified in a formal didactic elegiac treatise which (though it exploits much of the material of traditional elegy) shows clear signs of generic ascent from the *Amores*, not least through its constitution into three poetic books of quasi-epic length and continuity rather than the multi-poem books of the *Amores*; here the structure of the first two books of Callimachus' *Aitia* must be an important influence.[21] The *Ars* begins with some epic analogies for its speaker (*Ars* 1.5–8), adapts the metaphors and rhetorical and narratorial devices of the hexameter didactic of Virgil's *Georgics* and Lucretius' *De rerum natura*,[22] includes a lengthy catalogue of passionate heroines from Attic tragedy and Hellenistic/neoteric narrative poetry, a clear link with the *Heroides* (1.283–342),[23] and even parodies an archaic function of elegy, that of civic instruction, with a glance at the civic element of the contemporary didactic of the *Georgics*. Its opening couplet, with its explicit identification of the people of Rome as the addressee of its precepts (*Ars* 1.1–2), looks back with amusement on the moralizing advice handed down to the people of the Athenians in the archaic elegies of Solon (e.g. fr.37 West).

At the end of Book 2 the poet announces a switch of direction: Books 1 and 2 have advised males, now Book 3 will advise females, at their

---

[20] See Hintermeier (1993) and Kenney (1996).
[21] For the structure of the *Aitia* see the fundamental treatment by Parsons (1977).
[22] See Kenney (1958).
[23] This feature also goes back a long way in the tradition of hexameter didactic, to the Hesiodic *Catalogue of Women* – see Hollis (1977) 91.

request. This presents *Ars* 3 as a later sequel by popular demand after the publication of *Ars* 1–2; and Book 3 begins like Book 1 with epic analogies, comparing Roman women with the Amazons of Penthesilea (3.1–2). It is also in *Ars* 3 (343–6) that Ovid alludes explicitly and closurally to the achievements of his past work – stressing the didactic continuity of the *Ars* with the *Amores* and the innovative character of the *Heroides*, here proudly characterized as a literary mode unknown to other poets (3.346).

The *Remedia amoris* is a sequel to the *Ars*, billed as the antidote to the unhappy love possibly consequent on success in erotic pursuit (*Rem*. 9–16).[24] Though the *Remedia amoris* shares with the *Ars* a liberal use of the topics of hexameter didactic and epic book-length, we also find the equation familiar in traditional love-elegy between being a lover and writing elegy: when the poet claims to Cupid in the opening scene that he has always loved and is still loving now (*Rem*. 7–8), he is pointing not to his emotional biography but to his continuing commitment to erotic elegy in this poem. This links up with a particular feature of this poem: the *Remedia amoris* is self-consciously presented as the 'last' Ovidian work in love-elegy, with much authorial retrospection on his previous *oeuvre*. At *Rem*. 359–98, after advising lovers to concentrate on the physical frailties of their mistresses, the poet presents a substantial defence against potential critics for the colourful subject-matter of his poem: all great poets from Homer down have been subject to *inuidia*, and love-elegy is suitable for erotic matters, just as other poetic forms are suitable for different topics. The poet looks back specifically on his own work: 379–80 alludes to the *Amores*, and 395–6 makes the famous claim that Ovid has done for elegy what Virgil did for hexameter verse, i.e. he has matched in his elegiac output the variety (and ascent?) of the *Eclogues*, *Georgics* and *Aeneid*. This summary of the Ovidian elegiac career, and the awareness shown of other genres and their topics, both suggest a closural tone; and the closing personal section of this poem (*Rem*. 811–14), picking up in 811 the famous closing formula of the first collection of Horace's *Odes* (3.30.1),[25] seems to end a phase of the poet's career, not just a a single poem. Here, perhaps when the poet's literary career was turning towards the *Fasti* and *Metamorphoses*, we have a farewell to the 'lighter' love-elegy which his previous works had so strikingly diversified.

---

[24] On the *Remedia amoris* and the 'end of elegy' see above all the treatment by Conte (1994a) 35–66.

[25] It is clearly significant that Ovid uses the same phrase for the closure of his epic at *Metamorphoses* 15.871, again in imitation of Horace.

Elevating elegy – the *Fasti*

The programmatic opening of the *Fasti*[26] suggests both imagery and subject-matter associated with hexameter didactic (and already used in the *Ars amatoria*):[27] the poet asks Germanicus to steer his poetic ship (1.4) just as Virgil had asked Maecenas to aid his voyage over the literary sea (*Georgics* 2.41), and the stated syllabus of dates, their origins, and astronomy suggests an agenda strongly redolent of Aratus and other technical Hellenistic hexameter poets. But the mention of aetiology in the poem's first words ('times [of festivals] with their causes') promotes to centre stage another Hellenistic model for the poem's religious antiquarianism, the *Aetia* of Callimachus, already influential in the *Ars amatoria*. Here lies the prime justification for the poem's elegiac form: the Ovid of the *Fasti* is to follow the Propertius of Book 4 in seeking the status of the Roman Callimachus (Propertius 4.1.64), and though Callimachus' name is not directly uttered in the *Fasti*, its subject-matter and episodic form, often linked by dialogues between the poet and individual deities, irresistibly recall the first two books of the *Aitia*.[28] Like Propertius in his third and fourth books, Ovid in the *Fasti* identifies Callimachean imitation as one solution to elegy's need for generic ascent; and for both poets Callimachus, the supreme Greek elegist according to Quintilian (10.1.58), is strikingly reconstructed from an earlier character of a light, erotic, polished, anti-epic poet (Propertius 2.1.40, 2.34.32, *Am.* 2.4.19, *Ars* 3.329, *Rem.* 381,759) into a model for introducing into elegiacs some loftier didactic themes alien to traditional love-elegy.

This upwards move is encapsulated in the preface addressed to Augustus, at the head of Book 2,[29] suggesting an element of political conformism in directing a poem on the religious calendar to Augustus as head of the state religion. The poet self-consciously addresses his elegiac metre and stresses its ascent from mere erotic works, including even the more ambitious *Ars*: 2.3–4 'now for the first time, my elegiacs, you travel with greater sails – just now, I recall, you were a tiny kind of work', clearly looking back to the poet's recently concluded career of erotic elegy: 'greater sails' marks the ascent, using a navigational image typical of hexameter didactic. This drama of generic ascent, from love-elegy to elegiac Callimachean antiquarianism, is played out in particularly witty detail in the proem to *Fasti* 4, where Venus as patron goddess of the month of April is called upon to favour her poet's

---

[26] Probably revised in exile: cf. Fantham (1985).
[27] Cf. e.g. *Ars* 1.771–2 (poetic ship again); the image of the poetic voyage is also to be found in later Propertian elegy (3.3.22–4, 3.9.35–6).
[28] See esp. Miller (1982) and (1983).
[29] Possibly the original proem of the whole work: cf. Syme (1978) 21.

upward move.[30] Though greeted as the inspiration of both editions of the *Amores* (1 'mother of the twin Loves (*Amorum*)')[31] in an echo of the last poem of the *Amores*, where Ovid took leave of her in abandoning traditional love-elegy for tragedy (cf. *Amores* 3.15.1 'seek a new poet, mother of the gentle Loves (*Amorum*)'), Venus initially feels irritated at her invocation in this apparently allied but uncongenially loftier context (4.3), but relaxes when the poet claims that despite his larger themes he is still in her service (8) 'you are always my literary task (*opus*)'. This use of *opus* (by contrast with 2.4) suggests elegiac continuity, and the poet's reassurance of Venus suggests that her interests will not be far from the *Fasti*, which does indeed include a surprising number of erotic episodes for a poem on the Roman religious calendar.[32] It is important not to forget here that Callimachus' *Aitia* was the vehicle for his most famous erotic episode, that of Acontius and Cydippe (fr.67–75 Pf.), just as the *Fasti*'s many encomiastic passages on Augustus and his family pick up the courtly elements of Callimachus' work (e.g. the *Coma Berenices*, fr.110 Pf., and the *Victoria Berenices*, found in *Supplementum Hellenisticum* fr.254–69).[33]

As the *Fasti* is generically located 'above' love-elegy, so its elegiac form and antiquarian themes, laced with erotic colour, differentiate it 'downwards' from traditional epic. This literary taxonomy is further set out at the beginning of *Fasti* 3, where the poet, embarking on the month of Mars, invokes that deity and invites him to enter his poem.[34] Mars is specifically asked to remove his epic arms and armour, releasing his luxuriant hair from his helmet (1–2), a clear metapoetic symbol of descent into a softer, more elegiac role (given the common fixation of love-elegy with the mistress' hair),[35] and the god enters the poem not as the quintessential divinity of epic battles but as the seducer of Ilia, mother of Romulus, the story of whose dream and rape is then immediately narrated, with a clever variation on its famous source in Ennius' *Annales* (3.11–41).[36] This intergeneric drama, in which Mars descends to erotic activity, but in quasi-epic terms, clearly balances the scene with Venus at the beginning of Book 4, and evidently makes the same point about the *Fasti*'s liminal generic status: it is neither love-elegy, nor traditional epic, but something reflecting a dynamic interface between the two, closest to (but not identical with) Callimachean elegiac didactic.

---

[30] See the stimulating discussions by Hinds (1992) and Barchiesi (1997a) 53–61.
[31] See Barchiesi (1997a) 59.   [32] See Fantham (1983).
[33] On the probable positions of these poems in *Aitia* 3–4 cf. Parsons (1977).
[34] See the excellent discussion by Hinds (1992).
[35] Cf. e.g. Propertius 1.2.1, 2.1.7, Tibullus 1.89, [Tibullus] 3.8.9–10.
[36] See Skutsch (1985) 193–5.

Epic, elegy and generic variety – the *Metamorphoses*

The *Metamorphoses* stands as the sole surviving non-elegiac work in the extant Ovidian corpus.[37] Critics used to debate whether the *Metamorphoses* was an epic at all; but more recent scholars have rightly assumed that it meets epic criteria (being long, in hexameters, and treating mythological material), and have focused on the more fruitful question of precisely how the *Metamorphoses* negotiates its own complex position within the tradition of hexameter epic.[38] In terms of the generic ascent we have seen from *Amores* to *Fasti*, the *Metamorphoses*, though written alongside the *Fasti* chronologically, can be seen as the final stage; this is a reasonable inference both from its final programmatic self-characterization as ensuring the poet's eternal life (15.871–9), a claim not made in the *Fasti,* and by its climactic placing in the poet's catalogue of his works in *Tristia* 2 (555–62).

The *Metamorphoses* famously begins with an astonishingly brief four-line proem, identifying itself (1.4) as both 'continuous' (*perpetuum*) and 'fine-spun' (as the object of the verb *deducite*). This points to the tension evident in the poem between traditional, lengthy epic (its 15 books) and more polished, short and discontinuous Callimachean poetic practice (its 250 linked episodes); the proem, inverting the opening of *Amores* 1.1, dramatizes the generic move between elegy and epic, this time in the opposite direction.[39] The brevity of the proem (exactly matching that of Apollonius' *Argonautica*) and the metamorphic subject-matter and catalogue-frame of the poem also look to Hellenistic traditions, as does its overall concern with themes such as aetiology and paradoxography.[40] Book 1 begins with an Empedoclean/Lucretian-style cosmogonical narrative (the world's first metamorphoses), succeeded by the balancing metamorphosis-stories of the wicked Lycaon and virtuous Deucalion and Pyrrha, with the great flood and its consequences; it seems as if this poem is to be a didactic, moralizing poetic history of the world with a metamorphic slant.

This concern for self-location within the epic tradition continues throughout the poem. The *Metamorphoses*, 'fine-spinning', constantly refines traditional lengthy 'continuous' epic plots into briefer, often oblique episodes, which give unity to sections of the poem. These include the early history

---

[37] Apart from the lost tragedy *Medea*, there are some remaining fragments of an Ovidian hexameter translation of Aratus' *Phaenomena*, probably an early work (see Courtney (1993) 308–9); Pliny believed that Ovid wrote a work entitled *Halieutica* in exile on the fish of the Black Sea (Pliny *NH* 32.11, 152–3), but the extant hexameter work of that title is probably not by Ovid (see Richmond (1981) 2746–59).

[38] For recent stimulating work here see Knox (1986b), Hinds (1987), Solodow (1988), Myers (1994) and Tissol (1997).

[39] See Kenney (1976), Wheeler (1999) 8–30 and Feldherr in this volume, pp. 163–4.

[40] See Galinsky (1975) 1–14 and esp. Myers (1994).

of Thebes (3.1–4.603),[41] the Argonauts (7.1–158), the deeds of Theseus (7.404–end of Book 8) and Hercules (9.1–272), the *Iliad* and cyclic epics (12.1–13.622), and of course the history of Rome, especially using the *Aeneid* (13.623 to the end).[42] The last book also incorporates a reprise of didactic epic in the speech of Pythagoras (15.75–478), which in its Empedo-clean and Ennian tone forms a ring with the initial cosmogony of the opening book.[43]

The *Metamorphoses'* generic concerns do not of course restrict themselves to negotiating the poem's individual space within epic. It has been truly said that the poem 'handles the themes and employs the tone of virtually every species of literature',[44] and this generically multifarious character is often stressed. Particularly programmatic is the episode at 1.452–73. Here the first erotic episode of the work is explicitly introduced (1.452 *primus amor*, 'the first love'),[45] and an evidently metapoetical scene ensues in which Apollo asks Cupid what the latter, associated with love, is doing in 'his' supposedly martial epic (1.456).[46] Cupid shoots Apollo with an arrow. This confrontation between gods dramatizes the irruption of erotic/elegiac themes into the poem, and (like the opening of the *Metamorphoses* as a whole) evidently recalls and inverts the programmatic opening of the *Amores*, where Cupid shoots the poet in order to turn him from epic to elegy. The point is made that the erotic concerns of the *Amores* will be present in Ovid's epic, just as they had been present in the *Fasti* (see pp. 85–6 above); and the ensuing episode of Daphne adds instant corroboration, with Apollo playing the plaintive elegiac lover (compare e.g. 1.508 with the probably Gallan Virgil *Ecl.*10.48–9 and Propertius 1.8.7–8).[47]

Though elegy and the closely connected tradition of neoteric erotic narrative are important for the *Metamorphoses* (the other main episode of Book 1, that of Io, makes clear use of Calvus' lost *Io* – cf. 1.532 with Calvus fr. 9 Courtney), other literary genres are equally significant. Outside epic, elegy and Hellenistic/neoteric narrative, tragedy perhaps provides the most material: the epicization of Euripides' *Bacchae* in 3.511–733 and of his *Hecuba* in 13.399–733 are only two of the most notable examples.[48] The tradition of literary hymns is much mined, especially in the hymn to Ceres at 5.341–571, which (like the parallel narrative of the rape of Proserpina in

---

[41] See Hardie (1990).   [42] On 'Ovid's *Aeneid*' see most recently Hinds (1998) 107–19.
[43] See Hardie (1995).   [44] Solodow (1988) 18.
[45] Stephen Heyworth attractively sees *primus amor* as an echo of the opening of Propertius 1.1 'Cynthia was the first . . .', reinforcing the elegiac flavour here.
[46] See Nicoll (1980) and Knox (1986b) 14–17.
[47] See Knox (1986b) 14–17, Solodow (1988) 21.
[48] For full parallels see still Lafaye (1904).

Fasti 4.417–620) plainly incorporates much material from the *Homeric Hymn to Demeter*.[49] Pastoral scenes also occur, especially in the love-song of Polyphemus in *Metamorphoses* 13.235–68.[50]

The incorporation of other genres was of course not foreign to the epic tradition: the model of the *Aeneid* here is clear.[51] But the sheer range of other genres which are in some sense included in the *Metamorphoses*, and its occasional stress on this process of inclusion, suggests that generic multiplicity within a formally epic framework is particularly fundamental to the poem. This is another Hellenistic feature, following the generic variety and self-consciousness of works like Callimachus' *Aitia*, which incorporated elements from epic (fr.7 Pf.), epigram (fr.64 Pf.) and epinician poetry (*SH* 254–69) into its elegiac framework. Metamorphosis is the theme of the poem, both in terms of its formal content, and in terms of its generic variety. Genres appear and disappear and are transformed into each other through the long course of the poem, following its explicit programme (1.1–2): literary *forms* are transformed into new *bodies* of poetic work.

Elegy and epistolarity in exile – *Tristia, Ex Ponto, Ibis*

The Ovidian poetry written from exile presents a self-conscious rhetoric of poetic decline: the poet constantly tells his readers that this new work is inferior to what went before.[52] This proposition, accepted at face value by generations of critics, has been challenged and at least partly refuted by recent work which has re-evaluated the exile poetry.[53] In terms of generic complexity and drama, these poems certainly continue the concerns of the pre-exilic work at an equivalent or even greater level of intensity.

In general, the ten books of poetry certainly dated to Ovid's exile (five books of *Tristia*, one of *Ibis*, and four of *Ex Ponto*) constitute a double return in terms of the poet's career, to the genre of elegy and to the mode of epistolarity, explored so interestingly in the single *Heroides* (1–15);[54] indeed, many scholars, on plausible stylistic grounds, now add the paired *Heroides* (16–21) to the poems composed in exile.[55] As the title *Tristia*, 'sad things', suggests, the books from exile naturally share with the *Heroides* the

---

[49] See Hinds (1987). For further echoes of the Homeric Hymns in the *Met.* see Barchiesi (1999).
[50] See Farrell (1992) and more summarily Solodow (1988) 21–2.
[51] For the *Aeneid* as inclusive of other genres see e.g. Hardie (1986) 22.
[52] See Williams (1994) 50–9.
[53] See e.g. Kenney (1965), Hinds (1985), Williams (1994).
[54] On epistolary markers in the exile poetry see Stroh (1981) 2640–4, and on Ovidian epistolarity in general see Kennedy, ch. 13 in this volume.
[55] E.g. Knox (1995) 6, Reeve (1973) 330 n.1, Barchiesi (1996).

quintessential elegiac theme of lamentation: *lacrima*, 'tear', and its cognates occur 41 times in the *Tristia* and *Ex Ponto*, *tristis*, 'sad', and its cognates 55 times.[56]

Within the ten firmly exilic books, however, the first two books of *Tristia* show perhaps the most open generic self-consciousness. This is not surprising given their overt function, 'booking the return trip':[57] here the poet is concerned both to show diplomatic humility and repentance and to demonstrate through poetic pyrotechnics that he is still Rome's greatest living writer – both arguments for his return from Tomi.

Though the theme of the allegedly inferior quality of this new book, commensurate with the misery of its author's exile, is swiftly raised (1.1.11–14, 35–40), *Tristia* 1 seeks to claim a new and even ambitious literary space for itself. It is particularly concerned to differentiate exilic elegy from previous Ovidian erotic elegy: its theme is lamentation, not erotic pleasure (1.1.122) and it explicitly proclaims its difference from the disastrous *Ars* (1.1.67–8), commonly invoked in the exile poetry as a negative generic paradigm (cf. *Trist*.2, 3.1.4, 3.14.6, 5.12.48, *Pont*.1.1.2, 2.2.104, 3.3.37–8). The thematization of sorrow is repeated in other exilic programmatic contexts (cf. esp. *Trist*.5.1.3–4, *Pont*.1.1.15–16), as is the explicit differentiation from previous love-elegy (*Trist*.5.1.15–19). Particularly interesting is the rewriting of previous elegiac themes in *Trist*.1.6, the central poem of the book. Here Ovid's wife is addressed not only as a more respectable version of the elegiac mistress, gloriously perpetuated in the verse of the lover/poet (cf. *Amores* 1.3.19–26), a common theme of the conjugal elegies from Tomi (*Trist*.4.3.81–2, 5.14.1–6), but also as greater than the heroines of the *Heroides*: she will displace Penelope from the head of that collection (*Heroides* 1).[58]

If *Tristia* 1 is concerned to differentiate itself from love-elegy, it is also concerned to assimilate itself to epic. Ovid's voyage to Tomi in *Tristia* 1 can be explicitly compared to the *Odyssey* (1.5.57–84; cf. also 1.2.9), and is narrated in a manner which at its start strongly recalls the *Aeneid*, beginning *in medias res* with a dramatic storm with many verbal echoes of that of *Aeneid* 1 (1.2). The Virgilian analogy then continues with an emotional account of the hero's reluctant departure from his native city and wife (1.3, cf. *Aeneid* 2). 1.7 on the *Metamorphoses* brings Ovid's own epic into play, lamenting the poem's incomplete state as in *Tristia* 2, but again raises Virgilian parallels: the epic poem allegedly (19–22) burned by its author (but of course 'fortunately' preserved in other copies – 23–6) irresistibly recalls

[56] See n.13 above. [57] The title of Hinds (1985), very revealing on *Tristia* 1.
[58] See the treatment by Hinds (1985).

Virgil's supposed instruction for the combustion of the *Aeneid* (*Vita Donati* 38–9).[59] The *Metamorphoses* is here presented as the *Aeneid*'s equivalent, just as the *Aeneid* is echoed in this new style of elegy.

This concern with relations to other 'approved' contemporary genres, Ovid's assertion that he is as 'Augustan' a poet as Virgil, of course reaches its climax in *Tristia* 2, the single-poem book addressed to Augustus. This long epistolary self-defence can be seen as an Ovidian, elegiac counterpart of Horace's 'approved' hexameter epistle to Augustus (*Ep.*2.1), likewise concerned with the relationship between poetry and emperor.[60] The poem's main defensive proposition, that the *Ars* was not criminal, and erotically or morally no worse than other approved types of poetry (including generically elevated comparisons with Homer, Virgil and Greek tragedy – 371–408, 533–6), is supplemented by a climactic argument at 547–62. Here Ovid's more ambitious work is introduced as an argument for his essential worthiness, with the *Fasti* and the *Metamorphoses* presented as elevated in tone and full of praise of the *princeps* and his family.

The remaining books of the *Tristia* and the four books of *Ex Ponto* continue to differentiate Ovidian exilic elegy from previous love-elegy. The poems addressed to or longing for the poet's wife continue (as in *Trist.*1.6) the replacement of the disreputable mistress with a respectable wife (*Trist.*3.3, 4.3, 5.2, 5.5, 5.11, 5.14; *Pont.*1.4, 3.1). This can be varied by further back-reference to love-elegy: *Trist.* 3.3 also picks up the theme of an epistle to the mistress from the poet in distant illness (cf. also *Trist.*5.3), complete with morbidity and proleptic epitaph, from Tibullus 1.3, while *Trist.*3.7 addresses a further kind of mistress, the poet 'Perilla',[61] who combines the name of a famous elegiac mistress (cf.*Trist.*2.437–8) but has poetic talents which (like those of the book in which she features) are specifically respectable and non-elegiac (3.7.11–12). 'Respectable' revision of elegy is seen in other ways too: the end of *Pont.*1.4 inverts the famous end of *Amores* 1.13, with the coming of Aurora now desired for the poet to worship the imperial family, not deprecated as ending a night of love, while *Pont.*2.2.39–40 pathetically presents the exiled poet as an excluded petitioner in the language of the locked-out lover of elegy. Even the triumph-elegy of *Trist.*4.2, later apparently characterized by the poet as failed generic ascent to epic within exilic elegy (*Pont.*2.5.27–30; cf. *Pont.*3.4.83ff. on the problem of metre for describing a triumph), in fact picks up the model of Tibullus 1.7 as the elegiac poet's response to the deeds of a great man.

---

[59] See Hinds (1985).   [60] See Barchiesi (1997a) 29, (2001) 79–103.
[61] The name is surely a sobriquet in Ovid. I agree with Wheeler (1925) that 'Perilla' was Ovid's stepdaughter; for a contrary view see Luck (1977) 199.

Perhaps the most explicit rewriting of love-elegy in the later exile poetry comes in *Pont*.3.3.[62] There the poet sees a vision of Cupid, sadly changed from his smiling and generically transforming appearance in *Amores* 1.1 (cf. 3.3.13–20; cf. 3.3.31–2 with *Am*. 1.1.1–4). This is clearly a metapoetical statement about the 'decline' of Ovidian elegy in the exilic poems (cf. *Pont*.3.3.17 with *Trist*.1.1.1.12): Cupid, the inspiration of Ovidian love-elegy, revisits him in inferior form in his far-distant exile. The poet addresses him with condemnation of his own earlier, erotic poetry, especially the *Ars*, which led to such disaster and which prevented higher themes (3.3.35–40). Cupid replies by reiterating the defence of the *Ars* given in *Tristia* 2, fittingly repeating an elegiac argument, but goes on to hint at higher genres: his last visit to the Black Sea was to inspire Medea with love, a clear reference to the Argonautic epics (79–80), and he concludes by praising Tiberius' triumph and the imperial house, suggesting that his prayers at this joyous time may perhaps help the poet's cause (85–92); the suggestion is that Ovidian elegy can return to the encomiastic topics which earlier love-elegy excluded (cf. 35–6), if the poet himself returns to Rome to witness great imperial occasions.

Elsewhere, too, the later exile poetry continues to be aware of and employ both the full range of Ovidian elegy and more elevated modes and genres. The aetiology of the name of Tomi given in *Trist*.3.9 not only recalls the Callimachean aetiological flavour of the *Fasti* and *Metamorphoses*, but also narrates the dismemberment of Absyrtus, again from the epic Argonaut saga (cf. *Pont*.3.3); *Trist*.4.4, with an equally historical bent, recalls the tragic story of *Iphigenia in Tauris*, a story which appears again in *Pont*.3.2, where an aged Getic man, resembling the moralizing Lelex of *Metamorphoses* 8 as well as the local informants of the *Fasti*, tells it as the background to the great friendship of Orestes and Pylades. In *Pont*.4.7 we find a quasi-epic narrative of the governor Vestalis' capture of the city of Aegisos, reminding us that Greek poets such as Simonides could describe battles in elegiacs.[63]

Between the *Tristia* (AD 8–12) and *Ex Ponto* (AD 12–?16) in date comes the extraordinary *Ibis* (AD 10/11).[64] This one-book elegiac curse-poem is modelled on a lost (probably elegiac) curse-poem of the same name by Callimachus,[65] whom the poet also claims to be following in the work's

---

[62] On this poem see also Kenney (1965), Claassen (1991).

[63] On the epic colouring of the Ovidian poem see Williams (1994) 34–42; cf. Simonides *El*.3 W. (Artemisium) and 10–11 W. (Plataea), with the discussions in *Arethusa* 29.2 (1996).

[64] For the most recent and useful treatment see Williams (1996).

[65] See most conveniently Williams (1996) 15.

uncharacteristic obscurity (53–8). This attack on an enemy named only in bestial caricature as the unclean bird Ibis shows evident links with the generic tradition of archaic Greek iambus, a trait which no doubt goes back to the Callimachean original as well as Horace's more recent revival of it in the *Epodes*. Not only is the naming and shaming central to Archilochean iambus specifically invoked as a future punishment for Ibis should the anonymous attack of the *Ibis* be ineffectual (51–2), but at the beginning of the poem the poet announces that the peaceful nature of his previous elegiac output will now change in the taking up of invective arms (1–10). This is in effect a generic descent, iambus with its vulgar subject-matter and quasi-prosaic verse-form being perceived as 'low' since Aristotle. In fact, there is considerable continuity with Ovid's other work: this 642-line anonymous invective is in effect a kind of extension of the elegiac attacks on unnamed enemies or false friends found in the *Tristia* and *Ex Ponto* (*Trist.*1.8, 3.11, 5.8, *Pont.*4.3, 4.16), and the 'ferociously dense catalogue of sufferings'[66] wished on the hapless Ibis has much in common with the mythological learning of the *Metamorphoses* and *Fasti*. Again we have a generic experiment which fits well with the constant innovation of Ovidian poetics.

FURTHER READING

The most instructive generic debate in Ovidian criticism has centred on the comparison and contrast of the two Ovidian treatments of the myth of Persephone in *Fasti* 4.417–620 and *Metamorphoses* 5.341–661. The attempt of Heinze (1960; originally published 1919) to identify a clearly 'epic' narrative in the *Metamorphoses* version and an 'elegiac' version in the *Fasti* has been rightly countered, most creatively by Hinds (1987), which in a characteristically nuanced and intelligent discussion sees both versions as generically ambiguous, creatively problematizing the issue of genre.

Connected with this (and equally compulsory reading) is Hinds (1992), which looks at the instructive confrontations with epic in the programmatic passages of the *Fasti*. A connected debate is that on the genre of the *Metamorphoses*: here Hinds (1987), a good guide to what went before, is again vital in showing that generic problematization need not mean a lack of generic identity as an epic (where many critics had simply pronounced the *Metamorphoses* as being beyond generic classification). Knox (1986b), Farrell (1992), Myers (1994) and Hardie (1995) are all helpful in searching for the *Metamorphoses*' diverse literary affinities both epic and non-epic, while Nicoll (1980) presents an exemplary metageneric reading of a programmatic episode of the poem.

The most stimulating treatment of the issue of genre in the erotic elegiac works of Ovid is the chapter 'Love without Elegy' in Conte (1994a); though formally on the

---

[66] Hinds (1996) 1086.

Remedia amoris, it provides creative insights into Ovid's treatment of and variations on the 'elegiac code'. Jacobson (1974) contains much of interest on generic issues in the single *Heroides*; the paired *Heroides* 16–21 have much to offer here too (some material in Hintermeier (1993) 152–79, but more could be said). Hinds (1985) and Williams (1994) open up some stimulating perspectives on generic play in the *Tristia* and *Ex Ponto*, and this is again an area where much interesting work remains to be done. Most recently, Barchiesi (2001) contains much of interest on generic issues in Ovid.

6

ALISON SHARROCK

Gender and sexuality

Ovid has been called sympathetic to women.[1] While many modern feminists would be unhappy about this chivalric designation, there is no doubt that the Ovidian corpus provides a particularly rich site for gendered study. More than any other non-dramatic ancient poetry, male-authored as it overwhelmingly is, Ovid's work gives space to a female voice, in however problematic a manner, and to both male and female voices which reflect explicitly on their own gendered identity. It is also driven by a troubled relationship with the purveyors of Roman masculinity – the army, politics, Augustus, epic, and so on. Moreover, the poet – par excellence – of the fluidity of identity clearly provokes a gendered reading.

Unstable categories

Although sexual identity, in its modern form of a choice between homosexuality and heterosexuality, is not the driving force of ancient constructions of personality, the development and maintenance of Gender was a major preoccupation.[2] Engendering the self is as crucial as it is unstable in Ovid, poet of fluidity. The tidiest story of growing up to gendered identity is that of Iphis (*Met.* 9.666–797).[3] Before her birth, her father instructed that the child should be killed if it were a girl, but her mother saved her, and brought her up as a boy. On reaching adolescence, she was due to be properly and respectably married to someone with whom she herself was in love. The trouble

For this essay, I am especially grateful to Effie Spentzou and Patricia Salzman, from whom I have learned so much about Ovid and gender.
[1] See for example Wilkinson (1955) 86: '[Ovid] had also a tender side to his nature which gave him an interest in the weaker sex and a certain insight into what their feelings might be'; Griffin (1977) 59: 'Ovid actually liked women as a sex.' Despite the fact that such statements can look a little condescending in the present day, it seems to me that, with a bit of cultural translation, a valid point is being made.
[2] See Williams (1999), esp. 4–7, Gleason (1995).
[3] See Wheeler (1997) and (1999) 57 for an interesting connection with the other Iphis in the poem.

is that she and her bride are both women. Isis comes to the rescue, by turning her into a man. The story shows the anxieties surrounding the acquisition of gendered identity, and especially male gender. Precisely because its fantasy solution is so neat and nice, the difficulties in the interaction of nature and nurture in sexual identity are exposed as well as fudged. There are far more stories of the failure of entry into adult sexuality: Phaethon, Pentheus, Actaeon, Hermaphroditus, and most of all Narcissus. Narcissus embodies an essential paradox in desire: the lover desires union with the beloved, but desire requires distance. That lesson is painfully learned by the transgressive women Myrrha and Byblis, lovers of their father and brother respectively.[4] These too are forms of arrested development.

One of the oddest aspects of Roman sexuality to modern eyes is that male love, even in its most conventional manifestations, is not unproblematically masculine for the Romans. Masculinity is predicated not only on sexual performance but also on autarky, control of the self both internal (in the emotions) and external (in political liberty).[5] If the very thing that makes a man (sexual power) also unmakes him (by undermining his autarky), then gendered categories are never going to be easy and stable. It is very difficult to come to a sense of Roman constructions of femininity that do not tell us more about masculine attitudes to the Other (female, slave, foreigner) than they do about real Roman women, but since the lives of real Roman women will have been partly shaped by these masculine attitudes, such a sense is still useful. The category 'Woman' is crucially important, and perhaps at first sight simple, since you just need to look at the opposite of the ideal Man (start with 'soft, passive, and silent') – but in practice this simplicity is deceptive ('just like a woman'?).

Sexual performance is of course a part of the definition of virility, but even this virility is not without its anxieties. When Semele, mother of Bacchus, is tricked by Juno into asking Jupiter to make love to her in all his glory, the father of gods and men knows that his *uis*, his sexual power, will be too much for her (*Met.* 3.256–315). He tries to wear himself out first, by casting thunderbolts around. Even with these precautions, however, he cannot control himself, and Semele is burnt to a crisp. The story, almost too funny to be as troubling as it should be, nonetheless shows us how this very *uis* may be the cause of its own undoing. So it was also for Phaethon (*Met.* 1.747–2.332): this high-spirited boy overreached himself by demanding that his father, the Sun, give him proof of his paternity by letting him drive the Sun's chariot

---

[4] See Janan (1991).

[5] The gendered constructions of society in Roman culture exist not only in the relationship between the sexes but also in the interactions of power and identity in terms of slavery, class, and race.

across the sky. The boy himself, and nearly the whole world, is burned up when he cannot control the chariot's raging course. A thunderbolt from Jupiter stops him, but it is clear that the wild sexuality that runs out of control in the adolescent remains as the driving force also of the adult: while Jupiter is surveying the damage, fire courses through him at the sight of Callisto, the next victim of his sexual interest. In his loss of control over his sexual power, Jupiter is at once both hyper-masculine and feminized.

A man, to be a man, must be *durus* (hard), but love (for which he needs to be *durus*) will make him *mollis* (soft).[6] He must also be impenetrable. Historians of sexuality express something of the defining characteristic of Roman sexuality through the distinction between the active penetrator and the passive penetrated. Real men are not penetrated; 'women' are, as the notorious phrase *muliebria pati* ('to suffer female things') eloquently proclaims.[7] Among the many Ovidian stories illustrating this point, particularly telling is that of Caenis/Caeneus. Caenis was a virgin who was raped by Neptune. In recompense, she asks to cease to be a woman, so that she cannot suffer the same thing again. Neptune recognises the significance of her request, and makes her not only a man but also completely invulnerable to weapons, military as well as sexual (*Met.* 12.168–209).[8] We might illustrate the feminine alternative to such extreme masculine invulnerability through the story of Cyane (*Met.* 5.409–39). This nymph rose up from her pool to try and block the passage of Pluto with his stolen bride Proserpina, but her physical and verbal attempts to stop him were destroyed when the god hurled his spear into her pool, and through it opened up a way into the underworld. The pool stands here not just for Cyane but for all femininity; the spear is the raping phallus of masculine penetration.

But – these gendered norms don't tell the whole story. Time and again in Ovidian erotics, the lover, even when he is a rapist, is himself the victim of a wound. In the very first erotic adventure of the *Metamorphoses*,[9] Apollo the archer has been vaunting his masculine prowess in overcoming the monstrous Python, when he makes the mistake of provoking Cupid, claiming that the love-god's arrows have no place in a real man's epic (*Met.* 1.452–567). Cupid's reply is to shoot. Apollo is stricken with love; his beloved Daphne

---

[6] See Edwards (1993).   [7] See Williams (1999) 7.

[8] It is probably telling that both Caeneus and the other invulnerable man, Cycnus, are finally killed by being suffocated. Keith (1999) 234 sees death by suffocation as a return of the invulnerable super-men to female status. It seems to me, however, that the sheer excess required to suffocate them leaves the problems of masculinity and violence intact. Instead of a straightforward, forceful thrust into the opponent's body, the perplexed heroes are reduced to a frenzied crushing, almost like a travesty of a toddler's tantrum.

[9] So it is generally characterized, but Deucalion and Pyrrha comes first. Marriage is a badly neglected topic in Ovid, as I discuss further at the end of this chapter.

is shot with an antaphrodisiac and made to flee, and so begin the *MetAMORphoses*.[10] So began also the *Amores*: love poetry came into being when the poet, who was trying to wield the *arma* of epic (1.1.1), was instead himself penetrated by the arrow of Cupid, and received the *opus* – elegiac poetry and sex – which constitutes the *Amores*. The immediate result of Cupid's arrow is *Amores* 1.2, which is primarily concerned with portraying the lover as *inermis* (unarmed) and as wounded. The elegiac lover's classic (generic) desire is for entry to the beloved, and his classic song is the paraclausithyron (song before the locked door of the beloved), but as a poet he must constantly fail to penetrate the door; he must surrender to love (*Am.* 1.2.9–10) in the hopes that the promise of *Ars* 2.197 ('by yielding you'll leave as victor') will offer him some consolation. The point, then, is that even though Roman sexuality is constituted on the basis of penetrability or otherwise, nonetheless even the penetrator himself can be characterized as suffering a *uulnus* through being a lover, and so the gendered categories will not stay neatly separate.

Nowhere is this more true than in the discourse of poetics itself, since the act of writing is *both* an active, masculine activity (speech, *auth*ority), *and* also insecure in its masculine position by comparison with political and military activity. To be a love poet, in particular, is both to be virile and to be effeminate.[11] This paradox develops a particular poignancy for Ovid in exile: on the one hand, we have the elegiac limp and the failing poetic powers,[12] but on the other hand the sexiness of his poetry which caused his downfall is also what makes his exilic poetry attractive. Moreover, this is a heroic failure. Ovid in exile is Ulysses – an epic hero but weaker, more vulnerable to suffering than his *exemplum*. The terminology of wounding is again very active: Ovid has been wounded by his poetry, both literally hurt and in love; and wounded by Augustus, who has also been wounded by him.[13] The *uulnus* both gives and destroys his poetic *uires*. It is the *uulnus* itself which stimulates the poetry, gives it *materia*, as in erotic elegy, and yet it is the *uulnus* for which he seeks a cure through the poetry.

The erotodidactic poems, at first sight, take a very clear line on the constructions of gender, engendering the addressee in a manner far more explicit than most ancient poetry. This engendering happens not only in the division between *Ars amatoria* 1 and 2 (for men) and *Ars* 3 (for women) but also in the

---

[10] The outrageous bilingual wordplay is typically Ovidian. The proper derivation of the word 'meta-morphosis' is from Greek words meaning 'changing shape', not the Latin word for love.

[11] See Wyke (1995), Sharrock (1995), Wheeler (1999).

[12] Williams (1994), Rosenmeyer (1997).

[13] The erotic connotations of wounding are never far below the surface in the elegies from exile. In *Trist.* 2.568 Ovid singles himself out as the only poet whom his muse harms.

explicit rules and regulations about the appropriate dress and behaviour of the genders.[14] But all these clear-cut distinctions are nuanced, if not undercut, by the intrusion of a third party – the author – and by the problematizing of the gendered imagery. The young lover, learning to be an adult male, is himself seduced by the poet-teacher, and is taught to win by losing. Despite, or because of, the military and gladiatorial vocabulary, it seems that perhaps learning to be a lover is not the best and most manly way of learning to be a Roman man.

Who speaks?

Writing poetry, for Ovid, is not just *about* 'sexuality'; it is itself an erotic experience, in which it is impossible to distinguish clearly between sex and poetry. But despite all the instabilities and subversions of gender in the poet's voice and in Roman sexuality, the fact remains that poets are nearly all men, and Ovid is a man. This makes it all the more remarkable that so much space in the Ovidian corpus (*sic*!) is given to women. The *Heroides* are of particular interest here, for a crucial question is the extent to which we may be able to read a 'woman's voice'. What kind of gendered voice is produced by a male author speaking through a female mask, but completely subsuming his masculine authority into the female writing? The poems have no frame, no explicit sign from the author that we are really reading a male text.[15] Moreover, as is often noted, the poems partake of several 'feminine' features, such as repetition and absence.[16] Even if from one point of view this is (just) a reality effect, a more recuperative reading would see these poems as expressive of the feminine.[17] The temptation is to ask 'what does Ovid mean by this? – to make us hear Dido, or hear Ovid playing Dido?'[18] The same question arises when we try to confront more widely the very high profile of women in the corpus: is it friendly or not? How far is Ovid implicated in the exposure and objectification of women and denigrating violence towards them, perpetrated in and by his texts? The theoretical questions are too big

[14] See, for example, *Ars* 1.505–24, on how a lover should cultivate his appearance, but not too much, because all sartorial excess should be left to those who are not really men. In *Ars* 3, by contrast, most of the instruction is about cultivating the appearance. As often, the *Ars amatoria* treads an uneasy and playful line between opposition to and appropriation of conventional Roman mores. Ovid's advice has a lot in common with serious philosophical and moral writing on manly deportment. See Gleason (1995), esp. ch. 3.

[15] See Kennedy, ch. 13 in this volume, Farrell (1998).

[16] Rosati (1992), Spentzou (forthcoming), and on absence as 'feminine', Barthes (1990) 13–4. See also Harvey (1989).

[17] Indeed, the old 'sympathetic to women' judgement is perhaps an early twentieth-century version of such a reading: Cormier (1992).

[18] Desmond (1993).

to address here:[19] perhaps we may side-step them by looking at what the text does.

Woman are 'meant' to be silent. The suppression of women's voices, bodies, and sexuality is an all-too-common story in (ancient) culture and in the Ovidian corpus, where it is one of the meanings of metamorphosis.[20] We can see how the loss of humanity, autonomy, and speech is tied in with sexuality for women, in three early stories of rape and metamorphosis: Daphne, loved by Apollo and turned into a laurel tree, Io, loved by Jupiter and turned into a cow, Syrinx, loved by Pan and turned into pan-pipes. In each case, the changed woman is made to acknowledge her domination, by an act of para-speech that accentuates her loss of voice. The laurel tree nods assent to becoming a symbol for triumphs; the cow lows; the pan-pipes have music made through them by their player/lover. Io does also communicate by writing her name on the sand, in an attempt to hold on to her identity in the face of divine attempts to submerge it, but as Wheeler points out, her father takes this written communication as a sign of her loss of humanity through her loss of voice.[21] But these stories are mild compared with another set in which the voice and sexuality are violently entwined.

The most gruesome of these is the story of Philomela (*Met.* 6.424–674). After being raped by her barbarian brother-in-law, this eloquent Athenian virgin took him verbally to task, only to suffer a second, more absolute rape when he cut out her tongue, metaphorically castrating as well as deflowering her.[22] The resourceful Philomela still manages to find a way to communicate, by weaving a picture of her sufferings, and sending it to her sister. Her action here, again, reflects on the ambiguous gendering of the act of poetry, since weaving is a clear signifier both of Woman and of the poet, while the very fact of the communication is a challenge to Tereus' masculine domination.

---

[19] On this subject, Richlin (1992) is crucial. See also Curran (1978) and Sharrock (forthcoming).

[20] The loss of control in metamorphosis itself may be regarded as gendered and unstable: see Segal (1998).

[21] Wheeler (1999), especially 50–8. Wheeler sees writing in the *Metamorphoses* as particularly associated with the feminine, an association which would contribute to the problematic gendering of the author himself. Farrell (1998) 314 links the story of Io with the advice to Ovid's female pupil in *Ars* 3.617–18 to send a message, even if she is being watched by an Argus (who guarded Io). Writing becomes a way out of silence for women. On the significance of the proper use of the voice in developing gendered identity see Gleason (1995) chs. 4–6.

[22] See Richlin (1992). For a powerful feminist reading and appropriation of this story, see Joplin (1984=1991), who argues for a positive sense in the enabling power of the tapestry and its communication, as bringing to light all injustices against women (48). Segal (1994b) sets the issue of violent rape within the context of voyeuristic violence in Ovid and in Roman society more generally. Miller (1988) ch. 4 takes up the metaphorical force of weaving for the positive valuation of women's activity as writers.

The sequel is well known – Procne and Philomela kill, cook, and serve Procne and Tereus' son to his father, and the principals are all turned into birds. The story allows some measure of positive activity to these women, but only up to a point, for in the process of taking action and communication into their own hands, they turn into monsters, like their enemy.[23]

In the *Fasti*, a story of rape and mutilation stands at the foundation of Roman religion. The avoidance of ill-omened or inappropriate words was crucial to Roman ritual, and was under the tutelage of Tacita, the silent goddess. Her children were the Lares, the gods of the Roman household. This is how she came by them: Lara was a chatty nymph in early Latium, who told her sister Juturna of Jupiter's plan to capture and rape her, and told Juno of this next offence against her marriage. Jupiter therefore cut out her tongue and sent her down to the underworld, place of the silent, in the company of Mercury. But on the way, the soul-guider raped her, despite her mute appeals, and the Lares were the result. Her silencing and sexual domination are necessary to the foundation of Roman culture.

This story reflects a common calumny against women, that of excessive talkativeness. The most famous illustration of this pattern is Echo (*Met.* 3.355–401), whose story is one of several Ovidian myths to be appropriated by modern feminist thought.[24] Echo was punished, for keeping Juno talking while Jupiter pursued the nymphs, with a literalization of a normative situation for ancient women – she can only repeat, not initiate. This handicap is eloquently displayed in the story of her love for the beautiful boy Narcissus. But this is more than just a charming tale. Along with Pygmalion's statue,[25] Echo's shadowy semi-existence, mirrored and reflected in the male text rather than seen face-to-face, encapsulates the representation of women in (Ovidian) poetry generally. The elegiac woman is as much muse and poetry as she is flesh and blood; even in exile, the elegiac pattern remains in more respectable form. The role of *puella* is now shared between Augustus and Ovid's wife,[26] but remains as shadowy as before, an echo of the poet's voice.

---

[23] In this series of stories in the *Metamorphoses*, gender and race are tied up in each other. See Segal (1994), esp. 268–9, 276–7, and Joplin (1991).

[24] As is Philomela: Joplin (1984=1991), Marder (1992). For Echo, see Berger (1996), Spivak (1993); for Arachne, Miller (1988).

[25] See Sharrock (1991) and Hillis Miller (1990) 1–12. Liveley (1999) argues for the positive valuation of the statue as a woman, actively playing a role in her own metamorphosis, deliberately acting like an elegiac *puella*. This is typical of a new strand in feminist readings of classical literature, in which a 'releasing' reading offers a more positive evaluation of women's roles. My own answer to this approach is still that the woman of *Ars* 3 is 'womanufactured', but I expect to see more of this debate in the future.

[26] Rosenmeyer (1997).

The masculine order

The entire Ovidian corpus is in dialogue with the most powerful contemporary signifiers of the masculine order: Augustus, *arma* (war and epic), and political life.[27] It is a dialogue full of tensions, but it would be wrong to see it as a simple opposition between Roman masculinity and Ovidian difference.

The images for love which help to construct the elegiac world of the *Amores* and *Ars amatoria both* oppose *and* partake in the norms of Roman masculinity. The well-known figure *militia amoris* (the soldiery of love) is the most obvious example. *Amores* 1.9 'outrageously' compares the lover and the soldier down to the finest detail: it is outrageous because conventionally the lover is the exact opposite of the soldier, as the effeminate is of the super-masculine. But on the other hand Ovid is exactly right: his poetry is constantly showing us both the violence and the *uis* of love and also the vulnerability of violence. Again, in *Amores* 2.11 the lover is set up in opposition to the sailor, and yet in 2.12 he precisely is the soldier, only his is a victory *sine sanguine* ('without blood'). Even this itself is not so straightforward an opposition as it might seem, since 'blood' is very often used as a figure for sexuality.

The *Fasti* is, in some ways, Ovid's most Roman and even most masculine work. It also has almost as many rapes as the *Metamorphoses*. If it is useful to say that Augustan ideology appropriates to itself the discourse of positively-valued masculinity, and predicates that on Romanness (and Romanness on that), then we need to consider the construction of gender-difference in the work in which Ovid most of all confronts and perhaps conforms to 'Roman values', especially when he does so in elegiacs. The play and interplay with masculinity and intertextuality is most explicit in the opening of Book 2, where the little elegies have grown, but not into epic. Instead, they have developed this new genre of aetiological (patriotic? propagandistic?) elegy.[28] The phrase *haec mea militia est* ('this is my soldiering', 2.9) is a statement of the *Fasti*'s engagement with and opposition to epic, but it is also a commemoration of another famous line *militat omnis amans* ('Every lover is a soldier', *Am.* 1.9.1), and a reminder that the poetic pose, in erotic and in non-erotic elegy, is as much an appropriation of Roman masculinity as it is opposition to it. The proem to *Fasti* 2 continues to dwell on the *arma* the poet does *not* have. On the other hand, it also introduces the celebration of Augustus as *Pater Patriae*, the most patriarchal of all Roman designations of civic authority. This teasing refusal to tell us whether Ovid is being a man hits at the heart of the gendered oddity of the *Fasti*. Although Ovid

[27] For Roman attitudes to masculinity and soldiering see Alston (1998).
[28] Hinds (1992).

sets himself up as the poet of Augustan peace,[29] in which he is caught up in the ideology of Roman masculine social order and authority, the poem constantly undermines its own, Rome's, and Augustus' authority. The very choice of religion as a vehicle for celebrating the (masculine) status quo is itself not unproblematic, for the appropriation of religion in the service of the state and for the ordering of society on neat and clear gendered lines is full of contradictions inherent in the gendered complexity of the religion itself. And Ovid is the poet of contradictions.

Illustrative of this ambivalence is the story of the Roman cults of Cybele, the Great Mother of the gods. The Muse Erato gives Ovid lots of information about this strange Eastern goddess whose rituals have been integrated into Roman civic religion. Why, in the name of all that is holy, asks Ovid (I am paraphrasing a bit here), do we virile Romans celebrate within our manly culture a goddess whose priests are eunuchs? The answer is a myth (*Fasti* 4.223–46). Attis was a Phrygian boy loved 'chastely' by the goddess Cybele. He promised to remain a virgin, but broke his promise with a nymph, whom Cybele killed in vengeance. Attis castrated himself, in remorse for his broken pledge and the death of his beloved. The story plays on various psychological themes: the sexiness of virginity, the castrating mother, the boy who tries to grow up but fails. And that is meant to *explain* the presence of such a cult in Roman society? Foreignness and effeminacy act as signs of the risks to Roman masculinity, risks which must be controlled, but also they are somehow expressive of drives and desires which, to borrow the language of psychoanalytical film criticism, are more scopophilic than voyeuristic.[30]

Erato's sequel is the story of the goddess's reception into Rome,[31] a story full of emphasis on chastity and pious respect for motherhood. Most interesting is the role of Claudia, an aristocratic lady whose doubted chastity is exonerated by the goddess's favour. The East, the effeminate, the wild, the female, these things must all be controlled by civic religion, but religion contains (includes) as well as contains (keeps under control) these forces. Roman religion is about control of deviancy, but it is also about the expression of deviancy and is itself threatening to the very civic order it is enlisted to uphold. In choosing religion as the vehicle for his Roman Poem, Ovid exploits these ambiguities. When he calls Aeneas *Phryx pius* ('the pious Phrygian'), in close echo of the *Phryx puer* ('the Phrygian boy') who is Attis, he will not

[29] Hinds (1992), Newlands (1995).
[30] The terms have been made famous by, in particular, Mulvey (1975). To put it simply: the voyeuristic gaze is a controlling, dominating, active kind of looking, while scopophilia (literally, love of looking) is a more passive process, concentrated its pleasure on the act of looking itself rather than on the control of its object.
[31] Livy 29.10. On the function of Cybele and of Venus in Republican Roman constructions of femininity see Stehle (1989).

tell us whether the connection is subversive of Roman masculinity or expressive of the range of possible appropriations inherent in that monolithic but amorphous institution.

The gendering of genre is nowhere more at issue than in Ovid's one great extant foray outside elegy,[32] the *Metamorphoses*, written under the shadow of Virgil's *Aeneid*, which constructed (and deconstructed) the ideal of Roman masculinity and structured itself around the heart-rending force of sexual love. The problem of the interactions of virility and autarky, to which I referred earlier, is fundamental to the construction of the epic hero, who is both defined and undone by his *thumos*,[33] his driving force as man and hero. Ovid's odd epic poses the problem of the hero by both offering and denying the convention, giving us Aeneadae who can't stand the weather (13. 707), for example, and a Perseus who almost forgets to stay airborne when he sees the chained Andromeda (4. 677).[34] Likewise, Ovid's narrative of the Aeneas story is constantly getting side-tracked away from the right Virgilian path:[35] as the Aeneadae are driving their course between Scylla and Charybdis, what we actually hear about is not the manly prowess of the hero, but the transformation of Scylla, from the epic monster whom heroes after Odysseus must narrowly escape, into yet another Ovidian lovely girl, victimized by a god's sexual interest.[36] This teasing response is almost a form of coitus interruptus – to offer us masculine heroes, and then to retreat. Here, as elsewhere, we see Ovid's refusal to tie himself down and tell us what a man is, what a woman is, what a hero is.[37]

Differences

But 'gender', as Irigaray (1985) reminds us, is not another word for 'woman'. Inevitably in this chapter, I have raised and succumbed to a fundamental problem in the current state of gendered study: it is very common to run 'Gender' and 'Sexuality' together, and to lump 'Women' into the same conceptual pile, but to do so elides some important differences. Why should women's issues, any more than anything else about women, men, life, and everything, be tied in with sexuality and segregated from mainstream HIStory? These tendencies arise because people still think of maleness as normative, and so 'Gender' means 'different Gender', which means 'Woman',

---

[32] Effeminate elegy, with its limping pentameter: see Harrison, ch. 5 in this volume.
[33] I am grateful to Philip Hardie for this formulation.
[34] See Nagle (1988c), also Keith (1999).   [35] See Casali (1995) 63.
[36] Strictly speaking, Scylla is transformed *from* virgin *to* monster, but if we think of this in terms of the epic tradition it is the other way round. Ovid takes the story of the monster and turns it into a story of a lovely victim.
[37] I am grateful to Effie Spentzou here.

which – to complete the circle – means Sex (both sex-difference and erotic experience). Although I play along with this, I offer a tiny subversion of it by the inclusion of a small section on families and especially motherhood.

Very often in the Ovidian corpus, sexuality offers an alternative view of the world, most explicitly in the *Ars amatoria*, where sex is set up as an alternative to Augustan citizenship. Although the poem poses as denying that it teaches anything against the Augustan adultery laws, at almost every turn its presentation belies its protestation.[38] The didactic poem undermines marriage not so much because Ovid thinks adultery is a good thing, as in order to offer an alternative to Augustan social control. If in the *Ars amatoria* love seems to be an alternative to marriage, however, this is not true throughout the Ovidian corpus. Myth allows for a fudging of the realities of marriage and social control, and gives space for the exploration of a range of erotic loci, including married ones: for example, Baucis and Philemon, Pyramus and Thisbe, Ceyx and Alcyone, Cephalus and Procris, and even, albeit problematically, the exiled poet and his wife.

Myth allows space also for the examination of family matters rarely noticed elsewhere in ancient literature. I pick as an example a woman's account of the birth of her first child (*Met.* 9.275–323). Alcmene tells her pregnant granddaughter-in-law Iole (now married to Hercules' son Hyllas) about the birth of the great hero. She had been suffering for many days, but the birth was prevented by the malice of Juno. Lucina, goddess of birth, sat cross-legged on the altar with her fingers entwined. A clever servant-girl saw her there, rushed out to announce the birth (falsely) and so tricked the goddess into standing up, letting go, and allowing the birth to take place. Iole's reply likewise stresses the family. She tells the story of her sister Dryope's metamorphosis into a tree, including apparently unnecessary details about the woman's own mother and child. These stories constitute a foil to the epic masculinity of the greatest of heroes and offer an alternative view of the world.[39]

The driving force, the *uis*, of epic, inherently tends to occlude this 'feminized' viewpoint. Towards the end of the *Metamorphosis*, we see a gradual eliding of the female, the personal, the sexual, which culminates in the grand finale of the deification of Caesar and the projected deification of Augustus.[40] In all the ironic stress on the genetic significance of Caesar's fathering of Augustus (Octavian was adopted by his great-uncle in the Dictator's will), there is – there can be – no hint of the female role in procreation. Imperial ideology deletes woman. The one construction of femininity that does gain a place in the imperial patriarchal system is the conventional celebration of

[38] See Sharrock (1994b).   [39] See Segal (1998).
[40] One of the last sexual stories in the poem, that of Vertumnus and Pomona, has been subject to a feminist reading by Gentilcore (1995).

woman as the chaste channel for patriarchal progression. It looks at first sight as though Ovid obsequiously supports such a construction, in the one mention of maternity in this last section of the poem, when he speaks of Augustus' *prolem sancta de coniuge natam* ('child born from his holy wife', *Met.* 15.836) – until we remember that Tiberius is not the son of Augustus but of Livia's former husband, from whom the young Octavian removed her when she was pregnant with Tiberius.[41] Ovid thus provocatively exposes the deceptive imperial appropriation of conventional values.

But where does this leave women? Does Ovid expose or collude with this deletion of the female by imperial ideology? The question returns us to the issues raised earlier about the subversive effect of Ovidian appropriation of the masculine order. Violence has been appropriated for love, force for persuasion, epic for elegy.[42] If the lover is (not) a soldier, and the poet is (not) a statesman, then who wins in the struggle for interpretative control? Or need we think of it as struggle?

If love in Ovid is painful, it is also creative, for *uis* always has two sides, as we see in the story of Flora, told by herself, in the *Fasti*. The goddess of flowers was raped by the west wind Zephyrus, but she is quick to say she does not complain of this, or of her husband, and to point out the lovely fertility that is the result of her rape.[43] The monochrome has become colourful. A quick whip through various transgressive stories from the *Metamorphoses*, including Adonis, reminds us of this aspect of Ovidian sexuality – that the creative and the violent are closely knit up in each other. I do not think we should deny the beauty of Ovidian *uis*, whatever anxieties it might (rightly) raise in us.

FURTHER READING

Roman sexuality is just starting to catch up with its ancient Greek counterpart: four recent books on masculinity are important (Gleason (1995), the later essays in Foxhall and Salmon (1998a) and (1998b), and most fully Williams (1999)), while the collection by Hallett and Skinner (1997) on *Roman Sexualities* is crucial. It contains essays by D. Fredrick and P. Gordon which are of particular interest for this topic. Edwards (1993) is a very useful contribution to the cultural construction of gender at Rome.

Very many works on Ovid have some bearing on the matter, but there is no full-scale treatment either of the corpus or of individual works. There have been some excellent articles in the journal *Helios*, sadly hard to get hold of in Britain. In 1990

---

[41] I am grateful to Philip Hardie here.

[42] On the interactions of epic and elegy as erotic and gendered see *Amores* 2.18–19.

[43] See Newlands (1995) 122–3, who shows how, as an intermediary between *matronae* and *meretrices*, Flora acts as a counterpart to the poet of the *Fasti*, erotic and respectable at once (or not).

a special issue was devoted to feminist and other similar readings of Ovid. Kennedy (1993) is concerned with Roman elegy generally, and has a great deal of value on Ovidian sexuality. On the *Amores*, Keith (1994) is a good general piece, while the relevant chapters of Greene (1998) give a good sense of the state of play on such matters. For the interaction of gender and sexuality with race and class, Henderson (1991), (1992) is excellent, if difficult. The *Ars amatoria* has been oddly lacking in explicitly gendered treatments. For an approach interested primarily in poetics, Allen (1992) has a lot that is valuable, as does Gibson (1995) on winning girlfriends and influencing them. The *Heroides* are becoming big business in gendered reading: there is already Farrell (1998) and Desmond (1993), and we are set to see more in future (e.g. Spentzou (forthcoming)). On the *Metamorphoses*, the best overview is probably Segal (1998), while there is a great deal of value in Wheeler (1999). For a more traditional reading, one might try Anderson (1995). There are also large numbers of treatments of individual passages. Alison Keith and Michaela Janan have each produced a number of important articles, while on the specific issue of rape and representation Richlin (1992) is central, and on gender-instability Nugent (1990). Newlands' book on the *Fasti* (1995) is not explicitly concerned with gender and sexuality, but it is written from a feminist standpoint that produces excellent gendered readings of the poem. Fantham (1983) is one of the few works on the *Fasti* explicitly addressing issues of sexuality. Gendered readings of the exile poetry often, rightly, link the late poems with the earlier elegiacs, especially the *Heroides*. Exemplary in this regard is Rosenmeyer (1997), while O'Gorman (1997) is a wide-reaching treatment of gendered matters in historicist poetics in the *Ars* and *Heroides* as well as in the exile poems.

7

FRITZ GRAF

Myth in Ovid

Ovid on myth

Ovid's *Metamorphoses* was the book from which centuries of European culture drew their knowledge of Greek and Roman myth, and until the beginning of mythological studies in the eighteenth century, under the influence of the ethnographical discoveries and missionaries' reports, this work determined what myth had to be: fantastic stories about gods and heroes – or, as an early and sharp-tongued critic, Bernard de Fontenelle (1657–1757), described myth, 'un amas de chimères, de rêveries et d'absurdités'.[1] From our own understanding of myth, as shaped by the generations of scholars since the mid-eighteenth century, this has not always surprised and puzzled as much as it should have done: the deep seriousness of our own concept of what myths are – 'a traditional tale ... held to be not a passing enjoyment, but something important, serious, even sacred', 'traditional tales with immediate cultural relevance' – seems to clash violently with Ovid's irreverent playfulness, as he most often is perceived.[2] And although there is no doubt that the modern understanding of myth as something profound is a reaction to the earlier, less 'deep', way of thinking about myth as shaped by Ovid, it is by no means certain that playfulness and irreverence is all that there is to be said about Ovid's mythical narratives.[3]

In late Republican and early Augustan Rome, myths *(fabulae)* were universally understood as poetic fictions; this goes back to the late sixth century

---

[1] Bernard de Fontenelle, 'De l'origine des fables', *Oeuvres complètes 3*, ed. Alain Niderst (Paris 1989) 187.

[2] The definitions come from Burkert (1979) 1–4 and from Graf (1993a) 1–3; *ibid.* 9–34 for a history of research, and Neschke (1986) for a stimulating evaluation of myth in the *Metamorphoses*.

[3] von Albrecht (1981) 2328 puts the problem in a nutshell: 'Der Dichter, der dem Abendland die Welt des griechischen Mythos wohl am umfassendsten vermittelte, hatte selbst zum Mythos und zur römischen Wirklichkeit ein vielschichtiges und keineswegs unproblematisches Verhältnis'.

and its philosophical reaction to poetic narrations about the gods.[4] The Latin rhetoricians are unanimous in their definitions and refer, in their unanimity, back to their unknown Greek models. In their categorization of narrative texts, *fabula*, 'mythical narrative', is opposed to *historia*, 'historical narrative', and to *argumentum*, 'plot' (of a comedy *vel sim.*). These three types of texts are classified according to their content of truth: *historia* is a report of things that really happened, *fabula* and *argumentum* are fictions, but whereas *argumentum* shares with *historia* a clear orientation on real facts and thus is plausible, *fabula* 'is a text which contains neither true nor plausible things' and belongs especially to the tragic stage.[5] From his own perspective, that of a philosopher of religion, Varro concurs: among his three ways of 'speaking about the gods' (*theologia*), the 'discourse with mythical narratives' (*theologia mythice*) is the one that is used mainly by the poets, belongs to the stage, and meets open condemnation by the historian and philosopher because of its 'many things that are invented against the dignity and nature of the immortal gods'.[6] Varro, of course, shares this contempt with many ancient philosophers, from Xenophanes onwards, although it never meant that myth was entirely discarded – certainly not by the poets, nor in many other fields of ancient culture. Heroic myth was always understood as having a historical value and could be reconstructed as history, after the too fantastic and wild accretions had been pruned away, and it was used as a political argument well into imperial times and beyond.[7] Myths about the gods were read in an allegorical vein as referring to natural phenomena,[8] whereas heroic and divine myths could be read also as containing useful moralistic teaching – a reading favoured by teachers such as Plutarch and poets such as Horace.[9] While in these definitions traditionality, the modern shibboleth of myth, does not appear at all, it plays a certain role in other

---

[4] See the excellent discussion in Feeney (1991) 5–56.

[5] Cic. *De invent.* 1.27 *fabula est, in qua nec uerae nec ueri similes res continentur, cuiusmodi est 'angues ingentes alites, iuncti iugo'* (Pacuvius, *Medusa* fr. 397 Ribbeck) – one of the things Ovid then will call a *mendacium uatum* (*Am.* 3.6.15, Triptolemus' chariot), a *uotum puerile* (*Trist.* 3.8.3–4, Medea's, as in Pacuvius, immediately after Triptolemus'); *Rhet. Her.* 1.13 *fabula est, quae neque ueras neque ueri similes continet res, ut eae sunt, quae tragoedis traditae sunt.* The same classification is found in Quint. *Inst.* 2.4.2 and Isid. *Orig.* 1.44.5. This contradicts Aristot. *Poet.* 9.1–3, 1451a 37ff. who both assumes a basic historicity, at least as regards the names and, presumably, as regards the general outlines of the events, and plausibility.

[6] Varro, *Ant. rer. div.* frr. 6–11 Cardauns; the citation from fr. 7.

[7] For one specific case under Tiberius see Tac. *Ann.* 3.61–3; and Mehmet Fatih still tried to persuade the Romans to help him against Byzantium with a reference to their common Trojan origin. One should not call this way of dealing with myth 'euhemeristic', since Euhemerus explained solely divine mythology.

[8] This is not Varro's *theologia physice* which deals with philosophical cosmology: *Ant. rer. div.* fr. 8 Cardauns gives Heraclitus, Pythagoras and Epicurus as examples.

[9] Plut. *De aud. poet.* (and later Saint Basil *On the value of Greek literature*); Hor. *Epist.* 1.2.

contexts: mythical narrations go back to 'poets of old', Orpheus, Hesiod, Homer, and their ilk;[10] it was always clear that the narrations of tragedy had their source in epic poetry and were handed down from poet to poet.[11]

This had two consequences. First, traditionality of mythical narrative means intertextuality, in the sense that a later text is relying on and answering to an earlier one: Homer is the absolute 'master-text'. Oral mythical narratives were, if anything, 'minor myths';[12] antiquity did certainly not privilege oral tradition in the way that modern research on myth, still in the grips of its romantic past, does. Second, the tradition was not only open to change in point of detail:[13] an individual poet always had the freedom to create his own myth. Some of the aetiologies that conclude a Euripidean play might well be the poet's invention no less than the Platonic myths were Plato's invention. This need must have been felt even more urgently in Rome and Italy with their lack of literary traditions; Ennius and Virgil, who both walked boldly in Homer's footsteps, must have derived from this succession the legitimation to invent an Italian mythology – many otherwise unattested local myths in the *Aeneid* seem to be Virgil's own creation.[14] This should have bothered nobody: in a cultic context, the Augustan age could invent aetiological myths as readily as earlier centuries had and as later ones did, up to the *aition* for the Byzantine Brumalia that still relied on Romulus' actions.[15]

This is the horizon against which Ovid himself moves. To him, myths, *fabulae*, are poetic texts, written by specific or sometimes unnamed poets of the past. Several times, he alludes to the Homeric narration of how Hephaestus caught Venus and Mars *in flagranti* – it is a *fabula nota*,[16] as is the story of Arion and the dolphin[17] or of Achilles on Scyrus;[18] in the *Fasti*, the stories Ovid is about to tell are nearly always called *fabulae*.[19] Fictionality is not necessarily implied in this term. The story of Hephaestus, Venus and

---

[10] 'Poets of old': Ov. *Am.* 3.6.13; Hesiod and Homer already in Xenophanes B 17 DK, and, most famously, in Hdt. 2.58.

[11] See Aristot. *Poet.* 9.4, 1451b 24 (traditionality does not preclude changes).

[12] The term is Plato's, *Rep.* 377 C, the feeling is general in antiquity.

[13] Emphasized by Aristot. *Poet.* 9.4, 1451b 25.

[14] In this debated field, I follow the lead of Horsfall (1993).

[15] Augustan inventions: Scheid (1975) 352–63; (1990) 17–24; Bremmer (1993) 160–5. Brumalia: Malalas, *Chronogr.* 7.7 (Rhomos); cf. 7.9 (Brutus and the founding myth of the Consualia).

[16] *Am.* 1.9.40; *Ars* 2.561; *Met.* 4.189.   [17] *Ars* 3.326.   [18] *Ars* 1.681.

[19] *Fast.* 2.248 (a short catasterism); 2.248 *non faciet longas fabula nostra moras*, 'our story will not take long'; 3.304 (Faunus and Hercules) *fabula plena ioco*, 'a story full of humour'; 3,738 (Dionysus) *non habet ingratos fabula nostra iocos*, 'our story contains not unwelcome jokes'; 5.604, the constellation of Taurus is associated with a well-known *fabula*, that of Europa; 6.320, when the Fornacalia come up, the narrator checks himself: should he really tell the *fabula parua ioci* that is embarrassing for Priapus?

Mars regularly is said to be 'well-known in the entire sky', *fabula toto notissima caelo*:[20] the gods themselves thus legitimate the story – although the situation is somewhat ambiguous, because *fabula* is also 'gossip',[21] which could undercut its authority. Fictitiousness in the sense of lack of truth is expressly stated only when it serves the rhetorical strategy of the speaker. When his poems, as promised (in *Am.* 1.3), made his mistress so famous that he had to fear the threat of too many rivals, he tries to persuade everyone that all of this was only poetical fiction, as the many monsters of Greek myth were the product of too fertile minds: *exit in immensum fecunda licentia uatum,| obligat historica nec sua uerba fide* ('the fruitful freedom of singers goes out into unbounded space, it does not confine their words by historical truth': *Am.* 3.12.41f.). In a much more savage disclaimer in the *Amores*, he calls myths *ueterum mendacia uatum*, 'lies of the poets of old',[22] with the same devaluation of the hallowed concept of *uates* as in the former passage; and in the *Tristia*, he chastises himself because he still believes in stories about mythical marvels 'that no day ever will offer you', like a naive child.[23] This takes up the categories of the rhetoricians – and foreshadows the eighteenth-century understanding of myths as stories that belong to the childhood of humanity. But such a rejection of myth is only one possible reaction to its fictitiousness, and not the most common one: Ovid is much more complex than that, as will become clear from what follows.

Myth as example: love-poetry and poetry from exile

If myths are traditional tales with immediate cultural relevance, then mythical narration explains and, when necessary, legitimates cultural, societal and natural facts in a given society – cults and rituals, social structures, but also natural phenomena; the mythical history of a group defines its identity and place in the contemporary world. This function is not bound to a necessity for myths to be literally true: arguments of heroic mythology were often used in political discourse, and the use that Augustus and Virgil made of the myths of Aeneas shows clearly how mythical discourse was still perceived as full of meaning. Some of the heroic myths were read as *historia*, to use the

---

[20] This expression at *Met.* 4.189, but the other passages are phrased in a similar way.

[21] See esp. *Met.* 10.561: Venus begins her narrative of Atalanta: 'Perhaps you heard that a woman overcame men in fast running – that rumour was no myth, she really overcame them' (*non fabula rumor ille fuit, superabat enim*).

[22] *Am.* 3.6.13 – but the text then nevertheless uses myths as arguments in order to convince: see Davis (1980) 413–14.

[23] *Trist.* 3.8.11–12 *stulte, quid haec frustra uotis puerilibus optas,| quae non ulla tibi fert feretque dies?* ('Stupid man, why do you, with childish wishes, ask for things that no present or future day will bring you?')

term of the rhetoricians, including the myth of Aeneas' arrival in Latium, since the Trojan war was always historical. But even here, a literal reading proved difficult: Livy gives short shrift to the accounts of what happened before the foundation of Rome.[24]

Mythical narratives also provided a widely known language with which to talk about human relationships and human experience: not least Athenian tragedy had exploited this aspect of the traditional stories in hitherto unknown richness and depth, and archaic Latin tragedy must have followed suit; its importance for the knowledge of myths in Rome is difficult to assess, given its fragmentary state, but it certainly should not be underrated.[25] It is the *Heroides*, Ovid's innovative elegiac letters, that most directly explore this side of the mythical tales, giving voice to women in love, in specific situations as outlined in the literary tradition of mythical narration. The collection begins programmatically with a letter of Penelope to the still absent Odysseus, written shortly after Telemachus' exploratory visit to Nestor's court. It authenticates itself through a wealth of Homeric details, enriched by images 'from life' such as the vignette of a swaggering Trojan veteran who draws with wine a map of the battlefield on his table (*Her.* 1.31–6), and it marks its distance from the master-text not only by the elegiac exploration of Penelope's feelings, but also by the clever inclusion of the *Doloneia* into Nestor's account of the war, as narrated to Telemachus.[26]

But more important than the experiment of the *Heroides* is another function of mythical narrative. Its role as a discursive tool about emotion and experience made it as ideal for providing a template and standard in expressing new experience as for proving a point. This explains the frequent use of mythical *exempla* in a genre that had persuasion as one of its major rhetorical aims and dealt with experiences that were new in Roman literature: love elegy, from Catullus' marvellous poem 68 to Propertius.[27]

That is, however, far from being the only reason for Ovid's use of mythical *exempla*.[28] On one level, he continues earlier uses that were constitutive for the genre by which he defines himself so eloquently. Mythical *exempla* can still be arguments – in his paraclausithyron (*Am.* 1.6), the excluded

---

[24] Livy, *praef.* 6 *quae ante conditam condendamue urbem poeticis magis decora fabulis quam incorruptis rerum gestarum monumentis traduntur, ea nec adfirmare nec refellere in animo est* ('I intend neither to confirm nor to refute what poetical invention rather than undistorted tradition tells about the time before the foundation of the City'). Livy uses more or less technical language.

[25] See von Albrecht (1981) 2239.

[26] Virtually all ancient (i.e. presumably Alexandrian) Homerists agreed that bk. 10 'does not form part of the design of the Iliad', Hainsworth (1993) 151; Ovid might have known that, which adds to the cleverness of the passage.

[27] An overview in Canter (1933); for persuasion as a central goal in love elegy Stroh (1971).

[28] Davis (1980); Davisson (1993); Schubert (1992).

lover asks Boreas to blow away the door, 'if you really remember abducted Oreithyia' (53–4); the wish, not the myth, is burlesque. And *exempla* still seem to provide a template for the narrator's experience, including – but not limited to – love: his wrath, which led him to hurt his girl and disturb her coiffure (*Am.* 1.7), is compared to the madness of Ajax and of Orestes – and since his own madness had been much less disastrous, the comparison exonerates him at first from too great a feeling of guilt. But then another group of mythical *exempla* takes over: the speaker compares the beauty of his dishevelled mistress to the huntress Atalanta, to Ariadne on Naxus – and, finally, to Cassandra whom Ajax attacked in Minerva's temple, 'if she had not bound her hair in a fillet'(17). The sequence of *exempla* imperceptibly leads back to guilt. Atalanta, the mythical image for the mistress from Propertius 1.1, is simply beautiful and will be happily loved, but behind Ariadne lurks Theseus' treason (*periuri . . . Thesei*, 'treacherous Theseus' 15), behind Cassandra, Ajax' violence – no wonder that in the next line he addresses himself as *demens* and *barbare*, 'mad' and 'barbaric'. The effect is even stronger, when Cassandra's hair is held in place by her priestly fillet – a detail which Ovid must have invented, against a tradition which, from the Attic red-figured vases onwards, usually shows Cassandra with flowing hair, that sometimes gives an easy grip to her attacker.[29]

Whereas here the inner movement in the group of mythical *exempla* guides the reader through the zigzagging of the speaker's emotions, other *exempla* efficiently undercut what the speaker seems to pronounce, if only one reflects on the entire mythical story. In *Am.* 1.3 Ovid, only recently captured by his new mistress, tries to talk her into a permanent relationship – he is not rich, but he will stay true, and he is a poet. The argument is more than trite: he will make her famous with his song, as former poets made famous the loves of Io, Leda, and Europa. But the very triteness of the argument directs attention to the underlying incongruity: those relationships did not last very long, nor did they bring happiness to the women. This can be read either as somewhat inept courtship, a reading that makes fun of the tradition of mythical *exempla* as arguments for the lover, or as a discreet warning to the courted girl.[30] In any case, the allusion to the mythical narrative carries more meaning than Ovid's text discloses on its surface. Thus, although the mythical *exempla* still can function in their traditional ways, their distance from the tradition is unmistakable.

[29] Iconography: *LIMC* I. 1.339–49 (images where Ajax grips her hair: I. 2 nos. 53–7, 69f., 776f., 81, and the late Republican image no. 85). Literature: Virg. *Aen.* 2.403–4, Ov. *Am.* 1.9.38 (!). The deviation from tradition has been pointed out by many scholars (bibliography in Davis (1980) 416 n. 7), whose interpretation, though ('to make a joke of the use of mythological exempla generally'), overlooks the movement of the text.

[30] Davisson (1993) 270.

A specific Ovidian trick is to turn a story on its head, as a sort of *adynaton*. In the initial passage in the *Remedia amoris*, he gives a list of famous, but disastrous love stories that would never have happened, if he had been able to teach the people involved (Phyllis, Dido, Medea, Tereus, Pasiphae, Paris, Scylla, *Rem.* 55–66). This continues the use of mythical *exempla* in elegy as arguments in courtship, only that now Ovid courts someone who wants to be healed from love. If *Remedia* is also a discourse on love elegy, it shows the ambivalence of the use of myth.[31]

The use of mythical *exempla* gains a new and existential meaning in the elegies from Ovid's exile. In order to come to terms with his new and totally unexpected suffering, Ovid again finds in myth a template for his own experience. The first *exempla* in the collection of the *Tristia* are Phaëthon, victim of Jupiter's wrath, and Icarus, victim of his own temerity but one who left his name to a stretch of Mediterranean water (*Trist.* 1.79, 89) – excellent images for the poet who had envisioned himself, in the sphragis of his *Metamorphoses*, flying high and wide, and having left a work that would survive the wrath of Jupiter. The next mythical figures to enter are the two patient and suffering involuntary travellers Aeneas and Ulixes, both again exposed to divine wrath, but finally saved through divine protection (*Trist.* 1.2.7–9) – images of hope in the midst of unexpected disaster. Aeneas reappears only briefly in the *Epistulae ex Ponto*,[32] while Ulixes becomes a key figure for the entire exile.[33] But already in *Tristia* 1.5, where Ulixes reappears in a long comparison (57–84), Ovid states the insufficiency of myth adequately to cope with his experience: in distich after distich, he has his own sufferings outdo Ulixes' travels and ends with the insight that these calamities are fiction anyway, while Ovid's own are no *fabula*: reality exceeds by far the limits of what the mythic template can perform.[34] Similar evaluations of mythic stories appear elsewhere in the elegies – Jason's travels to another part of the Black Sea (*Pont.* 1.4.32–44) or historic and mythic exiles in a long catalogue (*Pont.* 1.3.61–82) are unable to equal Ovid's own grievous experience, and a list of mythic means of transportation that could help the return (*Trist.* 3.8.1–12) ends with the insight that fiction and grim reality are incompatible. Even though it breaks down as a paradigm, the mythic tradition still functions as a gauge; by its very breaking down, it sig- nals the new and unheard-of suffering of the exile, as it signals the end of love elegy: the very *exempla* that were useful in the world of urbane love

[31] Most of the myths used in *Rem.* 55–66 had already figured in *Am.* or *Ars*, which proves the point.

[32] Significant is 1.1.33–4 (again the first *exemplum*).

[33] See the contribution of Gareth Williams in chapter 14 of this volume.

[34] The same strategy, again with Odysseus, reappears in *Trist.* 3.11.61.

(the list of vehicles echoes an earlier one, in *Am.* 3.6.13–18) are no real help in understanding what is going on. Ovid's exile signals the end of mythology's usefulness.

Mythical aetiology: the *Fasti* and the *Metamorphoses*

Among the most elementary and most widespread functions of myth is aetiology – to explain and, by the very explanation, to organize natural and social phenomena by giving accounts of how they came into being in events of the distant past; often these myths legitimate social facts or human use of nature, and they were thus termed 'charter' myths by Bronislaw Malinowski.[35] Because aetiologies fulfil a cognitive or, as charters, a prescriptive need in an immediate present, they are constantly adapted to changing circumstances, even while their object remains the same;[36] entirely new stories might even be devised to explain the same object.

In evolved societies with a written tradition things become more complex. The different aetiological stories are preserved in the literary tradition and begin to compete with each other, and new forces influence the choice of variants and the change in traditional narrative. In societies in which the correct aetiology is part of orthodoxy, exegetes and allegorists take over. In others, where the collectivity of recipients is no longer society at large, but the group of like-minded *literati* and their patrons, literary or aesthetical strategies become the group concern that justifies choices of variants as well as changes and inventions in the tradition. Specific texts gain authority, and myths are chosen according to aesthetic values. Callimachus chose most of the stories told in his *Aitia* not for their relevance to Ptolemaic society, but for their aesthetic appeal, whereas the aetiology of the Nemean games in the *Victory of Berenice* is relevant to the court because of a victory of the queen's team, and the *Lock of Berenice* explains a recently found constellation through an aetiological metamorphosis that again concerns the queen and her court.[37]

Aetiological metamorphoses are a well-represented sub-type of aetiologies. They almost exclusively concern natural phenomena – animals, plants, rock formations, constellations; although the last already in antiquity are categorized as a separate group, catasterisms. In all cases, the phenomenon to be explained is understood as the result of a single change sometime in the

---

[35] Still important Kirk (1970) 254–7 and Kirk (1972); a good account of the history of the term in Loehr (1996) ch. 1.

[36] A concise account in Binder (1988) 264.

[37] *Victoria Berenices: Supplementum Hellenisticum*, ed. Lloyd-Jones/Parsons, frs. 254–9; *Coma Berenices*: Callim. fr. 110 Pf.

mythic past; only star myths refer to recent events – the transformation of an actual lock from the queen's head into the constellation, or of Caesar's soul into a comet.[38] The new object thus has some relationship to the object from which it changed; this gives free rein to any narrator's ingenuity in finding relevant correspondences and structures.

In Greece, the learned Hellenistic poets collected relevant myths and shaped them into collections that became master-texts for the Romans.[39] Their emphasis on poetical technique does not preclude an intense interest in narrative content: Callimachus' *Aitia* contained mainly aetiological myths about festivals, rituals and cult-images,[40] often drawn from local histories;[41] his younger contemporary Nicander of Colophon collected mythical metamorphoses; with the exception of the summaries in Antoninus Liberalis, only a few fragments of these *Heteroioumena* survived, and later similar collections, such as the *Ornithogonia* of Boios, a collection of bird metamorphoses, did not fare better.[42] We thus lack evidence to decide whether these poems were as loosely structured as Callimachus' *Aitia* or whether their structure already foreshadowed Ovid's *carmen perpetuum* with its historical organization.

In his two major poems, Ovid takes up both the Callimachean and the Nicandrian models. The latter provided the ancestry, though certainly not the poetology, for the *Metamorphoses*, while the *Fasti* followed Callimachus in their concentration on *tempora cum causis . . . lapsaque sub terras signa*, 'times with their causes . . . and the constellations that sink beneath the earth' – the aetiological myths of the Roman ritual calendar with its festivals, rites and cult images, and the constellations whose rising and setting accompanies the year. The reference to the prologue of the *Aitia* in *Fasti* 1.93f. is obvious enough and has been often remarked upon;[43] but Ovid goes on to depict Janus' surprising appearance in the (unCallimachean) colours of divine epiphany, thus signalling that for his poem religious experience is a relevant horizon.

The *Fasti* thus sprinkle Roman ritual aetiology with Greek star myths. The seventeen catasterisms are rather straightforward vignettes[44] in the tradition of Aratus' *Phainomena*, a poem that was very popular with both the Alexandrians and the Roman poets, from Cicero to Germanicus; Ovid's

---

[38] Lock: Callim. fr. 110 Pf.; Caesar: Ov. *Met.* 15.746–851.
[39] On their influence in general see Codrignani (1958).
[40] See the catalogue in Loehr (1996) 42–8.
[41] Xenomedes of Keos: Callim. fr. 75.54 Pf. (παρ᾽ ἀρχαίου Ξενομήδεος, 'from old Xenomedes'); 'old stories' (παλαιαὶ ἱστορίαι) of a certain Leandros, fr. 92.
[42] Forbes Irving (1990) collects and analyses all the Greek material; Nicander is discussed at 24–32, Boios at 33–37; see also Loehr (1996) 51–67.
[43] Cf. Callim. fr. 1.21–2 (already noted in Bömer's commentary ad loc.).
[44] At *Fast.* 2.248 Ovid remarks on the terseness of his narration: *non faciet longas fabula nostra moras*, 'our story will not take long'.

own *Phaenomena* is lost.[45] Rather more complex is the Roman mythology that gives the *causae* for the festivals, not least because we lack the rich intertextuality of Greek mythical narration; Virgil and Livy remain the best-known contexts, and both attest heavily to the Augustan reshaping of Roman mythology.[46] Ovid's mechanisms for attributing authority to his stories seem more necessary than ever, although, again, they follow Callimachean models: Ovid's narrator either is informed by the Muses or a divinity directly, or takes up the *persona* of an investigative historian, sometimes searching for information in scroll after scroll of old books, more often walking through his home-town and interrogating the native informants.[47] Roman ritual aetiology from the time of the annalists constructed a religious past that was coterminous with its history: the main aetiologies cluster around two figures and their epoch, Romulus and Numa; a few myths go further back, to the mythical Latin kings, and the Augustans add Aeneas and his epoch. Ovid follows these traditions. He has Janus explain why the old *aes* (bronze coin) is stamped with his head and a ship's bow by a story of how, during his reign, he received the exiled Saturnus who brought Eastern culture to the savage natives: the story with its unmistakably euhemeristic flavour – gods were beneficent kings who even put their portraits on their coins – looks Hellenistic, even if we cannot put a name to its inventor.[48] The roles that Evander and his mother Carmenta play build on Virgil's Evander, though with rather more emphasis on the mother, the ecstatic prophetess.[49] To the well-known epic narratives, Ovid often reacts either with brevity or with playful and even parodistic changes: his description of the *augurium* of Romulus and Remus, a stock narration since Ennius' *Annales*, is extremely short,[50] his account of Hercules' fight with Cacus, his answer to that brilliant Virgilian version of a piece of Augustan lore, is developed into a surrealistic monster-slaying,[51] and his Dido story, focusing on Aeneas' lust for the exiled Anna, is an ambivalent response to the Virgilian theme.[52] All this is as much intertextuality as mythology, although Ovid's inventiveness might have been stimulated by the erotic climate that characterized the rites of Anna Perenna. A similar reaction to ritual lies behind the sexual comedies that function as (untraditional) *aitia* for a sacrifice of the notoriously randy

---

[45] Five lines are preserved, *Fragm. Poet. Lat.* 112–13 Morel.   [46] Porte (1985).

[47] On the *persona* in the *Fasti* see Miller (1983) and Newlands (1992).

[48] It is repeated in Macrob. *Sat.* 1.7.21f.

[49] Carmenta and Evander: *Fast.* 1.465–586 (Carmentalia, with the story of Hercules and Cacus, utterly irrelevant for the festival, in 543–84); 5.91–8 (one of the *aitia* for the name of the month of May, presumably an Ovidian elaboration); 6.529–32 (Matralia).

[50] *Fast.* 4.813–18; see Ennius, *Ann.* 72–91 Skutsch; Livy 1.6.4; Dion. Hal. *Ant.* 1.86.2.

[51] *Fast.* 1.543–86, another Augustan stock topic: see Virg. *Aen.* 8.185–275; Liv 1.7.7; Prop. 4.9; Münzer (1911).

[52] Brugnoli (1992).

donkey (*Fast.* 1.391–440), the provocative ritual nudity of the *luperci* (2.303–358), aeschrology during the festival of Anna Perenna (3.675–96), and the paradoxical use of a donkey in the rites of chaste Vesta (6.319–48)[53] – all Ovidian inventions. Similarly, given the status of oral mythical tradition in antiquity, Ovidian inventions might hide behind the many stories that he purports to have heard personally, like the strange *aition* for the burning of a fox in the circus during the Cerealia, which Ovid had heard from an old host in Carseoli (*Fast.* 4.681–712),[54] or the second story in the aetiology for Anna Perenna that is not even introduced as *fabula*, but as *fama*, 'rumour', although with the paradoxical insistence on its plausibility.[55] This multiple aetiology – so embarrassing to a modern mind, but not rare in ancient scholarship[56] – thus plays with the traditions of the genre rather than giving several reliable traditions, as did Varro, who often refers to written authorities for multiple *aitia* and provides an authoritative name when he recurs to an oral source.[57]

Whereas the *Fasti* thus manifestly plays with the traditions of learned didactic poetry, the *Metamorphoses* moves in a different direction: its mythology constructs a cosmos that reaches from Chaos to Augustus. And although one of the main movements of its narration is the explanation of natural things – animals, plants, rock formations – through metamorphosis, it moves decidedly away from other kinds of aetiology. Even where Ovid's sources offered one, he changed the story, as in the case of Iphis, transformed from Nicander's myth of Leucippe, the *aition* of the cult of Leto Phytia in Phaestus, or the myth of Dryope, *aition* for a sanctuary of Apollo and its foot race,[58] or in the quaint little story of the Cypriot *Cerastae*, behind whom archaeology has taught us to see Cypriot bull masks.[59] Ovid mentions none of this. Although both the Iphis and the Dryope stories retain their local setting, the Iphis story develops into a rather intimate mother-daughter story that replaces Leto, the original local goddess, with Isis, the omnipresent divine helper (especially of women) in Ovid's own society.[60] And the Dryope story,

---

[53] Fantham (1983); for questions concerning the composition of the two donkey myths see Newlands (1995) 127–36.

[54] Le Bonniec (1966).

[55] *Fast.* 3.661–2 *haec quoque, quam referam, nostras peruenit ad aures|fama, nec a ueri dissidet illa fide*, 'the report that I'm about to relay also reached my ears, and it is not far from what we may take as true.' On such oral lore see Newlands (1992) 39–41.

[56] See esp. Miller (1992b) and Loehr (1996), against earlier and less convincing attempts.

[57] E.g. the *triceps historia* (not *fabula*) for the *lacus Curtius*, at *Ling. lat.* 5.148–50, or the two etymologies for Februarius, *ibid.* 6.34; oral witnesses: e.g. 6.21 the flamen Martialis M. Valerius Flaccus; 6.30 the pontifex maximus Q. Mucius Scaevola. No authorities for multiple aetiologies, e.g. at *Ling. lat.* 5.53, and regularly in Plutarch, *Qu. Rom.* and *Qu. Gr.*

[58] Leucippe: Ant. Lib.17, cf. Ov. *Met.* 9.666–797; Dryope: Ant. Lib. 32, cf. Ov. *Met.* 9.326–93; more in Loehr (1996) 152.

[59] *Met.* 10.220–37.   [60] Graf (1988).

while retaining the name of its heroine, grows into the pathetic account of the blunder of an innocent flower-picker. In their aetiology, the *Metamorphoses* strive for explanation of nature, not culture.

Ovid is in full command of his mythological tradition, wherever he picked it up; it has rightly become unfashionable to posit as his sources mythological handbooks, so favoured by nineteenth-century scholarship.[61] Of course, there could always have been other précis besides the ones we have by Parthenius to assist Roman poets, although they elude us – yet there is nothing to prevent us from assuming that Ovid read avidly and systematically. Even the overall arrangement of the work owes less to the structure of mythological handbooks than to that of universal histories like the one of Diodorus Siculus. And where he had to cope with overpowering master-texts, from which he could not easily get away, he again decided to be short and to elaborate the stories not told by them: witness the delightfully idiosyncratic duel between Achilles and Cygnus (*Met.* 10.75–167) before, and the fight over Achilles' armour (*Met.* 11.1–381) after, the part of the Trojan war that the *Iliad* covered, the history of Scylla before her meeting with Odysseus (*Met.* 14.1–74) and the transformation of Aeneas into Indiges (*Met.* 14.581–608).

In all of this, he shows the sheer, infinite adaptability of mythical narratives. They effortlessly elucidate complex emotional situations, as in the stories about the illegitimate love of Byblis (9.450–665, with a rather heavy-handed moralistic opening) and of Myrrha (10.298–502, with an even more pathetic warning) or the conjugal love of Ceyx and Alcyone (11.410–748, with a final comment by an observer), and they just as effortlessly analyse the new political constellation, beginning with a divine assembly in the style of an Augustan cabinet meeting (1.163–252) where the epic topos is slyly turned on its head.[62]

The divine assembly, of course, looks back to Virgil. Virgil's *Aeneid* not only became to the Augustans what the Homeric epics had been to the Greeks and Ennius' *Annales* to the late Republican Romans, but it also succesfully brought mythical narrative back to life as a tool to express seriously a new communal ideology, outbidding Livy's *Histories* with an account that gave a teleological sense to history's meandering course. Ovid reacted to this: one of the main themes of the *Metamorphoses* is the credibility of myth – both as a religious or ideological problem, and as a poetological one: how does fiction work, and how does it achieve such a powerful grip over its audience? Ovid's main tool in problematizing these traditional stories is the construction of his narrator: the narrator, an ever-present voice in these epic narratives, firmly believes in what he says. His second line already shows

---

[61] See Lafaye (1904) and Castiglioni (1906).   [62] Feeney (1991) 291.

it: it was the gods who did all this – *nam uos mutastis et illa*, 'since you have changed these things too'.[63] This attitude, of course, begs the question, at least when one takes the gods seriously, as the narrator emphatically does – and his next substantial intervention shows the problem: when, in the first metamorphosis that triggers off the chain of transformations (after the isolated Lycaon episode), the stones that Deucalion and Pyrrha throw on the authority of Themis turn into humans, he inserts a surprised and surprising comment: *quis hoc credat, nisi sit pro teste uetustas?* ('Who would believe this, if it were not sanctioned by antiquity?' *Met.* 1.400). The myth – and with it the workings of the gods involved in it – is implausible, and only guarantees its truth, the same antiquity that ordinarily was thought responsible for all sorts of distortions.

The topic returns explicitly in the centre of the poem. Achelous ends the tale of the Echinades and Perimele, five naiads transformed into islands in order to escape the river god's wrath. The audience is impressed. Only Pirithous 'laughs at the believers: "You tell a fiction and assume too much power for the gods, if they are able to give and take shapes"':[64] it is the guiding principle of the entire poem that is questioned, and with it the belief that the narrator stated in his second line. But at least the narrator's answer is obvious: Pirithous is the son of Ixion whom he had introduced into his poem as one of the sinners in Hades (*Met.* 4.461), and as such is himself 'of a savage mind', *mente ferox*; he provokes the opposition of the entire audience and is rebuked by Lelex, *animo maturus et aeuo* ('mature in spirit and age' 8.617), who refutes him with the highly edifying tale of Philemon and Baucis. Pirithous can only be wrong.

But things, of course, are not as simple as that: neither Pirithous nor the narrator nor the pious Lelex and his audience, whom his second tale touched even more (8.725) are absolute authorities. Another voice of dissent demonstrates this. The last book is dominated by a speech of Pythagoras, whose final doctrine, metempsychosis or reincarnation, again contradicts the entire poem: reincarnation makes metamorphosis an ongoing event as our divine souls migrate from our human bodies into birds and wild or tame animals (15.455–9). This negates the firm boundaries between gods, humans and animals that the narrator had erected in his account of creation in the first book, and jeopardizes all metamorphoses, whose entire point had been the definite and irrevocable change from one form into another one.[65] But

---

[63] See Feldherr in chapter 10 of this volume.

[64] *Met.* 8.614–15 *'ficta refers nimiumque putas, Acheloe, potentes | esse deos'*, dixit, *'si dant adimuntque figuras'*.

[65] 'Metamorphosis is as much concerned with reduction and fixity as with variability or complexity', Barkan (1986) 66; cf. Feeney (1992) 190.

again the narrator intervenes: he opens his report of Pythagoras' speech with the comment that his words, 'although learned, were not believed'.[66] And Pythagoras' most prominent pupil, he says, was king Numa (*Met.* 15.479): after Cicero's and Livy's stern refutation of any connection between the Roman king and the Greek philosopher,[67] this again sheds unfavourable light on the narrator. The question of narratorial authority is left unanswered.

The immense fame and influence of the *Metamorphoses* might, at a first glance, appear somewhat paradoxical. But perhaps they are not. Reacting to the *Aeneid*, Ovid brought myth to life in an even more seductive way, and the fact that the seducer intimated to the seduced what the two were doing, helped, as often, in the seduction.

FURTHER READING

The different aspects of myth in Ovid are treated in several recent monographs. While Porte (1985), Schubert (1992), Fabre-Serris (1995) and Loehr (1996) are all very thorough and scholarly, they are also conceptionally rather traditional; by far more stimulating, not only with regard to Ovid, is Feeney (1991). Works on myth in ancient culture abound, at least on Greek myth, and any selection is bound to be personal; a good introduction to the stories and their sources is Gantz (1993), while Graf (1993a) is an introduction to the history of scholarship and the functions of myth in Greece. Rome is less easy, since the discussion about what constitutes a Roman myth is wide open: see the contributions in Graf (1993b); a good narrative introduction is Gardner (1993). The relationship between myth and religion is even more open to debate: a brilliant introduction to Roman religion is Beard, North and Price (1998), and stimulating for Rome as well as for Greece is Veyne (1983).

---

[66] *Met.* 15.74 *docta quidem, sed non et credita.*
[67] Cic. *Rep.* 2.28f. *ficta*; Livy 1.18.2 *falso.*

8

STEPHEN HINDS

Landscape with figures: aesthetics of place in the *Metamorphoses* and its tradition

In Ovid's Cave of Sleep, three shape-shifting spirits (pre-eminent among the thousand sons of Somnus) fashion and enact dreams for kings and leaders: one has the power to assume human forms, one the forms of beasts, and a third, of diverse art (*diuersae artis*), the forms of 'earth, rocks, water, trees, all lifeless things' (*Met.* 11.642–3). As in Somnus' subterranean dreamworks, so in the epic *Metamorphoses* at large one of the privileged ingredients of Ovidian myth-making is the deployment of elements of natural setting: the poem constitutes a significant intervention in the history of landscape. Briefly put, Ovid's contribution to this history is to appropriate and renew the highly rhetorical and idealized tradition of landscape description as he inherits it, to enhance its self-consciousness, to mythologize its origins and accumulated generic associations, to extend the kinds of action which it stages, to exploit its potential for interplay between verbal and visual imagination, and to add a specifically cosmological accent by describing a metamorphic world in which the setting may always be more than just a setting. Partly because of the potency of his own appropriations, and partly because of the circumstances of transmission and survival which give him such prestige as a bearer of the classical tradition to medieval and early modern Europe, Ovid becomes a key collaborator in shaping aesthetics of landscape in later literature, as also in later visual art.[1]

Rhetoric, stereotype, archetype

> ... *Not that fair field*
> *Of Enna, where Proserpine gathering flowers*
> *Her self a fairer flower by gloomy Dis*

My thanks to Alessandro Barchiesi, Catherine Connors, Philip Hardie and Ann Kuttner for valuable advice on an earlier draft.

[1] Landscape noted in general treatments of *Met.*: Wilkinson (1955) 177–84; Viarre (1964) 90–6; Bernbeck (1967) 56–64; Galinsky (1975) 97–8; Fabre-Serris (1995) 266–76.

> *Was gathered, which cost Ceres all that pain*
> *To seek her through the world*; nor that sweet grove
> Of Daphne by Orontes, and the inspired
> Castalian spring, *might with this Paradise*
> *Of Eden strive* . . .
>
> (Milton, *Paradise Lost* 4.268–75)

Ovid's impact on western traditions of rhetorical landscape description has rarely been so paradoxically attested as in the climax of this famous set-piece encounter with the Garden of Eden, which draws attention to a cultural inheritance by claiming to reject or supersede it.[2] The ideal landscape, blessed with preternatural copiousness, its constituent elements predictable but admitting of infinite variations of detail, and configured more to the requirements of rhetoric than to the proprieties of climate and season: such is the pattern shared by Milton's Eden and by Ovid's 'fair field of Enna' (*Met.* 5.385–95), invoked above both as synecdoche for the tradition and as specific model:

> haud procul Hennaeis lacus est a moenibus altae,
> nomine Pergus, aquae: non illo plura Caystros
> carmina cycnorum labentibus edit in undis.
> silua coronat aquas cingens latus omne suisque
> frondibus ut uelo Phoebeos submouet ictus;
> frigora dant rami, Tyrios humus umida flores:
> perpetuum uer est. quo dum Proserpina luco
> ludit et aut uiolas aut candida lilia carpit . . .
> paene simul uisa est dilectaque raptaque Diti.

Not far from Henna's walls there is a lake of deep water, Pergus by name: not even Cayster's gliding streams produce more songs of swans. A wood crowns the waters ringing every side, and with its foliage as with an awning keeps off Phoebus' beams. The branches yield coolness, the moist ground yields purple flowers, and always it is spring. Within this grove while Proserpina was playing, and gathering either violets or white lilies . . . almost at once Dis saw, desired and carried her away.

In the classic discussion in his *European Literature and the Latin Middle Ages*, E. R. Curtius pares down to its essentials this rhetorical stylization of the lovely landscape in the Western tradition:

> . . . a beautiful, shaded natural site. Its minimum ingredients comprise a tree (or several trees), a meadow, and a spring or brook. Birdsong and flowers may be added. The most elaborate examples also add a breeze.[3]

---

[2] Cf. Kermode (1973) 264 and 284.   [3] Curtius (1953) 195. Cf. Schönbeck (1962).

If it be added that still water (i.e. pools or lakes) is as characteristic as running water (springs or brooks), and that the shade may come not just from a grove but from a cave (cf. *P.L.* 4.257–8 'umbrageous grots and caves | of cool recess'), some such menu can indeed be felt to underlie both the amplitude of Milton's description (*P.L.* 4.214–68) and the relative brevity of Ovid's.

No less essential to the sense of pattern is its sense of itself *as* a pattern. When Milton compares his Eden with Ovid's Enna, he self-consciously grounds his landscape description in a literary tradition of landscape descriptions. So too, in turn, when Ovid compares the water and singing birds of his Ennan landscape with the water and singing birds of the Cayster, he is invoking a template for his own landscape hardly less ancient for him than his is for Milton: the originary Greek location of the rape of Persephone/Proserpina (in Asia Minor rather than Sicily) in the *Homeric Hymn to Demeter*.[4]

The potency of Milton's evocation of the tradition of the ideal landscape comes in part from the fact that he is describing, in his and his readers' terms, the first of all the world's landscapes. The pattern at large derives its mythic quality from the fact that it is typically associated with, or implicitly derived from, settings which are primal or supernatural in terms of time or place, and associated in some way with divine presence: the Golden Age; the Elysian Fields; Mount Helicon. For Ovid to endow his Enna, seasonally, with 'perpetual spring' (*Met.* 5.391 *perpetuum uer est*) is to give it an archetypally Golden-Age climate – an archetype in which Milton reinvests through allusion to the Ovidian half-line at *P.L.* 4.268, directly before his overt mention of Enna. Indeed, Milton's locution ('while universal Pan ... | led on *the eternal spring*') may serve to reconnect *Met.* 5.391 with Ovid's own earlier phrasing of the Golden-Age archetype at *Met.* 1.107 *uer erat aeternum*. As for *Met.* 5.391 itself, its own investment in the archetype is by no means inert: 'perpetual spring' is precisely what will disappear from Enna, and from the earth as a whole, as a result of the rape of Proserpina: this myth is on its most common ancient reading an *aition* for the earth's seasonal cycle of vegetative growth, decay and rebirth.

This nexus of vernal reference in Ovid and Milton is symptomatic of what Curtius shows to be a pervasive negotiation between the natural and the supernatural inscribed in the landcape tradition, from Homer's Phaeacia ('a land of faery') onwards.[5] And when in due course the ideal landscape finds a home in a new and 'lower' genre, becoming the characteristic setting for poetic (and erotic) competition in Theocritean and Virgilian bucolic, that

---

[4] Hinds (1987) 26–7, 44–7.   [5] Curtius (1953) 185 for the quotation.

supernatural charge will endure as one of the main elements which gives to bucolic or pastoral poetry its sense of idealized ambience apart from the quotidian realities of life in a rural economy.

At some point soon before or after Ovid, the ideal landscape pattern begins to attract a name: *locus amoenus* (pleasant place, pleasance). An often-quoted passage in Horace's *Ars poetica*, deploring 'purple passages' of set-piece description, is open to two contrary interpretations in this regard (14–19):

> inceptis grauibus plerumque et magna professis
> purpureus, late qui splendeat, unus et alter
> adsuitur pannus, cum lucus et ara Dianae
> *et properantis aquae per amoenos ambitus agros,*
> aut flumen Rhenum aut pluuius describitur arcus.
> *sed nunc non erat his locus...*

Serious and ambitious designs often have a purple patch or two sewn on to give distinction – the description of a grove and altar of Diana, the winding of a stream rushing through pleasant fields, the river Rhine, a rainbow. But in that context there is not a place for them.

Either line 17 shows a formative moment in the prehistory of the technical term *locus amoenus,* or the term already exists and is sufficiently familiar to be obliquely evoked and even punned on (*lucus... per amoenos agros... non erat his locus*). And so too with the opening sentence of Virgil's description of the Elysian Fields (*Aen.* 6.638–9),

> deuenere *locos laetos et amoena uirecta*
> fortunatorum nemorum sedesque beatas

They reached the joyful places, the pleasant glades of fortunate woods, home of the blest.

– which to Servius at least, writing with hindsight, is a textbook instance of the term.[6]

Whether or not the ideal landscape yet has a formal place in contemporary taxonomies of style, the Horatian passage points to the fact that poets, like rhetoricians, have by Ovid's time a deeply ingrained habit of reifying the vivid description in general as a characteristic ornament or interruption of narrative or speech. Often but not always, what is in question when such

---

[6] To Servius on *Aen.* 6.638 and on 5.734 (quoted on p. 147) *amoena loca* carry a history of learned discussion going back to Varro: Maltby (1991) s.v. *amoenus.* The phrase is much used by Cicero, but never in a technical context comparable to Quint. *Inst.* 3.7.27 later: see *TLL* 1.1962–3, esp. 1962.57–67. Very suggestive for the idea of 'metaformular' awareness of the *locus amoenus* in Augustan poetry is Thomas (1982) 17, 24–6, 127–9.

overlapping terms as *enargeia, illustratio, descriptio* and (a survival into modern usage) *ekphrasis* are invoked is the set-piece description or praise of a place, and that often but not always an ideal place.[7] Furthermore, when a description of place interrupts or punctuates a narrative, as characteristically in Ovid's *Metamorphoses* and other epics, it has available a stereotyped entry formula to set it apart from its surrounding context, often couched in a 'timeless' present. *locus est* or more commonly *est locus* is the default opening ('there is a place . . .'), as in the first instance of the pattern in extant Latin poetry at Ennius, *Ann.* 20 (reprised by Virgil at *Aen.* 1.530),

> est locus Hesperiam quam mortales perhibebant[8]

or as in a famous Virgilian instance even earlier in the *Aeneid* (1.159)

> est in secessu longo locus . . .

typically picked up by a resumptive demonstrative or relative at the point of transition from description back into narrative (thus *huc* at *Aen.* 1.170). The initial *est locus* – which may lurk as a(nother) metaformular pun within Horace's *sed nunc non erat his locus*[9] – is regularly varied by the naming of the place or object described: *est specus, est nemus, stagnum est, fons erat.*

In the *Metamorphoses*, as in more sporadic examples in his non-epic works, Ovid brings to this 'ecphrastic' configuration something of the sensibility of an elegist, at once accentuating the formal scheme and opening it up to epigrammatic play. The rhetorical arrangement of the landscape elements may be stylized to the point of self-reference, as in *Fast.* 2.215 *campus erat, campi claudebant ultima colles* (a plain there was, a plain closed off by hills), where *claudebant* refers as readily to the stichic as to the topographical enclosure. Expectations of the entry formula may be manipulated in various ways: through postposition, as in *Fast.* 2.435–6 *monte sub Esquilio multis incaeduus annis | Iunonis magnae nomine lucus erat* (under the Esquiline mount, unfelled for many a year, named for great Juno a grove there was); through delegation to a character in *oratio obliqua*, as in *Met.* 4.772–3 *narrat Agenorides gelido sub Atlante iacentem | esse*

---

[7] Rhetorical terms for vivid description: Quint. *Inst.* 6.2.32 (citing Cicero); Vasaly (1993) 19–20, 89–91; Bartsch (1989) 7–10; Laird (1996) 91–4. *Ekphrasis* (ecphrasis) is nowadays used only for the set-piece description of landscapes (occasionally) and art objects (more usually; cf. now Webb (1999)); it has lost the broader range which it had in its Second Sophistic heyday.

[8] 'There is a place which mortals called Hesperia . . .'; (below) 'there is in a deep inlet a place . . . hither'; '. . . a cave/grove/pond/spring'.

[9] Laird (1996) 92.

locum ... (Perseus tells how lying beneath cold Atlas there is a place ...); through punning invocation of the default in the specific variation, as found at *both* ends of the Enna set piece quoted earlier: *Met.* 5.385 *haud procul Hennaeis lacus est* ..., 391 *quo* ... *luco*.[10] One of the first set-piece local descriptions in Ovid's career (*Her.* 12.67–9) offers one of his most mannered touches, an 'editorial' disruption of the 'timeless' ecphrastic present (by Medea, the poem's speaking voice, describing the scene of her and Jason's tryst in Colchis):[11]

> est nemus et piceis et frondibus ilicis atrum;
> uix illuc radiis solis adire licet.
> sunt in eo – fuerant certe – delubra Dianae

There is a grove, dark with pines and ilex fronds; thither the rays of the sun can scarcely find a way. There is in it – at any rate there *was* – a shrine of Diana

The subversion of the formula is immediately underscored as Medea returns to her direct address to Jason: *Her.* 12.71 *an exciderunt mecum loca?* 'Has the location (= the *est locus*) fallen from your memory along with me?'

Ovid applies the same kind of interest in formular play to the particular distillation of local description which is (or, if you will, which becomes) the *locus amoenus*. Since Curtius a passage from *Met.* 10 has been a byword here.[12] An *est locus*-type opening describes the landscape in which the Ur-poet Orpheus sits down, like a pastoral shepherd, to sing the songs of love and loss which will occupy the rest of Ovid's book. However, a crucial element is lacking to the standard setting: shade (88 *umbra loco deerat*). Orpheus' famous telekinetic powers put him in a unique position to address this problem. Using his lyre to summon to the spot a forest of twenty-seven species, meticulously catalogued by Ovid (*Met.* 10.90–106), he supplies the missing element, in effect adjusting the real world to fit the proprieties of the rhetorical one: 90 *umbra loco venit*.[13] The very amplitude of the grove thus summoned is itself part of the passage's rhetorical self-consciousness; such amplitude also becomes part of the Ovidian legacy to later traditions of landscape description.

Orpheus' fictive status as humankind's originary bard opens up a novel way of reading his virtuoso creation of shade at *Met.* 10.86–90: not as a belated play upon a well-established poetic *topos* or commonplace, but as an account of the *first invention* of the ideal landscape. Such a 'myth of origin' could illuminate Ovid's approach elsewhere in the *Metamorphoses* too. By

---

[10] Contrast Ovid's twin Enna ecphrasis at *Fast.* 4.427 *ualle sub umbrosa* locus est.
[11] Barchiesi (1992) on *Her.* 2.131–2.
[12] Curtius (1953) 194–5.
[13] 88 'shade was lacking to the place'; 90 (with a bold dative) 'shade came to the place'.

far the most notable concentration of landscape descriptions anywhere in Ovid occurs in the poem's first five books: Daphne, Io, Callisto, Actaeon, Narcissus and Echo, Pyramus and Thisbe, Salmacis and Hermaphroditus, the Muses, Proserpina, Arethusa – all these act out their stories in essentially interchangeable *loca amoena*. Ovid's framing of his epic as, in effect, a narrative recreation of the history of the universe allows him to recapitulate within its boundaries the history of the ideal landscape at large: thus, just as all *loca amoena* in the Greco-Roman tradition can be referred back *inter*textually to the *topoi* of the Golden Age, so all the closely-packed *loca amoena* of *Met.* 1–5 can be referred back *intra*textually to the *topoi* in Ovid's own recreation of the Golden Age in *Met.* 1.107–12. In such a perspective, it seems significant that the geographical location described in the poem's very first post-Golden Age *locus amoenus*, at *Met.* 1.568ff., is Tempe, the Thessalian home of Daphne's father Peneus, but also a real-world archetype of the perfect landscape: by Ovid's time *tempe* has passed into both the Greek and Latin languages as a common noun meaning 'a beautiful sequestered vale'.[14]

Part of what is distinctive about Ovid's engagement with the ideal landscape tradition in the *Metamorphoses*, then, is a strong in-built aetiological dimension: not only does he play with the stereotype, but (in keeping with the cosmic ambitions of the *Metamorphoses* as a whole) he shows a marked and repeated interest in locating and exploiting its mythic archetypes. Another place rich in this kind of aetiological potential is Arcadia, in mythological terms the oldest land in the world, and in literary historical terms the place constructed by Virgil as an archetypal milieu of pastoral.[15] In the contemporary *Fasti*, the dual associations of Arcadia as originary landscape and originary timescape impinge suggestively on a recurrent rural idyll of early Rome, through the immigrant figures of Carmentis and Evander. In the *Metamorphoses*, Arcadia comes up most strikingly in a myth treated in parallel in *Metamorphoses* and *Fasti*, the tale of Callisto, daughter of Lycaon and mother of the eponymous Arcas.

Although the Callisto myth does not constitute the earliest appearance of Arcadia in the *Metamorphoses* (as well as in Lycaon's own story we glimpse it, as a pastoral locale, in the nested myth of Pan and Syrinx), the refurbishment of the earth's landscapes necessitated by the cosmic conflagration of Phaethon allows Jupiter to *recreate*, as something both familiar and new, the

---

[14] *LSJ* s.v.; McKeown (1989) on *Am.* 1.1.15–16.
[15] Ovid's Arcadia as 'older than the moon': *Fast.* 1.469–70, with Bömer (1957–8) ad loc. Virgil's Arcadia as an archetypal pastoral milieu (even when stripped of added Renaissance associations): Hardie (1998) 25 and 61 (with bibl.).

archetypal Arcadian *locus amoenus* in which he will visit his erotic violence upon the nymph (2.405–8):

> . . . Arcadiae tamen est inpensior illi
> cura suae: fontesque et nondum audentia labi
> flumina restituit, dat terrae gramina, frondes
> arboribus, laesasque iubet reuirescere siluas.

Yet his own Arcadia is his more pressing care. He restores its springs and rivers, fearing as yet to flow; he gives grass to the ground, leaves to the trees, and bids the damaged woods grow green again.

As so often in the *Metamorphoses* (and not least in the book which begins with the 'cosmic icon' of the doors of the Sun's palace), the job of demiurge seems here to be interchangeable with that of (metamorphic) poet: like Orpheus later, Jupiter is here giving us what the imminent narrative needs, viz. a *locus amoenus* with all the usual fixings. As with Orpheus, Jupiter's manipulation of 'real' space tends to read as mimicry of the ecphrastic manipulation of rhetorical space, rather than *vice versa*.

This episode of divine scene-making complements and sharpens a second moment of meta-description later in the episode. We are still in Arcadia; and Diana and her nymphs are approaching a watered grove. This could be a cue for a set-piece description. Instead, the following (2.455–8):

> nacta nemus gelidum dea, quo cum murmure labens
> ibat et attritas uersabat riuus harenas.
> *ut loca laudauit,* summas pede contigit undas;
> *his quoque laudatis* 'procul est' ait 'arbiter omnis' . . .

The goddess reached a cool grove, through which a stream flowed its murmuring way and rolled about its well-worn sands. *When she had praised the place,* she dipped her foot in the waters. *Having praised these too,* she said 'No spy is near . . . '

A *locus amoenus*; but the self-conscious twist is that, before immersing herself in it, Diana herself *praises* it, step by step. The goddess rhetoricizes the moment of her own entry into the landscape, and thus usurps the poet's expected function: the italicized phrasing functions in a quasi-technical way to represent the set-piece *laudes* which are the poet's and rhetorician's stock-in-trade in such a context.[16] As it happens, the equivalent moment in Ovid's cross-referential version of the Callisto myth in the Fasti shows just what the

---

[16] *laus locorum*: Quint. *Inst.* 3.7.27; Persius 1.70–1 (prob. echoing Hor. *Ars poet.* 16–17). Contrast *Pont.* 1.3.51–4 on the 'unpraisability' of the grim landscape of Ovid's exile.

Metamorphoses passage might have looked like, had the poet done his own rhetorical work there too (*Fast.* 2.165–7):

> ut tetigit lucum (densa niger ilice lucus,
>   in medio gelidae fons erat altus aquae),
> 'hic' ait 'in silua, virgo Tegeaea, lauemur!'

When she had touched the grove (a grove there was, dark with thick ilex; in its midst a deep spring of cool water), she said 'Here in the wood, maid of Tegea, let us bathe!'

The deftly compressed ecphrasis, rendered the more emphatic by parenthetic postposition, constitutes a kind of authorial reclamation of and gloss on the twin version's displaced set-piece *laudes*. There is a further hint of meta-formular wit too: when read against the implied speech of the goddess in the *Metamorphoses* (*ut loca laudauit*), the *Fasti*'s Diana has claims to be a rhetor too, but one who (like a good slender elegist) merely 'touches on' her descriptive theme: *ut tetigit lucum*.[17]

Desire, violence, embodiment

There is a characteristic tension in the landscapes of the *Metamorphoses* between the beautiful setting and the sufferings which befall most of the characters who inhabit or enter it: in this sense, episode after episode takes the form of a 'paradise lost'. Ovid himself thematizes this tension in the case of the Persephone myth in *Met.* 5, by framing it as a (double-nested) narrative performed in the lovely environs of the newly-sprung Hippocrene by Muses whose joy in the security of that landscape (yet another of the poem's originary *loca amoena*) has recently been soured by an attempted rape perpetrated by Pyreneus. The Muses' own brush with sexual danger (which at first seems like an otiose digression) at once echoes and 'motivates' not only their mythic song's theme of violated chastity, but also its strongly marked emphasis upon the ideal landscape as the site in which that violence is enacted.

It is not surprising that modern readings should oscillate between seeing the poem's violence as redeemed by its stylized beauty, especially as distilled in its landscapes, and seeing its beauty as fatally corrupted by its violence.[18] A *Metamorphoses* whose violent myths unfolded in a dystopia might feel very different (think of the bleak ambience of myth in Ovid's own exile poetry);[19]

---

[17] OLD *tango* 10; note too Ovid's characteristic *locus/lucus* play.
[18] Segal (1969) 12 for the first position; Segal (1969) 92–3 and, more urgently, Richlin (1992) for the second.
[19] e.g. *Trist.* 3.9, *Ibis* passim. Actual recent adaptations of the *Met.* itself to modern urban

a *Metamorphoses* in whose *loca amoena* all mythic action was benign might feel very different. Many critics have seen a generic tension here: a combination of idyllic setting and idyllic action is more or less what pastoral offers, and Ovid's perversion of the latter is what makes his landscapes anti-pastoral.[20] True, up to a point. And yet even in the classic Virgilian form of pastoral itself the idyll is often out of the reach of the bucolic protagonists, lost, deferred or called into question; arguably the sense of a threat to harmony immanent in a harmonious setting is a constitutive feature of the landscape tradition at large.

In the case of Ovid's landscapes the violence is most often sexual, perpetrated within plots of courtship perverted or gone wrong; this is itself a kind of transformation of the gentle songs of erotic competition to which the pastoral landscape characteristically plays host. The emphasis on courtship reflects a mythic habit of locating myths of desire in desirable places which is at least as old as the myth of Persephone, and which comes to be programmed etymologically into the term *locus amoenus* itself through various kinds of derivation of *amoenus* from *amor*: thus Isidore, claiming the (pre-Ovidian) authority of Varro, *amoena loca Varro dicta ait eo quod solum amorem praestant et ad se amanda adliciant* (*Etym.* 14.8.33: Varro says that *amoena loca* are so called because they furnish only love (*amor*), and lure people into loving them).[21]

One context in which desire and violence come together is in an association of the poem's landscapes with the hunt.[22] Many of the figures who come to grief in these settings are acting out an age-old mythic paradigm whereby the hunter becomes the prey: either through literal reversal, as with Actaeon, or metaphorically, as with Daphne. Strikingly recurrent is the situation of predation upon a virgin devotee of Diana, whose embrace of the hunt constitutes a rejection of sexuality: Daphne, Syrinx, Callisto, Arethusa.[23] Here the 'hunter hunted' *topos* is at its most cruelly ironic, as the opposites in the nymph's world-view collapse into one another and (in an actualization of the venatic imagery so common in amatory poetry up to and including Ovid's own *Ars amatoria*) she becomes the sexual quarry of a predatory divine male.

Inasmuch as the ideal landscape pattern functions in the *Metamorphoses* as a recurrent setting for episodes of erotic desire and violence, such landscapes come to provide a narratological 'cue' for such action, especially

---

dystopia are Shakar (1996), a novel, and Iizuka (1999), a play; the former does locate a kind of beauty in its denatured cityscapes.

[20] Segal (1969) 74–85; qualifications in Parry (1964) 275, 280.
[21] Maltby (1991) s.v. *amoenus* for this and related passages.
[22] Parry (1964) esp. 269–74; Davis (1983).
[23] Davis (1983) 43–71, incl. discussion of two pointed anti-types, Salmacis and Pomona.

in the poem's first five books. In effect, this marks an intensification of an expectation already long programmed into the traditions of myth and landscape. Ovid may even editorialize on such an expectation back in *Ars amatoria* 3, in which Procris, relying on an informant, mistakes for a female rival (*Aura*) the refreshing breeze (*aura*) praised by her husband as he takes his siesta in an ideal landscape (ecphrastically described at *Ars am.* 3.687–96). In a sense, Procris' misinterpretation comes about because she is such a *good* reader of the landscape pattern, who knows exactly what kind of action to expect therein. As Ovid puts it (719), *credere quae iubeant, locus est et nomen et index*. What factors urge belief in her husband's erotic tryst? The informant; the name (Aura); and, metapoetically, the landscape's rhetorical *mise en scène* itself, the *locus est*-ness of the *locus amoenus*.

A suggestive line of work has consolidated this idea of narratological expectation by eliciting a strong *figurative* collusion in the *Metamorphoses* between landscape and action: on this reading the poem's plots of desire and predation are symbolically reflected and refracted in the very landscape elements themselves.[24] As to desire, this is partly a matter of the sheer emphasis upon sensuousness in the characteristic deployment of the ideal landscape. Thus C. P. Segal:

> In such an atmosphere the amorous pursuer will usually gain his ends, for the landscape itself is on his side. Midday heat, pleasant groves, water – the usual components of such settings – themselves imply the primacy of the senses over the mind.

As to predation, this can be felt to be inscribed in the ideal landscape's potential to turn frightening and uncontrollable when (as with the wilderness into which Jupiter invites Io at *Met.* 1.590–1) its groves thicken into pathless forests, its shade into darkness, its inherent numinousness into menace.[25] Segal again:

> [Ovidian landscapes] symbolize not only an inner world of free desires, but also a mysterious outer world where men meet an unwelcome and unexpected fate. They are akin to the sheltered pastoral bower; but they are also the ancestors of the dangerous wild wood of later literature.

However a landscape need not be palpably threatening in order to convey symbolic dangers of sex and violence: the most peaceful setting may

---

[24] Parry (1964) esp. 275–80; Segal (1969) (quotations at 8 and 15).

[25] On inherent numinousness cf. Ov. *Fast.* 3.295–6 *lucus Auentino suberat niger ilicis umbra, | quo posses uiso dicere 'numen inest'* (There was a grove under the Aventine dark with ilex-shade; at sight of it you could say, 'There is a divine presence here'); Isid. *Etym.* 17.6.6 *nemus a numinibus nuncupatum, quia pagani ibi idola constituerant* (*nemus* gets its name from *numina*, because, in times past, pagans set up their idols in groves).

hint at trouble to come. When Euripides' Hippolytus dedicates to Artemis 'a garland which I fashioned from an untouched meadow, where neither shepherd thinks it right to feed his flocks nor the iron has yet come ..., and Reverence [*Aidos*] cultivates it with streams of river water' (*Hipp.* 73–8), he lays symbolic claim to an ideology of abstinence; but in that act of plucking the flowers for the virgin goddess's garland he also accesses a repressed sexual dimension in the setting which presages his own undoing. Ovid echoes this passage's symbolism of abstinence in the clear and untouched pool to which he brings Narcissus, another extreme virgin, intensifying it into an emblem of Narcissus' selfishness and disengagement from pastoral society (*Met.* 3.407–10):

> fons erat inlimis, nitidis argenteus undis,
> quem neque pastores neque pastae monte capellae
> contigerant aliudue pecus, quem nulla uolucris
> nec fera turbarat nec lapsus ab arbore ramus.

There was a limpid pool, its waters silvery and bright, which no shepherds had ever touched, nor feeding mountain-goats, nor any other herd; which neither bird nor beast nor falling branch had ever disturbed.

This time the symbolic sequel is unmistakable. When Narcissus is touched by the desire and disappointment from which his solipsism has previously protected him, he violates the pool's clear surface with his own tears (474–6); the resultant break-up of his reflection anticipates his own imminent metamorphic erasure.

Such symbolism is especially potent when, as in the case of Narcissus' pool, the landscape itself undergoes a modification which in some way (pre)figures or doubles the crisis which takes place in it. One thinks here above all of the plucking of flowers from meadows (just touched on above). Flowers are traditionally associated both with virginal purity and with its vulnerability:[26] a strong symbolic nexus links the literal culling or harvesting of the earth's fruits on the one hand, and the sexual defloration or affectively charged death of a virgin on the other – nowhere more so than in the Persephone myth, its derivatives and its cognates, from the *Homeric Hymn to Demeter* to Moschus' *Europa*, Ovid's twin Proserpinas,[27] Milton's 'her self a fairer flower ...' (by implication, a reference to Eve as well as to Proserpine)[28] and beyond.

---

[26] Segal (1969) 33–8.
[27] Hinds (1987), 60 and 78–82; 88–90 on the associated pomegranate-plucking at *Met.* 5.535–6.
[28] [Carey and] Fowler (1968) on *P.L.* 4.270, comparing too 9.432 of Eve: 'her self, though fairest unsupported flower'.

An aspect of landscape symbolism peculiar to this poem (or at any rate to metamorphic myth) is the capacity of supernatural transformation to cause the symbolic and the literal to collapse fully into one another.[29] We have just seen a disturbance in a secluded pool operating as an emblem of Narcissus' sexual crisis. However, the symbolic stakes are even higher in the case of Cyane, the Sicilian water-nymph who in *Met.* 5 attempts to halt the abduction of Proserpina by standing up in her own pool to obstruct the chariot of Dis. The god's response is swift (421–4):

> ... in gurgitis ima
> contortum ualido sceptrum regale lacerto
> condidit; icta uiam tellus in Tartara fecit
> et pronos currus medio cratere recepit.

> Brandishing his royal sceptre with mighty arm he plunged it deep into the pool. The smitten earth made a path to Tartarus and received the down-plunging chariot in the midst of the abyss.

The penetration is of Cyane's pool rather than of Cyane herself. But the conventional symbiosis between a water-nymph and the element which she inhabits renders the boundary here between symbolic and literal violence inherently insecure (425–7):

> at Cyane, raptamque deam contemptaque fontis
> iura sui maerens, inconsolabile uulnus
> mente gerit tacita ...

> But Cyane, grieving for the abduction of the goddess and for the outrage to her own fountain's rights, bore a wound beyond consoling in the silence of her heart ...

In some ways this is the closest the *Metamorphoses* ever comes to describing the physical horror of actual rape. Cyane's 'wound' is specified by enjambment as a mental one, and *raptam deam* in 425 refers not to herself but to Proserpina; yet Ovid's affective phrasing leaves little room for doubt that more than a body of water has been violated here. As if to close off the possibility of restricting the trauma to the symbolic level, the episode now culminates in Cyane's supernatural dissolution into tears, which fuses her and her pool forever.

In the world of the *Metamorphoses*, the setting is always potentially more than just a setting:[30] any water, tree or bloom may not only symbolize or memorialize erotic victimhood, but actually embody a victim him- or herself.

---

[29] Cf. the bibl. on metaphor and metamorphosis cited on p. 176 n. 26.
[30] Barkan (1986) 89.

On one level this finds an epistemological context in the metamorphic principles of universal contiguity and flux expounded by Pythagoras in *Met.* 15 – which he applies, *inter alia*, to elements of landscape (261–355). But within the poem's mythic texture such an epistemology is all too closely bound up with the rupture of actual bodies; so that to plunge into *any* pool, to pluck *any* flower is to risk repeating an originary act of violence visited upon a now-metamorphosed victim. Such, precisely, is the experience of Dryope, for whom an innocent gathering of some lotus blossoms within a *locus amoenus* nightmarishly reopens the wound (and the story) of the nymph Lotis, who had lost her human form in fleeing the sexual predation of Priapus (*Met.* 9.344–5). The lesson which Dryope bequeaths to her unborn son, before being herself metamorphosed into another similarly vulnerable tree, is a paralysing one (380–1):

> stagna tamen timeat, nec carpat ab arbore flores,
> et frutices omnes corpus putet esse dearum.

Let him beware of pools, never pluck blossoms from trees, and think every bush to be the flesh of a goddess.

If all the figures who move through the landscapes of the poem were to acknowledge and experience this metamorphic logic (they do not), the whole economy of mythic setting and mythic action would collapse, and no character would ever enter a *locus amoenus* again.

For another Ovidian perspective on the embodiment of mythic victims in the landscape, we may turn to the contemporary *Fasti*. Here the goddess Flora presents herself as the proud owner of an originary flower-garden, from whose stunning variety of blooms derives all colour on the earth. Not uniquely among inhabitants of Ovidian landscapes, Flora experiences her garden *rhetorically*. Her own set-piece description (*est mihi . . . hortus*) is immediately followed by a disavowal of ability to compass her floral wealth in language (*Fast.* 5.213–14):

> saepe ego digestos uolui numerare colores
> nec potui: numero copia maior erat

Often did I wish to count the colours thus arranged, but could not: the resources were beyond measure

– where *digestos*, *colores*, *numero* and *copia* all resonate with the technical language of rhetorical and poetic style. More specifically, however, she presents herself as a metamorphic demiurge, claiming as her own work all the famous mythological transfigurations of wounded victims (the male ones, anyway) into floral form (221–8): Hyacinthus, Narcissus, Crocus, Attis,

Adonis. She seems entirely untroubled in her floral sublimation of these ephebic sufferings; in metaliterary terms the episode figures the stories of poignant death and transformation, evocatively for Ovid's pair-poem, as so many blooms on a poetic 'garland' of metamorphic song. Is this comfortable aestheticization to be ascribed to the poet of the *Metamorphoses* himself? Yes and no. Ovid certainly countenances some self-identification with the floral goddess, playfully associating her fragrance (in an implicit pun which becomes a favourite of Renaissance Ovidianism) with his own eponymous 'nose' for poetry (375–8 *floreat ... carmen Nasonis* 'that Naso's poem may flourish'; cf. *nasus, nasutus*).[31] But what abides from this episode's implied cross-reference to the *Metamorphoses* is the *contrast* between the insouciance of Flora's catalogue of floral victims and the depth of pathos visited upon the stories of many of those same blooms in the *Metamorphoses*. A more troubled form of aestheticism, then, in the latter case – but perhaps aestheticism none the less.

Art, vision, spectacle

Ovid has often, and justly, been described as a 'visual' poet; and seldom is the appeal to visuality stronger than in his set-piece landscape descriptions. It is not that such descriptions break new ground in their recreation of particular slices of nature, as apprehended by the eye (or by any other sensory organ): as with any other ancient poet (except perhaps Lucretius) the topography, however attractive, remains generic, specifications of light, colour and spatial relation are conventional ('shady', 'red and white', 'in a circle', 'on the right'), and the botany on display (whether or not 'perpetual spring' is invoked) is seasonally and climatically promiscuous. Rather the point is that Ovid's landscape descriptions characteristically involve *invitations to view*, whether channelled through the perceptions of characters who enter a setting ('s/he saw ... '), or more implicitly prompted by strong visual themes in the plots enacted therein (e.g. permutations of forbidden sight, desiring gaze and deluded vision in the highly charged landscapes where Actaeon, Narcissus and Pentheus meet their respective fates in the course of a single book).[32]

Furthermore, the invitation to view is often enhanced by specific analogies from visual art and architecture, in a way which both figures and externalizes the landscape's characteristic appeal to a constructed or *stylized* version of

---

[31] Newlands (1995) 109–10 (garland); Barchiesi (1997a) 134 (Naso pun).
[32] Leach (1988) 460–4 on *Met.* 3; Rosati (1983) 136–52 on a 'poetica della spettacolarità' in the *Met.* at large.

nature.[33] Consider for example the woodland grotto which constitutes the site of Actaeon's inadvertent voyeurism (*Met.* 3.157–60):

> ...in extremo est antrum nemorale recessu
> arte laboratum nulla: simulauerat artem
> ingenio natura suo; nam pumice uiuo
> et leuibus tofis natiuum duxerat arcum.

In the [valley's] most secret nook there is a sylvan cave, wrought by no artist's hand. But nature by her own talent had imitated art; for she had carved a natural arch from the living rock and soft tufa.

Such interplay as this between nature and art is not unique to Ovid; but it is perhaps especially marked in a poem which so frequently associates the work of the cosmic demiurge with that of poets (including the poet of the *Met.* himself), artists and other image-makers.[34]

These two aspects of Ovidian visuality (thematization of viewing, and appeal to visual art) come together at the pool of Narcissus, which endures for the reader (as for countless artists) as a visual experience in large part because Narcissus himself is represented as spending so long looking at it. So too the invitation to view along with Narcissus is sharpened when the poet has recourse to an analogy from sculptural art to describe how the youth appears to himself in the water (3.418–19):

> adstupet ipse sibi uultuque immotus eodem
> haeret, ut e Pario formatum marmore signum.

Spellbound by himself, he hangs there motionless in the same expression, like a statue shaped from Parian marble.

The *imago* in the pool (416) becomes a different kind of *imago* as Narcissus the viewer is immobilized (and himself objectified) by the spectacle of himself as art object; this thickening of the thematics of the gaze conditions and aestheticizes our own perception not just of Narcissus but also of the landscape which has made him its own.[35]

Among all landscape elements the pool, as a place where light is gathered and redirected, perhaps offers an especial stimulus to the visual imagination. Another episode in which a pool-scape, a beautiful youth and a desiring

---

[33] English 'landscape' is itself in earliest use a term used by painters: *OED* s.v.; Cosgrove (1984) 9, 16–18.

[34] Solodow (1988) 210–14.

[35] A suggestive intertext: Callistratus' ecphrastic description (*Stat.* 5; 3rd or 4th cent. AD) of a marble statue of Narcissus displayed by a woodland pool, with Elsner (1996b), esp. 250 on the passage as 'initially ambivalent about whether it is an ekphrasis of a landscape or of a work of art'.

gaze come together (perhaps the most sensuous in the whole poem) is that of Salmacis and Hermaphroditus. This time the water is translucent rather than reflective, and the youth is the object of another's gaze rather than of his own. But once again the invitation to view along with the characters is insistent, and once again the desiring gaze crystallizes at a crucial moment into an image of artistic connoisseurship – as, under the eyes of Salmacis, Hermaphroditus dives into the pool (4.353–5):

> desilit in latices alternaque bracchia ducens
> in liquidis translucet aquis, ut eburnea si quis
> signa tegat claro uel candida lilia uitro.

He dives into the waters and, swimming with alternate strokes, gleams in the limpid flow, as if one should encase ivory figures or white lilies in translucent glass.

As with the image applied to Narcissus, the object of the gaze is immobilized and aestheticized into a statue; but this time the water itself, figured as a precious glass envelope, has been transformed into art too. And the second half of the image further accentuates the interplay of landscape and art through its notable imagistic double-shift or transumption: desired youth into flower; flower into displayed art object.

In the *loca amoena* inhabited by Narcissus and Hermaphroditus, the stylization of visuality into art freezes the action, rendering the character (temporarily, in the case of Hermaphroditus) as static as the landscape he inhabits. However there is another way too in which the appeal to visuality can translate into an appeal to art: through the figuration of landscape as theatre.

The previous sections of this chapter have highlighted the way in which the ideal landscape functions in the *Metamorphoses* as a recurrent setting for (intensified) action, often further demarcated as such by an *est locus* formula which (in narratological terms) 'builds' the setting before inserting characters and plot into it. Add the kinds of appeal to visuality and to art just discussed, and the ideal landscape's strong literary historical association with pastoral competition and performance, and it is not surprising if this sense of a recurrent setting sometimes sorts itself into a specific image of the stage, thus mobilizing the mythological action as a sort of drama or theatrical spectacle.

Such an impulse is not exclusive to Ovid but belongs to the rhetorical landscape tradition at large. Thus it is that the massed trees of ideal groves before and after Ovid will sometimes sort themselves into the elevations or curves of theatre architecture (even as theatrical shapes and functions change). Here is the approach to Milton's Paradise (*P.L.* 4.137–42),

> ...and over head up grew
> Insuperable highth of loftiest shade,
> Cedar, and pine, and fir, and branching palm,
> *A sylvan scene*, and as the ranks ascend
> Shade above shade, *a woody theatre*
> *Of stateliest view* ...

a description which, within English poetry, evokes the 'stately theatre' of a wooded landscape at Spenser, *Faerie Queene* III v 39,[36] but also locates its point of rhetorical origin in the *siluis scaena coruscis | desuper* (backdrop of shimmering woods on high) of Virgil's dramatically configured Libyan harbour (*Aen.* 1.164).

The *Metamorphoses'* contribution is to adumbrate a distinctively Roman modification. In the set-piece description of Enna (p. 123 above), the grove which fringes the waters is said to shade them from the sun *ut uelo*, as if with an awning; the specification of the trees as forming a circle (*cingens latus omne*) renders that awning not theatrical but amphitheatrical – appropriately for the violent action which is about to be 'staged' beneath it.[37] In the Pentheus episode, opened up to metatheatrical effects by its allusion to Euripides' *Bacchae*,[38] the tree-girt plain where Pentheus encounters the Bacchic orgies is explicitly configured as a site for spectatorship from every side (*Met.* 3.709 *spectabilis undique*) – with Pentheus as a viewer who is fated himself to become a grisly spectacle. Both the configuration of the space and the climactic action which takes place therein – dismemberment, narrated with a further intensification of the language of the gaze (724–5 *ostendens, adspice, uisis*) – conspire to suggest, again, not so much the stage as the arena. However both theatricality and amphitheatricality find their clearest imagistic expression in the disruption of the landscape in which the doomed Orpheus performs his enchanting song to a 'theatre' of birds, animals and trees (11.22 *Orphei ...theatri*). The *locus amoenus* here is quite literally demolished as marauding maenads tear up trees and turf (29); and, in a startlingly contemporary simile which compares the imminent murder of the bard to a morning kill in a staged hunting show, the performance imagery slides into amphitheatricality (25–7):

---

[36] Cf. also *F.Q.* VI x 6; [Carey and] Fowler (1968) on *P.L.* 4.138–43.
[37] *OLD* s.v. *velum* 3; Hinds (1987) 33–5.
[38] Ovidian 'metatheatre': Curley (1999); Gildenhard and Zissos (1999), esp. 170–6.

> ...structoque utrimque theatro
> ceu matutina ceruus periturus harena
> praeda canum est...

...as when in the amphitheatre's morning sand a doomed stag falls prey to hounds.

The Roman *uenatio* thus evoked, combining as it does spectacle with a stylization of the woodland hunt, resonates at once jarringly and aptly with the *Metamorphoses'* characteristic articulation of the dangers of an untamed landscape.[39]

Painting, grotto, garden

A long-standing tradition of scholarship uses both the general visuality of Ovid's imagination and his ecphrastic invocations of visual art (most notably in the tapestry-weaving contest of *Met.* 6) to argue for the actual influence of works of painting or sculpture upon his mythological narratives;[40] and part of this has involved seeking the origin of Ovidian landscape settings in the taste for landscape and landscaped myth in contemporary Roman wall painting.[41] This unidirectional model of influence is now beginning to be replaced (or at least supplemented) by a more structural approach, which considers elements of parallelism and exchange between literary and painted landscapes in broader contexts of Roman aesthetic and cultural history.[42] The painted landscapes of Ovid's time are, like Ovid's own, rhetorically organized and governed by convention; they too contain elements of actual art and architecture which set off and render self-conscious their own artificiality; they too exploit a sense of numinousness, and show a grounding in a version of pastoral (especially in segments which modern critics characterize in terms of a 'sacral-idyllic' style); they too vary the inland grove with (equally formular) maritime schemes;[43] they too show an interest in landscape as a setting for archetypally Greek mythological action, and at times specifically in landscape as a *recurrent* setting for mythological action.

---

[39] Disturbing associations with Rome's 'fatal charades': see further on 'make-believe and violence' in chapter 2, pp. 39–42; and cf. Feldherr (1997) 42–4 on amphitheatricality in the Actaeon episode, a landmark discussion.

[40] Survey and critique by Viarre (1964), 29–140, useful though impressionistic; Solodow (1988) 224–6.

[41] Grimal (1938). [42] Leach (1988); Bergmann (1992).

[43] Maritime landscapes in the *Met.* are esp. (and aptly) concentrated where Aeneas' voyage moves the epic from Troy to Italy, in the Galatea/Scylla digression: cf. Segal (1969) 58–62.

A more structural or dialogic approach to relationships between Roman literature and art need not exclude new forms of positivism:[44] this may be the opportunity to turn the old question of painting's influence upon the *Metamorphoses* directly on its head, and to ask more energetically what influence the *Metamorphoses* itself may have exerted upon Roman painting in the later first century AD.

Consider a Vespasianic open-air fountain complex at the Pompeian 'House of Loreius Tiburtinus' (II 2.2), whose decoration includes twin panel-like frescoes of *Narcissus* and *Pyramus & Thisbe*, each depicted in a landscape: such a pairing is inconceivable without the *Metamorphoses*.[45] The story of the failed rendez-vous of Pyramus and Thisbe (of which four painted representations survive at Pompeii) has no known or likely currency at all outside the East until Ovid.[46] As for the Narcissus myth, while versions do circulate prior to and independently of Ovid, it would be perverse not to connect with the *Metamorphoses* an evident explosion of iconographic interest at Pompeii (some 50 paintings, including several of Narcisssus *and* Echo, apparently first linked by Ovid).[47]

It should be stressed, however, that to posit Ovidian influence on such an installation is not *necessarily* to posit (as above) new iconographic types 'scripted' in the wake of the *Metamorphoses*. Even if, individually, each of these two paintings were straight reproductions (with or without the landscape setting) from a standard Greek image repertoire, there could still be an Ovidian impulse behind the home-owner's or designer's *selection* of these mythic subjects over a host of others, and their *combination* into a compositional unit. (This is a point which can be applied, *mutatis mutandis*, to the consideration of Ovidian influence upon painted myths which are *not* Ovidian near-exclusives.) And viewers might read the mythic juxtaposition in the light of their reading of Ovid whether the allusion was originally intended or not. Greek art, like Greek poetry, necessarily acquires new meanings when reframed and consumed in Roman contexts.[48]

---

[44] *Pace* Leach (1988) 9 and 467.

[45] On this *euripus*, which also boasts Muse-statuettes and other paraphernalia of connoisseur-ship, cf. Zanker (1998) 145–56, with Plates 10.1–2 ('panels', in colour) and figs. 73–80; also Salza Prina Ricotti (1987) 169–72 on the identification of the area with the paired frescoes as a garden dining-room. The Vespasianic remodel of II 2.2, including these paintings (signed by a 'Lucius'), is in Zanker's view hack-work: this could strengthen the possibility that the *Met.* is by this date a routine source for visual art.

[46] *LIMC* s.v. on the Pompeian images, related and rich in Ovidian specifics. Pyramus in the East: Knox (1989).

[47] So *LIMC* s.v. 'Narkissos'. Pompeian Narcissi appear first in 'fourth style' work; nearly all are Vespasianic.

[48] Cf. the essays by Bettina Bergmann, Elaine Gazda and Ann Kuttner in Jones et al. (1995).

What makes this relatively neglected line of enquiry intuitively attractive is the extraordinary impact of the *Metamorphoses* upon painting and other visual arts *since* antiquity: the poem has exercised a larger and more pervasive influence upon the illustration of pagan themes than any other classical work, and early printed editions and paraphrases often designate it 'the painters' bible'.[49] Chapter 20 in this volume addresses this huge topic; all that needs to be emphasized in the context of the present chapter is the considerable importance of the interaction of *myth and landscape* in the artistic reception of the *Metamorphoses*.[50] In any given period, school or *oeuvre* there are of course a host of stylistic and iconographic reasons unconnected with the *Metamorphoses* which help to bring about and to shape this interaction; but it is not unreasonable to see Ovid's own emphases, encountered both directly and through the mediation of translators, adapters and book-illustrators, as a major catalyst. Given that by far the largest concentration of *loca amoena* in the poem occurs in the first five books, this involves some projection of the characteristic ambience of *Met.* 1–5 on to the poem as a whole: one may perhaps adduce a general tendency for the readerly reception of a very long work to be skewed disproportionately towards its earlier parts. In line with the pervasiveness of the emphasis upon landscape in the painterly reception of the *Metamorphoses* is the fact that some Renaissance book-illustrators of the poem draw garden backgrounds even for episodes where the text gives no warrant.[51]

For a glimpse of the interaction of Ovidian myth and Ovidian landscape in Renaissance painting, let us turn to Venice and to the '*poesie*', as he himself termed them, of Titian. Figures 1 and 2 reproduce *Diana and Actaeon* and *Diana and Callisto* (1556–9), two canvasses planned and still displayed as a pair. The Ovidianism of the Actaeon painting has received much attention;[52] in particular Panofsky's classic account of the artist's specific response to the interplay of art and nature in Diana's grotto at *Met.* 3.155–64 (key verses quoted on p. 137 above) merits quotation:

> Titian... took his clue from Ovid's description; but he reversed the accent. Instead of depicting a cave where the 'genius of nature' had imitated art, he depicted an architectural setting where art had followed the 'genius of nature'. For him and his contemporaries a Gothic vault, combined with a rusti-cated pier, was the man-made equivalent of what Ovid describes as a structure 'produced by nature in imitation of art'. And the ruined state of this structure,

49 Barkan (1986); Panofsky (1969) 140.
50 An important area also for Virgil-reception: Liversidge (1997) 99–101.
51 Hunt (1986) 43.
52 Panofsky (1969) 154–8 (quotation at 158); Barkan (1986) 200–1; Martindale (1993) 61–3; Sharrock (1996) 112.

Figure 1   Titian, *Diana and Actaeon*.

together with the inclination of the basin . . . , gives the impression that nature is reclaiming her own.

The incorporation into the pier of a stag's skull, the tracery of whose horns 'echoes' both the branching of the trees and the ribbing of the vault, not only deepens the dialogue between nature and art, but also adds a very Ovidian emphasis upon the interplay of setting and action: this iconographic hint transcends the pictorial moment to foreshadow Actaeon's imminent future (i.e. as a dead stag), and also effects a proleptic incorporation of the young man's metamorphic body *into* the setting where he is about to lose his human form.

Now consider the *Diana and Actaeon* in dialogue with its Ovidian pair-painting *Diana and Callisto*. The two subjects are of course inherently linked within Greco-Roman tradition as part of a set of myths about the inviolability of Diana's virginity. However, when that tradition passes through the filter of the *Metamorphoses*, what results is a peculiar intensification of existing

Figure 2   Titian, *Diana and Callisto*.

structural patterns, drawing these two stories more than ever before into the same imaginative space – and that space is, above all, a *locus amoenus*. An enhanced Ovidian sense of the grounding of myth in a recurrent landscape is what (directly or through intermediaries)[53] gives energy to Titian's pairing of Actaeon and Callisto, in which the very water seems to flow from one painting into the other, and in which everything – subject, iconography, composition, colour palette – is framed as virtuoso dialogue. It is almost superfluous for Titian to annotate the interplay between the two canvasses by including deer in bas-relief on the fountain in the Callisto painting, one of them fleeing from a huntress;[54] it is almost superfluous for the young Rembrandt to take the Ovidianism to its logical conclusion by playfully combining Titian's

---

[53] See Panofsky (1969) 140–1 and n.5 on the fifteen illustrated editions, translations and paraphrases of the *Met.* published at Venice in Titian's lifetime, including one in 1553 by his friend Lodovico Dolce; figs. 166–7 with 169–70 for Venetian book-illustrations of Actaeon and Callisto in stereotyped landscapes.

[54] Wethey (1975) 74.

twinned subjects on a single (1635) canvas, in which Actaeon and Callisto are confronted by Diana at the same time, in the same grove, and by the same pool.[55] The farther from Ovid's own account the interpenetration of the two landscapes proceeds, the more potently does it bear witness to the mythic legacy programmed by the Ovidian *locus amoenus*.

'All gardening is landscape-painting', runs an aphorism by Pope,[56] and a significant component in the early modern reception of Ovidian landscape is to be found in the actual gardens of the sixteenth century and later. We may take our bearings here from Roy Strong's suggestive invocation of the humanist vision of the garden as 'a place for fantasy about the classical world'.[57] The influence of Virgil in this area is great; but for a sense of magic in landscape the *Metamorphoses* reigns supreme, invoked both in its mythic particulars and as a synecdoche for the exuberance of classical paganism in general. Thus, on a 1645 visit to the gardens of the Villa d'Este at Tivoli, the diarist (and keen gardener) John Evelyn observed 'a long and spacious walk, full of fountains, under which is historicized the whole Ovidian Metamorphosis in *mezzo relievo* rarely sculptured'. John Dixon Hunt persuasively extends this habit of Ovidian reference to take in the interplay between nature and art characteristic of the Renaissance landscape gardener's way with water, rock and plant, often rendered explicitly metamorphic through tricks of plumbing: at the Villa d'Este stone mimics water and water stone in fountains shaped like staircases; elsewhere feats of hydraulic engineering cause visitors to be ambushed by random jets of water (the so-called *giochi d'acqua*), and (notably at Pratolino) garden sculptures to sing and move.[58]

Hunt lays especial emphasis on the power of water to create an atmosphere of Ovidian magic. Water, moving as well as still, will tend to be what most insistently draws the eye in a landscape; water is also, both in its fluidity and in its power to reflect and distort, the quintessentially metamorphic element. It would be interesting to know what proportion of all artistic visualizations of the *Metamorphoses* centre on water, from painting to garden art to Mary Zimmerman's remarkable theatrical adaptation of the poem in 1998–9 for a stage literally made of water.[59] Zimmerman's experiment returns us to the question of the Ovidian *locus amoenus* as a theatre, and this is another reason to set her work in dialogue with the art of the Renaissance landscaper: Hunt locates the Ovidianism of his fountains, grottoes and mythological sculptures (both animated and still) within a broader

[55] Panofsky (1969) 160 with fig. 171 on this Rembrandt in the collection of Prince Salm-Salm at Anholt.
[56] Quoted in Hunt (1992) 106.   [57] Strong (1979) 16.
[58] Hunt (1986) 42–58; quotation of Evelyn at 43.
[59] *Metamorphoses*: Lookingglass Theatre Company, Chicago 1998–9; toured Berkeley/Seattle/ L.A. 1999–2000.

context of self-conscious theatricality in the configuration of the Renaissance garden.[60]

A lost Elizabethan garden at Nonsuch Palace, Surrey, allows us to revisit Diana's grotto at *Met.* 3.155–64, this time under the heading of garden art. A traveller in 1599 describes a 'grove called after Diana' containing 'a rock out of which natural water springs into a basin, and on this was portrayed with great art and life-like execution the story of how the three goddesses took their bath naked and sprayed Actaeon with water.' Add that eye-witnesses mention a further aquatic device nearby, identified by Strong as a trick fountain for ambushing the unwary, and the implication of the visitor at Nonsuch in the 'garden theatre' of the Actaeon myth seems complete.[61]

This example affords a final transition back to antiquity. Already in the second century AD, the idea of treating *Met.* 3.155–64 as the blueprint for a fountain sculpture in a manmade grotto is in play: not in a garden, but in the indoor pool of an atrium; and not in an actual sculptural group, but in the elaborate ecphrastic imagining of such a group in the *Metamorphoses* of Apuleius. The passage in question (2.4), which allusively (re)inverts Ovid's *simulauerat artem natura* (*Met.* 3.157–8) in its own *ars aemula naturae* (art rivalling nature), constitutes a rich reading of Ovid's woodland pool, developing and complicating its conversations about nature and art, setting and spectatorship, verbal and visual representation.[62]

More broadly, the elaborate gardens of the Renaissance can serve as a reminder that Ovid's own experiments in the landscaping of myth and the mythologizing of landscape occurred in a culture which was itself no stranger to the stylization of landscape, not just in poetry and painting, but also in the interventions of actual garden design.[63] The Younger Pliny's discussions of his own property (avidly read by the landscape architects of the Renaissance) give an especially strong sense of Roman self-consciousness about interplay between nature and art in the planned garden – including, in a description of the prospect at his Tuscan villa, the idea of garden as amphitheatre.[64]

It may be noted that the Ovidian *Narcissus* and *Pyramus & Thisbe* decorating the fountain complex at the House of Loreius Tiburtinus are themselves, strictly speaking, elements of garden design; and (like Hunt's Renaissance examples) garden design which seems to find in the interplay

---

[60] Hunt (1986) 59–72, esp. 59.
[61] Strong (1979) 66–9. 'Three goddesses': other sources indicate (more correctly no doubt) Diana and two nymphs.
[62] See Slater (1998), a rich exploration.
[63] Cf. Rosati (1983) 70–7; Bergmann (1991); Kuttner (1999b), esp. 7–11 (with bibl.); *OLD* s.vv. *topia, topiarius*.
[64] Plin. *Ep.* 2.17 and 5.6 (*amphitheatrum aliquod immensum* at 5.6.7); on Renaissance readers Hunt (1986) 11–12.

of nature, art, myth and water-plumbing a peculiarly apt way to evoke the *Metamorphoses*. A different kind of garden Ovidianism can be glimpsed in Statius, *Siluae* 2.3, a playful poem which invents a myth to account for a strikingly shaped plane tree overhanging a pool in the real-life city garden of Atedius Melior. What Statius creates for his addressee is a classically Ovidian tale of the amorous pursuit of a Naiad, her refuge (with Diana's help) in the pool, and the god Pan's symbolic commemoration of his desire in the tree; the specifically Roman geography of Melior's property gives the myth a flavour of *Fasti* as well as of *Metamorphoses*. This is, of course, only a poetic conceit; but it shows with some vividness how an Ovidian sensibility *might* reshape a Roman's sense of landscape in general and actual landscape gardening in particular.

However, without the powerful Renaissance synecdoche which so often allows the *Metamorphoses* to stand in, not just for all classical myth, but for the whole classical world, a quest for particular Ovidian allusions in the actual gardens of ancient Rome (where retrievable) will probably yield only limited results. Instead, let us sketch a broader attempt to relate the Ovidian *locus amoenus* to the Roman construction and consumption of landscape at large.[65] Like Statius' more extended celebrations of rich private homes (*Silu.* 1.3 and 2.2),[66] *Siluae* 2.3 communicates a sense of the garden landscape as status symbol: the money lavished on it reflects the owner's wealth, the mythological allusions (whether in-built or supplied by the poet) his taste and education, and the very existence of the garden the élite leisure (*otium*) which he has to enjoy it. The possession of a mythological landscape painting sends the same kinds of message about taste and membership of an affluent and cultivated class. And at some level it may be possible to extend this sociology to the consumer of a poetic *locus amoenus* too.

Early in this chapter the etymologization of the *locus amoenus* as a place of love, *amor*, was noted; but it is symptomatic that a complementary etymology, attributed by Servius to Varro and by Isidore to Verrius Flaccus, derives it from the absence of agricultural *munia* ('functions', 'duties') with which it is often (though not always) associated: *'amoena' sunt loca solius uoluptatis plena, quasi 'amunia', unde nullus fructus exsoluitur* (*loca amoena* are places full of pleasure only, as it were *amunia* ['without function'], whence no produce is rendered).[67] This distinctly moralizing emphasis upon uselessness is of course just another way of describing *otium*; they are two

---

[65] Literature, leisure and landscape: cf. in general Williams (1973), esp. 13–34, 120–6; in Roman antiquity D'Arms (1970), esp. 46–8 and 132–3 on *amoenitas*; Connors (2000), esp. 499 on Martial 3.58.

[66] Myers (2000).

[67] Serv. *Aen.* 5.734. Cf. Serv. *Aen.* 6.638 (Varro); Isid. *Etym.* 14.8.33 (Verrius Flaccus); Maltby (1991) s.v.

sides of the same coin. The aestheticization of landscape, whether in the consumption of gardens, paintings or verse, is a distinctive prerogative of the leisured. Undoubtedly, one of the reasons for the enduring appeal of Ovid's *Metamorphoses* as a poem is that, despite all the mythopoeic emphasis upon crises visited upon fragile humans and other beings in its landscapes, the timeless beauty of those settings, the sense of them as a special, privileged space for the imagination, has for most readers lingered on, erasing or (perhaps in the end the same thing) stylizing the sufferings, and encouraging a kind of transcendent aestheticism. Such an embrace of beauty may always imply a measure of self-delusion, but it is not on that account hard to understand. Ovid himself was to miss the beauty of the Ovidian landscape in exile at Tomis (*Trist.* 3.10.75–6):

> aspiceres nudos sine fronde, sine arbore, campos:
> heu loca felici non adeunda uiro!

> You might behold naked fields, without leaf, without tree – a place, alas, to which no happy or productive man should come.

This couplet, in negating it, touches on much of what is precious in the *locus amoenus*:[68] the appeal to a shared, familiar, and specifically visualized arrangement of shade and foliage; a sense of the symbolic charge linking setting and inhabitant; an implicit belief in the mutual dependence of natural fertility and the fertility of the human imagination which describes it.

Let us return in this connection to E. R. Curtius, who first gave modern academic description to the rhetorical stylization of the lovely landscape in the western tradition, and who is himself in some ways the ultimate consumer of this cultural artefact. Curtius' quest for this, as for other *topoi*, was quite avowedly driven by a desire to identify a shared sense of beauty and culture unifying the Western tradition, as at once a bulwark against and a refuge from the ugliness of the Germany in which he stood in 1933:[69] his twentieth-century quest for the *locus amoenus* thus re-enacts an idealism and a belief in the power of beauty inherent to the *locus amoenus* pattern itself.

The problem is perhaps that such an appeal to transcendent beauty is more often apt to lull a sense of moral urgency than to stimulate it. And so it may

---

[68] The hexameter allusively recreates one of the rare dystopias in the *Met.* itself, the abode of Hunger at 8.789: Hinds (1985) 27 and n.39. Cf. Tomis as *locus . . . inamabilis* ('an unlovely place', i.e. the opposite of *amoenus*) at *Trist.* 5.7.43–4, with the *Met.*'s Underworld at 4.477, and Gareth Williams' discussion in chapter 14 below.

[69] Curtius (1953) vii–x, with 70–1 and 79–83 for his adoption of *topos* as a key term; cf. Martindale (1993) 24–5; Said (1993) 47; OCD³ s.v. 'topos'.

be for the history of the reception of the Ovidian *locus amoenus*. Despite some recent readings which would find the poem's beauty corrupted beyond redemption by its stories of injustice and violence, the aestheticizing valence in the landscapes of the *Metamorphoses* has proved largely irresistible, at once symptomatic and determinative of the consumption of all pleasure and pain enacted therein, for good or for ill

> Annihilating all that's made
> To a green thought in a green shade.
> (Marvell, *The Garden* 47–8)

FURTHER READING

On the *locus amoenus* pattern the seminal discussion is Curtius (1953), chapter 10 'The ideal landscape'. On vivid description as a category for ancient rhetoricians see Vasaly (1993) and Bartsch (1989), esp. chapter 1; the boundary between such description and narrative is theorized (with bibl.) by Fowler (2000) chapter 3. On the *est locus* formula see (with bibl.) Hinds (1987) 36–8 and nn., within an extended treatment of the landscape of Enna in *Met.* 5.

On interplay between landscape and action in the *Met.* Hugh Parry's succinct article (1964) is developed in different directions by Segal (1969) and Davis (1983). As to metamorphic 'embodiment' in landscape, Ovidian scholarship is now in dialogue with current discussions of the body as a site for constructions of and anxieties about identity, and as the *locus* for violence and desire: see Philip Hardie's overview of work on 'the self' in Hardie, Barchiesi, Hinds (1999) 5–9; also Keith (2000), esp. chapters 3 and 5; and Alison Sharrock's chapter 6 of this volume, with bibl. Richlin (1992) confronts both interpretative and ethical issues raised by the aestheticization of sexual violence in the *Met.*

On visuality in the *Met.* the major treatment is Rosati (1983); for the poem's overt appeals to visual art see Solodow (1988), chapter 6. The study of spectacle is a growing area of interest in Roman cultural studies: for the *Met.* see Philip Hardie's section on 'cultures of display' in chapter 2 of this volume; Feldherr (1997), esp. 42–4.

For the reception of the *Met.* in art, see Christopher Allen's chapter 20 of this volume with 'further reading'; on Titian see Panofsky (1969), chapter 6 'Titian and Ovid'; Barkan (1986), 175–206; and Martindale (1993) 60–4. For the *Met.* in Renaissance garden art see Hunt (1986), chapter 4 'Ovid in the garden'. The *Met.* receives limited attention in Leach's ambitious comparative study of literary and painted landscape at Rome (1988): 343–4, 348–52, 440–67. Recent work on actual Roman landscapes (esp. in villas, gardens and parks) has stepped up the level of dialogue between literary, art-historical and sociological approaches, and awaits an Ovidian dimension: exemplary are Bergmann (1991), and Kuttner (1999a). On the sociology of landscape at large Williams (1973) remains fundamental.

9

ALISON SHARROCK

Ovid and the discourses of love: the amatory works

All poets speak in quotations. In the decades immediately before Ovid wrote his love poetry, Propertius and Tibullus (and Gallus and Catullus before them) developed an elegiac genre in which the speaker is enslaved to a mistress, and chooses a life of decadence and devotion rather than civic and military success. The poems beseech and reproach the beloved, show her off to friends, and occasionally celebrate her and the relationship, rhetorically laying out in public the life of a young man in Augustan Rome: all this through a poetics which is clever, difficult, artistic, and stylized. Then Ovid did it again – differently. Much of Ovid's amatory work is infused with an aesthetics of repetition: of material, of style, of himself, and in his characters.[1]

All lovers speak in quotations. This precept of the modern erotodidact Roland Barthes was implicitly foreshadowed by Ovid when he outrageously reminds us that *militat omnis amans* ('every lover is a soldier', *Am.* 1.9.1):[2] that is, every lover enters into a discourse of erotic imagery in dialogue and in conflict with his society, literary, social, and political. Ovid's amatory works put private life on display – or rather, show us how private life is always already on display, a fiction played out for real, a reality fantasized. The discourses of love, the erotic as discourse, discourse as erotic – these things are at issue throughout the Ovidian corpus: in this chapter, I shall confine the discussion to the *Amores*, the *Ars amatoria*, and the *Remedia amoris*.

Ovid's three books of *Amores*, which once were five (so the poems claim when they introduce themselves), are a collection of short poems playing with the *topoi* of love elegy: the locked-out lover, the slave go-between, the traditional symptoms of love, the rich rival, the witch-bawd, infidelity, the military, political, and poetic alternatives, and even the occasional successful

---

[1] For help with thinking through this essay I am very grateful to Sergio Casali, Philip Hardie, John Henderson, and Duncan Kennedy. They may recognize that critics speak in quotations too.

[2] On this conceit see McKeown (1995).

erotic encounter.[3] Then he did it all again with the *Ars amatoria*, a didactic poem in elegiacs which teaches the reader how to be a good lover: how to catch a woman, how to keep her, and (addressed to women) how to catch and keep a man. And then yet again with the *Remedia amoris*, which teaches us how to be good at breaking up. In Ovidian aesthetics, and erotics, artfully judged familiarity can breed content.

Many of the issues in the discourse of Ovidian amatory poetry are raised by a poem which stands out as unusually explicit and plays with the reader's desire to know: *Amores* 1.5, in which the beloved Corinna pays a midday visit to the lover-poet. *Cetera quis nescit?* ('Who does not know the rest?') The poem plays around with light and half-light, hiding and sight, covering and uncovering. As Corinna teasingly plays at refusing to uncover herself, so Ovid-the-poet plays at refusing to uncover *himself*, his poetry, his sex, to the reader. Moreover, the poem presents Corinna as the *materia* and the *fons et origo* of erotic poetry, but also (it is almost the same thing) as the fetishized object of the gaze, the constructed thing, the fiction that guarantees the superior status of the speaker in the scale of realism.[4] He speaks, he looks, he touches, he writes.

Most of all, he tells – or doesn't. The biggest game with telling and not telling concerns the identity of Corinna. Is she 'real'? People have been asking this since Ovid's own day, according to the poet himself (*Ars* 3.538) – but of course he could be bluffing. He places Corinna in a catalogue with other elegiac women, as an example of how poetry can give fame (so love the poet for the sake of his poetry ...). But what use is fame based on a pseudonym?[5] And fame which, Ovid hints, derives from a mistaken reading of the *Amores*. Important work has been done to show how the beloved of elegy may be seen as a manifestation of the poetry itself, rather than as a real woman. When the poet, thinking of writing epic, is forced back into elegy by the *puella*'s erotic coaxing (*Am.* 2.1, 2.18), while the personified Elegy (3.1) and the sexy Muse (various in exile) are presented also as *puellae*, it is impossible to resist the implication that these girls are poems.[6]

But Ovid won't let us get away so easily from the tricks of realism and fiction, for *Amores* 3.12 plays a double bluff with the question of reality. The poet bewails the fact that his beloved is prostituted around the city, thanks

---

[3] For more on the elegiac nature of the amatory poetry see Harrison in chapter 5 of this volume. On the didactic poems, see Schiesaro, chapter 4 in this volume, particularly for the discourse of knowledge which is at stake there.

[4] On gaze-theory applied to Roman culture, including elegy, see Fredrick (forthcoming).

[5] *Ars* 3.536 plays around with fame, the reward for being loved by a poet, and names. See Kennedy (1993) 84–5 on pseudonyms.

[6] See especially Wyke (1989) and (1990); Cahoon (1985). The correlation between elegiac women and poetics is worked through by Keith (1994). For wider issues relating to women and writing/being written, see Gubar (1986).

to the fame of his poetry. At first sight, this looks like pretty clear support for the idea of the beloved as poetry, with the poet and his readers taking the roles of lover and rivals. But then the poem develops into a disquisition on poetic fictionality, arguing that everything in poetry is a lie, all made up, complete fiction. We poets can turn Niobe into stone, make Scylla a thief and turn her into the hideous sea-monster (conflating two Scylla-myths, by the metamorphic power of poetry) – and you persist in believing that I spoke the truth about my beloved? How naive! *Et mea debuerat falso laudata uideri | femina; credulitas nunc mihi uestra nocet* ('My woman ought to have been seen to be praised falsely; now your credulity is doing me harm', 3.12.43–4). Indeed so – except that the ostensible point of the poem is to protest at the excessive erotic popularity of the beloved, whom the poet wants to keep for himself. One level of rhetorical ploy going on here is to suggest the very reality of the beloved precisely in the attempt to deny it.

The poem may also be teaching us to read realism with care, realism as discourse. We (lovers, poets, readers, teachers, etc.) do manipulate discourse, but – from an Ovidian/Barthesian point of view – *we* are the effects of discourse, which shapes us and figures us as real. Ovid understood this well, and so manipulated (and was manipulated by) an apparent contradiction in love poetry: the lover's discourse desperately seeks sincerity, with a desire for immediacy and transparency seemingly incompatible with the necessary artifices of poetry. It may sound outrageously insincere when Ovid begs his beloved not to *be* faithful, but to act as if she were (*Amores* 3.14), but this too is part of the lover's discourse: 'if only I could avoid this suffering', so it goes, 'I'd be willing to undergo any indignities as long as I am granted a little love'. Moreover, this again is a poem about keeping things private (3.14.20). The contradiction of speaking publicly about privacy, of speaking sincerely (about insincerity) in a form full of conventions, is shown as essential to the workings of erotic discourse, for what Ovidian erotics expose is that the lover's desire for immediacy and transparency is mirrored in the reader's desire to understand, to enter and to belong. Poetic discourse constructs us as readers, just as erotic discourse constructs us as lovers.

Professor Ovid tells his pupil *est tibi agendus amans* (*Ars* 1.611): 'you must act the part of a lover' in order really to become one. It's easy to call Ovid cynical, and it is comments like this, together with the generic and traditional nature of many themes in Ovidian erotics, that have caused readers some discomfort over the question of the poet-lover's sincerity.[7] But Ovid foreknew

---

[7] Davis (1989) is a study of the varieties of acting and role-playing in the *Amores*. Although it gives, from an artistic point of view, a positive evaluation of Ovid's playful fictions, nonetheless it maintains the judgement of 'insincerity', for it argues that Ovid occasionally lets his mask drop, and shows us the reality of his feelings (see particularly ch. 4). It is not

this criticism. He instructs the reader-lover, first of all, *elige cui dicas 'tu mihi sola places'* ('choose someone to whom you can say "you alone please me"', *Ars* 1.42). Choose someone to be the recipient of your amatory discourse. On the one hand, this is an outrageous paradox, going to the heart of the conflict between love as a conscious, rational choice (therefore 'insincere') and as an irrational, overwhelming emotion (therefore 'sincere'), a contrast which informs the *Ars amatoria* in particular. But, on the other hand, the apparently awkward juxtaposition also shows how, in poetry as in life, motives and actions are complex. Moreover, the words put into the mouth of the aspiring lover are a direct quotation from Propertius (2.7.19). The lover is told, then, to 'choose someone with whom you can be an elegiac lover, with whom you can "be" Propertius'. While on the one hand this quotation constitutes a challenge to the elegiac autobiographical discourse of sincerity, on the other hand it also creates a new form of 'autobiography', one for an elegiac poet: choose a beloved, choose where to place yourself in the catalogue of elegiac poets. The amatory poetry runs the gamut of erotic discourses: declaration, desire, intimacy, celebration, conflict, absence, failure, repudiation. And of the metadiscourses: advice, fiction, realism, metapoetics. This is *agendus amans* ('acting the part of a lover'). But even if we think we know we are only acting, we may be trapped by the constructing power of discourse. However strong the pose of sophisticated detachment with which we approach the Ovidian erotic corpus, delighting in our knowledge that the question of sincerity need not trouble us, we had better watch out, because *fiet amor uerus qui modo falsus erat* ('love will become real which just now had been false', *Ars* 1.618).

Truth and falsehood, fiction and reality, secrets and publicity, sincerity and pose: these are the concerns of a lover, and are at issue throughout the amatory poetry, for they are central to the project of subjectivity which always raises crucial questions in Augustan poetry. How does a public discourse relate to the private I (and eye)? Why does a lover tell his secrets? – as Ovid complains in *Ars* 2.625–38. His own enigmatic claim about truth, honesty, and discretion in talking about love hardly settles the matter: *nos etiam ueros parce profitemur amores, | tectaque sunt solida mystica furta fide* ('I indeed only sparely proclaim my real affairs, and my mystic thefts are hidden under firm fidelity', *Ars* 2.639–40). Really? The refusal to tell secrets, to let us see fully what is going on, the pretence that we are spying on something private – all these things contribute to creating the poetic and erotic force of love poetry.

---

self-evidently clear to me that anger and abuse against slaves is any more or less real, any more or less a pose, than praise and concern (Davis, p. 102). A similarly positivist attitude to role-playing mars the discussion of *persona* in Stapleton (1996). See also Connor (1974). For a different attitude to Ovidian insincerity see Cahoon (1985).

In love poetry, a private matter is played out in the public domain. But in Augustan Rome, 'sex' is not left at home; it becomes a site for the construction of the individual self precisely because the self's relationship with society has been problematized by the coming of the principate, not only by the legislation about marriage and adultery which Augustus successfully introduced in 18 BC, but also more widely in the challenge the principate posed to Roman notions of manly autarky and freedom of speech (for upper-class males).[8] Ovid is constantly half-denying, half-proclaiming that he is really saying this stuff: *nos Venerem tutam concessaque furta canemus | inque meo nullum carmine crimen erit* ('I will sing safe Venus and allowed thefts and in my song there will be no crime', *Ars* 1.33–4); *en iterum testor, nihil hic nisi lege remissum | luditur* ('look, again I bear witness, no games forbidden by law are played here', *Ars* 2.599–600). Well, did he say it or didn't he?[9] For this game of playful denial Ovid invokes – and denies – his muse towards the end of *Ars* 2. She is to stay outside the bedroom; she isn't needed (*Ars* 2.705) because the lovers will know what to do and say without any instruction – this, followed by another 20-odd lines of intimate, public instruction about this intimate, private activity. 'Look at me not saying this!' The same thing happens in even more explicit terms in the parallel passage at the end of *Ars* 3. Ovid claims that *pudor* stops him from saying anything more (3.769), but Venus insists that he must finish the job (*opus*). With this, Venus drives to its climax the joke on *opus* as sex and as poetry which has been active throughout the amatory poetry.[10] And so finish it he does, with an extraordinary passage of advice on the varieties of sexual positions which suit different figures. There is a nice irony in the literary, even pompous erudition of the mythological *exempla* which are the vehicle for the instruction about sexual positions. Can you say these things or not?

Part of the erotic delight of poetry, especially subjective poetry, is the pretence that we are sneaking a look at something hidden. Ovid plays on that desire again in the context of secrets when he strikes a pose of pious indignation at anyone who would divulge the secrets of the mystery religions (*Ars* 2.601–24) – having just told the story of Mars and Venus, in order to encourage lovers to be relaxed about infidelity. Symbolic of this erotic covering and uncovering are the representations of Venus herself in this passage: at 2.613–14 we are reminded of the famous covering-cum-pointing gesture of Venus in art, but in the adulterous story Venus is presented as

---

[8] See in particular Wallace-Hadrill (1985). Our gut reaction that love and sex are 'private' must be a triumph of optimism over experience, since not only our national laws but also our popular culture deny that this is so. Yet the belief remains.

[9] As in the famous case some years ago as to whether a TV personality actually said **** when he enclosed the word in a conditional clause.

[10] See Kennedy (1993) 58–63.

unable to cover her *pudenda* because she is caught in Vulcan's trap (583–4). The attraction of the forbidden fruit is, of course, almost over-determined in erotic discourse.

It's this issue of desire for what is hidden that Ovid exposes in two more poems (outrageous poems, by the standards of naive, biosynthetic realism): *Amores* 2.19 and 3.4. The first complains about a husband who does not guard his wife well enough, and so fails to offer the lover sufficient challenge; the second complains that the husband's careful guard is pointless, and just makes his wife more desirable. Metapoetic readings of these poems, as referring to the writing of poetry as well as the furthering of an erotic relationship, seem almost inevitable, since the objectification of the beloved as 'poetry' is particularly in evidence.[11] For the poet to love, and the lover to write, there needs to be both an opportunity and a challenge. The poems also show how the lover's discourse is not just something between himself and the object of his desire. A third party comes into it as well: it might be a 'rival' or a 'friend' (or even both at once), but what is crucial about this 'other person' is that he breaks down the pseudo-barriers of intimate exclusivity which the discourse of love poses for the loving couple, but can never deliver.[12]

All this about doing private things in public hits at the heart of subjectivity in poetry. How does one 'speak love' when the material of 'love' and of 'poetry' comes already in inverted commas? The issue is intensified for Ovid, writing as he is in a tradition of subjective love poetry which is already well developed. Genre, topos, tradition – how can you say anything privately in the midst of that, when Propertius, Tibullus, and others now lost to us have been there before? Programmatic for such issues of repetition and privacy is the dinner-party in *Am.* 1.4, in which the poet instructs his beloved in the range of lovers' tricks for private communication. The point comes home to roost in *Am.* 2.5, when these techniques are turned against Ovid himself, as his beloved and another man engage in the same 'private' language. The supposedly private instructions, to be used as a secret language for communication which is exclusive to the lovers, even in the presence of a party-load of people, are given in public, in a public poem.[13] Communication through writing in wine on the table, through drinking from the same cup as the

---

[11] See Lateiner (1978). The argument is that the lover's desire for a challenge in his relationship is a reflection of the Callimachean poet's high valuation of difficulty in poetic production. The beloved is the poetry, more attractive in proportion to the difficulty of access.

[12] Another interesting 'other' is the witch (especially *Am.* 1.8), who is remarkably like Ovid himself. See Gross (1996) and Myers (1996).

[13] We ought to notice that the prequel to 2.5 is 2.4, a poem about Ovid's *ambitiosus amor*, which is excited by any kind of girl. He gives the game away, a bit, that this is also all about poetry, when he says that he likes tall girls and short ones ... *corrumpor utraque;* | *conueniunt uoto longa breuisque meo* (2.4.35–6). The reference to the elegiac couplet is, to say the least, obvious.

beloved, through pre-arranged body-language and touching under the table: this is hardly secret when *everyone knows* about these things.[14] The lover can speak and act only because there have been lovers speaking and acting before.

The subjective position of love poetry foregrounds the dynamics of communication and representation in the power-relations between speaker, subject, and reader. The *Amores* offer us a realist speaker who cannot simply be divorced from the 'I' of the individual poem, still less from the 'I' of the body of the poetry. The gap between lover and poet is paradoxically both more and less wide in Ovid's amatory poetry than in the elegiac tradition of Propertius and Tibullus: more ironically detached, and also more challengingly personal. While both lover and beloved are both artificial and realist, nonetheless he, we might say, 'seems real', but she 'seems like an illusion of reality', because the subjective nature of elegy creates a powerful realism for the speaker/poet, and a totalizing, objectifying, illusionism for the mistress, and moreover the speaker's realism is actually predicated on the mistress' objectification. If, for example, we take the first seven poems of Book 1 as a group, we can see a gradual unfolding of the story through the construction of the speaker and the unveiling of the mistress. The build-up from poetics to erotics, culminating in subjective self-absorption, successfully constructs the speaker as holding the power to be real, and the beloved as his object.

Notoriously, Ovid introduces the elements of elegy in reverse order. Where Propertius has *Cynthia prima* bringing love bringing elegy bringing elegiac couplets, in Ovid's schema the enforced elegiac couplet brings elegy bringing love bringing a beloved.[15] But it can be taken further. The collection starts with metre and the generic game of the foot with Cupid (in which the love god steals one metrical foot from Ovid's second line, thus turning his poetry from epic hexameters to elegiac couplets); then the *opus* (poetry and sex) with which the love god shot the poet catches hold of him, but still without an object (1.2); then comes the object, just about, in very nebulous terms (1.3), an object who is to be 'fertile material' for the poet, answering the *opus* of poem 1; then in poem 4 we seem finally to break out of the constraints of poetry and into the world of a Roman dinner party, as realism takes over (but note that a veil is still drawn over the mistress, 1.4.41–8); next – *ecce*

---

[14] See Wilkinson (1955) 143: 'Surely we have heard before, and more than once, of lovers communicating by writing on the table in wine, exchanging glances and signs, drinking from the side of the cup where the other has drunk, and touching hands.' Surely we have, although, as McKeown notes ad loc., the *topos* of secret language is considerably more common in Ovid than in the other elegists. My point here, however, is about *topoi* in general.

[15] See Buchan (1995).

Corinna uenit – comes a name, and a body constructed by the eye of the I. We may have reached a kind of erotic climax here, but there is still some way to go towards full-blown subjectivity. *Amores* 1.6 is the crucial next move – instead of going further *into* the relationship, as the movement of 3–4–5 might have encouraged us to expect, the poet-lover moves *out* onto the street, and into himself for a classic moment of elegiac self-absorption which hides the beloved. From there, we can move to the climax of subjectivity: the pain, the suffering, the guilt, the parody. But before we look at that poem, let's try that sequence again. These poems take us through a lot of ground in erotic discourse: Ovid starts as a poet, emulating Virgil and forced into a world he didn't choose; he becomes a lover surprised by his senses; then a lover declaring himself, though we are not sure who to; a jealous lover plotting; a successful lover; a desiring frustrated locked-out lover; an angry, crazy, remorseful lover. It's all there.

Amores 1.7 expresses the feelings of a man who has made a savage attack on his beloved, and is now filled with remorse, with the fear that his madness might be repeated, and with a desire for reconciliation. It's not hard to see an element of parody here, even before the final sting in the tail when the mistress is told simply to tidy up her hair, for the poem constitutes an exaggerated version of the self-flagellation and slightly worrying erotic violence that is found in Propertius and Tibullus. The *persona* Ovid adopts, then, must be quite separate from the poet himself, for that's how parody works. So it might seem – but this is not all that the poem does. The massive concentration on the Big Self which this poem presents, in the first person, denies us any easy splitting up of the poet from the *persona*. Moreover, it is with regard to this poem that Ovid makes one of his most explicit extra-generic comments, enticing and tempting us to read further between the lines and fill in the gaps of his self-presentation, to link the speaker of one work with the speaker of another. In *Ars* 2.169–72, playing now the role of teacher of love, Ovid refers again to this 'same incident', inviting us to learn by the example of his mishandling of his mistress. (Or was it?) We are tempted to ask: did he really hit her? Did he really tear her dress (he says not; he says she says he did)? Did he really just mess up her hair? The link between the poems creates a powerful sense of realism.

But this I – this Big Self – as soon as he sees the beloved, becomes an eye making erotic and aesthetic judgements which size the beloved up. She is moulded into being the embodiment of the 'lovely fault' (cf. *Rem.* 350),[16] and immediately becomes entangled in a web of literary and artistic

---

[16] See Cunningham (1958) for the argument that Ovid subscribed to the theory of the pleasant or appropriate fault, and applied it to the elegiac couplet. Here, I am moving the image from metre to mistress.

allusions.[17] She is like Atalanta (13–14), from Propertius 1; Ariadne (15–16), from Catullus 64; Cassandra (17–18), from *Aen*. 2. The beloved *is* a simile, whether of a mythological heroine or of nature (54–8); or joining the two in 51–2, where she is turned into a statue (the line evokes both the living rock in the hillside and the artistic creation hewn from it). Like Catullus' Ariadne (64.61), the beloved is frozen by her poetic creator, fixed by his gaze and by his aesthetic judgement into the form of a beautiful statue. The fact that it is the poet who is doing the looking (with a bit of connivance from the reader) makes him partake in an apparently living reality while the beloved becomes an image, a thing-to-be-looked-at. The emphasis on her silence (20–2) can only make his own voice louder.

Despite the fact that the *Amores* is so strongly focalized through the speaker-lover and his beloved, however, the 'private' Ovidian erotic world is actually quite crowded, with a range of other people who act as foils to the intimate relationship. One group, the slaves, provide in their powerlessness an interesting counterpart to the elegiac erotic ethos, which is founded on the figure of *seruitium amoris*, in and through which the lover-poet presents himself as eager (or forced) to throw away his manly Roman autarky and become a slave to a woman (e.g. 2.17).[18] Elegy offers an alternative world, where power relations supposedly work in the opposite direction from those of normal society. Slavery is thus a powerful metaphor for love, and the 'powerful' slave with control over the mistress's door looks at first sight like a neat and expressive inversion of the impotent lover. But just as the erotic 'slave' is actually the one constructing the relationship, so too the real slaves actually serve to underline the uneven power-relations of Ovidian erotics as much as of conventional Rome. Ovid-the-lover needs favours from the *ianitor* (1.6), Nape (1.11), Bagoas (2.2 and 2.3), and Cypassis (2.7 and 2.8),[19] but he can still make them dance to his tune.

The slaves of elegy have in common with the beloved *puella* also the manner in which they contribute to the realist illusion without themselves appearing real. They are part of the literary and cultural furniture, things for looking at and working with. By contrast, there are other characters in the *Amores* who seem to gain a realist status denied to the less-privileged: various addressees, who go by proper Roman names. There is Atticus in 1.9,

---

[17] The poem has been analysed by Morrison (1992) as a transgression of poetic genre, the poet's *furor* setting him up as an epic or tragic hero. This, I would say, both is and is not a parody.

[18] The image, as McKeown notes on 2.17.1 and 1.3.5, is much less common in Ovid than in the other elegists.

[19] On this diptych, see, crucially, Henderson (1991) and (1992). On slaves in Roman literature, see Fitzgerald (2000), especially the discussion (59–67) of elegiac slaves and their uncomfortable 'intrusions on [the] privacy' of free lovers.

Graecinus in 2.10, and Macer in 2.18. There is also 'Ovid's wife' in 3.13. What the wife (as an extension of Ovid-the-man), and still more the Roman friends have, along with the poet himself – P. Ovidius Naso – is realism. These Roman named men are invited to join with the poet (and the reader is allowed to tag along as well) and stand on the edges of the dramatic illusion of the elegiac erotic world. With Atticus we look at the figure of *militia amoris*. With Graecinus we play around with the ideas of exclusivity (the poem starts with a boast-cum-lament that the poet is in love with two women at once), of sexual and poetic potency (2.10.23–4) and especially of the interconnectedness of poetry and sex, when the poet hopes to die in the midst of the 'work' (sex) – this, as others have noted, in the midst of the work, the middle of the *Amores* (2.10.35–6).[20] With Macer, we enter into the generic battle for Ovid's poetic soul. His attempts to give up elegy for something more elevated are forestalled by the *puella*'s charming entreaty. But the *puella* of 2.18, even though she actually has some words to speak, is an embodiment of the poetry, and seems like an object of the poetic illusion. Macer, Ovid, and we, if we play the game as we are told to, have subjectivity, realism, and power.[21] Or so we are encouraged to think.

Another group of 'others' who are important in the lover's discourse are other lovers. In Ovid's amatory poetry, these are enormously important people for the construction of the erotic ethos: they are the rivals, the friends, and the recipients of Ovid's advice. It is when the 'natural' discourse of friendly advice meets the scientific discourse of didactic explication that love really becomes a communal matter. This is especially so since the *Ars amatoria* has always one eye on Virgil's *Georgics*, a didactic poem teaching its readers good societal relationships through the medium of skill in farming.[22] The power relations in erotodidaxis change also, for the reader is no longer an accomplice, or a spy onto Ovid's private erotic world, but rather himself (and, in a sense, herself) takes a step into that world, to become the recipient of Ovid's advice, and erotic attentions. The poet now tells us how to read, how to look at the world, how to engage with erotic discourse. The reader learns not only where to find a girl, how to choose, how to make the first approach, how to avoid giving expensive presents, and how to feel like a lover, but also how to read love poetry, how to write himself into the *Amores*.[23]

---

[20] See Henderson (1992) 81.
[21] I do not intend to say that the Roman men are 'really' more real than anyone else, but, rather, to move from the straightforward question of 'real or not?' into thinking about representation and realism as a mode of perception, as a discourse.
[22] On the relationship between the *Georgics* and the *Ars amatoria* Leach (1964) is still a classic.
[23] See Allen (1992).

Is this realistic, or 'just literary'? Certainly, it is literary, for the *Ars amatoria* is nearly as much obsessed with its own metapoetics as it is with *eros*. But also, it seems to me, the didactic form brings to the surface tensions of representation inherent in love poetry. The worldly-wise teacher, his naive pupil, and the universal subject-matter make this the most realistic of love poems, and yet to many people the idea that love is a skill which can be taught is also a patent absurdity. It is a joke on the rhetoric of knowledge, and yet love is presented from the very start as precisely a matter of knowledge (*Ars* 1.1). But Love keeps fighting back (*Ars* 1.9) and, like Daedalus (*Ars* 2.19–98), will not keep still while the Professor tries to beat it into shape and present it for us as a study-pack. The reader cannot really learn how to control love, but he might learn love's discourses: *cum dare non possem munera, uerba dabam* ('when I couldn't give gifts, I gave words', *Ars* 2.166).

Lovers are most likely to seek advice when things go wrong, so in steps Aunty Ovid with the answers to our problems, the *Remedia amoris*. This underrated, superbly sexy poem pulls off a brilliant coup, pretending to be the rhetorical 'other side' of the argument, and the ultimate retraction and denial of the world of erotic elegy, in preparation for greater things, but actually being a seductive song, which will draw us further into the world of Ovidian erotics. The poem, like the *Ars*, flirts with the discourses of medicine and philosophy, but in the end we cannot escape, because the rhetoric of renunciation is so crucial a part of erotic discourse. Much of Ovid's anti-erotic advice is likely to trap the unwary reader, as even the teacher admits. For example, the unhappy lover is invited to come on his mistress unawares, in the hopes of catching her out without *cultus* and so arousing disgust in himself (341–8). But, as Ovid says, *non tamen huic nimium praecepto credere tutum est: | fallit enim multos forma sine arte decens* ('it is not, however, safe to trust to this precept, for many have been deceived by beauty attractive without art', 349–50). The problem is that the discourse of *eros* constantly struggles with the rhetoric of renunciation: the images with which the reader-lover is invited to compare himself are those of wild *eros* – bull, fire, ranging torrent, thirst, hunt. Any contact with the world of *eros* is likely to cause a problem. For this reason, the lover is invited to avoid friends who will go on about love and make things worse (619–26).

Such a 'friend' is the poet himself. The very closeness of the *Remedia amoris* to the *Ars amatoria* and the *Amores* has contributed to the poor critical appraisal of it in much modern reading (it is 'more of the same'), but really this is the point. The poems present themselves *paruo discrimine* ('with little distinction'). The way the *Remedia* partakes in the discourse of the *Ars* can be seen most forcefully at the climax of each poem. The supposedly cured lover, by *Rem.* 785, is meant to be able to go past his mistress' door without a qualm. Now's the moment when, if you want to, you can do it (787): *nunc opus est celeri subdere calcar equo* ('now you need to apply the goad to the swift horse', 788). Where have we learned about that before? *Ars* 2.731–2: *cum mora non tuta est, totis incumbere remis,* | *utile et admisso subdere calcar equo* ('when delay is not safe, it is useful to press forward with full sails, and to apply the goad to the horse given its head'). In case we missed the allusion, Ovid gives us a second try at it two lines later (*Rem.* 790), telling us to use all speed to get past the house: *remis adice uela tuis* ('add sails to your oars'). We have to remember both *Ars* 2.731 *totis incumbere remis* and 2.725–6 *sed neque tu dominam uelis maioribus usus* | *desere* ('but you should not desert your mistress, using larger sails'). The context, in *Ars* 2, was the right management of mutually satisfying sex. If the lover has the opportunity, he must take his time to make sure that he and his mistress reach climax together; if not, he should press ahead like a rower or a rider in a race.

So, is the *Remedia amoris* really setting itself up as a didactic poem that *doesn't work*? At one level, yes: after all, if it really worked, in the sense of curing all lovers, it would be the end of erotic discourse, and almost the end of literature. Ovid himself makes this clear at 47–72, when he declares that if Dido, Pasiphae, Paris and others had read the *Remedia amoris*, their stories would have been insignificant. If the *Ars* didn't kill literature off (*Ars* 3.33–40), then the *Remedia* will surely finish the job, if we let it. The implications for Roman literature, and indeed Roman history, are momentous – if Dido had had no amatory difficulties, where would we be?

But, on the other hand, perhaps this is the final test for us, his pupils. If we can resist all the erotic enticements of this poem, then we really will have learned our lesson. Until we reach that moment of ataraxia, we still have the discourse of renunciation. As Ovid knew perfectly well: *qui nimium multis* *'non amo' dicit, amat* ('he who keeps telling everyone "I'm not in love", is', *Rem.* 648).

FURTHER READING

The *Amores* benefits from the extensive and highly learned, useful, and readable, but at the time of writing not fully published commentary of McKeown, in four volumes (the first containing text and general introduction). In addition, there is Barsby (1973) on *Amores* 1, Booth (1991) on *Amores* 2, Hollis (1977) on *Ars* 1, and Gibson (forthcoming) on *Ars* 3. The *Remedia amoris* has a commentary by Henderson (1979), but otherwise lacks significant modern scholarship. Among monographs, Kennedy's (1993) book on elegy is difficult but excellent, while Greene (1998) makes a valuable contribution to feminist reading of elegy, including Ovid. Allen (1992) is excellent both on the Ovidian poems themselves and on their later influence. Boyd (1997) is a rare full-scale treatment of the *Amores*, concentrating mainly on literary sources. Mack's general introductory book (1988) is a good starting place for all aspects of Ovid. On the *Ars*, there is a fine book in Italian (Labate, 1984). Myerowitz (1985) is particularly concerned with the poem as about 'serious play' and the interactions of nature and *cultus*, while Sharrock (1994a) looks at the aesthetics of repetition in *Ars* 2.

As regards articles, the chapters by DuQuesnay and Hollis in Binns (1973) make good readable introductions to the amatory works. Crucial to the reading of Corinna as poetry is Wyke (1989) and (1990), with also Greene (1998) and Keith (1994), while there have been several important pieces on Ovid's amatory poetry in *Helios*. Finally, on a topic which has always been in the background but never quite made it to centre-stage, Barsby (1996).

10

ANDREW FELDHERR

Metamorphosis in the *Metamorphoses*

As Gregor Samsa awoke one morning from uneasy dreams, he found himself transformed in his bed into a monstrous insect.

The first sentence in Kafka's *Metamorphosis*, a work whose moral serious-ness has sometimes seemed to place it at the opposite pole from Ovid's epic in the literature of transformation, is as baffling for the reader as the event it describes is for Gregor Samsa. As he has become a monstrous insect so we are immediately confronted with the question of how to make sense of and interpret this monstrous and bizarre subject. The first words, with their resemblance to the classic fairy tale beginning 'once upon a time', seem to offer one possibility: we can normalize this supernatural event by assuming the story belongs to a genre that doesn't ask us to take it seriously, and even rejoice in the distance that separates us from a fictional world where such things are possible. So for Samsa there is the fleeting possibility that he is still dreaming. But if the time when this event takes place is re-assuringly inde-terminate, other elements of the story bring it much closer to home. Gregor Samsa is too specific to be the name of a fairy tale prince, and the transfor-mation takes place in his own bed – it could indeed be ours. Throughout the story, the particularity with which Gregor's condition is described suggests a kaleidoscopic variety of strategies for making sense of it. Perhaps one of the most tempting is to neutralize its strangeness by treating it as a figure of speech, so that its significance becomes symbolic rather than literal. Gregor Samsa is merely like an insect – because of the alienating effects of bourgeois culture? because he is going through some psychological transformation? What we decide the image means matters less than the initial decision that it means something other than that one Gregor Samsa really did turn into an insect. After this move, the possibility of identifying with Samsa, seeing his condition as one that we somehow share, becomes much easier.

The opening lines of Ovid's poem make it even more explicit that the com-prehension of metamorphosis provides a crucial analogue for the reader's

ANDREW FELDHERR

experience of the poem:

> In noua fert animus mutatas dicere formas
> corpora: di coeptis (nam uos mutastis et illa)
> adspirate meis primaque ab origine mundi
> ad mea perpetuum deducite tempora carmen.
>
> (1.1–4)

> My spirit impels me to speak of bodies changed into new forms: gods, inspire
> my beginnings – for you have changed even those – and draw my song without
> breaks from the first beginning of the world to my own times.

The text itself, like the bodies it announces as its subject matter, has been transformed. Indeed the syntax of the opening sentence changes shape before the eyes of the reader, who might initially have taken the first line as a self-sufficient whole meaning 'my mind prompts a new venture, to speak of changed forms' but must reconstrue it upon seeing *corpora* (bodies) at the beginning of the second verse.[1] The kind of changes the poem exhibits on a larger scale include shifts in tone, subject matter, and even generic affiliation, among the 250 or so narratives of metamorphosis it contains. Thus in the first book we move suddenly from Apollo's destruction of the monstrous dragon Python to the story of Daphne, in which the same god figures not as a heroic bringer of order but as a lover, reminiscent of the protagonists of contemporary elegy. Yet this tale itself ends with a panegyric to Augustus and a glimpse ahead to the time when the laurel tree into which the resisting Daphne is transformed will adorn the emperor's triumphs.

Paradoxically, recognition of this metamorphic aspect of the text's construction has sometimes gone together with an undervaluation of the thematic centrality of transformation itself, which becomes a narrative leitmotif valuable solely because its omnipresence allowed the poem to travel freely among the varied stories of Greek myth. Indeed those occasions when the poet can be seen bending over backwards to slip a reference to metamorphosis into a story where it seems to have little place draw attention to his own invention and away from the story he is telling. Correspondingly, according to this view, the fairy-tale elements of metamorphosis distance the reader from the story by neutralizing the tragic and distressing. Thus in a story like that of Myrrha (10.298–502), who succumbs to sexual passion for her father, consummates it under cover of darkness, and is driven into exile when discovered, her final transformation into a myrrh tree acts as a kind of narrative *deus ex machina*. As opposed to the nightmarish overtones of Gregor Samsa's metamorphosis, Myrrha's leaves the real conflicts and consequences

---

[1] For the fullest treatment of these lines' shifting meaning, see now Wheeler (1999) 8–20.

of the human situation far behind.[2] Yet using Kafka's tale as a positive model reminds us that the choice of metamorphosis as a subject transforms a narrative in far more complex ways than simply providing for frequent changes of subject. Each individual metamorphosis opens up possibilities for contrasting responses: humour, terror, allegorization, even boredom. Of course these responses are largely conditioned by the text itself – if a story begins 'once upon a time', for example, we have a pretty strong clue about how to read it. On the other hand, the changing implications of metamorphosis among the many kinds of literary discourse in which it occurs make it a narrative element that invites contrasting readings and opens out interpretative possibilities. Ovid himself participates in this process by introducing multiple points of view on transformation itself as well as raising questions about the generic status of his work. Thus metamorphosis continually compels readers to refigure their relationship to the text, their understanding of the narratives it contains, and ultimately how it functions as a literary representation.

The tradition of using the metamorphosis theme to emphasize the *Metamorphoses'* essential lack of seriousness begins with Ovid himself, who in a later work tells us that his tales of transformation were 'not to be believed' (*Trist.* 2.64), a claim that highlights the first assumption a contemporary reader might bring to any such story. The rhetorical training that played such a crucial role in informing ancient responses to literature divided narratives into three classes according to their relationship to reality: histories (*historiae*) told what actually happened; *argumenta*, exemplified by the plots of new comedy, presented plausible stories, things that might have happened, and finally 'tales' (*fabulae*) describe events that are not only 'untrue, but separated even from the appearance of truth' because they are unnatural or impossible.[3] Illustrations of this last category often include tales of transformation.[4] Yet for all Ovid's overt acceptance of the 'fairy tale'

---

[2] For the classic statements of this position, see Fränkel (1945) esp. 97–100 and Galinsky (1975) 62–9.

[3] For examples of this classification see Sext. *Math.* 1.263, *Rhet. ad Her.* 1.13, Cic. *Inv.* 1.27, and Quint. *Inst.* 2.3.4 (quoted in the text); see Graf in this volume, p. 109.

[4] Thus Sextus (1.264) includes the tales 'of the companions of Diomedes changed into sea birds, of Odysseus changed to a horse, and of Hecuba to a dog', in this class, and Martianus Capella (550) presents the transformation of Daphne as a paradigmatic *fabula*. Ovid himself explicitly alludes to the generic distinction in an earlier poem (*Amores* 3.12) where he protests that poets should not be treated as if they were witnesses in a courtroom (19–20). He then proves his point that the 'licence of poets' is not constrained by the criterion of credibility that applies to the genre of history (*historica fide*, 42) by cataloguing the miraculous mythological stories to be found in their works. In most of these tales, the unbelievable element is precisely metamorphosis. Yet the context of the poet's plea not to be believed undercuts its ostensible message: Ovid has portrayed his (fictional) mistress in such terms that now everyone is in love with her and he himself is jealous. He therefore demands that his readers understand his

status of his narrative, other aspects of his poem suggest that in raising such traditional distinctions between fiction and reality he also challenges them. Thus while the second word of his poem, *nova*, which in Latin can mean not only 'new' but also 'strange' or 'unattested', perhaps hints at the miraculous nature of the stories to follow, the progress 'into the new' also points forward to the overall chronological schema of his work. This organizational pattern itself connects the 'fabulous' to the real world of the poet, the 'my times' that mark the poem's conclusion: rather than being limited to an undifferentiated mythical past, the miraculous transformations will be integrated into a framework that can also be described historically. Indeed throughout the poem, mortals will be punished precisely for failing to recognize that their capacity for metamorphosis allows the Olympian gods of legend to appear as unremarkably realistic figures. When, for example, the character Pirithous explicitly rejects a story as a fiction because it describes the gods changing shape,[5] he is admonished to be more careful with the story of Baucis and Philemon, which describes the punishment of those who failed to offer hospitality to gods disguised as mortals and the rewards of those who did.

In defining the place of his poem in the poetic tradition, Ovid challenges readers' expectations in another way by suggesting his allegiance to two kinds of poetry often opposed – and again his choice of metamorphosis as a topic accentuates this ambiguity. The verb *deducere* (1.4), used in the proem to describe how the gods 'draw out his song', was frequently used programmatically by Augustan poets to summon up the taste for short, elaborately refined poems codified above all by the Alexandrian Greek Callimachus (see also Harrison in this volume, p. 87). Yet in the same sentence Ovid describes his poem as *perpetuum*, continuous or unbroken, a translation of the Greek word used by Callimachus of the kind of chronologically arranged, loosely composed narratives that he defined his work against. While it is certainly possible to reconcile these characteristics, and as a Callimachean scholar has recently pointed out, no reader could bring against Ovid's poem the charges of monotony and sloppy construction that lay behind the rejection of 'continuous' poems, the reader continually experiences a tension between the epic architecture of the poem and the artful episodes of which it is made up.[6]

---

praise of her as false. For the poem's manipulation of the rhetorical categories of believable and unbelievable stories see McKeown (1979).

[5] '*ficta refers nimiumque putas, Acheloe, potentes | esse deos' dixit 'si dant adimuntque figuras.*' ('you retail fictions, Achelous,' he said, 'and you think the gods too powerful if they give and take away shapes.') (8.614–15) – lines that refer back to the *Metamorphoses*' programmatic description of its subject matter.

[6] Cameron (1995) 359–61.

The claims to alternative generic allegiances in these lines open up very different possibilities for understanding the poet's choice of metamorphosis as a subject. If we are to read the poem as a series of discrete, refined narratives such a topic would seem entirely appropriate.[7] Although their works are almost completely lost, Ovid's most important predecessors for building tales of metamorphosis into larger poetic units seem to have worked very much in the tradition of Callimachean brevity. In the second century BCE, for example, Nicander of Colophon, whose only surviving works are a pair of didactic poems about snakebites and antidotes, produced the *Heteroioumena (Transformations)*, in which he collected what seem to have been particularly obscure metamorphoses associated with the monuments and rites of far-flung cities and usually featuring local rustic divinities rather than the Olympian gods. While we are not in a position to tell what kind of larger structures Nicander used to organize his material, it is fairly clear that the poem was on a significantly smaller scale than Ovid's: five books, probably, as opposed to fifteen. Nothing can be said for certain about the scope, or even the date, of another source and antecedent of the *Metamorphoses*, the *Ornithogonia (Bird Origins)* of Boios, but his apparent aim of demonstrating that every species of bird was at one time a man again indicates a much more restricted canvas than Ovid's universal history.

By contrast to its suitability for these catalogue poems, the fabulous aspect of metamorphosis tales made them very difficult to reconcile with the aesthetic principles of serious epic, where supernatural solutions to human problems are pointedly avoided. In the Homeric poems, for example, stories of metamorphosis occur either in Odysseus' account of his wanderings, a narrative space reserved for all sorts of miraculous figures, or their very strangeness marks them out as communications from the gods, like the serpent and the bird's nest turned to stone mentioned in *Iliad* 2.301–29. And even these examples do not form a part of the poet's own narrative; they are described and interpreted by characters within the poem.[8]

In the works of Ovid's immediate epic predecessor, Virgil, the phenomenon of metamorphosis assumes a more prominent but deeply ambiguous role, one that in many respects looks ahead to its complex function in the *Metamorphoses*.[9] On the one hand Virgil seems to give an ideological dimension to Homer's reticence about transformation stories. Beyond raising questions about the plausibility of the narrative, metamorphosis suggests a

---

[7] For a general discussion of the treatment of metamorphosis in earlier literature, and detailed accounts of Nicander and Boios see Forbes-Irving (1990) 7–37. See also Hardie (1999a) for a discussion of metamorphosis as a way of commenting on the representational strategies of earlier epics.

[8] On the avoidance of the miraculous in Homer see Griffin (1977).

[9] For a fuller treatment of metamorphosis in the *Aeneid* see Hardie (1992).

world of unstable ephemerality that can only be at odds with the poem's motion towards the foundation of Rome as the centre of a stable cosmos, and indeed comes to be associated with the dehumanizing violence and immorality of Rome's civil wars. The bleeding bush that manifests the presence of Polydorus, a Trojan prince murdered by an avaricious and impious Thracian king, at the beginning of book 3, and the howling of the bestialized inhabitants of Circe's realm (*Aen.* 7.10–24) signpost regions where neither Aeneas' mission nor Virgil's narrative should go.[10] Virgil swerves just shy of metamorphosis in another sense when one of the poem's final similes figures Aeneas and Turnus, in the climactic duel that decides the fate of Italy, as battling bulls (*Aen.* 12.715–22). Animal rage and undifferentiated violence are hardly the stuff from which the reader expects the tapestry of Roman history to be woven. But since this is just a figure of speech, it can always be read as but a partial, imprecise image of the combatants, or even as a foil to them. Metamorphosis within Virgil's poem is not, however, merely the favoured *modus operandi* of the forces of darkness and dissolution. On the contrary, the victory of Aeneas, and by implication the emergence of Roman order from the chaotic final books of the poem, is in a sense a tale of metamorphosis, requiring the hero's transformation from the last remnant of a city doomed to fall to the founder of a civilization fated to endure. And in one important instance, his account of how the goddess Cybele saves the Trojan ships from destruction by turning them into nymphs (*Aen.* 9.77–122), Virgil highlights his inclusion of a miraculous transformation to make clear the special status of his epic. The passage has jolted Virgil's readers since antiquity, and even within the poem characters struggle to make sense of it.[11] The poet himself seems to hold the story at arm's length, presenting it as a legend, yet the transformation as an event is anchored in the plot of his epic.[12] But rather than regard Virgil's treatment of the episode as either half-hearted or misjudged, we can rather take it as a self-conscious deployment of the vexed status of metamorphosis within epic, alerting readers all too ready to dismiss the tale as fantasy that Aeneas' divinely guided foundation of Rome requires a different poetics than do the exploits of Homer's mortal

---

[10] For the re-emergence of these Circean dangers later in *Aen.* 7 see Putnam (1995) 100–20.

[11] Thus the ancient body of Virgilian commentary known as 'Servius Danielis' mentions two slightly different objections to the passage: one implies that the poet should never make up anything so remote from truth (3.46), and the other, though allowing poetic fictions, insists that they should have some precedent in earlier authors (9.81).

[12] The verb *fertur* ('it is said', 9.82) provides the most obvious sign of this authorial distancing – although even that can be treated as a learned reference to an earlier poetic authority. According to Servius Danielis, 'some have objected to this "fertur" because it denies authority to the tale; others have praised it as a sign that the poet was unwilling to lend authority to an unbelievable event.' (*Ad Aen.* 9.81).

heroes. As Ovid will later, Virgil here makes metamorphosis an occasion to reorient his readers' expectations of the poem.

If metamorphosis generally marks the limit of what is consistent with the moral seriousness of heroic epic, this is the line on which *Metamorphoses* dances. The poem's metre, size, and its incorporation of the Trojan and Roman subject matter of epic invite the reader to view the work in its entirety as a rival to those earlier works. Yet within that tradition, especially in the *Aeneid*, metamorphosis denoted a world of instability distinctly at odds with the clear and stable endings to which those works aspire – even if they notoriously fail to attain them. Should we read metamorphosis through epic eyes, with an even greater awareness of its essential unbelievability and trivializing effect? Can the epic form even save the work from itself by transfiguring its fabulous subject matter into a grand history of the Augustan world, just as Virgil allows metamorphosis a new role in his poem? Or is the work fundamentally an anti-epic, lending the gravity of the Homeric and Virgilian form to an antithetical vision of man's place in the cosmos? Or, a final alternative, should we simply avoid the question by allowing the poem to decompose itself into a Hellenistic assemblage of separate tales? Since Ovid often positions metamorphoses at the end of episodes, the transformations within the narrative tend to occur precisely where the structure of the work as a whole is most up for grabs. In deciding whether each metamorphosis marks an ending, or merely a transition, readers are continually confronted with the question of what kind of work they are reading.

To get a sense of what is at stake ideologically in the differing responses to metamorphosis offered by the poem, let us take a look at the poem's very first account of the transformation of a human being into an animal, the tale of Lycaon (1.209–43), an episode whose prominent position invites us to treat it as a paradigm for what is to come. This story follows after the poem's account of the formation of the cosmos, a process which involves not the creation of new substances out of nothing but rather a sorting into an ordered hierarchy of elements already present in the confused mass of primordial chaos. At first this story will seem to further the suggestion that metamorphosis itself serves as a tool for imposing a familiar, stable order on things, as opposed to representing the irruption of the unaccountable as it does in Kafka. Jupiter has heard of the impious behaviour of human beings, and in hopes of finding the story is false, he disguises himself as a mortal and descends from Olympus to investigate. When he enters Lycaon's realm, he gives signs of his divinity and begins to receive the worship of the people. The king, however, refuses to acknowledge Jupiter as divine and plots to prove him mortal by killing him in his sleep. He also kills a hostage and attempts to serve his cooked limbs to the god. In punishment, the god destroys the palace and Lycaon is driven into exile, at which point 'he wails and tries in vain to speak. His countenance takes upon itself all his madness; he turns his innate love of slaughter against sheep and even now rejoices in blood. His clothes turn into hair; his arms into legs. He becomes a wolf and preserves the traces of his old form. There is the same grayness, the same violent countenance. His eyes still gleam, and the appearance of bestiality remains.' (1.233–9)

Jupiter's account suggests that Lycaon has been quite literally put in his place. He had violated human norms by murdering a hostage and even attempted to usurp Jupiter's prerogative here by imposing his own test on the god. He subsequently undergoes a transformation that seems at once to punish his attempt to take on the god's role in the story and to express his own innate bestiality. (Notice that Jupiter never claims responsibility for the transformation, which appears to happen spontaneously, as if nature were simply taking its course.) Just as the creation of the world involved the separation of the lighter elements from water and earth, so here this wild beast who had somehow been grouped among men has finally been returned to his rightful category. The change that has taken place is merely one of form. And Lycaon's new shape not only more clearly reveals his essence, it also manifests and enforces the cosmic hierarchies he has violated. The wolf itself becomes a reminder of the consequences of behaving as either a beast or a god. There is also a more narrowly political significance to the metamorphosis. Before recounting this story Jupiter had been compared to the emperor Augustus, and the assembly of gods he addresses takes on the form of the Roman senate. The little epiphany of order that results from this metamorphosis, in which the natural world as we know it becomes a sign of the proper distribution of authority among gods and men, also serves as a reminder of the specifically Roman order that now, as Augustan artistic imagery so often implied, had embraced the cosmos itself.[13] The very name Lycaon derives from the Greek word for wolf (*lykos*), again suggesting that metamorphosis is above all a clarification of who he really is,[14] and that because of metamorphosis even verbal signs now more clearly represent the world. But of course in Ovid's text, Lycaon hasn't become a *lykos* but a *lupus*: metamorphosis as cosmic clarification depends upon the translation of Greek into Latin.

---

[13] For a good introduction to this pattern of imagery in the visual arts see Zanker (1988) 183–92 and Nicolet (1991) 29–56, and for an example of its development in literature see Hardie's (1986) 336–76 reading of the Virgilian shield of Aeneas.

[14] Solodow (1988) 174 defines 'clarification' as the central function of metamorphosis.

Such readings as this have produced a sense that the real emphasis in Ovid's poem of changes should be on stability. Far from suggesting a world of flux and shifting appearance, metamorphosis, which is always to be located in the past, results in a firm natural and political order in the present. The human beings who undergo metamorphosis, an emphatically final process that leaves no possibility of a return to their prior shape,[15] do not lose the enduring aspects of their being, rather they take on a form that reveals them – an idea that closely resembles influential stoic accounts of identity.[16] And indeed by narrating stories of this type, Ovid seems to be contributing to the semantic clarification and revelation that Jupiter sets in motion, by offering a world whose natural elements, like wolves, become transparent to human qualities and divine actions. But the very neatness of this interpretation results precisely from the tale's univocality and from the erasure of alternative points of view. Indeed this is the one story in the poem narrated by Jupiter himself, the ultimate representation of authority in the epic universe. Yet the metamorphosis that seems to provide such unanswerable closure in fact allows competing readings back into the text precisely because it makes the shutting down of alternative points of view so explicit. The first thing that happens to Lycaon is that he loses his power to speak – precisely the eloquence that allows Jupiter to tell his version of events. The last body parts mentioned are Lycaon's shining eyes, eyes that are depicted only as seen, not as seeing. Points of view opposed to Jupiter's would have been ready to hand for an informed reader of the text. For, as nearly as we can tell, no other account of Lycaon is so relentless in its condemnation of the king. Greek versions, in fact, present a highly ambivalent figure whose outrageous treatment of the gods is balanced by his role as a civilizing hero, an institutor of religious practices, whose name would be preserved not just by the wolf, but by the cult of Zeus Lykaios which he founded.[17] Even within Ovid's Jovian account, the boundaries between gods, humans, and animals seem dangerously permeable. Jupiter sets the plot in motion by his own shape-shifting, the assumption of human form – a disguise that anticipates the paradox of the final metamorphosis by simultaneously masking and revealing his divine nature. It might even be argued that Lycaon's outrage results less from his

---

[15] Though even to the 'rule' that metamorphosis for humans is irreversible, there are occasional exceptions like Mnestra, the daughter of Erysichthon (8.843–78). When her father sells her into slavery as a way of supporting his insatiable hunger, the god Neptune gives her the power to change shape as a way of escaping from her buyers.

[16] Dörrie (1959) connects the perpetuation of such an essence after metamorphosis with the view represented by the philosopher Posidonius (fr. 96) that each individual possesses a distinctive quality independent of his material existence.

[17] For earlier accounts of the Lycaon story see Forbes-Irving (1990) 90–5 and 216–18; see also Barkan's (1986) 24–7 integration of the legend of Lycaon the sacrificer with Ovid's story.

attempt to deprive the gods of the honour due them than from his scrupulous belief in the reality of appearances and his efforts to use those appearances to distinguish different orders of being. His very plot to kill Jupiter shows that he has taken his disguise seriously: far from attempting to dishonour the god, he assumes that the figure before him is a mortal impostor. And if Lycaon's error is really a failure to recognize that gods can disguise themselves as men, his experience is very relevant to Ovid's own readers who are making their first acquaintance with anthropomorphized gods in the work.[18] If they were to attempt to apply the same criterion of truth to their reading, then the entire epic machinery that underlies the moralizing/politicizing interpretation of the story would be called into question. To expose the gods as mere projections of human authority is to short-circuit their political use to glorify any individual human potentate – a central issue in Augustan iconography.[19]

Another tale from the first book reveals even more clearly how interpretation of the poem's thematic emphases hinges on the reading of a metamorphosis. When the nymph Daphne realizes that she will never win the foot-race against Apollo and will forfeit her virginity, she prays to be transformed and so to lose the external form (*figura*) that has caused her downfall by arousing the god's desire.

> Scarcely had she ended her prayer when a heavy sluggishness took possession of her limbs; her soft breast clothes itself in thin bark. Her hair grows into leaves, her arms into branches. Her foot once so swift cleaves to sluggish roots. A bough holds her face; only her beauty remains. (1.548–52)

Here the relationship between the new shape and the old becomes much more complicated. Far from fixing her in a state that permanently expresses her essential qualities, Daphne's metamorphosis strips her of the swiftness by which she has been characterized in the narrative; Ovid figures the transformation itself as a process of occlusion and possession. To try to read this metamorphosis according to the Lycaon paradigm by stressing the persistence of her beauty raises new problems, for it was her external attractiveness that warred against her desire to remain a virgin (*uotoque tuo tua forma repugnat*, 1.489). Indeed if anything has been preserved of Daphne it is the tragic discrepancy between her inner will and outer appearance. To read her metamorphosis as a clarification, then, implies that her essence lay in what she seemed to others to be rather than recognizing her as subject in her own right.

---

[18] For another adversarial reading of Jupiter's account of Lycaon see Anderson (1989); for the balance between contrasting readings in the story see Wheeler (1999) 171–81.

[19] For a discussion of how Ovid's hyper-anthropomorphized gods undercut imperial religious innovations see Feeney (1991) 205–24.

Such a reading is put forward by the divine interpreter within the poem, none other than Apollo himself, the god who pursued her on account of her form:

'Though you cannot be my wife, you will be my tree. My locks will always possess you, laurel, so will my lyre and my quiver. You will accompany the Latin chiefs when the joyful voice sings "Triumph" and the Capitoline witnesses long (triumphal) processions ... And as my youthful head is perpetually unshorn, so you will always retain the honour of leaves.'   (1.557–65)

Apollo's response to Daphne's metamorphosis in a sense completes the processes of the transformation by converting her form into a symbol, yet a symbol that recalls not so much who Daphne was as who Apollo is. It is his hair that her leaves are now made to recall, not her own once disordered tresses. Apollo's strategy also bears on the question of the poem's genre: by placing Daphne's transformation in an extensive historical context, recalling the broad temporal sweep proclaimed in the poet's prologue, and converting her into an instrument of praise, Apollo epicizes her story.[20] In doing so he fits it into the continuum prepared for by the poet himself, who introduced the story as an explanation for how the laurel tree came to be the sign of victory in the games that celebrated Apollo's conquest of the Python. Thus the tale that might have been thought to show how the god lost an archery contest with Cupid, and was forced to shed his typical attributes by assuming the role of a lover, becomes instead a celebration of his once and future triumphs. For Daphne, though, does her metamorphosis mark the beginning of her epic significance, or is it in fact the end of the story? Again her changed form holds the key. The final lines at first appear to close the gap between Daphne's perspective and Apollo's by suggesting that Daphne herself consented to the role Apollo offered her by nodding her bough 'as if it were a head'. But perhaps the bough is just a bough. In other words, perhaps Daphne's will has been masked completely by her new form, and the attempt to claim her participation in this future as though she were still there marks merely the final stage in her possession.

The readings offered so far suggest that the event of metamorphosis in Ovid mobilizes two coherent interpretations of the poem, and that the choice between them depends on the point of view adopted on the transformation itself. First, to focus on the new shape, which is often a form familiar from the actual experience of the reader, in several senses normalizes metamorphosis, subordinating a manifestly unbelievable process to an undeniably real product. The world is, reassuringly, not a place where metamorphosis

---

[20] For an introduction to the sophisticated pattern of generic play in this story see Nicoll (1980).

happens every day, and the very stories Ovid tells about wolves and laurel trees gives them a new significance as the manifest products of cosmic and political order and as *exempla* that perpetuate that order by recalling the consequences of violating it. In depicting metamorphosis from this perspective not only is Ovid in several senses doing the Lord's work, but he is also making his poem function like Virgilian epic, granting legendary events a privileged function for explaining the here and now, and conversely exalting the here and now by linking it to the grand sagas of past myth.[21] The reader's distance from the narrative, his recognition that this story by its nature must be a fiction, becomes anything but a disadvantage. Lycaon's tale, for example, readily lends itself to allegorization, an interpretative strategy that allows the dubious motives of Jupiter as character to fade from view. The alternative, to continue to recognize the human subjects of metamorphosis, dissolves the epic structure of the poem by making metamorphosis seem ultimately both inexplicable and very much the end of the story. Each transformation appears less a stage in the history of the cosmos than the shutting down of an individual consciousness, locked in opposition to the ordering forces of the universe. Here, far from retaining a comfortable position in the world after metamorphosis, the reader is drawn back into the unstable past, entering into the fiction rather than marking it off as such.

The pair of internal *Metamorphoses* that Ovid places at the beginning of his sixth book, in which the goddess Minerva and her human rival Arachne assemble stories of transformation for the two tapestries they weave in competition with each other, enshrine these polar alternatives for interpreting the process, for again the ideological differences between the two 'texts' result not just from the discursive use each artist makes of metamorphosis, but from the perspective they present on the process itself (6.1–145).[22] Minerva depicts four tales of metamorphosis, designed explicitly to warn Arachne of the dangers of rivalling the gods, symmetrically at the corners of a tapestry whose centrepiece shows her own triumph in a contest with Neptune for possession of Athens. In each case only the names of the victims and the final form they have assumed are indicated. By contrast the gods themselves are depicted in forms that, like the disguise Jupiter assumes in the Lycaon tale, are presented as at once anthropomorphized and authentic: 'His own appearance marks each god: Jupiter's is the image of a king' (6.73–4). In answer to Athena's use of metamorphosis as a warning against human presumption, Arachne presents a catalogue of the animal forms the gods

---

[21] On aetiology in Ovid see Myers (1994) and Graf (1988) 62.

[22] Leach (1974), Vincent (1994), and Feeney (1991) 190–4 offer particularly stimulating readings of this much discussed episode.

have used to deceive the victims of their lust. Here, rather than manifesting an essentially immutable hierarchy of powers, metamorphosis destabilizes such structures by revealing how the gods themselves can quite literally turn into beasts. Far from offering an absolute guide to behaviour, the visual forms that result from the god's metamorphoses highlight the shifting and uncertain nature of appearances; only the spatial settings of the crimes and the human faces of the victims preserve constant and reliable markers of identity.[23] A heavy emphasis in the account of Arachne's portrayal of these scenes falls on the verb *reddidit* (6.122) which here means 'render', but whose primary force is 'give back', as though her artistic depiction were returning countenances that these women had lost. While obviously this is not the case here – the victims she depicts never underwent metamorphosis – this nuance shows how Arachne's choice to portray rapes where the god changes form pointedly reverses the programmatic rape narrative of book 1, where the object of the god's passion does indeed lose her form. There the reader's 'recognition' of the victim under her new shape was a possibility that, if realized, radically reoriented his/her response to the tale. In Arachne's more one-sided presentation it is impossible not to see the rape victim as a human subject. Indeed Arachne's realistic descriptive technique – or rather Ovid's technique for presenting her depiction as narrative – works to draw the viewers into this world of deceptive fictions precisely by granting them access to the victim's point of view: thus in describing how the god Jupiter took on the form of a bull to abduct Europa, he comments that 'you would think it was a real bull', as if 'you' were Europa.

The tapestry's demonstration of the dependency between the work's competing ideological strands and the antithetical strategies of representation it employs takes us back to the point where we began, the analogy between making sense of the process of metamorphosis and interpreting the text that represents it. Here I want to go further by suggesting that changed appearances are even more closely connected to artistic representations of change. If metamorphosis produces an apprehensible trace of distant or incredible events in the real world of the readers, so too does a statue, a painting, or the book-roll before them. Thus metamorphosis becomes a way of dramatizing the act of representation itself and the alternative political valences the process of transformation acquires within the work apply also to what Ovid's own text is doing. As Solodow and others have shown, much of the poet's vocabulary for the product of metamorphosis, such as the word *imago*, overlaps with terms for artistic depictions.[24] And in cases of petrifaction, the

---

[23] *omnibus his faciemque suam, faciemque locorum | reddidit*, 6.121–2.
[24] Solodow (1988) 203–6; see also Anderson (1963).

frozen forms, like those produced by the head of Medusa (5.177–209), are essentially indistinguishable from statues. Another way of suggesting the same point is by alluding to the visual iconography of the figures described: so the second book ends with a description of Europa riding on the bull's back, her clothes billowing behind her in the breeze, precisely the aspect in which she was most commonly shown in actual paintings.[25] The connection between representation and the ordering, clarifying aspects of metamorphosis can apply to literary as well as visual representations. This becomes particularly clear when we examine the relationship between metamorphosis and metaphor. Niobe's transformation into a stone begins when she 'stiffens with evils' a common Latin metaphor. Thus not only does her final form again appear motivated by some essential quality of her experience – as Lycaon's innate bestiality makes him a wolf – it also offers a means for the figurative to become something more than figurative, for a trope to become reality.[26]

But as with the process of transformation itself, there is another side to the story. If metamorphosis figures the production of images it also resembles the subsequent transformation these images themselves undergo when they evoke the very figures they represent: just as the laurel tree can be read as Daphne, so an image or indeed a story of Daphne can be perceived as what it really is – a statue, painting or a text – or as the nymph it depicts. For statues and images do not only appear within the poem as the final products of metamorphosis, they also undergo metamorphosis by coming to life. Throughout the work, art and nature are notoriously unstable categories: elements of the natural world seem to aspire to the perfection and order of art, but the ultimate manifestation of artistic excellence is the illusion of reality.[27] So too the static, plastic images Ovid evokes ultimately contrast with the flow of the narrative in which they are embedded.[28] It thus seems better to speak of an oscillation between two processes: the distant and other becomes 'real' through translation into an artistic product, which in turn becomes 'real' in

---

[25] Kenney (1986) 390.

[26] For the relation between metaphor and metamorphosis see especially Pianezzola (1979), Barkan (1986) 20–5, and Hardie (1999a). The extension of this thesis, most fully developed by Schmidt (1991) is that Ovid's text invests reality with a set of metaphorical meanings, translating the world as it is into a storehouse of images which can be read as tropes for human qualities and experiences.

[27] See the examples collected by Solodow (1988) 210–14, in particular the description of the setting for Actaeon's encounter with Diana: 3.157–64. The conundrum of the priority of art over nature receives special attention already in the initial description of the ordering of chaos, where as Wheeler (1995) has shown, the terms in which the actions of the creator god are described are modelled on Homer's account of the crafting of the shield of Achilles.

[28] Cf. Hardie (1999a) for a complementary treatment of the effects of metaphor and allegory.

the opposite sense, in the sense that its illusion works, that it ceases to be a representation and gives the viewer/reader access to what it represents.[29]

The deployment of artefacts in the story of Phaethon illustrates just such an oscillation (1.747–2.366). Phaethon approaching the palace of the sun encounters a set of images that represent nothing less than the ordered cosmos whose construction we witnessed in the first book.[30] These images are embossed on the very door of the palace, and when Phaethon passes through it he moves into a world of animated artistic figures, beginning with his father himself, who with his radiate crown is not so much the sun as it really is as a symbol of the sun endowed with autonomous existence, very like the Tritons who represent the sea on the doors. So too on his wild ride through the cosmos, Phaethon will encounter the constellations not as clusters of stars but as the animals that represent them. The allotted boundaries between things are only restored when Phaethon is killed by Jupiter's thunderbolt, buried, and quite literally replaced by an inscribed tombstone. Thus the story achieves its ending, and the world returns to its regular form, when the one whose adventures animated the static image of the cosmos is himself transformed into a text. Yet this is not quite the end of the sequence of metamorphoses, for if the tombstone will not exactly come back to life, so powerfully does it evoke the absent figure it represents that Phaethon's mother actually treats it as a substitute for her lost son, covering it with tears and clasping it to her breast. So too the funerary rituals that his sisters undertake at his tomb prompt their own metamorphosis into poplar trees.

In an earlier chapter in this volume Thomas Habinek pointed out the paradoxical status of Ovid as at once a member of the Roman élite and as a subject, indeed a prominent victim, of the imperial order. This discussion of the poet's treatment of metamorphosis has pointed toward a corresponding set of ambiguities in the way the poet positions his audience in relation to the hierarchies depicted within the poem, and in how he portrays his own representation of that cosmos alternatively as a form of participation in the creation of the structured world we know, and as an exposure of the flux, change, and victimization that underlies it. My own experience as a reader of the work convinces me that an interpretation that privileges one tendency at the expense of the other remains fundamentally incomplete.

---

[29] Indeed one wonders whether the tapestries of Arachne and Minerva would have been quite so clear if they had depicted whole narratives rather than just scenes from narratives. Then Minerva might have had to show her criminals as human subjects, and conversely Arachne's work might have depicted the various civilizing heroes whose birth resulted from the gods' deceptions. For a fuller discussion of the relationship between metamorphosis and literary and artistic representation see Sharrock (1996).

[30] On this image see Brown (1987).

The challenge of comprehending metamorphosis means that each instance compels the reader to make a choice between different interpretations of the poem that bring into play all its discursive levels – the literary, the political, the theological. Some readers may make the same set of choices every time and achieve a remarkably consistent reading of the work, others will have more difficulty negotiating its transformations. Yet if such a proliferation of competing points of view seems but a new route to an impasse of equivocation all too familiar to students of Latin poetry, where every positive thesis the work advances about the world necessarily implies its own antithesis, Ovid's emphasis on metamorphosis suggests an antidote by refocusing our attention on the processes of representation and reading. Rather than search for the poem's political dimension in the propagation of a particular ideological stance, we might rather observe that the very task of interpreting Ovid's involves the vivid experience of contrasting perspectives on many different manifestations of authority. As the author can 'play god' by measuring his creation against the cosmos, so the reader can assume the role of Apollo, or of Daphne. By marking out the poem as a set of fictions, metamorphosis may indeed facilitate such play by reminding the reader of the distance that separates Ovid's text from the real centres of seriousness and significance in the Augustan world. Yet the same phenomenon also points out the poem's capacity to redraw the line between reality and mere representation and so between Ovid's cosmos and Augustus's. The fundamental ambiguity of metamorphosis thus at once reflects, and helps bring about, the transformation of Ovid's text into a dynamic locus for defining and codifying political and social roles.

FURTHER READING

Wheeler's (1999) application of reader-response criticism to the *Metamorphoses* offers a fuller development of many of the issues and approaches discussed here. Two more general book-length studies of the *Metamorphoses* presenting highly contrasting views of metamorphosis are Galinsky (1975) and Solodow (1988). Tissol (1997) and Ahl (1985), a still controversial book, explore in different ways the manifestations of metamorphosis in Ovid's language and style. Though they focus less directly on the metamorphosis theme, both Otis (1970) and Due (1974) offer stimulating book-length readings of the poem. The essential modern works on Ovid's manipulation of genre in the poem are Knox (1986b) and Hinds (1987). Barkan's (1986) dazzling history of metamorphosis in medieval and Renaissance culture commences with an extensive treatment of Ovid's poem. Feeney (1991) similarly includes an important chapter on Ovid, addressing both the poem's status as fiction and its relation to Augustan politics. For more on reception of the poem as a fiction, see the article by Konstan (1991), and, on ancient attitudes to fiction more generally, the collection edited by Gill and Wiseman (1993). On the relationship between metamorphosis and the body, see both the older article of Curran (1978) and Segal (1998). Forbes-Irving (1990) treats the religious and mythical aspects of metamorphosis in Greek culture and catalogues earlier versions of many of Ovid's tales. Antoninus Liberalis' *Metamorphoses*, a compendium of Hellenistic metamorphosis narratives that provides our evidence for the works of Nicander and Boios, is available in English translation by Celoria (1992). For those with the relevant languages, Rosati's (1983) treatment of illusion and representation, Schmidt's (1991) account of metamorphosis, and Galand-Hallyn (1994), on metamorphosis and poetic creation, are especially recommended.

ALESSANDRO BARCHIESI

Narrative technique and narratology in the *Metamorphoses*

N.'s fiction:

abnormal psychology	imagination
artist as protagonist	immortality
autobiography	incest
autocriticism	madness
cinematic influences	magician
cynicism	mirrors
death as theme	narcissism
deceptive mechanisms	open-ended narrative
double as theme	parody
flight as theme	
grief as theme	
illusion vs reality	

[from the index to A. Field, *VN – The life and art of Vladimir Nabokov*, London 1986]

The poet who minted Latin words like *narratus* 'narrative' and *narrabilis* 'narratable' is no passive participant in the modern debate about story-telling and its techniques, and the *Metamorphoses* is one of the indispensable readings for a theory of narrative, along with texts by authors like Cervantes, Sterne, Proust, James and Borges. Of course the contemporary interest in narratology can easily become a formalistic and technocratic *tour de force*; it is interesting that similar accusations have since antiquity been repeatedly voiced against Ovid himself. The striking revaluation of Ovid as a master in the second half of the twentieth century is inseparable from shifts in the theory and poetics of fiction – the rise of Queneau, Nabokov, Calvino, Eco, and Rushdie, the crisis of realism and naturalism, trends like postmodern poetics and magical realism. As I write now, this evolution of modern fiction, and Ovid's status as a new classic, are both *faits accomplis* (which means, ready for a change), and of course there are many other approaches to Ovid that are occluded rather than revealed by this new climate. However, the study of narrative and Ovidian poetics continue to be mutually illuminating, and they could take on a new lease of life, if only they both agreed to stop existing *in vacuo*, to get serious, to give up the pretence of autonomy, and take into account issues like power, gender, history, and identity – which they might do, since their opportunistic patron is Proteus, god of change. This chapter aims simply to show where the study of narrative technique in Ovid has reached at present, and will argue that the *Metamorphoses* are good to think with whenever one wants to learn more about how stories are constructed, and about the problems generated by theorizing on this topic.

Mostly *diegematikon*

The *Metamorphoses* is as much a web of narratives, acts of story-telling, as it is of stories. The act of story-telling is basic to the whole plot. When Longinus says that the *Odyssey* is 'mostly narrative' (*to pleon diegematikon*) he is opposing dramatic intensity and action (as seen in the *Iliad*) to a narrative mode defined by rambling curiosity and story-telling. With Ovid we can go further and say that the poem is 'mostly *about* narrative', if we consider the strategic importance of telling stories for the plot. The poet narrates, the characters, when they have an occasion to speak, tend to become narrators. Ovid develops the Odyssean tradition. A genre consisting in telling stories about actions becomes increasingly interested in the action of storytelling. The text not only consists of a mixture of narrative and mimesis, but also suggests the mimesis of a narrative. The attention claimed by internal narrators within the plot sensitizes readers to the point where we take very seriously the presence of a super-narrator within the text. Communication becomes a central theme of the myths of metamorphosis, and this is mostly a consequence of Ovidian innovations in inherited tales.[1] Action is frequently viewed at the point of its transmutation into the words (and images) of fame, report, hearsay, memorial.[2]

In the *Metamorphoses* the classic definition of *epos* as the interlacing of divine and human deeds develops into something like 'the interlacing of human and divine narratives'. Not coincidentally, the poem's first internal narrator is the most authoritative of characters, Jupiter (1.182–243),[3] and he is also the last voice to speak in the poem (a narrative in the future tense,

---

[1] Forbes-Irving (1990) 37, in a brief survey of ancient sources on metamorphosis, notes 'he does have special interests and particular ways in which he is likely to reshape the myths; for instance, there is a special emphasis on the relation between bodily transformation and speech which we do not find in the other sources'.

[2] See e.g. Rosati (1981) 306.

[3] He begins by alluding to the loftiest type of *epos*, Gigantomachy (cf. *Am.* 2.1).

15.807–42,[4] capping Jupiter's opening speech in the *Aeneid*, 1.257–96).
The author thereby shows great respect for the technique of a 'tale within a
tale': the subjects of the two stories allotted to the father of gods and men
are respectively the metamorphosis of a tyrant into a wolf and the metamorphosis of a universal leader into a star.

Relevance and functional status of internal narratives

If we compare Ovidian internal narrators with their predecessors in Greco-
Roman epic, we find that narrators have become less accountable for their
own role in the plot. Most internal narrators in the *Odyssey* and the *Aeneid*
are carefully positioned within the story: the poet takes responsibility for the
function and effect of inset tales, and balances the distribution of information between authorial narrative and first-person narratives in the mouths
of characters.[5] In the *Metamorphoses*, as a part of a general trend towards
licentia (poetic anarchy), the narrative economy is constantly threatened by
an impulse towards expenditure, conspicuous consumption, and dispersion.
The plan of the work, as in previous epics, is both unitary and fragmentary
but in ways that are significantly new and anomalous. The titular subject,
transformation, being endlessly repeatable and variable, guarantees inclusion but does not account for selection. The attribution of individual tales
to different narrative voices is sometimes well motivated,[6] but is often
unpredictable or random. The tradition offers no safe guidance: a story
can be (re)told because it has a long tradition that commands respect, or
shortened and even omitted because it has a long tradition that threatens
boredom.

The time scale is also a problem for the ordering of narrative: this *epos* has
the longest time span ever in ancient literature, from the age of chaos before
the world was invented (*ante* being the first word after the *proemium*, 1.5),

---

[4] The epic poet is able to narrate about past, present, and even future, in the last instance
both as *vates* and in conformity with Hesiod's and Plato's influential ideas about narrative
(cf. Laird (1999) 51–2).

[5] I develop this contrast in Barchiesi (1997b).

[6] Some internal narrators perform stories that have obvious relationships to their identity and
traditional biography. Other stories may offer clues that generate metaliterary implications
when taken together with their 'authors' or addressees. The narrator of the Erysichthon
episode (8.726–78), based on a Callimachean model, is a river in flood (Achelous, 8.549–59:
see Hinds (1988) 19), a famous symbol in Callimachean polemics. Theseus (8.726) is especially pleased by a tale (Philemon and Baucis, 8.618–724) that alludes to a famous poem
about himself, the Callimachean *Hecale* (see Kenney (1986) p. xxviii). Orpheus offers a new
version of Cinna's *Zmyrna* (10.304–51: see Courtney (1993) 218–20 on Cinna's fragments);
Orpheus and Cinna are both famous for the manner of their death, both dismembered by
a frantic mob. Tales about human-into-bird transformation sometimes culminate in images
of thinning bodies, *macies* (11.793; 14.578), perhaps a reference to the master of avian
metamorphosis in Latin poetry, Aemilius *Macer* (Mr 'Thin').

to the moment when the author pens the final lines and the time of the story collapses into the time of its composition (*iamque* being the signal of closure at 15.871). This means that the author has a licence to include every conceivable event within the primary narrative (with the partial exception of the age of Augustus, whose status in the plot is liminal and terminal, in that the last event reported by the narrator is Jupiter's prophecy of that age). As a result flashback and flashforward are not seen to be motivated by structural economy. In the case of Homeric and Virgilian epic, whose plots have a rigorously limited time-span, the author uses internal narrators like Odysseus and Aeneas, or Teiresias and Anchises, whose memory or foreknowledge can grant access to the time, past or future, external to the span of the main story. In particular the *Aeneid*, set in the eleventh century before Augustus but looking forward to him, has access to modern Rome only through moments of prophecy and foreboding. In the *Metamorphoses* the reason why a certain event is related through recollection or prophecy (instead of the 'unmarked' mode of third-person narrative) is often opaque. In the jargon of narratology, the whole of universal history is potentially material for internal prolepsis or analepsis, so that there can be no external prolepses (flashforwards) or analepses (flashbacks), with the single exception of Jupiter's concluding prophecy.[7]

The image of the author that emerges from these clues is that of one who has as much power and authority over his plot as the Virgil of the *Aeneid*, that is, a lot of it, but who is much less accountable for individual choices and effects of planning. The distance between narrative act and plot tends to be variable, while the Virgilian narrator is routinely concerned to have characters perform narratives that require involvement and direct interest on the part of narrators and audiences. The extensive use of reported speech makes no clear distinction between what is being told and what is being performed in song: Ovid elides the strong traditional distinction between two forms of reported discourse, tales and songs,[8] and even features, on one occasion, a written source, the letter of the appropriately named Byblis. But in

---

[7] According to Genette's terminology, flashbacks (analepsis) and flashforwards (prolepsis) can be external or internal, that is they can be related either to a time-span that is not covered, or a time-span that is covered, by the main narrative. But it is fair to note that the cognate distinction between heterodiegetic and homodiegetic is even more deeply problematic in the poem: if we grant that every prolepsis or analepsis is internal, we have considerable problems in deciding, as a next step, which ones are homodiegetic (that is, linked to the main storyline) versus heterodiegetic (that is, centrifugal). The problem is, quite simply, that the idea of a 'main storyline' with its unspoken implications of unity, function, and coherence is contested as our reading of the text progresses.

[8] The two categories are often very close to each other in heroic epic (see Segal (1994a) and Mackie (1997) on the *Odyssey*) but in Homer, Apollonius and Virgil the rule seems to be that long tales can be quoted verbatim while tales being reported as songs will be offered in resumé.

fact all these modes of discourse – narrative, song, and writing – are absorbed within an overarching presence of textuality. The dimension, structure, and tone of the narrative are a constant reminder that the book format, 'thrice five volumes of changed shapes' (*mutatae, ter quinque volumina, formae, Trist.* 1.1.117, 3.14.19), is the condition that makes literary communication possible.

It is also hard to see any thematic or occasional motivation for a prefer-ence between homodiegetic and heterodiegetic mode:[9] stories of supernatural and praeternatural subjects – and in this poem this means roughly the whole subject-matter – are not tied to preferential narrative strategies. In traditional epic there is a sense that some stories are more suited for authorial narra-tive and some for internal narrators. We see the gods shattering the walls of Troy through the eyes of Aeneas, and Odysseus is our witness for far-off cannibals. Ovid's reports of metamorphosis are indifferently seen from the vantage points of the author, of characters witnessing the miracle, and even from the much less panoramic viewpoint of the characters undergoing metamorphosis.

If we consider the agendas of individual narrators, we notice a curious law of diminishing returns. In spite of the fact that they are all working for Ovid, and so profitable to the collective economy of the poem, the internal narrators are normally unrewarded. Whenever stories are told with a view to an immediate and practical effect,[10] be it consolation, seduction, admonition, blackmail, persuasion or warning, they fail: they cannot be said to be effective according to the intentions of their authors, and the only clear example of a narrative that achieves a practical result is when Mercury's story of Syrinx lulls the vigilant Argo to sleep (1.713: clearly, *inter alia*, an in-house joke for the professional community of tale-writers). Considering the ancient polarity between utility and pleasure in literature, we might say that the implicit result is that we are left with just the pleasure principle to get on with – except that the dimension and quality of the work is scandalously at odds with a purely hedonistic approach. The late appearance of Pythagoras and his attempt to explain how the universe works is an ironical comment on this disproportion between ambitious scale and entertaining function, and the final triumph of metempsychosis is a hint that metamorphosis could stand accused of being useless knowledge. Readers convinced by this lecture in Greek theory will have to go back and reconsider the entire story: why was

---

[9] The choice is between a mode where the narrator is a character in the story (homodiegetic) and a mode where the narrator is absent (heterodiegetic). For reasons why the older opposi-tion between first-person narrative and third-person narrative is not effective see chapter 5 on 'Voice' in Genette (1980).

[10] Barchiesi (1997b). The issue is related to Tarrant's (1995) 'failure of rhetoric' approach.

the focus on Bodies (Metamorphoses) if there is so much more to tell on the subject of the adventures of Souls (Metempsychoses)?

Problems of the narrative voice

The narrator's voice in this poem is notable for laying bare and making visible conventions that are formalized, taken for granted, and naturalized in the poetic genre of *epos*, or in narrative texts in general. Some examples follow, inevitably a selective choice, but all sharing a high level of consciousness of the conventions and shortcomings of the narrative medium. The *Metamorphoses* is almost the only known epic in which direct speech, in the process of unfolding, takes into account reactions of other characters without any editorial comment by the narrator.[11] Hardly any other epic poet allows himself a situation such as the following (14.322–24): 'if you have a look at this statue here, you will see what the hero of my story looked like.' The internal narrator breaks the epic convention whereby internal addressee and general addressee together enjoy shared information and shared access to the storyworld, this adjustment of information being part of the narrator's task. Perhaps rather less surprisingly, no other epic poet has speakers who comment on sudden bodily change that affects them while they are speaking.[12] Epic, which is basically a report of actions and speeches, tends to regulate the traffic by having either action or speech in progress at a given time. Ovidian speakers are used to this convention and can surprise us by pointing out changes of scenery and even bodily changes which intervene and develop even as they deliver their speech. This 'live' approach to literary discourse is at home in classical poetry about occasions (e.g. 'mimetic' poems about festivals) but not in the epic tradition.

It is normally assumed that narrative and direct speech can be cleanly distinguished from each other in epic. In theory, this separation is based on a number of vulnerable conventions and suspensions of disbelief, such as (i) the idea that characters speak in verse and (when they are e.g. ethnic Greeks) in a language not their own; (ii) that these really are their own words; (iii) that the narrator confines himself to the insertion of unexceptional editorial pointers like *ait*, 's/he said'. With regard to the second assumption, a delicate problem in both epic and historiography, consider the end of the speech of Boreas at 6.702, 'such were the words Boreas spoke – or words not less grand than these' (*haec Boreas aut his non inferiora locutus*). As for the third, Ovid is the only extant ancient poet to challenge the convention regarding shifts of voice through a diabolically simple device, exemplified at *Her.* 16.83

---

[11] Albert (1988) 225.   [12] Albert (1988) 220.

'ne'c ait = et ait 'ne'; or *Met.* 1.456 *'quid'que 'tibi . . .' dixerat*; or *Met.* 6.262–3
'di'que 'o communiter omnes' dixerat. The *-c*'s and *-que*'s that link direct discourse to the narrative are authorial, not uttered by the character, yet by the
Latin grammar they coalesce with the previous word, and can be taken apart
only through an artificial use of a modern device, the quotation mark. Ovid
reaches a breaking point in the evolution of an epic style whose originary
norm had been the Homeric separation of narrative and speech guaranteed
by sizable and autonomous introductory and closing formulas.[13] Later writers, especially Callimachus, Theocritus and the Roman poets, had made the
boundaries thin and variable, and started to exercise pressure on the written
medium's distinction between narrative and speech. In short, the blurring of
the institutional divide between authorial voice and mimesis of speech gives
more than a hint that both voices are being mediated through writing.[14]

At least one Ovidian narrator comments on the complex nature of
narrative time, a compromise between the rhythm of narrative and the
implied pace of the events: at 10.679–80 Venus says that she will cut short
the story, so that speech (*sermo*) will not be slower than the event conveyed
by the speech, a foot-race. But the context is paradoxical: Venus has just said
that she has been slowing down Atalanta's running with a couple of supernatural tricks, and the style (*sermo*) of the passage demonstrates that poetry
itself can do surprising tricks, for example describe the slowing down of a
fast runner in a line consisting purely of swift dactyls (10.678): *impediique
oneris pariter grauitate moraque* ('I slowed her up equally with the weight
of her burden and by the delay'). The analogy between writer and Olympic
god is here extended to their power of manipulating events: Venus is both
reporting on a situation and creating it, and the author likewise – except that
he has only words to work with.

Story and narrative

The *Metamorphoses*, a plural title, defy the normal strategies of *reductio ad
unum*, as deployed not only in literary criticism, but in the less sophisticated
practice of summaries and abstracts. Plot-resumés were already a common
feature of Ovid's literary culture (e.g. those prefixed to Attic dramas, or those
found in criticism, rhetoric, mythography) but Ovid forestalls, through size,
complexity, and variety, any such attempt to summarize his own poem. Even

---

[13] Only a dozen out of 1369 Homeric speeches lack formal introductions, and only four speeches
begin or end within a line (see in general Fantuzzi (1988), 47–85 on the whole Greek tradition
down to the third century BC).

[14] Kahane in Bakker and Kahane (1997) 116–17 comments on pauses, interstices of silence,
deictic shift, change of person, epiphany and movement across time as features of epic in
performance.

productions as sophisticated as modern printed editions seem powerless. Introductions and prefaces, normally the institutional sites for sketching and summarizing contents, fully able to cope with many other poems and novels of comparable length, never tell us the plot or story of the *Metamorphoses*. Significantly, the function is usually fulfilled by appending glossaries and alphabetical resumés by proper name, and the poem cries out for non-linear, hypertextual publication. A long 'pluralistic' poem not without influence on this Ovidian poetics, Callimachus' *Aitia*, was circulated in Hellenistic times in learned editions with summaries accompanying every new *aition*,[15] but even this drastically fragmentary segmentation is difficult to apply to the Ovidian text.[16] We cannot gain an overview of the story as a whole, and even when we turn to the individual tales, beginning as they do in mid-sentence and mid-hexameter, straddling book divisions, and framing each other, they resist separation and reordering. It must be significant that Ovid writes in the wake of the traditions not just of Alexandrian poetry but also of the exegesis of Alexandrian poetry.

This quality of the text has the important effect of challenging one of the most delicate and controversial concepts of narratology, the possibility of distinguishing a neutral, invariant 'core' story, in opposition to its many (actual or virtual) narrative realizations and variants.[17] The Ovidian narrative wants simply to stick to its 'story', whatever it is, and contests the distinction.

Narrative voices and levels

From my comments on internal narrators at p. 181 it is easy to understand why critics want to assert that there is really only one narrative voice in the epic, Ovid's voice as the supernarrator.[18] Yet Colin Burrow (this volume, p. 305), for example, draws attention to a passage within a two-tier inset story, where Venus is describing someone and addressing her narratee Adonis (10.578–9): 'face and body bare – like mine – or like yours, if you were to become a woman'. This simple sentence is a compression of three modes of desire: woman desires man, man desires woman, man desires man; and it is hardly irrelevant that we are in the presence of three concentric narrators: (i) Ovid; (ii) Orpheus, who has just turned from being

---

[15] On the relationship between hypothesis (plot summary of a text of poetry) and mythographic hypomnema (collection of potted stories in prose) see Lightfoot (1999) 225; on scholia and summaries of the *Aitia*, Cameron (1995) 120–6.

[16] Alan Cameron in a forthcoming book on Greek mythography in the Roman world argues that the attempt in Lactantius' *Narrationes* is in fact conditioned by the traditions of Callimachean interpretation.

[17] Problems involved: Herrnstein Smith (1981); Laird (1999).

[18] See Solodow (1988) 37.

a loving husband to being a proponent of pederasty; (iii) Venus, motivated by her desire for Adonis – and of three levels of addressee: (i) Ovid's
readers with their various love interests; (ii) Orpheus' non-human listeners;
(iii) Venus' beloved Adonis. So can we make a case for the various 'narrating
instances' being more significant than is usually assumed? Arethusa will be
our guide.[19]

It's hot in Arcadia, and Arethusa, undressed, is floating in a pool of miraculous transparency: even pebbles on the bottom are visible. While the water
exposes her nudity, the lonely virgin hears a raucous voice of male desire;
after a moment of shock, she realizes that the aggressor is one and the same
as the water that envelops her body. This unsettling epiphany is likely to
test every reader's position with respect to gender and the gaze, sexuality
and narrative in the *Metamorphoses*. It is of course disappointing to read
this glamorous episode through the routine of narratology, and yet, from the
present point of view, I must remind my readers that in this much discussed
section of book 5:

> Ovid narrates (5.250–678) that
> Pallas (Minerva) visits the Muses and one of them (5.268) narrates
> (5.269–678) that
> Calliope in a singing contest, refereed by a group of Nymphs, (5.316)
> sings that
> Ceres loses Proserpina and finds her again (5.341–662), and Arethusa
> (5.572–642) narrates her own story to Ceres . . .
> Ovid narrates (to the reader) that a Muse narrates (to Pallas) that
> Calliope narrates (to the referees) that Arethusa narrates (to Ceres)
> that:

>> " " " "nescio quod medio sensi sub gurgite murmur
>> territaque insisto propiori margine fontis.
>> 'quo properas, Arethusa?' suis Alpheus ab undis,
>> 'quo properas?' iterum rauco mihi dixerat ore . . ." " " "
>>
>> 5.597–600

---

[19] 'Narrating instance' is J. Lewin's translation of Genette's phrase 'instance narrative' (Genette
(1980)). In possibly one of the first Genettian moments of Ovidian criticism, Hinds (1987)
164 n. 25 glosses the French formula with 'relationships between "frame" and inset narrative', 'importance of internal narrator, audience and setting to the stories'.

On the limits of the 'only one narrative voice' approach see Barchiesi (1989). For important
readings of the Ceres episode see Leach (1974); Hinds (1987), esp. 164–5; Nagle (1988d);
Cahoon (1996); Johnson (1996); Rosati (1994); Zissos (1999). My reading, designed in
the mid-90s for an Ovidian conference at Sulmona, is independent of Johnson, Rosati and
Zissos (all of them independent of each other), but there are several points of contact, which
is encouraging in such a tangled area. My approach is mostly interested in the aporia created
by attempts to privilege one internal narrator or audience over another.

' ' ' 'I heard an indistinct noise under the middle of the water; terrified I stood on the nearer bank of the river. 'Where are you rushing to, Arethusa?' said Alpheus from his waves, 'Where are you rushing to?' he said again with his raucous voice . . .' ' ' ' '

In other words, the raucous voice of the river god is the fifth level, that is the fourth internal level, in a narrative that displays the maximum of complexity ever reached in a classical narrative. Now there is no obligation to think that a technical interest in the form of narrative will occlude other points of view: when we observe that the story of Arethusa is controlled by three female narrators, a Muse, Calliope and the nymph herself, we can begin to sense what is shared in their respective 'narrating instances'; and it is even more interesting to notice that the two male voices involved in the story-telling are top and bottom of the sequence, which proceeds from the invisible Ovid via three virgin goddesses to another, much less articulate, male speaker.

But unfortunately my mission is to focus on technical narratology. Lest my approach become entirely idle, I should like my readers to agree that the very existence of five levels of utterance is something of a scandal in the ancient epic tradition. We have mentioned that Virgil and Homer are concerned to motivate their use of internal narrators, at least if we use the parameters of function and unity to read their texts.

Now Arethusa too, as a narrator, had voiced a concern about her role (5.499–500): 'there will come a timely moment for my narrative' (*ueniet narratibus hora | tempestiua meis*). In fact Ceres is not in the carefree mood which had been recognized by the Muse and by Minerva as a precondition for listening to the whole of the Ceres story:

> 'sed forsitan otia non sint,
> nec nostris praebere uacet tibi cantibus aures.'
> 'ne dubita uestrumque mihi refer ordine carmen!'
>
> 5.333–5

'But perhaps you are not at leisure, and do not have the time to lend your ears to my singing.' 'Do not hesitate, but give me your song in full'

– and Arethusa will tell her own story later, when the time is right (5.576 *fluminis Elei ueteres narrauit amores*).[20] Yet she is not laying down a general rule that constrains other narrators as well. As we will see, a few lines before this episode, the narrative voice – that is Ovid + the anonymous

---

[20] A story that surfaces, sinks, and reappears is only too apt for this hydrological freak, and we also notice the uncommon tmesis in *hac Arethusa tenus* (5.642), where Arethusa, true to her flowing habit, pops up, and rules are bent in grammar as in nature.

Muse + Calliope – lingers on the story of the virtuous Cyane and thus rel-
ativizes Arethusa's subsequent claim that her story – a story very similar to
that of Cyane, another nymph persecuted by a rapist and sympathetic to
Proserpina's misfortune – should not awkwardly interrupt the striving of
Ceres towards her narrative *telos*. If Arethusa is laying down a general rule,
why is Cyane's story narrated at all? A reader may consider that a general
rule would not fit all addressees of a story. A narrative (like the Ovidian
poem) that does not focus on one individual addressee does indeed face the
problem of reconciling different types of desires and expectations.

Arethusa's introduction to the story reminds us that Ovidian characters
have inherited features, and that it may be rash to overlook their earlier history. In her rare previous appearances in extant Latin verse, Arethusa had
twice been summoned to be responsive to a tale of *amores*: 'begin [the
poet addresses Arethusa]: let us tell of Gallus' troubled love' (*incipe;
sollicitos Galli dicamus amores*, Virg. *Ecl.* 10.6); 'starting with Chaos she
[Clymene, Arethusa being one of the audience] listed the numerous loves of
the gods' (*aque Chao densos diuum numerabat amores*, Virg. *Geo.* 4.347).
Perhaps she has learned from those occasions, or perhaps Virgil presupposes some poetic tradition where Arethusa is a protagonist. Anyway, the
presence of Arethusa in the audience in *Georgics* 4 is recalled by Ovid,
who models her first appearance in *Metamorphoses* 5 on the same Virgilian
episode:

> sed ante alias Arethusa sorores
> prospiciens summa flauum caput extulit unda
> *Geo.* 4.351–2

But before her other sisters Arethusa looked out and raised her head above the
surface of the water.

> tum caput Eleis Alpheias extulit undis
> *Met.* 5.487

Then Alpheus' nymph [Arethusa] raised her head above the water.

Moreover, the Virgilian idea of nymphs as audience for Clymene is also
relevant to the frame for the Ceres story, since the original song by Calliope
had been performed before a similar audience. (The relationship of Nymphs
to Muses is not a new problem in ancient poetics.)[21]

Do those referees matter to the Ceres story in their identity as nymphs? We
might suspect that they are water nymphs, since they swear by rivers: '"let

---

[21] Stehle (1997) 203 on Hesiod's Muses: 'The Muses appear at the beginning to be nymphs ...
Nymphs are dangerous.' See below on Muses and Nymphs in Virgil and perhaps Gallus.

the nymphs decide the contest!'" . . . 'the chosen nymphs swear by the rivers' (*'dirimant certamina nymphae!'* . . . *electae iurant per flumina nymphae, Met.* 5.314; 316). The question 'what kind of stories do nymphs like?' is not extremely promising *per se*, but in the world of this epic you end up learning answers to questions you never thought to ask:

> ad pelagi Nymphas pelagi gratissima Nymphis
> ibat et elusos iuuenum narrabat amores.
>
> *Met.* 13.736–7

She, the favourite of the sea-nymphs, used to visit the sea-nymphs and tell them stories of her escapes from love-struck young men.

Apparently what the nymphs like are *amores*, in the very specific sense of stories where girls successfully elude rapists. This is just what Arethusa offers in book 5: 'she told of the former loves of the river of Elis' (*fluminis Elei ueteres narrauit amores*, 5.576), with a specific twist on the model of *Georgics* 4, 'starting with Chaos she [Clymene] listed the numerous loves of the gods' (*aque Chao densos diuum numerabat amores, Geo.* 4.347). Now the story that Arethusa tells is of her successful escape (so it would appear) from Alpheus (only here in the whole mythological tradition is the rape frustrated),[22] and in fact the whole Proserpina story, that is the story Calliope tells to the jury of nymphs, is very much a *maius opus*, 'greater work', in the same tradition.

So the inset Arethusa story has a triple bearing on the threefold narrative frame: (i) it introduces a story which commands attention because of its parallelism with the Proserpina story,[23] (ii) a story which is of interest to the nymphs and also (iii) a story which is of interest to Pallas, as we shall see. Moreover, Arethusa has a decisive role in the Proserpina story. It is she who gives the definitive clue to Ceres; in the parallel version of the story in the *Fasti* she was rather the occasion for the rape, and is for some reason called *frigida*: 'cold Arethusa had invited the mothers of the gods' (*frigida caelestum matres Arethusa uocarat, Fast.* 4.424). But Arethusa is not the only helper in the epic version who is a water nymph: we have already met the beneficent Cyane, praised by Calliope with surprising emphasis: 'Cyane, most famous of the Sicilian nymphs' (*inter Sicelidas Cyane celeberrima nymphas, Met.* 5.412), and ready to do anything to help Proserpina and her searching mother: 'she came to Cyane as well . . . [although she could not speak] yet she

---

[22] Forbes Irving (1990) 305–6 discusses the Arethusa story as exceptional in the metamorphic tradition and points out that Ovid is our only witness for her successful escape (but there is a discordant note in the epithet *Alpheias* at 5.487).

[23] See Hinds (1987) 92–3.

gave clear signs' (*uenit et ad Cyanen . . . signa tamen manifesta dedit*, 5.465; 468).[24]

After Cyane, and before Arethusa, the Sirens are featured both for their metamorphic experience and for their help in the search for Proserpina. Again the epic version has some unusual details, and those details reveal something of a pro-nymph bias: according to Hyginus (*Fab.* 141) the Sirens had been metamorphosed as revenge for not helping Demeter. The bias is clear if we compare Ovid's version with that of Apollonius of Rhodes. Ovid calls them *Acheloides* (5.552), *doctae Sirenes* (5.555), and stresses the vocal charms of these daughters of a Muse (according to Apollonius' genealogy, *Argon.* 4.895–6):

> ne tamen ille canor mulcendas natus ad aures
> tantaque dos oris linguae deperderet usum,
> uirginei uultus et uox humana remansit.
>
> *Met.* 5.561–3

> But so that their tongues should not lose that power of song designed to charm men's ears, such a great vocal gift, they retained their maidens' faces and human voice.

In Apollonius' version the emphasis on song and charm is completed by an emphasis on murder:

> . . . where the melodious Sirens, the daughters of Achelous, charm and murder with their sweet song whoever moors at their island. Beautiful Terpsichore, one of the Muses, lay with Achelous and gave birth to them, and there was a time when they attended the fair daughter of Demeter, before her wedding, with their medley of songs.   *Argon.* 4.893–7

After the unsuccessful attempts of Cyane and the Acheloides (Sirens) it will be, as we have seen, another water nymph, Arethusa, who solves the mystery: '"these eyes of mine saw your Proserpina there"' ('*uisa tua est oculis illic Proserpina nostris*', *Met.* 5.505). I conclude that Ovid is not simply narrating his own version of the Proserpina myth; rather, his own version is coloured by the particular version which Calliope performed on a particular occasion and for a special audience, a jury of nymphs. The narrative cannot be cleanly severed from its 'narrating instance'.

But this is hardly the end because as we have seen there is one more 'narrating instance' to examine. The voice of Calliope, who narrates for the nymphs, is dubbed by the voice of one unspecified Muse narrating for

---

[24] This positive role again has no parallel in the *Fasti* version, where, as Hinds (1987) 82–3 notes, *praetereo* is an arch cross-reference to the heroic cameo of Cyane in the epic: *praeterit et Cyanen . . .* (*Fast.* 4.469).

Pallas. Is it conceivable that this narrative situation too has an effect on what is being told? That involves asking another awkward question: what kind of stories does Pallas Athena like? One might guess that Pallas has a preference for stories where chastity conquers. In the following book she will destroy the stories of divine *amours* on Arachne's tapestry, with its images of lust, violence, and even representations of what looks like zooerasty. In the present situation, she is visiting Helicon, seat of the Muses, who are represented as fellow-virgins: *uirgineumque Helicona petit* (5.254), and who have successfully resisted the sexual aggression of mad Pyreneus – this is the rare story which a Muse immediately reports to Athena: 'everything scares the virgins' minds' (5.274); 'he tried to rape us, but we escaped' (5.288). After this prologue the main narrative will be concerned not only with Proserpina's lost virginity but also with Pallas' resistance to Venus:

> 'Pallada nonne uides iaculatricemque Dianam
> abscessisse mihi? Cereris quoque filia uirgo,
> si patiemur, erit ...'   5.375–7

'Don't you see that Pallas and the archer Diana have already rebelled against me? The daughter of Ceres will also be a virgin, if I allow it to happen ...'

and with Arethusa's exceptional success in preserving her maiden identity against Alpheus: 'I thought it a crime to please a man ... I escaped to Ortygia' (5.584; 640).

A Demeter and Persephone story should have an Eleusinian episode and this Ovidian story is exceptional, when compared not just with the *Homeric Hymn to Demeter* but also with Ovid's own alternative version in the *Fasti*, in dodging the Eleusinian adventure, which establishes Demeter's centrality in Attica; interestingly, the Muse makes it clear that Athens is Pallas' city from the very start: '[Ceres] directed her light chariot to the city of Pallas' (*Tritonida ... in urbem*, 5.645),[25] and the next book of the *Metamorphoses* will show how much Pallas cares about this privilege.

We can thus make a case that Pallas has a vested interest in the story she listens to, and that traces of her presence are visible in the narrative. Is the anonymous Muse too perceived as a particular voice? We know that she is re-performing Calliope's song, and the Muses are famous for their mnemonic power. We have seen that Calliope's situation as a narrator influences her poetics; but now we can add that the anonymous Muse also manipulates the story, for example in negotiating the competing claims of Demeter and Athena to the land of Attica. So can we suggest that the unnamed Muse has some kind of identity? It is awkward that we don't know who she is:

---

[25] Contrast *Fast.* 4.502–62.

she could be any of the eight Muses other than Calliope, who is the narrator of the inset story as well as – one is tempted to add – the Muse of epic. The only tenuous trace I have been able to follow would connect this nameless Muse with the elegiac poet Cornelius Gallus.[26] As is well known, the beginning of Calliope's song is a repetition of a famous elegiac text by Gallus:

'utinam modo dicere possim
carmina digna dea: certe dea carmine digna est.'
Met. 5.344–5

'if only I can sing songs worthy of a goddess; to be sure the goddess is worthy of a song.'

...tandem fecerunt carmina Musae
quae possem domina dicere digna mea
Gallus fr. 1 Courtney[27]

At last the Muses have created songs that I can sing as worthy of my mistress.

In fact there is a corresponding trace in the outermost 'narrating instance', because when Ovid introduces the anonymous Muse he uses two expressions – the hexameter ending *una sororum*, and *chorus* used of the nine sisters – which share their first appearance in extant Latin poetry in a famous passage about Gallus and the Muses:

...quam sic adfata est una sororum:
'o nisi te uirtus opera ad maiora tulisset
in partem uentura chori Tritonia nostri...'
Met. 5.268–70

One of the sisters addressed her thus: 'Pallas, you who would have been one of our choir, had your virtue not raised you to greater deeds ...'

tum canit, errantem Permessi ad flumina Gallum
Aonas in montis ut duxerit una sororum
utque uiro Phoebi chorus adsurrexerit omnis.
Virg. *Ecl.* 6.64–6

---

26 Gallus also has links with the narrator of the inmost inset tale, Arethusa: she is invoked at the beginning of *Eclogue* 10 (above, p. 190), and there has been discussion as to whether this reflects models in Gallus or in Greek bucolic poetry; *Ecl.* 10.9–12 (cf. 7.21) also suggests a tradition of poetry where nymphs and Muses are interchangeable.

27 This allusion is denied by Courtney (1993) 267, but the two texts are linked by the shared intention of winning over a *domina*, and the striking alliteration of the Ovidian passage D-P-C-D-D-C-D-C-D must be explained, I think, as a teasing remake of the blunt and archaizing triple consecutive alliteration D-D-D in Gallus.

Then he sang of how one of the sisters led Gallus, wandering by the waters of Permessus, up to mount Helicon, and of how the whole choir of Apollo rose in honour of the man.

Now the location of the Ovidian episode, Helicon with its fountains Hippocrene and Aganippe, is sacred to a succession of poetic memories – Hesiod, Callimachus,[28] Ennius, Gallus, Virgil the bucolic poet, and Propertius. Perhaps the layering of the two Muses reflects this stratification. Perhaps the anonymous Muse has a Gallan tinge because she is retelling, and thus manipulating, a tale by Calliope the Muse of epic: one is not surprised that the final effect, in a manner that reflects the general poetics of the *Metamorphoses*, is that epic cannot be easily kept clean of elegiac thumbprints.

But my main point has been that Ovidian narrative is not free from the traces left by a multitude of narrative voices. The collector of stories, the ultimate narrator Ovid, is in fact our only protection against the deafening effect of the echo-chamber of *Fama*; but the final result, the poem, cannot escape the interference of its many echoes and inflections:

FAMA

nocte dieque patet; tota est ex aere sonanti,
tota fremit uocesque refert iteratque quod audit.
. . . .
    ueniunt, leve uulgus, euntque
mixtaque cum ueris passim commenta uagantur
milia rumorum confusaque uerba uolutant;
e quibus hi uacuas implent sermonibus aures,
hi narrata ferunt alio, mensuraque ficti
crescit et auditis aliquid nouus adicit auctor.
              Met. 12.46–58[29]

---

[28] In the Heliconian prologue to the *Aitia* Callimachus mentioned not only several Heliconian hydronyms and the aetiology of Hippocrene, but also the idea of a 'tenth Muse' (fr. 2a, 5–15 Pf.; cf. *Met.* 5.270).

[29] Typically, references to *Fama* establish a polarity between an author's dependence on and innovation within a previous tradition, but in this poem, where the richness of tradition becomes difficult to master, the main effect is to stress the reader's dependence on the author as the only force able to control background noise and give a narrative shape to this interplay of competing narrators. Cf. Hinds (1996) 1085: 'He engages with an unprecedented range of Greek and Roman writing; every genre, not just epic, leaves its mark in the poem's idiom. But in the final analysis the *Metamorphoses* renders its sources superfluous: with its many internal narrators and internal audiences, with its repeated stress on the processes of report and retelling whereby stories enter the common currency, the primary intertextual reading which the poem insists on is one internal to itself.' Cf. also Kenney (1986) p. xxv 'So far from sending us back to his models, indeed, Ovid has rendered them expendable.'

Day and night [the House of *Fama*] lies open; it is made all of sounding bronze, it is all abuzz, and it reports what men say and repeats what it hears.... The fickle mob come and go, and thousands of invented rumours mingled with truths wanders everywhere, tossing about a babble of words; some of them fill idle ears with talk, others carry stories to other parts. The scale of the fiction grows, and each new author adds something to what he has heard.

The process of generation and transmission of stories in the House of *Fama* is described by the author at the beginning of his new account of the much-broadcast Trojan war. The first and last word of the paragraph about *Fama* is, in true ring-composition, a form of *orbis* (12.39, 12.63), both 'world' and 'cycle', with a teasing reminder that the story has become world-famous through the repetitive epic Cycle. The notion of *auctor* is wittily split into competitive meanings, three of them current in normal Latin usage: a seller (one who controls a good to be sold); a creator; a guarantor; while the fourth is suggested by the contextual association with *nouus* and *adicit*, and by the etymology from *augeo* 'augment': 'someone who increases, adds to something'. In Roman culture, stories regularly need an *auctor*, but for Ovid it is thought-provoking that the word can describe the producer of a text, the guarantor of a pre-existing information, or the latecomer who brings a little something new to add to the series of fictions.

We are back, via a different route, to the familiar notion of Ovid as a privileged narrator in his poem. What makes Ovid so special and powerful in comparison with the many inventors and retailers of stories competing for attention? Even more, we wonder how we are to locate the frame that controls the work, and whether we can tell it apart from the picture. Perhaps the *Fama* image is part of the Trojan story, perhaps it is external to it, and it is not even definitively clear whether Ovid as an authorial voice is part of the opus or of the frame. This dilemma will easily point readers towards issues of ethics and power.

As I approach the end of this enquiry I raise some broader issues, ones impossible to resolve within the limits of narratology, but made inescapable by the study of narrative.

1. Mythological competence. How do we assess the relationship of one individual tale to other pre-existing or even potential versions of the same story? Critics normally react to this question with the 'learned' poet approach, but this is just one response. We might say that Jupiter's unparalleled description of Lycaon as a monster implies the regular alternative version where Lycaon is a pioneer of the Arcadian cult of Jupiter. Or is Ovid criticizing that version / criticizing Jupiter? (see Feldherr in this volume, p. 171). The *Metamorphoses* also challenges a related distinction, that between

intertextual and intratextual implications. The poem is as rich in literary allusions as any other text in the Alexandrian tradition, but it is also so rich in myths that it 'renders its sources superfluous' (so Hinds, quoted in note 29).

2. Another important result is to question the very essence of what makes a story individual and, to use Ovid's neologism, *narrabilis*, 'narratable'. The sheer size of the poem and its alternation of short and long narratives is a constant invitation to compare and contrast, and the question about what makes a character (different from another) is never far from the surface.

3. The authority of the primary narrator is established not by naturalizing epic conventions, but by laying bare the conventions. The challenge to the audience is that belief can be renegotiated at any moment without breaking the contact between narrator and addressee: this is what Ovid proudly claims in his definition of the poem as bodies transformed *in non credendos ... modos* (*Trist.* 2.64).

4. Our entire appreciation of the poem is based on implied ideas of unity and relevance, but in the act of reading it those ideas are constantly questioned and revised.

Coda. Retracing the Trojan war

In the *Aeneid* Aeneas narrates to Dido, at the dinner-table, how the epic tradition begins: right before the fall of Troy, the Greek army has vanished, and the Trojans are left with traces, memories, and interpretations on an empty, scarred coast:

> iuuat ire et Dorica castra
> desertosque uidere locos litusque relictum:
> hic Dolopum manus, hic saeuus tendebat Achilles;
> classibus hic locus, hic acie certare solebant.
>
> *Aen.* 2.27–30

They take pleasure in going out and looking at the Greek camp, the deserted places and abandoned shore: this was where the Thessalians used to pitch their tents, and there the cruel Achilles. This was the place for their fleet, and here they used to fight in battle.

In Ovid's *Heroides* Penelope writes to Ulysses that the Greek heroes have been re-evoking the same story for their wives, who have never seen the war itself. Troy has been utterly destroyed, and what Virgil described as traces *in situ* is now a diagram on a dinner-table (the narrative frame for Virgil's inset story):

> atque aliquis posita monstrat fera proelia mensa,
>> pingit et exiguo Pergama tota mero:
> 'hac ibat Simois; haec est Sigeia tellus;
>> hic steterat Priami regia celsa senis.
> illic Aeacides, illic tendebat Ulixes;
>> hic lacer admissos terruit Hector equos.'
>
>> *(Her.* 1.31–6)

When the tables had been set someone would give a show of the fierce battles, painting the whole of Troy with a few drops of wine. 'This is where the Simois flowed; this is the land of Sigeum; this was where old Priam's lofty palace stood. This was where Achilles pitched his tent, and there Ulysses; this was where the mangled Hector terrified the horses into bolting.'

The precise allusion to Virgil makes it impossible to decide whether this is a trace of the Trojan war or of Virgil's text about that war. In the meantime, according to Ovid's *Ars amatoria*, Ulysses has been retelling and redrawing the same story in many different versions, but for the wrong lady, Calypso:

> haec Troiae casus iterumque iterumque rogabat:
>> ille referre aliter saepe solebat idem.
> litore constiterant: illic quoque pulchra Calypso
>> exigit Odrysii fata cruenta ducis.
> ille leui uirga (uirgam nam forte tenebat)
>> quod rogat, in spisso litore pingit opus.
> 'haec' inquit 'Troia est' (muros in litore fecit):
>> 'hic tibi sit Simois; haec mea castra puta.
> campus erat' (campumque facit), 'quem caede Dolonis
>> sparsimus, Haemonios dum uigil optat equos.
> illic Sithonii fuerant tentoria Rhesi:
>> hac ego sum captis nocte reuectus equis.'
> pluraque pingebat, subitus cum Pergama fluctus
>> abstulit et Rhesi cum duce castra suo.
>
>> *Ars am.* 2.127–40

Again and again she asked for the story of the fall of Troy; he often told the same story in different words. They were standing by the sea; there too fair Calypso asked about the bloody fate of the Thracian general. By chance he was holding a light stick; with the stick he drew on the firm sand a picture of what she asked for. 'Here,' he said, 'is Troy' (and he drew walls on the shore); 'imagine that this is the river Simois, and that this is my camp. There was a field' (and he drew a field) 'which we spattered with the blood of Dolon, as he went out on patrol in the hope of winning Achilles' horses. That was where the tents of Thracian Rhesus were; this was the route that I took back at night after capturing the horses.' He was drawing more, when a sudden wave swept away Troy and Rhesus' camp, general and all.

Here the shoreline (from the beginning of *Aeneid* 2) and the insatiable female addressee (from the end of *Aeneid* 1) collapse the Carthaginian frame and the Trojan inset story in Virgil, but the deictic drawing includes the *Heroides* as well. We are back to a sandy shore, but very far away from Troy and Ithaca: once again the sequence of deictics (*hic, haec, hac* etc.) points the reader both towards an absent reality being imagined in the text, and towards an absent model text, by Virgil, or perhaps two texts, by Virgil and Ovid, if this passage is also an allusion to Ovid's earlier epistles. The model of textual fixation and transmission – the various instances of 'here' now being sketched out on pages imitating each other – is to be contrasted with a boundless flux of momentary reenactments.

The problems of narrative in Ovid can be seen as expressions of a deeper concern with the act of representation: this poet, after all, has pioneered not only words like *narrabilis* 'narratable' and *narratus* 'narrative', but also words like *imitamen* 'imitation', *simulamen* 'simulation', *simulans* 'imitative'. Latin poetry in this age responds not only to Greek poetry but to the traditions of philosophy, art criticism, and rhetoric. To speak about 'narrative technique' is often to occlude these wider implications. Similarly, the study of allusion and imitation in Ovid should not be restricted to techniques and literary agendas. I therefore refer my readers to other chapters in this volume (particularly those by Tarrant and Hinds), as well as to the works listed below.

FURTHER READING

Foundational studies of narratology: Bal (1985); Genette (1980).

Works on classical literature with an emphasis on theories of narrative and their impact on interpretation and link with textuality (necessarily, a very selective list): Winkler (1985); Fusillo (1985); Sharrock and Morales (2000); Laird (1999); Doherty (1995); Fowler (2000) (a survey on classics and narratology by D. Fowler is forthcoming in Harrison (2001).

Studies of Ovidian poetry with an interest in narrative technique and/or theory: Rosati (1981) 297–309, (1983), (1994); Hinds (1987); Nagle (1988d); Barchiesi (1989), (1997b), (2001); Keith (1992a); Holzberg (1997a); Wheeler (1999), offers the most comprehensive and up-to-date discussion. Philip Hardie's forthcoming projects on *Fama* and on Ovid's poetics of illusion (2002) are also relevant to this chapter. Several papers in Hardie, Barchiesi, Hinds (1999) are also of interest, as are all the papers quoted in my note 19.

12

CAROLE NEWLANDS

Mandati memores: political and poetic authority in the *Fasti*

Ovid's *Fasti*, his elegiac poem on the Roman calendar, begins where his *Metamorphoses* leaves off, in present, imperial time. The *Fasti* has sometimes simply been plumbed as a random source of historical or anthropological knowledge. But as a poem about Rome and its complex imperial present as well as its past, the *Fasti* offers important insights into the mentality of Roman society at a crucial juncture of cultural development in the late Augustan age. Indeed, it raises questions that remain important today, for the poem explores the authority of the sources by which national myths are constructed and time and speech are controlled.

The *Fasti* has often been read as a work of national celebration, the product of some thirty years of Augustan peace.[1] Yet the latter part of Augustus' régime was hardly the 'golden age' projected by Virgil in the *Aeneid*. Beset by dynastic troubles, military failures abroad and discontent at home, Augustus had begun to place restrictions on freedom of speech.[2] As Denis Feeney has argued, the very title of the poem, *Fasti*, advertises its concern with the conditions for lawful *(fas)* speech.[3] The *Fasti* demonstrates its acute awareness of the political pressures that beset investigation into national history and custom in the late Augustan period; it provocatively foregrounds the ideological management of 'truth.' The *Fasti* invites us to ask not only how we read, but why, perhaps, it matters.

Beginnings

Ovid probably worked on the *Fasti* and the *Metamorphoses* simultaneously, between AD 2 and 8.[4] Like the *Metamorphoses*, the *Fasti* is an aetiological poem that is strongly marked by generic play.[5] Yet in the *Fasti* the quest

---

[1] Recently Herbert-Brown (1994); Fantham (1998) 42.
[2] On the stressful political conditions of the later Augustan principate see Wiedemann (1975).
[3] Feeney (1992).   [4] Hinds (1987) 10–11.
[5] Hinds (1987), (1992); Myers (1994) on the *Metamorphoses*.

for origins is directed towards understanding Rome. The poem's opening dedication to Germanicus, imperial heir and nephew of Tiberius (1–26), immediately suggests a political orientation at variance with that of the *Metamorphoses*, which concludes with a superb gesture of independence from the emperor Augustus.[6]

Indeed, the *Fasti* poses particular problems in critical understanding. In structure it is episodic, disjunctive, and apparently incomplete, for its six books cover only the first six months of the year; the poem ends halfway through the calendar in June. Did Ovid lack scholarly resources in Tomis? Or had Ovid in fact completed the poem but defiantly erased Augustus' special months of July and August? Ovid's words in exile about the poem's form (*Trist.* 2.549–52) remain enigmatic.[7] Although Ovid made revisions to the *Fasti* at Tomis, we do not know their true extent.[8] The beginning of the poem too is problematic. Under Tiberius Ovid added the new proem to Germanicus, placing the original proem to Augustus at the start of Book 2.[9] Do we then approach the *Fasti* as an Augustan work, or as a post-Augustan work that is strongly marked by the experience of exile?[10]

Despite such difficulties, in the past two decades the *Fasti* has at last earned critical acclaim as a learned, sophisticated, and also playful work.[11] Moreover, the Roman calendar has been recognized as a document central to the construction of Roman identity; its vital concern was the exposition of new and changing ideas of 'Romanness'.[12] It offered Ovid a flexible form in which to explore different constructions of Roman identity.[13]

Indeed, the *Fasti* intimately responds to a critical period of Roman intellectual and political development that Andrew Wallace-Hadrill has argued was in effect 'a cultural revolution'.[14] Under Augustus, learned specialists working in the service of a relatively monolithic state were displacing the educated aristocracy, who had been the traditional preservers and transmitters of knowledge. Time was among the important areas of knowledge in which, due to the calendrical reforms of Julius Caesar and Augustus, authority was relocated from the control of the aristocracy to mathematicians and antiquarians, academic experts whose knowledge was aligned with Augustus' political needs.[15] Verrius Flaccus' learned commentary and calendar, the *Fasti Praenestini*, was a product of this Romano-centric interest

---

[6] Hardie (1997), esp. 194.
[7] Peeters (1939) 63–103; Bömer (1957) 17–22; Fantham (1998) 3–4.
[8] Bömer (1957) 17–18; Fantham (1985) 257–66 and (1992) 166–70.
[9] On the two proems see Bömer (1958) 79.
[10] Barchiesi (1997a) argues that the *Fasti* was profoundly shaped by the experience of exile.
[11] See the review articles of Miller (1992a) and Fantham (1995).
[12] Beard (1987); Feeney (1998) 124–5.   [13] Feeney (1998) 123–33.
[14] Wallace-Hadrill (1997).   [15] Wallace-Hadrill (1997) 16–18.

in investigating and controlling time and in promoting Augustus' family, whose festivals augmented the calendar.[16] The topography of Rome itself was dramatically reshaped to promote imperial interests.[17] An obelisk erected within the imperial complex on the Campus Martius to serve as a gigantic sundial provided an ostentatious sign of Augustus' authority over time itself.[18] By such means, Andrew Wallace-Hadrill comments, Augustus succeeded in 'turning all Roman time into Augustan time'.[19]

As a poem about time, Ovid's *Fasti* participates in this cultural revolution and yet also stands apart from it. Located firmly within the tradition of Hellenistic aetiological poetry as well as within that of Roman antiquarianism, the poem both represents and contests imperial control over time. The *Fasti* is strongly marked by Ovid's personal journey through the Roman year; Roman time is also Ovidian time.

In the opening couplet of the poem, the poet announces his pursuit of different temporal sequences, civic, religious, and cosmological (1–2):

> tempora cum causis Latium digesta per annum
> lapsaque sub terras ortaque signa canam.

I shall sing of the special occasions organized through the Latin year, their origins too, and the constellations that rise and set below the earth.

While *tempora* 'times' includes historical events worthy of commemoration as well as religious festivals, second in importance to *tempora* are *signa*, astronomical signs. In this opening couplet Ovid suggests that his subject is no less than time itself in all its earthly and celestial complexity.

With *causis*, the Latin word for 'origins' (in Greek *aitia*), Ovid announces his attempt to understand the present through uncovering the links with the past; he places his subject within a sophisticated Callimachean framework of aetiological investigation.[20] The first line of the *Fasti* also plays off the programmatic first elegy of Propertius' Book 4, where, at line 69, the poet announces a new poetic topic of 'sacred rites, days, and the former names of places' *(sacra diesque canam et cognomina prisca locorum)*.[21] Ovid follows Propertius in the challenging task of writing about national themes in a metre traditionally considered light, the elegiac; likewise he experiments with a

---

[16] Peeters (1939) 52–4; Degrassi (1963) 107–45.   [17] Zanker (1988) 108–66.
[18] Buchner (1982); Schütz (1990).   [19] Wallace-Hadrill (1987) 226.
[20] Miller (1982); on the influence too of Callimachus' *Hymns* see Miller (1980) and (1982) 407–9; Fantham (1998) 11–15.
[21] Cf. *Fast.* 1.7–8: *sacra recognosces annalibus eruta priscis | et quo sit merito quaeque notata dies* ('you will recognise sacred rites unearthed from ancient annals and the special distinction of particular days').

wide variety of voices and tonal effects as well as subjects, thereby resisting any univocal approach to his subject.[22]

In Book 4 Propertius avoids the subject of astronomy, for the astronomer Horus warns him that the constellations are a source of personal danger (4.1.150). The stars, however, are a prominent theme of Ovid's *Fasti*. Aratus' *Phaenomena* as well as Virgil's *Georgics* provided Ovid with literary precedents for the poetic treatment of astronomy, although these works' interest in the stars is scientific rather than aetiological.[23] The stars of Ovid's *Fasti* are not tied to the collective process of human labour and the battle against nature. Rather, through the myths of their origins, they bring passion and eroticism into the *Fasti* in a substantial way. Indeed, in an age in which political leaders exploited astronomy to augment their power, star myths often provide through striking textual juxtapositions a new, provocative perspective upon Roman culture.[24] The *Fasti* thus derives much of its complex texture as a work of art from its interplay among different sources of temporal reference, including the Roman and the Greek.

In transferring the calendar to the private form of the book roll, the poem invites intimate, learned scrutiny as a literary text and leisurely reading in a non-linear manner.[25] Indeed, the apparent disjunction in the *Fasti* between elegiac form and national subject is mirrored in the two types of learned readership we can construct for the *Fasti*, each with different expectations and needs: the imperial audience, and the audience of devoted readers of Ovid's elegiac poetry. This latter audience is constructed in the text as expecting a broad palette of tonal effects, wit and humour among them.

The difficulty of Ovid's task in the *Fasti*, the negotiation between different audiences as well as the expansion of the elegiac genre to new national themes, is highlighted in the dedicatory address to Augustus at the start of Book 2. Here the poet, referring to his earlier elegiac career, implicitly includes his broader readership in his address to Augustus (7–8):

> idem sacra cano signataque tempora fastis:
> ecquis ad haec illinc crederet esse uiam?

> Still the same, I sing of sacred rites and the special occasions marked in the calendar: who could have thought I would take this road?

---

[22] See for instance Newlands (1995), Barchiesi (1997a); for a dissenting view Herbert-Brown (1994).

[23] On connections however in Ovid's Vestalia with Stoic cosmological exegesis and allegory see Gee (1997).

[24] Newlands (1995) 27–50; Gee (2000).   [25] Newlands (2000).

What does Ovid mean here with the paradoxical juxtaposition of *idem* and *sacra*? [26] Despite his new role as antiquarian, is the poet the same person as before, and is only the object of his investigations different? Does he promise here all the devices of the former love poet – such as irony, wit, and self-deprecatory and irreverent humour – now applied to religion and history? Yet if so, would such an approach please his addressee Augustus, whose heavy hand of wrath fell upon the *Ars amatoria*?

With the metaphor of the road (*uiam*), time and space are fused in the imagining of Ovid's poetic career and progress through the Roman year as an adventurous journey. [27] Ovid leaves ambiguous what he means by *idem*, 'the same', I suggest, in order to express the elusive identity of the traveller who is traditionally open to change and experimentation – and also is often displaced and disoriented.

Thus Ovid turns to several guides to help him decode the complexities of the Roman past. Through dialogues with various informants, human and divine, that the poet meets on his travels through the Roman year, the *Fasti* dramatizes the quest for origins. Random encounters on the road lend an air of happenstance to the *Fasti*. In trying to make sense of time, the *Fasti* uncovers the disorderliness of the past and the often arbitrary nature of links between past and present.

Significantly, although aetiology attempts to bridge the rupture between past and present, these are frequently in conflict in the *Fasti*. [28] Indeed, the processes of selection, emphasis, and textual juxtapositions draw attention to the disjunctions within Ovidian time. The origin of the Lares Compitales, for instance, whose cult was closely tied to Augustus' genius, is explained through a brutal myth of mutilation and rape (*Fast.* 2.583–616). [29] Different versions of the past too compete with one another. Janus' opening celebration of early Italy as a Golden Age under Saturn (*Fast.* 1.231–54) is questioned by the later, grimmer account of Saturn as a god who demanded human sacrifice (*Fast.* 5.625–32).

Days that have accrued different meanings, a particular feature of Ovid's *Fasti*, highlight the tension between past and present time. On the Ides of March, a day of celebration for the ancient goddess Anna Perenna and also the anniversary of Julius Caesar's assassination, Republican and Augustan time confront one another. But whereas the festival of Anna Perenna is discussed at length (523–696), the assassination of Julius Caesar concludes the day with a mere fourteen lines (697–710). Ovid's *Fasti* demonstrates the importance of Republican popular festivals, where licence of speech and

---

[26] Miller (1991) 23–4.   [27] Bakhtin (1981) 125–6, 243–5   [28] Bing (1988).
[29] Suet. *Aug.* 31.4; Bömer (1958) 301–2.

behaviour was preserved.[30] But the structural manipulation of the Ides of March also emphasizes the troubling gap between the carnivalesque popular festivals and the new state occasions of carefully doctored history that threaten to displace them.

Narrators

Though personalized in form and method, the *Fasti* performs important work in antiquarian research and the exploration of Roman cultural identity. Indeed, the poem represents a way of thinking that is central to Roman religious thought. For example, in his investigation of origins of festivals and cults, the poet frequently offers different explanations without deciding among them. Multiple exegesis is a feature of antiquarian research and religious thinking; it is not specific to the aetiological methods of Ovid's *Fasti*.[31]

Janus provides an initial paradigm for Ovid's approach to the problem of interpreting time (*Fast.* 1.63–288).[32] Through this dualistic god of beginnings, Ovid gives dramatic form to the aetiological method of investigation. Overcome with fright at the god's sudden epiphany, the poet's hair stands on end, his heart almost stops (97–8). Janus humorously exploits his bizarre shape, offering to the poet's view his two faces (95–7), and yet courteously speaking only from the front-facing mouth (100). Since he sees both forward and backward, Janus provides an initial conciliatory voice that smoothly links past and present and belies the disjunctions to come. Thus while he admires the virtuous early days of Italy, he enjoys the prosperity of imperial Rome (189–226; 229–55).

Yet Janus is not without ambiguity. He provides various, incompatible explanations for his dualistic shape (102–44). Certainly, multiple exegesis is at home in antiquarian research (see also Schiesaro, ch. 4 above, pp. 65–6). But it is surely one thing for an antiquarian to provide multiple explanations, quite another for the subject of research itself to do so. For if the god of beginnings himself does not know the reason for his shape, what hope is there for any sure investigation of origins? Indeed, as god of origins, Janus programmatically dramatizes at the start of a poem about origins the unreliability of authority, even when it is divine.[33]

Ovid's *Fasti* then dramatizes and personalizes antiquarian methodology. Ovid constructs for himself a poetic 'I', who employs a wide range of stylistic registers, at times serious and deferential, at other times witty and irreverent.

---

[30] Johnson (1978); Newlands (1996).
[31] Scheid (1992) 118–24; Miller (1992b) 12–14; Feeney (1998) 127–31.
[32] On the programmatic importance of Janus see Barchiesi (1991) 14–17; Hardie (1992) 72–4.
[33] See Hardie (1992) 74.

Unlike the confident narrator of the *Ars amatoria*, he claims no secure knowledge and competence.[34] Sometimes he is in command of sophisticated antiquarian debate, at other times – and increasingly towards the poem's end – at a loss in his investigations of Rome's customs and past.[35] Ovid thus appears as both subject and audience, for he frequently surrenders his poetic authority to that of more 'expert' informants – not the ancient literary and antiquarian authorities drawn upon by his contemporaries such as Verrius Flaccus, but, following Callimachus, fictionalized informants, both human and divine, who have their own set of values and invite the reader to examine the discursive traditions that shape different versions of knowledge.[36] The Roman antiquarian's investigation of origins was intimately involved with the impulse to celebrate the contemporary imperial city of Rome.[37] Ovid, however, creates a dramatic distance from his research. His essentially deauthorized stance is, in part, a comic device that encourages the interplay of different perspectives upon Roman history and cult.

Moreover, the many narrators that Ovid consults demonstrate biases that undermine their reliability.[38] These biases are shaped by social and institutional as well as personal forces. For instance, although the account of the Parilia in Book 4 (807–62) is characterized by a wide variety of alternative explanations, overall it is aligned with Augustan interests. For over time the Parilia has accumulated meaning; it is not merely a pastoral festival but celebrates the birthday of Rome. Thus the deified Romulus, Rome's founder, inspires Ovid's account (808). And he sponsors an exculpatory account of Remus' murder that lays the blame on a guard Celer, not Romulus (835–56). Clearly social and institutional pressures as well as personal factors shape this reinvention of the past. In particular, Romulus' 'heir' Augustus, invoked in the proem to Book 4 (19–20), forms part of the book's external audience – hence the need to remove the stain of fratricide and set the discussion firmly within the context of the Augustan restoration.[39]

In an age that was inventing Rome as an empire controlled by Augustus' desire for a 'universalizing culture', the *Fasti* performs the important work of revealing the political and social management of 'reality'.[40] Whereas Augustus, late in his rule, was closing off options for discussion and dissent, Ovid's *Fasti* attempts to keep open a dialogue about Rome and the nature of Roman identity. What have been deemed the 'faults' of the *Fasti* – in

34 On the confident narrator of the *Ars amatoria* see Sharrock (1994a).
35 Newlands (1995) 79–80.
36 Foucault (1971), esp. 178–95; Rutledge (1980); Miller (1983); Newlands (1995) 51–86.
37 See Graf (1992), especially 24–5.
38 On Ovid's self-interested informants see Harries (1989).
39 See Graf (1992) 22–5.   40 Wallace-Hadrill (1997) 22.

particular, its episodic nature and its panegyrical elements – can be seen as a function of an ambitious, innovative narrative strategy seeking to scrutinize the myths of the present as well as the past in a more nuanced way than, perhaps, the elegiac poet had hitherto explored. As a written, literary work, the *Fasti* offers a different experience of time and of the calendar from that of daily lived experience or indeed from that of the antiquarian researcher devoted to the solution of individual problems. Ovidian time challenges and eludes certainties and universals.

The art of the *Fasti* is thus necessarily that of juxtaposition rather than fluent narrative development. Different episodes are selected and organized so that particular textual juxtapositions create new relationships, new conditions of meaning. Partly as a consequence of this deliberately disjunctive mode, the poem, as its opening couplet programmatically suggests, is profoundly intertextual. The *Fasti* is frequently in dialogue with other works of literature, both Greek and Latin, and with Ovid's own earlier works. Yet in this very allusiveness and its synthesis of cultural elements the poem is, it could be suggested, most profoundly Roman.

Erato

The Muses are traditionally the supreme sources of poetic authority. In the *Fasti* Ovid draws upon the Muses several times for information, following the precedent of Callimachus' *Aitia*, whose first two books are organized as a conversation with the Muses. Callimachus' encounter with the Muses is based on a dream that he was transported to Mount Helicon.[41] Ovid on the other hand meets the Muses directly, and they appear most prominently in the poem's second half.[42] They are not, however, unimpeachable sources of knowledge. At the start of Book 5 (1–110) three of them debate the origin of the month's name, *Maius*, without reaching any consensus.[43] The poet, aware that a partisan vote could cause offence to those who are the staple of his creative existence, refuses to resolve the debate (108–10). The Muses appear again at the end of the poem, summoned to explain the origins of the temple of Hercules Musarum (*Fast.* 6.797–812). But Clio's speech is compromised, for it ignores the temple's important Republican founder, M. Fulvius Nobilior, and praises its restorer, L. Marcius Philippus, who had close connections with the imperial family.[44]

The most prominent appearance by a Muse occurs in Book 4, where Erato is consulted about the cult of Magna Mater (179–372). Erato most fully

---

[41] Callim. *Ait.* fr. 2.   [42] In the first half only *Fast.* 1.657–62; *Fast.* 2.271–82.
[43] See Barchiesi (1991); Newlands (1995) 73–7.
[44] Newlands (1995) 209–36, esp. 230–1; Barchiesi (1997a) 259–72.

perhaps reveals the social and political constraints under which even the Muses must work in Augustus' Rome. Moreover, her appearance in the middle of the *Fasti* as we have it raises larger questions about the design of Ovid's seemingly episodic poem.

The Magna Mater was brought to Rome in 204 BC, thus within the time of written records.[45] She was among the first foreign deities to be brought to Rome and incorporated into the state religion, although Romans were not allowed to participate in the exotic aspects of her cult.[46] Her importance in the *Aeneid*, to which Peter Wiseman drew attention, reflects her significance as the goddess of Roman victories who simultaneously confirmed Rome's Trojan origins.[47] Her temple was restored by Augustus; it was situated opposite his Palatine house within the precinct of Victoria.[48]

Erato's explanation of the cult of the Magna Mater takes place in the heart of the city streets, *urbis per medias . . . uias* (*Fast.* 4.186), during the goddess's tumultuous procession. Ovid here plays off Lucretius' description of the rites of the Magna Mater in *De rerum natura* 2 (598–660).[49] The dramatic situation also evokes that of *Amores* 3.2, where Ovid presents himself as a spectator of the procession of the gods in the Circus.[50] In *Amores* 3.2 Ovid is in charge both of the representation of the procession and of the internal drama of seduction that he wittily directs. In the *Fasti* he is not in the enclosed space of the Circus, but on the streets, an observer of an exotic procession where he no longer has control over events. Terror renders him virtually inarticulate (4.189–90):

> Quaerere multa libet, sed me sonus aeris acuti
> terret et horrendo lotos adunca sono.

> I want to ask a lot of questions, but the sound of the shrill bronze terrifies me
> and the curved flute with its dreadful sound.

Terret wittily undercuts the authority of the Lucretian narrative, which aims to dispel irrational fear. Lucretius has failed Ovid as teacher here.[51] Instead, Ovid defers to the goddess herself and through her to Erato. In comic demonstration of his aphasia, he produces a brief request for information, *da, dea, quem sciter* ('grant, goddess, someone to inform me,' 191) – the rare

---

45 Basic discussion of the Magna Mater in Vermaseren (1977). For her advent in Rome see Gruen (1990) 5–33. For Ovid's use of literary sources see Miller (1991) 82–90. On the Romanization of her cult see Beard, North and Price (1998) 96–8.
46 Dion. Hal. *Ant.* 2.19.3–5.   47 Wiseman (1984) 123–8.   48 *Res gestae* 19.
49 Miller (1991) 82–5 argues that since the procession was not part of the state cult, Ovid may be conflating different aspects of the cult here. See also Lambrechts (1952) 143–5; Summers (1996) 342–3.
50 Miller (1991) 87.
51 On Lucretius' treatment of the Magna Mater see Summers (1996).

use of *sciter* suggesting a reverence of tone.[52] Ovid thus reshapes Lucretian and his own earlier elegiac material in his creation of a new didactic poet for the later Augustan age, one who defers to higher sources of authority that nonetheless turn out to be unreliable or 'contaminated' in various ways. Ovid no longer has complete control of the Muse whom he appropriated in the *Ars amatoria* (2.16). Erato, the Magna Mater's chosen informant, is in the service of the state, for she is ordered (*iussit*, 192) to speak and does so 'mindful of the goddess' command' (193).

Ovid's dramatic situation at the procession of the Magna Mater stands in marked contrast too to his viewing of the popular festival of Anna Perenna (3.523–42). The people celebrate this ancient goddess with sexual and verbal freedom; the stories that Ovid tells to explain the identity of the goddess (543–696) give a privileged space to uninhibited speech.[53] By contrast, in the procession of a goddess appropriated by Augustus, sexual licence or deviancy is restricted to the eunuch priests, while the poet himself loses his voice.

Erato tells three stories to explain the cult, all of which exist in famous earlier versions: the birth of Jupiter (197–214), narrated both in Callimachus' *Hymn to Zeus* and Lucretius' *De rerum natura* 2.633–9; the castration of Attis (221–46), the topic of Catullus 63; and the bringing of the Magna Mater to Rome (291–347), a story made famous by Livy (29.11–14). Erato's versions promote the interests of the Magna Mater as a goddess of new Augustan significance. The last two stories make prominent the theme of chastity, an important Augustan preoccupation, while the first story promotes the interests of motherhood.[54]

Hugh Parker has argued that these three myths sequentially represent the gradual Romanization of the goddess, transformed from exotic divinity to respectable, mother goddess and guardian of matronly chastity.[55] Yet the controlling voice of Erato is complex. Her authoritative status is qualified both by her social position as granddaughter of the Magna Mater, herself a 'protegée' of Augustus, and by the institution of the goddess's festival, the Megalensia. Yet Erato is also chosen as narrator since she represents the interests of love poetry. Her name refers to tender love, *teneri nomen amoris habet* (196); her primary audience is an elegiac poet who has dedicated Book 4 to Venus, who, as both goddess of love and foundress of the Augustan *gens*, likewise has her foot in two camps.[56] Erato then embodies the conflicting erotic and nationalistic agendas of the *Fasti*.

[52] Bömer (1958) 223; Fantham (1998) 130.   [53] Newlands (1996).
[54] Eg. *Fast.* 4.201–3 *questa est, totiens fecunda nec umquam | mater* ('she complained that she was so often fertile yet never a mother').
[55] Parker (1997) 125–41.
[56] Discussion of the proem to Book 4 in Barchiesi (1997a) 53–60.

Erato's divided loyalties are perhaps seen most clearly in her treatment of chastity. In Erato's account of the madness of Attis, for instance, the Magna Mater is given a rational motive for her punishment of Attis, his breaking of an oath of chastity (225–30). When Attis exclaims at *Fasti* 4.239, *merui! meritas do sanguine poenas* ('I have deserved this! I pay with blood the punishment I have deserved'), the figure of repetition draws attention to this revision of Catullus' story, which gives no explanation for the goddess's anger.[57]

The story of Claudia Quinta is organized around a deviant centre of interest, not the goddess's reception in Rome by leading dignitaries of state, as in Livy's version, but the miraculous proving of Claudia's virtue.[58] Nonetheless, as Muse of love and erotic poetry, Erato ambivalently represents Claudia as an elegiac *puella* (307–10):

> Casta quidem, sed non et credita: rumor iniquus
> laeserat, et falsi criminis acta rea est;
> cultus et ornatis uarie prodisse capillis
> obfuit, ad rigidos promptaque lingua senes.

She was in fact a chaste woman, contrary to her reputation: an unfair rumour had wronged her, and she was accused of a crime she had not committed; her elegance and her attractive hairstyle were held against her, and her tongue that was ready to answer back to disapproving old men.

Erato here adopts an urbane perspective. Only senile moralists object to elegant female adornment.[59] The Claudian *gens* was known for its hardy virtue.[60] Yet Claudia Quinta is perhaps modelled on a later Clodia, Catullus' Lesbia, herself the object of rumour and the butt of old men's tongues, which in poem 7 Catullus urges her to ignore. The typology of the elegiac mistress characteristically rests on a combination of elegance and feigned virtue. The preciosity of Claudia here in this elegiac poem keeps doubts about her chastity teasingly in play.

Livy's account of the coming of the Magna Mater to Rome prioritizes the role of Scipio Nasica, who is chosen by the senate to receive the goddess from the ship. Claudia Quinta is merely one of his matronly entourage who receive the goddess on land, a devout act that alone rehabilitated her reputation.[61] Her story in the *Fasti*, by contrast, is vividly dramatic. The ship is grounded in the mouth of the Tiber but Claudia alone frees it with the 'slightest tug'

---

[57] On the common use of this figure of repetition in Ovid's poetry see Wills (1996) 310–25.

[58] Barchiesi (1997a) 196.

[59] On the relationship to Propertius 1.2.1 see Barchiesi (1997a) 197.

[60] Ovid, *Fast.* 4.305 claims the descent of Claudia Quinta from the Sabine Clausus (cf. *Aen.* 7.706–9). On Livia's genealogical link to Claudia Quinta see Littlewood (1981) 384–5; such a connection may be too early for Ovid's *Fasti*.

[61] Livy 29.14.12.

(*exiguo … conamine*, 325), thanks to divinely granted strength. Erato comments on this miracle with the droll aside that the dramatic stage proves its truth, *mira, sed et scaena testificata loquar* ('I shall speak of miracles, but they are attested by the stage').[62] The reference to the stage makes elegant acknowledgment of the fact that the Megalensia was one of the great dramatic festivals of Rome, and, indeed, the first of the year.[63] The story of Claudia Quinta probably formed one of the historical dramas, *praetextae*, that were commonly performed on such occasions, and that formed an important source for Ovid's *Fasti*.[64] By providing a miracle drama that focuses on chastity, Erato reflects an important social and political issue of the Augustan age. But the dramatic stage was particularly the site of verbal and sexual licence.[65] At the authenticating moment of Claudia Quinta's chastity, Erato draws attention to its dubious and texualized provenance. Indeed, Erato's discussion of the Magna Mater is characterized by a number of dramatic asides that draw attention to the fictionality of the stories she tells.[66]

The discussion of the Magna Mater is preceded by the star sign of the Pleiades and an explanation of why only six out of these seven stars are regularly seen (165–78). The juxtaposition is a significant one. For this brief mythological excursus allows the poet to provide an unconventional transvaluation of chastity. Six of the sisters slept with gods; the seventh, the only one to marry, is, according to the first of two alternatives offered, obscured by the shame of such a lowly act (175–6):

> Septima mortali Merope tibi, Sisyphe, nupsit;
> paenitet, et facti sola pudore latet.

The seventh of the Pleiades married you, Sisyphus, a mortal man; she is sorry she did, and she alone hides out of shame for her deed.

Pudor is surprisingly redefined here as the shame that attends marriage. The Pleiades provide a contrapuntal perspective upon chastity, which is shown to be a contingent, not an absolute value, one subject to ideological appropriation. We are thus prepared, in a sense, for Erato's nuanced approach, with her shifts between moral disapproval and urbanity as she responds both to the elegiac poet's request and to the Magna Mater's command.

Strangely, the Muses, who are rarely summoned in the *Fasti*, are here invoked to account for a cult that was documented in historical records. Their elevated invocation at line 193, *pandite, mandati memores, Heliconis alumnae* ('reveal, mindful of your command, graduates of Helicon'),

---

[62] For an allegorical reading of the miracle see Staples (1998) 119; the vindicated chastity of Claudia Quinta neutralized the ritual danger imposed by the arrival of the Magna Mater.
[63] Barchiesi (1997a) 196.   [64] Wiseman (1979) 94–9 and (1998) 22–51.
[65] See *Fast.* 3.535–8.   [66] Barchiesi (1997a) 194–7. See also *Fast.* 4.203–4; 267.

corresponds to the invocation that prefaces the arrival of Aesculapius in Rome at the end of the *Metamorphoses: pandite nunc, Musae, praesentia numina uatum* ('reveal now, Muses, divinities who watch over poets', *Met.* 15.622).[67] Similar forms of address ironically introduce the arrival of foreign deities to Rome within historical time.[68] Yet whereas the epic Muses belong to the poets, in the *Fasti* the Muses are subject to the deity's command (*mandati memores*, 193). The Muses of the *Fasti* emblematize the greater constraints placed upon the speech of many of the narrators of the *Fasti*. In imperial Rome, even well documented history, it seems, must be carefully presented under the supervision of higher authorities.

Yet, though 'mindful of the goddess' command', Erato has an uncertain memory. Despite the existence of written records, she does not know who founded or first restored the temple of Magna Mater. She knows only that the temple once bore the name of Metellus and has now been restored by Augustus – *Augustus nunc est, ante Metellus erat* (348) – an unhelpful statement, since there were at least four possible Metelli who could claim to be the first restorer of the temple at the end of the second century BC.[69] There is, moreover, no final glorification of the Augustan restoration.[70] Rather, the alternation of *nunc* and *ante* suggests a fluidity in temporal relations – a sort of 'here today and gone tomorrow' mentality that marks the instability of memory.[71] Indeed, these concluding lines to the story of the coming of Magna Mater to Rome, the great moment of cultural authentication for the divinity of the Augustan *gens*, are marked with uncertainty. Erato dramatizes and problematizes the search for origins and the status of authority. She is an appropriate, divided Muse for Ovid's poem of the late Augustan age.

Yet even as Ovid plays with didactic authority in the *Fasti*, he promotes his literary authority as the pioneer of a new kind of elegiac poetry. The episode of the Magna Mater draws attention to the textualization of her history; the patriotic story of her accommodation to Roman and particularly Augustan social values is told through the lens of a capacious literary history whose works and writers have provided Ovid with different perspectives upon the Magna Mater to refashion and contest: Lucretius, Callimachus, Catullus, Virgil, Livy, and the historical dramas of the festival stage. The poem's dialogue with these authors makes the reader aware of the importance of literature as a means of keeping open the discourse about what constitutes 'truth' and how and by whom it is constructed. In conclusion, I

---

[67] Cf. *Aen.* 7.641.   [68] See Barchiesi (1991) 5.   [69] Fantham (1998) 161.
[70] On the fire of AD 3 that destroyed the temple see Val. Max. 1.8.11; Tac. *Ann.* 4.64; Littlewood (1981) 382–5.
[71] The following day in the calendar likewise asserts the instability of memory with its notification of the temple of Publica Fortuna. But which temple, of three possible candidates, is not made clear. See Fantham (1998) 164–5.

wish to look at the way in which the *Fasti* inserts itself self-consciously into Roman *literary* as well as national history, a history traditionally conceived through epic and historical writings as patriotic and celebratory. In Book 4, the discussion of the Magna Mater participates in a rewriting of literary history in which elegy and drama contribute provocatively to a new shaping of national consciousness.[72]

Journeys and endings

Politically, the journey of the Magna Mater to Rome was enormously symbolic.[73] East and West were linked in the appropriation of a foreign goddess. In the Augustan age her journey too could be seen to authenticate the emperor's supreme position in Rome and his claim to divine descent and protection.

In the *Fasti*, however, the journey of the Magna Mater is represented as a journey through Rome's literary as well as national history. Specifically, the goddess retraces the voyage of Virgil's Aeneas.[74] She heads from Troy (277–86) past Crete (285), round Sicily (286–7), and up past Sardinia (289) to the mouth of the Tiber (291).

Yet included prominently in this Virgilian journey are places with self-referential and elegiac resonance. The first identified site is the Hellespont, *longaque Phrixeae stagna sororis* ('the long straits of Phrixus' sister,' 277–8), named here specifically after the sister of Phrixus, whose story is told in Book 3 of the *Fasti*, 853–76. Similarly, when Erato summarizes the myth of Daedalus and Icarus (283–4),

> transit et Icarium, lapsas ubi perdidit alas
> Icarus et uastae nomina fecit aquae.

> she crosses the Icarian Sea too, where Icarus lost his wings that slipped off his arms and gave his name to the vast sea,

we are reminded of Ovid's versions of this myth in the *Ars amatoria* (2.21–96) and the *Metamorphoses* (8.183–235), both of which end with Icarus' naming of the sea. The Troad too is not only the Troad of *Virgil's Aeneid*; it is also the Troad of Catullus, Ovid's predecessor in elegiac experimentation, who lost his brother there. Erato's *Rhoeteum rapax* ('rapacious Rhoeteum,' 279)

---

[72] As Hinds (1998) 132 has argued, 'every allusion made by a poet . . . mobilises its own ad hoc literary historical narrative.'

[73] See Gruen (1990) 33: 'Romans adopted the myth of Trojan origins rather than other reconstructions of their past, for through that myth they could do more than link themselves to Hellas – they could differentiate themselves from her.'

[74] See Bömer (1958) 232–4.

sums up Catullus' line about his brother in poem 65.8, *Troia Rhoeteo quem subter litore tellus | ereptum nostris obterit ex oculis* ('snatched from our eyes below the Rhoetean shore and crushed under Trojan soil'). And Catullus 65, moreover, is a work that demonstrates its awareness of literary genealogy.[75]

The Magna Mater then journeys through places made famous by Rome's poets, not only Virgil, but also, particularly, Catullus and Ovid. Here Ovid offers a new perspective upon the great patriotic journey of the Magna Mater by employing it, I suggest, as a trope for literary history as seen from the complex perspective of an elegiac Muse writing on national themes. The journey rests upon a new literary genealogy for Rome in which elegiac as well as patriotic values are fundamental. This is a landscape of personal loss, of human affection and grief, as well as one of nationalistic endeavour. Significantly, in his opening praise of Venus in *Fasti* 4, Ovid makes the imperialistic assertion that the first poetry was love elegy, not epic or nationalistic discourse (109–10): *primus amans carmen uigilatum nocte negata | dicitur ad clausas concinuisse fores* ('the lover is said to be the first to have sung to closed doors poetry composed in the wakeful hours of the night denied to him').[76] Ovid thus constructs a new literary-historical genealogy for Rome in which elegy plays a foundational role.

In particular, as Muse in charge of memory (however unstable) and love, Erato performs the important task of demonstrating one form of 'truth', the important place that Ovid holds within the literary-historical genealogy he constructs for himself in the *Fasti*. In the journey of the Magna Mater there is for once no uncertainty about names or origins. Indeed, our attention is drawn to the power of poetry to memorialize. Icarus' fall gave the sea his name; but it is from Ovid's texts that we know of this fall.

Curiously, by appearing towards the start of the second half of the extant poem, Erato occupies the same middle position in the *Fasti* as she does in Apollonius' *Argonautica* and Virgil's *Aeneid*, where she begins Books 3 and 7 respectively.[77] The link with earlier literature marks the creative tension embodied in Ovid's Erato who, at a very Augustan moment in the *Fasti*, advertises her erotic as well as her patriotic affiliations.[78] Moreover, her positioning here in Book 4 of a six-book poem provides evidence of a possibly more deliberate structure to the *Fasti* than has often been thought.

In the textualized journey of the *Fasti* the Magna Mater reaches Rome and her home on the Palatine hill, next to Augustus. Book 4 of the *Fasti* ends with Augustus triumphantly esconced on the Palatine with Apollo and

---

[75] Hunter (1993b).   [76] Barchiesi (1997a) 58–9.
[77] Ap. Rhod. *Argon.* 3.2; Virg. *Aen.* 7.37.   [78] Hunter (1993a) 180–1.

Vesta (951–4). But the poet's own journey through the Roman year ends before it reaches Augustus' months of July and August, thereby resisting, perhaps, the nationalistic teleology, the dominance of Augustus' construction of Roman history and time.

In this poem of questions, the presence of Erato in the middle of the poem presents perhaps the most tantalizing question of all: is the poem's fragmentary state part of a formal design? Whatever we may be inclined to argue on this point, the poem's apparent incompletion serves one of its goals – to maintain openness to divergent readings. In the dynamic interplay among varying perspectives within the *Fasti*, Ovid's national poem offers its own version of Roman identity and time based on cultural pluralism and open debate. And the existence today of different critical responses to Ovid's poem undoubtedly points to the remarkable textual openness of his *Fasti*.

FURTHER READING

Commentaries: Frazer (1929); Bömer (1957–8); Fantham (1998) on Book 4.

Review articles: Miller (1992a) and Fantham (1995).

Literary studies: for the traditional view that the *Fasti* is little more than a versified almanac see Fränkel (1945). The seminal article by Ralph Johnson (1979), occurring one year after a new Teubner text of the *Fasti*, edited by Alton, Courtney, and Wormell (1978), sparked a serious reconsideration of the *Fasti* in literary studies. The new papyrological evidence for Callimachus' *Aitia* also made possible a greater understanding of its influence on the *Fasti*. See Miller (1980, 1982, 1983, 1992b). Miller (1991) has shown the considerable extent to which Ovid's earlier elegiac poetry also informs his treatment of Roman religion and cult in the *Fasti*. By examining the myth of Proserpina in Book 4 of the *Fasti* Hinds (1987) goes beyond Heinze's (1919) argument that the *Fasti* is a paradigmatic elegiac text; rather, the poem represents a bold, creative experimentation with generic convention.

Politics: McKeown (1984) denied that the poem had a political dimension. Critics have subsequently disagreed with his argument. Feeney (1992) points out that the poem's title advertises its intimate concern with the limits placed upon speech in the later Augustan period. Hinds (1992), examining the political implication of generic play in the *Fasti*, relates it directly to the subtle undermining of Augustan myths and icons. For Newlands (1995), the poem's inconcinnities and playfulness represent a form of resistance to Augustus' appropriation of Roman culture. Barchiesi (1997a) argues that the *Fasti* constructs its own Augustan world, eluding the emperor's social control through its witty and often irreverent versions of Roman myth and history. Herbert-Brown (1994) provides an important voice of critical dissent. She argues that the *Fasti* is laudatory in intent, a key text nonetheless for understanding the development of ruler cult and the dynastic politics of the late Augustan period.

The Roman calendar: Michels (1967) provides thorough information on the form and function of the Republican calendar; Scullard (1981) describes the festivals of the Roman year. Beard (1987) demonstrates the calendar's importance for the construction of Roman identity and thus draws attention to the social and political significance of Ovid's poem. Wallace-Hadrill (1987), investigating the political function of the Julian calendar and the changes made by Augustus, argues that Ovid's poetic version could not incorporate Augustus into a system of Hellenized values so at variance with the emperor's ideas of nationhood. Gee (1997 and 2000) deals with astronomy and argues that the *Fasti* engages closely with Greek scientific and Stoic interpretive traditions; at the same time Roman political power and the stars are closely connected.

Roman religion and the *Fasti*: the value of the *Fasti* as a source for Roman religion and history has frequently been debated. Feeney (1998) has argued that the *Fasti* is important for understanding Roman religious mentality. Wiseman (1998) has drawn attention to the value of the *Fasti* as a source for Roman dramas and mimes originally performed at religious festivals.

13

DUNCAN F. KENNEDY

Epistolarity: the *Heroides*

In Book 3 of his *Ars amatoria*, Ovid rounds off a survey of authors put forward as suitable reading for the would-be female lover with a characteristic claim that his works will bring him immortality. Perhaps, he surmises, his name will be ranked with those of Sappho, Propertius or Virgil; perhaps 'somebody will say: "read the cultured poems of our maestro, in which he draws up the battle-lines of the sexes"' – the *Ars amatoria* itself – '"or the *Amores*, or recite a *Letter* in an assumed voice; this type of work, unknown to others, he pioneered"' (*uel tibi composita cantetur EPISTVLA uoce; | ignotum hoc aliis ille nouauit opus*, 3.345–6). The nature of Ovid's claim for this last work – universally agreed to be what we have grown accustomed to call the *Heroides* – continues to generate considerable scholarly debate.[1] It is unlikely that the poet who was to go on to write the *Metamorphoses* would seek to claim that the emergence of any form – still less the invention of a literary one – takes place *ex nihilo*. The epistle of Penelope to Ulysses, which stands first in the collection of fifteen as we currently have it and may have been put in first place by Ovid himself as a programmatic gesture,[2] is itself a transformation of Homer's *Odyssey*, and the lament voiced by a heroine abandoned by her lover had had a long history in various generic manifestations in Greek and Latin literature, notably Euripidean tragedy and Alexandrianizing epic. Nor need we assume that the poet whose grandest theme was to be continuity in change would

---

[1] Classical scholars in particular have long wondered whether Ovid was already familiar with the third poem of Propertius' fourth book of elegies, in which a seemingly contemporary Roman woman (given, in accordance with the prevailing convention of erotic poetry, the Grecizing name 'Arethusa') writes a love-letter to her absent soldier husband 'Lycotas'. The precise literary chronology of this period is likely to remain uncertain, and if Ovid did know the fourth book of Propertius (the latest datable reference in which is 16 BC), then he is also likely to have been aware of the publication three years earlier of the first Book of Horace's *Epistles* – profound explorations in verse of the potential of epistolary form (see de Pretis (1999)), though scarcely ever mentioned in this context, perhaps because they are not love letters and are resolutely 'masculine' in ethos.

[2] See Hinds (1985) 28.

expect that the literary type to which he gave its initial form, as the epistolary lament of a heroine separated from her lover, would remain unaltered in its subsequent manifestations. The so-called 'single epistles' give rise in time to the 'double epistles' in which heroes and heroines exchange letters – Paris and Helen (*Her.* 16 & 17), Leander and Hero (*Her.* 18 & 19), and Acontius and Cydippe (*Her.* 20 & 21). Persistent scholarly doubts about the Ovidian authorship of some of the single[3] (and sometimes also the double)[4] epistles point to an assumption that Ovid had immediate imitators, a belief encouraged by Ovid's own statement (*Am.* 2.18.27–8) that his friend Sabinus penned replies from their menfolk to his own heroine's epistles.[5] The epistle of Sappho (*Her.* 15) does not come down to us in the same manuscript transmission as the rest of the single epistles,[6] and many scholars assume either that it is not the epistle Ovid refers to in *Amores* 2.18.26 and 34, or that these references are themselves interpolations. The dynamism of this tradition suggests that we might look for its subsequent manifestations not simply in the vogue for translations of the *Heroides* into the vernacular from the Middle Ages onwards (e.g. that of Planudes into Byzantine Greek in the thirteenth century, or the *Bursario o las Epístolas de Ovidio* of Juan Rodríguez in the mid-fifteenth, the first complete translation of all the single and double epistles),[7] or for close imitations of its verse epistle form and heroine authors, often adapted to non-classical subjects (e.g. Drayton's *England's Heroicall Epistles* or Pope's *Eloisa to Abelard*).[8] The tradition of 'female complaint',[9] the Spanish *novela sentimental* of the fifteenth century[10] and the epistolary novel, especially in the eighteenth century,[11] have long been acknowledged to carry Ovid's stamp.

Seen in the light of developments that he could not have known, Ovid's claims for the *Heroides* do not seem fantastic or immodest. Although the would-be female lover in the *Ars amatoria* is instructed to *sing* these poems, and so practise the role of the lover lamenting her abandonment with her voice adjusted to the part she is to play (*composita . . . uoce*),[12] Ovid refers to them specifically in terms of their form, *epistula*. The reference in the

---

[3] For a brief discussion see Knox (1995) 5–14.
[4] For a brief discussion see Kenney (1996) 20–6
[5] The letters of Sabinus that are printed in Renaissance editions of Ovid were penned by Angelo Sabino.
[6] It was first placed in its present position as the last of the single epistles in the edition of Daniel Heinsius (1629); see R. J. Tarrant in Reynolds (1983) 272.
[7] Rodríguez excludes the epistle of Sappho, which he may not have known, but added three that he himself composed, and by default attributes them to Ovid (see Brownlee (1990) 39). Literary imposture is written into epistolary heroinism from the start.
[8] See Dörrie (1968).   [9] See Kerrigan (1991).   [10] See Brownlee (1990).
[11] See e.g. Day (1966), Mylne (1981).
[12] For this sense of *composita* see Fränkel (1945) 190 n.1.

previous couplet to the title of his earlier work, the *Amores*, makes at least plausible the suggestion that he gave these poems to the world not as the *Heroides* but as the *Epistulae heroidum*. For much of the nineteenth and twentieth centuries (a period in any case marked by a dramatic decline in the critical fortunes of Ovid,[13] not least in contrast with the eighteenth),[14] Ovidian scholarship was prone to downplay the epistolary form. In his introduction to Arthur Palmer's commentary of 1898, Louis Claude Purser asserts: 'The Epistles are *really* soliloquies, the epistolary setting being little more than a mere form which gives an apparent reason for these soliloquies being committed to writing at all', fretting that 'it is a poor kind of facetiousness to make merry over the epistolary setting' and 'shallow wit to object to Ariadne's letter to Theseus because there was no regular postal service between Naxos and Athens'.[15] In 1955, L. P. Wilkinson writes that '[t]he choice of epistolary form for what are *really* tragic soliloquies was not entirely happy.'[16] It was common practice to treat the poems as '*suasoriae* in verse', the *suasoria* being the rhetorical school exercise (at which Ovid is said to have excelled) advising a particular mythological or historical character to pursue a particular course of action. Although this remains of relevance to many accounts of the immediate literary context of the poems,[17] it helped to underpin a negative view of the *Heroides* as repetitive exercises on a single theme. As late as the 1960s and 1970s, critics who saw themselves as generally sympathetic to Ovid could still speak of 'the wearisome complaint of the reft maiden, the monotonous reiteration of her woes'.[18] The commonplace of monotony was sometimes reinforced by approving echoes of Dryden's complaint about 'wit out of season' in the preface to his translation of 1680. Howard Jacobson put it thus: 'The wit and humour that are now and then present in the *Heroides* degenerate at times into little else than cleverness, sometimes rather ludicrous cleverness.'[19] Much though Jacobson wants to like and admire the *Heroides*, his book is pervaded by a profound sense of disappointment.

Retrospectively from the present, an antipathy to rhetoric together with an insensitivity to discursive difference (characteristic, perhaps, of a realist epistemology which largely failed to accommodate the works of Ovid in a positive manner), and a determinedly masculine condescension pervade this lengthy episode in the poems' reception, which, as we begin to leave it behind, seems ever more strikingly an aberration from the largely enthusiastic reception the poems met with in earlier times. The dramatic reversal in critical estimates of the *Heroides* in the past generation or so arises not

---

[13] See Vance (1988). [14] See Trickett (1988). [15] Palmer (1898) xi; emphasis mine.
[16] Wilkinson (1955) 86; emphasis mine. [17] See Schiesaro in this volume, pp. 71–2.
[18] Otis (1970) 17. [19] Jacobson (1974) 8.

simply from a closer attention to epistolary form,[20] but also a heightened awareness of, and investment in, the distinctive aspects of letter-writing as a discursive mode, as a model of communication and as a subject-position. Derrida's *La Carte postale*[21] itself cast in an epistolary form as a series of postcards addressed to his unnamed lover, draws attention to the way that letter-writing can suggest a mode, epistolarity, not reducible to formal elements of style or generic category: 'the letter, the epistle . . . is not a genre but all genres, literature itself' (*'la lettre, l'épître . . . n'est pas un genre mais tous les genres, la littérature même'*).[22] This can serve to remind us that in English ('letters'), as in Latin (*litterae*), the same term can embrace epistles and writing more generally, and that epistolarity as an analytical term can be applied not only to works that formally identify themselves as letters (such as the *Heroides* or the *Epistulae ex Ponto*) but also to those (such as the *Tristia*) which have some of the characteristics of letters (e.g. separation of writer and addressee) or are concerned to explore issues of communication more generally. Derrida's own use of epistolary form highlights the performative aspects of language in an effort to deconstruct received distinctions between amatory and scholarly discourse, between criticism and creation, and to question the conventional relegation of love letters to the margins of discourse (thereby interrogating marginalization from the margins in the role of one marginalized).[23] The capacity of epistolarity to render generic categories permeable diachronically as well as synchronically has facilitated the tracing of fresh literary genealogies back to Ovid of the kind that Linda Kaufmann, for example, proposes for works such as Vladimir Nabokov's *Lolita* (1955), Roland Barthes' *Fragments d'un discours amoureux* (1977) or Margaret Atwood's *The Handmaid's Tale* (1986). The latter, she writes, 'has been compared thematically to *The Scarlet Letter* and to "fearsome future" novels like *1984*, but its epistolary origins can be traced to the *Heroides*, for like Ovid's heroines Offred narrates from exile, a ceaseless reiteration of her desire and despair.'[24] There is a useful corrective here: 'reiteration' rather than 'repetition' offers an invitation, not a disincentive, to view the *Heroides* collectively, even syntactically. What a more hostile tradition of reception tropes as 'monotony' may be alternatively construed as an important and lasting feature of Ovid's innovation, a poetics of 'writing in isolation' which has at its heart a cry, destined to be repeated, demanding (but not confident of receiving) an *adequate* response.

In considering further the 'epistolarity' of the *Heroides*, we might organize our thoughts around the question: what is their destination? At one level, the question has a deceptively straightforward answer: their addressees.

[20] See Kirfel (1969).   [21] Derrida (1980).   [22] Derrida (1980) 48.
[23] See Kaufmann (1992) 96–7.   [24] Kaufmann (1992) 223.

Penelope writes to Ulysses (though she protests that she does not know where he is); Ariadne writes to Theseus (though she is alone on a desert island with no means of conveying her letter to him) and so on. The writers turn to written missives to overcome a separation from their addressees which the letter attempts, with greater or lesser success, to bridge. As Terry Castle puts it, 'the letter symbolizes and reifies communication while it does not necessarily embody it'.[25] Some are physically separated from their addressees by forces outside their control, such as war or its attendant politics (Penelope (1); Briseis (3); Hermione (8); Laudamia (13)), whilst others have been, or consider themselves, abandoned (Phyllis (2); Dido (7); Deianira (9); Ariadne (10); Medea (12)). Others still may be physically close to the objects of their love but 'separated' from them by social convention (Phaedra (4)), or by the consequences of its transgression (Canace (11)). Paris actually writes to Helen while staying with her in the palace of her husband Menelaus at Sparta (16). It emerges from his letter that his previous attempts to seduce her in person have been rebuffed, and so he resorts to writing to her.

However, the addressee is not only spatially, but temporally absent. Penelope does not know where Ulysses is; she writes a letter to give to every passing sailor who visits Ithaca in the hope that he will be able to give it to Ulysses (*Her*.1.59–62). The implication of her words is that she does not know *when* Ulysses will read it.[26] The letters reflect an awareness of that absence whilst simultaneously working to eliminate it: this is what Janet Gurkin Altman refers to as the 'bridge/barrier' function of a letter.[27] Epistolary discourse must manipulate both space and time in order to overcome these barriers so as to make communication relevant rather than anachronistic at the moment when the letter is read. Paris, as it transpires from Helen's reply (*Her*. 17), succeeds; but we may surmise that many of the authors of the single epistles, at least in so far as their formal addressees are concerned, fail.

However, the destination of the letters cannot simply be reduced to the addressee formally identified. Gareth Williams has recently argued that the relationship of daughter and mother looms larger in Hermione's letter to Orestes (*Her*. 8) than that of husband and wife, with the result that 'the complexities of her tangled relationship with Helen make for a psychological drama in which Orestes (*qua* addressee) is a relatively peripheral player'.[28] Similarly, the destination of Hypsipyle's letter to Jason (*Her*. 6) is as much

[25] Castle (1982) 43.
[26] The particular letter that *we* read as *Heroides* 1 seems to be written to be given to a 'stranger' who is Ulysses returned to Ithaca in disguise; see Kennedy (1984).
[27] Altman (1982).
[28] Williams (1997) 130; see also his analysis of the relationship of Canace and her father Aeolus (*Her*. 11), again not the addressee of her letter: Williams (1992).

his current object of desire, Medea, with whom Hypsipyle is so obsessed that she comes to take on her characteristics and even her identity. Fantasizing revenge for the wrongs she feels, she exclaims: 'I would have drenched my face with the blood of your mistress, and your face, which she took away from me with her poisons. I would be Medea to Medea!' (*Medeae Medea forem*, 6.149–51). These letters have an *intended* destination, but the moment and circumstances of their arrival can be, in epistolary terms, no less important than the moment they are written (or sent), and this is not necessarily in the writer's control, and can have effects that the writer neither foresees nor would desire.[29]

The figure of the addressee/reader is thus a complex one, and the circulation of their letter can be wider than their writers intend, or wish, or imagine (this can be a source of anxiety: the writer of the letter ever has to contemplate the consequences of its publication). But there is another level at which these considerations hold. These are not only the heroines' letters: they are Ovid's *Heroides*, and at that level their destination is the reader who feels addressed by these poems, whether that be a contemporary of Ovid's, Dryden translating the *Heroides* in the seventeenth century or readers at the start of the twenty-first century – and beyond, for the relationship so established, as we shall see, is not wholly determined or foreclosed. Ovid, like Penelope, could not know what the circumstances would be in which his various letters would be read. As we have seen, at this level the *Heroides* have 'failed' as well as 'succeeded' as acts of communication: some readers have felt that these writings do not (in the classic trope of 'presence') 'speak' to them, or at least not in particular ways that matter to them: in so far as the barrier has not been bridged and readers do not feel that the poems 'address' them and their present concerns, they tend to resort to a historicizing mode of trying to (re-)construct what the writer *must have* intended. The barriers not bridged become those that serve to distinguish 'past' and 'present' in any mode of reception.[30] We need to keep these two levels of authorship, and their interaction, in mind in what follows. *Mutatis mutandis*, what is said of the heroine or hero and their readers can be interestingly predicated of Ovid and his, and vice versa.

The need or impulse to write a letter is the product of particular circumstances which the letter often explicitly acknowledges.[31] Letters thus involve writing 'to the moment,'[32] and this can serve to associate them with spontaneity, sincerity and authenticity of emotion, an aspect often admired

---

[29] See e.g. Kennedy (1984), Williams (1992).

[30] In this way also, 'la lettre, l'épître . . . n'est pas un genre mais tous les genres, la littérature même' (Derrida (1980) 48).

[31] For further implications of this see Kennedy (1984), esp. 413–16.

[32] The phrase comes from Samuel Richardson's introduction to his epistolary novel *Clarissa*.

by readers of works in the tradition of epistolary heroinism and often seen also as discursively feminine.[33] There is a continuing critical debate about whether this is to be accepted at face value in the case of the *Heroides*. The positive case has been argued most recently, against the critical commonplace that the 'rhetorical' nature of the letters marks them as insincere, by Joseph Farrell. The heroines, he says, 'no matter how rhetorically they express themselves, and even when they do not know it, are to be generally understood as speaking fom the heart.'[34] The exception, he says, is Phaedra (*Her.* 4), whose purpose is to deceive the object of her desire. However, sincerity is judged not solely in terms of the feelings or the intention of the moment, but, as Farrell's own parenthesis 'even when they do not know it' implies, in the light of subsequent events. Many of the heroines are, they have come to realize, the victims of deception, and, as writers, can be assumed to have a heightened sensitivity to rhetoric – not least the rhetoric of sincerity and deception – as a result. Writing to the moment can (even in the case of Phaedra) involve speaking from the heart, but the epistle is ever caught up in the logic of its temporality, as it attempts to bridge the 'present' of writing and the 'future' of reading, and to elide that tense distinction. Writing to the moment, and uncertain of the outcome of their situation or the response to their missives – however strong their desire for a particular response or outcome – the heroines (and heroes) fantasize events turning out as they choose and imagine responses, both to the reception of their letters and to acts they imagine: the addressee is, as Roland Barthes suggests, absent in a physical but present in an allocutory sense,[35] so that the anticipated reading is written into the text. As Janet Gurkin Altman says, in no other genre do readers 'figure so prominently within the world of the narrative and in the generation of the text'.[36] The writer's perception of her addressee and of his anticipated response therefore shapes her discourse and the way in which she constructs her identity, and her most fervent wish is that desired and actual responses will 'correspond', that no *unwelcome* distinction will be perceived between the 'present' of reading and the 'past' of writing. The writers of the single epistles are generally more concerned with reunion than reply; Penelope's opening sentiments ('but don't write anything back to me; come yourself!', *Her.* 1.2) are programmatic for this collection.[37] For the writers of the double epistles, however, the situation is more complex, for a favourable response may fulfil their more immediate desire by presaging the physical union they ultimately crave. As Paris writes (collapsing the temporal

---

[33] See Kaufmann (1992) 105.   [34] Farrell (1998) 318.
[35] Barthes (1979) 15.   [36] Altman (1982) 37.
[37] Contrast the final couplet of Sappho's letter (and of the modern collection of single epistles), which specifically asks for a reply (*Her.* 15.219–20).

barrier which separates the moment of inscription from the moment of reading), the fact that Helen *has* received his letter gives him hope that he might be likewise received (*Her.* 16.13–14). Helen's first response, she reports, was to treat his letter as tantamount to physical violation (*Her.* 17.1–4). Leander pictures himself *as* his letter, arriving at its intended destination, in the hands of his beloved, whose imagined response is all he could wish for. As it strives to achieve immediate presence, and the effacement of its materiality as text or sign, his letter is driven back on that materiality as a surrogate, even a fetishized substitute, for presence, as Leander imagines it kissed, fondled and subjected to even more passionate signs of physical love (*Her.* 18.15–18). The body's fluids become the most potent trope of presence, and blots, whether made by tears (*Her.* 3.3) or blood (*Her.* 11.1–2), are felt to carry a meaning that the letters they efface cannot aspire to. The epistles seek to make textual a surrogate for sexual intercourse, but in troping text as sex, physical absence loops back to emphasize a palpable sense of the potential gap between signifier and signified, fantasy and reality, the desired and actual response to the text.

In the case of the *Heroides*, as we have seen, another reader is always at hand, the reader of Ovid's poems (often referred to as the 'external' reader), who imposes a further perspective beyond that of the heroines and heroes or their formal addressee, and often finds in their words a fuller significance than they are in a position to grasp when they write them. The time of reading is thus crucial to the perceived meaning of the text. Thus Oenone reminds Paris that he had carved this epigram on a poplar tree as an earnest of his everlasting love (*Heroides* 5.29–30):

> cum Paris Oenone poterit spirare relicta,
> ad fontem Xanthi uersa recurret aqua.

> When Paris shall be able to leave Oenone and still draw breath, the waters of the river Xanthus will turn and run back to their source.

What for Paris as he wrote is a trope of impossibility (*adynaton*) and, for Oenone at the moment when she reports it, a token of his insincerity and betrayal, is, for the 'external' reader at a much later stage, an ironic fore-shadowing, since, by abandoning Oenone for Helen, Paris sets in motion the events of the Trojan war, which will include the incident narrated in *Iliad* 21 when Achilles slaughters so many Trojans that their bodies block the channel of the Xanthus. What the external reader will experience as 'foreshadowing' will not be so for the writers, who, however, if they look forward from their present in the belief or dread that the event they refer to will happen, may see it as an omen (*Her.* 13.135) or a dream (*Her.* 19.195–204), or express it as a prophecy (*Her.* 17.237–40) or a threat (*Her.* 12.207–8).

This raises issues of temporality and intertextuality, for the external reader's knowledge comes from what are often termed Ovid's 'source' texts – Homer, Euripides, Callimachus, Virgil and so on. The heroes and heroines who write these letters are not simply 'mythological' or 'legendary' but 'literary': many of the letters have an obvious specific canonical text or texts with which they correspond in both dramatic and verbal detail, and it is possible that, had more ancient literature survived, all would be seen to enjoy such a relationship. The heroines' stories, when we come to read their letters, are, in this sense, already written, and in versions more or less canonized in the literary tradition. The epistolary form freezes them at a moment *within* the story, foreseeing or desiring a particular 'end' to their stories, which may or may not approximate to the 'end', the outcome or consequences, with which the external reader is familiar. The writers experience, we may say, the circumstances of their stories at the moment when they write as open and contingent, whereas the external reader, in a privileged position beyond the end, sees them as working out a sequence of events already determined, and so as facilitating or struggling against their destiny – against the destination, that is, to which, at the end of the story, the external reader feels it has been directed all along. The meaning, and effect, of their letters, however strongly willed by their writers, remains anxiously contingent upon events, and it is against this end that the external reader reads their desire as 'fantasy'. When the end anticipated by the writer does not correspond to the end assumed by the external reader, the result is a sense of irony, tragic or humorous as the case may be. The 'source' texts we assume in and for our intertextual reading serve to determine the ironies we experience in the letters. So, if we assume Virgil's *Aeneid*, as well as the Homeric poems, as an intertext for the letter of Helen, the end, the outcome or consequences, against which the external reader assesses Helen's forebodings should she elope with Paris to Troy acquire all the more ironic resonances (*Her.*17.245): *nec dubito quin, te si prosequar, arma parentur*, 'nor do I doubt that, were I to follow you, war would be prepared'. The external reader with Homer in mind could take *arma* ('war') here as the Trojan war, but with Virgil in mind could see the resonances of the word extending into the wanderings of Aeneas and beyond into Roman history – even to the composition of the *Aeneid* itself, of which *arma* is, of course, the first word and surrogate title. It is therefore the so-called 'source' text which both suggests to the external reader contingencies of meaning in the letters and provides a sense of closure on those perceived contingencies.

It is from the 'source' text that the external reader may feel confident of what 'really' happened, and in this way of reading it acts therefore as an authority, taken, maybe, even as the 'objective' account of events. But a consequence of this is to see the legendary author's perspective as not only 'subjective' but subject precisely to that authority. At this point gender issues and power relations tend to make themselves felt. This intertextuality has two temporal aspects, however, which relate to the two 'authors' of any of these epistles, the heroine/hero and Ovid. If we regard Ovid as the author, then the 'source' texts (Homer, Euripides, Virgil and so on) are temporally anterior to the epistle, which then echoes them. However, if we regard the heroine/hero as the author, then a chronology of authorship is established in which the legendary heroines and heroes have temporal priority: the so-called 'source' texts are 'forestalled' by the legendary authors of the *Heroides*, and it is Homer, Euripides or Virgil who 'echoes' *them*. There can be a subtle subversiveness to this procedure. The Dido of *Heroides* 7 contradicts Virgil, and does so, in terms of her 'authorial' chronology, 'before' Virgil writes.[38] Works such as the *Aeneid* from this perspective come to look like ('later') appropriations or recuperations of the legendary authors' words, and work either 'for' or 'against' what we then construe as the legendary authors' intentions and self-fashionings. The heroines, in particular, have a 'mythic' or prototypical quality to them (Penelope the faithful, Helen the adulterous wife, for example). Allowing them to write in their 'own' words, and, vitally, 'to the moment', gives them the opportunity to subvert the timeless abstractions they have become. The *Heroides* work to unravel the phenomenology of myth itself, and the role in myth-formation of 'classic' texts. In *Heroides* 17.141–4, Helen protests that adultery is something new to her:[39]

> sum rudis ad Veneris furtum, nullaque fidelem –
> di mihi sunt testes – lusimus *arte* uirum.
> nunc quoque, quod tacito mando mea uerba libello,
> fungitur officio littera nostra nouo.

> I am not an expert in the theft of love, and – the gods are my witnesses – have never deceived my faithful husband with any intrigue. Even now, this very act of entrusting my words to a secret letter is a new kind of writing.[40]

The 'new kind of writing' of which Helen speaks concerns the deception of a *uir* and is characterized by the term *ars*. Helen's words, written to the moment, pinpoint the origin of a myth, that of Helen the prototype of the adulterous wife, a myth of which she is not aware, and would, as her oath suggests, disown if she were; but her words also provide a myth of origin,

---

[38] See Desmond (1993); also Tarrant in this volume, p. 25.
[39] I am grateful to Martin Brady for permission to summarize his exposition of this passage.
[40] For the translation I have adapted that of Kenney (1996) 137, ad loc.

and she does seem vaguely conscious and excited by it (intrigue is not only the subject but the tone of her words), for she presents herself as the author of a letter which adumbrates a fresh genre – one that was to issue forth in Ovid's own *Ars amatoria*. Similarly, when Paris carves an elegiac couplet on the poplar tree, we can see him as a proto-elegiac lover – his 'later' appearance in the *Iliad* serves to 'epicize' or 'heroize' (but also arguably to 'reduce'?) a figure fashioning himself as already elegiac – and also as a proto-elegiac *author*, devising the tropes which Ovid himself, as 'heir' to the elegiac tradition, was 'later' to take up, in defiance of the prevailing assumption of the priority, literary and historical, of epic.[41] Within this style of reading, concerns of literary genealogy and generic affiliation are thematized by the legendary authors of the *Heroides* themselves. The legendary authors can then be seen to be caught up in the politics of literary canon formation, with its attendant ideological pressures. But this temporal perspective can operate on a metaliterary level as well. Reading the literary canon 'forwards towards the present' rather than 'backwards from the present' works to reverse not only ideological hierarchies, but also literary ones. As with the waters of Xanthus, we can find, against our expectations, the flow of literary influence need not be one way, and, rather than talk of 'sources', we might think of meaning as not simply 'arising' out of one or other of the texts, as the river metaphor suggests, but as a result of a 'correspondence' between them, with all that that can imply at the epistolary level. This correspondence between texts, even as it emphasizes and manipulates the separation between texts, works to bridge that barrier, making the text of Homer 'present' in that of Ovid, of course, but also that of Ovid no less 'present' in Homer.

Each of these letters has, as we have seen, two notional authors, the legendary figure and Ovid, and one or the other tends to be privileged in any reading. Florence Verducci's otherwise timely defence of the humour of the *Heroides* ('The rule of Ovid's *Heroides* is the rule of indecorum, of wit in conception no less than in language, a wit which is not his heroine's own but the token of the poet's creative presence in the poem')[42] could be criticized as being at the expense of the heroine as writer. Similarly, the recent emphasis on the intertextuality of the *Heroides* has arguably focused attention on Ovid as manipulator of the literary tradition and seen him as ventriloquizing his literary concerns through the heroine or hero. A gender issue is often felt to be at stake here by those critical of these approaches: a concentration on the Ovidian voice muffles what is distinctive about the voice of the *heroine* in

---

[41] Barchiesi (1993) has several other analyses of this type; see also Barchiesi (1997a) 58–9 on elegy as (for Ovid) the original form of poetry.

[42] Verducci (1985) 32.

particular, relegating her and her concerns, authorial as well as erotic, once more to the margins. Attempts to recuperate that voice are currently under way,[43] a process complicated when two 'voices' are simultaneously inscribed in a text. In what sense is voice or authorship distinctively female (or male)? Because it comes from a woman? Can we treat the heroines as examples of *écriture féminine*? Or as ever exiled by patriarchy from a language that is not their own, like Briseis struggling to write Greek in her 'barbarian hand' (*Her.* 3.2)? But this runs the opposite risk of writing Ovid out of the letter entirely. In the *Ars amatoria*, as we have seen, Ovid (an interested party, to be sure) treats the reading of the *Heroides* as practice in role-playing, part of his pupil's acculturation of herself as a lover. If we may translate that into the terms of Roland Barthes,[44] the *Heroides* can thus be located as part of a lover's discourse in which its readers situate themselves as amatory subjects. This is not an exclusively female activity; the role-playing suggested to the female in Book 3 of the *Ars amatoria* is recommended no less to the would-be male lover in Book 1 (611–15). The heroines self-consciously model themselves on and identify with each other, when the circumstances of one are known to another, as in the cases of Hypsipyle and Medea or Phyllis and Ariadne. And, as we have seen, intertextualist readings can attribute a formative, even originary, role to the heroine in the development of amatory discourse. A Barthesian approach involves seeing Woman (and Man) as an effect of writing rather than an intrinsic essence, and gender therefore as situational. Biological sex does not wholly determine the roles one may play. As Barthes puts it:

> Historically, the discourse of absence is carried on by the Woman: Woman is sedentary, Man hunts, journeys; Woman is faithful (she waits), man is fickle (he sails away, he cruises). It is Woman who gives shape to absence, elaborates its fictions, for she has time to do so; she weaves and she sings; the Spinning Songs express both immobility (by the hum of the Wheel) and absence (far away, rhythms of travel, sea surges, cavalcades). It follows that in any man who utters the other's absence *something feminine* is declared: this man who waits and who suffers from his waiting is miraculously feminized. A man is not feminized because he is inverted but because he is in love. (Myth and utopia: the origins have belonged, the future will belong to the subjects *in whom there is something feminine*.)[45]

In an intertextually resonant moment, Barthes' comments evoke Penelope (the programmatic figure of Ovidian epistolary heroism, we may recall) to

---

[43] See Seeck (1975) who attempts to isolate the authorial 'I' of the letters; and Spentzou (forthcoming).

[44] On the issues raised by this see Kennedy (1993) 64–82.

[45] Barthes (1979) 13–14; emphasis Barthes'.

underpin *his* 'myth' of 'origins'. Although *A Lover's Discourse* is not formally composed as a series of letters, Barthes nonetheless plays with the epistolary mode because, in the words of Linda Kaufmann, 'from the *Heroides* to Héloise, from *Letters of a Portuguese Nun* to *Clarissa*, [the epistle] has traditionally been considered the feminine mode par excellence',[46] and this is a subject position and cultural mode the authorial 'I' of Barthes' treatise wishes to inhabit: 'The necessity for this book is to be found in the following consideration: that the lover's discourse is today *of an extreme solitude.*'[47] In this scheme, desire is associated with absence: 'But isn't desire always the same, whether the object is present or absent? Isn't the object *always* absent?'; 'Like desire, the love letter waits for an answer'.[48] It is from within such an interpretative paradigm that Patricia Rosenmeyer treats Ovid's choice of the letter form for the exile poems 'not only as an allusion to, but also an authorial statement of identification – on some level – with his earlier epistolary work, the *Heroides*. The *Heroides* may be read as letters from exile... in which Ovid pursues his fascination with the genre of letters and the subject of abandonment through literary characters; the *Tristia* take that fascination one step further as the author himself, in letters to loved ones, writes from the position of an abandoned hero of sorts.'[49] From this perspective, the heroines provide the tropes which the exiled Ovid inhabits, and the hierarchy of authorship so often attributed to the *Heroides* is reversed in the exile poems.

But if the 'authors' of the *Heroides*, the heroine and Ovid, are analytically separable in and for the agenda of any particular reading, they remain functionally intertwined: it is in their interplay, their correspondence even, that the *Heroides* achieve their distinctive form. When Briseis says at the beginning of her letter that it is written with difficulty in Greek by her barbarian hand, and the blots which Achilles will see are made by her tears (*Her.* 3.1–3), we may be conscious that we are reading a poem in Latin elegiac couplets, and in a clean and legible copy. Joseph Farrell has suggested that 'we must posit some intermediary – a translator, an interpreter, a *hermeneutes* – between the writer and ourselves.'[50] As Farrell observes, problems of translation become a basic constitutive generic element in the later tradition of epistolary heroinism (e.g. *Les Lettres portugaises* (1669), published in French, purport to be a translation from the Portuguese), and the implicit Ovidian editor is often replaced by an explicit one who presents the correspondence. He

---

[46] Kaufmann (1992) 103.
[47] Barthes (1979) 1; emphasis Barthes'. On abandonment as a specifically 'female' condition, see Lipking (1983) and (1988).
[48] Barthes (1979) 15, 158; emphasis Barthes'.   [49] Rosenmeyer (1997) 29.
[50] Farrell (1998) 335.

also notes how the Latin word for 'blot' (*litura*) can also signify 'erasure' or 'editorial correction'.[51] The Ovidian author becomes troped as reader, and a particular kind of reader: scholarly concerns such as translation, textual emendation and authenticity become thematized within the text, and Farrell looks to future work which will trace 'the web of ironies created by Ovid's anticipation of the hermeneutic processes to which his text would inevitably be subjected.'[52] Farrell wants to associate this kind of reading with Ovid himself, but if Ovid is seen as a scholar, what sort of scholar committed to what kind of hermeneutic processes? A textual critic emending the text, as Farrell suggests? A feminist revealing the forces of appropriation and recuperation to which 'his' heroines have been subjected? Where might this list end? Theoretically it will never end, since the process of interpretation will continue to be reconfigured. Practically it ends in the preferred style of interpretation of each reader in that reader's here-and-now.

So, when we consider the relationship of Ovid and *his* addressee, the reader or critic of his poetic epistles, Ovid takes on the discursive situation and role of the heroine. The indeterminacy of space and time which separates writer and addressee is every bit as pronounced as it is in the case of the legendary writers and their beloveds. We figure Ovid as writing at a particular moment, temporally frozen, intending, desiring or willing meanings for his epistles, attempting to anticipate or determine those meanings, seeking to gain an adequate response from his reader. However, the meaning of his text remains anxiously contingent upon the end which will determine it. But what is that end? What is it that provides closure on *these* contingencies of meaning? What governs our sense that the ends we attribute to Ovid are or, ironically, are not fulfilled? At the level of the heroines' correspondence, the closure was provided by what was termed (if problematically) the 'source' text. If we are to know what Ovid was 'trying to do', 'succeeded in doing' or 'failed to do', we similarly need to have a 'source' text of some kind or other which we assume gives us a 'true' or 'objective' account of things. At this level, the 'source' text is our take on reality, which may be embodied in a corpus of texts which are presented as authoritative (e.g. Barthes, Ovid's *Ars amatoria*), but which is otherwise more surreptitiously provided by the grid of our theoretical assumptions – those ideas, terms and models we deem to be objectively and transhistorically true about reading, interpretation, history, love and so on (and which guide our choice, and our mode of reading, of those 'source' texts too). In recent scholarship, we may point to the discourses of intertextuality, genre, gender and above all epistolarity, which configure Ovid (as Farrell explicitly does) as already interested in and practising some or other

[51] Farrell (1998) 336 n.58.   [52] Farrell (1998) 338.

of the (eagerly contested) concerns which underpin scholarly readings. The construction of temporality involved seems oddly familiar: the text of the *Heroides* is organized as being 'prior' to those of the epistolary novelists of the eighteenth century and beyond, or of *The Handmaid's Tale* or *La Carte postale*, as temporally anterior, therefore, to the 'source' texts which provide closure on the contingencies of its meaning: Ovid is configured as a proto-novelist or a proto-poststructuralist writer, already, but not yet, manipulating the categories of, say, *écriture feminine* or the lover's discourse, just as Helen is already, but not yet, manipulating the tropes of the *Ars amatoria*. We may recall once more the issue of destination, and consider its association with the notion of destiny. The poems have their meaning when they arrive at the point to which we assume they have been directed, when we feel addressed by them. The meaning they happen to have in any such contingent reading thus becomes the meaning regarded as determinate and inherent in the text. Contingency and desire become closely linked, as do determination and satisfaction. The *Heroides* fashion a literary mode which allows us to resolve and separate the subject positions of desire and its (possible) satisfaction, of contingency and (possible) determination, and then to occupy both those subject positions through simultaneous identification with the complex and composite figures of the writer and the reader.

The relationship between Ovid and his reader is, historically, never fully determined or foreclosed. Other readers will succeed us, and can we foresee how the *Heroides*, and our readings of them, will be configured twenty, one hundred, two thousand years hence? This puts us in turn in the discursive position occupied by the heroine and by Ovid before us. Writing to this moment, it is possible to feel that a postmodernist sense of the inadequacy of language – the slippage between signifier and signified, the dialectic of presence and absence, the relativization of the roles of writer, reader and critic – and the lament over that inadequacy finds in epistolarity and epistolary tropes a congenial mode which is suited to its own sense of belatedness (every missive is a postscript to the already written, every reading a re-reading) and enacts its uncertainty of what is to come after (*post*).[53] Writing to this moment waits upon the response of the future.

FURTHER READING

The *Heroides* are now fairly well served by commentaries with the publication of Knox (1995), containing *Her.* 1, 2, 5, 7, 10, 11, 15; and Kenney's *Ovid Heroides* XVI–XXI (1996); Palmer (1898; repr. Hildesheim, 1967) covers all the poems and remains useful. For those with Italian there are now detailed commentaries on 1–3

[53] See Kaufmann (1992) 264–5.

by A. Barchiesi (1992); on 9 by S. Casali (1995); on 12 by F. Bessone (1997) and on 18–19 by G. Rosati (1996). On epistolarity, key theoretical works are Altman (1982) and MacArthur (1990). Kaufmann (1986) and (1992) are particularly useful for the way they are prepared to rethink the tradition of epistolary heroinism and Ovid's relationship to it. For an older survey of this tradition see Dörrie (1968). Two major critical works on the *Heroides* remain useful: Jacobson (1974) and Verducci (1985); but the most influential work of recent years has been in article form: see especially Kennedy (1984); Barchiesi (1993); Hinds (1993); Farrell (1998).

14

GARETH WILLIAMS

Ovid's exile poetry: *Tristia, Epistulae ex Ponto* and *Ibis*

Ovid's sudden banishment from Rome in AD 8 was precipitated by two admitted causes, *carmen et error* (*Trist.* 2.207), the second of which – an apparently 'innocent' misdemeanour (cf. e.g. *Trist.* 3.5.49–52, 3.6.29–36, *Pont.* 1.6.21–6), possibly political in nature – receives only passing mention in the exile poetry and remains mysterious despite the speculations of modern theorists.[1] Whatever the truth of the matter, this *error* appears to have compounded the disfavour which Ovid had already incurred by the publication (c. 1 BC–AD 2) of the risqué *Ars amatoria* ('The Art of Love'), harmless on a 'sensible' reading (that naturally urged by Ovid in his defence of the poem in *Tristia* 2, addressed directly to Augustus) but fatally out of step with official tastes, themselves shaped by the programme of moral reform undertaken by Augustus (including legislation in c. 18 BC promoting marriage and curbing adultery).[2] If the *Ars amatoria* immediately aroused hostility in high places, Ovid's *error* may have supplied the pretext in AD 8 for a late but devastating retaliatory blow: relegation to Tomis (modern Constanza, on the Romanian coast of the Black Sea), a penalty less severe than *exilium* (which would have deprived him of Roman citizenship and property)[3] but still extreme in its deracinating physical and psychological effects. Two collections of exilic elegies, the *Tristia* ('Sorrows') in five books (fifty poems, AD 9–12) and the *Epistulae ex Ponto* ('Letters from Pontus') in four (1–3 were published together in AD 13, 4 probably posthumously; forty-six poems in all), chronicle Ovid's maladjustment to life in Tomis.[4] A third major production, the elegiac *Ibis* (c. AD 12),[5] elaborately curses an unnamed enemy at Rome (pseudonymously termed Ibis). A long introductory section (1–250) gives way to a vast catalogue of obscure imprecations drawn from the byways of mythology, history and legend (251–638); conventionally dismissed

---

[1] Surveyed by Thibault (1964); for the political angle updated see Green (1982a) 49–59 and (1982b).

[2] See for the legislative details Green (1982a) 71–2.   [3] Evans (1983) 4, 27.

[4] Chronology: Syme (1978) 37–47.   [5] Date: Williams (1996) 132 n. 52.

by modern critics as a self-indulgent *jeu d'esprit*, an impotent weapon whose only utility lay in distracting Ovid from meditation on his exilic grief, the poem is nevertheless open to reassessment as an important counterpoise – a contrived explosion of manic rage – to the melancholy which pervades the rest of the exilic corpus.

Ovid's declared motive for persevering with poetry in Tomis is practical utility (*utilitas*):[6] destroyed by the Muses (in the form of the *Ars amatoria*), he nevertheless finds exilic solace in their company (cf. *Trist.* 4.1.19–52, 4.10.115–22); by maintaining communication with his friends at Rome he performs an act of *utilitas officiumque* (*Pont.* 3.9.56), of utilitarian appeal for help in seeking his removal from Tomis and of duty (*officium*) according to the code of personal *amicitia*; and while he doubtless corresponded in prose as well as in verse, the gift of poetic celebration stood to reward loyal friends (*named* celebration at least in the *Epistulae ex Ponto*; anonymity is the rule in the earlier and less certain times of the *Tristia*, where fear of endangerment through association with him reins in Ovid's impulse to name his addressees).[7] Beyond these declared motives, however, the exile poetry, itself a radically new departure in the Roman elegiac tradition, stands alone in classical Roman literature as an unprecedented meditation on the state of exile itself, on the psychological pressures bearing upon an individual isolated from the native land, the family, friends and the (literary) culture which define his entire being – an isolation potentially compounded by a secondary form of exile: either alienation from his new cohabitants, or yet further alienation from Rome if he learns, however reluctantly, to adapt to his foreign circumstances. This ambiguous condition as 'a poet between two worlds',[8] Rome and Tomis, sharply distinguishes Ovid's exilic writings from the most obvious Roman parallels. While Cicero's letters from exile (58–57 BC) yield significant parallels for Ovid's description of his own sufferings (the similarities may or may not be coincidental),[9] Cicero lacks the more introspective tensions which surface in Ovid's gradual resignation to exile as a *permanent* condition; and Seneca's Stoic response to exile on Corsica (AD 41–9) – not least his fusion of the doctrine of 'citizenship of the universe' with the traditional consolatory topos that an exile can make any land his

---

6 See for broader discussion Nagle (1980) 71–82.
7 Cf. *Trist.* 3.4.63–6, 4.5.13–16. *Tristia* 2 (to Augustus) and 3.7 (to Perilla) are exceptional, as are *Pont.* 3.6 and 4.3 (no named addressees). But for the anonymity of the *Tristia* as strategic in other ways see Evans (1983) 58 (the collection acquires 'a generality of appeal' by not addressing named individuals), with Williams (1994) 104–6 (Ovid emphasizes moral rather than named identity), and Oliensis (1997) 178 (Ovid's silences 'dramatize how exile has jammed the works of *amicitia*', also delivering an oblique reproach to Augustus).
8 Fränkel (1945).
9 Similarities: Nagle (1980) 33–5; but cf. Kenney (1992) p. xvii n. 5 (that Ovid read Cicero's letters 'is on balance unlikely').

own (*Consolation to Helvia* 8.5–6)[10] – lacks in its impassivity the emotional drama, and arguably therefore the greater human interest, of Ovid's writings (a different side is shown at *Consolation to Polybius* 18.9, where Seneca offers a more anguished account, Ovidian in colour but transparently strategic, of his alleged sufferings in exile).[11]

Despite Ovid's insistence on the sincerity of his exilic voice (cf. *Trist.* 3.1.5–10, 5.1.5–6, *Pont.* 3.9.49–50), recent scholarship has become increasingly alert to the exaggerations which aggravate his plight in Tomis, by his account a town located in a war-stricken cultural wasteland on the remotest margins of empire. Historical research tells a different story: Ovid's Tomis is populated by the Thracian Getae, but there is no evidence to suggest that its Greek language and culture, originating from its Milesian foundation, were fatally eroded by the crude Getic presence which he describes; while inscriptional evidence indicates that Tomis was indeed threatened by sporadic attack in a still turbulent region (Moesia was brought under firm Roman control only late in the first century BC), Ovid clearly exaggerates the scale of the unrest; and other discrepancies abound,[12] encouraging some modern sceptics to suspect that he never in fact set foot in Tomis and may even have invented the entire exile (an intriguing possibility, but the burden of proof remains with the doubters).[13] True, Ovid's readers in distant Rome, many of whom presumably had little or no direct experience of Moesia, might have been impressionable to an extent; on a practical level, greater sympathy for his plight might be won by exploiting Roman ignorance of a distant region; but his distortions are also the 'sincere' outpourings of a *persona* whose inner crisis is naturally expressed in terms of hyperbolical excess, so that the loss of equilibrium in Ovid's exilic self becomes reflected in the extremes of the broader environmental picture which he draws.

In Virgil's third *Georgic* (339–83) Italy represents the balanced climatic centre between the polarized extremes of Scythia to the north and Libya to the south. The Virgilian picture of Scythia, itself traditional (extending back at least to Herodotus),[14] provides an important model for Ovid's exilic landscape in, e.g., *Trist.* 3.10: by being able to 'confirm' through direct observation the general character of Virgil's Scythia, Ovid creates the illusion that his first-hand experience of the place commands special trust; but whereas Virgil surveys the Libyan and Scythian extremes from the Roman centre, the

---

[10] Cf. Green (1994) pp. xlvi–xlvii.
[11] See Griffin (1976) 62 and n. 3 with Degl' Innocenti Pierini (1980) 114–22.
[12] See Habinek (1998) 158 and 219 n. 15 for bibliography.
[13] E.g. Fitton Brown (1985); for the history of the theory see Claassen (1999) 34. Cf. Habinek (1998) 218 n. 9: 'the ideological force of his depiction of the Tomitans and of himself would not be categorically different if the whole project were fictitious'.
[14] See Hartog (1988) 12–33 with Thomas (1982) 51 and 66 nn. 68–9.

more poignant effect of the Virgilian presence in *Trist.* 3.10 is to emphasize by contrast Ovid's *dislocated* perspective as he views the world from its margins. That Tomis was not strictly in Scythia, named as his exilic destination at, e.g., *Trist.* 1.3.61, is irrelevant to his creative vision, which also extends to portraying his Tomitan landscape as a negation of the literary Golden Age (war is constant, the earth sterile, the people of Iron Age hardness) and as an alternative underworld – a natural setting given Ovid's frequent equation of exile with death (e.g. *Trist.* 5.9.19, *Pont.* 1.8.27, 4.9.74). The region is Stygian in its bleak (*tristis*) and cheerless (*inamabilis*) character (*Trist.* 5.7.43–4; for *inamabilis* of the underworld cf. *Met.* 4.477, 14.590, for *tristis* Virg. *Aen.* 4.243, 6.438, Hor. *Carm.* 3.4.46).[15] If, moreover, Rome marks the global median point in contrast to extreme Scythia, Ovid exploits in a predictable way the familiar correlation drawn in antiquity between human character and climate:[16] in contrast to the balanced Italian character, the Scythians are as coarse (*crudi*), wild (*feri*) and hard (*duri*) as their environment, their harsh character reflected in their wild appearance (unshaven at *Trist.* 5.7.18, the very opposite of Roman neatness; cf. *Ars am.* 1.518) and in the menacing arms which they always carry (*Trist.* 5.7.15–16).

Already in *Tristia* 1 Ovid's description of his storm-tossed journey into exile (*Trist.* 1.2, 1.4) symbolically expresses his inner turmoil (cf. *animique marisque | fluctibus, Trist.* 1.11.9–10 'turbulent waves of both mind and sea').[17] The epic storm rages with unbelievable violence at all but the emotional level, allowing Ovid to achieve a 'realistic' effect despite (and through) the hyperbole; his unmeasured description represents a lack of balanced focus in his traumatized *persona*, an effect sustained when he goes head-to-head with Ulysses in a point-by-point comparison of sufferings at *Trist.* 1.5.57–84 and easily wins on all counts (Ovid again triumphs over Ulysses at *Pont.* 4.10.9–30, and over Jason in a similar syncrisis at *Pont.* 1.4.23–46; myth itself is exhausted in his promotion of the greater myth of his own incredible but all too 'real' hardships.[18]) After arrival in Tomis, the epic scale of his sufferings (*ultima nunc patior, Trist.* 3.2.11 'now I endure the worst extremes') is in direct proportion to his emotional as well as physical distance from Rome (cf. *Trist.* 3.4b.52–3 'alas, how near to me is the last land in the world! But far off is my homeland . . .'), and the environmental extremes he describes (e.g. *Pont.* 2.7.31 'no race in the entire world is more fierce than the Getae', 63–4 'no land more dismal than this lies under either pole', 72 'the Sarmatian coast is frozen with eternal cold') reflect the strained perspective from which they are viewed rather than reality. 'The mind and

---

[15] More examples and discussion in Nagle (1980) 23–32.
[16] See Johnson (1960) with Williams (1994) 16–18.   [17] Cf. Dickinson (1973) 162–3, 167–8.
[18] For the line cf. Davisson (1993) 224–37.

body find relief in a mild climate' (*Pont.* 2.7.71), but in the absence of any such moderation (*temperies caeli*) Ovid loses the delicate balance of his constitution and succumbs to constant sickness (cf. *Trist.* 3.3.3–14, 3.8.23–34, 4.6.39–44, *Pont.* 1.10.3–14 etc.), his sufferings at e.g. *Trist.* 5.13.3–6 ('I have contracted in body my illness of mind, that no part of me may be free from torment . . .') as extreme as the 'excessive cold' (*non modico frigore*, 6) which leaves him ironically 'scorched' (*uror*, 5) by fever. His ailing health also serves as a physical metaphor for the alleged decline of his poetic abilities in exile; the sterility of his creative *ingenium* (*Trist.* 3.14.33–6, 5.12.21–2) is reflected on a larger scale in the barren landscape of Tomis (*Trist.* 3.10.71–4, *Pont.* 1.3.51–2, 3.1.19–24), where his mental worry (*anxietas animi*, *Pont.* 1.10.36) and consequent poetic failure ('poems are happy work and require peace of mind', *Trist.* 5.12.3–4) are themselves conditioned by the general restlessness of the region (cf. *male pacatis* of the 'barely pacified' Getae at *Trist.* 5.7.12 and *Pont.* 2.7.2).

The loss of centre in Ovid's exilic self is partially redressed by his mental travels back to Rome and by his visual memory in Tomis of the city, his family and the friends he has left behind.[19] By visiting in his mind's eye the familiar sights of Rome (*Pont.* 1.8.33–8) he creates the illusion of a continuing presence there; even late in his exile he still participates in Roman civic life by 'attending' the consular inaugurations of Sextus Pompeius and Graecinus, occasions graphically pictured at *Pont.* 4.4.27–46 and 4.9.9–56; an exile in all but mind ('I shall use my imagination, which alone is not exiled', *Pont.* 4.9.41), he enters the city still to converse with Cotta Maximus (*Pont.* 3.5.49–50); in *Trist.* 4.2 he is 'there' to witness in vivid ecphrastic detail (19–56) the triumphal procession which he predicts for Tiberius in anticipation (1–2) of the latter's successful German campaign of AD 10 – indeed a triumph of the imagination (cf. 57–9 'although exiled, all this I shall see in my mind's eye – the only way. My mind is entitled to go to that place which is forbidden to me; it ranges freely over boundless lands . . .'), as it preempts by two or so years the real event in AD 12.[20] But while in *Trist.* 4.2 Ovid shares as a fellow citizen in witnessing at the hub of empire the subjugation of distant and troublesome peoples, *his* Getae in *his* remote Pontus remain relatively untamed, their respect for Rome apparently minimal ('the great majority of these people cares nothing for you, most beautiful Rome, and has no fear of Italy's armed strength', *Pont.* 1.2.81–2). The comfort which Ovid derives from his mental travels is offset by his

---

[19] Nagle (1980) 91–7 assembles examples.
[20] Tiberius' Pannonian triumph (23 October AD 12); awarded in AD 9 but postponed because of the *clades Variana* in Germany (hence Tiberius' avenging campaign), it is celebrated in *Pont.* 2.1.

inevitable return to this exilic reality; the consolation which he derives from his visual memory of his wife (*Trist.* 3.4b.59 'before my eyes is the image of my wife, as if she were present') is offset by her still painful absence (60–1). While the close personal and literary friendships which he shared with the likes of Atticus (*Pont.* 2.4) and Graecinus (*Pont.* 2.6), Pompeius Macer (*Pont.* 2.10) and Tuticanus (*Pont.* 4.12, 14) are sustained by his poetic communications from exile, this contact with Rome merely reinforces his lack of real companionship and cultural opportunity in Tomis. In these and many other ways Ovid is simultaneously present in and absent from both Rome and Tomis, Getic influence now taking hold ('I think I could write in Getic measures', *Trist.* 3.14.48), his Roman side resisting, not least through a stubborn commitment to Latin letters.

As for many exiles ancient and modern,[21] Ovid's linguistic isolation in Tomis compounds his estrangement from home with a secondary form of alienation from his new cohabitants. Forced to communicate only by gesture (*Trist.* 5.10.36), Rome's greatest living poet appears uncivilized by Getic standards ('*I'm* the barbarian here, understood by nobody', 37), his Latin words an object of ridicule (38); the hallowed name of *Romanus uates* ('the bard of Rome', *Trist.* 5.7.55) means nothing in Tomis, where (whatever the pretensions of Augustan imperialism) Roman language and culture are apparently no more recognized than Roman arms are feared (*Pont.* 1.2.81–2). The penalty he pays in exile for the 'corrupting' *Ars amatoria* is a form of solitary linguistic confinement, his Latin powerless to exercise any kind of influence among the uncomprehending Tomitans; and yet a more sympathetic reading of the *Ars amatoria* suggests that Ovid's Latin is misunderstood not only in Tomis but also, in a different way, by that austere section of his Roman readership which originally found fault with the *Ars*. That fault leads to a more radical poetic failure in Tomis, as he claims to be losing his grasp of Latin because he has no one to converse with in his native tongue (cf. *Trist.* 4.1.89–90, 5.2.67); barbarian words consequently creep into his diction (*Trist.* 3.1.17–18, 3.14.49–50), contaminating the Latin verses which he struggles to produce in Tomis, his creative *ingenium* crushed by the weight of his exilic sufferings (*Trist.* 1.1.35–48, 1.11.35–6, *Pont.* 4.2.15–16); hence also his rejection of the basic canons of technical (Horatian) *ars* in his failure to polish and correct his exilic verses (*Trist.* 5.1.71–2, *Pont.* 1.5.17–18, 3.9.13–32).[22] But while Ovid's insistence on his poetic decline long served to confirm the judgement of his harsher modern critics, the fact remains that his writing shows no real signs of deterioration from its pre-exilic standard.[23]

---

[21] See Doblhofer (1986).

[22] For the important Horatian dimension see Nagle (1980) 128–30.

[23] Important analysis in Luck (1961).

The pose is strategic, sympathy partly its goal; but Ovid also 'concentrates in a concern about language ... the anxieties about intercultural contact that absorb the attention of colonizers everywhere',[24] his repeated insistence on his failing literary powers gradually strengthening the illusion that his failure is real. 'His exile books grow into their trope: "decline" becomes decline',[25] at least in the sense that Ovid's *persona* succumbs to its own growing (if misguided) conviction; he relies on the sustained quality of his verse for the neurosis of phantom decline to be properly staged.

Ovid's claims that he is losing his Latin in Tomis reach their climax in *Pont.* 4.13, where he reports that he has recited before an enthusiastic local audience a Getic poem in Latin metre on the apotheosis of Augustus. Whether or not the report is true (there is no surviving evidence of any such poem, and good reason to doubt its existence),[26] Ovid's feat of cross-cultural invention – the medium is as unique (or as monstrous?) as the Augustan phenomenon which it celebrates – symbolically marks an extreme stage in his gradual 'gétisation'[27] at Tomis, while his Getic audience's positive response (35–6) to his imperial praises also signals its allegiance to Rome and to Tiberius (27–8) as Augustus' successor. But these bilateral signs of cultural interaction, with the Getae finally constructed as willing imperial subjects (Ovid's Getic production may thus advertise 'the potential role of poetry and poets in the process of pacification'),[28] cannot disguise the more bizarre aspects of the scene, not least the incongruous spectacle of the 'uncivilized' Getae (*inhumanos*, 22) attending a poetic recitation in the first place, and then shaking their quivers (35) and murmuring (36) in polite appreciation of Ovid's performance. And despite his exuberant show of loyalty to the imperial house, his tone is complicated by hints of innuendo: how appropriate to the status of the imperial family is Ovid's celebration of Augustus in 'barbarian words' (*barbara uerba*, 20)? When he has a local tribesman state that so loyal a supporter should have been restored by Augustus (37–8), does Ovid imply that the Getae have a sympathetic sensibility which the emperor himself lacked? The tension generated in *Pont.* 4.13 by these and other such implications[29] unsettles Ovid's overt celebration of Augustus, an all-powerful but inevitably remote figure when viewed from the poet's isolated and vulnerable Tomitan perspective; hence the more widespread ambivalence which characterizes Ovid's exilic treatment of his persecutor and yet also his only possible saviour.

At *Trist.* 2.213–38 Ovid prepares the way for his defence of the *Ars amatoria* by claiming that the poem is hardly worthy of Augustus' attention, burdened as he is by much more important responsibilities abroad (225–32)

[24] Habinek (1998) 162.   [25] Hinds (1998) 90.   [26] Williams (1994) 91–2.
[27] Lozovan (1958) 402.   [28] Habinek (1998) 161.   [29] Williams (1994) 98.

and at home (233–4). The passage recalls Horace's similar approach to Augustus in *Epistles* 2.1, where the poet is tactfully aware that by detaining the emperor he interferes with the public interest both at home and abroad ('you protect our Italian state with arms, you equip it with morals and reform it with laws' *res Italas armis tuteris, moribus ornes,* | *legibus emendes,* 2–3). The crucial difference between the two passages, however, is that Horace views Augustus and his responsibilities from the impregnable safety of Rome itself, while Ovid is in relatively close proximity to the eastern troublespots which he describes (225–30).[30] From the latter's different perspective the Augustan myth of universal supremacy (promoted in the *Res gestae*) is in conflict with the Pontic 'reality', which is apparently beyond the limits of the Augustan peace (cf. *Pont.* 2.5.17–18, 2.7.67–8), the 'true' state of the region unknown: 'although a god knows everything,[31] Caesar knows nothing of the real nature of this extreme region' (*Pont.* 1.2.71–2). From the Ovidian standpoint Augustus' vaunted reputation for restraint (e.g. *Trist.* 1.9.25 'none is more moderate', 2.27, 41–2, 147) and clemency (e.g. *Trist.* 2.43–50, 4.4.53–4, 5.2.35–6, 5.4.19–22, *Pont.* 1.2.121–3) must count for little, and the exile's repeated allusions to those qualities must be a potential embarrassment as long as the emperor remains unbending. These and the many other implied criticisms of Augustus which recent scholarship has detected in the exile poetry[32] do not amount to a sustained and committed 'anti-Augustan' campaign on Ovid's part; but they nevertheless set Augustus' Roman public image (reaffirmed by the seemingly abject flattery of, e.g., *Trist.* 5.2.45–60, *Pont.* 2.8, 3.6.7–50) against the 'reality' which Ovid sees from his detached perspective of physical insecurity (no Augustan peace) and indefinite confinement (no hint of Augustus' famous clemency) in Tomis. The tension resulting from this conflict – easily resolved if Augustus answers Ovid's prayers – empowers the *Tristia* and *Epistulae ex Ponto* as a form of commentary on the 'real' nature and limitations of Augustan rule; every plea to the emperor is a test of his legend.

There are flashes of sharper defiance, none more explicit than Ovid's proud claim in *Trist.* 3.7 that his poetic talent (*ingenium*) and the immortal fame it has won him lie beyond Augustus' control (47–52);[33] his assertion of his own lasting renown carries with it the implicit diminution of the emperor's secular power. In *Tristia* 2 Ovid's long defence of the *Ars amatoria* against

---

[30] Emphasized by Habinek (1998) 156–7.

[31] For Augustus' identification with Jupiter cf., e.g., *Trist.* 1.3.37–40, 1.5.77–8, 2.37–40.

[32] Staple bibliography in Evans (1983) 181 n. 4, Evans himself notably playing down this subversive element (10–30; cf. Williams (1978) 97 'Here [sc. in the exile poetry] is the finished creation of an Augustan poetic mystique of ruler worship').

[33] Much quoted; Evans (1983) 17–19 and 182 n. 20 for further bibliography.

the charge of immorality directly confronts Augustus with a series of appeals and arguments notorious for their barely concealed irony and irreverence. Given the emperor's immense responsibilities at home and abroad (213–36), is it any surprise that he has never read the *Ars amatoria* (237–8)? But then how can the emperor condemn a work of which he has no first hand experience? And (245–52) how can Ovid be guilty of corrupting married women when he explicitly excludes them from his readership, in lines (*Ars am.* 1.31–4) which are reproduced with minimal change at *Trist.* 2.247–50? The subtle humour of *Ars am.* 1.31–4, where Ovid parodies solemn religious ritual by banishing the uninitiated *matronae* from his risqué proceedings ('Far off with you, you respectable ladies of nice little headbands (badge of modesty!) and long foot-reaching skirts ...'), passes unrecognized at *Trist.* 2.247–50, where his bare literalism offers a glaringly insensitive (hence suspiciously Augustan?) reading of his own poetry.[34] Augustus' literary sensibility is also held up to almost open ridicule when, in lines 361–2, Ovid argues that though he is not the only poet to have written on erotic themes, he alone has been punished for it. In his ensuing survey of the Greco-Roman poetic tradition (363–470) Ovid makes his inevitable point: if Augustus is going to incriminate the *Ars amatoria*, then why not take action against any other salacious work? What is the *Iliad*, for example, if not a poem about adulterous love (371–2), the *Odyssey* about a woman surrounded by ardent suitors while her husband is absent (375–6)? And yet who would dream of taking action against such poems? Ovid's reading of literary tradition in lines 363–470 is of course hopelessly one-sided, but Augustus would be well advised not to press the point if and when he ever read *Tristia* 2: in this *reductio ad absurdum*[35] Ovid offers him an object lesson in how (not) to read the *Ars amatoria*, or any other poem for that matter, with unbalanced prejudice.

These and other provocative arguments in *Tristia* 2 show Ovid's Muse to be only partially subdued and transformed by exile. She remains mischievous, justifying his anxiety in lines 3–4 ('why do I turn again to the Muses so recently condemned, my cause of guilt? Or is one well-earned punishment too little?') and in danger of fulfilling more than his/her good intentions in 21 (*Musa ... quam mouit, motam quoque leniet iram* 'the Muse who stirred it will also soften the anger that has been provoked'): in soothing Augustus' anger she may yet seek playfully to needle him again, exacerbating the broader tensions which characterize Ovid's exilic relationship with her. If in the exile poetry Ovid's wife (addressed in e.g. *Trist.* 1.6, 3.3, 4.3 and 5.14)

---

[34] Williams (1994) 206–8.   [35] Evans (1983) 16 after Wilkinson (1955) 311.

supplants the traditional Roman elegiac mistress (Corinna in the *Amores*), his love/hate relationship with the Muse (another exilic version of Corinna) also modifies the familiar elegiac *topos* of love's sweet torture (cf. *Am.* 3.11b.1–2 'love on this side and hate on that are wrestling and pulling my fickle heart in different directions; but, I think, love is winning'). Even though his Muse has destroyed him, he remains infatuated with poetry (*carmen demens carmine laesus amo*, *Trist.* 4.1.30 'although ruined by verse, in my madness I still love verse'), a constant source of alleviation in Tomis (cf. 49–50); hence his continued devotion to the Muses whom he curses (*Trist.* 5.7.31–3 'although I sometimes curse my poems when I recall the harm they have done me, and curse my Muses, after I have duly cursed them still I cannot live without them'). These oscillations between love and hate[36] are themselves symptomatic of the more general state of instability which characterizes so many of Ovid's exilic relationships, both with his Roman correspondents and with his Tomitan neighbours; the poet between two worlds is inevitably assailed by doubts about his standing in either. Hence his suspicion that the Tomitans insult him when they speak of him in their native language, which he can barely understand (*Trist.* 5.10.39–40); hence his many appeals to his Roman friends for their continued support, loyalty and communication (cf. *Trist.* 1.9.65, 3.6.19–24, 4.5.17–24, 5.3.47–58 etc.), and his need for reassurance that his wife still remains devoted to him (*Trist.* 4.3.11–20); hence the emotional chaos which threatens to erupt if and when his confidence in his closest friends is shown to be misguided. 'I shall sooner believe that the gorgon Medusa's head was garlanded with snaky locks, . . . that there is a Chimaera . . . a Sphinx and Harpies . . .; all these I shall sooner believe than that you, dearest friend, have changed and laid aside your love for me' (*Trist.* 4.7.11–20): after Ovid delivers a mild rebuke (1–10) to his anonymous friend for failing to send word since his arrival in Tomis two years before, these *adynata* (impossible occurrences) convey the monstrous effect of the inconceivable suddenly made real, his imagination running riot in response to the unthinkable prospect of his friend's disloyalty.[37] The artistically contrived paranoia of *Trist.* 4.7 is only one (albeit extreme) example of the nervous uncertainty resulting from the attritional effects of displacement – a condition illustrated at the outset by the tentative manner in which Ovid sends his first exilic book back to Rome (*Trist.* 1.1.21–30, 73–88, 101–4). The condition reaches fever pitch in the *Ibis*, Ovid's ultimate act of revenge after the warning shots which he delivers to the unnamed enemy (or enemies) addressed in *Trist.* 1.8, 3.11, 4.9 and 5.8.

---

[36] See further Lieberg (1980) 20 n. 138.

[37] *Adynata* in the exile poetry: Williams (1994) 118–21 with 119 n. 35 for bibliography.

In the great catalogue of obscure maledictions which dominates the second half of the *Ibis* (251–638) Ovid explores every possible avenue of death for Ibis, his pseudonymous enemy (the name is taken from Callimachus' curse-poem, now lost, on which Ovid models his own; cf. 55–60). Now speared by the barb of a sting-ray in the manner of Telegonus, Odysseus' son by Circe (567–8), now throttled as was Anticlus in the Trojan horse (569–70), now crushed to death in a mortar like the philosopher Anaxarchus (571–2), Ibis is killed in these and countless other bizarre ways only to find himself still living at the end of the poem and under threat of a yet more horrific iambic assault if he continues to persecute the poet (639–44). The Hellenistic tradition of curse poetry had already inflicted on its targets exotic punishments announced in language of intimidating obscurity,[38] but Ovid's catalogue, very possibly unprecedented in length, is no slavish replica of its Hellenistic prototypes. Whether or not Ibis ever existed (A. E. Housman's firm dismissal of him as a fiction[39] has not entirely killed him off in modern scholarship), and whatever his 'true' identity (many different names have been canvassed, none with anything approaching certainty),[40] the fact remains that this enemy, real or imagined, has nothing to fear as soon as (if not before) Ovid acknowledges that Ibis will survive the present onslaught (*postmodo, si perges . . .*, 53 'afterwards, if you will persist . . .'). After Ovid's placid opening announcement that he is forced against his will and nature to take up arms against a persistent enemy (1–10), the poem quickly gains momentum as he warms to his task, a new apprentice who looks to Callimachus as his guiding model in how to curse (55–66). But Ovid's prayer for support to every god that ever existed (67–88) – itself an early sign of insecurity – gives way to a bizarre series of manoeuvres: Ibis is readied for human sacrifice in lines 97–106, then made a social and global outcast in a stream of maledictions (107–26) apparently endorsed by a divine sign from Apollo (127–8) – all this as a mere prelude for much worse to come! The maledictions reach their climax in the catalogue (251–638), where the imbalance between the scale of Ibis' original offences (11–22) and the scale of his punishment grows vaster as Ovid descends ever further into a dream-like fantasy of revenge. Already in *Trist.* 5.7 cursing features prominently in the self-expression of the poet in exile, with the Muses his victim (31–3, cited on p. 242 above; cf. *Trist.* 4.1.101–2 for his destroying his poetic efforts in Tomis in fits of manic burning); Ovid's *persona* needs the emotional outlet which cursing provides, even though he knows that the gesture is futile, that he achieves nothing beyond the satisfaction of (pointless) revenge. Viewed from this perspective, the *Ibis*

---

[38] See generally Watson (1991) 79–193.   [39] (1920) 316 = (1972) 1040.
[40] For candidates see La Penna (1957) pp. xvi–xix with Watson (1991) 130 n. 344 for updated bibliography.

is no awkward appendage to the rest of the exilic corpus, or merely a *jeu d'esprit* which enabled Ovid to fill his hours in Tomis; in manic contrast to the all-pervading melancholy of the *Tristia* and the *Epistulae ex Ponto*, the curse makes an important (even necessary) contribution to the psychological 'wholeness' of the collection.[41]

The obsessive tendencies which are such a striking feature of Ovid's *persona* in the *Ibis* find important precedents in the *Metamorphoses*, where various characters share aspects of the same general mentality. So Aglauros: once bitten by jealousy (2.798–805) she can only feed her obsession until she is devoured by it (805–11); even when turned to stone (819–31) she still shows her state of mind in her livid discolouration (832).[42] In his different way Ovid's *persona* is frozen in a potentially devouring obsession in the *Ibis*, his endless cycles of *exempla* in the catalogue amounting to a form of psychological imprisonment after his metamorphosis into a warring avenger (cf. 1–10, 45–54). Ovid's post-transformation grief in the *Tristia* and *Epistulae ex Ponto*, still keenly felt even in his Tomitan 'death', also resembles that of a number of figures in the *Metamorphoses*, Niobe prominent among them, still weeping after her transformation into rock (6.310–12) – a parallel modified by Ovid at *Pont.* 1.2.29–30 to aggravate his own 'worse' condition in exile ('Happy Niobe! Although she saw so many deaths, she lost the power of feeling when she was turned to stone by her misfortunes'). Beyond the *Metamorphoses*, the many thematic and structural similarities between the exile poetry and the *Heroides* are accompanied by powerfully suggestive psychological links,[43] not least the 'psychic gratification'[44] which both Ovid in Tomis and various of the authoresses seek to derive from their necessary but potentially wasted effusions. Already in the *Amores* the tribulations of the 'excluded lover' also foreshadow the experience of the excluded poet in exile, the latter's insomnia, pallor, loss of appetite and general physical condition replacing (and aggravating) the more familiar erotic elegiac torments.[45] Another significant Ovidian theme first glimpsed in the *Amores* is that of the self-destructive potential of one's own art, as when Ovid claims to be vulnerable to his own teachings in the *Ars amatoria* (*ei mihi, praeceptis urgeor ipse meis, Am.* 2.18.20 'alas! I am tormented by my own precepts'; cf. *Am.* 1.4.46, 2.19.34). Various examples of artists harmed or destroyed as a direct or indirect result of their own supreme talent are found in the *Metamorphoses* (e.g. Arachne, 6.1–145, Marsyas, 6.383–400, Daedalus, 8.183–235). Personal obsession also leads to self-destruction (e.g. Phaethon, 2.150–332, Aglauros, 2.708–832, Narcissus, 3.339–510, Erysichthon, 8.823–878); and

---

[41] For this approach see Williams (1996).   [42] See further Williams (1996) 87–8.
[43] See Rahn (1958) and now Rosenmeyer (1997).   [44] Jacobson (1974) 372.
[45] Nagle (1980) 43–70 collects and analyses the transformed erotic motifs.

Ovid's alienation as a poet between two worlds is suggestively paralleled by (at least) Actaeon in *Metamorphoses* 3, transformed into a stag but still human in feeling (201–3), an absent but present witness of his destruction through his own hounds (242–52). Given this fascination with the theme of self-destruction, and given his long interest in the psychology of exile and estrangement, Ovid's own experience – the disastrous consequences of his art/*Ars* and his alienated existence in Tomis – touches upon significant pre-occupations in his earlier career; in his artistic arrangement of exile Ovid is banished by Augustus to strangely familiar psychological territory, a coincidence which significantly narrows the divide between the *Tristia, Epistulae ex Ponto* and *Ibis* and his pre-exilic *oeuvre*.

FURTHER READING

Commentaries: on *Tristia*, Luck (1967–77), in German; in English, Owen on *Trist.* 1 (1902; 3rd edn.), *Trist.* 2 (1924) and *Trist.* 3 (1893; 2nd edn.); on *Epistulae ex Ponto* 4.1–7 and 16, Helzle (1989), in English; Green *Ovid: The Poems of Exile* (1994) offers valuable notes on both collections; *Ibis*: La Penna (1957), in Italian.
Historical aspects: Syme (1978); Podosinov (1981) and (1987).
Literary studies: for stylistic analysis, Luck (1961); articles: Kenney (1965); Dickinson (1973); Hinds (1985); (1993); eight articles in *Ramus* 26 (1997), a volume devoted to the exile poetry; Habinek (1998) 150–69.
Book-length studies: Nagle (1980); Evans (1983); Videau-Delibes (1991); Claassen (1999). *Ibis*: Watson (1991); Williams (1996).

3
RECEPTION

15

RAPHAEL LYNE

Ovid in English translation

Thenne it is a gret thynge to hym that secheth to know thentendement
of Ovyde and he ought tendyne & sette hys hye corage to contynuel
estudye & to take payne & dilygence to rumyne and chewe hys cudde
and enqyre that the sayd poete hath devysed and dysputed of
natures or of maners and of gestes.
(William Caxton, 'Proheme' to *Ovyde hys Booke of
Methamorphose*, c. 1483)[1]

I could go on and on with these scientific facts.
If it wasn't so late I'd tell you a whole lot more.
(Michael Longley, 'According to Pythagoras')[2]

There are sections taken directly from his work in the poetry of Chaucer and
Gower, but translation of Ovid into English as a distinct process starts in
the cradle of printing, with William Caxton's version of the *Metamorphoses*
in 1483 and Wynkyn de Worde's *Flores de Arte Amandi* in 1513. It traces
a path through the history of publishing, its latest manifestations being
phenomena of the modern industry: the Loeb parallel text, the Penguin
Classic, and the Faber and Faber poetry volume. Arthur Golding's translation of the *Metamorphoses* (1565–7) is one of several translations in his
period: Turbervile's *Heroides* (1567), Churchyard's *Tristia* (1572), and
Underdowne's *Ibis* (1569) follow soon after. Each text has its own origins,
Golding's being dedicated to the Earl of Leicester under whose patronage
various translation projects were under way.[3] However, they can all be
connected to a conjunction of affordable print, an aspirant vernacular culture, and a ready readership.[4] George Sandys' monumental *Metamorphoses*
translation (1621–6) also comes amid a period of translation: Gower's 1640
Festivalls (*Fasti*), and the various works of Wye Saltonstall in the 1630s
(*Heroides*, *Tristia*, and the first English *Ex Ponto*) stand out among others.

---

[1] Caxton (1968) I 14ʳ.   [2] In Hoffman and Lasdun (1994) 288.
[3] See Rosenberg (1955).   [4] See Bennett (1965) 87–111.

Sandys' translation, though, represents a new relationship between print and Ovidian translation because, in the 1632 version, it is a lavishly illustrated folio dedicated to the King.

The opportunism of printers is often evident: the posthumous appearance of Marlowe's apparently youthful version of the *Amores* with Sir John Davies' *Epigrams* carries the classic spurious imprint 'Middlebrough' (in Holland) and has no indication of Marlowe's authorization. Thomas Heywood complains bitterly (in the preface to his 1613 play *The Brazen Age*) that his version of the *Ars amatoria* has been published against his will.[5] The most successful conjunction of poetic talent and publishing acumen comes in the *Metamorphoses* organized by Samuel Garth in 1717. This harnesses the talents of Dryden and others in a translation which to some extent is a collective effort but, from the publisher's important perspective, is a complete thing in itself. Something comparable has more recently been achieved in the 1994 collection *After Ovid*. In the nineteenth century the economy of classical texts focused on the schoolroom. Translations of all Ovid's works appear in such exotically named series as Kelly's Classical Keys, Bohn's Classical Library, the Tutorial Series, Aids to the Classics, Gibson's Interlinear Translations, and the Hamiltonian System. The most successful series to emerge from these, the Loeb Classical Libary, is still a staple. What emerges from the many ways in which Ovid has been translated is a sense of how various the responses to his work have been. Not surprisingly the most important translations of Ovid have been (thus far) of the *Metamorphoses*, and the nature of this work has contributed to the variety of response. Its existence as an ambiguously organized whole, or as a collection of arresting episodes, frequently leads to tension as translators opt into or out of the grand design. It is testimony to the complexity of Ovid's reception that, while there has been much great translation of Ovid, there is not quite an agreed dominant equivalent to Dryden's Virgil or the Homers of Chapman and Pope.

Perhaps fittingly the start of the story is a false start. It is not even certain that Caxton ever printed his version: it survives in a unique manuscript which, again fittingly, has spent most of its life in two parts (and now resides in two libraries even though the volumes share one display case, thanks to the rigorous rules governing the Pepysian Library at Magdalene College, Cambridge). One piece of evidence that the text may have been printed comes in the preface to his *Golden Legend* (1483), where there is a list of works 'parfourmed and accomplisshed' by Caxton. It includes the *Metamorphoses* among other works which certainly were printed. More importantly, Caxton's version is not truly a translation of Ovid at all: in fact it is

---

[5] Heywood (1874) 167.

the author's very literal translation of a variant of the *Ovide Moralisé* which Caxton almost certainly came across while working in Colard Mansion's print shop in Bruges (a text of which is found in British Library MS Royal 17.E.iv). This version does not explore the allegorical extremities of other strains of the medieval tradition of reading Ovid as a source of moral wisdom: it prefers drawing lessons for life in a material world to reading through the veil of allegory for Christian truths. What it shares with the earlier tradition is distance from the Latin text: the stories of the *Metamorphoses* are presented in paraphrase with lengthy moral explanations. This can be seen in the case of Actaeon:

> Noble sygnificacyon may be had by the mutacyon of Acteon. Hit was so that Acteon entremeted of huntynge and to hold houndes whyche amynusshed hys goodes and empoverd hym. He sawe Dyane naked bathyng her self. Whych had also holden longe huntynge and syn lefte it and dyde no more. But not wyth-stondynge that he lefte huntynge yet he helde always hys meyne and hys houndes wythoute labour and despended al that he had and becam poure and a beggar and for this cause his propre houndes ete and devoured hym. By this ensample and hystorye every man may note and marke that it is a peryllous thinge for to holde peple and meyne withoute som bysenes. For it may never come to good ende, how wel it be delectable. (Bk III, Cap. 7)

Typically this barely deviates from the French text, and its most distinctive vocabulary – 'entremeted', 'amynusshed', 'his propre houndes' – all derives directly from French: 'sentremist', 'admendrist', 'ses propres chiens'. The lesson taught by the story is a stern economic one, banal in comparison with the imaginative variety of Petrus Berchorius, who includes the idea that the transformation of Actaeon into a stag is a figure for the incarnation of Christ.[6]

Christopher Martin has argued that, even with the intervening stages, some of the vividness of Ovid's writing comes through in Caxton's prose.[7] More certainly Caxton is the first English writer to encounter a central problem in translating Ovid, even if he does not actually translate his text. A Christian tradition of interpreting stories inevitably conflicted with a 'humanist' interest in studying texts. This did not always result in a lack of harmony, but it could result in a kind of doublethink. Writers professed one unimpeachable religious mode of reading but seem to modern readers to translate with different priorities in mind. In Caxton this conflict does not materialize, but in translating he repeats revealing scruples about his alleged source:

> In the begynnyng of this worlde unto the comynge of Jesu Cryst the poetes have made many fyxyons and fables whych semed to some but of lytyl

---

[6] See Berchorius (1979) 90ʳ.   [7] Martin (1998) p. xxvi.

effect. But ther is nothyng but it is good and of grete proufyt to them that can drawe and take the sens and fruyt therof. For the trouth therof lyeth coverid under the fables. Of which I can not speke with oute recytynge of them.

(Book I, Preface 'Thordenance for to have the understandynge of this booke')

Caxton is defensive generally, about un-Christian literature, and specifically, about the problematic aspects of Ovid's tales. He goes on to encourage the reader to correct him if he has gone wrong in any respect. Most interesting here is the development of an old argument about the veiled value of pagan stories to a point where a blunt truth leaks out: 'Of which I can not speke with oute recytynge of them'. Caxton does not follow this to its conclusion and does not take on the Latin poem.

But Golding, in many ways the inheritor of the same set of scruples, does, and in his work the interaction of text and interpretation is sharper. His translation is undoubtedly a monument: read by Shakespeare and Spenser, it conveys a spirited Ovid with all his range of emotion and diversity of plot. It is a monument which may well have amused Ovid greatly. The urbanity which suffuses Ovid's work is sometimes accompanied by a kind of detachment: not a cool lack of emotion, but rather an enigmatic distancing of feeling which is the consequence of consummately witty artistry. Golding encounters stories in a very different way, delivering every twist and turn in as whole-hearted a manner as possible. Ovid likens blood gushing from Pyramus' wound to water bursting from a pipe, and Golding's version is unabashed:

> And when he had bewept and kist the garment which he knew,
> Receyve thou my bloud too (quoth he) and therewithall he drew
> His sworde, the which among his guttes he thrust, and by and by
> Did draw it from the bleeding wound beginning for to die,
> And cast himselfe upon his backe, the bloud did spin on hie
> As when a Conduite pipe is crackt, the water bursting out
> Doth shote it selfe a great way off and pierce the Ayre about.
>
> $(4.143-9)^8$

In Ovid this sheds ironic light on the epic simile, as its self-conscious gaucheness puts further strain on the brittle *gravitas* of this tragic tale. Golding's metre, the fourteener, shares too many features with the ballad form not to amplify this further. As in this story, it often welcomes Ovid's more melodramatic effects. So Pyramus becomes a hero who is both less logical (more absurd and hyperbolic) and more logical (more in keeping with the general tone) – and the same can be said of the difficult simile of the burst

---

[8] Reference to Golding (1965).

pipe. Golding may barrel through the fine points of irony, but he registers all the pace and gusto of Ovid's narration (and adds some of his own).

Golding is often seen as a willing inheritor of the tradition of the *Ovide Moralisé*, and in some parts of the work its precepts are accommodated. The 1567 edition has an Epistle to the Earl of Leicester which offers anticipatory moralizations of many stories. It seems reasonable to say that the Earl, under whose patronage Golding translated both Ovid and Calvin – perhaps the most unlikely combination ever attempted – might have appreciated the clarity of the Epistle's readings, such as of the tale of Arachne:

> Arachnee may example bee that folk should not contend
> Ageinst their betters, nor persist in error to the end.
>
> (121–2)

A modern perspective on this reading might feel that this limits a story which actually displays the capricious and self-serving nature of Minerva's justice – and indeed that it seems not so much a moral as an amoral lesson in how to avoid catastrophe in an unjust world. The important thing is that when Golding approaches the story itself his translation does not show the heavy imprint of a moral reading. Whatever defensive claims are made in the Epistle and the Preface 'Too the Reader', the relentless excitement and irreverent variety of the *Metamorphoses* are not dampened.

The feature of Golding's style which gives his translation its character is his use of words with many English resonances. Instead of attempting to convey the atmosphere and paraphernalia of a vale in Thessaly, or a mountainside in Thrace, he conjures up images of a countryside closer to home. This is evident in Golding's expansive treatment of Ovid's description of the Golden Age:

> The fertile earth as yet was free, untoucht of spade or plough,
> And yet it yeelded of it selfe of every things inough.
> And men themselves contented well with plaine and simple foode,
> That on the earth of natures gift without their travail stoode,
> Did live by Raspis, heppes and hawes, by cornelles, plummes and cherries,
> By sloes and apples, nuttes and peares, and lothsome bramble berries,
> And by the acornes dropt on ground, from Joves brode tree in fielde.
> The Springtime lasted all the yeare, and Zephyr with his milde
> And gentle blast did cherish things that grew of owne accorde,
> The ground untilde, all kinde of fruits did plenteously avorde.
>
> (1.115–24)

Several details are added and what were five fruits in Ovid become twelve. In the *Metamorphoses* there is little real interest in the texture of this rustic plenty except inasmuch as it plays a part in the set-piece description of the first Age. For Golding, however, there is a wealth of detail to be conjured up here: detail which derives neither from Ovid, nor from a vision of classical eating habits. These are English fruits, and this is an English *Metamorphoses*, even if the classical 'Zephyr' still blows. In the Preface Golding promises to deliver an Ovid who speaks English as if it were his own tongue: he carries this commonplace through further than most. What results is a work which sits well with the patriotic strain in Leicester's patronage, and with the ambitions on behalf of their native tongue shared by many renaissance writers.[9]

Just as one can perceive in Golding a certain patriotic edge to his project, it has proved possible for some readers to deem Sandys' Ovid a national triumph, as in Michael Drayton's poem to his friend Sir Henry Reynolds:

> Then dainty *Sands* that hath to *English* done,
> Smooth sliding *Ovid*, and hath made him run
> With so much sweetnesse and unusuall grace,
> As though the neatnesse of the *English* pace,
> Should tell the Jetting *Lattine* that it came
> But slowly after, as though stiffe and lame.
>
> (157–62)[10]

Drayton is not above a note of cultural jingoism, and the accusation of pride in the adjective 'jetting' is typical (the *OED* defines this obsolete sense as 'ostentatious in gait or demeanour; strutting; boastful; vaunting'). His observation on the possible superiority of the English Ovid to the original is based on a stylistic judgement, and it does credit to Drayton's literary judgement that he praises this early successful exploration of the English heroic couplet.[11] This metre subsequently became dominant in English epic (and especially in English translation of both Latin hexameters and elegiac couplets). Sandys' couplets achieve an elegant compression which contrasts with Golding's relative verbosity, as seen in this extract from the story of Echo:

> Yet then, as now, of words she wanted choyce;
> But only could reiterate the close
> Of every speech. This *Juno* did impose.
> For, often when she might have taken *Jove*,
> Compressing there the Nymphs, who weakely strove;
> Her long discourses made the Goddesse stay,
> Untill the Nymphs had time to run-away.
> Which when perceiv'd; shee said, For this abuse

---

[9] See Lyne (1996). [10] Drayton (1931–41) III 230.
[11] On Sandys' style, see Pearcy (1984) 71–99.

> Thy tongue henceforth shall bee of little use.
> Those threats are deeds: She yet ingeminates
> The last of sounds, and what she hears relates.
>
> (p. 89)[12]

Short clauses mimic Latin absolutes; combined with the connecting relative pronoun ('Which when perceiv'd') the sentence structure seems designed to convey a classical sophistication. This extract also shows Latinate vocabulary which is particularly characteristic of this translation: 'reiterate', 'ingeminates' (translating *ingeminat*), and the use of 'compress' to mean 'to embrace sexually'. Some is prompted by etymological equivalents in Ovid, but not all: Sandys seems to aim at a translation-language which approaches the Latin not through Golding's flagrant Englishness but through a linguistic stretch towards its source. This has the opposite atmospheric effect from Golding: Sandys' Ovid seems urbane, witty, elegant, but once in a while, in comparison, staid.

What makes Sandys' Ovid a particularly unusual text is that the greater part of it was completed in the New World, while the translator was working as Treasurer in the Jamestown colony. Before he departed in 1621, Books 1–5 had appeared, and the project was not, it appears, put on hold even during the uncomfortable journey across the Atlantic:

> Yet amongst the roreing of the seas, the rustling of the Shrowdes, and Clamour of Saylers, I translated two bookes, and will perhaps when the sweltring heat of the day confines me to my Chamber gain a further assaye. For which if I be taxt I have noe other excuse but that it was the recreacion of my idle howers. (Letter to Sir Samuel Wrote, 28th March 1623)[13]

Given the nature of his employment and the difficult circumstances in Virginia in the early 1620s, it is only natural that Sandys should be tactful about what may have been a significant use of his time. Sandys' biographer R. B. Davis puts the situation positively: 'if American literature is a fusion of European intellect and American environment, Sandys' Ovid may well be included in it.'[14] However this 'fusion' remains nebulous. Sandys' commentaries are full of anecdotes and travellers' tales, as well as the more familiar scholarly materials of mythography.[15] On many occasions he strikes a personal note in connecting an Ovidian myth to something he has heard or, in some cases, witnessed. A significant number of these have an American context, but the translation itself appears almost insulated from the turmoil around it, except for one moment in Book 15 when a marginal note says

---

[12] References to Sandys (1632).   [13] Kingsbury (1906–35) IV 66.
[14] Davis (1973) 13; see also Davis (1955).   [15] On which see Pearcy (1984) 39–60.

'such have I seene in America' against Pythagoras' reference to shells having been found on dry land (p. 497). The interplay between a classical text and a New World does not result in any obvious or glib *rapprochement*. The translation is stylish and faithful and interesting, and yet it is hard not to feel that something of the energy of Golding (and Ovid) is lacking in Sandys' sophisticated poise.

Just as the *Metamorphoses* translations of Golding and Sandys are the monuments of periods of busy translation in English, Samuel Garth's 1717 volume, printed by Tonson, comes amid another flowering of the art, centred (as is Garth's book) on the talents of John Dryden (who had died in 1700).[16] Multi-authored volumes of the *Heroides* and *Amores*, and the *Ars* and *Remedia*, are dwarfed not least by the physical scale of the 1717 folio. Garth praises the 'Ingenious Gentlemen' responsible for it in his Preface but perhaps the greatest ingenuity is his, in deploying the efforts of Dryden, Addison, Tate, Gay, Pope, Congreve, and Rowe, as well as those of eleven others including himself.[17] The Garth Ovid is united by principles – as he says, 'neither to follow the Author too close out of a Critical Timorousness, nor abandon him too wantonly through a Poetick Boldness' (p. lviii) – and by the heroic couplet metre. Although segmented and in some books the work of several writers in close proximity, what results is a grandiose and unified design. Inevitably it has high points, many of which are Dryden's:

> He felt again, his fingers made a print;
> 'Twas flesh, but flesh so firm, it rose against the dint:
> The pleasing task he fails not to renew;
> Soft, and more soft at ev'ry touch it grew;
> Like pliant wax, when chafing hands reduce
> The former mass to form, and frame for use.
> He would believe, but yet is still in pain,
> And tries his argument of sense again,
> Presses the pulse, and feels the leaping vein.
>
> (p. 327)[18]

This version of the metamorphosis of Pygmalion's statue is remarkable in its receptiveness to the delicate ambivalence of Ovid's version.[19] The rhyme of 'Print' and 'Dint' is an effective way of enforcing the awkward physicality of the story, as a misogynist gropes a statue into life. Dryden's particular innovation is the move into elegant abstraction amid the complex wax simile, where 'mass' and 'form' and 'use' leave one wondering, as one should, where

[16] See Hopkins (1988b) on the roles of Garth and Tonson, and especially that of Dryden as the originator of the project. Also Hopkins (1988a).

[17] Garth (1998) p. lxiii.   [18] Garth (1998) has 'chasing' for 'chafing'.

[19] See Brown (1999) 133–9.

the personality is in the person this statue becomes. Here Dryden is sensitive to nuance and deploys words with Ovidian care. Elsewhere he is necessarily efficient in conveying drama. Between the two great rhetorical set-pieces by Ajax and Ulysses in Book 13 there is a tiny bridging passage which gives just enough context:

> He said: a murmur from a multitude,
> Or somewhat like a stifled shout ensu'd:
> 'Till from his seat arose *Laertes'* son,
> Look'd down a while, and paus'd, e'er he begun;
> Then, to th' expecting audience, rais'd his look,
> And not without prepar'd attention spoke:
> Soft was his tone, and sober was his face;
> Action his words, and words his action grace.
>
> (p. 420)

The momentous 'He said' and the indefinable noise of an undecided and expectant crowd (brilliantly amplifying Ovid's *ultima murmur*) provide the perfect setting for the measured excellence of Ulysses' build-up. The couplet which ends this linking passage is so well-turned as to risk triteness, but it manages to convey through its own practice how effective and composed rhetoric can be.

This is a translation with great style, and style is a priority throughout. Garth's Preface makes only a cursory survey of the allegorical and moral potential of the *Metamorphoses* (pp. li–lvi) and spends far more time out-lining features of Ovid's style and the variety of content. But while Dryden manages to trace the twists and turns of his model's wit, other translators fare a little less consistently. One low point is William Congreve's negotiation of Orpheus' song (which is, admittedly, a minefield for the imitator):

> Let me again *Eurydicè* receive,
> Let Fate her quick-spun thread of life re-weave.
> All our possessions are but loans from you,
> And soon, or late, you must be paid your due;
> Hither we haste to human-kind's last seat,
> Your endless empire, and our sure retreat.
> She too, when ripen'd years she shall attain,
> Must, of avoidless right, be yours again:
> I but the transient use of that require,
> Which soon, too soon, I must resign entire.
>
> (p. 316)

In comparison with Sandys' inventive coinings and pseudo-Latinisms 'avoidless' seems contrived. The real problem here is Congreve's failure to resolve the difficulty of the scene he is tackling, in which a semi-divine poet persuades the forces of Hell. Whereas Virgil decorously avoids ventriloquizing him in *Georgics* 4, Ovid has him deliver a lengthy speech in ironically plain style. This version fails to deliver the simple argument with clarity, or to achieve the far more difficult task of approaching a tone worthy of Orpheus. Congreve seems to want to give eloquence to Orpheus, and ends up caught between two stools.

After the Garth-Dryden version, translation of Ovid does not produce any comparable achievements until the late twentieth century. This is not least due to the diminished status of Ovid during this period: he becomes a writer still much read in schools, and one much recalled as a source of stories, but in comparison with Virgil he is judged lacking in moral or artistic seriousness. It is true that this is not a particularly auspicious period in the translation of Virgil either.[20] According to Norman Vance the Garth volume 'had no real rivals throughout the nineteenth century' and it remained in print into the 1800s.[21] Lee Pearcy has argued that both the reading of Ovid and the idea of translation found in Dryden's poetry and criticism dominated the years which followed.[22] In the eighteenth century in particular, perhaps partly as a reaction to the serious classicism of Dryden, stories from the *Metamorphoses* were given a burlesque treatment which to some extent they had always anticipated, as in William Meston's 1720 version of Phaethon. Perhaps the most intriguing of the century's extravagant creations is the version of the debate of Ajax and Ulysses written by Robert Forbes in a broad Aberdeen dialect.[23] By the time the shadow of Dryden had waned in the late nineteenth and early twentieth centuries, classical translation no longer commanded the literary high ground.

In recent years literary translation has shown signs of revival, and Ovid has benefited from this more than most classical authors. This is partly the result of a revitalized sense of the value of Ovid's poetry. It is also the result of a convenient schism between different kinds of translation, which has opened up a creative space modern writers seem keen to explore. David Slavitt, translator of the *Metamorphoses* and the exile poetry, has described this division:

> What I was aiming for is a text that is lively and readable in English, and if that meant taking liberties, I allowed myself that privilege. After all, the Latin poems remain, and faithful, literal translations are available to those who wish to consult them.[24]

[20] See Burrow (1997) 30–4.   [21] Vance (1988) 224.
[22] Pearcy (1984) 100–38.   [23] See Martin (1998) 285.   [24] Slavitt (1990) p. vi.

The distinction between texts which one reads and ones which one would 'consult', between the literary and the literal, only began to predominate in the twentieth century. It is a problematic but nevertheless convenient demarcation between translations which are involved in the poetic reputations of two writers, and those which trade only with one: that of the author being translated. Slavitt is often highly visible in his work in moments of anachronism:

> My horses, twitching their ears, spooked by this monster, broke
> into a frenzy and dashed.... I tried my best to restrain them,
> control their course with the reins as we bounced along on that beach,
> and thought I might yet subdue them and bring them back to their senses,
> but the axle of one of the wheels of my car hit a huge boulder
> that wrenched the hubcap off. We lost our wheel, and the car
> flipped and threw me over. (15.512–8)[25]

Slavitt elides the story of Hippolytus in *Metamorphoses* Book 15 with that of a young joyrider, almost casually transforming a chariot into a motor car. His anachronisms do not come across as punchlines partly because they are neatly contained within a generally successful attempt at English hexameters, but mostly because they have an Ovidian ability to supply vividness and ironic alienation at the same time. The features for which Slavitt is best known are his added notes of internal commentary, attacking or defending or categorizing what is being done, in some ways responding expansively to things which in the Latin poem are implied by negotiation with well-worn convention. One of his interventions is good advice for Congreve, as seen above:

> But it's risky, even for Ovid, to try to do Orpheus' voice.
> What poet, what bard or *Dichter*, does not doubt his powers,
> know how clumsy and thick-tongued he is? To perform as the proto-
> poet? The task is daunting, and Ovid turns our attention
> from cause to effects. (10.34–8)

The intertextuality with Virgil gives Ovid's treatment of Orpheus' speech an extra *frisson*, and Slavitt seems to want to breathe some life back into this interaction. As he says, Ovid moves swiftly on to describe the success of Orpheus' song, leaving it to the reader to consider what has passed. Slavitt makes a subtly nuanced decision to linger at this point.

One of the landmarks of Ovid in modern English is the collection *After Ovid*, which emulated Garth in bringing together an even larger number

---

[25] References to Slavitt (1994).

of poets to translate or respond to the *Metamorphoses* (or most of it). The collection has highs and lows, and it features some acts of ingenious anachronism. Tom Paulin offers Cadmus as William Whitelaw (p. 86) and as 'Descartes with a scalpel' (p. 85), amongst other guises, as he finds resonances with the hero's battle with the dragon in Irish politics and questions of political liberty. William Logan gives Niobe 'a Hermès handbag in the Stop and Shop' (p. 147) as he transforms her into an urban interloper in rural New England. Jo Shapcott's 'Peleus and Thetis' is sharpened by a modern sexual politics which provides a prism through which to view the rape which resulted in Achilles' birth (p. 264). Every good translation, of course, is an interpretation, and many of those in *After Ovid* shed light on subtle nuances of the original. Christopher Reid's brief 'Deucalion and Pyrrha' discovers wistfulness:

> Since when, we have always found
> something hard, ungracious,
> obdurate in our very natures,
> a strain of that very earth
> that gave us our abrupt birth;
> but a pang, too, at the back
> of the mind: a loss . . . a lack . . .
>
> (p. 27)

In Ovid the tone of this neat conclusion is that of an aetiological magician pulling away a curtain to reveal the stony origins of stony humanity. Reid's sense of separation from the earth sits no less easily with Ovidian urbanity than Golding's jaunty rusticity, but it reveals something buried within the brittle bones of the story of Deucalion and Pyrrha. The closing couplet does not derive from Ovid, but his story does not wholly hide the reserves of emotion which it leaves artfully untapped. Michael Longley's several contributions to *After Ovid* strike a note of poignancy more than once: he transforms Pygmalion into a figure for pity, humorous condescension, and (to some extent) for revulsion as the statue resembles a kind of pornography ('Ivory and Water', p. 244). Again there is a sense more of discovery than of imposition as one aspect of Ovid's hero is drawn out. In the *Metamorphoses* the misogynistic sculptor strikes an absurd pose as he lavishes gifts on a statue, and Longley resolves Ovid's delicate ambivalence into an ultimately thwarted bittersweetness: the dream of his statue melts away into water.

As a response to the variety and structural complexity of the *Metamorphoses* the multi-authored volume is a solution which offers distinctive possibilities, but in this case poets' different styles and reputations necessarily amplify the disjointedness of the experience of reading stories which were already often tenuously bridged. Some of the *After Ovid* translators make a virtue of this necessity and (as Ovid does) dwell on the patchwork nature of this mythology. Amy Clampitt emphasizes the half-ending of the story of Medea:

> A fugitive
> once more, she called on her winged beasts, sprung
> from the stock of Titans, and flew straight to
> the city of Athena, where King Aegeus
> (the story goes on being awful), to be brief,
> made the mistake of making her his wife.
>
> (p. 179)

This draws attention to the partial telling of the story: something Ovid achieves by brusqueness, an imitator needs to register more deliberately. It might be argued that this volume takes the subtly brittle connections between stories in the *Metamorphoses* and crudely snaps them: over the page starts James Lasdun's unconnected 'The Plague at Aegina': 'Cephalus at Aegina, not a face | Familiar on the skiffs or landing place'. However, the arrangement of the different elements of *After Ovid* results in felicitous overlaps and stylishly-managed connections, as well as staccato schisms. Charles Tomlinson ends one extract 'And so ends The Tale of Dryope Transformed', with the next (Fleur Adcock's 'Iphis and Ianthe') starting 'But that's nothing to what happened in Crete' (pp. 218–19). There is something distinctly Ovidian about the myriad kinds of dialogue between stories.

Some of the extracts in *After Ovid* were, soon after, incorporated into Ted Hughes' *Tales from Ovid*, in which Hughes proves receptive to the original's shifts in tone. However, there is one way in which this translation is persistently not Ovidian, and that is in its avoidance of his model's characteristic understatement. Ovid often leaves things implicit, perhaps to the point of negligence, subjugating local climaxes to a greater momentum. Hughes lingers over the possibilities of individual moments, as in the grim climax of Myrrha's story:

> The next night father and daughter did it again
> In the pitch darkness.
> The same, night after night. On the ninth night
> Cinyras made a mistake.
> He let curiosity take over.
> He prepared a lamp. That he lit
> And held high, as she lay there,
> Revealing the form and the face

Of his bedmate –
His daughter.

Now all the guilt was his.
Too huge and elemental
For words
His anguish
Was a roar throughout the palace.

(p. 126)[26]

The things which Hughes seems to add to Ovid – the 'mistake', the quality of the 'guilt', and the rhetorical drama of the moment of revelation – add to his version. Their presence, though, sacrifices the tone of an original which is tantalizingly ambiguous. It is somewhat inadequate to say that Ovid lets events speak for themselves, although this is part of it; perhaps it is better to say that what Hughes misses is a chasm of potential – horrific or ironic, sometimes both – which opens up through characteristically Ovidian understatement.

The title of *Tales from Ovid* implies that it will not take on the epic structure of the *Metamorphoses*. There is no attempt at the speech of Pythagoras, which does appear in *After Ovid* in Michael Longley's affectionately bathetic version, and there is (as in *After Ovid*) no translation of the Roman-historical finale. Hughes does translate the opening sequence of the *Metamorphoses*, including the creation of the world (the same text opens *After Ovid* as well), and here too his characteristic expansion of Ovid is evident:

Before sea or land, before even sky
Which contains all,
Nature wore only one mask –
Since called Chaos.
A huge agglomeration of upset.
A bolus of everything – but
As if aborted.
And the total arsenal of entropy
Already at war within it.

(p. 3)

The touches which amplify the tone here ('agglomeration of upset', 'bolus of everything', 'arsenal of entropy') both add something to Hughes' text and miss something in Ovid's. The poetic temperature is raised by such strong language, but in the *Metamorphoses* there is a point to the relative coolness, as Ovid is pacing himself, allocating rhetorical energy on his own terms.[27]

[26] References to Hughes (1997).   [27] See Henderson (1999).

Here, at the beginning of the work, Hughes may be guilty of wanting too much too soon: at the end, though, he does resort to understatement. For although *Tales from Ovid* does not end as the *Metamorphoses* does, it does reach a distinct end, with the pathos of Pyramus and Thisbe:

> And the two lovers in their love-knot,
> One pile of inseparable ashes,
> Were closed in a single urn.

(p. 254)

Hughes' version of Ovid ends with this poignant picture of unity in death which is also a poignant rescue of a positive note from a tragic story. The tales in the collection are not arranged in their *Metamorphoses* order and this seems a deliberate and appropriate place to end: proposing a conclusion which is unifying and thematic rather than historical and prophetic about the poet's future glory. Hindsight enhances this impression, since *Tales from Ovid* was published so close to the end of the poet's life and the reassessment of his career and in particular his relationship with Sylvia Plath ('inseparable ashes'?). In a way Hughes' translation is most valuable because of an apparent discrepancy in style: his dialogue with his source is not afflicted with the 'timorousness' Garth feared. Indeed, he discovers Hughesian moments in the *Metamorphoses* much as Golding unearths English settings for the myths.

FURTHER READING

A wide range of Ovidian translation can be found in Martin (1998), and Poole and Maule (1995). The landmark *Metamorphoses* translations before the twentieth century are those of Arthur Golding (1567), George Sandys (1632), and the collaborative version of 1717 organised by Samuel Garth and starring John Dryden. In recent years three important new versions have appeared: David Slavitt's full version (1994), Ted Hughes' translation of extracts (1997), and the Faber collection edited by Michael Hofmann and James Lasdun (1994) and featuring the work of a constellation of modern poets.

Brown (1999) and Martindale (1988) cover the full historical range of Ovidian influence and English translations. Pearcy (1984) focuses on Renaissance versions, as does Lyne (2001). Henderson (1999) looks at the most modern translations.

16

JEREMY DIMMICK

Ovid in the Middle Ages: authority and poetry

Ovid in the Middle Ages is an *auctor* perpetually falling foul of authority. As *auctor* he is more than an author in the modern sense: he is 'a man of gret auctorite' (Chaucer's phrase),[1] learned in moral philosophy, natural science and philosophy, as well as the unchallenged expert on love and the most important resource for students of classical mythology. Nonetheless, *carmen* continues to be coupled with *error* throughout his medieval reception; however culturally central he becomes, he is never fully restored from his Augustan exile, and remains an archpriest of transgression, whether sexual, political or theological. It is in this powerfully ambivalent role of the *auctor* at odds with *auctoritas*, just as much as (and indeed inseparable from) his expertise on mythology and sexuality, that he is most precious to the poets. This chapter will explore a selection of medieval readers and reinventors of Ovid to reconstruct some of the personal and more institutional agendas that the reading of his works could generate, in both secular and religious discourses.

A small, unassuming passage of seemingly-incidental description can serve as our jumping-off point. It is deployed by the twelfth-century poet Marie de France in the *lai* of 'Guigemar', the first in a collection of short French narratives purporting to be drawn from oral Breton tradition; it serves at once to signal Ovid's presence in the *lai* and to dramatize his repudiation. A beautiful, noble lady is married to an aged, jealous lord who keeps her imprisoned in a tower by the sea; guarding her is the eunuch priest of a chapel evidently consecrated to Venus, and the walls of her heavily eroticized chamber are decorated with the goddess's imagery:

> Venus, la deuesse d'amur,
> Fu tresbien [mise] en la peinture,
> Les traiz mustrez e la nature
> Cument hom deit amur tenir

---

[1] *The House of Fame* 2158, in Chaucer (1987).

E lëalment e bien servir;
Le livre Ovide, ou il enseine
Coment chascun s'amur estreine,
En un fu ardant le gettout
E tuz iceus escumengout
Ki ja mais cel livre lirreient
Ne sun enseignement fereient.[2]

Venus, the goddess of love, was finely depicted in the painting. The character and nature of love were shown there, how one should be faithful to love and serve it loyally and well. The book where Ovid teaches how everyone should take control of love she threw into a burning fire, and she excommunicated all who might ever read this book or follow its teaching.

It is not clear exactly what Ovid's offence is, or which book is being burned. His crime must be one of infidelity – the contrast with the preceding lines demands it – but its interpretation, and hence the meaning of the painting, remains contested. The key word is *estreine*: later in the *lai* it refers to the literal tightening of a belt which can only be undone by a true lover (572); Marie also uses it of a lovers' embrace ('Equitan' 207). Here it has been read negatively as the constraining of desire taught in the *Remedia amoris*: Venus would thus be recapitulating Cupid's fear that Ovid has turned traitor.[3] Equally, though, the reference could be to the *Ars amatoria*'s instruction on how to master love, with its presupposition of sexual infidelity.[4] If we consider the iconography, like the entire complex in which the lady is imprisoned, to be the husband's design, then the burning of the *Ars* serves to reinforce his control over his wife's body, suborning the goddess of love herself to serve his interest. The image can be claimed by other interests, however: they may express the lady's resistance to the erotic control exerted by her husband (*estreine* in the sense of 'grasp' or 'force').[5] Fidelity is indeed to be the virtue that drives the *lai* – not, however, fidelity to a husband.

As the *lai* progresses it becomes clear that the lord's interpretation is going to lose out: hermeneutic control over the painting fails as radically as physical control over his wife. The hero Guigemar gains access to the tower, and in so doing, ensures that the destruction of one Ovidian text has paved the way for the entrance of another. Guigemar descends from the world of the *Metamorphoses*, a chaste hunter indifferent to the women who pursue him,

---

[2] 'Guigemar' 234–44, in Marie de France (1995). The collection is generally dated to the 1160s–1180s (*ibid.* pp. ii–viii).
[3] So Marie de France (1995) 167; cf. Allen (1992) 168 n.29, Whalen (1996).
[4] Braet (1978) 24. Hanning (1981) 44 sees 'the whole Ovidian system' of erotic calculation as the target.
[5] Greimas (1992) s.v. *estraindre*, senses 1 and 2.

and mortally wounded by his own agency – part Hippolytus, part Actaeon, part Narcissus.[6] His arrow kills a hind, but rebounds and strikes him in the thigh; the dying animal curses him to die unless he is cured by a woman who will suffer more for love of him, and he for her, than any before them. Eros is transformed from the *Metamorphoses'* agent of destruction to one of redemption: 'Guigemar', archly dewy-eyed, promotes pure, mutual, and adulterous passion as its sole moral and social value. Marie, no less than the jealous husband, is appropriating and revising both elegiac love and Ovidian mythology.

Yet *Guigemar's* moral triumph of adulterous love is immediately answered by a tale of unbending severity ('Equitan'), in which adulterers are punished by death at the hands of a royal husband who incarnates the vengeful power of outraged authority. Moral and social values in the *Lais* have become contingent rather than absolute, driven by perspective and particular interest; its arts of love are answered by remedies, juxtaposing contrarieties with little prospect of synthesis. Ovid for the Middle Ages stands as the single most important window into this imaginative world of secular contingency, power, passion, and the scope and limits of human art. If Ovid is an *auctor*, he is one who reveals *auctoritas* to be a power-source, exploited and contested, rather than the stable, central authority of Scripture, and Marie's ecphrasis reveals this at an intimately allusive level. Her playful, unpredictable anatomies of the relationships between personal desire, socially-inscribed authority and art rightly acknowledge Ovid as kindred spirit and competitor. The possessive husband's tower, with its effort at containing and controlling Ovid's book, is a prototype for all medieval efforts to appropriate him, deploying (and where necessary critiquing) the poems and their author to serve their own interests and neutralize competing ones. The husband's loss of command, his cuckolding mocked by an iconographic programme of his own devising, is equally instructive: no one reading, however strenuously enforced, manages to eliminate its rivals.

Ovid's books have a habit of surviving their burning. The supposed destruction of the *Metamorphoses* on their author's departure into exile is part of its myth of epic origins, and perhaps Marie's image recalls this.[7] One medieval reconstruction of the composition of the *Fasti* has it that it too was destroyed at the same time, with the first six books reconstructed from memory in exile, and rededicated to Germanicus. Others claimed that Books 7 to 12 were suppressed by the patristic Church as idolatrous, or for blasphemously applying to Julius and Augustus Caesar prophecies which were

---

[6] Spence (1996) 128–36.
[7] Ov. *Trist.* 1.7.11–30; see Tarrant, in Martindale (1997) 61.

properly of Christ.[8] A central, indispensable author for the Middle Ages, he remained an acutely combustible one.

Several constituencies could regard Ovid's books as fit for burning. Christine de Pizan (*c.*1363–*c.*1430) takes them as a threat to the dignity of women: for her, Ovid is the father of a tradition of clerical misogyny in love poetry whose chief modern son is Jean de Meun in the *Roman de la Rose*. Like Marie, she has him condemned by the gods of love themselves: Cupid in the *Epistre au Dieu d'amours* condemns *Ars amatoria* and *Remedia amoris* alike.[9] According to Christine's distinctively embroidered version of his life in her *Livre de la cité des dames*, Ovid was banished for his dissipation, promiscuity and corrupting influence, but recalled from exile by a powerful clique of young Roman men; failing to learn his lesson, he was eventually punished with castration, as though a prototype Abelard. Frustrated at his inability to indulge his vices any longer, he wrote the *Ars* and *Remedia* out of malice, to turn other men against women.[10] Christine's detestation of Ovid does not make her unwilling to borrow from him; on the contrary, she does so repeatedly, and in a consciously revisionist spirit, appropriating mythological protagonists and narratives from the *Metamorphoses* for her own arguments.[11]

Male clerical tradition has its own grounds for attack, not surprisingly encountered earlier and more often than the feminist critique. The twelfth-century theologian William of St Thierry neither deigns nor needs to name the *doctor artis amatoriae* who corrupted natural love rather than teaching it, and was eventually obliged to recant. William's treatise *De natura et dignitate amoris* is presented as a counterblast, an *Ars amatoria* for the Christian soul, thereby bearing reluctant witness to the twelfth-century explosion of interest in Ovid. Love, for William, is a natural force analogous to gravity, but one which nonetheless requires an art to teach it: the soul must now relearn what was originally natural to it in Paradise.[12] The scandal of Ovid here is that he stands so close to the proper function of the *magister Amoris*, yet subverts it utterly.

His poetic allure remains strong for his detractors: even the aptly-named *Antiovidianus*, an anonymous fourteenth-century Latin poem from Italy, casts itself into Ovid's own medium of elegiac couplets, and concedes, adapting his own words, that his Muse was more fertile than all other poets': *nam quod temptabas scribere versus erat* ('for whatever you tried to write, it came

---

[8] Alton (1930) 123, Ghisalberti (1946) 41, Minnis and Scott (1991) 362.
[9] *Epistre* 281–92, 365–78, in Fenster and Erler (1990).
[10] 1.9.2, translated in Christine de Pizan (1999) 20–1.
[11] Brownlee, in Brownlee and Huot (1992) 234–61, Kellogg (1998), Wisman (1997).
[12] 1.1–3 in William of St Thierry (1953), translated in William of St Thierry (1981).

out verse').[13] The poem is a stylish and energetic denunciation, representing everything Ovid wrote as pernicious and unfit for consumption, and culminating with a burning not of the books but of their author, in the fires of hell. Yet the *Antiovidianus* cannot deny the poetic gift on which, indeed, its own writing depends: poetic talent is here quite divorced from ethical or philosophical reliability. Indeed, there is a case for seeing the poem less as the denunciation it purports to be, more as a rhetorical challenge to a set of by-now-traditional pedagogic strategies that sought to make Ovid a respectable, upright citizen of the literary commonwealth. The poem's insistence, for example, that Ovid's *Remedia* is as poisonous as the original disease spread by the *Ars*, or that the *Heroides*, however they may praise Penelope's virtue, are themselves 'whorish poems' (*meretricia carmina*, 73), runs directly counter to the mainstream scholarly approach.

Like much of medieval Ovidian tradition, these strategies were formulated in the twelfth century, in this case by schoolmasters seeking to justify his presence in the curriculum. Conrad of Hirsau, writing in the first half of the century, faces the question squarely in his *Dialogus super auctores* between a master and a student. Why, the latter asks, should Christ's pupil 'submit his tractable imagination' to Ovid? Even if there is gold amid the dung, the treasure-seeker is polluted by the contact.[14] If Conrad's master remains cautious in his response, the well-known tradition of *accessus ad auctores*, basic introductions to the study of an author, confidently justify Ovid's presence in the curriculum. Poetic texts generally belong under moral philosophy: ethics provides a set of implicit norms of behaviour, which poetry dramatizes. The *Heroides* in particular are kept under control by this approach, so that for all their domination by sexually-charged, passionate, female voices, they are controlled by a male moralist's invisible hand. Penelope, by being placed first, articulates a standard of conjugal love by which all the ensuing heroines can be measured. Accordingly, the *Heroides* map out an anatomy of love, with the chaste love of marriage set against species of foolish or criminal desire.[15] This overly tidy schematization does provide some useful categories for poets, and it has been plausibly argued that the *Roman d'Eneas*, for one, constructs its large-scale contrasts between Dido and Lavine (Virgil's Lavinia, promoted to a starring role as Eneas' true lover) on such a basis.[16] Indeed, Marie's *lais* show something of the same anatomizing instinct, juxtaposing incompatible models of love, but they also

---

[13] *Antiovidianus* 382, in Burdach and Kienast (1929); cf. Ov. *Trist.* 4.10.26. Stroh in Albrecht and Zinn (1968) 567–80 traces the verse's medieval and modern reception.
[14] Huygens (1970) 114.
[15] Huygens (1970) 31. The Ovidian *accessus* are translated in Elliott (1980).
[16] Nolan (1989).

suggest that the project of an anatomy of love held more imaginative appeal to poets than the rigid ethical framework that was supposed to contain it. The *Antiovidianus* gives the latter short shrift: Ovid's meretricious voice is less a moralist's than that of the *anus* (73–4) – the aged Dipsas of *Amores* 1.8, who had come to found a long line of such figures, from the twelfth-century comedy *Pamphilus* to Jean de Meun's La Vieille and beyond.[17] For all the shocked disapproval deployed by the speaker of the *Amores*, her voice is dangerously close to his own.[18]

With the *Ars* or the *Amores*, it is harder to construct an ethical reading than for the *Heroides*, and the *accessus* are more inclined to present the *Ars* as a genuine how-to manual, proper amatory didactic, or as entertainment. If it still belongs under moral philosophy, it does so only because it considers *mores*, specifically the behaviour of young women, since if you know their ways, you know how to keep them. The potential for 'ethics' as a philosophical category to become separated from any didactic intention is clear from the bald statement of one introduction to the *Amores: Intentio eius est delectare. Ethicae supponitur* ('its intention is to entertain. It belongs under ethics').[19]

Exactly where the art of love belongs in clerical discourse is explored with quietly comic resourcefulness in a remarkable version of the *Ars* in French prose, complete with a commentary so straight-faced that it has been read quite straight by its editor and translator.[20] The *Art d'amours*, whose original version (first third of the thirteenth century) comprised only Books 1 and 2 of the *Ars*, is automatically marginal to academic culture by virtue of its vernacularity, but it lays claim to a genuine, Latinate scholarly authority with its careful mythological glossing. At the same time, it undermines that authority's foundations. Its unquestioned premise is that the art of love is perfectly proper for clerics to pursue, unlike such black arts as sorcery, divination or gambling. To refuse to love women is a sin, as surely as homosexuality or the mad, suicidal despair of the unskilful lover (*Accessus* 96–109). While aristocrats learn it by nature, and the common people by habitual practice – that is, foolishly and arrogantly imitating their betters – clerics have to turn to books (30–41). It is implied, then, that this is a book for clerics; the tradition of comic debates on the respective merits of knights and clergy as lovers (the latter generally victorious) lies in the background.[21] The commentary is

---

[17] *Pamphilus* is edited in Bate (1976) 61–89; a published translation is Garbaty (1967). Guillaume de Lorris and Jean de Meun (1992) 12385–4719, translated in Guillaume de Lorris and Jean de Meun (1983).

[18] Myers (1996) confirms and develops the *Antiovidianus*' perception, in Tibullus and Propertius as well as Ovid.

[19] Huygens (1970) 36.   [20] Ed. Roy (1974), trans. Blonquist (1987).

[21] A famous example is the *Altercatio Phyllidis et Florae* (text and translation in Caverly (1980)). Haller (1968) reads the poem as 'Ovidian satire'.

inclined to represent love as the great social and discursive leveller. Its most striking feature is its frequent recourse to snatches of French verse which it claims to draw variously from aristocratic songs and popular proverbs, to parallel and reinforce Ovid's advice. By calling on voices from the other two estates, aristocratic and demotic, the commentary implicitly places Ovid's pragmatic, secular wisdom on the same level as popular proverb or dance-song. The commentary strips away his specifically textual, clerical authority, while seeming to reinforce it through formal commentary. As a vernacular offshoot from the scholarly tradition, the *Art d'amours* enjoys the revelation that Latin textual authority is by no means of a different order to the authority of vernacular verse: it revels in the self-exploding nature of Ovid's didactic posture in the *Ars*, and offers an inspired recreation of it on the margins of scholarly propriety.

The commonest way of rationalizing the place of the *Ars* in the canon, however, was to point out that Ovid himself paid dearly for it. The apparent retreat from ethically-slanted reading is essentially tactical, since that reading is about to stage a come-back in the form of an elaborate penitential narrative. The *Remedia amoris* is transformed into a genuine retraction of the *Ars*. Considering that Ovid begins the work by reassuring Cupid that it is no such thing (1–40), and we have seen more than one medieval writer clearly aware of this, the reading of the *Remedia* as properly remedial proved oddly persistent; as a narrative pattern, the structure of an offence and an attempt at restitution had a special imaginative hold. The structural pattern of sequel-as-refutation is visible, indeed, even within the *Art d'amours*: a second author added a version of Book 3 towards the end of the thirteenth century, and is more a rival and corrector than a disciple, most obviously in providing the book for women which his predecessor had denied them. The earlier commentator explicitly warns against allowing the book to fall into female hands (2327–51), when it offers details on the dangerous love-potions to which Ovid merely alludes (*Ars* 2.99–106). The continuation begins with an implicit rebuke to his predecessor by justifying the provision of the art to female readers (which, as Pierre Col points out in his defence of Jean de Meun, is at least feasible in the vernacular).[22] In another respect, however, the levelling of hierarchies in Books 1 and 2 is distinctly resisted: Book 3 drops the quotations from songs, and prefers to cite proverbial wisdom within the learned matrix of Solomon or Boethius.

This principle of construction, in which texts and parts of texts seem to shift restlessly between continuity and a direct competition for interpretive command, is pervasive in medieval Ovidian works. An extreme case

[22] Hicks (1977) 105.

is Andreas Capellanus' famous *De amore*, dating perhaps from the 1180s. Among its manuscript titles is *De arte amandi et de reprobatione amoris* ('the art of loving and the condemnation of love'), the modification of Ovid's terminology marking a stark internal opposition. A later alteration attempts to identify these two *amores* as different species, honourable and dishonourable ('honeste amandi . . . inhonesti amoris'), but this tidying-up misrepresents a text that resists all attempts to reduce it to a single argument.[23]

Where the translators of the *Art d'amours* dispute the propriety of female readers, Andreas deploys male and female voices as part of the *De amore*'s internal warfare. He directs the work to a specific male reader, a friend suffering from love, but in Book 1, women's voices are used to articulate a rational resistance to male desire.[24] This book is dominated by a series of dialogues of attempted seduction played out between different social classes, in none of which is the man actually successful. Andreas later represents various noblewomen, including Marie, Countess of Champagne and Eleanor of Aquitaine, as sound judges of propriety in love (2. 7). But Book 3 drowns out these voices with an increasingly hysterical tirade against sexuality and, especially, against women. Sexual love is the creation of the devil, chastity that of God; no woman has ever sincerely loved either her husband or her lover, or indeed possessed a single virtue (3.38–39, 65–112). Violent contrariety has become the basic method of the text, in its internal stresses and its precise inversions of Ovid: in place of two books of arts for men and one for women, Andreas' first book mounts its resistance to the *Ars* in women's voices, but he demonizes them in his third. The lower-class interlocutor of dialogue D in Book 1 (*mulier plebeia*) offers a rebuke to her would-be seducer which stands as a programme for the whole work:

> In tuis videris sermonibus tanquam cancer in ambulando retrogradus, quod nunc negare contendis quod statim audaci lingua . . . firmaveras.   (1.188)

> In your speeches you seem to have a backwards gait, like a crab, for you're now striving to deny what you were a moment ago affirming in rash terms.

The teaching and the condemnation of love are both subordinate to the dynamic driving the work, a far-from-edifying theatre of rhetorical and psychological extremes in which self-contradiction and retrograde motion are governing principles.

Subtler and more indefinite, the *Roman de la Rose* is probably the most influential of all the works inspired by this Ovidian art of construction by contrarieties. Like the *Art d'amours* it is the work of two authors with different agendas at opposite ends of the thirteenth century, Guillaume de Lorris

---

[23] Andreas Capellanus (1982) 1–3.   [24] Calabrese (1997) 8–15.

and Jean de Meun. Guillaume explicitly represents his work as a new art of love from the outset (37–9), and his central mythological image is a reinvention of Ovid's Narcissus.[25] Before he enters the garden of love, the narrator-protagonist is an antitype of Narcissus: washing his face in a river (rather than a static, self-enclosed pool), he sees through the clear water to the gravel bed; no reflection interposes (103–23). At the heart of love's garden itself, however, he looks into the perilous fountain of Narcissus (1422–1619), at the bottom of which are two crystals which seem to be images of the eyes of either Narcissus or the lover, or of some fusion of the two into a single, self-enwrapped agent of erotic vision in which the Rose, and the whole universe of the garden, are reflected. It remains unclear from Guillaume's incomplete narrative what closure this might generate – whether Amant is doomed to become another Narcissus, absorbed into the original narrative, or whether the poem's goal is to recall him from it.

Jean de Meun constructs a lineage of love poets founded directly on *Amores* 3.9, naming only Guillaume and himself as the modern heirs of elegy's 'apostolic succession' (E. K. Rand's phrase), Tibullus, Gallus, Catullus and Ovid (10511–620).[26] The impression of smooth continuity is deceptive: his vast continuation, for all that it promises explanation (10607–8) and at least delivers narrative closure, divided critical opinion early and lastingly. The divisions run along familiar lines: while Christine de Pizan condemns it as amoral and misogynistic, its defenders claim it as the work of an ironic moralist, constituting a *Remedia amoris* rather than an *Ars amatoria*. Pierre Col, one of Christine's opponents in the debate, insists that Jean describes the storming of the castle of Jealousy so as to forewarn its defenders, and even offers anecdotal evidence that the cure could work.[27] As with Andreas Capellanus, Jean's argument cannot be reduced to singularity; he sets off against each other competing spokespersons, most of them with some genuine claim to authority or experience – among them the pragmatic, secular and elegiac know-how of Ami (7233–10010) and La Vieille (12389–4723), male and female adherents respectively of the *Ars amatoria*, between whom the advice of Ovid's three books is divided.[28] Each readily functions as *Remedia*, however; Ami quotes extensively from the competing voice of a jealous husband, mounting misogynist tirades from within the voice of amatory experience. Jean also develops his own mythological master-image from the *Metamorphoses*, a Pygmalion to counter Guillaume's Narcissus. The

---

[25] For fuller accounts see Harley (1986), Steinle (1989).
[26] Rand (1925) 9; see also Fleming in Brownlee and Huot (1992) 81–100.
[27] Hicks (1977) 105.
[28] Bouché (1977) helpfully tabulates Jean's direct borrowings from Ovid, which are concentrated in these speeches.

result is a ceaseless process of Ovidian and anti-Ovidian invention and exegesis which inexorably drew in early and more recent readers as participants.[29]

The acutely unstable relationship between *Ars* and *Remedia* in medieval readings could be stabilized to a degree by appealing to a wider biographical context. That 'the life of our poet ... was bisected' (Rand again) dominates medieval lives of Ovid, and shaped the way his whole output was read.[30] Biographical accounts tend to divide his career into those works which got him into trouble and those in which he tried and failed to extricate himself. This group of 'remedial' texts regularly expands to include the *Heroides* and *Remedia* as well as the elegies from exile. The *Fasti* and *Metamorphoses* too were sometimes regarded as efforts to recapture the cultural high ground after the *Ars* had outraged Roman public opinion in general, or Augustus in particular.[31] The life of Ovid that prefaces the *De vetula* (a text discussed below) teases out a clear political line in which Ovid incurs Augustus' wrath primarily because of the *Ars*, and attempts to win back his grace with the *Remedia*. The *Fasti*, written in exile, is dedicated to Germanicus in the hope that his mediation will earn forgiveness from Augustus, while the *Metamorphoses* honours Caesar's ancestors with the same intent.[32]

Even the *Amores*, more surprisingly, are touched by this approach: they generally circulated in manuscript as *Liber sine titulo* ('book without a title'), and some speculated that Ovid left them untitled so as not to call casual attention to their erotic subject matter. One version has it that he was commanded by Augustus to produce a five-book epic on his war against Antony and Cleopatra, and disguised his failure to do so by leaving his new erotic work unnamed. As well as offering some sort of explanation for Ovid's prefatory reference to a five-book poem that has become three, this suggestion draws attention to the recurring displacement of epic by elegy established from the outset (*Am.* 1.1, cf. 2.1), and in particular to 3.12.15–16, where 'Caesar's deeds' constitute one of the epic themes to have been displaced by Corinna. One *accessus* dismisses such suggestions as 'trivial and of no value' (*frivole ... et nulle*), but goes on to argue that Ovid left the work untitled when he was exiled, so as not to associate the poems too closely with the notorious *Ars* and earn them proscription.[33] If both the *Amores* and *Heroides*

---

[29] For Jean's Pygmalion (20801–1218) see Poirion (1970), Cahoon (1986). On early reception and interpretation, see especially Huot (1993).
[30] Rand (1925) 8.
[31] Huygens (1970) 31–6, *Vulgate Commentary*, *accessus* 98–103 in Coulson (1991), Alton (1930) 123.
[32] Ed. Robathan (1968) 42.
[33] Ghisalberti (1946) 12; Huygens (1970) 36, where the aborted epic is a *Gigantomachia* (cf. Ov. *Am.* 2.1.11–22).

are placed after the *Ars* in Ovid's career, this one poem becomes a kind of literary original sin, from whose consequences everything else he wrote becomes a series of increasingly desperate (and consistently misfiring) defensive or corrective reactions.

This biographically-inspired reading generates a distinctly Christian narrative pattern of sin, punishment and a long effort to recover the state of grace that is Rome, but it lacks the proper Christian conclusion. One *accessus* to the *Fasti*, explaining the dedication to Germanicus as intended to help reconcile poet and *princeps*, comments: *Vtilitas huius libri nulla legitur fuisse, quia ab exilio numquam legitur rediisse* ('we read that this book was of no benefit at all, for, we read, he was never recalled from exile').[34] The most fantastical elaborations of the story thrive on tragic closure: the fourteenth-century Italian commentator Giovanni del Virgilio, having cited the standard opinion that Ovid died in exile, adds an alternative version in which he was eventually recalled to Rome, only to be suffocated by the crowds that had gathered to welcome him.[35] One last time, and in his moment of triumphant vindication as the most famous poet of his age, he is the victim of his own *ingenium*.[36]

The proximity of Ovid to his Christian readers, and the spiritual gulf that separates them, are both dramatized in a powerful anecdote preserved and discussed in at least two thirteenth-century Latin versions.[37] It tells of two *clerici* who visit Ovid's tomb in Tomis, praise him as a model of eloquence, and ask each other what they consider his best and worst lines. A voice from the tomb answers their question, offering two verses from the *Heroides*: respectively, Helen's *Est virtus placitis abstinuisse bonis* ('there's virtue in refusing goods that please', *Her.* 17.98), and a version of Phaedra's dismissal of conventional morality, *Omne iuvans statuit Iupiter esse pium* ('Jupiter established that the good is whatever gives pleasure', cf. *Her.* 4.133).[38] So far, Ovid is being much more cooperative with his censorious readers than in the distant model for the anecdote, the story in Seneca's *Controuersiae* 2.2.12 that the three verses his friends would soonest see suppressed were exactly those Ovid would not part with. The gap separating the poet from his critical readers seems to have been eliminated: in fact, the disembodied voice

---

[34] Alton (1930) 123.

[35] Ghisalberti (1946) 41, translated in Minnis and Scott (1991) 363. On Giovanni see Ghisalberti (1933).

[36] See also Raphael Lyne's 'Love and exile after Ovid' in chapter 17 of this volume.

[37] Edited by Bischoff (1952) from Freiburg, University Library, MS. 380, and Wright (1842) 43–4, 225 from London, British Library, MS. Harley 219.

[38] Wright's version substitutes *licitis* for *placitis* ('even goods that are permitted'), further 'improving' the sentiment.

has become a species of Echo, capable only of reproducing the sentiments of its interlocutors.

The clerics are suitably impressed, and begin to pray for Ovid's soul, but the voice speaks again, and with a will of its own: *Nolo pater noster; carpe, viator, iter* ('I don't want "Our Father"; traveller, be on your way').[39] The Harley version explains that Ovid knew himself damned, and that prayer could not help him. The *nolo* has more force than that, however; it is a positive refusal, and the Freiburg version reacts angrily against it. It adds a coda insisting that Ovid was in fact saved: in his extreme old age, he was converted by St John of Patmos and became a great preacher, as befits one who by his own account had learned the local vernacular (the scribe quotes *Tristia* 5.12.58). Finally, as bishop of Tomis, he died for the faith and is known as St Naso. We must therefore believe that the voice from the tomb was counterfeited by the devil, envious at having lost Ovid, who had for so long been in his power.[40] The first sign of Ovidian resistance to Christian appropriation here generates an even more extravagant effort at claiming him. Its corollary, though, is that the voice from the tomb, speaking Ovid's own verses, must be demonic. The fantasy of a conversion at the end of his life is of only limited help: it leaves his authentic words pagan. At best, they are dim adumbrations of the truths a converted Ovid comes to perceive, at worst a set of dangerous errors. Ovid remains trapped as 'a poet between two worlds' and, unlike Fränkel's, not necessarily tending in the right direction.[41]

One way to carry him over the threshold was to invent the truly Christian poem he never wrote. The *De vetula* is the longest piece of medieval pseudo-Ovidiana, probably written in Paris in the mid-thirteenth century and often, though insecurely, attributed to Richard de Fournival.[42] The poem comes complete with an elaborate prose *accessus* that offers a full and largely reliable biography before departing into fiction: it presents the *Vetula* as Ovid's long-lost final work, a poetic testament which he had placed in his tomb in the hope that it would be returned, with his bones, to Rome after the death of Augustus. A circumstantial account of its rediscovery follows, with the volume found in the tomb, undamaged by age. The hagiographic miracle of incorruption is here applied to the text: having become a disembodied, sepulchral voice in the *Nolo pater noster* story, Ovid's authentic body is now

---

[39] The line is not, of course, a quotation, but perhaps cf. the pseudo-Ovidian *Nux* 136 for *carpe uiator* in this metrical position.
[40] Wright (1842) 44; Bischoff (1952) 272–3.
[41] Fränkel (1945) esp. 2–3, 21–3, 163. I am grateful to Philip Hardie for this point.
[42] Robathan (1968) 1–5.

materialized as a book, that can be carried triumphantly back via Byzantium to the west.[43]

The poem that follows stands as Ovid's true *Remedia amoris*: in exile, despairing of temporal hope, he recalls his past way of life and how he was converted from it – a comic narrative of sexual disgust in which he is tricked into sleeping with the old woman who was supposed to be his go-between. Ironically, this work which purports to be the final corrective to Ovid's literary and sexual misdeeds was itself subject to censorship; several manuscripts omit these two books of elegiac comedy, two of them explaining: *propter multa quae intersunt scurrilia* ('because of the many scurrilous things contained there').[44] In Book 3 'Ovid' reveals the true remedy for secular despair, *lux doctrine*, the light of learning and of specifically Christine doctrine (3.1–18): he reveals his knowledge of Christ, the Virgin, and the future resurrection of the dead – significantly outdoing Virgil's fourth *Eclogue* – and denies that the polytheism of the *Metamorphoses* was any more than pandering to public opinion (3.611–796).[45]

The fact that the recollections of Ovid's elegiac misdeeds were themselves subject to censorship reveals again the limitations of conversion to redeem Ovid's canonic works, and underlines a distinct tendency towards backsliding. It seems that the most strenuous efforts to convert him reveal the fragility of the enterprise; and Dante (1265–1321), who places Statius in purgatory as a secret Christian who dared not confess his faith (*Purg.* 21), does not offer Ovid the same lifeline.[46] The question of what Ovid can offer to a Christian epic repeatedly nags at the *Commedia*, nonetheless, and Dante's answer seems at first glance discouraging. Initially, his presence is muted, even inert, primarily because too many of his possible roles seem to have been annexed by Virgil, whom Dante claims from the outset as his master and *autore* (*Inf.* 1.85). Virgil so incarnates the poetic calling that Homer, Horace, Ovid and Lucan pay honour to him with a single voice (*Inf.* 4.79–93); when Dante names his poem as *la mia comedìa*, it is in the context of Virgil's allusion to his own epic, *l'alta mia tragedìa* (*Inf.* 21.2, 20.113). Even when the punishments of hell first take on a literally metamorphic character, in the wood of the suicides in Canto 13, the primary model remains Virgilian (the transformed Polydorus in *Aen.* 3.19–48). Finally, if Ovid (as well as

---

43 The twin metamorphoses of Ovid's poetic self into 'eternal voice and perishable book' are explored by Farrell in Hardie, Barchiesi, Hinds (1999) 127–41. Thanks are again due to Philip Hardie for this reference.

44 Sidney Sussex College, Cambridge, MS. Delta 3.11; Jesus College, Cambridge, MS. Q.G.22, both fifteenth-century (Robathan (1968) 30).

45 Cf. Conrad of Hirsau (Huygens (1970) 115), who infers from *Met.* 1.32 that Ovid was a closet monotheist, unwilling publically to acknowledge the true God either from blindness or fear. See Wright, in Hardie, Barchiesi, Hinds (1999) 71.

46 The *Commedia* is cited from Dante (1970–75).

Lucan and Virgil) is addressed in Canto 25, it is to be silenced. Dante's audacious exchange of form and matter between the thieves has no reason to envy the poet of the *Metamorphoses* (25.94–102).[47]

Ovid, then, should be a poet of infernal mutation who can be safely left behind as 'a curator of the fallen world in all its hideous permutations'.[48] Politically, too, Dante's imperial loyalties make Ovid, the Augustan exile, a distant second-best compared with the poet of Aeneas' Roman destiny who 'lived at Rome under the good Augustus' (*Inf.* 1.71). Yet numerous modern studies have concurred that he fails to be left behind, even (indeed especially) in *Paradiso* where Virgil's guidance has been superseded. He becomes a crucial poetic model precisely because of the disordered, transgressive power of the Ovidian imagination.[49] If, in the *Purgatorio*, Dante ranges himself on the side of the Muses against the challenge of the Pierides, and neutralizes the threat of Arachne by incorporating her into an ordered, moralized ecphrasis (*Purg.* 1.7–12, 12.43–5), at the start of *Paradiso* he assimilates himself to another Ovidian challenger, Marsyas (*Par.* 1.13-21). To serve as a vessel for the divine poetic power of Apollo, Dante must invite the flaying of Marsyas; his position as mortal poet setting out to describe heaven is by its nature transgressive. This, moreover, is only the first of a string of mythological revisions drawn from the *Metamorphoses* by which Dante moulds himself in the course of the *Paradiso*. In a sense, this confirms a secret Ovidian quality that has always been there, since, where Virgil's more abstract functions revolve around reason, Dante's narratorial *persona* has always been driven by desire – albeit the rarefied love of Beatrice rather than the elegiac posture.[50] In political terms, too, Dante's posture begins to move towards Ovid's, as in canto 17 of *Paradiso* his exile from Florence is predicted, while the political hope invested in the Roman empire wanes.

These mixed signals suggest that Ovid has a real role, and one less limited than the official programme of the *Commedia* cares to acknowledge; there is real force in Curtius' passing observation that Dante's work more closely resembles the *Metamorphoses* than any other epic in the sheer size of its cast,[51] as well as its construction as a *perpetuum carmen* built from small narrative units. In that sense, the *Commedia* is certainly more Ovidian than Virgilian. Even so, the exploitation of Ovid requires caution and indirection, for, unlike the scholarly *accessus*, the *Paradiso* is not primarily

[47] On this much-discussed passage see in particular Ginsberg (1991), Sowell (1991) 35–49, Barkan (1986) 156–8.
[48] Hawkins, in Sowell (1991) 21.
[49] E.g. Kleiner (1994) 130–6; Hawkins, in Sowell (1991) 25–31; Brownlee (1986).
[50] The hypothesis that Ovid directly influenced the troubadours was proposed by Schrötter (1908); a more recent contribution is Cahoon (1989).
[51] Curtius (1990) 365.

attempting to bring Ovid under control, but to exploit his status as the master of transgression, exile and marginality as Dante designs his own perilous itinerary.

Dante's *Commedia* has raised two issues to which I will devote the rest of this chapter. The first is the possibility that, with appropriate interpretive safeguards, the Christian devotional imagination may be able to benefit from the pagan fables of the *Metamorphoses* – a possibility which was most confidently realized in the practice of allegoresis. This rather abstract appropriation of Ovid as fabulist to serve the interests of the Christian interpretive community stands at the opposite extreme from a second, much more personal, appropriation also visible in the *Commedia*: the partial reinvention of an author's own poetic *persona* out of Ovid's authorial self-projection. Often, as in Dante, the relationship between Ovid and Virgil becomes part of the process of creating a poetic stance; in fact, this relationship turns out to be at least as problematic as that between Ovid and Christ.

The practice of allegorical reading has traditionally been the most notorious strand of medieval exegesis. Rather than convert the poet, after the manner of the *Vetula*, allegory converts the text by means of a consciously transformatory reading method. In the tenth century Theodulf of Orléans somewhat grudgingly concedes that for all their many vanities (*frivola multa*), the fables of the poets can be read by the philosophical reader as integuments – poetic veils to conceal esoteric truth from unworthy eyes.[52] For some interpreters, indeed, the allegories were placed there by the poet: we have already met the argument that Ovid was a closet monotheist whose poetic machinery of pagan gods conceals his real beliefs. Arnoul of Orléans, the twelfth-century pioneer among Ovid commentators of allegorical interpretation, holds to this view: philosophy acts as a master discourse held in common by pagan and Christian readers, and a source of *rapprochement* between them.[53]

If this approach sometimes credits Ovid with the didactic intention behind the philosophical sense, elsewhere there is a marked theoretical orientation towards reader-response rather than intentionalism. The two great 'moralized Ovids' of the fourteenth century aim to serve the interests of two species of Christian reader: the vast, anonymous *Ovide moralisé* (in French octosyllabic couplets) fosters a species of devotional meditation; Pierre Bersuire's Latin prose *Ovidius moralizatus* is for the use of preachers seeking *exempla*, narrative illustrations.[54] Bersuire and the *Ovide* have in common the emphasis on the commentator's *ingenium*, rather than the

---

[52] Godman (1985) 168–70. [53] On Arnoul see Ghisalberti (1939).
[54] Bersuire (1962); de Boer, de Boer and Van 'T Sant (1915–38).

poet's: they open up the text to multiple (but not competing) readings. Otherwise they differ radically, for all the long tradition of confusing them. Bersuire offers brief summaries of the narratives and throws out suggestions for Christian allegories as options for the preacher; his allegories are designed to end in a *sententia* which is usually scriptural.[55] Ovid's Latin, not quoted verbatim, is rendered subordinate and almost invisible before the Latin of the Vulgate.

The *Ovide moralisé*, by contrast, very rarely quotes scripture after its Prologue. What it wants from the Bible is a master narrative, rather than master texts – a narrative of sin and redemption which centres, obsessively, on the Incarnation of Christ as the ultimate metamorphosis. This core repertory of sacred storytelling is reimagined time and again in the prism of different pagan fables. Ultimately, the project of the *Ovide* is one that plays as fast and loose with the Bible as with Ovid: it seeks to invest the single, central narrative of Christian history with the mythographic richness that the pagan *fabulae* possess in such enviable profusion, and to turn that narrative into the ultimate vernacular romance. For the *Ovide* is more than a translation and commentary on the *Metamorphoses*: it is a vernacular *summa* of an entire tradition – not just a French *Ovidius maior*, but an *Ovidius maximus*.[56] It incorporates earlier French adaptations, including the *Philomena* sometimes attributed to Chrétien de Troyes (6.2183–3840). Its expanded account of the Trojan War brings in material from the *Heroides*, and more unlikely sources: when Paris has made his judgement in favour of Venus (11.1473–2400), she provides him with commandments of love which précis the *Ars amatoria*, and the whole scene seems to be modelled on Amant's homage to the god of love in Guillaume de Lorris' *Roman de la Rose*.

One unexpected result of this creation of an Ovidian and post-Ovidian museum, under Christian curatorship, is that the commentary provides a safe, circumscribed space in which the earlier, secular tradition of Ovid in French can continue to thrive. One reason this is possible is the fact that the narratives themselves are not regarded as intrinsically didactic. As Demats and others have pointed out, the commentary guards the moralizing function jealously to itself.[57] In fact the 'fables' lose all authority, by being shown to deviate as much from historical as from moral truth: frequently, the commentary begins by reconstructing a demythologized 'original' history which poetic *ingenium* has falsified. Meanwhile the *ingenium* of the commentator draws us back towards another true history, the spiritual history of fall and redemption played out in the macrocosm and in the individual soul.

---

[55] Hexter (1989), Reynolds (1990) 89–90.
[56] See Copeland (1991) 116–9.   [57] Demats (1973) 107, 113; Copeland (1992) 124–6.

The process of re-imagining is itself consciously metamorphic: there is a marked tendency for the commentary to change the moral polarity, so to speak, of the actors. Where Orpheus detests heterosexual love and chooses the love of young boys – a preference which can be expected to call forth moral condemnation – one of the allegorical readings makes him Christ, who loves the innocent and is disgusted at the 'female' weakness of sinners (10.556–77). This lurking misogyny is often a part of the process of transformation: in particular, female victims of divine rape are regularly transformed into figures of sin, often specifically sexual lust.[58] The *Ovide*'s running concern to expose what lies beneath a specious appearance makes it deeply suspicious of a beautiful, innocent-seeming heroine such as Callisto, even when the actual narrative has been wholly sympathetic to her; the moral allegory makes of her a hypocrite whose chastity was merely for show (2.1365–819). Yet the process can also work in reverse: Myrrha's incestuous love for her father can make her a type of the Virgin Mary (10.3478–795). The traditional critique of its 'forced' allegories is beside the point: the *Ovide* exuberantly foregrounds the work of its own *ingenium* by creating the most drastic incongruities between pagan and Christian narratives, as well as locating their structural congruences. Meanwhile, in the space between these two 'true' histories – the secular history from which popular and poetic traditions have departed, and the sacred narrative to which the commentary directs them – the Ovidian fable paradoxically retains its disruptive and playful force, precisely because it no longer bears the weight of any didactic programme. If the apparatus of the *Ovide moralisé* looks initially like a straitjacket, there is a case for seeing it as a liberator.[59]

Certainly as a translation the *Ovide* seems to have given the *Metamorphoses* a new lease of life in the vernacular. Machaut and his contemporaries and successors turned to it regularly as a narrative source, but without imitating its hermeneutics.[60] In England, it may have been known to the two great Ovidians of the reign of Richard II, Gower (d.1408) and Chaucer (d.1400).[61] Again, neither shows much sympathy with its commentary. Gower's approach to the integumental tradition is distinctly secular and philosophical in slant, while Chaucer's orbit is even more eccentric to the moralizing project.

John Gower's credentials as an Ovidian are formidable; his ten-thousand-line Latin satire, the *Vox clamantis*, is in unrhymed elegiac couplets – according to Rigg, the first substantial Anglo-Latin poem in that medium for a century – and its first book, in particular, is suffused with quotations that

---

[58] E.g. Io and Syrinx (1.3830–4150), Callisto (2.1695–2006), Proserpine (5.2947–3028), and even Procne and Philomena (6.3719–840).

[59] For the opposing view see Allen (1992) 56.   [60] Blumenfeld-Kosinski (1997) 136–70.

[61] Gower: Mainzer (1972). Chaucer: Meech (1931), Minnis (1979); cf. Cooper, in Martindale (1988) 74–5.

span the entire range of Ovid's work.[62] In the English verse of his *Confessio Amantis* the influence is narrative and structural. A tale collection framed by the dialogue of a lover with his confessor, the *Confessio*'s most important narrative source is the *Metamorphoses*. There is also a profound structural congruence between the two poems, beyond the general principle that they create an integrated, articulate whole out of fragmented narrative materials. Gower's Prologue centres on a meditation on the declining world, represented through the sequence of metals familiar from Book 1 of the *Metamorphoses*, and given an apocalyptic edge by being fused with its biblical analogue in Daniel 4. In a sense, Gower's Prologue fuses books 1 and 15 of Ovid's epic by presenting a world of restless flux, but one whose trajectory is inevitably for the worse. The remainder of the poem, with a combination of confessional dialogue, narrative and commentary, explores the psychological dimension, in particular, of this state of disorder and decay, and seeks out remedies in both self and society. One end result is a new philosophical statement, placed near the end of the poem and structurally analogous with Pythagoras' speech in *Metamorphoses* 15.[63] Gower, however, has substituted Aristotle for Pythagoras, and the change has major implications. Where Pythagoras revels in the exhilaration of flux, and Gower's Prologue laments it, Aristotle creates an ordered, scientific system. The philosophical framing with which the *Confessio* seeks to work towards its closure is only partly generated out of Ovidian resources; it is also an anti-Ovidian move in the poem. The stories adapted from the *Metamorphoses*, unvarnished and often bleak accounts of sexual obsession and violence, constitute a demonic world within Gower's poem, whose challenge to its rationalist leanings must be accommodated as well as resisted. Gower's *Metamorphoses* are contained and to a degree deployed by more stable discourses, but work to destabilize them in turn.

In the poem's closure, the result is a near-total inversion of Ovid's: Gower has substituted a secure Aristotelian system for the Pythagorean celebration of metamorphosis, but cannot generate the same certainty in the political sphere. The *Confessio*, like the *Metamorphoses*, ends with praise of a prince, just as each has a philosopher who advises a prince: Gower's Aristotle appears as the tutor of Alexander (where Ovid's Pythagoras teaches Numa), and Richard II stands in the place of Caesar as the recipient of a closing panegyric. Ovid's ending is a perilous juxtaposition: the apotheosis of Rome,

---

[62] Rigg (1993) 287. The *Vox* is edited by Macaulay in Gower (1899–1902) IV; translation by Stockton, Gower (1962), whose notes, incorporating Macaulay's, identify most of the Ovidian allusions.

[63] Harbert, in Martindale (1988) 87; Bennett (1986) 416–17. Somewhat analogous is Simpson (1995) 141–4, comparing the opening moves of the *Confessio* and the *Amores*; see further Simpson (1999).

with its promise of perpetual endurance, is left to fend for itself alongside Pythagorean scepticism of any such claim.[64] Gower's ending is no less so, for there are two different conclusions (and introductions), dating from only a couple of years apart, in the earlier of which Richard II is both dedicatee and object of praise, in the other simply absent.[65]

If Gower works at a considerable remove from the mainstream of 'philosophical' Ovids, Chaucer engages with it only at the level of parody, if at all. *The Book of the Duchess*, among his early dream visions, moves away from the whole didactic premise of the moralizing tradition, for which Chaucer presents himself as ill-equipped in any case. Driven by insomnia to reach for a 'romance' in which he reads, and retells, the tale of Ceyx and Alcyone (Ov. *Met.* 11.410–748), his first response is one of literalistic scepticism, doubting the existence of Morpheus: 'For I ne knew never god but oon' (237). His second response is a personal identification with the narrative, praying 'in my game' (238) to the god of sleep for his own sake. This personalizing rather than moralizing is of a piece with his version of the Alcyone story, which is driven by a 'pittee' and 'routhe' which 'I that made this book' orchestrates (96–7). This intensely affective mode of reading is sustained throughout; Chaucer has abandoned the didactic proposition of literature altogether, in favour of the cultivation of aestheticized, melancholic memory, 'sorwful ymagynacioun' (14). Immediately after his mock-prayer he falls asleep, the book as his pillow – a fictive Morpheus turns out to have real power – and in the dream which follows, there is only one, abortive attempt at didacticism. His interlocutor, the grieving knight in black, assures him that 'nought all the remedyes of Ovyde' could banish his sorrow (568); Chaucer nonetheless tries out the remedy of patience, with a stock of examples against suicide including several from the *Heroides*, but without making any impact (714–44). If Chaucer's pity for Alcyone becomes part of a larger programme, it is still sorrow and sympathy that drive the text, articulated through an allegorical knight who stands in for a real patron – the widower John of Gaunt.[66] The burden of Ovidian allusion here has become thoroughly subjective, an integument of passion rather than of doctrine.

The harmony of shared pity that governs the *Book of the Duchess* is altogether absent from one of Chaucer's later Ovidian projects, and its fictive patron much less tractable. The *Legend of Good Women*, edgy and

---

[64] Barkan (1986) 84–8.
[65] The motives behind the revisions are disputed: e.g. Nicholson (1988), Simpson (1995) 293–4, Stow (1993).
[66] See Hanning (1986) 122–41, Hardman (1994).

abrasive, returns us to a world of authority violently appropriated by a tyrannical god of love.[67] Chaucer's role in the *Duchess* was one of sympathetic audience; here he is personally under threat, and the *persona* he develops runs closely parallel with Ovid's as he encounters an intractable monarchical power, and must bend his pen accordingly. It is a fittingly ironic inversion that a Chaucerian *Remedia amoris*, rather than an *Ars amatoria*, should be the cause of his problems: Cupid chooses to read Chaucer's *Troilus and Criseyde* as a heretical attack on love's power, a *dissuasio* based on the supposed infidelity of women.[68] The penance is an inspired parody of the moralizing tradition: on the orders of Cupid and his queen, Alcestis, Chaucer borrows the Christian narrative form of hagiography, and converts it for the use of amatory paganism. (The title by which Chaucer refers to the work in the catalogue of the *Man of Law's Prologue* makes the parody clearer: 'the Seintes Legende of Cupide', *Canterbury Tales* 2.61.) The work will be a new *Heroides*, founded on the passive suffering of haplessly virtuous heroines. It is also a new *Ars amatoria* of a distinctly chastened kind, a 'craft of fyn lovynge' (F.544) based on matrimonial fidelity and self-sacrifice, as embodied by Alcestis herself.

Indeed, the *Legend* seems to reinvent Ovid's elegiac corpus in its entirety. Cupid stipulates that the first heroine should be Cleopatra, without giving any reason, and I suspect a covert allusion here. We have already encountered the suggestion that Ovid's failure to produce an epic of Augustus' war against Antony and Cleopatra was one of his literary sins, disguised by leaving the *Amores* untitled; most of the 'Legend of Cleopatra' is in martial mode and gives as much space to Antony's world of military honour as to the fate of the queen. Chaucer seems to be making good Ovid's omission, as though to repair the damage done by the *Amores*, but at the same time to underscore the parallel between his outraged Cupid and Ovid's irate Augustus. His portrait of a wilful, arbitrary kingship literally places love and majesty on a single throne; but, as Ovid says of Jupiter's abduction of Europa, 'sovereignty (*maiestas*) and love do not suit well together, nor remain long in one abode' (Ov. *Met.* 2. 846–7; cf. Chaucer's *Franklin's Tale* 764–6). It is perhaps no coincidence that one of the most subtly wrought and covert classical allusions in all Chaucer's work is to the rape of Europa, in the Prologue to the *Legend* (F.112–114). Ovid has provided the model for an oblique but penetrating account of the strained relationships that can obtain between poets and princes, weaving its way secretively through the sexual politics that more evidently dominate the *Legend*.

[67] Kiser (1983), Simpson (1998).
[68] *Troilus* and its source in Boccaccio's *Il Filostrato* are themselves profoundly shaped by the pattern of *Ars* and *Remedia*; see Nolan (1992) 119–246.

Chaucer's partial recreation of his poetic *persona* on the basis of the disgraced Ovid, desperately writing his way back to grace while covertly recording his continuing recusancy, forms part of a long tradition. Ovid's self-presentation as exile seems, indeed, to be the earliest aspect of his work to capture medieval imaginations. Peter Godman traces it as a *leitmotif* in the Latin poets at the Carolingian court – in particular, in Modoin of Autun (nicknamed Naso in this poetic circle) and Theodulf of Orléans, the latter exiled under Charlemagne's successor Pippin.[69] Hildebert of Lavardin, writing in the late eleventh and early twelfth centuries, cunningly fuses Ovid's voice with Boethius to mount a scathing attack on his own personal sub-Augustus, while rising above secular disappointment. The abuses of tyrants are part of the inconstancy of created things, a sign of the rule of fortune, permitted by providence. Ostensibly correcting Ovid's complaint by offering a philosophical *remedium*, he also gets to participate in that complaint.[70] Especially rich is the work of Hildebert's contemporary Baudri, abbot of Bourgeuil.[71] Much of his poetic *persona* is founded on Ovidian *nequitia*, and the kinship is pressed home with a pair of 'new' *Tristia*, a pair of letters along the lines of the double *Heroides*, between Ovid at Tomis and a Roman friend, Florus. Baudri's project here is to make explicit the bitter animosity which Ovid's own epistles are careful to disguise. These are private letters in which the correspondents can mount a robust apologia, can speak openly of *iniustam duri Cesaris iram* ('the *unjust* wrath of implacable Caesar', my italics), can insist that Ovid's poetry was never the real reason for his exile, a private act of vengeance founded on misinformation. He can even confess that the high-flown panegyrics were merely tactical, flattering in hopes of a recall.[72] Baudri gives us a sophisticated reading of the subtext of Ovid's poems from exile, and a robust self-defence under colour of Ovidian imitation.[73]

Florus lets slip that the false suspicion which incurred Augustus' wrath was that of adultery with his wife, a popular explanation for the *error* that compounded the *carmen*. One of the more bizarre, fourteenth-century elaborations of the story has it that Ovid was observed climbing up to Livia's bedroom by none other than Virgil, who sabotaged his ladder. Ovid broke his leg on the way down, and hated his fellow poet from then on; this is why, when he praises his contemporaries, he snubs Virgil with a mere *Vergilium tantum uidi* ('Virgil I only saw', Ov. *Trist.* 4.10.51).[74]

With or without active sabotage, Virgil always seems to stand as the centre to which the medieval Ovid is marginal. Modoin of Autun's *Egloga* begins

---

[69] Godman (1987) 93–148.   [70] 'Nuper eram locuples', poem 22 in Hildebert (1969).
[71] Here I am much indebted to Bond (1989), (1995).
[72] Baudri (1979) 97.13, 98.111–12.   [73] Bond (1995) 42–69.   [74] Ghisalberti (1946) 50.

with a dialogue between an old established court poet and an ambitious newcomer, in which the *senex* cites Ovid as a warning of what happens to poets who are insane (*demens*) enough to incur Caesar's wrath. The *puer* responds with a catalogue of poets whose verse brought them prosperity; at the head of the list is Virgil, who came to Rome after losing his estates and regained them by his poetry.[75] This fiction of a smooth course to prosperity on the sails of a linear poetic career is the perfect antitype to the characteristic Ovidian course of reversal, severance and marginalization. This distance from an 'official', central Rome, identified (far too simply, of course) with Virgil and Caesar, is part of what makes Ovid uniquely intimate with medieval poets. It seems that Ovid is required even to make sense of Virgilian narrative, as in the well-known case of the twelfth-century *Roman d'Eneas*.[76] One of the founders of the new wave of *roman antiques* that revolutionized heroic narrative, the *Eneas* is consciously revisionist: it thinks of the process of empire-building in terms of dynastic marriages, and its public narrative must be articulated as much in erotic as in martial terms. Accordingly, Ovid's elegiac versions of epic become an indispensable hermeneutic ally in interpreting the *Aeneid*. This process can cut both ways: Baudri of Bourgeuil, as well as his new *Tristia*, wrote a new pair of letters for Paris and Helen, by no means 'exact imitations' of Ovid, but a systematic reopening of negotiations between Ovid and Virgil.[77] Writing in hexameters, he places his epistles chronologically earlier than the *Heroides*, as though to forestall Ovid's black comedy, and seeks to restore Helen, in particular, to a genuinely tragic dignity. Persuaded into the elopement only by a fatalistic belief in oracles, she becomes a counter-Aeneas, an unwilling exile driven by fate and the gods towards a war which she can foresee. *Virgilii grauitas, Ouidii leuitas* are the qualities Baudri praises in fellow-poet Godfrey of Rheims (99.8); they are working out their differences in his own work too.

The process of renegotiation and competition between the poets is still ongoing in Chaucer, where Dido takes Helen's place as chief locus of conflict, both in the *Legend of Good Women* and the earlier *House of Fame*.[78] Venus' temple in Book 1 of the *House of Fame* rather resembles the lady's chamber in Marie de France's 'Guigemar', in that it presents an iconographic programme whose interpretation runs out of control. As mother and patroness of Aeneas, Venus presides over Chaucer's epitome of the *Aeneid*, which he sees depicted on the temple walls. The retelling is famously taken

[75] Godman (1985) 24.60–75.

[76] Ed. Salverda de Grave (1925–29); trans. Yunck (1974). On Virgil and Ovid in the *Eneas* see Baswell (1995) 168–219, Blumenfeld-Kosinski (1997) 15–51, Nolan (1992) 75–118.

[77] Poems 7 and 8 in Hilbert's edition. The quoted phrase is from Fyler (1979) 19; the Virgilian strand is discussed by Albrecht (1982), and Bond (1995) 62.

[78] See Baswell (1995) 220–69 and Dronke (1986).

over, however, by Dido, and by Venus' other role as goddess of love. In this guise it is Ovid not Virgil who is 'Venus clerk' (1487). The 'Epistle of Ovyde' temporarily supplants the 'Eneydos' (378–9) as Chaucer launches into a catalogue of betrayed Ovidian heroines. Within a temple full of 'ymages | Of gold' (121), Chaucer has conjured the moral: 'Hyt is not al gold that glareth' (272). Ovid provides a model for an authorial rebellion in which Chaucer can claim emancipation even from Ovid himself: in the speech of Dido which dominates his miniature *Aeneid*, 'Non other auctour alegge I' (314). The return to Virgil's official Aeneas is a brief and perfunctory gesture of obedience. In the *Legend of Good Women*, meanwhile, where the demand for authorial loyalty and obedience is pressingly explicit, Chaucer likes to cite multiple sources for his narratives, perhaps as part of his covert resistance. Ovid's authority repeatedly offsets or supplements someone else's – Livy in 'Lucrece', Guido delle Colonne, the prose historian of Troy, in 'Hypsipyle and Medea'. In the 'Legend of Dido', the Virgilian public narrative is again modified and increasingly supplanted by Ovid's female-dominated alternative, to the extent that the legend ends with an extract of her letter to Aeneas, added as though an afterthought when her death has already been narrated. A tale that began with a Dantesque offering of 'glorye and honour' to 'Virgil Mantoan' (924) ends with a direction to 'rede Ovyde' (1367).

Ovid is the ideal guide in reclaiming, questioning and revising the cultural authority of the ancients, precisely because he is himself already engaged in the effort of reclamation and problematization. His perspective on Virgil and on Augustus' Rome is already retrospective, as well as being generically and, in the end, geographically displaced. As such he becomes the model for all future efforts to recapture, reinvent or pick apart the central authority of Rome, as well as providing the most troubling of cautionary tales. His sheer variousness, as well as the varied personal and institutional interests that impelled his medieval readers, ensured that no single Ovid dominated critical or poetic traditions. His authorship constituted a locus where discursive authority could be explored, asserted and disputed; the result was a rich and complex network of readings, claims, counter-appropriations, repudiations and retractions, in which Ovid's works never ceased to thrive.

FURTHER READING

There has never been an Ovidian equivalent of Comparetti's *Vergil in the Middle Ages*, and as Elliott (1978) says, 'a comprehensive survey of Ovid's influence will probably never be written' (3). There are numerous general studies on a smaller scale, mostly older: Rand (1925) is witty and immensely readable; there are great riches in Wilkinson (1955) 366–98, and Robathan's survey in Binns (1973) 191–209 is thorough. Essential supplements, though not in English, are Battaglia (1959) and

Munari (1960). A wealth of material *ad indicem* for medieval Latin poetry can be found in Raby (1934), Curtius (1990) and Dronke (1968).

The best starting point for a wide-ranging sampler of modern critical approaches is an Ovidian issue of *Mediaevalia* 13 (1989 [for 1987]), a number of whose articles are cited in my notes. Studies of the reception of particular texts include Stapleton (1996) on the *Amores*, Allen (1992) on the *Ars* and *Remedia*, and for the *Metamorphoses* the highly influential Barkan (1986), and several essays in Hardie, Barchiesi, Hinds (1999). Individual mythic protagonists have also attracted attention, including Narcissus (Knoespel (1985)) and Apollo and Daphne (Barnard (1987)).

Academic and pedagogic traditions have attracted much attention in recent years, though few commentaries have been published. Alton (1960–61) and McGregor (1978) offer accessible introductions. Hexter (1986) is a seminal study of commentaries on the *Ars, Ex Ponto* and *Heroides*. Coulson has studied, and edited in part, the thirteenth-century 'Vulgate' commentary on the *Metamorphoses* (1991), while McKinley (1996) compares commentaries on *Met.* 10. Viarre (1966) studies Ovid's role as natural philosopher in the twelfth and thirteenth centuries.

Amongst a good deal of minor pseudo-Ovidiana, Lebek (1978) is worth singling out, a clever piece of clerical satire appended to *Met.* 1's Deucalion and Pyrrha. F. W. Lenz edited many pseudo-Ovidian pieces, to which references are collected in Albrecht and Zinn (1968) 546–66; see also Dronke (1976) and Lehmann (1927).

Ovid's impact on vernacular poetry makes itself felt across Europe; the present chapter's neglect of Germany (where Albrecht von Halberstadt produced the first vernacular *Metamorphoses*) can be made good by Stackmann (1966), and of Spain by Schevill (1913); see in particular Juan Ruiz (1999), and Parker (1991). For French translations of Ovid, Lucas (1970) is a useful summary; in Italy, my account of Dante needs to be supplemented by Boccaccio (Hollander (1977), Brownlee (1989)) and Petrarch's *Trionfi* and *Rime* (Monti (1990), Sturm-Maddox (1985), Hardie (1999b)).

For Chaucer and Gower, Minnis (1991) is a superb study of poetic *auctoritas* and its lapses. Fyler (1979) offers a rather general but interesting study of the long-observed affinity between Chaucer and Ovid; Calabrese (1994) is also valuable. For Gower, Simpson (1995) and (1999) are indispensable, a significant advance from such earlier studies as Hiscoe (1985) and Harbert (1988). Simpson also offers challenging accounts of medieval Virgilian and Ovidian models of poetics; further ramifications of their relationship are traced by Baswell (1995) and Desmond (1994).

17

RAPHAEL LYNE

Love and exile after Ovid

Aston Cokayne's *The Tragedy of Ovid* is the only English play which tells the story of the Latin poet's exile and death in Tomis. In the final scene the focus turns to the poet's suffering as he receives a letter from his wife, with the news that her efforts to arrange his return have failed. Ovid connects this to news in another letter:

> Besides, my friend Graecinus,
> (A Roman of high note) hath writ me word
> The Gracious Princess Julia, our great Empress
> And my best Friend is, in Trimerus, dead.
> One of these News were much too much to strike
> My poor and Crazy body into my Grave:
> But joyning both their Poysonous stings together;
> I needs must to the world this Truth impart,
> That Ovid dies here of a broken Heart.
>
> (5.6.56–64)[1]

And Ovid does indeed die then and there. His relationship with Augustus' grand-daughter Julia is treated decorously by Cokayne, but at this point Ovid's grief and the possibility of ambiguity in the word 'friend' connect his exile and the stories of unlawful love in his Roman past. In the play the traditional equation of Julia and Corinna is given credence, but the poet's adoration for the princess is said to be an honourable thing, more or less ('if I er'e enjoy'd her, it was through | Her craft; I taking her to be another,' 4.3.21–2). The link between his exile and the erotically-centred *persona* of his love poetry is explored further in a soliloquy:

> Sure I was born when all the glorious Starrs
> Were met in Councell to contrive a Mischief.
> Under pretence of my Loose youthfull studies,

---

[1] Reference to Cokayne (1662). Line references from the text at Chadwyck-Healey's Literature Online database, <http://lion.chadwyck.co.uk>.

For the composing of my Art of Love.
In my declining years (when I expected
Ease, and a quiet Life) I was exil'd
From Rome, and here confin'd to end my daies.
(4.3.1–7)

Cokayne portrays a pathetic Ovid, who plays a kindly but rather detached part in the amorous goings-on of other Tomitan residents and visitors. Love calls for deceit and cleverness here and there, and Ovid helps out, but he lines up alongside the good and the abused in the play's brutal moments. The strongest link between one phase of his life and the other comes in the person of Cypassis, former maid to Julia, and known from the *Amores*. How Cokayne's licentious bawd, constantly trying to fix up her daughter Spinella, relates to her namesake in Ovid's works, is unclear. In *Amores* 2.7 Ovid denies Corinna's charge of infidelity with Cypassis, only to have 2.8 describe this very thing. None of this is mentioned in *The Tragedy of Ovid*, leaving the impression that this Ovid is not settling easily into a role – that his story is in fact rather difficult to tell, composed as it is of vivid *personae* which do not all fit together. In this respect Cokayne's play serves as an instructive introduction to a distinctive quality in the reception of Ovid.

The spectre of Ovid's career, as well as specific works, often influences later writers. Moreover, the influence of the love poetry, for example, is sometimes more easily seen in terms of responses to the authorial *persona* than to the poems themselves. M. L. Stapleton has traced the presence and the insistence of Ovid's version of himself as lover from antiquity to the Renaissance, the many facets of what it offers to imitators serving as testimony to the vivid effectiveness of Ovid's construction of an image of himself in his poetry.[2] Also important are the bare and poignant anecdotes and facts of Ovid's biography, whether it is seen as a cautionary tale or an example of tyrannical injustice, and for this reason the exile-poetry's *persona* also plays a prominent role (see also Dimmick, ch. 16). Many 'Ovidian' works, then, show the influence of an idea of the poet as much as of an idea of the poem, although distinguishing between the two is not always possible or necessary. The fortunes of the various *personae* vary, but writers consistently find in Ovid images of how an author and his work fit into the world: this affects characters within works and authors' own self-presentations.

The two key *personae*, the lover and the exile, connect because some excesses of the former may have helped create the problems of the latter, and because the latter looks back nostalgically to the former. The connection

[2] Stapleton (1996).

contains a tough lesson for poets which is learned in different ways in different periods. As Gareth Williams explores elsewhere in this *Companion*, there are a variety of reasons to connect the love poetry and the exile poetry, as Ovid revives the techniques of the amatory mode when framing his suit to Augustus and his longing for Rome.[3] So the possibility of a dialogue between the two *personae* is there from the beginning, and at key points in the reception of Ovid's works later writers respond to their connection. In the Middle Ages, the Renaissance, and perhaps also the twentieth century, Ovid's *personae*, and the poetic career behind them, have their zeniths, but the points at which their values are diminished are all part of the story: the casual, amoral, threatened, subversive, fragile qualities found there are bound to fall flat sometimes (although they have a pathos and an ultimate triumph in posterity which can be irresistible).

Boccaccio saw Ovid and Dante both enacting a tripartite career – poets of love, transformation, and exile – but with Dante crucially reversing the Ovidian model, rescuing himself from his version of exile by embracing a poetry of divine love. As Janet Smarr suggests, Boccaccio uses these suggestive parallels as a means of figuring his own career and its divisions.[4] Louis Martz describes John Milton as a 'poet of exile' and sees the poetics of exile as a founding material of *Paradise Lost*, but avoids making many specific links between the epic (which borrows extensively from the *Metamorphoses*) and the exile poetry itself.[5] Edmund Spenser could be thought of in similar terms, with Ovid's career the silent, perhaps unmentionable, subtext to a career more obviously focused on a Virgilian model. The different *personae* and portrayals of Ireland in his work create dynamics of exile which often veer close to Ovidian territory.[6] Patrick Cheney, interestingly, sees Marlowe reacting instead to the orthodox Virgilian pattern in Spenser's case, and founding for himself an Ovidian 'counter-national' career plan, moving from amatory poems to tragedy and then to epic.[7]

Ovid's career, then, can be the wrong model, but the one which nevertheless offers a compelling pattern. This could be the case with Robert Herrick, whose *Hesperides* opens with a clue – a portrait frontispiece with a tellingly large nose. Within the collection other poets make obvious reference points: Virgil, perhaps, for pastoral, or Horace, for the pleasure of rural *otium*. Alongside them Ovid keeps coming to mind, as a forerunner in exile in 'Dean-bourn, a rude river in Devon', but also as an enthusiast for erotic love: it does not seem coincidental that it is 'Corinna' who is 'going a-Maying'

[3] See also Nagle (1980) 42–70.   [4] Smarr (1991).
[5] See Martz (1986), particularly pp. ix–xvii.
[6] See McCabe (1991); also, more generally, Burrow (2001).   [7] Cheney (1997).

in Herrick's poem.[8] It might be possible to attempt something similar with Shakespeare, a writer of witty love poems and plays who moves on to tackle weighty tragic and romantic transformations: the only things missing are the poems Shakespeare might just have sent to London from his retirement in Stratford (or from London to his family). Less fanciful than this is the astute recognition by Jonathan Bate that the emotional dynamics of Ovid's love for his mistress in the *Amores* and his wife in the *Tristia* may combine in the way the poet describes the fair youth of the Sonnets.[9]

Another good example of this elusive structure of career-influence is Petrarch, a poet who meditates upon metamorphic and amatory themes again and again, but who could also be seen as living out his whole career to a quasi-Ovidian template as lover and exile. Bartlett Giamatti sees Petrarch in a constant state of separation, divided by time rather than space from his intellectual origins in classical literature.[10] Giamatti does not explore a relationship with the *Tristia* , but Ovid may serve nevertheless as a potential predecessor. Certainly one could argue that Petrarch's poems explore myriad forms of disjuncture and separation. Philip Hardie has shown that his reading of the *Metamorphoses* in fact reinvents it in the terms of *Amores* and *Tristia*, love and exile.[11] In Petrarch's work Ovidian themes in love poetry take an important step into vernacular literature, a step which involves assimilation at Ovid's expense. The classic *topoi* of his loving *personae* become so familiar that they barely need a specific source (something which, interestingly, gradually becomes true of both Ovid and Petrarch). One account of the role of Ovid in the Spanish Renaissance, for example, refers to 'that evasive less tangible indebtedness to the Ovidian inheritance'.[12]

Lost evidence such as the 1160s *Ars amatoria* translation of Chrétien de Troyes would probably only clarify slightly the gradual assumption of Ovidian love themes into a post-classical European tradition. In the Middle Ages the image of Ovid was transformed no less radically than the *Metamorphoses* when it was rewritten as the *Ovide Moralisé*. Readings of different works made him adopt the roles of dangerous immoralist, tragic exile, natural or ethical philosopher, medical doctor (the *Remedia amoris* even being read by monks to dampen their desires), and magician, but perhaps his most acclaimed role was one he initiated for himself, the *praeceptor amoris*.[13] The influence of this figure in the Middle Ages even extends into the works of the wandering Troubadours, taking the characteristics of the urban

---

[8] Herrick (1648) 28.   [9] Bate (1993) 95.   [10] Giamatti (1984) 12–32.
[11] Hardie (1999b).   [12] Schevill (1913) 199.
[13] On 'Ovid's Transformations' in the Middle Ages see Rand (1925) 131–43; see also Wilkinson (1955) 366–98.

poet-lover on a European tour.[14] In Chaucer's *House of Fame* Ovid is awarded a high place on somewhat different grounds:

> And next hym on a piler was,
> Of coper, Venus clerk Ovide,
> That hath ysowen wonder wide
> The grete god of Loves name.
>
> (1486–9)[15]

A 'clerk' is a scholar, and what is praised specifically here (and perhaps with some irony) is Ovid's hard-working study on behalf of love rather than his practice of it. John Fyler captures the importance of the love-poetry's *persona*: 'from that work [*Metamorphoses*] Chaucer takes stories, but from the love poems he adopts a cast of mind.'[16] Chaucer tends to conflate poetry and biography in a typically medieval way, as has been described by Michael Calabrese.[17] Other texts, such as the eleventh-century Latin 'Liebesconcil' (Love-Council), share the lover-scholar motif, but take it further:

> Lecta sunt in medium   quasi euangelium
> Precepta Ouidii   doctoris egregii
> Lectrix tam propicii   fuit euangelii
> Eua de Danubio,   potens in officio
> Artis amatoriae,   ut affirmant aliae.[18]

> In the middle [of the council] the precepts of Ovid, that excellent expert, were read as if they were a Gospel. Eva of the Danube was the reader of so beneficial a gospel, she herself a powerful player in the business of the art of love, as the other women would confirm.

Here the *precepta* of Ovid are read *quasi evangelium*, as part of a holy text of love. It seems right to register a slight ironic blasphemy here, but also to recognize the esteem in which Ovid's guidance was held: he is one of the upholders of the good order of love which those excommunicated at the end of the 'Liebesconcil' have broken. The combination of irony and esteem is perhaps an early indication that unabashed abasement before Ovid the lover could not last forever: one *praeceptor* could be emulated by a legion of new *praeceptores* with fresh things to say about new eras of sexual politics and social life.

In the French Renaissance Ronsard's *Amours* contain in their title a connection with the *Amores*, but their myriad influences, Petrarch and neo-Latin elegy as well as Ovid, make it difficult to discern the presence of a specifically Ovidian love *persona* as opposed to one which had been

---

[14] See Schrötter (1918).   [15] Reference to Chaucer (1987).   [16] Fyler (1979) 17.
[17] Calabrese (1994) 11–32. See also Ghisalberti (1946).   [18] Waitz (1849).

assimilated into tradition. In the English Renaissance Ovid certainly plays a role in the background of Donne's love poetry, but this learned writer knows his Propertius and Tibullus as well, and he is influenced by a Petrarchan tradition which has itself incorporated Ovidian elements.[19] Donne also manages to define for himself a *persona* as a lover which, in its unstinting self-assertion, eclipses other *personae*.[20] After the English Restoration the rakishness of Ovid metamorphoses into that of the Earl of Rochester, with the poet's lax morality and mild self-deprecation magnified into extraordinary flights of lust and self-mockery, taking Ovid's impotence theme to the extreme in 'The Imperfect Enjoyment', a lavish imitation of *Amores* 3.7. Rochester in fact translated *Amores* 2.9, but (crucially) the Ovidian edge of his *persona* is one of its tamest features.[21]

The characteristic libertine pose of Rochester is paralleled in Restoration drama, and there too it evokes the spirit of Ovid. E. K. Rand saw a broader influence on the era's urbane comedy: 'there has never been a finer monument to Ovid's placid irony than *The Way of the World*'.[22] Ovid is also a more than plausible source for the genre's love of the city's *cultus*, and antipathy towards the countryside. Harriet can tease Dorimant in Etherege's *The Man of Mode* that 'all beyond Hyde Park's a desert to you', but he replies, perhaps ruefully, that 'now my passion knows no bounds'.[23] These plays can result in the unsettling of the most Ovidian figures, although *The Way of the World*'s closing lines show that this is not at the expense of wit:

> From hence let those be warned, who mean to wed;
> Lest mutual falshood stain the bridal-bed:
> For each deceiver to his cost may find,
> That marriage frauds too oft are paid in kind.[24]

The moral tone attempts a solution of the problem caused by a city full of Ovidian lovers, but the play depends on their presence. Mirabell here discovers an irony that is implicit in the structure of the *Ars amatoria*: everything can be worked from both sides. Restoration Comedy seems to have assimilated the Ovidian *persona* so fully that it seems clumsy to think of it in terms of imitating individual works. In addition, Restoration Comedy manages to accommodate Ovid's more daring moments within its depiction of respectable social life. After a while, true loucheness begins to find Ovid almost naive. Byron captures this in *Don Juan* by rhyming Ovid as a 'tutor' with 'neuter':

---

[19] See Gill (1972), Peacock (1975), Revard (1986).
[20] See Lerner (1988) and Carey (1960), particularly 180–99.
[21] For Rochester's version of *Amores* 2.9, see Martin (1998) 232.
[22] Rand (1925) 166.   [23] Etherege (1979) 5.2.138–41.   [24] Congreve (1971) 5.1.560–3.

Oh Love! of whom great Caesar was the suitor,
  Titus the master, Antony the slave,
Horace, Catullus, scholars, Ovid tutor,
  Sappho the sage blue-stocking, in whose grave
All those may leap who rather would be neuter.

(2.1633–7)[25]

Byron's apostrophe is deeply ironic and he cannot take Ovid's role as *praeceptor* seriously. Ovid does not take his own role seriously either, but the irony of his presentation of his *persona* is replaced here by an uncongenial stereotype. Ovid the lover finds himself in a backwater: the characteristics of his amatory *persona* are assumed into vernacular culture and translated into facets of Petrarchanism, rakishness, and many other forms of love. The Roman poet who still wants to teach his precocious pupils attracts their scorn as well as their respect.

The combination of Ovid's *personae*, however, seems to have an enduring power. During the Renaissance the vitality of the lover *persona* is sometimes enhanced by the harnessing of its narratives to those of the exile poetry, as explanations of Ovid's exile had always done. In the English 1590s the two *personae* relate in delicate and complex ways, as in George Chapman's *Ovids Banquet of Sence* (1595), which brings them into uneasy contact. This poem focuses on the poet's illicit love for the Emperor's daughter (*sic*) Julia, and extracts voyeuristic pleasure and metaphysical musing from the gradual exposure of all his five senses to her physical presence. Just as things reach the most intimate stage Ovid is interrupted (as he interrupts himself at *Amores* 1.5.25) and the poem dissipates with a knowing closing stanza:

But as when expert Painters have displaid,
To quickest life a Monarchs royall hand
Holding a Scepter, there is yet bewraide
But halfe his fingers; when we understand
The rest not to be seene; and never blame
The Painters Art, in nicest censures skand:
So in the compasse of this curious frame,
  Ovid well knew there was much more intended,
  With whose omition none must be offended.

(1045–53)[26]

Chapman's poem is very deliberately wrought, exploring the relationship between perceptions, representation, and artistry. It is also a satirical

---

[25] Reference to Byron (1980–93).   [26] Donno (1963) 242.

reflection on the fashion for erotic Ovidian epyllia then current: it teases the reader and then retreats into arch reference to all the things which the poem does not say. There is, however, a large thing which is also unmentioned and which lurks in the background: the affair with Julia is one traditional explanation of Ovid's exile, and Chapman's poem can evoke the whole Ovidian life story. The poem might then be one scene in a tragic fall, with discovery and relegation waiting for the final act. The connection is delicately and distantly implicit, but the position of the poem, and its treatment of the value of artistry, is deliciously precarious as a result.

Ovid features as a character in Ben Jonson's *Poetaster* (1601), a play which centres on a plot in which Horace (a thinly veiled version of Jonson himself) overcomes his detractors (thinly veiled versions of Marston and Dekker). Ovid's role is in a parallel plot involving his illicit love for Julia and an ill-judged pageant of the gods which is interrupted by the Emperor, who decides to exclude Ovid from the court. This plot is subtler and less biased than the other, and Jonson proves somewhat ambivalent towards a poet with whom he shares little temperament. Some have seen Jonson as essentially condemning Ovid, but it is possible to see an inconsistent response, as if Jonson regrets Ovid's parting.[27] Anne Barton makes an interesting connection between Jonson's uncertain feelings about Ovid and his uncertainty in imitating *Romeo and Juliet* when writing his own play's scene of parting (4.10).[28] Ian Donaldson has pointed out that Ovid's recitation of Marlowe's translation of *Amores* 1.15 (1.1.43–84) may be a note of sympathetic memory for the dead poet whose translation had recently been condemned and burned.[29] It seems that Jonson's portrayal of Ovid allows, at the very least, for some regret at the misapplication of the poet's wit. The soliloquy given to Ovid for him to describe his exile, however, does not strike the highest tragic note:

> As in a circle, a magician, then
> Is safe, against the spirit, he excites;
> But out of it, is subject to his rage,
> And loseth all the vertue of his arte:
> So I, exil'd the circle of the court,
> Lose all the good gifts, that in it I joy'd.
>
> (4.8.10–15)[30]

Jonson's Ovid is excluded from his love's presence, but is not sent to Tomis. An Ovidian insistence that it is only worth living in the highest urban echelons

---

[27] In Jonson (1995) 19–23 Tom Cain argues that Jonson is rejecting the lawless metamorphic verse of the 1590s; Mulvihill (1982) argues that Ovid in *Poetaster* is corrupted by circumstances rather than vice versa.
[28] Barton (1984) 84–5.   [29] Donaldson (1997) 206–9.   [30] Quoted from Jonson (1995).

lacks the plangent force of true *Tristia*. This denies the story the dignity of tragedy, perhaps, but it also refuses to punish its hero to the full force of the law. This may be a telling instance of Ovid's life-story seeming too close for comfort, Jonson himself having been imprisoned for sedition and slander in *The Isle of Dogs* (1597). *Poetaster* comes between this experience and that of *Eastward Hoe* (1605), which contained an anti-Scottish passage for which Jonson was again imprisoned and narrowly avoided having his ears and nose slit. Jonson's version of Ovid, then, may be that of someone who knows that the life of a poet can be dangerous (and interestingly the other author punished for the *Eastward Hoe* episode was George Chapman).

The third figure in this group of English quasi-Ovids is one of the co-authors of *The Isle of Dogs*, Thomas Nashe, who left London during the aftermath and wrote *Lenten Stuffe*, a digressive prose work which never quite makes explicit its Ovidian pattern (wit deprived of its natural urban location). His commentary on the habits of Yarmouth (his destination) is constantly informed by Ovid's fate, even though Nashe rarely courts pathos wholeheartedly. It is in another work, *Summer's Last Will and Testament*, that Nashe indulges an Ovidian tone in expressing displacement. This play centres on dying Summer's decision as to who should inherit his wealth. He is helped in his contemplation of the candidates by Will Summers, Henry VIII's fool. After his epilogue Will quotes Ovid's *Tristia*: *Barbarus hic ego sum, quia non intelligor ulli* (I am a barbarian here, because nobody understands me).[31] Given that this play manages to combine a pageant-like quality with a lament for a happier time in which revelry was not threatened by plague and puritan constraints, Nashe's voice joins his character in expressing the Ovidian sentiment.

It is not only in England that writers find ways of mapping their own predicaments on to Ovid's. In the French Renaissance there are intense direct encounters with the exile poetry, in the works of Marot and Magny, and especially in those of Joachim Du Bellay. His *Regrets* are *Tristia* written from Rome rather than back to Rome, an irony rarely far from view. Du Bellay confronts a recurring issue in responses to Ovid's exile *persona*, namely the potentially awkward cultural dynamics on which it is based. Non-Roman writers have to find ways around their non-Romanness. In his *Antiquitez de Rome* Du Bellay struggles with the legacy of classical Rome and the spectral voices of its great poets, when faced with the ruined city before him – the city in which Ovid's lover *persona* thrived. The *Regrets* emulate Ovid's personal reflection on his exile:

---

[31] Nashe (1958) III 295 (lines 1954–5).

Malheureux l'an, le mois, le jour, l'heure & le poinct,
Et malheureuse soit la flateuse esperance,
Quand pour venir icy j'abbandonay la France:
La France, & mon Anjou, dont le desir me poingt.

(XXV, 1–4)[32]

The year, the month, the day, the hour and the moment were all unhappy, and
so were my flattering expectations, when I abandoned France to come here:
France, and my Anjou – oh, how I want to go back there!

In this example Du Bellay is imitating Petrarch's *Canzoniere* 61 ('Benedetto
sia 'l giorno e 'l mese et l'anno') but inverts its mood.[33] In doing so he revisits
but also inverts geographically the classic situation of Ovid's exile. In other
poems his meditation on the *Tristia* develops the problem of his diverging
national allegiance and poetic inheritance:

Un peu de mer tenoit le grand Dulichien
D'Ithaque separé, l'Appenin porte-nue
Et les monts de Savoye à la teste chenue
Me tiennent loing de France au bord Ausonien.
Sterile est mon sejour, fertile estoit le sien,
Je ne suis pas des plus fins, sa finesse est cogneue:
Les siens gardans son bien attendoient sa venue,
Mais nul en m'attendant ne me garde le mien.
Pallas sa guide estoit, je vays à l'aventure,
Il fut dur au travail, moy tendre de nature:
A la fin il ancra sa navire à son port,
Je ne suis asseuré de retourner en France:
Il feit de ses haineux une belle vengeance,
Pour me venger des miens je ne suis assez fort.

(XL)

A small amount of sea separated the great Dulichian from Ithaca, but the cloud-
bearing Apennines and the snow-capped mountains of Savoie hold me far from
France on the Ausonian bank. My stay has been fruitless; his was packed with
incident. I am not one of the subtlest, while his subtlety is well-known. He
had people looking after his interests and awaiting his return, while nobody is
waiting for me and looking after mine. Pallas was his guide, while I trust to
chance. He was hardened by labours, while I am tender by nature. In the end
he anchored his ship at his port, while I am by no means assured that I will get
back to France. He wreaked a fine vengeance on his enemies: I am just not
strong enough to avenge myself on mine.

---

[32] References to Du Bellay (1970).   [33] See Petrarch (1976).

Du Bellay emulates Ovid's comparison of himself with Ulysses (*Tristia* 1.5.57–84), and adds another level to the mapping of one journey on to another. In this sonnet he bypasses Ovid to establish his own relationship with Homer's hero – but creates a double irony in repeating Ovid's self-consciously self-pitying comparison. What also comes through is the characteristic anxiety of Du Bellay's dealings with the Roman world: like Petrarch he finds himself feeling nostalgia in more than one direction. Goethe's *Römische Elegien* also play on the reversal of Ovidian *topoi* in the poet's travel to Rome, but add something to Du Bellay in their enjoyment of Rome's seamier side – courting at times the flavour of Ovid's love poems. One aspect of the appeal of the exile *persona* may be that it enables writers to express both the problems they have which parallel Ovid's, and the sense of separation that they have from their source.

The problem of reconciling a Roman sense of separation from the imperial centre with a wish to give some potential to the other parts of the world is found in one aspect of the twentieth-century vision of Ovid's exile. Two novels based on his life rewrite the mood of the exile poetry in a fundamental way, depicting an Ovid who ends up reconciled with Tomis and its language. Christoph Ransmayr's *The Last World* (*Die letzte Welt*) tells the story of Cotta, addressee of six of the *Epistulae ex Ponto*, who goes to Pontus to find out what has happened to his friend.[34] He discovers a bewitching landscape populated by people who share names with figures in the *Metamorphoses*. Ovid, it seems, has become more and more joined to the landscape, an experience Cotta begins to undergo himself:

> His first thought was of Naso, who – he was sure – slept night after night like this in these mountains, a Roman who had exchanged not only the columned halls of the empire, but also the stone roof of his last refuge for this open sky. He no longer feared the wilderness.[35]

Ovid has left behind him a poem and a landscape which have blurred into one another. For Ransmayr's characters leaving Rome is not separation from *cultus* but from bureaucracy and autocracy. David Malouf's *An Imaginary Life* depicts a similar transformation in Ovid's attitude to his surroundings. In this novel the exiled poet becomes fascinated by a wild boy who lives outside even the barbarous confines of Tomis. The anxiety about language in the exile poetry is taken further as Ovid begins to realize more and more the irrelevance of his old language as he tries to teach the boy Getic. While one part of him continues to write letters home in a

---

[34] Kennedy, ch. 19 in this volume, discusses *The Last World* in more detail. Wishart (1995), which is set in Rome, also focuses on the mystery of Ovid's exile.
[35] Ransmayr (1990) 141.

hollow performance, another begins to learn a language of nature from the wild boy:

> When I think of my exile now it is from the universe. When I think of the tongue that has been taken away from me, it is some earlier and more universal one than our Latin, subtle as it undoubtedly is. Latin is a language for distinctions, every ending defines and divides. The language I am speaking of now, that I am almost speaking, is a language whose every syllable is a gesture of reconciliation. We knew that language once. I spoke it in my childhood. We must discover it again.[36]

The interaction of old and new cultures is a regular theme in Malouf's novels and while *An Imaginary Life* does not share the Australian setting of *Remembering Babylon* or *Harland's Half-Acre*, it shares their Australian interest in the intrusion of one culture into a new landscape full of old rules and its own mythology. Malouf creates *Ovidius Australiensis*, a figure who discovers the value in a new world. Indeed, his version of the landscape around Tomis seems quite Australian, and Gareth Griffiths has connected the integration of humans and nature which Ovid discovers with the Australian Aboriginal landscape of Bruce Chatwin's *Songlines*.[37] Malouf has been grouped with other Australian writers who suffer from what is called a 'Tomis Complex'.[38] On his journey Chatwin actually carries 'the Penguin Classics edition of Ovid's *Metamorphoses*' and likens the Songlines to the 'totemic geography' of classical mythology.[39] Both Malouf and Ransmayr rescue Ovid from despair, and fictionalize a life beyond the consistent tone of the exile poetry. In a way, though, both writers are overcoming a problem in Ovid's exile as it bears on later writing, a problem present also in Du Bellay. In overcoming Ovid's despair at his separation from Rome, they also overcome the possibility of their own barbarity in comparison with him.

These two novels strive to find a solution caused by the implications of Ovid's exile, and in doing so offer some kind of solution to Ovid's problem as well. Often, in modern poetry, the image of Ovid allows for articulation of modern versions of exile: the internal political banishment of Osip Mandelstam in his 1922 *Tristia*, or the various forms of exile (political, religious, cultural, emotional) recounted by the Irish poems discussed on these Ovidian terms by John Kerrigan.[40] In modern writing the exile *persona* seems still to offer poets arresting if uncomfortable images of their own possibilities. Perhaps social changes, or the extended development of the tradition, prevent the lover *persona* from doing so, but this is evidence

---

[36] Malouf (1978) 98.   [37] Griffiths (1992) 438–40.   [38] Pana (1993).
[39] Chatwin (1987) 75, 117.
[40] Kerrigan (1992). See also Kennedy, ch. 19 in this volume, on Joseph Brodsky.

of how fundamentally the Ovidian lover has been taken into later traditions. Paradoxically the relative disappearance of the lover *persona* may show how avidly it has been dealt with. Far more than Virgil, more also than Horace, Ovid remains a poet who influences through life as well as work: or rather, as one whose works prompt such a poignant, fleetingly vivid picture of the life behind them, that their reception has this special quality.

FURTHER READING

Ovid the lover and the exile has a varied career as an English literary character. In the Renaissance Ben Jonson's Elizabethan *Poetaster* (ed. Cain [1995]) and Aston Cokayne's Restoration *The Tragedy of Ovid* (London, 1662) put him on the stage, while George Chapman's poem *Ovids Banquet of Sence*, found in Donno (1963), makes him the central character in a partly philosophical, partly erotic poem. In the modern era several novels have featured Ovid, including David Malouf's *An Imaginary Life* (1978) and Christoph Ransmayr's *The Last World: With An Ovidian Repertory* (1990).

Criticism germane to the reception of the lover and exile *personae* is as varied as the reception itself. Rand (1925), and especially Wilkinson (1955), remain useful surveys of the long tradition of Ovidian reception. Allen (1992) and Stapleton (1996) trace the influence of Ovid's portrayal of love. Exile is less systematically covered, though Giamatti (1984) discusses the general ground well, and various critics have explored the ramifications of Ovidian exile in later writers: Kerrigan (1992), Martz (1986), Pana (1993), and Smarr (1991).

18

COLIN BURROW

Re-embodying Ovid: Renaissance afterlives

Ovid was the most imitated and influential classical author in the Renaissance. This is not surprising, since many of the central preoccupations of his work seem almost to have been calculated to appeal to imitators. He is interested in how texts survive, and in their physical frailty. His writing also repeatedly meditates on the relationship between continuity and change in the universe, in individual lives, and within a poetic *oeuvre*. This passage from an epistle to his wife in the *Tristia* brings out all of these concerns:

> atque utinam pereant animae cum corpore nostrae,
> effugiatque avidos pars mihi nulla rogos!
> nam si morte carens vacua volat altus in aura
> spiritus, et Samii sunt rata dicta senis,
> inter Sarmaticas Romana vagabitur umbras,
> perque feros manes hospita semper erit.
>
> (*Trist.* 3. 3. 59–64)

> And here I wish my soul died with my breath
> And that no part of me were free from death,
> For, if it be immortal, and outlives
> The body, as *Pythagoras* believes,
> Betwixt these *Sarmates' ghosts*, a *Roman* I
> Shall wander, vexed to all eternity.
>
> (trans. Henry Vaughan)[1]

Here Ovid becomes his own first imitator. He reflects on the transmission and survival of his own texts and of his own body, and at the same time he consciously recalls and modifies his earlier work. He revisits the discourse of Pythagoras in *Metamorphoses* 15 (a section of the poem which the majority of early modern readers believed contained the philosophical core of the poem) and reconsiders it in the light of his present exile. Immortality becomes

---

[1] Text from Vaughan (1983).

a source of horror, and oblivion a consummation devoutly to be wished. In the same poem he transforms the optimistic ending of the *Metamorphoses*, which promises that 'As far as the limits of Roman power extend I shall be read', and reflects instead on his own bodily frailty, and on the probability that he will die far from the centre of culture and patronage. The poem deliberately creates a sense of historical and spatial distance from its author, even to the extent of reproducing an inscription for his tombstone. It is designed to make its Roman readers think of Ovid as a disembodied voice from the past, who is transforming his own works as he looks back at them.

The main aim of this chapter will be to show that Ovid's Renaissance imitators took up these and other cues left by Ovid to his readers. Their readings and imitations of Ovid are acutely influenced by Ovid's own reflections on imitation and re-embodiment. And this is something distinctive to the period from about 1500 onwards – although it is hard to draw hard distinctions between 'Medieval' and 'Renaissance' responses to Ovid, since many of what are traditionally thought of as 'Medieval' features of his reception (such as allegorical commentaries) persist well into the seventeenth century, and many of what are often thought to be 'Renaissance' responses to his work (such as the use of Ovidian narratorial *personae*) can be found in Chaucer and Gower. But between 1500 and 1700 there are some broad shifts of emphasis. Commentators begin to draw attention increasingly to the rhetorical surface of Ovid's work. And Ovid's self-consciousness about how his texts will survive and how they will be reread in the light of new circumstances come to play a central part in his reception. Humanists who regarded themselves as the heirs of Greece and Rome also frequently thought of themselves as exiled from the sources of learning and civilization. They might seek to re-embody the sources of their knowledge, but would still often record their sense of distance from their literary originals. In these respects they are deeply indebted to Ovid. As Raphael Lyne shows in chapter 17, Petrarch's *Rime sparse* build on the two main aspects of Ovid's elegiac work: Petrarch's endless longing for Laura derives from Ovid's *persona* in the *Amores*; and Ovid's spatial removal from the source of civilization in the *Tristia* is transformed by Petrarch into a temporal isolation from the founts of Roman culture.[2]

Ovid provided his Renaissance imitators with a rich stock of metaphors which they could use when describing their own activity in reviving the past. Renaissance poets who wished to lay claim to the authority of classical literature could claim to re-embody, metamorphose, or even metempsychose Ovid. Book 15 of the *Metamorphoses* also provides one of the richest classical models for poetry which at once dwells on the destructive power of time,

---

[2] Giamatti (1982). For other aspects of Petrarch's Ovidianism, see Vickers (1981–2).

and which seeks to wrest poetic immortality from its ravages. This combination of concerns makes Ovid the most potent classical influence on writers at work between 1500 and 1700. He seems almost to have anticipated their desire to produce writing which presents itself both as acutely vulnerable to the passage of time and as a renewal of past literature. Shakespeare's sonnet 60 is in these respects the classic statement of Renaissance Ovidianism:

> Like as the waves make towards the pebbled shore,
> So do our minutes hasten to their end,
> Each changing place with that which goes before,
> In sequent toil all forwards do contend.
> Nativity, once in the main of light,
> Crawls to maturity, wherewith being crowned
> Crookèd eclipses 'gainst his glory fight,
> And Time that gave doth now his gift confound.
> Time doth transfix the flourish set on youth,
> And delves the parallels in beauty's brow,
> Feeds on the rarities of nature's truth,
> And nothing stands but for his scythe to mow.
> > And yet to times in hope my verse shall stand,
> > Praising thy worth, despite his cruel hand.

The poem closely follows *Metamorphoses* 15. 178–85: 'As every wave drives other forth, and that that comes behind | Both thrusteth and is thrust itself: Even so the times by kind | Do fly and follow both at once, and evermore renew', as Golding renders it. Shakespeare collapses together Pythagoras' discourse on change and Ovid's own final prophecy that his poem will be immortal. The poem also quietly asserts that followers can take Ovid one step further: 'In sequent toil all forwards do contend' both records the ceaseless mobility of time and suggests that those who follow can move things on. It goes forward from Ovid even as it closely echoes his phrasing (*sequuntur*, *Met.* 15. 183). This aspiring optimism is damped a little in the couplet: can abstract praise of someone's 'worth' compensate for the destruction of the body? Will a poem actually withstand the physicality of Time's destructive power? The poem ends in an uneasy balance between loss and recuperation which is typical of responses to Ovid in this period: Ovid is revived and imitated, but with a lasting impression that texts may be weak opponents to Time's destructive energy. As we shall see, re-embodying Ovid in this period brings with it the hope of a revival: it also brings with it a sense of bodily frailty and impermanence.

Ovid, however, had many forms in early modern Europe: he was allegorized in commentaries, plundered for rhetorical ornaments in text books, plagiarized in mythological handbooks, read as smut, transformed into highly self-conscious narrative art, and drilled into schoolboys almost every day of their lives. School-children in England and Europe were encouraged to learn Latin verse composition by translating verses of Ovid into the vernacular, and then translating them back into Latin prose. They would then be required to structure their prose translation into a metrical and rhetorically shaped approximation of their original, so that (ideally) they might 'have made the very same' poem as Ovid originally wrote.[3] Like the best kind of schoolmaster, though, Ovid gave his students a sense that there was more to life than the curriculum: biographies of Ovid, prefixed to editions of his poems from the 1490s, frequently relate that the poet himself was a reluctant pupil, who rebelled against his training in the law. Many of his readers and imitators presented Ovid as someone who you would want to read under the desk in the back row of the classroom: Johannes Secundus began his cycle of erotic neo-Latin Elegies (posthumously printed in 1539) by explaining that he chose erotic subjects for his poems (which imitate the *Amores* and the decidedly un-schooly *Ars amatoria*) in order to prevent grammarians using his works as school texts.[4] Montaigne described how he would hide himself away with the *Metamorphoses*, eagerly absorbing its fables: 'The first taste or feeling I had of books, was of the pleasure I took in reading the fables of Ovid's *Metamorphoses*; for, being but seven or eight years old, I would steal and sequester my self from all other delights, only to read them.'[5]

The wicked pleasures of Ovidianism were pursued by many English writers in the 1590s. Ovid enabled writers from the period to sound respectably learned even while they described undressing with their mistress – as Donne does in 'To his Mistress Going to Bed'. Through the late 1580s and '90s narrative poets, especially those with connections with the theatre, used tales from Ovid's *Metamorphoses* to construct what was effectively a new genre of short erotic narrative poems (often called 'epyllia' or minor epics by modern critics).[6] These are usually presided over by narrators who have learnt from Ovid to be by turns ironically detached and passionately engaged. Several of the tales transformed into epyllia derive from sections of the *Metamorphoses* which draw attention to relationships between the tales and their tellers. Book 10, which contains the tales told by Orpheus, was especially popular. Narrated by Orpheus, the archetypical poet, Book 10 is rich in stories which ponder the effects of art, such as the tale of Pygmalion, the artist who makes his creation come to life. Because Ovid's Orpheus is in Ovid's version a lover

---

[3] Brinsley (1612) 193.   [4] Nichols (1979) 486.   [5] Montaigne (1603) 88.
[6] On which see Keach (1977), Hulse (1981), Lanham (1976).

of boys he also tells tales which soften the hard distinctions between male and female bodies. At one point Orpheus, the lover of boys, relates how Venus, who is in love with Adonis, a boyish young man, relates how Hippomenes falls for the boyish runner-girl Atalanta. When

> He saw her face and body bare, (for why the Lady then
> Did strip her to her naked skin) the which was like to mine,
> Or rather (if that thou wert made a woman) like too thine:
> He was amazed. (Golding, 10. 673–6)

Golding's translation misses the anticipatory flicker of metamorphosis in the original which enables the narrator to unsettle our view of Atalanta's body: Ovid's Venus says to her Adonis 'like mine, or like yours *if you were to become* a woman' (*si femina fias*); and at that moment a reader's sense of who desires whom is in turmoil, since the narrator is both Venus, a woman in love with a boyish young man, and Orpheus, a lover of boys who, one suspects, would quite like it if the androgynous Atalanta were to become a boy. Readers of Ovid in the 1590s were acutely sensitive to Ovid's ability to unsettle our views of bodies and their genders. Marlowe's *Hero and Leander* (written some time soon before his death in 1593) takes from Ovid a delight in the polymorphousness of both narrative art and sexual desire. It is presided over by an Ovidian ironical narrator who is able to desire anyone, male or female, and who seems intent on disturbing the relationship between the rigid physical embodiment of gender and the potential multiplicity of forms which can be taken by sexuality. Marlowe's description of the moment when the god Neptune laps around the body of Leander as he swims the Hellespont is quintessentially the Ovid of the 1590s in England. Marlowe makes his Neptune both a god and the physical matter of the sea, which laps over the body of Leander. This enables him to make his readers, most of whom would have been men, feel their bodies melt into desire for the male youth:

> He watched his arms, and as they opened wide,
> At every stroke, betwixt them would he slide
> And steal a kiss, and then run out and dance,
> And as he turned, cast many a lustful glance,
> And threw him gaudy toys to please his eye,
> And dive into the water, and there pry
> Upon his breast, his thighs, and every limb,
> And up again, and close beside him swim,
> And talk of love: *Leander* made reply,
> 'You are deceived: I am no woman, I.'
>
> (667–76)

Re-embodying Ovid here means more than just reincarnating him: it means thinking about how the physical form of the human body may relate or not relate to the polymorphousness of sexual desire. Francis Beaumont's *Salmacis and Hermaphroditus* of 1603 develops Marlowe's fascination with the fusions and confusions of gender: its epigraph to the reader hopes 'my poem is so lively writ | That thou shalt turn half-maid with reading it'. Marlowe shares this aim of mining within his reader's bodily desires.

In 1598 Francis Meres wrote that 'the sweet witty soul of Ovid lives in mellifluous and honey-tongued Shakespeare',[7] and Shakespeare is the most famous Elizabethan re-embodiment of Ovid. His Ovidian career began with the narrative poem *Venus and Adonis* (1593) and continued the next year in graver mood with *Lucrece* (which derives from Ovid's tale of Lucretia's rape by Tarquin in the *Fasti*). Both poems add richly Ovidian rhetorical set-pieces – lengthy complaints and persuasions to love – to their originals. Shakespeare's variation on the theme of Venus and Adonis omits the long inset tale of Atalanta and Hippomenes, which Venus tells to Adonis in order to delay his departure for the hunt; but its main narrative revels in the reversals and confusions of gender which, as we have seen, are unleashed by that tale. Venus is a manly woman who can tuck Adonis under one arm and his horse's reins under the other, and it is she who uses all the traditional rhetoric of male seduction. Adonis meanwhile remains poutily silent, an ephebe on the boundary between boyhood and manhood. Sexual desire in its Ovidian form blurs boundaries between physical bodies: when Venus finally wins a kiss she seems set to become another Salmacis, fusing with her lover's flesh ('Incorporate they seem, face grows to face', 540), before Shakespeare remembers the Ovidian association between sexual desire and the hunt, and 'her face does reek and smoke' with the savagery of a bird enjoying its prey. Shakespeare's narrative poems suggest that sexual desire brings about emotional metamorphoses which are more significant than their physical counterparts: it turns Tarquin into a wolfish rapist, and transforms the goddess of love herself for a moment into a vulture-like predator.

These Ovidian experiments with the multiple forms of sexual desire were possible on the page, but on the Elizabethan stage there were clearer limits to what could and could not be done with bodies. Since female roles were in this period played by boys it was of course possible for the imagination of an audience to flicker between the female role and the ephebic actor, and this form of imaginative hermaphroditism is a vital part of the effect of many of Shakespeare's comedies. It is, however, impossible onstage to metamorphose an actor into an animal or plant (although the actor who plays Bottom does pop on an ass's head when he has retired to the tiring

---

[7] Smith (1904) II, 317.

house). Nonetheless Ovid does dominate Shakespeare's early career as a dramatist. *Titus Andronicus* (probably composed within a year of *Venus and Adonis*) is an extended meditation on the tale of Philomela from Book 6 of the *Metamorphoses*. Shakespeare's Philomela figure is Lavinia, who is raped by not just one but two Tereuses. The play is set in a fictional period in late imperial Rome, and this post-classical milieu colours the ways in which characters within it respond to Ovid. They often behave as though they are themselves distantly remembering his works and seeking, like monstrous parodies of humanist imitators, to overgo Ovid's carnal excesses. For the two rapists Chiron and Demetrius the tale of Philomela has a clear moral: if you are to imitate Tereus and rape someone you should cut off their hands as well as cutting out their tongue so they cannot emulate Philomela and weave a record of your crime. Lavinia comes onstage, raped and mutilated, tongueless and handless. She is the starkest portrayal of a non-metamorphosed, mutilated body in the entire Shakespeare canon: she is denied the release of metamorphosis by the cruel conventions of the stage. Lacking the release provided by words, and lacking the potential for revenge provided by Philomela's weaving, Lavinia can only rely on others to speak for her. Marcus, her uncle, tries:

> Fair Philomel, why she but lost her tongue
> And in a tedious sampler sewed her mind:
> But, lovely niece, that mean is cut from thee.
> A craftier Tereus, cousin, hast thou met,
> And he hath cut those pretty fingers off
> That could have better sewed than Philomel.
> (*Titus Andronicus* 2. 4. 38–43)[8]

Many readers and viewers of this scene have found the references to Ovid in Marcus's speech gruesomely inappropriate to the horror he is witnessing. But this is in its gruesome way a profoundly thoughtful Renaissance re-embodiment (or dismemberment) of Ovid: as Ovid's Philomela is re-embodied in a newly excessive form an audience is made to think about whether or not a classical tale is an adequate vehicle to carry her suffering. Can quoting Ovid seem any more than an excuse for failing to respond to what Lavinia has undergone? This question implies a profound temporal exile from Ovid, which is characteristic of Renaissance responses to his writing: his texts, half-remembered from Marcus's schooling, are not adequate to represent living, bodily suffering. A good humanist like Marcus seems obscenely insensitive when he quotes his texts in response to theatrical re-embodiments of the suffering related in the *Metamorphoses*.

---

[8] Quotations from Shakespeare (1986).

However there is also a secondary, recuperative, set of questions raised by Lavinia's plight and Marcus's Ovidian response to it. When you see pain of this kind is there *any* way of grasping it? Isn't the gap between Marcus's references to Ovid and the plight of Lavinia a reflection of a divide that always exists between suffering and efforts to give it words? Shakespeare uses a humanist's sense of exile from Ovid to articulate the necessary distance between a sufferer and a tragic spectator. No text is a sufficient vehicle to capture the suffering endured by Lavinia. Although gruesome and often unsteady in its craftsmanship, *Titus* is asking questions about what it means to re-embody Ovid, and it is using those questions to reflect on problems which are central to the *Metamorphoses*: the poem is fascinated by the ways in which extreme pain might expose the inability of human bodies to express it, and *Titus* metamorphoses that concern into a historical question: can we re-embody the suffering enacted in past texts?

In plays written in the 1590s Shakespeare tends to present Ovid as archaic in two distinct ways: he is the source of primitively gruesome tales, and he is also the author of old, half-remembered stories. This does not diminish his power over the early Shakespeare, however. At the end of *A Midsummer Night's Dream* Bottom and his friends perform a botched version of the tale of Pyramus and Thisbe. The theatrical style of their performance is pointedly outmoded, just as the subject of the story they enact displays a more primitive violence than the actions of the Shakespearean drama within which it is set. Ovid is not, though, irrelevant in the *Dream* because he is archaic. Far from it: the Ovidian tale of Pyramus and Thisbe, of filial disobedience, elopement and death, casts a retrospective darkness over the preceding action of the play. Even if the onstage audience thinks the Ovidian drama presided over by Bottom is hopelessly outmoded, the offstage audience might see that the whole play is haunted by an ancient, threatening presence of Ovid which it is labouring very hard to turn into comedy.

By about 1600 the reputation of Ovid was undergoing significant changes. No Renaissance reader could forget that Ovid was banished for a poem and a crime (*carmen et error*, Trist. 2. 1. 207): medieval *accessus* and printed Renaissance lives of the poet frequently speculated on what the 'error' was. Politian's elegy on the death and exile of Ovid (composed in the 1490s) frequently found a place among the prefatory matter of editions of Ovid's work, and was translated by Wye Saltonstall in his 1633 translation of the *Tristia*. The *Tristia* themselves were often among the first Latin poems studied at school. And the figure of Ovid whose physical exile anticipated the temporal exile of humanist writers from their sources came to be central to his reception. The first English translation of the *Fasti* by John Gower (1640) is presented as not just an imitation but as a metempsychosis of Ovid ('On this book, Reader, lay thy hand and swear, | Ovid himself is Metamorphos'd here').[9] It goes on to relate a detailed biography of Ovid the poet of exile, founded on extensive quotation from the *Tristia*. By the 1640s in England Ovid among the Getes had become an established literary character with whom many poets claimed a close resemblance this side metempsychosis. Henry Vaughan's translations of the exile poetry (in *Olor Iscanius*, printed in 1651) intensify the personal miseries of Ovid, and invite identifications between Ovid's state of exile in Tomis and Vaughan's own unhappiness at the destruction of the English Church during the Civil War.

The exile of Ovid had begun to shape responses to the poet by the late 1590s. Touchstone in *As You Like It* 3. 3. 5–6 (c. 1600) jokily makes a comparison between his sylvan exile and Ovid's ('I am here with thee and thy goats as the most capricious poet honest Ovid was among the Goths'). His joke shows that the figure of Ovid among the Getes or goats or Goths played as great a part in the mythology of the poet in the early seventeenth century as his huge nose for 'smelling out the odorous flowers of fancy' (*Love's Labours Lost* 4. 2. 116). But the first major literary representation of the moment of Ovid's exile in England was Ben Jonson's *Poetaster* in 1601, and this, as Raphael Lyne shows in chapter 17, marks a delicate stock-taking of earlier responses to Ovid. Ovid is physically re-embodied in *Poetaster*: he is brought onstage at the start of the play as a paradigm literary rebel, and is eventually banished for impersonating the gods.[10] The play insistently attempts to differentiate Jonson's ethical response to classical literature from the exuberant immorality of *Hero and Leander* and *Venus and Adonis*. Coming on the back of a clamp-down in 1599 on erotic and satirical verse, the play in part aimed to end the dominant eroticized reading of Ovid.

And this was one of the most influential literary campaigns in the English Renaissance. Donne probably ceased calling his poems elegies in around 1600. Donne is also likely to have begun and abandoned his satirical mini-epic of metempsychosis, 'The Progress of the Soul', which relates the successive reincarnations of the soul of the apple eaten by Eve, in around 1601. By 1603 Michael Drayton had revised some of the more sumptuous Ovidian details out of his historical epic *Mortimeriados*, and had composed the last of his anglicizations of the *Heroides*. *Poetaster* also coincides with the marked reduction in explicit allusions to Ovid in Shakespeare's plays.[11] But Ovid was by no means completely banished in 1601. Changed anew, he again becomes a major presence in Shakespeare's work around 1609, at about the same time

---

[9] Isaac Tinckler's dedicatory epistle in Gower (1640), sig. ¶4[b].
[10] See Jonson (1995) 19–23.
[11] Although see Bate (1993) ch. 5 for the view that many of the tragedies are *imitationes* of Ovidian tales.

as Thomas Heywood's dramatizations of tales from the *Metamorphoses* were being performed at the popular playhouse the Red Bull. Shakespeare's imitations of Ovid late in his career recall the sections of the *Metamorphoses* which had fascinated him from the 1590s, but these episodes are reshaped by new preoccupations. Ovid retains sinister associations with rape and archaic violence, but acquires equally strong associations with the power of the imagination. The tale of Philomela, for instance, casts a dark shadow over *Cymbeline*. When Iachimo spies on Imogen as she sleeps he describes her in terms which recall Shakespeare's responses to Ovid from fifteen years before. He refers to both the Ovid of *Lucrece* ('Our Tarquin thus | Did softly press the rushes') and to that of *Titus Andronicus* (Imogen has been reading the *Metamorphoses* and the book is open at 'The tale of Tereus' (2. 2. 45)). But although *Cymbeline* returns to the Ovidian tales so gruesomely re-embodied in Shakespeare's earlier works, it transforms them completely. The tale of Tereus and Philomel is physically registered in a book onstage, but it is not physically re-enacted. The assault on Imogen becomes purely imaginary. Iachimo makes notes on what he sees and persuades her husband Posthumous he has indeed slept with her. The ravishing detail of his description is enough to make actual carnal seduction unnecessary. Allusion to Ovid turns into illusion.

That emphasis on the power of the imaginary is Shakespeare's equivalent in the late plays for the literary self-consciousness of Ovid. He transforms Ovid's literary self-consciousness into theatrical self-consciousness. So at the end of *The Winter's Tale* a 'statue' of the supposedly dead Hermione miraculously comes to life, and rewrites the tale of Pygmalion in a key of high theatrical knowingness. This tale (another of those told by Orpheus, the poet who famously fails to revive the dead) shows Ovid at his most writerly, as he teasingly makes readers participate in the transformation of the statue. The statue becomes grammatically 'she' when it acquires a feminine pronoun (*hanc*, *Met*. 10. 267); then Pygmalion gives it/her soft pillows *tamquam sensura*, as if she could feel them – but also as if she *will*, since *sensura* is a feminine future participle (*Met*. 10. 269). These minute effects of grammar defy transposition to the stage. But the finale of *The Winter's Tale* demands a similarly attentive participatory magic from its audience. Given that there was a vogue for masques which contained actors who played statues in 1613,[12] and given that an audience might believe Hermione to be dead indeed, the balance between illusion and living art is shared by Leontes and his offstage audience. Neither quite knows what they should be seeing or feeling. Are they supposed to believe that the actor before them is pretending to

---

[12] Armitage (1987).

be a statue? Or that the actor is pretending to be a person pretending to be a statue? Is Pygmalion being re-embodied before them?

> Still methinks
> There is an air comes from her. What fine chisel
> Could ever yet cut breath? Let no man mock me,
> For I will kiss her. (5. 3. 77–9)

The art of re-embodying Ovid could scarcely be enacted on more levels: Leontes at once fears that he is 'mocked with art' and hopes that he will turn into Pygmalion; an audience hopes to see the Pygmalion story brought to life, and perhaps worries that the actor playing a statue will sneeze or wobble. And then – if you are prepared to believe it – a statue comes to life.

The revival of the dead Hermione is not an entirely comfortable event, however, since it is given distinct overtones of necromancy (as Leontes says, 'If this be magic, let it be an art | Lawful as eating', 5. 3. 110–11). And this remark raises a wider element in Ovid's influence on Renaissance writing. He offers, as we have seen, a set of metaphors to describe what imitators are doing; but these metaphors of revival and re-embodiment often have sinister doubles. Reviving the dead could be miraculous and beneficial; but it could also be sacrilegious or necromantic. Christian poets reviving a pagan work of fiction are acutely responsive to this dilemma. It is registered at the end of *The Tempest*, when Prospero renounces his magic art. He quotes and revives Ovid's Medea:

> the strong-based promontory
> Have I made shake, and by the spurs plucked up
> The pine and cedar; graves at my command
> Have waked their sleepers, oped, and let 'em forth
> By my so potent art. But this rough magic
> I here abjure. (5. 1. 46–51)

The passage stands out from its context as an ostentatious imitation of Medea's invocation before she rejuvenates the aged Aeson in *Metamorphoses* 7. 198–218. Some critics have wished to deny that there is any point in comparing Prospero to Medea, and have seen the speech as just a set-piece display.[13] The strange detail that 'graves at my command | Have waked their sleepers' (which corresponds closely to what Medea says in *Met.* 7. 206) does not on the face of it relate to anything the play has shown of Prospero so far, and seems an undigested relic of Medea's speech: graves have not liter-ally waked their sleepers in the course of the play. But Prospero *has* revived

---

[13] Martindale (1990) 23; but see Bate (1993) 9–10.

the past and brought the dead back to life in a metaphorical way: his own previous experiences have been re-enacted in a drama which is itself substantially revived from Virgil and Ovid. Ferdinand, supposed dead, has been returned to his father; Prospero, also supposed dead, has come back to life. Shakespeare attempts to transpose Medea's literal claim to have revived the dead into something imaginary. But this transformation of Ovid does not completely cancel out the voice of Medea, and her claim literally to have opened graves and revived the dead. The whole speech registers a fear that the act of re-embodying Ovid is not simply beneficial, and that the necromantic violence of the pagan text could take over its modern imitator. This is just a momentary ripple of unease in *The Tempest*. For writers within the epic tradition, however, it points to an area of consistent anxiety. As the next section will show, the wish to re-embody Ovid is often accompanied by a fear that Ovid will come to dominate his Christian imitators.

Through the sixteenth century Ovid had been championed as a classical model for a kind of epic poetry which had multiple heroes and multiple tales. Giraldi Cinthio's defence of the mode of romance uses Ovid as precedent for its structural freedom: 'abandoning Aristotle's laws of art with admirable mastery, he commenced the work at the beginning of the world and treated in marvellous sequence a great variety of matters.'[14] Epic poets in the earlier sixteenth century are relatively at ease with their Ovidian heritage: Ariosto's *Orlando furioso* (1532) revels in an interwoven Ovidian multiplicity of plots, and responds with direct humour to Ovid's tales.[15] But for epic poets in the later sixteenth century there was an increasing fear that multiplicity of stories might be accompanied by the structural and ethical disintegration of heroic poetry and even of heroism itself. Spenser's *Faerie Queene* (1590–6) is particularly anxious about this structural and moral problem, and this in turn has an immeasurable effect on the way that Spenser responds to Ovid. He is presented from the very start of Spenser's poem as a poet of potentially corrupting multiplicity. In Book 1 the Redcrosse Knight ventures into the wood of Errour. Having passed an ostentatiously Ovidian catalogue of trees, he encounters Errour herself, a monstrous spawn of Ovid:

> And as she lay vpon the durtie ground,
>> Her huge long taile her den all ouerspred,
>> Yet was in knots and many boughtes vpwound,
>> Pointed with mortall sting. Of her there bred
>> A thousand yong ones, which she dayly fed,

---

[14] Cinthio (1968) 20.   [15] Javitch (1976).

Sucking vpon her poisonous dugs, eachone
Of sundry shapes, yet all ill fauored:
Soone as that vncouth light vpon them shone,
Into her mouth they crept, and suddain all were gone.

(1. i. 15)

Throughout this chapter we have seen how Ovid permeates the descriptive techniques and the narrative material of early modern writers. He also frequently influences the ways in which writers think about their own activity as imitators and revivers of pagan antiquity. Spenser's description of Errour shows how Ovidian material could be associated with malign as much as with benign rebirths. She, a monstrous imitation of Ovid's Scylla, spews up an unending generation of offspring. She is a grisly parody of rebirth. And she prompts an allusion to Ovid's account of the spontaneous generation of worms from the mud of the Nile ('Huge heapes of mudd he leaves, wherein there breed | Ten thousand kindes of creatures, partly male | And partly female of his fruitfull seed', 1. i. 21; compare *Met.* 1. 422–33). Ovid is more or less identified at this stage of Spenser's poem with a temptation to wander after vain desires, and with a ceaseless multiplication of not quite human forms. Ovidian locales are repeatedly associated with sinister revivals of the dead and with a temptation to wander endlessly away from moral obligations: Aesculapius, who is discovered in a richly Ovidian lair, attempts to bring back Sans Joy from the grave in 1. v. It is from the unmistakably Ovidian cave of sleep that Archimago conjures up a phantasmal version of his lady Una who leads Redcrosse away from his quest into a world of duplicity and delusion.

Spenser's Ovid is by no means all darkness, however. The fecundity of Ovid has both a nightmarish and a beneficent dimension. On the one hand it generates creatures such as Errour which have an energy that chokes with its own vitality; on the other hand it offers a potentially benign and renewable image of the universe as endlessly vital. And at the centre of *The Faerie Queene* this aspect of Ovid generates the endless rebirths and renewals described in the Garden of Adonis in III. 6. Spenser's Adonis occupies a garden which is the source of all life. He lies among a bed of flowers, each of which recalls an irreversible Ovidian metamorphosis. He himself, however, changes endlessly:

There wont faire *Venus* often to enioy
    Her deare *Adonis* ioyous company,
    And reape sweet pleasure of the wanton boy;
    There yet, some say, in secret he does ly,
    Lapped in flowres and pretious spycery,
    By her hid from the world, and from the skill

> Of *Stygian* Gods, which doe her loue enuy;
>   But she her selfe, when euer that she will,
> Possesseth him, and of his sweetnesse takes her fill.
>
> And sooth it seemes they say: for he may not
>   For euer die, and euer buried bee
>   In balefull night, where all things are forgot;
>   All be he subiect to mortalitie,
>   Yet is eterne in mutabilitie,
>   And by succession made perpetuall,
>   Transformed oft, and chaunged diverslie:
>   For him the Father of all formes they call;
> Therefore needs mote he liue, that liuing giues to all.
>
> (III.vi.46–7)

Here Book 15 of the *Metamorphoses* enters the poem with a thrill of life. In *Metamorphoses* 10 Adonis is irreversibly transformed into a flower: here he takes on the endless vitality described by Pythagoras in Book 15. Ovid is, as it were, his own antidote: the Ovidian universe of change is transplanted on to the end of one of Ovid's stories of irreversible metamorphosis in order to make it live anew. (Spenser may well have noted that at the end of Ovid's version of the story Venus predicts the repeated delight which will come from the flowering of the metamorphosed Adonis each year.) There is no irreversible metamorphosis in this world, just endless renovation. While Spenser describes this Ovidian revival he is also thinking about his own poetic transformation of Ovid: he makes Ovid perpetual by transplanting the changeful cosmos of the end of the *Metamorphoses* on to the end of one of Ovid's tragic tales of change. His Adonis lives.

This is not simply an optimistic re-embodiment of Ovid, nor is it simply an allegory of the prospect of permanent life offered to a Christian reader. The Garden of Adonis shares the sense of textual and bodily fragility which plays such a central part in Renaissance responses to Ovid. Time is present in the Garden, doing his work as *edax rerum*, and reminding us that this world too is subject to destructive influences. Spenser hints that readers of the poem inhabit a world temporally exiled from the perfection of the garden, and that that ideal world may be an illusionistic fiction ('sooth it seemes they say'). He wishes simultaneously to revive Ovid and to register our distance from the world of perfection which is constructed from Ovidian sources.

At the end of *The Faerie Queene* (as it has come down to us – like Ovid's *Fasti* it is left ostentatiously incomplete) there is another imitation of Ovid which both revitalizes its original and registers its author's and its readers' temporal exile from a world of perfection. In the *Mutabilitie Cantos*, which are the core of an incomplete seventh book of the poem, Spenser retells the story of Actaeon. In his version an Irish wood-god Faunus spies on Diana. Faunus is not metamorphosed and torn apart by his dogs as Ovid's Actaeon is, however; he is simply clad in deerskin and chased. He lives on. Diana, however, violates the Irish landscape in revenge, turning it into a wasteland full of wolves and robbers:

> Since which, those Woods, and all that goodly Chase,
> Doth to this day with Wolues and Thieues abound:
> Which too-too true that lands in-dwellers since haue found.
>
> (VII. vi. 55)

The story ends the poem with a flavour of Ovidian exile: Spenser spent most of his adult life in Ireland, in a place he regarded as barbarous, and which was far removed from the court for which he wrote. The allusion to the tale of Actaeon, to whom Ovid compares himself in *Tristia* 2. 1. 105, may mark a faint identification between Spenser and the figure of Ovid in exile.[16] And the tale makes its readers share in that exile in a temporal form: we are occupants of the world after Diana has worked her vengeful metamorphosis on the Ovidian world of nymphs and fauns. The final books of *The Faerie Queene* emphasize that even if Ovid can generate the mythic perfection of the Garden of Adonis, he is also the poet of spatial and temporal exile.

John Milton stands at the end of this tradition of self-conscious imitations of Ovid. Ovid was one of the three works he most frequently wished to have read to him in his blindness (the others were Isaiah and Homer), and Ovid is the strongest classical influence on his writing.[17] His early Latin elegies interweave the exile poetry into the fabric of Ovid's earlier writing, skipping easily from allusions to the *Amores* to echoes of the *Tristia*.[18] The figure of Echo resounds through the music of *Comus*. But it is in *Paradise Lost* that Milton thinks most deeply about what it might be to re-embody Ovid, and, like so many of his predecessors, he works on those concerns through stories which explore both the vulnerabilities and the vitality of the body. Ovid is present both in the accounts of the creation of the universe and in the near demonic parody of that creativity which animates his description of Chaos.[19] As in *The Faerie Queene* Ovid manages to occupy both the core of what is beneficent in the poem, and to generate much of what is potentially threatening. That Ovid is poised dangerously on the cusp between good and

---

[16] Holahan (1976), McCabe (1991).   [17] Martz (1986) 203.
[18] See, for example, Elegy 1, lines 17–24; Elegy 3, line 2; Elegy 4, lines 1–4.
[19] Martz (1986) 212–13.

evil is illustrated by the closest imitation of Ovid in the poem, Eve's account to Adam of her creation:

> As I bent down to look, just opposite,
> A shape within the watery gleam appeared
> Bending to look on me, I started back,
> It started back, but pleased I soon returned,
> Pleased it returned as soon with answering looks
> Of sympathy and love; there I had fixed
> Mine eyes till now, and pined with vain desire,
> Had not a voice thus warned me, 'What thou seest,
> What there thou seest fair creature is thy self,
> With thee it came and goes: but follow me,
> And I will bring thee where no shadow stays
> Thy coming, and thy soft embraces, he
> Whose image thou art, him thou shall enjoy
> Inseparably thine, to him shalt bear
> Multitudes like thyself, and thence be called
> Mother of human race': what could I do,
> But follow straight, invisibly thus led?
>
> (*Paradise Lost* 4. 460–76)

The echoes of Ovid's tale of Narcissus are precise (see *Met.* 3. 420–36), even to the extent of faithfully reproducing the tense of Ovid's mocking comment on Narcissus' image ('with thee it came' translates the perfect tense of the Latin's *uenit*). It seems as though Milton has followed the injunction of early modern school-teachers to produce 'the very same poem' when imitating Ovid. Fidelity to Ovid, however, carries a high price. Eve might become a mere echo, as it were, of Narcissus, in love with herself and unable to participate in her historical role as the mother of the human race. Milton has an urgent and theologically motivated need to transform Ovid. He does so by resorting to two of his most deeply valued notions: the first is that of conversation, which he regards as the chief goal of married union. Here he transforms Ovid's mocking narratorial aside into a gently directive address to Eve: he makes her listen to the voice of her creator as Narcissus cannot.[20] The second value Milton imposes on Ovid is a Spenserian imperative to breed, which is linked with a very distinctive Miltonic stress on the moral value of recognizing the autonomy of other beings. Love for Milton is a moral wager which requires you to take a risk on the unpredictable freedom and independence of another person. Eve learns to take that wager, and so escapes from simply replicating the fate of Ovid's Narcissus.

---

[20] See DuRocher (1985) 88–93.

Milton is not here simply imposing his vision on Ovid's. He is also attempting to have a conversation with his Latin source by delicately suggesting that from the slightest shifts in the emphases of his original he can create a literary work which is founded on entirely different moral and literary priorities. Eve's story of her creation, in which she slowly learns the need to love something which is different from herself, has its metapoetic double: Milton is directly acknowledging how like he is to Ovid by all but quoting him; he is also gently severing himself from the earlier poet's way of representing human desire. He is affirming that he is no mere echo of Ovid, but a new voice which transforms the values of his original even as he closely echoes his words, and which can transform Ovidian perversities into the original companionate marriage.

The person who frequently – indeed frenziedly – does re-enact Ovidian tales is Milton's Satan. An exile from heaven (and the Ovid of the *Tristia* is never far from his laments against his treatment by his *princeps*), he transforms himself into a small zoo's worth of different animals in his efforts to spy on Adam and Eve, turning from tiger to toad with the slipperiness of Proteus. When he finally returns to hell to receive the plaudits of the devils for having engineered the fall of man he is forcibly transformed into a snake. It is as though he is eventually trapped by Ovid, his metamorphic master. He is entrapped too by the kind of narcissistic self-regard which is Milton's darkest association with Ovid. Eve moves beyond the fate of Narcissus into a world of conversation, but Satan never achieves that kind of liberating ethical metamorphosis of Ovid. In Book 2 he meets his daughter Sin, with whom he has had an incestuous union. From this union grew Death, whose birth causes Sin to metamorphose into a snake-tailed prototype of Ovid's Scylla:

> The one seemed woman to the waist, and fair,
> But ended foul in many a scaly fold
> Voluminous and vast, a serpent armed
> With mortal sting: about her middle round
> A cry of hell hounds never ceasing barked
> With wide Cerberean mouths full loud, and rung
> A hideous peal: yet, when they list, would creep,
> If aught disturbed their noise, into her womb,
> And kennel there, yet there still barked and howled,
> Within unseen. Far less abhorred than these
> Vexed Scylla bathing in the sea that parts
> Calabria from the hoarse Trinacrian shore.
>
> (*Paradise Lost* 2. 650–61)

Satan's creation imitates and vauntingly overgoes Ovid's Scylla, which is 'Far less abhorred than these'. In its excess, however, Satan's creation of Sin is endlessly self-destructive: what it creates from Ovid is not just a landmark on the Trinacrian shore, but Death, a universal, permanent force of destruction. Sin's conviction that she is an original creation is also mistaken, since no reader could miss her sources in both Ovid's Scylla and Spenser's Errour. Through the figure of Sin Milton offers a fearful image of what imitative poets might do with Ovid: they might re-embody Ovid in a destructive parody of the creative processes of child-birth. And they might mistakenly claim originality and priority for what is in fact an imitation. There is no Renaissance response to Ovid so gruesomely memorable as Milton's Sin, and none so darkly self-conscious about the dangers of seeking to re-embody him.

Histories of the influence of classical literature in the Renaissance have an unhealthy tendency to end with Milton. The extremely delicate calibrations between indebtedness and individuation which characterize Milton's responses to Ovid are not found in later writers, but this does not mean that with Milton we enter the iron age of post-Ovidian gloom. Certainly by the 1720s many of the negative critical views of Ovid which have only relatively recently been outgrown (his supposed lack of seriousness, his incongruous humour) were well established and frequently voiced. The translations of Ovid by many hands, such as Samuel Garth's volume of 1717, were, however, phenomenally popular through the eighteenth century. Affection for Ovid remained widespread even at the low point in his critical reputation. One means of accommodating this awkwardly contradictory attitude to Ovid was to associate him with the mock-heroic (a mode to which Ovid has some originating claim, via his deliberately off-key performance of the *Aeneid* in *Metamorphoses* 13–14, and through his descriptions of the battles of the Lapiths and the Centaurs). Ovidian *loci* were frequently drawn on in mock-heroic narratives as types of the creaky machinery of epic: Boileau's *Le Lutrin* (1674) takes the cave of sleep from Ovid as its model for the boudoir of Slumber; Garth's mock-heroic *The Dispensary* (1699) begins in the unmistakably Ovidian asylum of the God of Sloth. Even Pope, whose scorn for English translations of Ovid was vocal, drew a crazy form of Ovidianism into his mock-heroic mode: the Cave of Spleen in the *Rape of the Lock* tells how 'Unnumbered Throngs on ev'ry side are seen | Of Bodies chang'd to various forms by *Spleen*' (4. 47–8; compare *Met.* 1.1–2). This strand of Ovidianism responds to Milton's association between Ovid and the Underworld, and picks up both his and Spenser's suspicion that Ovid might spawn dark monsters of the imagination. But it also responds to the extraordinary imaginative vitality of Milton's Ovid, who whether he belongs to heaven or to hell always has the energy to spawn 'Unnumbered Throngs' of bodies. Ovid does not die as a literary influence after Milton: he lives on, metamorphosed.

FURTHER READING

The most informative overview of Ovid's afterlife in the Renaissance is Barkan (1986). Hollander (1981) has a wealth of thoughts about how figures and themes in Ovid influence his imitators, and Lanham (1976) shows how the poet nourishes a fluid, rhetorical conception of selfhood in the period. Unsurpassed still on the educational use of Ovid at the time is Baldwin (1944), which remains the first port of call for anyone interested in what went on in early modern classrooms.

Clark (1994) contains many of the epyllia discussed, as well as a helpful bibliography. Hulse (1981) and Keach (1977) remain the most accessible critical studies of the Elizabethan minor epic. Their treatment of gender seems now a little innocent, on which Smith (1991) offers some valuable thoughts.

Many studies of Ovid's influence on individual writers are outstanding on Ovid himself. Notable in this respect is Bate (1993). Martindale (1990) is a learned and approachable guide to Shakespeare and Ovid, and Martindale (1986) is the best introduction to Milton's responses to Ovid. DuRocher (1985) is valuable on Milton's use of the *Metamorphoses*, but neglects (as do most of the works mentioned so far) the foundational role played by exile poetry in Renaissance responses to Ovid. The same goes for the valuable chapters in Martz (1986), and, for that matter, Burrow (1988). For more detailed discussion of how Ovid's imitators draw on his own language of imitation, see Burrow (1999).

19

DUNCAN F. KENNEDY

Recent receptions of Ovid

The task of mapping Ovid's presence in the twentieth century, let alone a theoretical consideration of what might constitute that presence, has hardly begun. The *Metamorphoses* holds pride of place in the recent reception of Ovid, it may be granted; but in what ways is its presence to be defined? In a thematics of corporeal transformation, such as we see in Kafka's *Metamorphosis* or David Garnett's *Lady into Fox*? In explicit acknowledgement of the poet and his work? Extravagant (and sometimes perplexing) claims are made by, and on behalf of, writers and artists of the twentieth century for the influence of Ovid on their work. Notoriously in his note on line 218 of *The Waste Land*, T. S. Eliot invokes the figure of Tiresias, quotes 19 lines from the story told of him in Book 3 of the *Metamorphoses*, and suggests that 'although a mere spectator and not indeed a "character", [Tiresias] is yet the most important personage in the poem, uniting all the rest . . . What Tiresias *sees*, in fact, is the substance of the poem.'[1] James Joyce prefaced his *Portrait of the Artist as a Young Man* with a quotation from Ovid's *Metamorphoses*, and he makes the reading of Ovid's poem one of the formative factors in the education of its protagonist, Stephen Daedalus, but if we broaden our terms of reference to include a more general discourse of metamorphosis – manifested, for example, in the capacity of language through metaphor to 'create as well as describe metamorphosis'[2] in its objects of reference – Joyce's work (and not only his) can be seen to take on a more pervasive Ovidian character. Ezra Pound's knowledge of Ovid's text may have been patchy, but he did assert on behalf of his *Cantos* 'that a great treasure of verity exists for mankind in Ovid and in the subject matter of Ovid's long poem, and that only in this form could it be registered.'[3] In Pound's assertion of a transcendent 'verity' manifested in the *Metamorphoses* and in the 'form' of the *Cantos*, one senses the trope of metamorphosis at

---

[1] See Medcalf (1988) 234, who sees the note as Eliot's irony at the expense of prospective commentators on his poem.
[2] Brown (1999) 190.   [3] Pound (1938) 299; cf. Henderson (1999) 304–6.

play. The *Metamorphoses* is not claimed as the *origin* or the *source* of this verity, rather each work is an historical embodiment or incarnation of it. This might recall for some Walter Benjamin's theory of translation which holds that truth is defined by its *translatability*. Benjamin's model for this is the interlinear version of the scriptures: truth does not inhere in any one instantiation, but is sensed in its capacity to be accommodated to different versions;[4] *mutatis mutandis*, the same claim could be made for the 'Ovidian'. Indeed, in the past decade it is through prestigious and popular translations and adaptations of the poet's works, notably the collection *After Ovid* and Ted Hughes' *Tales from Ovid*,[5] that Ovid has been brought back from the margins of cultural consciousness. When Hughes claims of Ovid that '[t]he right man had met the right material at the right moment',[6] he contextualizes that claim by associating the composition of the *Metamorphoses* with 'that unique moment in history – the moment of the birth of Christ within the Roman Empire',[7] thus seeing Ovid as present at, if perhaps not conscious of, the emergence of a new historical order. The temptation to see Hughes in the process of constructing himself as the right man meeting the right material at the right moment is hard to resist, and has not been resisted by many reviewers of his work.[8] There is a *fin-de-siècle* feel to some of these most recent receptions. The title *After Ovid* evokes not only the language of translation and adaptation, but also a postmodern sense of belatedness, and uncertainty that anything will retain its current shape. But the obverse of this is Hughes' anticipation of newness mediated through his identification with a figure he construes as straddling the point of transition between an old world and a new one.

If we are seeking to insert the *Metamorphoses* into history, then it is salutary to recall the ways in which metamorphosis can serve to organize the way we think about history. Writing about the reception of Ovid constantly appeals to, and structures itself around, the issues and questions, ontological and epistemological as well as historical, that metamorphosis as a trope explores: continuity and discontinuity; development; identity and identification; appearance and reality. The following account of Ovid's influence and reputation by Sarah Annes Brown can serve to highlight some of the ways in which writing a history of the reception of Ovid tropes its task as metamorphosis:

> It would be possible to trace the Ovidian line's continuation into a great deal
> of twentieth-century culture – such a project might include the discourses of

---

[4] Benjamin (1970) 69–82.   [5] See Lyne, ch. 15, 259–63.
[6] Hughes (1997) p. vii.   [7] Hughes (1997) p. x.
[8] See however MacDonald (1999), esp. 65–6, for a dissenting view.

psychoanalysis and postmodernism as well as artistic developments such as surrealism and magic realism . . . Critics and teachers may take some of the credit for this welcome resurgence of interest in the *Metamorphoses* among creative writers. Long marginalised by the academy, Ovid has finally been reabsorbed into the mainstream. The rehabilitation of the *Metamorphoses* can be traced back to L. P. Wilkinson's *Ovid Recalled* (1955), and then to a steadily increasing number of important critical studies, including such diverse volumes as Galinsky's *Ovid's Metamorphoses* and Solodow's *The World of Ovid's Metamorphoses*.[9]

The project is construed as tracing the continuity of an identity, a quality of sameness (here 'the Ovidian line'), across discontinuities seen as changes of form (here 'the discourses of psychoanalysis and postmodernism as well as artistic developments such as surrealism and magic realism'). The hypothetical mode in which this passage is framed suggests the open-endedness of a project framed in this way: the 'Ovidian' *can* be configured (i.e. 'shaped') in different ways, as we have seen above, and will *continue* to be so. Are we to emphasize the similarities or differences between what artists on the one hand and critics and teachers on the other do? Or between periods we may wish to assert as distinct, for example modernism and postmodernism? Brown opts to emphasize discontinuity when she traces back the 'rehabilitation' of Ovid in academic circles to Wilkinson's justly appreciated book of 1955, the title of which plays neatly on the poet's exile so as to promote its desired critical re-evaluation; others might trace it back to Hermann Fränkel's under-appreciated and no less significantly entitled *Ovid: A Poet Between Two Worlds* of 1945. Others still whose main concerns lie in Ovid's place in the interaction between the philosophical and rhetorical traditions in Western thought would see the publication in 1976 of Richard Lanham's *The Motives of Eloquence* as marking a key moment of change. These dates show how easily, and how problematically, discussions of 'transformation' can slide into appeals to 'origins'. The appeal to 'origins' won't go away, but in a discourse of transformation, what interests are at stake in any appeal to a particular phenomenon as an origin? The issue is particularly delicate in any appeal to Ovid's *Metamorphoses* as 'origin' – any appeal, therefore, to the 'original' meaning of the poem, or assertion that such-and-such was what 'Ovid really meant' – for such an appeal will retrospectively configure the poet and his text in such a way as to reflect the interests of that particular appropriation.

The challenges involved in writing the history of the recent reception of Ovid can be dramatized by considering three of those very receptions, those

[9] Brown (1999) 217.

of Christoph Ransmayr, Salman Rushdie and Joseph Brodsky, in which the 'Ovidian' is invoked, but also interrogated. The scenario of Ransmayr's *The Last World* (originally published in German in 1988) at one level appeals to historical familiarity and a specific historical setting. When unconfirmed reports of the poet's death filter back to Rome, Cotta (a figure recognizably historical to readers of Ovid as the addressee of six of his *Epistulae ex Ponto*) sets out to find the poet in the place of his exile, Tomi, and to discover more, if he can, about his masterpiece, the *Metamorphoses*, burnt by the poet just before he went into exile. But the world the novel represents disorients familiar (or, it may be, received) senses of historical time and place. When Cotta arrives at Tomi in search of the person who is insistently referred to not as 'Ovid' but as 'Naso', he finds a 'town of iron', described in brutally 'realistic' terms which suggest a decaying post-industrial city: we initially see Cotta through the curious gaze of one of Tomi's inhabitants as he tries to make out a fading timetable on a rusting bus stop. The town is peopled, moreover, with what appear to readers of the novel to be reflexes of characters from the *Metamorphoses*: the local butcher is called Tereus, the weaver Arachne, the travelling film projectionist Cyparis. Our sense of 'reality' is disrupted by a mixture of characters we might otherwise regard as *either* 'historical' *or* 'imaginary', but that are here interacting. Categories we may have thought of as distinct have here become permeable. Cotta's Rome seems no less strange to the reader of the conventional historical novel. The mansion Naso left to go into exile lies, we are told, in the Piazza del Moro, and contains a billiard-room. Naso's banishment is associated with a speech he made at the opening of a stadium before 'a bouquet of shiny microphones'.

The techniques of realism, as we have been made familiar with them by critics such as Roland Barthes,[10] are present in abundance, but the juxtapositions of modes of reference we have come to associate with different periods disrupts our sense of time and subverts rather than underpin the realist pretensions of the representation. The description of Cotta's Rome in terms of modern topography, names and material detail suggests both an Augustan and a twentieth-century totalitarian régime, and assimilates the two: that is, it suggests that, together with the manifest *changes* over time, there emerges an *identity* that links the two: history is troped as metamorphosis. We might say (which is to hazard another such assimilation) that Ransmayr's mixture of the 'imaginary' and the 'historical', of the 'past' and the 'present', has ample precedent in Ovid's *Metamorphoses*, for example when the gods assembling for a council summoned by Jupiter are compared in a simile to the senators hurrying to the Palatine Hill to attend upon Augustus

---

[10] See Barthes (1974).

(*Met*.1.167–76). In Ransmayr's novel, events (or persons or texts, for that matter) are not historical *per se*: they *become* 'historical', gain their historical significance, through their interpretation and appropriation *over time*. In this way, everyone involved in the interpretation of an event, as time goes by, is a kind of author trying to (re-)construct what 'really' happened. Thus, in relation to Naso's burning of his *Metamorphoses* 'there were so many explanations. A book burning – a desperate, enraged man acting without thinking. A matter of insight – the censor was right, and he laid his own hand to the ambiguities and blunders. A precautionary measure. A confession. A deception. And so on.'[11] A relatively *stable* interpretation of Naso's destruction of his work (which is not to say it is 'true') does emerge over the course of time: 'because as years passed by there was no trace of a manuscript that people had long thought to be in safe hands, the suspicion gradually grew in Rome that the fire on the Piazza del Moro had not been set out of despair, not to serve as a beacon, but indeed to destroy.'[12] The author of the *Metamorphoses* is but one interpreter among many, and has very limited control over the interpretation of his texts or of the events in which he is an agent. Short extracts from the work have been recited by Naso before his banishment, but there is little agreement about what the *Metamorphoses* is about. 'A *roman-à-clef* about Roman society' becomes a current theory in the wake of the beating-up of a rich Genoese shipping magnate popularly identified with a staged depiction of Midas excerpted from Naso's work. But, we are told,

> Naso broke his silence only once, when he let it be known in a newspaper article that the figure of *Midas* had been travestied beyond recognition on the stage of the wrecked theatre … He had in fact never attempted to dramatize Roman reality by trite analogy … But because this remained the only explanation Naso ever provided, it was dismissed as conventional caution and hardly noted.[13]

So too with the banishment. Naso fails to observe the formalities of address in his speech at the opening of a stadium, and this is noted by a pervasive state apparatus which reports it to the bored emperor, who reacts only with a wave of his hand. The activity of interpretation itself becomes folded back into the novel's 'historical' action:

> A motion of the hand. The sign was passed on and sank only very slowly down through the levels of government. By way of precaution, the apparatus embraced all interpretations … Somewhere in those depths, then, somewhere very close to real life, a presiding judge *rendered* an opinion. It was shortly

[11] Ransmayr (1990) 8.   [12] Ransmayr (1990) 9.   [13] Ransmayr (1990) 33.

before his lunch break, and he dictated it to an apathetic clerk in the presence of two witnesses. A motion of His hand meant *begone*. *Out of my sight!* Out of sight of the emperor, however, meant the end of the world. And the end of the world was Tomi.[14]

'Reality' in *The Last World* is not only subject to fantasy, imagination and interpretation, it is structured, even constituted, by it. Naso's banishment sets in motion an intensified appropriation of both the poet and the meaning of his works, which serves over time to reconfigure 'official' historical judgements about them. Although Naso had never had any contacts with the opposition, 'virtually all opposition factions claimed him, mentioning and quoting him on their placards and in their flyers so frequently that for Roman officialdom his removal must have seemed unavoidable in retrospect.'[15] Opposition support for Naso is based not on sympathy for the man or admiration for his work but on his new political usefulness:

> A famous broken victim of dictatorial cruelty could prove much more useful to the goals of the resistance than a reprieved, or worse, a happy man. Besides which, the sombre greys of the cliffs above Tomi suited a persecuted *Poet of Freedom* far better than a luxurious villa on the elegant Piazza del Moro, than fountains and gardens in the shade of century-old trees.[16]

Naso's death furthers the process of his transfiguration into a martyr of the resistance, and this in turn prompts the state apparatus to reclaim him as a counter-measure: 'And once they had claimed him, might not the catacomb dwellers hesitate in future to honour this Naso as a martyr, particularly if a monument were erected to him at the behest and in the name of the emperor?'[17] This emphasis on the contingencies of politics and history offers a challenge to assumptions that final or determinate meanings can be attributed to things, events, persons, texts, facts outside of the continuing process of their interpretation and appropriation, and the ideological interests they 'in turn' represent, for if history is troped as metamorphosis, 'facts' never exist in themselves, but 'figure' other things. Ransmayr's fable factors in time and circumstance to an epistemological tradition that has tended to screen them out. The identity of the text does not float free of history but is realized in and through it, and *shapes* it in turn – down to the present and beyond, for Ransmayr's novel (and my take on it) are part of this continuing process. If history is troped as metamorphosis, let us recall the words of Johannes Fabian cited by Thomas Habinek in an earlier contribution to this volume ('The important thing in tales of evolution

---

[14] Ransmayr (1990) 42; emphases Ransmayr's.   [15] Ransmayr (1990) 76.
[16] Ransmayr (1990) 76.   [17] Ransmayr (1990) 83.

remains their ending') together with Habinek's gloss on the finality of metamorphosis ('the only changes that matter are those that produce the world as currently configured').[18] Within history, of course, the only ending we experience – other than by an explicitly *imaginative* anticipation – is that defined by the moment we call the 'present'. To 'trope' history *as* metamorphosis is a mise-en-abyme, perhaps, but the abyss on whose edge we stand and into which we are invited to take a vertiginous look is the endlessness of time, past and future. That, of course, does not free us from the desire, or the ideology, of original meaning and of stable meaning in the 'present', and of this Cotta may serve as a symbol. He is searching not only for Naso, we may recall, but for the text of his *Metamorphoses*. Naso proves an elusive figure in Ransmayr's novel. Cotta never finds him, and he may well be dead, but Cotta senses his presence – or perhaps the enduring presence of the *Metamorphoses* – powerfully. The novel plots Cotta's realization that the 'reality' he inhabits is a reflection of that text. While Cotta is constantly seeking out and sometimes coming across fragments of the text's physical inscription, his experience is being thoroughly shaped – transformed, even – by an act of construction and poiesis he will never be able to claim to have 'read' in its entirety.

If history is thus troped as metamorphosis, then what we experience as the 'reality' of the past is the effect of authors' constructions of similarity and difference, be they poets, critics, novelists or historians. This in turn can foreground 'realism' as a problematic and unstable concept, both in and out of fiction, and it is historical realism and its association with political authority that comes under searching scrutiny in Ransmayr's novel. It is perhaps the forthright claim to *knowledge* that distinguishes realism from other aesthetic modes, as Fredric Jameson has argued,[19] and so makes it the dominant aesthetic of historical scholarship and other discourses in which the authority of the 'real' is mobilized politically. In magical realism, reality is reconfigured as the realm of common practice, of what is generally taken to be the case. As a result, knowing where the limits of 'reality' are may mean knowing how far we want to look, as Cotta's search for the presence of Ovid can remind us. Ransmayr's 'Ovidian repertory' in the last twenty-five pages of the novel (a parody of the glossaries often found in historical novels) graphically dramatizes this in its parallel entries. Two columns summarize each name twice, respectively as 'Characters in the Last World' and 'Characters in the Ancient World', the right hand column giving us a more familiar 'realist' historical configuration. The facts in the left column are obviously made up; but how, and by whom, are those in the right made up?

[18] Cf. above p. 52.   [19] See Jameson (1992) 158.

The conventions of realism in the right column, as they cancel their own *fictive* qualities, allot to the authorial role an ideological position of passivity, in which texts are believed to reflect a pre-existent 'real', and to events a meaning in themselves awaiting discovery and transcription. Realism strives to ontologize its objects of reference, to see them as 'things', strictly demarcated by their 'nature' from other things. In particular, it observes a boundary between 'past' and 'present', even if, on reflection, we can detect that the 'past' is in some way acting as a surrogate for, or is constructed in terms of, the preoccupations and interests of the 'present'; it disowns its *appropriation* of events. Ransmayr's novel works to dissolve such boundaries so as to make this process of appropriation evident. History, the meaning of events and texts and persons, it is suggested, is not comprehensible outside this continuing process of appropriation and reception. Magical realism presents worlds constructed partially in accordance with realist literary techniques that have become thoroughly conventional, but in which fantastic happenings are narrated as a norm, and not discriminated in the narrative from what we might otherwise regard as 'real'. In magical realist texts, the 'fantastic' is not a simple or obvious matter, but it is an ordinary or everyday matter; conversely the 'real' – the ordinary and familiar – can begin to appear neither simple nor obvious. The most fantastic things have actually been believed or asserted by live people somewhere (in his reception, Ovid has after all been 'moralized' and 'Christianized', which can seem every bit as bizarre to some minds as an Ovid 'magically realized' can, no doubt, to others). This doesn't make these things true, but it may make them real. On the other hand, those interpretations of the past which seem to be most 'real' to us are not thereby to be taken uncritically as 'true'. When appropriations (i.e. suggested links between past and present) convince us of their 'reality', they become, simply, 'appropriate', aspects of what appears to us as Reality in the metaphysical sense. The distinctiveness of metamorphosis as a trope is that, as we have seen in our reading of Ransmayr, it can blur distinctions between history, ontology and epistemology, resisting reduction to any one.

Ransmayr's novel thus uses Ovid and the *Metamorphoses* to explore the capacity of description to summon 'reality' into being, a theme taken up also in another magical realist novel published in the same year which appeals to Ovid both in its composition and its reception. Salman Rushdie's *The Satanic Verses* opens with its two protagonists, Gibreel Farishta and Saladin Chamcha, in freefall from a hijacked Air India Jumbo jet which has just exploded over England. As they fall, they collide with one another, and 'the force of their collision sent them tumbling end over end, performing their geminate cartwheels all the way down and along the hole that went to Wonderland; while pushing their way out of the white came a succession of cloudforms, ceaselessly metamorphosing, gods into bulls, women into spiders, men into wolves.' Hybrid cloud-creatures, we are told, press in on them from all around – gigantic flowers with human breasts, winged cats, centaurs – and 'Chamcha in his semi-consciousness was seized by the notion that he, too, had acquired the quality of cloudiness, becoming metamorphic, hybrid, as if he were growing into the person whose head nestled now between his legs and whose legs were wrapped around his long, patrician neck.'[20] The opening metamorphic moment in this tale is characteristically mediated by a literary allusion which blends Lewis Carroll's *Alice* and Ovid's stories of Jupiter and Europa, Arachne and Lycaon, the first of many such hybrid allusions which will link works as diverse as the *Thousand and One Nights*, the Bible and its associated literature (for this will be a 'fortunate fall') and, notoriously, the Qur'an. The association of cloudiness with hybridity, which gives Chamcha a sense that he too is metamorphosing, recalls Ovid's designation of centaurs as 'cloud-born' (*nubigenae*, *Met.* 12.211). As Saladin Chamcha (whose father's name is 'Changez')[21] finds himself turning into a foul devil with a goatish body, his friend Haji Sufyan, who is harbouring him in his B&B in London, attempts to give some philosophical consolation:

Sufyan, kindly fellow that he was, went over to where Chamcha sat clutching at his horns, patted him on the shoulder, and tried to bring what good cheer he could. 'Question of mutability of the essence of the self,' he began, awkwardly, 'has long been subject of profound debate. For example, great Lucretius tells us, in *De Rerum Natura*, this following thing: *quodcumque suis mutatum finibus exit, continuo hoc mors est illius quod fuit ante.* Which being translated, forgive my clumsiness, is "Whatever by its changing goes out of its frontiers," – that is, bursts its banks, – or, maybe, breaks out of its limitations, – so to speak, disregards its own rules, but that is too free, I am thinking ... "that thing", at any rate Lucretius holds, "by doing so brings immediate death to its old self". However,' up went the ex-schoolmaster's finger, 'poet Ovid, in the *Metamorphoses*, takes diametrically opposed view. He avers thus: "As yielding wax" – heated, you see, possibly for the sealing of documents or such, – "is stamped with new designs And changes shape and seems not still the same, Yet it is indeed the same, even so our souls," – you hear, good sir? Our spirits! Our immortal essences! – "Are still the same forever, but adopt In their migrations ever-varying forms." '[22]

---

[20] Rushdie (1988) 6–7.
[21] Chamcha's own name may recall that of Kafka's Gregor Samsa, as Stephen Hinds has suggested to me.
[22] Rushdie (1988) 276–7.

The passage Sufyan cites is from the speech of Pythagoras about the transmigration of souls in Book 15 of the *Metamorphoses* (169–72), and he enthuses 'For me it is always Ovid over Lucretius . . . Your soul, my good poor dear sir, is the same. Only in its migration it has adopted this presently varying form.' Caught uncomfortably between the models of the self represented by 'Lucretius' and 'Ovid', Chamcha is at this moment disposed to side with 'Lucretius', but as the story progresses and Chamcha loses his goatish form and is reconciled with his father back in Bombay, 'Ovid' prevails.

In a twist on the words of Ovid's Pythagoras, however, Chamcha's metamorphosis is not unassociated with his geographical and cultural migration. His father had sent him as a boy to school in England, where Chamcha, an accomplished mimic who does voice-overs for television advertisements, mutates into an Englishman. A 'real' Englishman or an 'imitation' one? Shape-shifters raise the issue of who they 'really' (often reduced, rather problematically, to the question of who they 'originally') are, and realist attitudes associate their role-playing with deception: the ill-omened Jumbo jet from which Chamcha falls has the flight number 420, which is also the number of the statute in the Indian legal code forbidding fraud and imposture. After his fall from the disintegrating airliner, he is arrested as an illegal immigrant, beaten up in the police van and forced to eat his goatish excrement, a process that speeds up his physical transformation. As a fellow immigrant tells Chamcha, 'They have the power of description, and we succumb to the pictures they construct.'[23] As described by the establishment, the immigrant is a bestial embodiment of evil, and in this book in which reality is called into being and determined by description, Chamcha's devilish form is strikingly literalized as a cultural construct – a construct, moreover, which can conceive of the identity of the people it categorizes as 'immigrants' only in terms of their origins, not what they might (have) become. Metamorphosis is here appropriated as an anti-racist discourse. In his defence of *The Satanic Verses* in the wake of the *fatwa* against him issued by the Ayatollah Khomeini in February 1989, Rushdie suggests that 'a book is a version of the world; if you don't like it write another version'.[24] *The Satanic Verses* is, he says 'a migrant's-eye view of the world';[25] 'what the . . . disruption of reality teaches immigrants', he writes elsewhere, is 'that reality is an artifact, that it does not exist until it is made, and that, like any other artifact, it can be made well or badly, and that it can also, of course, be unmade.' The world which Rushdie would write into being has a strong postcolonialist agenda which finds its rationale in 'the very experience of uprooting, disjuncture and metamorphosis . . . that is the migrant condition,

---

[23] Rushdie (1988) 168.   [24] Rushdie (1991) 412.   [25] Rushdie (1991) 394.

and from which, I believe, can be derived a metaphor for all humanity.' He continues:

> *The Satanic Verses* celebrates hybridity, impurity, intermingling, the transformation that comes of new and unexpected combinations of human beings, cultures, ideas, politics, movies, songs. It rejoices in mongrelization and fears the absolutism of the Pure. *Mélange*, hotchpot, a bit of this and a bit of that is *how newness enters the world*. It is the great possibility that mass migration gives the world, and I have tried to embrace it. *The Satanic Verses* is for change-by-fusion, change-by-conjoining. It is a love-song to our mongrel selves.[26]

Such a work is construed as necessarily anti-authoritarian: 'Human beings understand themselves and shape their future by arguing and challenging and questioning and saying the unsayable; not by bowing the knee, whether to gods or to men.'[27]

Given its interest in strategies of representation and its sense of realism as a historically evolving style, one of the appeals of magical realist fiction is 'its impulse to re-establish contact with traditions temporarily eclipsed by the mimetic constraints of nineteenth- and twentieth-century realism.'[28] In critical treatments of the literary affiliations of magical realism, mention is frequently made of works such as the *Decameron* and *Don Quixote*, less often of Ovid, though this may be in part the result of Ovid's critical eclipse over the past two centuries (which can, of course, be associated with those very mimetic constraints). In a book which is top-heavy with intertextual reference, Rushdie's preferred sources are the artists of metamorphosis and exile, including many who have, whether by design or accident, fallen foul of authority: Ovid jostles for attention with figures as diverse as Apuleius, Borges, Bulgakov, Calvino, García Márquez, Joyce, Pynchon. Literary history is no less an artifact than anything else; whilst magical realism's perceived 'origins' in Latin America have often led to its being thought of as a Third World literary phenomenon, they have also led to its being criticized as a gesture of compliance towards the First World's dominant literary concerns. For the Rushdie of *The Satanic Verses*, Ovid's *Metamorphoses* are amongst the First World's canonical works which can be assigned an honoured place within a literary and ideological tradition self-consciously reconfigured as no longer simply 'European' or 'Western' but 'multi-cultural'. Ovid becomes once more a poet between two worlds.

Ransmayr, I have suggested, reminds us that in thinking about texts and their interpretation, we must consider factoring in time and circumstance.

---

[26] Rushdie (1991) 394; emphasis Rushdie's.   [27] Rushdie (1991) 394–5.
[28] Zamora and Faris (1995) 2.

As we have seen, one proposition of magical realism is that if texts 'create' reality – whether that is how their authors see them or not – those texts actively caught up in the processes of appropriation Ransmayr explores may over time increasingly seem to 'reflect' it. The two years that saw the transformation of *Die letzte Welt* into *The Last World* included the *fatwa* pronounced on Rushdie for the alleged blasphemy of *The Satanic Verses*, and in his review of the English translation of Ransmayr's novel,[29] which he reads as 'a parable of the ability of art to survive the breaking of the artist', Rushdie assimilated himself to the figure of the exiled Ovid, implicitly casting Khomeini as the Emperor Augustus ('Artists, even the finest of them all, can be crushed effortlessly at any old tyrant's whim') in a drama about tyranny and the censorship of art in which 'the Sword wins almost all the battles, but the Pen re-writes all these victories as defeats.' This, Rushdie ruefully concedes, 'is not, of course, much consolation for the author in the ruin of his life'. Rushdie's Ovid, just like Rushdie himself (for the identification is here almost total), is therefore obliged to play the long game in the hope that the world, and its history, will be transformed by his writings. In the meantime, the victimized writer must resort to repeated defences of his work. Rushdie's essay 'In Good Faith'[30] (which it is tempting to liken to Ovid's second book of the *Tristia*) grapples to understand the accusation against his work without abandoning the terms in which he has always sought to understand and present it, and he interprets the hostility against him as a failure on the part of his opponents to understand what he was doing. '*He did it on purpose* is one of the strangest accusations ever levelled at a writer. Of course I did it on purpose. The question is, and it is what I have tried to answer: what is the "it" that I did?'[31] Rushdie appeals to his own intention and understanding of his work, and interprets the criticisms levelled at *The Satanic Verses* as a gigantic category mistake. But if reality were to be, at least here and now, as Ransmayr describes it, then the artist, whether Rushdie or Ovid, is not in sovereign control of what 'it' is. In trying to understand and dramatize his own position by assimilating it to the fate of Ovid as he configures it, Rushdie appeals to a Manichean vision of politics and art: 'Of all the opposed pairs of ideas by which human beings have sought to understand themselves, perhaps the oldest and deepest-rooted are the eternally warring myths of stasis and metamorphosis. Stasis, the dream of eternity, of a fixed order in human affairs, is the favoured myth of tyrants; metamorphosis, the knowledge that *nothing holds its form*, is the driving force of art.'[32] Rushdie appears content to follow Ransmayr

---

[29] Rushdie (1991) 291–3.   [30] Rushdie (1991) 393–414.
[31] Rushdie (1991) 410.   [32] Rushdie (1991) 291.

here in suggesting that, of all Ovid's works, it is the *Metamorphoses* that carries the most powerful political and historical charge, but in his identification with Ovid, he has an understandable desire in the circumstances in which he finds himself to resolve the dialectic between similarity and difference and trope history not as metamorphosis but as ideological conflict, the collision of two realities which won't interact. Rushdie concludes, in a tangible moment of foreboding and self-pity, 'As for Ransmayr's vision of art conquering defeat by remaking the world in its own image, one can celebrate its optimism, while continuing to feel more concerned about Publius Ovidius Naso, banished from his own people, buried by a strange sea in an unknown grave.'[33]

The temptations and dangers of collapsing the tension between similarity and difference in historical identification are explored through another major recent reception of Ovid. 'The current interest in the literature of exiles has to do, of course, with the rise of tyrannies', writes Joseph Brodsky (1940–1996), himself exiled permanently from the Soviet Union in 1972. 'Approached on the subject,' he says, 'an exiled writer will most likely evoke Ovid's Rome, Dante's Florence and – after a small pause – Joyce's Dublin.'[34] Brodsky's involvement with the figure of the exiled Ovid begins in 1964, after his trial for 'social parasitism', with an unfinished poem 'Ex Ponto: The Last Letter of Ovid to Rome'. Brodsky's place of internal exile in 1964–5 was the White Sea, at the diametrically opposite end of *his* empire from Ovid's on the Black Sea, but no less 'on the edge of space',[35] and this curious inversion of Ovid recurs in his writing up to his death. The exiled writer is an obsessively retrospective creature, he notes, liable to stick in his writing to the familiar material of his past, producing sequels to his previous work. Hence he associates Ovid's exilic writing with Rome, and this reference serves to signal Brodsky's particular take on Ovid and exile, for 'good old exile ain't what it used to be'. Nowadays, Brodsky argues, exile involves escape from the worse to the better:

> The truth of the matter is that from a tyranny one can be exiled only to a democracy ... It isn't leaving civilized Rome for savage Sarmatia anymore, nor is it sending a man from, say, Bulgaria to China. No, as a rule what takes place is a transition from a political and economic backwater to an industrially advanced society with the latest word on individual liberty on its lips. And it must be added that perhaps taking this route is for an exiled writer, in many ways, like going home – because he gets closer to the seat of the ideals which inspired him all along.[36]

---

[33] Rushdie (1991) 293. [34] Brodsky (1995) 27.
[35] Polukhina (1989) 198. [36] Brodsky (1995) 24.

For the exiled Brodsky, heir to the poetic tradition of Osip Mandelstam, who championed the idea of a 'world culture' based on the classical poets in the face of official hostility to literature,[37] travelling to Rome was, ideologically, a return home. In his 'Roman Elegies' and his essays, an ironic reversal of Ovid's situation is a pervasive theme: he, the Russian-Jewish poet, is a Scythian or Hyperborean, a barbarian coming to Rome from another empire which has succeeded Rome. 'Empire' in Brodsky's poetry represents 'a universal realm with no distinct geographical or historical boundaries; it is impersonal, alienating, godless – in opposition to the free, or freedom-seeking individual',[38] and the imagery of the Roman Empire, its legions and statuary, provides the framework for working through these ideas in his poetry. In a poem from 1972, the year of his exile, entitled 'Letters to a Roman Friend', and addressed to a figure called 'Postumus', Brodsky evokes the Horatian theme of *carpe diem*, complete with instructions for a dinner party and payments for the hetaerae. The poem contains extensive echoes of the classical poets, but though the figure of Ovid is evoked, it is supplanted by that of Martial, the provincial who withdrew from Rome and returned to Spain:

> If one's fated to be born in Caesar's Empire
> let him live aloof, provincial, by the seashore.
> One who lives remote from snowstorms and from Caesar
> has no need to hurry, flatter, play the coward.[39]

And yet, by the end of what is a letter, we realize its place of dispatch is 'Pontus'. For all that he wishes to distance himself from Ovid and what he sees as some of the more negative manifestations of his exilic writings, the figure of Ovid remains irresistible, in the end eclipsing the Horatian role he has adopted in the poem. Horace elsewhere acts as a foil for Ovid in Brodsky's continuing struggle not to collapse his identity into that of the Roman poet he most admires, but to construct their sameness in terms of contrast as much as comparison. In his 'Letter to Horace', written in 1994 and prompted by a re-reading of the *Odes*, it is Ovid, not Horace, who continually barges to the front of Brodsky's thoughts, to the extent that Brodsky feels obliged to apologize to Horace for treating him in this way in a letter addressed to him. But he resists any too close identification: 'No matter how similar my circumstances may now and then appear to his in the eye of some beholder, I won't produce any *Metamorphoses*. Besides twenty-two years in these parts won't rival ten in Sarmatia. Not to mention that I saw my Terza Roma crumble... But even as a young pup, kicked out

---

[37] Polukhina (1989) 14.   [38] Kline (1990) 62; cf. Polukhina (1989) 198.
[39] Brodsky (1980) 53.

of my home to the Polar Circle, I never fancied myself playing his double. Though then my empire looked indeed eternal, and one could roam on the ice of our many deltas all winter long.'[40]

What is lacking in his relationship with the Roman poets is a sense of reciprocity; he can read Horace's poems, but Horace can never read his.[41] As he remarks elsewhere, 'While antiquity exists for us, we, for antiquity, do not. We never did, and we never will. This rather peculiar state of affairs makes our take on antiquity somewhat invalid.'[42] The 'Letter to Horace' is a meditation on this asymmetrical relationship, and on the attractions and pitfalls it presents: 'Nowhere does time collapse as easily as in one's mind. That's why we so much like thinking about history, don't we?'[43] He begins it by reminding Horace of the anecdote from Suetonius which recounts that Horace lined his bedroom with mirrors so that he could watch himself making love, a fetishization of the self that Brodsky matches with an erotic anecdote of his own from the days he spent in Rome. The mirror thus provides a figure, and, in the terms in which it is presented, a seductive one for thinking about the relationship of the present to the past; the images returned are immediate, and reflect our every mood, desire and action. Brodsky's reminiscences will summon up for some another author of latter-day 'Roman Elegies', Goethe, who found in Rome, in sexual pleasure and in beating out the rhythm of the elegiac couplet on his mistress' bare back, a formula which could dissolve the temporal distance between him and the classical elegists. For Brodsky also, metre transcends temporal barriers and creates the particular bond he feels with Horace: 'Two thousand years – of what? By whose count, Flaccus? Certainly not in terms of metrics. Tetrameters are tetrameters, no matter when and no matter where ... When it comes to collapsing time, our trade, I am afraid, beats history.'[44] Collapsing time is, however, precisely the danger as Brodsky sees it, and Ovid, whilst in no way the equal of Horace in his metrical versatility, provides a corrective figure which makes him the greater artist in Brodsky's eyes: 'metamorphosis is not a mirror'.[45] Metamorphosis insists upon a dialectic of continuity *and* change, sameness *and* difference, and that identification *of* (something or someone) and identification *with* (something or someone) will never be the end of the story: 'To put it bluntly, Naso insists that in this world *one thing is another*. That, in the final analysis, reality is one large rhetorical figure and you are lucky if it is just a polyptoton or a chiasmus.'[46] In certain circumstances, of course, certain metaphors may seem inescapable because we believe, or are made to believe, that there is no other way of understanding the world; that way realism lies. Brodsky's

[40] Brodsky (1995) 433.   [41] Brodsky (1995) 439.   [42] Brodsky (1995) 267.
[43] Brodsky (1991) 441.   [44] Brodsky (1995) 440.   [45] Brodsky (1995) 455.
[46] Brodsky (1995) 452.

remarks are shot through with the privileging of language and the associated anti-realist trends that have played such a prominent role in the thought of the last quarter of the twentieth century, and it is in such terms that, for Brodsky, (his) Ovid can be the man for the moment and metamorphosis its preferred trope: 'to him the world was language: one thing was another, and as to which was more real, it was a toss-up.'[47] Ovid, he asserts, offers a vision that the reality we inhabit is not a room of mirrors that encloses us in our own images, but can – will – change, for '[w]ith Naso the tenor is the vehicle, Flaccus, and/or the other way round, and the source of it all is the ink pot. So long as there was a drop of that dark liquid in it, he would go on – which is to say, the world would go on.'[48] The open-endedness of this view, and its claims for the enduring presence of Ovid in the power invested in language, chime happily with the closing lines of the *Metamorphoses* (15.877–8) in which Ovid predicts that he will have mention on people's lips and, if the prophecies of poets have any truth, he will live in their talk:

> ore legar populi, perque omnia saecula fama,
> siquid habent ueri uatum praesagia, uiuam.

FURTHER READING

There is nothing on Ovid's reception in the twentieth century comparable to Ziolkowski (1993) on *Virgil and the Moderns*, and the need for a major work on this scale is becoming ever more apparent, as many important areas of reception remain largely uncharted. Brown (1999), especially chapters 10–12, offers a number of thought-provoking case-studies. For some stimulating ideas on Ovid's relation to Modernism see Medcalf (1988). Henderson (1999) offers a keen analysis, prompted by the publication of Ted Hughes' *Tales from Ovid*, of the place the *Metamorphoses* has in the cultural consciousness of the twentieth century. For Brodsky and Ovid see Brodsky (1995); Polukhina (1989), esp. ch. 5; Loseff and Polukhina (1990), especially G. L. Kline, 'Variations on the theme of exile' (56–88), and G. Nivat, 'The ironic journey into antiquity' (89–97); Burnett (1999).

[47] Brodsky (1995) 452.　　[48] Brodsky (1995) 452.

20

CHRISTOPHER ALLEN

Ovid and art

Ovid was the most important literary source for mythological subjects in the art of the Renaissance and the subsequent centuries. 'No other classical author,' as Panofsky wrote, 'treated so great a variety of mythological subject matter and was so assiduously read, translated, paraphrased, commented upon and illustrated.'[1] No other great poet of antiquity, indeed, had made the recounting of myth the main purpose of his work. The *carmen perpetuum* of the *Metamorphoses*, which will be the focus of this essay,[2] became a kind of handbook whose influence can be found everywhere in the painting and sculpture of the early modern period. Svetlana Alpers goes so far as to say: 'The "painter's bible", as the name implies, was first of all the most popular and convenient source for mythological narratives. In this sense, "Ovidian" is simply synonymous with mythological, although some of the frequently represented myths, such as Cupid and Psyche, and Diana and Endymion, are not found in Ovid's compendium.'[3]

As these last remarks suggest, however, the apparent ubiquity of Ovidian influence can disguise the difficulty of explaining precisely what we mean by an 'Ovidian subject'. To put the matter schematically, we could say that the field of mythological painting is both broader and narrower than the field of the Ovidian text. It is broader because Ovid may be supplemented by material from other authors (including his own sources), and even stories he does not tell may find themselves generically grouped under his label. On the other hand it is narrower because many of his tales are never painted, and because for various reasons artists draw selectively on his text in picturing the myths they do choose to deal with. Often both these processes of addition and subtraction are combined, especially in large-scale iconographic programmes,

---

[1] Panofsky (1969) 140.
[2] Although the *Metamorphoses* was by far the most important of Ovid's works for visual artists, the *Fasti* were also referred to in certain cases: cf. Panofsky (1972a) 61 n. 73, and Wind (1968) 114–17.
[3] Alpers (1971) 151.

where material from Ovid and other sources is taken apart and reassembled to serve a specific iconographic purpose.[4] Under these circumstances, it is less useful to prove that an Ovidian passage can be taken as the necessary and sufficient explanation of a given painting than to understand why Ovid held such a pre-eminent place among the available literary sources. The answer to this question, of course, will lie not simply in the abundance of information to be found in the *Metamorphoses*, but in the literary character of the poem itself.

This essay will ask first why the art of the early modern period was attracted to mythological subjects in general, and why Ovid became so important a literary source for these stories. Next it will consider how artists used material from his poem, and what implicit rules determined which subjects or episodes were suitable or unsuitable for pictures. Finally, the rise and fall of mythological – or Ovidian – subjects in painting will be briefly surveyed. For reasons of space, I shall confine my discussion essentially to the art of painting, only incidentally referring to the important question of book illustrations. I shall also concentrate on the period from the Renaissance to the French Revolution, which sees Ovidian subjects return to life after the medieval period, and then at length fade again into allegorical codes or vacuous ornament.

The appeal of Ovid as a source for artists

The twentieth century tried hard to forget that the art of painting is inherently concerned with the telling of stories. The avant-garde not only ridiculed the traditional hierarchy which made 'history' painting the highest genre of the art, but promoted the paradoxical view that painting comes closest to its 'essence' when it abandons the representation of the world altogether. These modernist dogmas would have been incomprehensible to the painters of any earlier century. The Byzantine-derived predecessors and contemporaries of Giotto knew that their task was to make visible the figures of God and the saints, and to recount the sacred stories in compact and memorable form. In the Renaissance this narrative intention was doubled by a descriptive one: it was not enough for the painter's figures to be narratively intelligible and graceful, they had to evoke the world as actually seen by the eye – or more precisely by an 'eye' conceived as the geometrical abstraction of a viewpoint. This invention of a viewing subject and of an objective world contributed to the emergence of modern science and eventually led to the nineteenth-century

---

[4] On programmes see Gombrich (1972) 6–7, and 75: 'It may well have been the pride of the authors of the programmes to make their instructions a closely-woven texture of "authentic" classical descriptions.' See also Panofsky (1969) 140 on Titian's willingness to 'supplement the text with other sources'.

crises in mimetic painting. For the time being, however, it infused the art of painting with an unprecedented energy and created that momentum without which art history would scarcely exist: the world was to be seen anew, and the great stories were all to be reimagined in new terms.

The stories which the artists of the Renaissance had inherited, however, were almost exclusively those of the Old and New Testaments, of the history of the Church and the lives of the Saints. It was rich and varied material, and theological dogma did not rule out imaginative storytelling. Religious subjects were, nonetheless, undeniably limited in their range. They emphasized the transcendent finality of human existence, and excluded some of the dimensions of experience that most appealed to Renaissance sensibility. There was not much room for sexual love in any of its manifestations, nor indeed for the martial and civic virtues admired by the ancients, except where these were in the service of the City of God. Human life in general was inevitably considered within the wider framework of divine providence. The medieval world was intelligible from the point of view of God and the meaning of any religious subject was similarly prescribed; there might be room for expressive nuance in a *quattrocento* Virgin and Child, but there was no real ambiguity about the picture's significance.

Renaissance artists never ceased to reinvent the stories of Christianity, but the revival of classical mythology vastly enlarged the scope of human experience and even of metaphysical imagination available to them and to their patrons. Mythology was most obviously appealing in its rich repertoire of love stories. Whether ostensibly concerning gods or men, the human interest was immediate and universal, the human point of view inescapable. At the same time, the myths of the ancients were felt to be pregnant with moral and cosmological significance. However grudgingly, the Church conceded that some understanding of God's purpose had been granted to the pagan philosophers and poets, and that concession was greatly enlarged in the thinking of the Renaissance.[5] The ancient authors had, however, guarded their deepest spiritual doctrine 'with enigmatic veils and poetic dissimulation', as Pico della Mirandola wrote.[6] The searchers after hidden wisdom thus set

---

[5] As late as the end of the seventeenth century the Oratorian Père Thomassin could vindicate the study of ancient myths on these grounds, in a work significantly entitled *Méthode d'étudier et d'enseigner chrétiennement et solidement les lettres humaines par rapport aux lettres divines et aux Écritures* (Paris, 1681–82): 'St Clement of Alexandra wholeheartedly subscribed to the same view, namely that philosophy, in which are to be included the poets, was given by God to the Greeks to prepare them for the Gospels, much in the way that the Old Testament was given to the Hebrews to the same end' (vol. 1, 224, quoted by Thuillier (1996) 182). The Church could not but accept such a view at least implicitly, since from Augustine to Aquinas its own intellectual culture was drawn almost entirely from the heritage of the ancients.

[6] 'Pico della Mirandola planned to write a book on the secret nature of the pagan myths which was to bear the title *Poetica theologia*. "It was the opinion of the ancient theologians," he

themselves to interpreting the sometimes extravagant stories of mythology, and the Neoplatonists overlaid erotic or even violent tales – the rape of Europa or Ganymede, or the flaying of Marsyas – with moral or mystical interpretations: the soul being carried off by the divine, or being stripped of its muddy vesture of decay.[7] The result, as any student of Renaissance iconography knows, was a highly ambivalent attitude towards mythological material: paradoxical, almost flirtatious and yet finally serious. It seems that the playful uncertainty, the imaginative game of hypothetical, alternative or parallel metaphysics (and morals), was an essential part of the appeal of mythology for people accustomed to stories that left no room for indeterminacy.

For the artists of this period, Ovid's *Metamorphoses* was not simply a convenient reference book, but a vital source – a fount of inspiration, like the poetic waters of Hippocrene or Castalia. Dante used this image when he encountered Virgil at the outset of his journey into the underworld: *or se' tu quel Virgilio, e quella fonte,* | *che spandi di parlar sì largo fiume?*[8] – 'are you then Virgil, and that fount that poured forth so broad a river of speech?' In the same way, Ovid was a living model of mythological narration. He not only includes every detail that might help the reader to visualize the events he describes, but deliberately adopts the most vivid and even sensationalistic way of telling each tale. Galatea herself narrates how Polyphemus caught sight of her 'in the lap of Acis'; and Achelous recounts in graphic terms his own violent defeat and humiliation at the hands of Hercules.[9] Ovid's storytelling endows the mythologies with an actuality that no manual or reference book could achieve, and that is his principal virtue. He appears not to attempt the high seriousness of Homer, Virgil or the Greek tragedians, and generations of critics have chided him for what they took to be frivolity.[10] From the point of view of the painter, however, this may actually be another, and related virtue. The myths are scattered and usually treated in allusive fashion by these more august poets, and they are embedded in meanings that are specific to the works in which they figure. Ovid, on the other hand, recounts the stories of his *carmen perpetuum* with enormous gusto but with very little sense of any ulterior meaning or finality. Animating them with a powerful imaginative life, he retains a certain neutrality which makes them ideally suited to serve as raw material for painters.

said ... "that divine subjects and the secret Mysteries must not be rashly divulged ... That is why the Egyptians had sculptures of sphinxes in all their temples, to indicate that divine knowledge, if committed to writing at all, must be covered with enigmatic veils and poetic dissimulation"' (Wind (1968) 17).

[7] See Edgar Wind's discussion of the Flaying of Marsyas, (1968) 171–6.
[8] Dante, *Inferno* 1.79–80.   [9] Ovid, *Met.* 9.1–88.   [10] See Hopkins (1988a) *passim*.

At the same time, the combination of the dramatic and the deadpan in Ovid's narrative style contributes to that sense of artifice or fiction that Philip Hardie has discussed above (39–40). Many of Ovid's most characteristic devices are both vivid and self-consciously artificial, like the use of internal narrators. Some of these are treated as extended performances – notably those of the Muses or of Orpheus – which may in turn contain subsidiary voices (thus Orpheus has Venus tell Adonis the story of Atalanta and Hippomenes: see Barchiesi in this volume, 187–8). The sense of immediacy they evoke can be suddenly deflated by a touch of irony, as when Galatea observes that Polyphemus' voice was as deep as a giant's should be. Ovid's style is characterized by such shifts from pathos to humour, from engagement to detachment.

If the 'neutrality' of Ovid's storytelling suits the specific needs of painters, his 'fictional' ambivalence corresponds to the general Renaissance attitude to mythology discussed above. Ovid's poem draws us into a world in which nature is pervaded by mystery and the supernatural, in which familiar things have miraculous origins, and above all in which their external forms are subject to magical transformation. The metamorphoses that conclude most of Ovid's tales belong to a world in which nature is mutable, whether spontaneously or under the influence of divine intervention. Time and again, the appearance and physical being of an individual give way under the pressure of excessive passions and appetites, evil actions, or accidental transgressions against the gods. Most often he is changed into the image of his true nature, or of what has become a fixed and irreversible attitude. A period as fascinated by symbolic codes and emblematic devices as the Renaissance could not but be drawn to a process through which an individual is corporeally changed into a emblem of himself.

It is not surprising that the period of Ovid's greatest influence in early modern art extended from the later fifteenth to the middle of the seventeenth centuries. Modern science was beginning to take shape but had not yet made all other forms of knowledge obsolete. This is the period in European intellectual life with which modern philosophers feel least comfortable, the transition between medieval scholasticism and the systematic articulation of scientific method. To modern eyes, Renaissance philosophers turn to nature with a new attentiveness, but combine their proto-scientific observations promiscuously with magic, occultism and syncretistic theology. The theme of metamorphosis is at home in this intellectual climate. Nature has become a living force: it is no longer reducible, as in scholastic thought, to the 'creation' of a transcendent mind, but nor is it yet the mechanical model of Descartes. Metamorphosis implies that nature is animate, that bodies can change their forms, and that spirit and matter can still act on each other.

The constraints of decorum

But much as the idea of metamorphosis may have appealed to the sensibility of our period, not all of Ovid's stories, and not all episodes in the stories, were suitable for painting. Although the doctrine (if it can be called that) of *ut pictura poesis* implied that painting should draw its inspiration from poetry, and that any subject that was appropriate for one art was similarly good for the other, the rules of decorum were actually far narrower for the visual arts than for the literary.[11] Decorum (another unfamiliar concept in modern art) impinged on the practice of painting in two ways. What we might call relative decorum dictates that the artist shall be faithful to the source text; shall also, more generally, take care to be historically and archaeologically accurate; and at the most general level of all, shall observe appropriate discriminations of sex, age, rank, and so forth. Absolute decorum, on the other hand, prohibits the display of the violent, the repulsive and the obscene. The underlying principle of absolute decorum is that the integrity and dignity of the human body are to be preserved. Such rules were neither rigid nor uniformly applied. Exceptions were made for countless martyrdoms of the saints, and other scenes of violence authorized by sacred texts (like the decollation of Holofernes), although even this licence varied from one place and time to another. The same is true of profane subjects, but the rules are generally more strictly observed, since mythological subjects are governed by less authoritative texts and are ostensibly for pleasure (and didactic utility), but not for the propagation of faith.

The general effect of these more or less tacit principles of decorum was that the human body could very seldom be shown actually undergoing metamorphic change. One of the few exceptions that came to be accepted was the transformation of Daphne into the laurel tree. An early image by Pollaiuolo shows Apollo – in the guise of a young Florentine – clasping a similarly contemporary Daphne, as her upper arms turn into two leafy branches [Figure 3]. Charming as this version is, however, it is neither classical in form, nor does it really rise to the challenge of describing, as Ovid does, the transformation of a girl's body into a tree. On the other hand, the illustration of this scene in Michelle de Marolles' *Tableaux du Temple des Muses* of 1655 follows the poet with a literalism that would have been quite unacceptable in contemporary painting. Daphne is shown rooted to the ground in mid-flight, her skin visibly hardening into bark. The effect is touching in verse, but the illustration looks like something from a manual of dermatology. The best known of all versions of the myth, however, the youthful Bernini's marble

---

[11] For all of these issues, see the forthcoming edition of Dufresnoy, *De arte graphica*, by F. Muecke, Y. Haskell and the author.

Figure 3   Pollaiuolo, *Apollo and Daphne*.

group in the Villa Borghese [Figure 4], ingeniously manages to evoke the pathos of Daphne's transformation without compromising the beauty of her body: the tree begins to close around her graceful form, and only the fingers and toes actually begin to change into twigs with diaphanous leaves.

In many other subjects, the metamorphosis is only alluded to discreetly, or else other episodes of the story are shown, and we are left to imagine the transformation itself. Thus in Poussin's early *Narcissus*, the youth lies languidly by the pool, while the new-born flower appears around his head. Echo, behind him, is more clearly changing into stone, but this transformation involves no distortion of her form. In the later version of the myth Poussin inserted into his *Birth of Bacchus*, he goes much further in evoking Narcissus' death, or more exactly his resorption into the earth. Frequently, as in the *Cephalus and Procris* or *Acis and Galatea* [Figure 5] Poussin shows a moment of the story that does not involve transformation at all. This is all the easier where the metamorphosis, as so often, takes place not as the climax of a story but as its *dénouement*.

Such is not the case with the myth of Diana and Actaeon. Nonetheless, the version that Titian painted for Philip II [Figure 2: see Hinds in this volume, 142–3], like most subsequent treatments of the myth, avoids dealing with the transformation itself by concentrating on the moment of transgression which is its cause. Actaeon is seen accidentally discovering the goddess and her nymphs bathing, and we are left to imagine Diana's vengeance and the hero's death. Once again, however, the artist treats the same theme much more boldly in a later work: in the London National Gallery picture Actaeon is seen with a stag's head and antlers, the exception which reminds us how rare such composite forms are in Renaissance painting [Figure 6].[12] It is notable, however, that although Titian appears more faithful to the text in this case, or at least less reluctant to omit something that might have been considered horrifying or grotesque, he is simultaneously less faithful to it in other respects. There are no nymphs in this composition, and Diana is seen apparently shooting the half-changed Actaeon with her bow, bringing about his death in this case directly rather than indirectly.[13]

It is hard to imagine such an image being painted except by an artist as distinguished and self-confident as Titian, and in a city like Venice, which

[12] In Francesco Albani's version of the same subject (Louvre), Actaeon is unchanged except for a tiny and discreet pair of antlers growing from the top of his head. On the other hand, Charles Le Brun painted the transformation of the Pierides (Ovid, *Met.* 5.294–320 and 662–78) – their arms turning into magpie wings – and other such scenes in the Salon des Muses at Vaux-le-Vicomte.

[13] Despite Panofsky (1969) 163, there is no other reasonable way of interpreting this picture, even though the goddess does not appear to be aiming clearly at Actaeon, and there is no visible arrow.

Figure 4   Gianlorenzo Bernini, *Apollo and Daphne*.

Figure 5 Nicolas Poussin, *Acis and Galatea*.

Figure 6 Titian, *Diana and Actaeon*.

was not inclined to be doctrinaire about the practice of art. There are other transformations, however, which are completely unthinkable in painting, as we can see by looking at the plates in illustrated Ovids and other mythological publications. In the metamorphosis of Phaethon's friend Cycnus in Marolles' *Tableaux*, for example, the young man still has human legs, while the upper part of his body has turned into a swan. Still more bizarre is the plate of Tithonus (a non-Ovidian subject), where the amorous Aurora is seen embracing her lover, now an ancient man with long white hair and beard. The bounds of decorum have already been overstepped in this inappropriate mingling of ages, but there is much worse: from the waist down Tithonus has developed the long abdomen of an insect and his cicada legs are beginning to wrap themselves around the goddess [Figure 7].

If the process of transformation is tacitly excluded whenever it would make the body look ridiculous or disgusting, decorum does not forbid the representation of such authorized semi-human creatures as centaurs and satyrs. They are of course long-established hybrids in an otherwise anthropomorphic mythology, but it is also significant that they retain much or most of the human figure, including the head and face, virtually unchanged.[14] The Minotaur, in contrast, as the figure of a man with the head of a bull, is far more monstrous: it is the seat of reason itself that is compromised. Canova's 1781 sculpture and G. F. Watts' disturbing painting of 1885 [Figure 8] are almost unprecedented. Rubens' sketch of Lycaon with a wolf's head, for the Torre de la Parada [Figure 9], is as exceptional as Titian's Actaeon (Rubens also painted, for the same series, a very unorthodox Minotaur with a bull's *body* and human *face*). Decorum also permits the depiction of gods in their metamorphic disguises, for once again the human form is not compromised, but only replaced, and such miraculous substitution is in any case more acceptable in the case of a god. Thus Zeus can embrace Io in the form of a cloud, carry off Europa as a bull, or impregnate Danaë with the future hero Perseus in a shower of gold.

In practice, therefore, different standards of decorum apply to literature and the visual arts. Language is a more abstract medium, and we can read with pleasure about things that would shock or disgust us if presented before our eyes. The greater immediacy of the visual was recognized by Horace, who observed that those things we hear have a less stimulating effect on us – *segnius irritant animum*[15] – than those we see, and the distinction was taken up by later theorists, such as Pietro da Cortona and Boileau, culminating

---

[14] See the interpretation of Botticelli's *Pallas and the Centaur*, in Gombrich (1972) 70–2 and n.
[15] Horace, *Ars poet.* 180.

Figure 7   *Aurora and Tithonus*, plate for M. de Marolles, *Tableaux du temple des muses* (1655).

Figure 8   George Frederick Watts, *The Minotaur*.

Figure 9   Peter Paul Rubens, *Lycaon changed into a wolf.*

in the writings of Caylus, Burke and Lessing in the eighteenth century.[16] Horace, indeed, had explicitly said that many things that may be spoken should be hidden from the eyes, and although he was discussing messenger speeches on the stage, two of his examples are more obviously painterly than theatrical – Procne turning into a bird, Cadmus into a snake.[17]

The differentiation between a decorum for writing and a decorum for painting helps to explain an anomaly to which I have so far alluded only implicitly. If the illustrator of a book can depict events that would be inconceivable in a painting, it is because he is not operating within the jurisdiction of painting, but within that of the book. His work is conceived as an extension of the text and benefits from the greater latitude allowed to literary compositions. Thus the great illustrated Ovids, like Salomon's in 1557 or Sandys' in 1640, display not only the metamorphoses of Lycaon and Actaeon [Figure 10], but the Lycian peasants who are turned into frogs, Ocyrhoe who is turned into a horse, and numerous other transformations into animals, plants or birds. Book illustrations allow us to identify the elusive category of significant absence in painting.

In recognizing that the difference between illustration and original composition (for want of a better term) is inherently one of principle, not simply one of degree, we are also brought to appreciate another factor that complicates the relation between the artist 'inspired by' Ovid and the 'source text'. In the broadest terms, it is that the illustrator *serves* the text, while the artist *uses* the text. An artist may also perform the role of an illustrator in other circumstances, as Poussin did in the series of drawings from Ovid that he made for the poet Marino before leaving Paris for Rome. In the drawing of Acis and Galatea, Poussin has tried to convey as clearly as he can both the physical situation and the contrasting passions of the protagonists at the moment when Polyphemus catches the lovers in the forest, just before Galatea sees him [Figure 11]. A few years later, in Rome, Poussin painted the beautiful picture that is now in the National Gallery of Ireland, no longer a sensationalistic and literal narrative, but a poetic meditation on desire, reciprocity and loneliness [Figure 5]. Poussin's understanding of the story

[16] Cortona and Ottonelli (1652) 30; Boileau (1966) 170; Burke (1990) 149–61; Lessing (1766) *passim*. In his *Tableaux tirés de l'Iliade* ..., the Comte de Caylus explicitly states that the decorum (*bienséance*) for painting is not the same as the decorum that applies to poetry: he admits that the revolt of the gods described at *Iliad* 1.396–406 would make a good subject for a picture, but adds: 'Yet it must be agreed that this art has a decorum peculiar to itself, and that it must avoid these kinds of subject ... The poet can tell of a number of things that the painter must not represent' (Caylus (1757) 15). Significantly, the subject in question is in breach both of relative decorum (Zeus is the greatest of the gods and it is undignified, and therefore essentially inaccurate, to show him protected by a giant) and of absolute decorum (the giant is a monster, because he has a hundred hands).

[17] Horace, *Ars poet.* 183–4, 187.

Figure 10   Plate for Book III of George Sandys (ed.), *Ovid's Metamorphoses Englished, Mythologiz'd and Represented in Figures.*

Figure 11   Nicolas Poussin, *Polyphemus, Acis and Galatea*. Drawing made for Marino.

has deepened both in a greater familiarity with Ovid's text and its own sources, and in an independent reflection on the significance of the subject. Thus Polyphemus is now seen, as Theocritus describes him (*Idyll* 11), seated high on a headland, looking out to sea, finding consolation in music. But Poussin has ignored the explicit indications of his ugliness given in both the Hellenistic and the Augustan poets, and, like Annibale Carracci a generation earlier, judged that in painting at least the deformity of a single eye is sufficiently pathetic. He has actually heightened the pathos by giving the Cyclops the ideal proportions of the Laocoön.

Such a painting epitomizes much of what I have said about the importance of Ovid as a source of information for painters, and the qualifications we should bear in mind in speaking of 'Ovidian subjects'. It is frequently Ovid's talent as a storyteller, I would suggest, that first motivates the artist or the patron, or both, to plan a picture on a given mythological subject. He provides an abundance of detail, the storytelling is vivid to a fault, he establishes a mood which is at once magical and ironic, a floating, fictional environment in which the mythic imagination is allowed free play. Either artist or patron or literary adviser may add material from other classical authors, or from mythological handbooks and commentaries, but it is arguably the storytelling core that holds these erudite fragments together. At the same time, however, not all of the stories are suitable: the rules of decorum exclude some altogether, and limit the way others may be presented. Finally, the artist is not concerned simply to illustrate the text, for all its appeal, but to make a work that answers to several kinds of intention or expectation, of which fidelity to Ovid's poem is but one.

The evolution of Ovidian subject-matter

It remains to consider the history of 'Ovidian' subject-matter over the course of the early modern period. The ancient gods had never been quite forgotten in the rise of Christianity and the fall of the Roman empire. They were inextricably woven into the fabric of a culture that had been largely assimilated by the Church, and it was monks who recopied Greek and Latin books during centuries when no-one else could even read them. The gods and other figures of mythology lived in the minds of a far greater part of the population, however, through their role in astronomy and astrology, which flourished in the high Middle Ages, as Hellenistic speculation about the planets and the divinities attached to them was rediscovered through Arab authors. Not surprisingly, renewed interest in the planetary divinities was followed by a rediscovery of Ovid. Medieval versions of the *Metamorphoses*, however, are comprehensively christianized. The most famous and influential was the anonymous French *Ovide moralisé* of the early fourteenth century, an immensely long paraphrase with relentless Christian glosses in the text itself (see Dimmick in this volume, 278–80).[18]

Thinkers of the Renaissance were naturally less sympathetic to such Christian readings, even though they were open to syncretistic interpretations of ancient wisdom. Rabelais made fun of the idea that Ovid had intended to allegorize the sacraments of the Church.[19] The Renaissance was more inclined to resort to a combination of Hellenistic and late antique interpretations: from the euhemeristic explanation of myth as an amplification of historical realities, to Neoplatonic or other philosophical or occultist readings of myth as the vehicle of a hidden truth. From the sixteenth century, ethical interpretations begin to predominate. It must be recognized, however, that the concerns of the editors and mythographers only partly match those of contemporary artists, and in general exhibit a considerable time-lag in sensibility. The commentaries retain for years Christian readings inherited from the Middle Ages, and even later the trite moralities they propose manifestly have little relevance to the spirit of a Renaissance *Danaë* or *Rape of Europa*.

In spite of the renewal of interest in antiquity, however, mythological subjects are not particularly common in the art of the early Renaissance. They begin to appear in minor genres, like the painted panels of *cassoni*, the grand wedding-chests that were prominent items of household furniture in quattrocento Florence. In paintings, they are initially confined to artists with a particular philosophical or literary bent, and who are working for similarly inclined patrons: Botticelli, Piero di Cosimo or Mantegna. Botticelli's *Birth of Venus* and *Primavera*, like his *Pallas and the Centaur* [Figure 12] or *Mars and Venus*, belong to a very particular Neoplatonic environment in Florence, and are in any case allegories rather than narratives. Mythology, together with other aspects of classical civilization, begins to be part of the broader culture of the educated classes with the High Renaissance. Raphael is a central figure in this process of familiarization: engravings such as *The Judgement of Paris* [Figure 13] as well as the fresco of the *Parnassus*, the decorations of the Farnesina and other works set a new and definitive standard for the picturing of the gods, just as his compositions in the Stanza della

---

[18] This was followed by a mythological handbook by the English writer Neckham (otherwise known as the Mythographus Vaticanus Tertius), which in turn was used as a reference-work by Boccaccio in his *De genealogia deorum*, a far more classical work than the French poem. Boccaccio's friend Pierre Bersuire (Berchorius) then composed a prose commentary in Latin, the *Ovidius moralizatus*. The preface to this work, which briefly discussed the attributes of each of the gods, was later published separately in various versions, as the *Libellus*. These works are the basis of the late-medieval handbooks of ancient mythology. (My summary is drawn from a long note in Panofsky (1972b) 78 n.2).

[19] Seznec (1980) 89.

Figure 12   Botticelli, *Pallas and the Centaur*.

Figure 13   Marcantonio Raimondi, engraving of *The Judgement of Paris* after Raphael.

Segnatura had established a synthesis of classical form and natural observation in the representation of the human body.[20] Raphael's contribution, in fact, was less to bring 'Ovidian' subjects into general currency than to develop the figural language in which they would become familiar. His pupil Giulio Romano, although far less subtle an artist, applied this language to countless mythological subjects at the Palazzo del Te in Mantua.

The enjoyment of Ovidian subjects as pleasurably poetic, enhanced rather than overwhelmed by symbolic meanings, culminates in the work of Titian.[21] The philosophical significance of his paintings, some already mentioned, seems harmoniously subsumed into their *prima facie* appeal as discreetly erotic human stories. But the sixteenth century also sees a proliferation of gratuitously complex symbolic painting, epitomized by Bronzino's *Allegory* or the sometimes unintelligible mythologies painted at Fontainebleau by Rosso and Primaticcio and their followers. At the same time the painters of Mannerism often resort to inherently obscure texts or rarely-depicted incidents in their quest for novelty. It is against this background that we should consider the great ceiling frescoes of the Galleria Farnese, painted by Annibale Carracci and his brother Agostino in the last years of the sixteenth century and the first years of the seventeenth [Figure 14].

G. P. Bellori, in his life of Annibale, proposes an elaborate Neoplatonic interpretation of the Gallery as evoking the struggle and reconciliation between the Celestial Venus and the Earthly Venus. The explanation is less convincing, however, than his reading of the Hercules stories in the Camerino, Annibale's earlier work in the Palazzo Farnese, whose centrepiece is the *Choice of Hercules*. The Gallery seems rather to illustrate the old theme of love's victory over men and gods alike: not only is Zeus shown bewitched by desire, but Venus herself falls prey to irresistible desire for Anchises, as the *Homeric Hymn to Aphrodite* recounts at length.[22] The subjects are partly (but not exclusively) Ovidian, and the tone of the ensemble is quite consonant with what we have seen to be the poet's own sensibility: his love of story-telling, his way of combining vivid immediacy with ironic distance.

[20] Incidentally, although the Judgement of Paris was not an Ovidian subject, Raphael's print was successful enough to have a literary description of the subject by Nicolas Renouard added to French Ovids of the seventeenth century. See Allen (1970) 197.

[21] 'No other major artist interested in mythological narratives relied so largely on Ovid, and from a single phrase of the text drew visual conclusions of such importance' (Panofsky (1969) 140).

[22] *Ho. Hy. Aphrod.* 45–290: cf. Alpers (1971) 166–7. Venus' footstool is inscribed with the Virgilian phrase *genus unde Latinum* (*Aen.* 1.6) reminding us of the fateful consequences of this coupling, and in this light certain other subjects relating to the progress of the Trojan War (Mercury and Paris, Juno and Jupiter) could be understood in relation to the ultimate founding of Rome. The programme as a whole, however, cannot be reduced to such an intention: the destiny of Rome is only one of many disparate manifestations of the power of love.

Figure 14 Annibale Carracci, *Triumph of Bacchus and Ariadne.*

More important than the question of textual source, however, is the fact that the Carracci have avoided rare or eccentric subjects. They have concentrated on the 'loves of the gods' from Ovid, from Homer or Virgil, or from the cycle of Hercules. All their protagonists are central figures from the mythological tradition, and the subjects are both familiar and appealing. Returning to the example of Raphael and Titian, they helped to constitute a central corpus of mythology, which would become a narrative *lingua franca* for the painters of succeeding generations.

The two most important mythological painters of the seventeenth century, Rubens and Poussin, are both heirs to the Carracci, although each deals with his inheritance very differently. Poussin is the last and greatest representative of the philosophical interpretation of mythology. He is intellectually drawn to an ideal of order, but his temperamental inclination is to emphasize the tragic (this is one reason why even in his earliest, most Titianesque pictures, he is less interested in Zeus's many affairs with mortal girls than in the loves of the goddesses for human youths, which, as Calypso complains in the Odyssey, almost always end unhappily). Poussin's central themes, as I have suggested elsewhere,[23] belong to a Stoic cosmology which allows him to co-ordinate a number of subjects from mythology with others from the Old and New Testaments. The order of nature is based on the immanence of mind or Logos in the material world. Poussin is attracted to those figures – Bacchus, Moses and Christ – who epitomize the incarnation of Logos, and he is concerned with the difficulties and resistance which they encounter, especially in the circumstances of their births and infancies. The incarnation of the Logos is threatened by death or obscure chthonian forces, sometimes figured by a snake, as in his highly original *Orpheus and Eurydice* [Figures 15 and 16], although the human experience of death may, as he suggests in the equally unexpected *Birth of Bacchus*, be compensated by the birth of the god [Figure 17]. The same connection of death and illumination is evoked in the *Landscape with Orion*. Poussin even pondered the fifteenth book of the *Metamorphoses*, more seldom visited by painters, and produced an early but mysterious painting of *Numa Pompilius and the Nymph Egeria*, in which the legendary king is seen plucking the Golden Bough under the nymph's guidance [Figure 18]. This apparent conflation of Ovid and Virgil, perhaps suggested (at this early stage in his career) by the artist's learned patron, Cassiano del Pozzo, appears to associate Numa's instruction in the Pythagorean mysteries with Aeneas' revelation of the cycles of reincarnation during his visit to the underworld in *Aeneid* 6. Much later, Poussin will similarly combine the Ovidian story of Orpheus and Eurydice with the Virgilian account, centred on Aristaeus, in *Georgics* 4.

[23] Allen (1996) *passim.*

Figure 15 Nicolas Poussin, *Orpheus in Hades*. Drawing made for Marino.

Figure 16 Nicolas Poussin, *Orpheus and Eurydice*.

Figure 17 Nicolas Poussin, *The infant Bacchus entrusted to the nymphs of Nysa; the death of Echo and Narcissus.*

Figure 18 Nicolas Poussin, *Numa Pompilius and the nymph Egeria.*

Poussin was by far the most original interpreter of ancient mythology. He was not only a *peintre-philosophe*, creating elaborate moral and cosmological meditations, but a *peintre-poète*, for whom the figures of myth were living presences. The contrast with Rubens in this respect is striking. Although the latter was also deeply attracted to Stoic philosophy, he remained an essentially Christian and Catholic artist. There is no room in his world of belief for the ancient gods to become numinous again as they do in Poussin. For most of Rubens' career, they are transformed into a cast of allegorical *figurants*, accompanying Marie de' Medici at every step of her vast painted biography, or demonstrating a straightforward moral lesson in *Minerva defending Peace from Mars*. Minerva, we know, stands for the force of reason and wisdom in such paintings, and we are never even tempted to imagine that the rather heavy young Flemish woman who embodies her may be a goddess. Late in his life, Rubens undertook a series of specifically Ovidian subjects, some of which have already been mentioned. The commission was to decorate the Torre de la Parada, the Spanish king's hunting lodge. Rubens executed over forty oil sketches of 'Ovidian subjects' that were realized as full-scale paintings by his assistants.[24] Rubens ignores the philosophical interpretation of the Ovidian stories, and the greatest originality of these works, as Alpers has convincingly suggested,[25] is that he seeks to rediscover them, in something like Ovid's own spirit, as human narratives. It is the comic and the pathetic aspects of the stories that appeal to him. The fact that he found inspiration for these works in the illustrated Ovids of the second half of the sixteenth century – whereas the traditions of painters and illustrators were generally separate – is not only to be explained by the need to produce a very large number of compositions very quickly, but also reflects his sympathy for images more directly derived from the text itself.

Rubens' late Ovidian narratives were, however, much less influential than his reduction of the classical gods to a grand allegorical rhetoric. The Baroque painters used them to decorate the ceilings of palaces, endlessly flattering the real or imagined virtues of their patrons. It was the beginning of a new age in which art would increasingly be mobilized in the service of the state. At the same time, the rapid rise of scientific rationalism was sapping whatever numinous charge the myths might still possess. The new Cartesian rigour razed the whole complex if rather ramshackle intellectual edifice of the Renaissance,

[24] 'Of the sixty-three mythological works painted for the Torre, forty-one depicted narratives from Ovid's *Metamorphoses*, twelve more either depicted myths referred to though not narrated by Ovid, or myths not told at all by Ovid in the *Metamorphoses*, nine were non-narrative works with mythological or allegorical figures, and one subject remains unidentified' (Alpers (1971) 78).

[25] Alpers (1971) 166–73.

with its ambiguous boundaries between the poetic, the theological and the scientific.

The consequences of these changes were first experienced in France, which succeeded Rome as the centre of European art in the later seventeenth century. The Academy (founded in 1648 but really only active from the 1660s) and its leader Charles Le Brun struggled, unawares, with deep contradictions that ultimately vitiated their work. Their doctrine was ostensibly founded on the standards of their greatest national painter, Poussin, but their practice was, of necessity (since they were engaged in decorating palaces), much closer to the models established by Rubens, although the latter was officially considered a dangerous example to follow. The gods in the planetary rooms at Versailles are thus completely bland, while Louis XIV is accompanied, in the Hall of Mirrors, by a Rubensian cast of allegorical attendants: Hercules, Minerva, Mars, and so forth. One of the last French mythologies to retain any sense of poetry is Charles de la Fosse's *Clytie turned into a sunflower*, from a series of 27 Ovidian subjects ordered by Louis XIV for the Trianon in 1688.[26]

Pomp without imagination led to an inevitable reaction in Rococo art. Ovidian reminiscences make only tentative appearances in the work of Watteau: a bathing girl, natural rather than ideal in appearance, is supplied with a bow mainly, it seems, in order to remind us of Actaeon's transgression, and to introduce a suggestion of voyeurism. Boucher also painted the Bath of Diana, as well as two versions of the story of Europa, but in general the mythological subject has become less a narrative than the occasion for a display of female nudes. Thus Ovid's characters limp through the early eighteenth century, and when Neoclassicism calls for a return to seriousness, they are ignored in favour of more elevated subjects from Homer, Virgil or Roman history. The influential amateur and scholar, the Comte de Caylus, in the middle of the century, even published a book in which the *Iliad*, the *Odyssey* and the *Aeneid* are fully analysed into subjects for painters. In the nineteenth century Ovid's stories suffer the indignity of being embalmed by the *pompiers* while the *avant-garde* sneers at the very idea of painting anything so outmoded. Twentieth-century painting, as I have already mentioned, rarely has the desire or the means to deal with mythological subjects.

The twentieth century actually witnessed a great renewal of interest in mythology, motivated by anthropology and psychoanalysis. Neither of these, however, contributes to the currency of mythological stories as a central vehicle of our culture. Anthropology traces myth back to its primitive origins, stripping away the very layers of literary interpretation which have made

---

[26] Versailles, Grand Trianon. The painting is reproduced by A. Mérot, *La peinture française au dix-septième siècle* (Paris, 1994) 292.

the Greek myths more complex and humanly resonant than the countless folk tales whose interest is limited to their own tribe. Psychoanalysis similarly diminishes the properly human and social interest of myth, reducing it to the mapping of individual neurosis. These reductive and ultimately anti-humanistic readings of myth are not only unhelpful to artists but diametrically opposed to Ovid's lively, passionate and humorous storytelling.

FURTHER READING

The literature on mythological subjects in art and on the symbolic systems derived from myth is immense. Two of the most reliable guides to this field are Erwin Panofsky and Sir Ernst Gombrich. In Panofsky and Saxl (1933) Panofsky already outlines some of his central theses, which are further developed in Panofsky (1972b). Further important studies are Panofsky (1970) and (1972a). Panofsky (1969) contains a valuable essay on Titian and Ovid. Panofsky's early work was also a starting-point for Seznec (1980). Many of Gombrich's essays on the subject are gathered in Gombrich (1972), although others are to be found in later volumes of his writings. Those who wish to gaze more deeply into the bottomless well of Neoplatonic speculation in the Renaissance may consult Wind (1968). Allen (1970) is a rich if occasionally idiosyncratic study, as its subtitle states, of 'allegorical interpretation in the Renaissance'. At the opposite extreme, Llewellyn (1988) is a concise introduction to the subject of Ovid in the visual arts. Alpers (1971) is invaluable both for Rubens and for the history of Ovidian subjects in general. Allen (1996) is an attempt to offer a synthetic view of Poussin's treatment of mythological and scriptural material. Blunt (1967) remains the foundation of modern work on Poussin, although there are many more recent essays and books of varying quality. A valuable recent essay on mythology in the art of the Baroque period is Thuillier (1996). An exceptionally valuable primary source for Rubens, Poussin and Annibale Carracci is Bellori (1672), especially because Bellori followed the advice of his friend Poussin and included detailed discussion of particular works by each artist. For mythological subjects in the work of particular artists other than those discussed in this essay, readers should refer to recent monographs or exhibition catalogues. Several studies of the illustrations to editions of the *Metamorphoses* (with which I have not been directly concerned) will be found listed at the end of the article on Ovid in *The Dictionary of Art*, ed. J. Turner (1996). Another reference book that will be helpful is the *Oxford Guide to Classical Mythology in the Arts* (2 vols, 1993): articles on mythological figures are arranged alphabetically, each comprising a chronological list of works of literature, painting, etc. connected with that figure from the Middle Ages to the present. A number of websites are now also dedicated to Ovid and to the illustrated editions of his work, including one at the University of Marburg(http://www.fotomr. uni-marburg.de/ovidserv/Ausgaben.htm) where the Sandys and other plates may be viewed, and another at the University of Virginia Library (http://etext.virginia. edu/cgi-local/ovid/ovid1563.html). The University of Erlangen has an extensive site including much critical work on Ovidian texts as well as links to sites dealing with illustrations (http://www.phil.uni-erlangen. de/~p2latein/ovid/start.html).

DATELINE

Some of these dates, in particular those for the earlier works of Ovid, are necessarily approximate or speculative.

BC

753	Legendary foundation of Rome
510	Traditional date of expulsion of kings and foundation of the Republic
270	Callimachus, Theocritus, Aratus active
100	Birth of Julius Caesar
84	Birth of Catullus
70	Birth of Virgil, 15 October
65	Birth of Horace
63	Birth of Octavian; consulate of Cicero
55	Death of Lucretius
54	Death of Catullus
49	Civil War begins
46	Dictatorship of Caesar
44	Assassination of Caesar by Cassius and Brutus, 15 March
43	Birth of Ovid, 20 March; death of Cicero
42	Battle of Philippi: defeat and deaths of Cassius and Brutus
39–8	Completion of Virgil's *Eclogues*
31	Battle of Actium; defeat of Antony and Cleopatra
29	Virgil completes *Georgics* and begins *Aeneid*
28	Propertius, Book 1
27	Octavian receives title 'Augustus'; Tibullus, Book 1
26	Death of Gallus
25	Ovid begins *Amores*
23	Horace, *Odes* 1–3 published
22–1	Propertius, Book 3; publication of original first book(s) of *Amores*

20	Horace, *Epistles* 1
19	Death of Virgil, 21 September; death of Tibullus
15	Birth of Germanicus; first collection of *Heroides*
13	Horace, *Odes* 4 and *Epistles* 2 completed
12–7	Second edition of *Amores*
8	Deaths of Horace and Maecenas
2	Exile of elder Julia; Augustus receives title 'Pater Patriae'
2 BC–AD 2	Publication of *Ars amatoria*, *Remedia amoris*, and double *Heroides*

AD

2	*Metamorphoses* and *Fasti* in progress
4	Augustus adopts Tiberius
8	Exiles of Ovid and younger Julia
9–12	*Tristia*; *Ibis*
12	Tiberius' Pannonian triumph
13	*Ex Ponto* 1–3
14	Augustus dies, succeeded by Tiberius
17/18	Death of Ovid in exile

SELECTED DATES IN THE RECEPTION OF OVID

Some of these dates are necessarily approximate or speculative.

1185	Andreas Capellanus, *De Amore*
1230	Guillaume de Lorris, *Roman de la Rose*
1280	Jean de Meun's continuation of *Roman de la Rose*
1310	*Ovide moralisé*
1321	Dante, *Divina Commedia*
1340	Bersuire, *Ovidius moralizatus*
1380	Chaucer, *House of Fame*
1390	Gower, *Confessio amantis*
1532	Ariosto, *Orlando Furioso*
1567	Golding's translation of the *Metamorphoses*
1590	Spenser, *The Faerie Queene*, Books 1–3
1593	Shakespeare, *Venus and Adonis*; Marlowe, *Hero and Leander*
1596	Spenser, *The Faerie Queene*, Books 4–6
1601	Ben Jonson, *Poetaster*
1611	Shakespeare, *The Tempest*
1632	Sandys' translation of the *Metamorphoses*

1674	Milton, *Paradise Lost*
1717	Garth's collaborative translation of the *Metamorphoses*
1945	H. Fränkel, *Ovid: A Poet between Two Worlds*
1997	Ted Hughes, *Tales from Ovid*

WORKS CITED

Adams, J. N. (1982) *The Latin Sexual Vocabulary*. London

Ahern, C. F. Jr. (1989) 'Daedalus and Icarus in the *Ars amatoria*', *Harvard Studies in Classical Philology* 92: 273–96

Ahl, F. (1985) *Metaformations: Soundplay and Wordplay in Ovid and Other Classical Poets*. Ithaca

Albert, W. (1988) *Das mimetische Gedicht in der Antike*. Frankfurt

Albrecht, M. von (1981) 'Mythos und römische Realität in Ovid's "Metamorphosen",' *Aufstieg und Niedergang der römischen Welt* 2 31:4: 2328–42

   (1982) 'La correspondance de Pâris et d'Hélène: Ovide et Baudri de Bourgueil', in R. Chevallier, ed. *Colloque présence d'Ovide*, 189–93. Paris

   (1988) 'Les dieux et la religion dans les "Métamorphoses" d'Ovide', in D. Porte and J.-P. Néraudau, eds., *Res Sacrae. Hommages à Henri Le Bonniec*, 1–9. Brussels

Albrecht, M. von, and E. Zinn, eds., (1968) *Ovid*. Darmstadt

Alexiou, M. (1974) *The Ritual Lament in Greek Tradition*. Cambridge

Allen, C. (1996) 'Enfants et serpents: la religion de Poussin', *XVIIe Siècle* 191: 229–40

Allen, D. C. (1970) *Mysteriously Meant: The Rediscovery of Pagan Symbolism and Allegorical Interpretation in the Renaissance*. Baltimore and London

Allen, P. L. (1992) *The Art of Love: Amatory Fiction from Ovid to the 'Romance of the Rose'*. Philadelphia

Alpers, S. (1971) *The Decoration of the Torre della Parada* (Corpus Rubenianum Ludwig Burchard Part IX). London

Alston, R. (1998) 'Arms and the man: soldiers, masculinity, and power in Republican and Imperial Rome', in Foxhall and Salmon (1998a) 205–23

Alter, R. (1975) *Partial Magic. The Novel as a Self-conscious Genre*. Berkeley, Los Angeles, London

Althusser, L. (1971) 'Ideology and ideological state apparatuses: notes towards an investigation', in *Lenin and Philosophy and Other Essays*, trans. B. Brewster, 121–73. New York

Altman, J. G. (1982) *Epistolarity: Approaches to a Form*. Columbus

Alton, E. H. (1930) 'The mediaeval commentators on Ovid's *Fasti*', *Hermathena* 20: 119–51

   (1960–61) 'Ovid in the mediaeval schoolroom', *Hermathena* 94: 21–38, 95: 67–82

Alton, E. H., Wormell, D. E. W., and Courtney, E., eds., (1978) *P. Ovidi Nasonis Fastorum Libri Sex*. Leipzig

Anderson, W. S. (1963) 'Multiple change in the *Metamorphoses*', *Transactions of the American Philological Association* 94: 1–27

(1976) 'A new pseudo-Ovidian passage', *California Studies in Classical Antiquity* 7: 7–16

(1982) *Essays on Roman Satire*. Princeton

(1989) 'Lycaon: Ovid's deceptive paradigm in *Metamorphoses* 1,' *Illinois Classical Studies* 14: 91–101

(1995) 'Aspects of Love in Ovid's *Metamorphoses*', *Classical Journal* 90.3: 265–9

Andreas Capellanus (1982) *On Love*, ed. and trans. P. G. Walsh. London

Armitage, D. (1987) 'The dismemberment of Orpheus: mythic elements in Shakespeare's romances', *Shakespeare Survey* 39: 123–33

Auguet, R. (1972) *Cruelty and Civilization: The Roman Games*. London

Bakhtin, M. (1981) 'Forms of time and chronotope in the novel', in *The Dialogic Imagination*, trans. M. Holquist, 84–258. Texas

Bakker, E. and Kahane, A., eds. (1997) *Written Voices, Spoken Signs*. Cambridge, Mass.

Bal, M. (1985) *Narratology*. Toronto

Baldwin, T. W. (1944) *William Shakspere's Small Latine and Lesse Greeke*, 2 vols. Urbana

Barchiesi, A. (1989) 'Voci e istanze narrative nelle Metamorfosi di Ovidio', *Materiali e Discussioni* 23: 55–97

(1991) 'Discordant Muses', *Proceedings of the Cambridge Philological Society* 37: 1–21

(1992) *P. Ovidii Nasonis Epistulae Heroidum 1–3*. Florence

(1993) 'Future reflexive: two modes of allusion and Ovid's *Heroides*', *Harvard Studies in Classical Philology* 95: 333–65

(1996), review of Kenney (1996) in *Bryn Mawr Classical Review* 96.12:1

(1997a) *The Poet and the Prince. Ovid and Augustan Discourse*. Berkeley, Los Angeles, London

(1997b) 'Poeti epici e narratori', in G. Papponetti, ed., *Metamorfosi*, 121–41. Sulmona

(1999) 'Venus' masterplot: Ovid and the Homeric Hymns', in Hardie, Barchiesi, Hinds (1999) 112–26

(2001) *Speaking Volumes. Narrative and Intertext in Ovid and Other Latin Poets*. London

Bardon, H. (1958) 'Ovide et le baroque', in Herescu (1958) 75–100

Barkan, L. (1986) *The Gods Made Flesh. Metamorphosis and the Pursuit of Paganism*. New Haven and London

Barnard, M. E. (1987) *The Myth of Apollo and Daphne from Ovid to Quevedo: Love, Agon, and the Grotesque*. Durham, N. C.

Barolini, T. (1989) 'Arachne, Argus, and St John: transgressive art in Dante and Ovid', *Mediaevalia* 13: 207–26

Barsby, J. A. (1973) *Ovid's Amores, Book 1*. Oxford

(1996) 'Ovid's *Amores* and Roman comedy', *Papers of the Leeds Latin Seminar* 9: 135–57

Barthes, R. (1974) *S/Z*, trans. R. Miller. London

(1979) *A Lover's Discourse: Fragments*, trans. R. Howard (repr. Harmondsworth, 1990). London

Barton, A. (1984) *Ben Jonson, Dramatist*. Cambridge

Bartsch, S. (1989) *Decoding the Ancient Novel*. Princeton
(1994) *Actors in the Audience. Theatricality and Doublespeak from Nero to Hadrian*. Cambridge, Mass. and London
(1997) *Ideology in Cold Blood. A Reading of Lucan's Civil War*. Cambridge, Mass. and London
Baswell, C. (1995) *Virgil in Medieval England. Figuring the 'Aeneid' from the Twelfth Century to Chaucer*. Cambridge
Bate, J. (1993) *Shakespeare and Ovid*. Oxford
Bate, K., ed. (1976) *Three Latin Comedies*. Toronto
Battaglia, S. (1959) 'La tradizione di Ovidio nel medioevo', *Filologia Romanza* 6: 185–224
Baudri of Bourgeuil (1979) *Baldricus Burgulianus, Carmina*, ed. K. Hilbert. Heidelberg
Beard, M. (1987) 'A complex of times: no more sheep on Romulus' birthday,' *Proceedings of the Cambridge Philological Society* 33: 1–15
Beard, M., North, J., and Price, S. (1998) *Religions of Rome*. Cambridge
Becher, I. (1988) 'Augustus und seine Religionspolitik gegenüber orientalischen Kulten', in G. Binder, ed., *Saeculum Augustum* Bd. 2 *Religion und Literatur*, 143–70. Darmstadt
Belanco, G. B. (1672) *Vite de' pittori, scultori ed architetti*. Rome
Benjamin, W. (1970) *Illuminations*, trans. H. Zohn. London
Bennett, H. (1965) *English Books and Readers 1558–1603: Being a Study in the History of the Book Trade in the Reign of Elizabeth I*. Cambridge
Bennett, J. A. W. (1986) *Middle English Literature*, ed. D. Gray. Oxford
Berchorius, P. (Pierre Bersuire) (1979) *Metamorphoses Ovidiana Moraliter [...] Explanata* (repr. of 1509 edn). New York
Berger, A.-E. (1996) 'The latest word from Echo', *New Literary History* 27.4: 621–40
Bergmann, B. (1991) 'Painted perspectives of a villa visit: landscape as status and metaphor', in E. Gazda, ed., *Roman Art in the Private Sphere*, 49–70. Ann Arbor
(1992) 'Exploring the grove: pastoral space on Roman walls', in J. D. Hunt, ed. *The Pastoral Landscape* (Studies in the History of Art 36), 21–46. Washington
Bernbeck, E. (1967) *Beobachtungen zur Darstellungsart in Ovids Metamorphosen* (Zetemata 43). Munich
Bersuire, P. (1962) *Reductorium morale, liber xv, cap. ii–xv. Ovidius moralizatus*, ed. D. Van Nes and J. Engels. Utrecht
Bessone, F. (1997) *P. Ovidii Nasonis Heroidum Epistula XII: Medea Iasoni*. Florence
Binder, G. (1988) 'Aitiologische Erzählung und augusteisches Programm in Vergils "Aeneis",' in G. Binder, ed., *Saeculum Augustum* Bd. 2 *Religion und Literatur*, 255–87. Darmstadt
Bing, P. (1988) *The Well-Read Muse*. Göttingen
Binns, J. W., ed. (1973) *Ovid*. London and Boston
Bischoff, B. (1952) 'Eine mittelalterliche Ovid-Legende', *Historisches Jahrbuch* 71: 268–73
Blonquist, L. B., trans. (1987) *L'Art d'amours (The Art of Love)*. New York and London
Blumenfeld-Kosinski, R. (1997) *Reading Myth. Classical Mythology and its Interpretations in Medieval French Literature*. Stanford
Blunt, A. (1967) *Nicolas Poussin*. London

Boileau, N. (1966) *Oeuvres Complètes*. Paris

Bömer, F., ed. (1957) *P. Ovidius Naso. Die Fasten* I. *Einleitung,Text and Übersetzung*. Heidelberg

(1958) *P. Ovidius Naso. Die Fasten* II. *Kommentar*. Heidelberg

Bond, G. A. (1989) 'Composing yourself: Ovid's *Heroides*, Baudri of Bourgeuil and the problem of persona', *Mediaevalia* 13: 83–117

(1995) *The Loving Subject. Desire, Eloquence and Power in Romanesque France*. Philadelphia

Bonner, S. F. (1949) *Roman Declamation in the Late Republic and Early Empire*. Liverpool

Booth, J. (1991) *Ovid Amores II*. Warminster

Bouché, T. (1977) 'Ovide et Jean de Meun', *Le Moyen Age* 83: 71–87

Boyd, B. W. (1997) *Ovid's Literary Loves: Influence and Innovation in the Amores*. Ann Arbor

Braet, H. (1978) 'Note sur Marie de France et Ovide (Lai de *Guigemar*, vv. 233–244)', in J. de Caluwé, ed., *Mélanges de philologie et littérature romanes offerts à Jeanne Wathelet-Willem*, 21–5. Liège

Braund, S. M. and Mayer, R., eds. (1999) *amor: roma. Love and Latin Literature* (Cambridge Philological Society Supplement No. 22). Cambridge

Bremmer, J. N. (1993) 'Three Roman aetiological myths,' in Graf (1993): 158–75

Brink, C. O. (1982) *Horace on Poetry. Epistles Book* II: *The Letters to Augustus and Florus*. Cambridge

Brinsley, John (1612) *Ludus Litterarius: or, The Grammar Schoole*. London

Brodsky, J. (1980) *A Part of Speech*. Oxford

(1995) *On Grief and Reason*. London

Brooks, P. (1984) *Reading for the Plot: Design and Intention in Narrative*. New York

(1993) *Body Work. Objects of Desire in Modern Narrative*. Cambridge, Mass. and London

Brown, R. (1987) 'The Palace of the Sun in Ovid's *Metamorphoses*', in M. Whitby, P. Hardie, M. Whitby, eds., *Homo Viator: Classical Essays for John Bramble*, 211–20. Bristol

Brown, S. A. (1999) *The Metamorphoses of Ovid: Chaucer to Ted Hughes*. London

Brownlee, K. (1986) 'Ovid's Semele and Dante's metamorphosis: *Paradiso* xxi–xxiii', *MLN* 101: 147–56

Brownlee, K. and Huot, S. eds. (1992) *Rethinking the 'Romance of the Rose'. Text, Image, Reception*. Philadelphia

Brownlee, M. S. (1989) 'The counterfeit muse: Ovid, Boccaccio, Juan de Flores', in K. Brownlee and W. Stephens, eds., *Discourses of Authority in Medieval and Renaissance Literature*. Hanover and London: 109–27

(1990) *The Severed Word: Ovid's Heroides and the Novela Sentimental*. Princeton

Brugnoli, G. (1992) 'Anna Perenna', in G. Brugnoli and F. Stok, eds., *Ovidius*, 21–45. Pisa

Buchan, M. (1995) 'Ovid Imperamator: beginnings and endings of love poems in *Amores* and empire', *Arethusa* 28: 53–85

Buchheit, V. (1966) 'Mythos und Geschichte in Ovids Metamorphosen I', *Hermes* 94: 80–108

Buchner, E. (1982) *Die Sonnenuhr des Augustus*. Mainz

Burdach, K. and Kienast, R. (1929) *Aus Petrarcas ältestem deutschen Schülerkreise.* Halle and Berlin

Burke, E. (1990) *A Philosophical Enquiry into the Origin of our Ideas of the Sublime and Beautiful.* Oxford

Burkert W. (1979) *Structure and History in Greek Mythology and Ritual* (Sather Classical Lectures 47). Berkeley, Los Angeles, London

Burnett, L. (1999) 'Galatea Encore' in L. Loseff and V. Polukhina, eds., *Joseph Brodsky: The Art of a Poem,* 150–76. London and New York

Burrow, C. (1988) 'Original fictions: metamorphoses in *The Faerie Queene*', in Martindale (1988) 99–119

(1997) 'Virgil in English translation', in Martindale (1997) 21–37

(1999) '"Full of the maker's guile": Ovid on imitating and on the imitation of Ovid', in Hardie, Barchiesi, Hinds (1999) 271–87

(2001) 'Spenser and classical traditions', in *The Cambridge Companion to Spenser,* ed. Andrew Hadfield: 217–36. Cambridge

Byron, George Gordon, Lord (1980–1993) *The Complete Poetical Works,* ed. J. J. McGann, 7 vols. Oxford

Cahoon, L. (1985) 'A program for betrayal. Ovidian *nequitia* in *Amores* 1.1, 2.1, and 3.1', *Helios* 12: 29–39

(1986) 'Raping the rose: Jean de Meun's reading of Ovid's *Amores*', *Classical and Modern Literature* 6: 261–85

(1988) 'The bed as battlefield: erotic conquest and military metaphor in Ovid's *Amores*', *Transactions of the American Philological Association* 118: 293–307

(1989) 'The anxieties of influence: Ovid's reception by the early troubadours', *Mediaevalia* 13: 119–55

(1996) 'Calliope's Song: shifting narrators in Ovid, *Metamorphoses* 5', *Helios* 23: 43–66

Calabrese, M. A. (1994) *Chaucer's Ovidian Arts of Love.* Gainesville

(1997–8) 'Ovid and the female voice in the *De amore* and the *Letters* of Abelard and Heloise', *Modern Philology* 95: 1–26

Cameron, A. (1968) 'The second edition of Ovid's *Amores*', *Classical Quarterly* n.s. 18: 320–33

(1995) *Callimachus and His Critics.* Princeton

Canter, H. V. (1933) 'The mythological paradigm in Greek and Latin poetry', *American Journal of Philology* 54: 201–24

Carey, J. (1960) *The Ovidian Love Elegy in England.* Ph. D. diss. Oxford

Carey, J. and Fowler, A., eds. (1968) *The Poems of John Milton.* London

Casali, S. (1995) 'Altre voci nell' *Eneide* di Ovidio', *Materiali e Discussioni* 35: 59–76

Castiglioni, L. (1906) *Studi intorno alle fonti e alla composizione delle Metamorfosi di Ovidio.* Pisa

Castle, T. (1982) *Clarissa's Ciphers: Meaning and Disruption in Richardson's Clarissa.* Ithaca and London

Caverly, D. (1980) 'The Debate of Phyllis and Flora', *Allegorica* 5: 50–79

Caxton, W. (1968) *The Metamorphoses of Ovid Translated by William Caxton,* 2 vols. New York

Caylus, C.-P., Comte de (1757) *Tableaux tirés de l'Iliade, de l'Odysée d'Homère et de l'Enéide de Virgile.* Paris

Works cited

Celoria, F. (1992) *The Metamorphoses of Antoninus Liberalis: A Translation with Commentary.* London

Chatwin, B. (1987) *The Songlines.* London

Chaucer, G. (1987) *The Riverside Chaucer*, gen. ed. L. D. Benson. Boston

Cheney, P. (1997) *Marlowe's Counterfeit Profession: Ovid, Spenser, Counter-Nationhood.* Toronto

Christine de Pizan (1999) *The Book of the City of Ladies*, trans. R. Brown-Grant. London

Cinthio, Giraldi (1968) *On Romances*, trans. Henry L. Snuggs. Lexington

Citroni, M. (1995) *Poesia e lettori in Roma antica. Forme della comunicazione letteraria.* Rome and Bari

Claassen, J.-M. (1991) 'Une analyse stylistique et littéraire d'Ovide (*Epistulae Ex Ponto* 3.3). Praeceptor amoris ou praeceptor Amoris', *Les Etudes Classiques* 59: 27–41

(1999) *Displaced Persons: The Literature of Exile from Cicero to Boethius.* London

Clark, S., ed. (1994) *Amorous Rites: Elizabethan Erotic Narrative Verse.* London

Clausen, W. V. (1987) *Virgil's Aeneid and the Tradition of Hellenistic Poetry.* Berkeley, Los Angeles, London

Clauss, J. J. (1989) 'The episode of the Lycian farmers in Ovid's *Metamorphoses*', *Harvard Studies in Classical Philology* 92: 297–314

Clemente, G. (1981) 'Le leggi sul lusso e la società romana tra il III e il II secolo a. C.', *Società romana e produzione schiavistica* 3: 1–14; 301–14

Codrignani, G. (1958) 'L'aition nella poesia greca prima di Callimaco', *Convivium* 26: 527–45

Cokayne, Aston (1662), *The Tragedy of Ovid.* London

Coleman, K. M. (1990) 'Fatal charades: Roman executions staged as mythological enactments', *Journal of Roman Studies* 80: 44–73

Commager, S. (1962) *The Odes of Horace.* New Haven and London

Congreve, William (1971) *The Way of the World*, ed. B. Gibbons. London

Connor, P. (1974) 'His dupes and accomplices: a study of Ovid the illusionist in the *Amores*', *Ramus* 3: 18–40

Connors, C. (2000) 'Imperial space and time: the literature of leisure', in O. Taplin, ed., *Literature in the Greek and Roman Worlds*, 492–518. Oxford

Conte, G. B. (1986) *The Rhetoric of Imitation: Genre and Poetic Memory in Virgil and Other Latin Poets*, ed. C. Segal. Ithaca and London

(1994a) *Genres and Readers.* Baltimore

(1994b) *Latin Literature: A History*, trans. J. B. Solodow. Baltimore and London

Cooper, H. (1988) 'Chaucer and Ovid: a question of authority', in Martindale (1988) 71–81

Copeland, R. (1991) *Rhetoric, Hermeneutics, and Translation in the Middle Ages. Academic Traditions and Vernacular Texts.* Cambridge

Cormier, R. J. (1992) 'Tisbé, Dané, and Procné: three Old French/Ovidian heroines in quest of personal freedom', in R. Dotterer and S. Bowers, eds., *Sexuality, the Female Gaze, and the Arts: Women, the Arts, and Society*, 102–14. Selinsgrove

Cortona, P. da and Ottonelli, G. (1652) *Trattato della pittura e scultura.* Florence

Cosgrove, D. (1984) *Social Formation and Symbolic Landscape.* London

Coulson, F. T. (1991) *The 'Vulgate' Commentary on Ovid's Metamorphoses: The Creation Myth and the Story of Orpheus.* Toronto

Works cited

Courtney, E. (1993) *The Fragmentary Latin Poets*. Oxford

Cunningham, M. P. (1958) 'Ovid's poetics', *Classical Journal* 53: 253–9

Curley, D. (1999) *Metatheater: Heroines and Ephebes in Ovid's Metamorphoses*. Ph. D. diss. Univ. of Washington, Seattle

Curran, L. C. (1972) 'Metamorphosis and anti-Augustanism', *Arethusa* 5: 71–91
(1978) 'Rape and rape victims in the *Metamorphoses*', *Arethusa* 11: 213–41

Curtius, E. R. (1953) *European Literature and the Latin Middle Ages*, trans. W. Trask (repr. with afterword by P. Godman, Princeton, 1990). London

Dalzell, A. (1996) *The Criticism of Didactic Poetry: Essays on Lucretius, Virgil, and Ovid*. Toronto

Dante Alighieri (1970–75) *The Divine Comedy*, trans. with comm. by C. S. Singleton, 3 vols. in 6. Princeton

D'Arms, J. (1970) *Romans on the Bay of Naples*. Cambridge, Mass.

Davis, G. (1980) 'The problem of closure in a *carmen perpetuum*: aspects of thematic recapitulation in Ovid *Met.* 15', *Grazer Beiträge* 9: 123–32
(1983) *The Death of Procris: Amor and the Hunt in Ovid's Metamorphoses*. Rome

Davis, J. T. (1980) '*Exempla* and anti-*exempla* in the *Amores* of Ovid', *Latomus* 39: 412–17
(1989) *Fictus Adulter: Poet as Actor in the Amores*. Amsterdam

Davis, R. B. (1955) *George Sandys: Poet Adventurer*. London
(1973) *Literature and Society in Early Virginia 1608–1640*. Baton Rouge

Davisson, M. H. T. (1993) '*Quid moror exemplis?* Mythological *exempla* in Ovid's pre-exilic poems and the elegies from exile', *Phoenix* 47: 213–37

Day, R. A. (1966) *Told in Letters: Epistolary Fiction Before Richardson*. Ann Arbor

de Boer, C., de Boer, M. G., Van 'T Sant, J., eds. (1915–38), *Ovide moralisé. Poème du commencement du quatorzième siècle*, Verhandelingen der Koninklijke Akademie van Wetenschappen te Amsterdam, Afdeeling Letterkunde, n.s. 15, 21, 30.iii, 37, 43. Amsterdam

Degl' Innocenti Pierini, R. (1980) 'Echi delle elegie ovidiane dall' esilio nelle *Consolationes ad Heluiam* e *ad Polybium* di Seneca', *Studi Italiani di Filologia Classica* 52: 109–43

Degrassi, A. (1963) *Inscriptiones Italiae*. Vol. 13.2. Rome

Demats, P. (1973) *Fabula. Trois études de mythographie antique et médiévale*. Geneva

de Pretis, A. (1999) *Epistolarity in the First Book of Horace's Epistles*. PhD diss. University of Bristol

Derrida, J. (1980) *The Post Card. From Socrates to Freud and Beyond*, trans. A. Bass. Chicago and London

Desmond, M. (1993) 'When Dido reads Vergil: gender and intertextuality in Ovid's *Heroides* 7', *Helios* 20: 56–68
(1994) *Reading Dido. Gender, Textuality, and the Medieval 'Aeneid'*. Minneapolis

Dickinson, R. J. (1973) 'The *Tristia*: poetry in exile', in Binns (1973) 154–90

Doblhofer, E. (1986) 'Die Sprachnot des Verbannten am Beispiel Ovids', in Stache, Maaz, Wagner (1986) 100–16

Doherty, L. E. (1995) *Siren Songs: Gender, Audiences and Narrators in the Odyssey*. Ann Arbor

Donaldson, I. (1997) *Jonson's Magic Houses*. Cambridge

Donno, E. S., ed. (1963) *Elizabethan Minor Epics*. London

Dörrie, H. (1959) 'Wandlung und Dauer: Ovids Metamorphosen und Poseidonios' Lehre von der Substanz', *Altsprachliche Unterricht* 4.2: 95–116

(1968) *Der heroische Brief*. Berlin

Drayton, Michael (1931–41) *The Works of Michael Drayton*, vols. 1–4 ed. J. W. Hebel, vol. 5 ed. K. Tillotson and B. H. Newdigate. Oxford

Dronke, P. (1968) *Medieval Latin and the Rise of European Love-Lyric*, 2 vols. in 1, 2nd edn. Oxford

(1976) 'Pseudo-Ovid, *Facetus*, and the arts of love', *Mittellateinisches Jahrbuch* 11: 126–31

(1986) 'Dido's lament: from medieval Latin lyric to Chaucer', in Stache, Maaz, Wagner (1986) 364–90 (repr. in P. Dronke [1992] *Intellectuals and Poets in Medieval Europe*, 431–56. Rome)

Du Bellay, Joachim (1970) *Oeuvres Poétiques*, ed. Henri Chamard, 8 vols. Paris

(1974) *Les Regrets et Autres Oeuvres Poétiques*, ed. M. A. Screech, 2nd edn. Geneva

Due, O. S. (1974) *Changing Forms: Studies in the Metamorphoses of Ovid*. Copenhagen

Duff, J. W. (1964) *A Literary History of Rome in the Silver Age, from Tiberius to Hadrian*. London

DuQuesnay, I. M. le M. (1973) 'The *Amores*', in Binns (1973) 1–48

DuRocher, R. J. (1985) *Milton and Ovid*. Ithaca and London

Edwards, C. (1993) *The Politics of Immorality in Ancient Rome*. Cambridge

(1994) 'Beware of imitations: theatre and the subversion of imperial identity', in J. Elsner and J. Masters, eds., *Reflections of Nero: Culture, History and Representation*, 83–97. London

Elliott, A. G. (1978) 'Orpheus in Catalonia: a note on Ovid's influence', *Classical Folia* 32: 3–15

(1980) '*Accessus ad auctores*: twelfth-century introductions to Ovid', *Allegorica* 5: 6–48

Elsner, J., ed. (1996a) *Art and Text in Roman Culture*. Cambridge

(1996b) 'Naturalism and the erotics of the gaze. Intimations of Narcissus', in N. B. Kampen, ed. *Sexuality in Ancient Art. Near East, Egypt, Greece, and Italy*, 247–61. Cambridge

(1998) *Imperial Rome and Christian Triumph*. Oxford

Etherege, George (1979) *The Man of Mode*, ed. J. Barnard. London

Evans, H. B. (1983) *Publica Carmina: Ovid's Books from Exile*. Lincoln and London

Fabian, J. (1991) 'Of dogs alive, birds dead, and time to tell a story', in J. Bender and D. Wellbery, eds., *Chronotypes: The Construction of Time*, 185–204. Stanford

Fabre-Serris, J. (1995) *Mythe et poésie dans les Métamorphoses d'Ovide. Fonctions et significations de la mythologie dans la Rome augustéenne*. Paris

Fantham, E. (1982) *Seneca's Troades. A Literary Introduction with Text, Translation, and Commentary*. Princeton

(1983) 'Sexual comedy in Ovid's *Fasti*: sources and motivations', *Harvard Studies in Classical Philology* 87: 185–216

(1985) 'Ovid, Germanicus and the composition of the *Fasti*', *Papers of the Liverpool Latin Seminar* 5: 243–81

(1992) 'The role of Evander in Ovid's *Fasti*', *Arethusa* 25: 155–71

(1995) 'Recent readings of Ovid's *Fasti*', *Classical Philology* 90: 367–78

(1996) *Roman Literary Culture from Cicero to Apuleius.* Baltimore and London

(1998) *Ovid Fasti Book IV.* Cambridge

Fantuzzi, M. (1988) *Ricerche su Apollonio Rodio.* Rome

Farrell, J. (1992) 'Dialogue of genres in Ovid's "Lovesong of Polyphemus" (*Metamorphoses* 13.719–897)', *American Journal of Philology* 113: 235–68

(1997) 'Towards a rhetoric of (Roman) epic?,' in W. J. Dominik, ed., *Roman Eloquence. Rhetoric in Society and Literature*, 131–46. London and New York

(1998) 'Reading and writing the *Heroides*', *Harvard Studies in Classical Philology* 98: 307–38

(1999) 'The Ovidian *corpus*: poetic body and poetic text', in Hardie, Barchiesi, Hinds (1999) 127–41

Feeney, D. C. (1991) *The Gods in Epic: Poets and Critics of the Classical Tradition.* Oxford

(1992) '*Si licet et fas est* . . . : Ovid's *Fasti* and the problem of free speech under the Principate', in Powell (1992) 1–25

(1993) 'Epilogue. Towards an account of the ancient world's concepts of fictive belief', in C. Gill and T. P. Wiseman, eds., *Lies and Fiction in the Ancient World*, 230–44. Exeter

(1998) *Literature and Religion in Rome.* Cambridge

(1999) '*Mea tempora*: patterning of time in the *Metamorphoses*', in Hardie, Barchiesi, Hinds (1999) 13–30

Feldherr, A. (1997) 'Metamorphosis and sacrifice in Ovid's Theban narrative', *Materiali e Discussioni* 38: 25–55

(1998) *Spectacle and Society in Livy's History.* Berkeley, Los Angeles, London

Fenster, T. S. and Erler, M. C., eds. and trans. (1990) *Poems of Cupid, God of Love. Christine de Pizan's 'Epistre au dieu d'Amours' and 'Dit de la Rose', Thomas Hocclevei's 'The Letter of Cupid', with George Sewell's 'The Proclamation of Cupid'.* Leiden

Fish, S. (1990) 'Rhetoric', in F. Lentricchia and T. McLaughlin, eds. *Critical Terms for Literary Study*, 203–22. Chicago and London

Fitton Brown, A. D. (1985) 'The unreality of Ovid's Tomitan exile', *Liverpool Classical Monthly* 10.2: 18–22

Fitzgerald, W. (2000) *Slavery and the Roman Literary Imagination.* Cambridge

Forbes-Irving, P. M. C. (1990) *Metamorphosis in Greek Myths.* Oxford

Foucault, M. (1971) *The Archaeology of Knowledge*, trans. A. M. Sheridan Smith. New York

Fowler, D. P. (2000) *Roman Constructions. Readings in Postmodern Latin.* Oxford

(forthcoming) *Unrolling the Text.* Oxford

Foxhall, L. and Salmon, J., eds. (1998a) *When Men were Men: Masculinity, Power, and Identity in Classical Antiquity.* London and New York

eds. (1998b) *Thinking Men: Masculinity and its Self-Representation in the Classical Tradition.* London and New York

Fränkel, H. (1945) *Ovid, a Poet between Two Worlds.* Berkeley and Los Angeles

Frazer, J. G. H. (1929) *Publii Ovidii Nasonis Fastorum Libri Sex.* London

Frécaut, J.-M. (1972) *L'Esprit et l'humeur chez Ovide.* Grenoble

Fredrick, D. (ed.) (forthcoming) *The Roman Gaze: Vision, Power, and the Body in Roman Society.* Baltimore

Fusillo, M. (1985) *Il tempo delle Argonautiche.* Rome

Fyler, J. M. (1979) *Chaucer and Ovid*. New Haven and London

Galand-Hallyn, P. (1994) *Le reflet des fleurs: Description et métalanguage poétique d'Homère à la Renaissance*. Geneva

Galinsky, K. (1969) 'The triumph theme in the Augustan elegy', *Wiener Studien* 82: 75–107

(1975) *Ovid's Metamorphoses: An Introduction to the Basic Aspects*. Oxford and Berkeley

(1989) 'Was Ovid a Silver Latin poet?', *Illinois Classical Studies* 14: 69–89

(1996) *Augustan Culture. An Interpretive Introduction*. Princeton

(1999) 'Ovid's *Metamorphoses* and Augustan cultural thematics', in Hardie, Barchiesi, Hinds (1999) 103–11

Gantz, T. (1993) *Early Greek Myth. A Guide to Literary and Artistic Sources*. Baltimore

Garbaty, T. J. (1967) '*Pamphilus, de amore*: an introduction and translation', *Chaucer Review* 2: 108–34

Gardner, J. F. (1993) *Roman Myths*. Austin

Garth, Samuel (1998) *Ovid's Metamorphoses Translated by John Dryden and Others*, with an introduction by Garth Tissol. Ware

Gee, E. (1997) '*Parva figura poli*: Ovid's Vestalia (*Fasti* 6.249–468) and the *Phaenomena* of Aratus', *Proceedings of the Cambridge Philological Society* 43: 21–40

(2000) *Ovid, Aratus and Augustus. Astronomy in Ovid's Fasti*. Cambridge

Genette, G. (1980) *Narrative Discourse*, trans. J. Lewin. Oxford

Gentilcore, R. (1995) 'The landscape of desire: the tale of Pomona and Vertumnus in Ovid's *Metamorphoses*', *Phoenix* 49.2: 110–120

Ghisalberti, F. (1933) 'Giovanni del Virgilio espositore delle *Metamorfosi*', *Giornale Dantesco* 34: 1–110

(1939) 'Arnolfo d'Orléans: un cultore di Ovidio nel seculo XII', *Memorie del Reale Istituto Lombardo, Classe di lettere e scienzi morali e storiche* 24: 155–234

(1946) 'Mediaeval biographies of Ovid', *Journal of the Warburg and Courtauld Institutes* 9: 10–59

Giamatti, A. B. (1982) 'Hippolytus among the exiles: the romance of early humanism', in M. Mack and G. de Forest Lord, eds., *Poetic Traditions of the English Renaissance*, 1–23. New Haven and London

(1984) *Exile and Change in Renaissance Literature*. New Haven and London

Gibson, R. K. (1995) 'How to win girlfriends and influence them: *amicitia* in Roman love elegy', *Proceedings of the Cambridge Philological Society* 41: 62–82

(forthcoming) *A Commentary on Ovid Ars Amatoria III*. Cambridge

Gildenhard, I. and Zissos, A. (1999) '"Somatic economies": tragic bodies and poetic design in Ovid's *Metamorphoses*', in Hardie, Barchiesi, Hinds (1999) 162–81

Gill, C. and Wiseman, T. P., eds. (1993) *Lies and Fiction in the Ancient World*. Exeter

Gill, R. (1972) '*Musa Iocosa Mea*: thoughts on the *Elegies*', in A. J. Smith, ed., *John Donne: Essays in Celebration*, 47–72. London

Ginsberg, W. (1991) 'Dante, Ovid, and the transformation of metamorphosis', *Traditio* 46: 205–33

Gleason, M. W. (1995) *Making Men: Sophists and Self-Presentation in Ancient Rome*. Princeton

Godard, B. (1993) 'Intertexuality', in I. R. Makaryk, ed., *Encyclopedia of Contemporary Literary Theory: Approaches, Scholars, Terms*, 568–72. Toronto

Godman, P. (1985) *Poetry of the Carolingian Renaissance*. London
  (1987) *Poets and Emperors. Frankish Politics and Carolingian Poetry*. Oxford
Golding, Arthur (1961) *Shakespeare's Ovid: Being Arthur Golding's translation of the Metamorphoses*, ed. W. H. D. Rouse. London
  (1965) *Ovid's Metamorphoses: The Arthur Golding Version*, ed. J. F. Nims. New York
Gombrich, E. (1972) *Symbolic Images*. London
Gower, J. (1899–1902) *The Complete Works of John Gower*, ed. G. C. Macaulay, 4 vols. Oxford
  (1962) *The Major Latin Works of John Gower*, trans. E. W. Stockton. Seattle
Gower, John, trans. (1640) *Ovids Festivalls, or Romane Calendar*. Cambridge
Graf, F. (1988) 'Ovide, les Métamorphoses, et la véracité du mythe', in C. Calame, ed., *Métamorphoses du mythe en Grèce antique*, 57–70. Geneva
  (1992) 'Römische Aitia und ihre Riten: das Beispiel von Saturnalia und Parilia', *Museum Helveticum* 49: 13–25
  (1993a) *Greek Mythology. An Introduction* Baltimore
  ed. (1993b) *Mythos in mythenloser Gesellschaft. Das Paradigma Roms* (Colloquia Raurica 3). Stuttgart and Leipzig
Green, P. (1982a) *Ovid: The Erotic Poems*. Harmondsworth.
  (1982b) '*Carmen et error*: πρόφασις and αἰτία in the matter of Ovid's exile', *Classical Antiquity* 1: 202–20
  (1994) *Ovid: The Poems of Exile*. Harmondsworth
Greene, E. (1998) *The Erotics of Domination: Male Desire and the Mistress in Latin Love Elegy*. Baltimore
Greene, T. M. (1982) *The Light in Troy: Imitation and Discovery in Renaissance Poetry*. New Haven and London
Greimas, A. J. (1992) *Dictionnaire de l'ancien français. Le Moyen Âge*. Paris
Griffin, A. H. F. (1977) 'Ovid's *Metamorphoses*', *Greece & Rome* 24: 57–70
Griffin, J. (1977) 'The Epic Cycle and the uniqueness of Homer', *Journal of Hellenic Studies* 97: 39–53
Griffin, M. T. (1976) *Seneca: A Philosopher in Politics*. Oxford
Griffiths, G. (1992) 'Culture and identity: politics and writing in some recent post-colonial texts', in A. Rutherford, ed., *From Commonwealth to Post-Colonial*, 436–43. Sydney
Grimal, P. (1938) 'Les Métamorphoses d'Ovide et la peinture paysagiste à l'époque d'Auguste', *Revue des Études Latines* 16: 145–61
Gross, N. P. (1996) '*Amores* 1.8: whose amatory rhetoric?', *Classical World* 89.3: 197–206
Gruen, E. S. (1990) *Studies in Greek Culture and Roman Policy*. Leiden
  (1996) 'The expansion of the empire under Augustus', *Cambridge Ancient History*, vol. 10, 147–97. Cambridge
Gubar, S. (1986) 'The blank page and the issue of female creativity', in E. Showalter, ed., *The New Feminist Criticism: Essays on Women, Literature and Theory*, 292–313. London
Guillaume de Lorris and Jean de Meun (1983) *The Romance of the Rose*, trans. C. Dahlberg. Hanover and London
  (1992) *Le Roman de la Rose*, ed. with modern French trans. A. Strubel. Paris
Habinek, T. (1997) 'The invention of sexuality in the world-city of Rome', in Habinek and Schiesaro (1997) 23–43

(1998) *The Politics of Latin Literature: Writing, Identity, and Empire in Ancient Rome.* Princeton

Habinek, T. and Schiesaro, A., eds. (1997) *The Roman Cultural Revolution.* Cambridge

Hainsworth, B. (1993) *The Iliad. A Commentary*, gen. ed. G. S. Kirk, vol. 3. Cambridge

Haller, R. S. (1968) 'The *Altercatio Phyllidis et Florae* as an Ovidian satire', *Mediaeval Studies* 30: 119–33

Hallett, J. P. and Skinner, M. B., eds. (1997) *Roman Sexualities.* Princeton

Hanning, R. W. (1981) 'Courtly contexts for urban *cultus*: responses to Ovid in Chrétien's *Cligès* and Marie's *Guigemar*', *Symposium* 35: 34–56

   (1986) 'Chaucer's first Ovid: metamorphosis and poetic tradition in *The Book of the Duchess* and *The House of Fame*', in L. A. Arrathoon, ed. *Chaucer and the Craft of Fiction*, 121–63. Rochester

Harbert, B. (1988) 'Lessons from the great clerk: Ovid and John Gower', in Martindale (1988) 83–97

Hardie, P. R. (1986) *Virgil's Aeneid: Cosmos and Imperium.* Oxford

   (1988) 'Lucretius and the delusions of Narcissus', *Materiali e Discussioni* 20: 71–89

   (1990) 'Ovid's Theban history: the first anti-*Aeneid*?', *Classical Quarterly* 40: 224–35

   (1991) 'The Janus Episode in Ovid's Fasti,' *Materiali e Discussioni* 26: 47–64

   (1992) 'Augustan poets and the mutability of Rome', in Powell (1992) 59–82

   (1993) *The Epic Successors of Virgil: A Study in the Dynamics of a Tradition.* Cambridge

   (1994) *Virgil: Aeneid IX.* Cambridge

   (1995) 'The speech of Pythagoras in Ovid *Metamorphoses* 15: Empedoclean epos,' *Classical Quarterly* 45: 204–14

   (1996) 'Virgil: a paradoxical poet?', *Papers of the Leeds Latin Seminar* 9: 103–21

   (1997) 'Questions of authority: the invention of tradition in Ovid *Metamorphoses* 15', in Habinek and Schiesaro (1997) 182–98

   (1998) *Virgil* (*Greece & Rome* New Surveys in the Classics 28). Oxford

   (1999a) 'Metamorphosis, metaphor, and allegory in Latin epic', in M. Beissinger, J. Tylus, S. Wofford, eds., *Epic Traditions in the Contemporary World: The Poetics of Community*, 89–107. Berkeley

   (1999b) 'Ovid into Laura: absent presences in the *Metamorphoses* and Petrarch's *Rime Sparse*', in Hardie, Barchiesi, Hinds (1999) 254–70

   (2002) *Ovid's Poetics of Illusion.* Cambridge

Hardie, P. R., Barchiesi, A., and Hinds, S. E., eds. (1999) *Ovidian Transformations: Essays on Ovid's Metamorphoses and its Reception* (Cambridge Philological Society Supplement No. 23). Cambridge

Hardman, P. (1994) 'The *Book of the Duchess* as a memorial monument', *Chaucer Review* 28: 205–15

Harley, M. P. (1986) 'Narcissus, Hermaphroditus, and Attis: Ovidian lovers at the *Fontaine d'Amors* in Guillaume de Lorris's *Roman de la Rose*', *Publications of the Modern Language Association* 101: 324–37

Harries, B. (1989) 'Causation and the authority of the poet in Ovid's *Fasti*,' *Classical Quarterly* 38: 164–85

(1990) 'The spinner and the poet: Arachne in Ovid's *Metamorphoses*,' *Proceedings of the Cambridge Philological Society* 36: 64–82

Harrison, S. J., ed. (2001) *Texts, Ideas and the Classics*. Oxford

Hartog, F. (1988) *The Mirror of Herodotus. The Representation of the Other in the Writing of History*, trans. J. Lloyd. Berkeley and London

Harvey, E. D. (1989) 'Ventriloquizing Sappho: Ovid, Donne, and the erotics of the feminine voice', *Criticism* 21: 115–38

Hawkins, P. S. (1991) 'The Metamorphoses of Ovid', in Sowell (1991) 17–34

Heinze, R. (1919) 'Ovids elegische Erzählung', *Berichte der Sächsischen Akademie zu Leipzig, Philologisch-historische Klasse* 71.7. Leipzig [repr. in R. Heinze *Vom Geist des Römertums*, ed. E. Burck, 3rd edn. (1960) 308–403. Stuttgart]

Helzle, M. (1989) *P. Ovidii Nasonis Epistularum ex Ponto Liber IV: A Commentary on Poems 1 to 7 and 16*. Hildesheim

Henderson, A. A. R. (1979) *Remedia Amoris P. Ovidi Nasonis*. Edinburgh

Henderson, J. G. W. (1991) 'Wrapping up the case: reading Ovid, *Amores* 2, 7(8), I', *Materiali e Discussioni* 27: 37–88

(1992) 'Wrapping up the case: reading Ovid *Amores*, 2, 7(8), II', *MD* 28: 27–83

(1997) 'Not wavering but frowning: Ovid as isopleth (*Tristia* 1 through 10)', *Ramus* 26: 138–71

(1999) 'Ch-Ch-Ch-Changes', in Hardie, Barchiesi, Hinds (1999) 301–23

Herbert-Brown, G. (1994) *Ovid and the Fasti: An Historical Study*. Oxford

Herescu, N. I., ed. (1958) *Ovidiana: Recherches sur Ovide*. Paris

Herrick, Robert (1648) *Hesperides*. London

Herrnstein Smith, B. (1981) 'Narrative versions, narrative theories', in W. G. T. Mitchell, ed., *On Narrative*, 209–33. Chicago

Hexter, R. J. (1986) *Ovid and Medieval Schooling. Studies in Medieval School Commentaries on Ovid's 'Ars Amatoria', 'Epistulae ex Ponto', and 'Epistulae Heroidum'*. Munich

(1987) 'Medieval articulations of Ovid's *Metamorphoses*: from Lactantian segmentation to Arnulfian allegory', *Mediaevalia* 13: 63–82

(1989) 'The *Allegari* of Pierre Bersuire: interpretation and the *Reductorium morale*', *Allegorica* 10: 51–84

Heywood, Thomas (1874) *The Dramatic Works of Thomas Heywood*, ed. J. Payne Collier, 6 vols. London

Heyworth, S. J. (1994) 'Some allusions to Callimachus in Latin poetry', *Materiali e Discussioni* 33: 51–79

Hicks, E., ed. (1977) *Le Débat sur le 'Roman de la Rose'*. Paris

Higham, T. F. (1958) 'Ovid and Rhetoric,' in Herescu (1958) 32–48

Hildebert of Lavardin (1969) *Hildeberti Cenomannensis episcopi Carmina minora*, ed. A. B. Scott. Leipzig

Hillis Miller, J. (1990) *Versions of Pygmalion*. Cambridge, Mass. and London.

Hinds, S. E. (1985) 'Booking the return trip: Ovid and *Tristia* 1', *Proceedings of the Cambridge Philological Society* 31: 13–32

(1987) *The Metamorphosis of Persephone. Ovid and the Self-conscious Muse*. Cambridge

(1988) 'Generalizing about Ovid,' *Ramus* 16: 4–31

(1992) '*Arma* in Ovid's *Fasti*', *Arethusa* 25: 81–153

(1993) 'Medea in Ovid: scenes from the life of an intertextual heroine', *Materiali e Discussioni* 30: 9–47

(1996) 'Ovid,' in *Oxford Classical Dictionary*, 3rd edn., 1084–7. Oxford

(1998) *Allusion and Intertext. Dynamics of Appropriation in Roman Poetry.* Cambridge

(1999a) 'First among women: Ovid, *Tristia* 1.6 and the traditions of "exemplary" catalogue', in Braund and Mayer (1999) 123–42

(1999b) 'After exile: time and teleology from *Metamorphoses* to *Ibis*', in Hardie, Barchiesi, Hinds (1999) 48–67

Hintermeier, C. M. (1993) *Die Briefpaare in Ovids Heroides* (Palingenesia 41). Stuttgart

Hiscoe, D. W. (1985) 'The Ovidian comic strategy of Gower's *Confessio Amantis*', *Philological Quarterly* 64: 367–85

Hoffman, H. (1985) 'Ovid's *Metamorphoses: carmen perpetuum, carmen deductum*', *Papers of the Liverpool Latin Seminar* 5: 223–41

Hofmann, M. and Lasdun, J., eds. (1994) *After Ovid. New Metamorphoses.* London

Holahan, M. N. (1976) '*Iamque opus exegi*: Ovid's changes and Spenser's brief epic of mutability', *English Literary Renaissance* 6: 244–70

Hollander, J. (1981) *The Figure of Echo: A Mode of Allusion in Milton and After.* Berkeley and London

Hollander, R. (1977) *Boccaccio's Two Venuses.* New York

Hollis, A. S. (1973) 'The *Ars Amatoria* and *Remedia Amoris*', in Binns (1973) 84–115

(1977) *Ovid Ars Amatoria Book 1*. Oxford

(1990) *Callimachus Hecale*. Oxford

Holzberg, N. (1997a) *Ovid. Dichter und Werk*. Munich

(1997b) 'Playing with his life: Ovid's autobiographical references', *Lampas* 30: 4–19

(1999), rev. B. W. Boyd, *Ovid's Literary Loves*, *Classical Review* 49: 59–60

Hopkins, D. (1988a) 'Dryden and Ovid's "wit out of season"', in Martindale (1988) 167–90

(1988b) 'Dryden and the Garth-Tonson *Metamorphoses*', *Review of English Studies* 39: 64–74

Horsfall, N. (1979) 'Epic and burlesque in Ovid, *Met*. viii. 260ff.', *Classical Journal* 74: 319–32

(1993) 'Mythological invention and *poetica licentia*', in Graf (1993b) 131–42

Housman, A. E. (1920) 'The *Ibis* of Ovid', *Journal of Philology* 34: 222–38

(1972) J. Diggle and F. R. D. Goodyear, eds., *The Classical Papers of A. E. Housman*, 3 vols. Cambridge

Hughes, T. (1997) *Tales from Ovid*. London

Hulse, C. (1981) *Metamorphic Verse: The Elizabethan Minor Epic*. Princeton

Humphries, R. (1955) trans. *Ovid's Metamorphoses*. Bloomington

(1957) trans. *Ovid: The Art of Love*. Bloomington and London

Hunt, J. D. (1986) *Garden and Grove*. London

(1992) *Gardens and the Picturesque*. Cambridge, Mass.

Hunter, R. (1993a) *The Argonautica of Apollonius*. Cambridge

  (1993b) 'Callimachean echoes in Catullus 65', *Zeitschrift für Papyrologie und Epigraphik* 96: 179–82

Huot, S. (1993) *The 'Romance of the Rose' and its Medieval Readers. Interpretation, Reception, Manuscript Transmission*. Cambridge

Huygens, R. B. C., ed. (1970) *Accessus ad auctores. Bernard d'Utrecht. Conrad d'Hirsau, 'Dialogus super auctores'*. Leiden

Iizuka, N. (1999) *Polaroid Stories*. Woodstock

Irigaray, L. (1985) 'Any theory of the "subject" has always been appropriated by the masculine', in *Speculum of the Other Woman*, trans. G. C. Gill, 133–46. Ithaca

Jacobson, H. (1974) *Ovid's Heroides*. Princeton

James, P. (1986) 'Crises of identity in Ovid's *Metamorphoses*,' *Bulletin of the Institute of Classical Studies* 33: 17–25

Jameson, F. (1992) *Signatures of the Visible*. New York and London

Janan, M. (1988) 'The book of good love? Design versus desire in *Metamorphoses* 10', *Ramus* 17: 110–37

  (1991) 'The "Labyrinth and the Mirror": incest and influence in *Metamorphoses* 9', *Arethusa* 24: 239–56

Javitch, D. (1976) 'Rescuing Ovid from the moralisers: the liberation of Angelica, *Furioso* X', in A. Scaglione, ed., *Ariosto 1974 in America*, 85–98. Ravenna

Johnson, J. W. (1960) 'Of differing ages and climes', *Journal of the History of Ideas* 21: 465–80

Johnson, P. (1996) 'Constructions of Venus in Ovid's *Metamorphoses* V', *Arethusa* 29: 125–49

Johnson, W. R. (1970) 'The problem of the counter-classical sensibility and its critics', *California Studies in Classical Antiquity* 3: 123–51

  (1978) 'The desolation of the *Fasti*', *CJ* 74: 7–18

Jones, C., Segal, C., Tarrant, R., Thomas R., eds. (1995) *Greece in Rome: Influence, Integration, Resistance (Harvard Studies in Classical Philology 97)*. Cambridge, Mass.

Jonson, Ben (1995) *Poetaster*, ed. Tom Cain. Manchester

Joplin, P. K. (1984) 'The voice of the shuttle is ours', *Stanford Literary Review* 1: 25–53 [repr. in L. A. Higgins and B. R. Silver, eds., *Rape and Representation* (1991), 35–64. New York]

Joshel, S. (1997) 'Female desire and the discourse of empire: Tacitus's Messalina', in J. Hallett and M. Skinner, eds., *Roman Sexualities*, 221–54. Princeton

Juan Ruiz (1999) *The Book of Good Love*, trans. E. D. MacDonald. London

Kaufmann, L. S. (1986) *Discourses of Desire: Gender, Genre, and Epistolary Fictions*. Ithaca and London

  (1992) *Special Delivery: Epistolary Modes in Modern Fiction*. Chicago and London

Keach, W. (1977) *Elizabethan Erotic Narratives*. New Brunswick

Keith, A. M. (1992a) *The Play of Fictions: Studies in Ovid's Metamorphoses Book 2*. Ann Arbor

  (1992b) '*Amores* 1.1: Propertius and the Ovidian programme', in C. Deroux, ed. *Studies in Latin Literature and Roman History* VI, 327–44. Brussels

  (1994) '*Corpus eroticum*: elegiac poetics and elegiac *puellae* in Ovid's *Amores*', *Classical World* 88: 27–40

(1999) 'Versions of epic masculinity in Ovid's *Metamorphoses*', in Hardie, Barchiesi, Hinds (1999) 216–41

(2000) *Engendering Rome*. Cambridge

Kellogg, J. L. (1998) 'Transforming Ovid: the metamorphosis of female authority', in M. Desmond, ed., *Christine de Pizan and the Categories of Difference*, 181–94. Minneapolis and London

Kennedy, D. F. (1984) 'The epistolary mode and the first of Ovid's *Heroides*', *Classical Quarterly* 34: 413–22

(1992) '"Augustan" and "anti-Augustan": reflections on terms of reference', in Powell (1992) 59–82.

(1993) *The Arts of Love: Five Studies in the Discourse of Roman Love Elegy*. Cambridge

Kenney, E. J. (1958) '*Nequitiae poeta*' in Herescu (1958) 201–9

(1965) 'The poetry of Ovid's exile', *Proceedings of the Cambridge Philological Society* 11: 37–49

(1969a) 'On the "Somnium" attributed to Ovid', *AGON* 3: 1–14

(1969b) 'Ovid and the law,' *Yale Classical Studies* 21: 241–63

(1973) 'The style of the *Metamorphoses*', in Binns (1973) 116–53

(1976) 'Ovidius prooemians', *Proceedings of the Cambridge Philological Society* 22: 46–53

(1982) 'Ovid' in E. J. Kenney and W. Clausen, eds., *Cambridge History of Classical Literature* vol. II *Latin Literature*, 420–57. Cambridge

(1986) Introduction and notes to Melville (1986)

(1992) Introduction and notes to Melville (1992)

(1994) *P. Ouidi Nasonis Amores, Medicamina faciei femineae, Ars amatoria, Remedia amoris*. Oxford

(1996) *Ovid: Heroides XVI–XXI*. Cambridge

Kermode, F. (1973) *Renaissance Essays*. London

Kerrigan, J., ed. (1991) *Motives of Woe: Shakespeare and 'Female Complaint'*. Oxford

(1992) 'Ulster Ovids', in N. Corcoran, ed., *The Chosen Ground: Essays on the Contemporary Poetry of Northern Ireland*, 237–69. Bridgend

Kingsbury, S. M., ed. (1906–35) *The Records of the Virginia Company of London*, 4 vols. Washington

Kirfel, E.-A. (1969) *Untersuchungen zur Briefform der Heroides Ovids*. Bern and Stuttgart

Kirk, G. S. (1970) *Myth. Its Meaning and Function in Ancient and Other Cultures* (Sather Classical Lectures 40). Berkeley

(1972) 'Aetiology, ritual, charter. Three equivocal terms in the study of myths', *Yale Classical Studies* 22: 83–102

Kiser, L. J. (1983) *Telling Classical Tales. Chaucer and the 'Legend of Good Women'*. Ithaca and London

Klein, U. (1967) '"Gold"- und "Silber"-Latein', *Arcadia* 2: 248–56

Kleiner, J. (1994) *Mismapping the Underworld. Daring and Error in Dante's 'Comedy'*. Stanford

Kline, L. (1990) 'Variations on the theme of exile', in Loseff and Polukhina (1990) 56–88

Knoespel, K. J. (1985) *Narcissus and the Invention of Personal History*. Ithaca and London

Knox, P. E. (1985) 'The Epilogue to the *Aetia*', *Greek Roman and Byzantine Studies* 26: 59–65

(1986a) 'Ovid's *Medea* and the authenticity of *Heroides* 12', *Harvard Studies in Classical Philology* 90: 207–23

(1986b) *Ovid's Metamorphoses and the Traditions of Augustan Poetry*. Cambridge

(1989) 'Pyramus and Thisbe in Cyprus', *Harvard Studies in Classical Philology* 92: 315–28

(1995) *Ovid Heroides. Select Epistles*. Cambridge

Konstan, D. (1991) 'The death of Argus, or what stories do: audience response in ancient fiction and theory', *Helios* 18: 15–30

Kristeva, J. (1968) *Theorie d'Ensemble (Tel Quel)*. Paris

Kuttner, A. (1999a) 'Culture and history at Pompey's Museum', *Transactions of the American Philological Association* 129: 343–73

(1999b) 'Looking outside inside: ancient Roman garden rooms', *Studies in the History of Gardens and Designed Landscapes* 19: 7–35

Labate, M. (1984) *L'arte di farsi amare: modelli culturali e progetto didascalico nell'elegia ovidiana*. Pisa

(1987) 'Elegia triste ed elegia lieta. Un caso di riconversione letteraria', *Materiali e Discussioni* 19: 91–129

Lafaye, G. (1904) *Les Métamorphoses d'Ovide et leurs modèles grecs*. Paris

Laird, A. (1996) '*Vt figura poesis*: writing art and the art of writing in Augustan poetry', in Elsner (1996a) 75–102

(1999) *Powers of Expression, Expressions of Power: Speech Presentation and Latin Literature*. Oxford

Lambrechts, P. (1952) 'Les fêtes "phrygiennes" de Cybèle et d'Attis', *Bulletin de l'Institut historique belge de Rome* 27: 141–70

Lanham, R. A. (1976) *The Motives of Eloquence. Literary Rhetoric in the Renaissance*. New Haven and London

La Penna, A. (1957) *Publi Ovidi Nasonis Ibis*. Florence

Lateiner, D. (1978) 'Ovid's homage to Callimachus and Alexandrian poetic theory (*Amores* 2.19)', *Hermes* 106: 188–96

Leach, E. W. (1964) 'Georgic imagery in the *Ars amatoria*', *Transactions of the American Philological Association* 95: 142–54

(1974) 'Ekphrasis and the theme of artistic failure in Ovid's *Metamorphoses*', *Ramus* 3: 102–42

(1988) *The Rhetoric of Space: Literary and Artistic Representations of Landscape in Republican and Augustan Rome*. Princeton

Lebek, W. D. (1978) 'Love in the cloister: a pseudo-Ovidian metamorphosis (*Altera sed nostris eqs.*)', *California Studies in Classical Antiquity* 11: 109–25

Le Bonniec, H. (1966) 'Les renards aux Céréalia', in *Mélanges J. Carcopino*, 605–12. Paris

Lee, A. G. (1958) 'The authorship of the *Nux*', in Herescu (1958) 457–71

(1968) *Ovid's Amores*. London

(1990) *Tibullus: Elegies*. Leeds

Lehmann, P. (1927) *Pseudo-antike Literatur des Mittelalters*. Leipzig

Leigh, M. (1997) *Lucan: Spectacle and Engagement*. Oxford

Lerner, L. (1988) 'Ovid and the Elizabethans', in Martindale (1988) 121–36

Lessing, G. E. (1766) *Laokoon*. Berlin

Lewis, C. S. (1936) *The Allegory of Love: A Study in Medieval Tradition*. Oxford

Lieberg, G. (1980) 'Ovide et les Muses', *Les Etudes Classiques* 48: 3–22

Lightfoot, J. L. (1999) *Parthenius of Nicaea*. Oxford

Lipking, L. (1983) 'Aristotle's sister: a poetics of abandonment', *Critical Inquiry* 10: 61–81

(1988) *Abandoned Women and Poetic Tradition*. Chicago and London

Littlewood, R. J. (1981) 'Poetic artistry and dynastic politics: Ovid at the Ludi Megalenses (*Fasti* 4. 179–372)', *Classical Quarterly* 31: 381–95

Liveley, G. (1999) 'Reading resistance in Ovid's *Metamorphoses*', in Hardie, Barchiesi, Hinds (1999) 199–215

Liversidge, M. (1997) 'Virgil in art', in Martindale (1997) 91–103

Llewellyn, N. (1988) 'Illustrating Ovid', in Martindale (1988) 151–66

Loehr, J. (1996) *Ovids Mehrfacherklärungen in der Tradition aitiologischen Dichtens*. Stuttgart and Leipzig

Loseff, L. and Polukhina, V., eds. (1990) *Brodsky's Poetics and Aesthetics*. London

Lozovan, E. (1958) 'Ovide et le bilinguisme', in Herescu (1958) 396–403

Lucas, R. H. (1970) 'Mediaeval French translations of the classics to 1500', *Speculum* 45: 225–53

Luck, G. (1961) 'Notes on the language and text of Ovid's *Tristia*', *Harvard Studies in Classical Philology* 65: 243–61

(1967) *P. Ovidius Naso: Tristia, Band I – Text und Übersetzung*: Heidelberg

(1977) *P. Ovidius Naso: Tristia, Band II – Kommentar*. Heidelberg

Ludwig, W. (1965) *Struktur und Einheit der Metamorphosen Ovids*. Berlin.

Luhr, F.-F. (1980) 'Nova imperii cupiditate: zum ersten Kapitel der Weltgeschichte des Pompeius Trogus', *Grazer Beiträge* 9: 133–154

Lyne, R. (1996) 'Golding's Englished *Metamorphoses*', *Translation and Literature* 5: 183–200

(2001) *Ovid's Changing Worlds: English Metamorphoses 1567–1632*. Cambridge

MacArthur, E. J. (1990) *Extravagant Narratives: Closure and Dynamics in the Epistolary Form*. Princeton

McCabe, R. (1991) 'Edmund Spenser, poet of exile', *Proceedings of the British Academy* 80: 73–104

MacDonald, P. (1999) review of Hughes (1997). *Translation and Literature* 8: 65–73

McGregor, J. (1978) 'Ovid at school: from the ninth to the fifteenth century', *Classical Folia* 32: 29–51

Mack, S. (1988) *Ovid*. New Haven

McKeown, J. C. (1979) 'Ovid *Amores* 3.12', *Papers of the Liverpool Latin Seminar* 2: 163–177

(1984) 'Fabula proposito nulla tegenda meo: Ovid's *Fasti* and Augustan Politics', in A. J. Woodman and D. A. West, eds., *Poetry and Politics in the Age of Augustus*, 169–87. Cambridge

(1987) *Ovid: Amores I: Text and Prolegomena*. Liverpool

(1989) *Ovid: Amores II: A Commentary on Book One*. Leeds

(1995) 'Militat omnis amans', *Classical Journal* 90: 295–304

(1998) *Ovid: Amores III: A Commentary on Book Two*. Leeds

Mackie, H. (1997) 'Song and storytelling: an Odyssean perspective', *Transactions of the American Philological Association* 127: 77–95

McKinley, K. (1996) 'The medieval commentary tradition 1100–1500 on *Metamorphoses* 10', *Viator* 27: 117–49

Mainzer, C. (1972) 'John Gower's use of the mediaeval Ovid in the *Confessio Amantis*', *Medium Aevum* 41: 215–29

Malouf, David (1978) *An Imaginary Life*. London

Maltby, R. (1991) *A Lexicon of Ancient Latin Etymologies*. Leeds

Marchesi, C. (1910) 'Leggende romane nei "Fasti" di Ovidio', *Atene e Roma* 13: 110–119, 170–183 [= *Scritti minori di filologia e di letteratura*, Firenze, 1978, II 761–87]

Marder, E. (1992) 'Disarticulated voices: feminism and Philomela', *Hypatia* 7.2: 148–66

Marie de France (1995) *Lais*, ed. A. Ewert, introd. G. S. Burgess. London

Marolles, M. de (1655) *Tableaux du temple des muses*. Paris. [facsimile edition: S. Orgel, ed., 'Renaissance and the gods' no. 31. New York and London, 1976]

Martin, C., ed. (1998) *Ovid in English*. Harmondsworth

Martindale, C. (1976) 'Paradox, hyperbole and literary novelty in Lucan's *De Bello Civili*', *Bulletin of the Institute of Classical Studies* 23: 45–54

(1986) *John Milton and the Transformation of Ancient Epic*. London

ed. (1988) *Ovid Renewed. Ovidian Influences on Literature and Art from the Middle Ages to the Twentieth Century*. Cambridge

(1993) *Redeeming the Text: Latin Poetry and the Hermeneutics of Reception*. Cambridge

(1997) *The Cambridge Companion to Virgil*. Cambridge

Martindale, C. and M. (1990) *Shakespeare and the Uses of Antiquity: An Introductory Essay*. London and New York

Martz, Louis L. (1986) *Milton: Poet of Exile*. New Haven and London

Mattern, S. (1999) *Rome and the Enemy: Ideas of Warfare and Empire from 31 BC to AD 235*. Berkeley, Los Angeles, London

Mayer, R. (1982) 'Neronian classicism', *American Journal of Philology* 103: 305–18

(1999) 'Love it or leave it: Silver Latin poetry', in Braund and Mayer (1999) 143–57

Medcalf, S. (1988) 'T. S. Eliot's *Metamorphoses*: Ovid and *The Waste Land*', in Martindale (1988) 233–46

Meech, S. B. (1931) 'Chaucer and the *Ovide moralisé* – a further study', *Publications of the Modern Language Association* 46:182–204

Melville, A. D., trans. (1986) *Ovid. Metamorphoses*. Oxford

(1992) trans. *Ovid. Sorrows of an Exile*. Oxford

Mérot, A. (1994) *La peinture française au dix-septième siècle*. Paris

Michels, A. K. (1967) *The Calendar of the Roman Republic*. Princeton

Millar, F. (1993) 'Ovid and the *Domus Augusta*: Rome seen from Tomoi', *Journal of Roman Studies* 83: 1–17

Miller, J. F. (1980) 'Ritual directions in Ovid's *Fasti*: dramatic hymns and didactic poetry', *Classical Journal* 75: 204–14

(1982) 'Callimachus and the Augustan aetiological elegy', *Aufstieg und Niedergang der römischen Welt* II 30.1: 371–417

(1983) 'Ovid's divine interlocutors in the *Fasti*', in C. Deroux, ed., *Studies in Latin Literature and Roman History* III, 156–92. Brussels

(1991) *Ovid's Elegiac Festivals*. Frankfurt

(1992a) 'Introduction: research on Ovid's *Fasti*', *Arethusa* 25: 1–10

(1992b) 'The *Fasti* and Hellenistic didactic: Ovid's variant aetiologies,' *Arethusa* 25: 11–31

(1993) 'Ovidian allusion and the vocabulary of memory', *Materiali e Discussioni* 30: 153–64

Miller, N. K. (1988) *Subject to Change: Reading Feminist Writing*, New York

Milton, John (1998) *Paradise Lost*, ed. A. Fowler, 2nd edn. London

Minnis, A. J. (1979) 'A note on Chaucer and the *Ovide moralisé*', *Medium Aevum* 48: 254–7

(1991) '*De vulgari auctoritate*: Chaucer, Gower and the men of great authority', in R. F. Yeager, ed., *Chaucer and Gower. Difference, Mutuality and Exchange*, 36–74. Victoria, BC

Minnis, A. J. and Scott, A. B., eds. (1991) *Medieval Literary Theory and Criticism c. 1100–c. 1375. The Commentary Tradition*, rev. edn. Oxford

Momigliano, A. (1987) 'The origins of universal history', in *On Pagans, Jews, and Christians*, 31–57. Middletown

Montaigne, Michel de (1603) *Essayes*, trans. John Florio. London

Monti, R. C. (1990) 'Petrarch's *Trionfi*, Ovid and Vergil', in K. Eisenbichler and A. A. Iannucci, eds., *Petrarch's Triumphs. Allegory and Spectacle*, 11–32. Ottawa

Morgan, K. (1977) *Ovid's Art of Imitation: Propertius in the Amores*. Leiden

Morrison, J. V. (1992) 'Literary reference and generic transgression in Ovid, *Amores* 1.7: lover, poet, and *furor*', *Latomus* 51: 571–89

Most, G. W. (1992) '*Disiecti membra poetae*: the rhetoric of dismemberment in Neronian poetry', in D. L. Selden and R. J. Hexter, eds., *Innovations of Antiquity*, 391–419. New York and London

Muecke, F., Haskell, Y., and Allen, C. (forthcoming) *Dufresnoy, De arte graphica*. Geneva

Muller, D. (1987) 'Ovid, Iuppiter und Augustus. Gedanken zur Götterversammlung im ersten Buch der Metamorphosen', *Philologus* 131: 270–88

Mulvey, L. (1975) 'Visual pleasure and narrative cinema', *Screen* 16.3: 8–18

Mulvihill, J. D. (1982) 'Jonson's *Poetaster* and the Ovidian debate', *Studies in English Literature 1500–1900* 22: 239–55

Munari, F. (1960) *Ovid im Mittelalter*. Zürich

Münzer, F. (1911) *Cacus der Rinderdieb*. Basel

Murgatroyd, P. (1994) *Tibullus: Book 2*. Oxford

Myerowitz, M. (1985) *Ovid's Games of Love*. Detroit

Myers, S. (1994) *Ovid's Causes. Cosmogony and Aetiology in the Metamorphoses*. Ann Arbor

(1996) 'The poet and the procuress: the *lena* in Latin love elegy', *Journal of Roman Studies* 86: 1–21

(1999) 'The metamorphosis of a poet: recent work on Ovid', *Journal of Roman Studies* 89: 190–204

(2000) '*Miranda fides*: poet and patron in paradoxographical landscapes in Statius' *Silvae*', Materiali e Discussioni 44: 103–38.

Mylne, V. (1981) *The Eighteenth Century French Novel: Techniques of Illusion*, 2nd edn. Cambridge

Nagle, B. R. (1980) *The Poetics of Exile: Program and Polemic in the Tristia and Epistulae ex Ponto of Ovid* (Collection *Latomus* 170). Brussels

(1988a) 'A trio of love-triangles in Ovid's *Metamorphoses*', *Arethusa* 21: 75–98

(1988b) 'Erotic pursuit and narrative seduction in Ovid's *Metamorphoses*', *Ramus* 17: 32–51

(1988c) 'Ovid's "reticent" heroes', *Helios* 15.1: 23–39

(1988d) 'Two miniature *carmina perpetua* in the *Metamorphoses*: Calliope and Orpheus', *Grazer Beiträge* 15: 99–125

Nashe, Thomas (1958) *The Works of Thomas Nashe*, ed. R. B. McKerrow, 5 vols. Oxford

Neschke, A. (1986) 'Erzählte und erlebte Götter. Zum Funktionswandel des griechischen Mythos in Ovids "Metamorphosen"', in R. Faber and R. Schlesier, eds., *Die Restauration der Götter. Antike Religion und Neo-Paganismus*, 133–52. Würzburg

Newlands, C. (1992) 'Ovid's narrator in the *Fasti*', *Arethusa* 25: 33–54

(1995) *Playing with Time: Ovid and the Fasti*. Ithaca and London

(1996) 'Transgressive acts: Ovid's treatment of the Ides of March', *Classical Philology* 91: 320–38

(2000) 'Connecting the disconnected: reading Ovid's *Fasti*', in Sharrock and Morales (2000) 171–202

Nichols, F. J. (1979) *An Anthology of Neo-Latin Poetry*. New Haven and London

Nicholson, P. (1988) 'The dedications of Gower's *Confessio Amantis*', *Mediaevalia* 10: 159–80

Nicolet, C. (1991) *Space, Geography, and Politics in the Early Roman Empire*. Ann Arbor

Nicoll, W. S. M. (1980) 'Cupid, Apollo, and Daphne (Ovid *Met.* 1.452ff.)', *Classical Quarterly* 30: 174–82

Nivat, G. (1990) 'The ironic journey into antiquity', in Loseff and Polukhina (1990) 89–97

Nolan, B. (1989) 'Ovid's *Heroides* contextualized: foolish love and legitimate marriage in the *Roman d'Eneas*', *Mediaevalia* 13: 157–87

(1992) *Chaucer and the Tradition of the Roman Antique*. Cambridge

Nugent, S. G. (1990) 'This sex which is not one: de-constructing Ovid's Hermaphrodite', *Differences* 2.1: 160–85

O' Gorman (1997) 'Love and the family: Augustus and Ovidian elegy', *Arethusa* 30.1: 103–24

O' Hara, J. J. (1996) 'Vergil's best reader? Ovidian commentary on Vergilian etymological wordplay', *Classical Journal* 91: 255–76

Oliensis, E. (1997) 'Return to sender: the rhetoric of *nomina* in Ovid's *Tristia*', *Ramus* 26: 172–93

O'Neill, K. (1999) 'Ovid and Propertius: reflexive annotation in *Amores* 1.8', *Mnemosyne* 52: 286–307

Oppel, E. (1968) *Ovids Heroides: Studien zur inneren Form und zur Motivation*. Diss. Erlangen-Nürnberg

Otis, B. (1970) *Ovid as an Epic Poet*, 2nd edn. Cambridge

Owen, S. G. (1893) *Ovid Tristia Book III*, 2nd edn. Oxford

(1902) *Ovid Tristia Book I*, 3rd edn. Oxford

(1924) *Ovid : Tristium Liber Secundus*. Oxford

Palmer, A. (1898) *P. Ovidi Nasonis Heroides*. Oxford

Pana, I. G. (1993) 'The Tomis complex: versions of exile in Australian literature', *World Literature Today* 67: 523–32

Panofsky, E. (1969) *Problems in Titian, Mostly Iconographic.* New York
(1970) *Meaning in the Visual Arts.* Harmondsworth (1st edn. 1955)
(1972a) *Studies in Iconology.* New York (1st edn. 1939)
(1972b) *Renaissance and Renascences in Western Art.* New York (1st edn. Stockholm, 1960)

Panofsky, E. and Saxl, F. (1933) 'Classical mythology in medieval art', *Metropolitan Museum Studies* 4: 228–80 (repr. as *La mythologie classique dans l'art médiéval,* Paris 1990)

Parker, H. (1997) *Greek Gods in Italy in Ovid's Fasti.* Lampeter

Parker, M. (1991) 'The text as mediator: Ovid and Juan Ruiz', *Comparative Literature Studies* 28: 341–55

Parry, H. (1964) 'Violence in a pastoral setting', *Transactions of the American Philological Association* 95: 268–82

Parsons, P. J. (1977) 'Callimachus' *Victoria Berenices*', *Zeitschrift für Papyrologie und Epigraphik* 25: 1–50

Peacock, A. J. (1975) 'Donne's Elegies and Roman love elegy', *Hermathena* 119: 20–9

Pearcy, L. (1984) *The Mediated Muse: English Translations of Ovid, 1560–1700.* Hamden

Peeters, F. (1939) *Les 'Fastes' d'Ovide: Histoire du texte.* Brussels

Pennacini, A. (1988) 'Retorica', in *Enciclopedia virgiliana* IV, 457–60. Rome

Petrarch (1976) *Petrarch's Lyric Poems: The Rime Sparse and Other Lyrics*, ed. and trans. R. M. Durling. Cambridge, Mass.

Phillips, C. R (1992) 'Roman religion and literary studies of Ovid's *Fasti*', *Arethusa* 25: 55–79

Pianezzola, E. (1979) 'La metamorfosi ovidiana come metafora narrativa', *Quaderni del circolo filologico-linguistico padavano* 10: 77–91

Plass, P. (1988) *Wit and the Writing of History. The Rhetoric of Historiography in Imperial Rome.* Madison and London

Podosinov, A. V. (1981) 'Ovid as a source for the history of West Pontus', *Vestnik Drevnej Istorii. Revue d'Histoire Ancienne, Moskva* 156: 174–94
(1987) *Ovids Dichtung als Quelle für die Geschichte des Schwarzmeergebiets.* Constanza

Poirion, D. (1970) 'Narcisse et Pygmalion dans le *Roman de la Rose*', in R. J. Cormier and U. T. Holmes, eds., *Essays in Honor of Louis Francis Solano*, 153–65. Chapel Hill

Polukhina, V. (1989) *Joseph Brodsky: A Poet for our Time.* Cambridge

Poole, A. and Maule, J., eds. (1995) *The Oxford Book of Classical Verse in English Translation.* Oxford

Porte, D. (1985) *L'Étiologie religieuse dans les Fastes d'Ovide.* Paris

Pound, E. (1938) *Guide to Kulchur.* London

Powell, A., ed. (1992) *Roman Poetry and Propaganda in the Age of Augustus.* London

Pratt, M. L. (1992) *Imperial Eyes: Travel Writing and Transculturation.* New York

Putnam, M. C. J. (1995) *Virgil's Aeneid: Interpretation and Influence.* Chapel Hill

Quinn, K. F. (1982) 'The poet and his audience in the Augustan age', *Aufstieg und Niedergang der römischen Welt* II 30.1: 75–180

Raby, F. J. E. (1934) *A History of Secular Latin Poetry in the Middle Ages*, 2 vols. Oxford (repr. 1999)

Rahn, H. (1958) 'Ovids elegische Epistel', *Antike und Abendland* 7: 105–20

Rand, E. K. (1925) *Ovid and his Influence*. London

Ransmayr, C. (1990) *The Last World: With An Ovidian Repertory* [*Die letzte Welt*], trans. John Woods. London

Rawson, E. (1985) *Intellectual Life in the Late Roman Republic*. London

Reeve, M. D. (1973) 'Notes on Ovid's *Heroides*', *Classical Quarterly* 23: 324–38

Reid, J. D.(1993) *Oxford Guide to Classical Mythology in the Arts*, 2 vols. Oxford

Revard, S. (1986) 'Donne and Propertius: love and death in London and Rome', in C. J. Summers and T.-L. Pebworth, eds., *The Eagle and the Dove: Reassessing John Donne*, 69–79. Columbia

Reynolds, L. D., ed. (1983) *Texts and Transmission. A Survey of the Latin Classics*. Oxford

Reynolds, W. D. (1990) 'Sources, nature, and influence of the *Ovidius moralizatus* of Pierre Bersuire', in J. Chance, ed., *The Mythographic Art. Classical Fable and the Rise of the Vernacular in Early France and England*, 83–99. Gainesville

Richlin, A. (1992) 'Reading Ovid's rapes', in A. Richlin, ed., *Pornography and Representation in Greece and Rome*, 158–79. Oxford

Richmond, J. A. (1981) 'Doubtful works ascribed to Ovid', *Aufstieg und Niedergang der römischen Welt* II 31.4: 2744–83

Rigg, A. G. (1993) *A History of Anglo-Latin Literature 1066–1422*. Cambridge

Robathan, D. M., ed. (1968) *The Pseudo-Ovidian 'De vetula'*. Amsterdam

  (1973) 'Ovid in the Middle Ages', in Binns (1973) 191–209

Rosati, G. (1981) 'Il racconto dentro il racconto: funzioni metanarrative nelle "Metamorfosi" di Ovidio', in *Atti Convegno Letterature Classiche e Narratologia*, 297–309. Perugia

  (1983) *Narciso e Pigmalione. Illusione e Spettacolo nelle Metamorfosi di Ovidio*. Florence

  (1992) 'L'elegia al femminile: le Heroides di Ovidio (e altre Heroides)', *Materiali e Discussioni* 29: 71–94

  (1994) 'Introduzione', in *Ovidio. Le metamorfosi*. Milan

  (1996a) *Heroidum Epistulae XVIII–XIX. Leander Heroni, Hero Leandro*. Florence

  (1996b) 'Sabinus, the *Heroides* and the poet-nightingale: some observations on the authenticity of the *Epistula Sapphus*', *Classical Quarterly* 46: 207–16

Rosenberg, E. (1955) *Leicester, Patron of Letters*. New York

Rosenmeyer, P. (1997) 'Ovid's *Heroides* and *Tristia*: voices from exile', *Ramus* 26.1: 29–56

Roy, B., ed. (1974) *L'Art d'amours. Traduction et commentaire de l'*'*Ars amatoria*' *d'Ovide*. Leiden

Rushdie, S. (1988) *The Satanic Verses*. London

  (1991) *Imaginary Homelands: Essays and Criticism 1981–1991*. New York and London

Rutledge, E. (1980) 'Ovid's informants in the *Fasti*', in C. Deroux, ed., *Studies in Latin Literature and Roman History* II (Collection Latomus 168): 322–31

Said, E. (1993) *Culture and Imperialism*. New York

Salverda de Grave, J.-J., ed. (1925–29) *Eneas. Roman du xiie siècle*, 2 vols, Les classiques français du moyen âge, 44, 62. Paris

Salza Prina Ricotti, E. (1987) 'Water in Roman garden *triclinia*', in E. B. MacDougall, ed., *Ancient Roman Villa Gardens* (Dumbarton Oaks Colloquium on the History of Landscape Architecture 10), 135–84. Washington

Salzman, M. (1998) 'Deification in the *Fasti* and the *Metamorphoses*', in *Studies in Latin Literature and Roman History* IX, ed. C. Deroux (Collection *Latomus* 244), 313–346. Brussels

Sandys, George (1632) *Ovid's Metamorphoses Englished, Mythologiz'd, and Represented in Figures*. London

Scheid, J. (1975) *Les frères Arvales. Recrutement et origine sociale sous les empereurs julio-claudiens*. Paris

(1990) *Romulus et ses frères. Le collège des frères arvales, modèle du culte public dans la Rome des empereurs*. Paris

(1992) 'Myth, cult and reality in Ovid's *Fasti*', *Proceedings of the Cambridge Philological Society* 38: 118–31

Schevill, R. (1913–16) 'Ovid and the Renascence in Spain', *University of California Publications in Modern Philology* 4: 1–268

Schiesaro, A. (1997a) 'The boundaries of knowledge in Virgil's *Georgics*,' in Habinek and Schiesaro (1997) 63–89

(1997b) 'L'intertestualità e i suoi disagi', *Materiali e Discussioni* 39: 75–109

Schmidt, E. A. (1991) *Ovids poetische Menschenwelt: Die Metamorphosen als Metapher und Symphonie*. Heidelberg

Schönbeck, G. (1962) *Der locus amoenus von Homer bis Horaz*. Diss. Heidelberg

Schrötter, W. (1908) *Ovid und die Troubadours*. Halle

Schubert, W. (1992) *Die Mythologie in den nichtmythologischen Dichtungen Ovids* (Studien zur klassischen Philologie 66). Frankfurt

Schütz, M. (1990) 'Die Sonnenuhr des Augustus auf dem Marsfeld', *Gymnasium* 97: 432–57

Scullard, H. H. (1981) *Festivals and Ceremonies of the Roman Republic*. Ithaca

Seeck, G. A. (1975) 'Ich-Erzähler und Erzähler-Ich in Ovids Heroides. Zur Entstehung des neuzeitlichen literarischen Menschen' in E. Lefèvre, ed., *Monumentum Chiloniense. Studien zur augusteischen Zeit (Festschrift Erich Burck)*, 436–70. Amsterdam

Segal, C. P. (1969) *Landscape in Ovid's Metamorphoses: A Study in the Transformations of a Literary Symbol* (*Hermes* Einzelschrift 23). Wiesbaden

(1994a) *Singers, Heroes and Gods in the Odyssey*. Ithaca

(1994b) 'Philomela's web and the pleasures of the text', in I. J. F. de Jong and J. P. Sullivan, eds., *Modern Critical Theory and Classical Literature*, 257–80. Leiden, New York, Köln

(1998) 'Ovid's metamorphic bodies: art, gender, and violence in the *Metamorphoses*', *Arion* 5.3: 9–41

Seznec, J. (1980) *La survivance des dieux antiques*, 2nd edn. Paris (1st edn. in English, *The Survival of the Pagan Gods*, 1953)

Shakar, A. (1996) *City in Love: The New York Metamorphoses*. Normal, Ill.

Shakespeare, William (1986) *The Complete Works*, ed. S. Wells and G. Taylor. Oxford

Sharpe, J. (1993) *Allegories of Empire: The Figure of Woman in the Colonial Text*. Minneapolis

Sharrock, A. (1987) 'Ars Amatoria 2, 123–142. Another Homeric scene in Ovid', *Mnemosyne* 40: 406–12
  (1991) 'Womanufacture', *Journal of Roman Studies* 81: 36–49
  (1994a) *Seduction and Repetition in Ovid's Ars Amatoria II*. Oxford
  (1994b) 'Ovid and the politics of reading', *Materiali e Discussioni* 33: 97–122
  (1995) 'The drooping rose: elegiac failure in *Amores* 3.7', *Ramus* 24: 152–80
  (1996) 'Representing metamorphosis', in Elsner (1996) 103–30
  (forthcoming) 'Looking at looking: can you resist a reading?', in Fredrick (forthcoming)
Sharrock, A. and Morales, H., eds. (2000) *Intratextuality. Greek and Roman Textual Relations*. Oxford
Simpson, J. (1995) *Sciences and the Self in Medieval Poetry. Alan of Lille's 'Anticlaudianus' and John Gower's 'Confessio Amantis'*. Cambridge
  (1998) 'Ethics and interpretation: reading wills in Chaucer's *Legend of Good Women*', *Studies in the Age of Chaucer* 20: 73–100
  (1999) 'Breaking the vacuum: Ricardian and Henrician Ovidianism', *Journal of Medieval and Early Modern Studies* 29: 325–54
Sinclair, P. (1995) *Tacitus the Sententious Historian. A Sociology of Rhetoric in Annales 1–6*. University Park, Penn.
Skutsch, O. (1985) *The Annals of Quintus Ennius*. Oxford
Slater, N. (1998) 'Passion and petrifaction: the gaze in Apuleius', *Classical Philology* 93: 18–48
Slavitt, D. (1990) *Ovid's Poetry of Exile*. Baltimore and London
  (1994) *The Metamorphoses of Ovid, Translated Freely Into Verse*. Baltimore and London
Smarr, J. L. (1991) 'Poets of love and exile', in Sowell (1991) 139–51
Smith, B. R. (1991) *Homosexual Desire in Shakespeare's England*. Chicago
Smith, G. G., ed. (1904) *Elizabethan Critical Essays*, 2 vols. Oxford
Smith, R. A. (1997) *Poetic Allusion and Poetic Embrace in Ovid and Virgil*. Ann Arbor
Solodow, J. B. (1988) *The World of Ovid's Metamorphoses*. Chapel Hill
Sowell, M. U., ed. (1991) *Dante and Ovid. Essays in Intertextuality*. Binghamton
Spence, S. (1996) *Texts and the Self in the Twelfth Century*. Cambridge
Spenser, Edmund (1977) *The Faerie Queene*, ed. A. C. Hamilton. London
Spentzou, E. (forthcoming) *Reading Characters Read: Transgressions of Gender and Genre in Ovid's Heroides*. Oxford
Spivak, G. (1993) 'Echo', *New Literary History* 24: 17–43
Stache, U. J., Maaz, W., Wagner, F., eds. *Kontinuität und Wandel: Lateinische Poesie von Naevius bis Baudelaire; Franco Munari zum 65. Geburtstag*. Hildesheim
Stackmann, K. (1966) 'Ovid im deutschen Mittelalter', *Arcadia* 1: 231–54
Staples, A. (1998) *From Good Goddess to Vestal Virgins*. London and New York
Stapleton, M. L. (1996) *Harmful Eloquence: Ovid's Amores from Antiquity to Shakespeare*. Ann Arbor
Stehle, E. (1989) 'Venus, Cybele, and the Sabine women: the Roman construction of female sexuality', *Helios* 16: 143–64
  (1997) *Performance and Gender in Ancient Greece*. Princeton
Steinle, E. M. (1989) 'Versions of authority in the *Roman de la Rose*: remarks on the use of Ovid's *Metamorphoses* by Guillaume de Lorris and Jean de Meun', *Mediaevalia* 13: 189–206

Stow, G. B. (1993) 'Richard II in John Gower's *Confessio Amantis*: some historical perspectives', *Mediaevalia* 16: 3–31

Stroh, W. (1971) *Die römische Liebeselegie als werbende Dichtung*. Amsterdam

(1981) 'Tröstende Musen: zu Ovids Exilgedichten', *Aufstieg und Niedergang der römischen Welt* II 31.4: 2638–84

Strong, R. (1979) *The Renaissance Garden in England*. London

Sturm-Maddox, S. (1985) *Petrarch's Metamorphoses. Text and Subtext in the 'Rime sparse'*. Columbia

Summers, K. (1996) 'Lucretius' Roman Cybele', in E. N. Lane, ed. *Cybele, Attis and Related Cults*, 337–65. Leiden

Summers, W. C. (1910) *Select Letters of Seneca*. London

Syme, R. (1978) *History in Ovid*. Oxford

Tarrant, R. J. (1978) 'Senecan drama and its antecedents', *Harvard Studies in Classical Philology* 82: 213–63

(1981) 'The authenticity of the Letter of Sappho to Phaon (*Heroides XV*)', *Harvard Studies in Classical Philology* 85: 133–53

(1995) 'Ovid and the failure of rhetoric,' in D. Innes, H. Hine, C. Pelling, eds., *Ethics and Rhetoric. Classical Essays for D. Russell on his Seventy-fifth Birthday*, 63–74. Oxford

Theodorakopoulos, E. (1997) 'Closure: the book of Virgil', in Martindale (1997) 155–65

Thibault, J. C. (1964) *The Mystery of Ovid's Exile*. Berkeley and Los Angeles

Thomas, E. (1959) 'Some reminiscences of Ovid in later literature', *Atti del Convegno Internazionale Ovidiano* vol. I, 145–71. Rome

Thomas, R. F. (1982) *Lands and Peoples in Roman Poetry: The Ethnographic Tradition* (Cambridge Philological Society Supplement No. 7). Cambridge

(1985) 'From *recusatio* to commitment. The evolution of the Virgilian programme', *Papers of the Liverpool Latin Seminar* 5: 61–73

Thuillier, J. (1996) 'La mythologie à l'âge "baroque"', in S. Georgoudi and J.-P. Vernant, eds., *Mythes grecs au figuré: de l'antiquité au baroque*, 167–87. Paris

Tissol, G. (1997) *The Face of Nature. Wit, Narrative, and Cosmic Origins in Ovid's Metamorphoses*. Princeton

Trickett, R. (1988) 'The *Heroides* and the English Augustans', in Martindale (1988) 191–204

Vance, N. (1988) 'Ovid and the nineteenth century', in Martindale (1988) 215–31

Vasaly, A. (1993) *Representations: Images of the World in Ciceronian Oratory*. Berkeley and Oxford

Vaughan, Henry (1983) *The Complete Poems*, ed. A. Rudrum, rev. edn. Harmondsworth

Verducci, F. (1985) *Ovid's Toyshop of the Heart: Epistulae Heroidum*. Princeton

Vermaseren, M. (1977) *Cybele and Attis: The Myth and the Cult*. London

Vessey, D. (1973) *Statius and the Thebaid*. Cambridge

(1999) 'The defeat of love', in Braund and Mayer (1999) 158–73

Veyne, P. (1983) *Les grecs, ont-ils cru à leurs mythes? Essaies sur l'imagination constituante*. Paris

Viarre, S. (1964) *L'image et la pensée dans les Métamorphoses d'Ovide*. Paris

(1966) *La Survie d'Ovide dans la littérature scientifique des XIIᵉ et XIIIᵉ siècles*. Poitiers

Vickers, B. (1988) *In Defence of Rhetoric*. Oxford

Vickers, N. J. (1981–2) 'Diana described: scattered woman and scattered rhyme', *Critical Inquiry* 7: 265–79

Videau-Delibes, A. (1991) *Les Tristes d'Ovide et l'élégie romaine: une poétique de la rupture*. Paris

Vincent, M. (1994) 'Between Ovid and Barthes: ekphrasis, orality, textuality in Ovid's "Arachne"', *Arethusa* 27: 361–86

Waitz, G., ed. (1849) 'Das Liebesconcil', *Zeitschrift für Deutsches Alterthum*: 160–7

Wallace-Hadrill, A. (1985) 'Propaganda and dissent? Augustan moral legislation and the love-poets', *Klio* 67: 180–4

(1987) 'Time for Augustus. Ovid, Augustus and the *Fasti*,' in M.Whitby, P. Hardie, M. Whitby, eds., *Homo Viator: Classical Essays for John Bramble*, 221–30. Bristol

(1997) '*Mutatio morum*: the idea of a cultural revolution', in Habinek and Schiesaro (1997) 2–22

Watson, L. C. (1991) *Arae: The Curse Poetry of Antiquity*. Leeds

Way, M. (1998) *Violence and Elite Speech in Plautus*. Diss. Berkeley

Webb, R. (1999) 'Ekphrasis ancient and modern: the invention of a genre', *Word & Image* 15: 7–18

West, M. L. (1974) *Studies in Greek Elegy and Iambus*. Berlin

Wethey, H. (1975) *The Paintings of Titian III: The Mythological and Historical Paintings*. London

Whalen, L. E. (1996) 'A medieval book-burning: *objet d'art* as narrative device in the *Lai* of *Guigemar*', *Neophilologus* 80: 205–11

Wheeler, A. L. (1925) 'Topics from the life of Ovid', *American Journal of Philology* 46: 1–28

Wheeler, S. M. (1995) '*Imago mundi*: another view of the creation in Ovid's *Metamorphoses*', *American Journal of Philology* 116: 95–121

(1997) 'Changing names: the miracle of Iphis in Ovid *Metamorphoses* 9', *Phoenix* 51.2: 190–202

(1999) *A Discourse of Wonders: Audience and Performance in Ovid's Metamorphoses*. Philadelphia

Wiedemann, T. (1975) 'The political background to Ovid's *Tristia* 2', *Classical Quarterly* 25: 264–71

Wight Duff, J. A (1964) *Literary History of Rome in the Silver Age. From Tiberius to Hadrian*. London, 3rd edn. (1st edn 1927)

Wilkinson, L. P. (1955) *Ovid Recalled*. Cambridge

William of Saint-Thierry (1953) *Deux traités de l'amour de Dieu. De la contemplation de Dieu. De la nature et la dignité de l'amour*, ed. with French trans. M.-M. Davy. Paris

(1981) *The Nature and Dignity of Love*, trans. T. X. Davis, introd. D. N. Bell. Kalamazoo

Williams, C. A. (1999) *Roman Homosexuality: Ideologies of Masculinity in Classical Antiquity*. Oxford

Williams, G. D. (1992) 'Ovid's Canace: dramatic irony in *Heroides* 11', *Classical Quarterly* 42: 201–9

(1994) *Banished Voices: Readings in Ovid's Exile Poetry*. Cambridge

(1996) *The Curse of Exile: A Study of Ovid's Ibis*. Cambridge

(1997) 'Writing in the mother-tongue: Hermione and Helen in *Heroides* 8 (a Tomitan Approach)', *Ramus* 26: 113–37

Williams, G. W. (1978) *Change and Decline. Roman Literature in the Early Empire.* Berkeley, Los Angeles, London

Williams, R. (1973) *The Country and the City.* Oxford

Wills, J. (1996) *Repetition in Latin Poetry. Figures of Allusion.* Oxford

Wind, E. (1968) *Pagan Mysteries in the Renaissance*, 2nd edn. London

Winkler, J. J. (1985) *Author and Actor: A Narratological Reading of Apuleius' The Golden Ass.* Berkeley and Los Angeles

Wiseman, T. P. (1979) *Clio's Cosmetics.* Leicester

(1984) 'Cybele, Vergil, and Augustus', in T. Woodman and D. West, eds. *Poetry and Politics in the Age of Augustus*, 117–28. Cambridge

(1998) *Roman Drama and Roman History.* Exeter

Wishart, David (1995) *Ovid.* London

Wisman, J. A. (1997) 'Christine de Pizan and Arachne's metamorphoses', *Fifteenth Century Studies* 23: 138–51

Woodman, A. J. (1998) *Tacitus Reviewed.* Oxford

Wright, N. (1999) 'Creation and recreation: medieval responses to *Metamorphoses* 1.5–88', in Hardie, Barchiesi, Hinds (1999) 68–84

Wright, T., ed. (1842) *Latin Stories from Manuscripts of the Thirteenth and Fourteenth Centuries.* London

Wyke, M. (1989) 'Mistress and metaphor in Augustan elegy', *Helios* 16: 25–47

(1990) 'Reading female flesh: *Amores* 3.1', in A. Cameron, ed., *History as Text*, 113–43. London

(1995) 'Taking the woman's part: engendering Roman elegy', in A. J. Boyle, ed., *Ramus Essays in honour of J. P. Sullivan*, 110–28. Bentleigh, Victoria

Yunck, J. A., trans. (1974) *Eneas. A Twelfth-century French Romance.* New York and London

Zamora, L. P. and Faris, W. B., eds., (1995) *Magical Realism: Theory, History, Community.* Durham N. C. and London

Zanker, P. (1988) *The Power of Images in the Age of Augustus*, trans. A. Shapiro. Ann Arbor

(1998) *Pompeii: Public and Private Life*, trans. D. Schneider. Cambridge, Mass.

Zetzel, J. E. G. (1983) 'Re-creating the canon: Augustan poetry and the Alexandrian past', *Critical Inquiry* 10: 83–105

Zingerle, A. (1869–71) *Ovidius und sein Verhältniss zu den Vorgängern und gleichzeitigen römischen Dichtern.* Innsbruck

Ziolkowski, T. (1993) *Virgil and the Moderns.* Princeton

Zissos, A. (1999) 'The rape of Proserpina in Ovid *Met.* 5.341–661: internal audience and narrative distortion', *Phoenix* 53: 97–113

Zissos, A. and Gildenhard I. (1999) 'Problems of time in *Metamorphoses* 2', in Hardie, Barchiesi, Hinds (1999) 31–47

Zwierlein, O. (1999) *Die Ovid- und Vergil-Revision in Tiberischer Zeit* Vol. 1, *Prolegomena.* Berlin and New York

Note: references in **bold** refer to illustrations.

Index

Index